3182 lines of alliterative v[e]
Hwæt we gardena in ge
Printed often, since Ke[m]   (‑‑‑‑)
under the title

BEOWULF

for
John Davey

BEOWULF
an edition
with
relevant shorter texts

Bruce Mitchell
Fellow Emeritus of St Edmund Hall, Oxford

Fred C. Robinson
Douglas Tracy Smith Professor of English,
Yale University

including

'Archaeology and *Beowulf*'
by Leslie Webster
Department of Medieval and Later Antiquities,
British Museum

 Blackwell
Publishing

© 1998 by Bruce Mitchell and Fred C. Robinson

350 Main Street, Malden, MA 02148-5018, USA
108 Cowley Road, Oxford OX4 1JF, UK
550 Swanston Street, Carlton South, Melbourne, Victoria 3053, Australia
Kurfürstendamm 57, 10707 Berlin, Germany

First published 1998 by Blackwell Publishers Ltd, a Blackwell Publishing company
Reprinted 2000, 2002

Library of Congress Cataloging-in-Publication Data

Beowulf: an edition with relevant shorter texts / [edited by] Bruce
Mitchell and Fred C. Robinson: including Archaeology and Beowulf by
Leslie Webster.
    p. cm.
Includes bibliographical references.
ISBN 0–631–17225–4 (acid-free paper)—ISBN 0–631–17226–2 (pbk:
acid-free paper)
1. Epic poetry, English (Old). 2. English language—Old English, ca.
450–1100—Texts. 3. Epic poetry, English (Old)—History and criticism.
4. Epic poetry, English (Old)—Criticism, Textual. 5. Archaeology, Medieval.
6. Beowulf. I. Mitchell, Bruce, 1920– . II. Robinson, Fred C.
III. Webster, Leslie. Archaeology and Beowulf.
    PR1580.M57   1998   97–47428
    829'.3–dc21   CIP

A catalogue record for this title is available from the British Library.

Set in 10.5 on 12 pt Ehrhardt
by Joshua Associates Ltd, Oxford
Printed and bound in the United Kingdom
by T. J. International Ltd., Padstow, Cornwall

For further information on
Blackwell Publishing, visit our website:
http://www.blackwellpublishing.com

Contents

Foreword

Believing as we do that some knowledge of Old English is desirable for all serious students of English literature; that the literature of the Anglo-Saxons is indeed, as has recently been claimed, 'literature of the highest order'; and that *Beowulf*, with its complex blend of heroic and Christian, is one of the outstanding works in the corpus, we offer here a new edition of that poem. It is designed to give maximum help to those reading the poem for the first time, and consists of four parts with supporting apparatus – illustrations, facsimile pages, a map, bibliography, and glossary:

  I Introduction
 II Text and Notes
III How We Arrived at our Text
IV The Background

Since we visualize a readership which already has some acquaintance with what were to the Argentinian poet Jorge Luis Borges

> the elemental words
> Of a language that in time would flower
> In Shakespeare's harmonies,

we have agreed the following aims:

1 first and foremost, to provide the help needed for an understanding of the text;
2 to keep the notes as simple as possible, so that we do not goad the reader into asking 'So what?';
3 to reduce emendation to a minimum;
4 not to repeat in the notes what is in the glossary;
5 to discuss phonological and metrical problems, and variant readings, only when they may affect the meaning of the poem. But, as IIIA shows, we do not attempt to conceal the existence of these and related problems;
6 to discuss archaeology in IVC (kindly written for us by Leslie Webster of the British Museum), and what Klaeber calls 'the fabulous elements' and 'the historical elements' in the introduction or in the rest of IV, with references in the notes to the relevant numbered sections;

7 to adopt a detached and impersonal presentation and to avoid imposing
   our own ideas or those of others, about the 'meaning' or the 'significance'
   of individual passages or of the poem, apart from a short section in which
   we individually explain our own differing views on *Beowulf*. Such
   problems of judgement and literary interpretation we leave to the
   student and the teacher.

A study of the contents list will throw further light on our aims.

The title we originally proposed – *'Beowulf': A Student's Edition* – was
independently trumped by George Jack in 1994 with his *'Beowulf': A
Student Edition*. In this dilemma we lack the courage displayed by P. G.
Wodehouse and have changed our title to *'Beowulf': An Edition*:

> A word about the title. It is related of Thackeray that, hitting upon
> *Vanity Fair* after retiring to rest one night, he leaped out of bed and
> ran seven times round the room, shouting at the top of his voice.
> Oddly enough, I behaved in exactly the same way when I thought of
> *Summer Lightning*. I recognised it immediately as the ideal title for a
> novel. My exuberance has been a little diminished since by the
> discovery that I am not the only one who thinks highly of it. Already I
> have been informed that two novels with the same name have been
> published in England, and my agent in America cables to say that
> three have recently been placed on the market in the United States.
> As my story has appeared in serial form under its present label, it is
> too late to alter it now. I can only express the modest hope that this
> story will be considered worthy of inclusion in the list of the
> Hundred Best Books Called Summer Lightning.

It is a pleasant duty to thank all those who have helped, advised, and
encouraged us. We are grateful to those who studied our specimen pages
and replied to the questionnaire which accompanied them: Carl Berkhout,
Robert Bjork, George Brown, George Clark, Daniel Donoghue, James Earl,
Christine Fell, Roberta Frank, Allen Frantzen, Malcolm Godden, Jim
(J.R.) Hall, Nicholas Howe, Sarah Larratt Keefer, Calvin Kendall, Ted
Leinbaugh, Roy Michael Liuzza, Jerome Mandel, Bernard Muir, Shigeru
Ono, Marijane Osborn, Phillip Pulsiano, Jane Roberts, Geoffrey Russom,
Paul Beekman Taylor, Joseph Trahern, Ruth Waterhouse, Gernot Wie-
land, and David Yerkes. We are conscious of special obligations to Alfred
Bammesberger, Jim Hall, Sonia Chadwick Hawkes, Susan Irvine, Kevin
Kiernan, Jan Peder Lamm, Andrew P. Scheil, Leslie Webster, and Laura
Williams; to Trevor Mason for the map and for the illustration on p. 39; to
those named on p. iv; to Margaret Aherne, Fiona Sewell, Patricia Bird, and
Vera Keep; to the unjustly anonymous helpers at Blackwell Publishers,
Joshua Associates, and T. J. International; to each other and to our wives
Mollie and Helen; and to John Davey, whose encouragement and

enthusiasm are recognized in our Dedication. And finally, in further acknowledgement of debts admitted in our preliminary note to the text, we thank all the Old English scholars and students, living and dead, who have contributed to this book.

We hope and wish that, as you embark on your reading of *Beowulf*, your efforts will prosper – *Wel þe þæs geweorces!* – and that in time you may wish to write in your copy the translation by Alastair Reid of the poem which Jorge Luis Borges wrote in his:

> At various times I have asked myself what reasons
> Moved me to study while my night came down,
> Without particular hope of satisfaction,
> The language of the blunt-tongued Anglo-Saxons.
> Used up by the years my memory
> Loses its grip on words that I have vainly
> Repeated and repeated. My life in the same way
> Weaves and unweaves its weary history.
> Then I tell myself: it must be that the soul
> Has some secret sufficient way of knowing
> That it is immortal, that its vast encompassing
> Circle can take in all, can accomplish all.
> Beyond my anxiety and beyond this writing
> The universe waits, inexhaustible, inviting.

Acknowledgements

The authors and publishers offer grateful acknowledgements to the following for permission to reproduce copyright material:

Penguin Books, for two quotations from *Jorge Luis Borges: Selected Poems 1923–1967* (1972, reprinted 1985); Oxford University Press, for extract from Bruce Mitchell's note on *ealuscerwen* in *Review of English Studies* 43 (1992); Columbia University Press, for extracts from *Anglo-Saxon Poetic Records*, George Krapp and Eliot Dobbie, eds, copyright 1953 Columbia University Press; and J. M. Dent, for extracts from G. N. Garmonsway, J. Simpson and H. E. Davidson, *'Beowulf' and its Analogues* (London, 1968).

Illustrations: City of York Museums Service, York Castle Museum (front cover); Copyright IRPA-KIK Brussels (back cover); Sheffield Arts and Museums Department (half-title); British Library (frontispiece, six facsimile pages); © Sonia Chadwick Hawkes (figure 2); Simon James / Royal Archaeological Institute, *Archaeological Journal* (figure 3); The Board of Trinity College Dublin (figure 4); British Museum, London (figures 5a, 5b, 13, 15, 16, 17a, 17c, 17d, 18 and 20); Copyright Eva Wilson (figures 6, 7, 8); Antikvarisk-topografiska arkivet, Stockholm / photo Iwar Anderson (figures 9, 14); Dominic Tweddle (figure 11); Northamptonshire County Council (figure 12); The Board of Trustees of the National Museums and Galleries on Merseyside (figures 17b, 21); Rijksmuseum van Oudheden, Leiden (figure 19); R. M. Williams (figure 22); Sheffield Arts and Museums Department (Part One); photo © British Museum (Part Three); photo © British Museum (top), photo Suffolk County Council for M.o.D. (bottom) (Part Four).

The publishers apologize for any errors or omissions in the above list and would be grateful to be notified of any corrections that should be incorporated in the next edition or reprint of this book.

Illustrations

The illustrations appear between pages 185 and 186.

For details of the manuscript facsimile pages see Contents. The front cover shows the York Helmet, the back cover the back of the Brussels Cross. The boar from the Benty Grange helmet appears on the half-title page and the capital B on p. 39 is from the Ramsey Psalter, British Library Harley MS 2904, folio 4.

Map: The Geography of *Beowulf*

The map is based on that in Klaeber's edition of *Beowulf* by kind permission of George G. Harrap and Company. The names of the less important tribes are given in upper and lower case.

The village of Lejre (south-west of Roskilde on the island of Zealand) is often identified with the seat of the Scylding kings. It has been marked as the site of Heorot.

Mitchell and Robinson's *Beowulf: An Edition* has all of the features one hopes to find in a classroom edition: glossary, notes, copious but clear explanatory material. But it is more than an edition. It is a distillation of decades of affectionate attention to the poem by two of the top scholars in the field. From the smallest of details like punctuation to the broadest interpretations, Mitchell and Robinson display an abiding respect and admiration for the magnificent artistry of *Beowulf*.

Professor Daniel Donoghue, Harvard University

PART ONE

Introduction

Helmet with boar crest and inlaid silver cross,
Benty Grange, Derbyshire, seventh century

A   The Manuscript

§1 *Beowulf* is preserved in a single manuscript in the British Library in London. Since the early seventeenth century it has been known as MS Cotton Vitellius A. xv,[1] or, more informally, simply as 'the *Beowulf* manuscript'. Since the vast majority of Old English manuscripts perished during the Anglo-Saxon period and in the centuries immediately following, it is by lucky chance that this one is still extant. There may once have been many copies of the poem, but only Cotton Vitellius A. xv survives. Palaeographers have determined from characteristics of the scribal hands that wrote the text that the manuscript was copied down in the late tenth century or perhaps the first decade of the eleventh.

§2 Originally the poem *Beowulf* seems to have been the last in a series of narratives about wondrous creatures gathered together to make the book that is Cotton Vitellius A. xv. The first text in the manuscript is a fragmentary homily on St Christopher in Old English prose. The saint is said to have been twelve fathoms tall and is in other respects quite out of the ordinary, and so he qualifies as a wondrous creature. *The Wonders of the East* and a putative *Letter of Alexander to Aristotle*, both also in Old English prose, follow. Like *The Passion of St Christopher* these are translations of Latin texts which tell of marvellous creatures and places. *Beowulf* follows *Alexander's Letter*, and the last leaf of *Beowulf* is scuffed in a way that suggests that it was for a time the final page in the collection of narratives. But a fragment of another vernacular poem on the apocryphal Old Testament heroine Judith has been added to the collection following *Beowulf*. It is written by the same scribe who wrote the last portion of *Beowulf*, and so these five texts would appear to have been gathered

[1] 'Cotton' is the name of the collector, Sir Robert Bruce Cotton (1571–1631), who owned and named the manuscript. Cotton kept his manuscripts in bookcases, each of which had a bust of a Roman emperor (or other notable) on top of it. The *Beowulf* manuscript was kept on shelf A of the bookcase surmounted by a bust of Emperor Vitellius. It was the fifteenth book (xv) on shelf A. This volume actually comprises two separate and unrelated manuscripts, *Beowulf* and the four texts accompanying it (all written at about the same period) and a completely unrelated twelfth-century manuscript which Cotton had bound together with it. When one examines the volume in the British Library, it is the later manuscript, beginning with an Old English version of the *Soliloquies* of St Augustine, that one encounters first, the *Beowulf* manuscript beginning only some ninety leaves into the volume.

together in the scriptorium where they were copied out. We may say, then, that *Beowulf* is preserved in a book containing texts about marvellous creatures combined with a narrative about a heroic woman saving her nation in Old Testament times. Taking note of the contents of the manuscript in which *Beowulf* is found provides us with just about the only context we have for judging what the poem may have meant to its original audience – i.e. it was one of a group of stories about men and monsters.[2]

§3 What do we know about the history of this manuscript? Before it came to rest in the British Library, where it is now displayed as a chief treasure of the English nation, the *Beowulf* manuscript belonged to Sir Robert Bruce Cotton (1571–1631), who kept his library in a building ominously named Ashburnham House. Fire swept through the library in 1731, and the *Beowulf* manuscript was badly singed, as a glance at any of the facsimiles of manuscript pages in the text following will show. Before Cotton owned the manuscript, it had passed through the hands of Lawrence Nowell, a sixteenth-century antiquary who signed his name on the first surviving leaf of the St Christopher homily, dating the signature 1563. Nowell or a contemporary also wrote the word *feared* (i. e. 'terrified' in sixteenth-century English) over the Old English word *egsode* in l. 6 of *Beowulf*, thus showing that this part of the text was being read with understanding at this time. Before the manuscript came into Nowell's possession it had probably lain in a monastic library since monastic libraries are where most of the manuscripts from Anglo-Saxon England reposed between 1066 and the Reformation. We know that during this period someone took an interest in the *Beowulf* manuscript, for two readers have scribbled a few Middle English translations (or 'modernizations') of Old English words in the interlinear spaces of *The Wonders of the East*. We know nothing about the manuscript's history before this time. Some, it is true, have speculated that *Beowulf* ll. 1357–76 was a source for a somewhat similarly phrased description of hell by a tenth-century homilist,[3] but it is hazardous to assume a direct connection between two similar passages when so much has been lost.

§4 We may be sure that Cotton Vitellius A. xv is not an author's holograph but rather a scribe's copy made from a pre-existing exemplar. Wax tablets rather than vellum and ink would have been what an author would probably use to compose a text, but aside from this there are numerous indications in the manuscript that it is a copy of a copy. Two different scribes wrote out the texts. Scribe A copied *St Christopher*, *The Wonders of the East*, *Alexander's Letter*, and ll. 1–1939 (through the word *scyran*) of *Beowulf*. The remainder of *Beowulf* and all of *Judith* are written in

[2] Andy Orchard, *Pride and Prodigies: Studies in the Monsters of the Beowulf-Manuscript* (Cambridge, 1995) provides a discussion of the monster-theme of Cotton Vitellius A. xv together with text and translations of *The Wonders of the East* and *The Letter of Alexander to Aristotle*.

[3] Richard Morris, ed., *The Blickling Homilies*, Early English Text Society o.s. 58, 63, 73 (London, 1880), pp. 208–10.

the hand of scribe B. (See the facsimile on p. 113 below and count down three lines in order to see where scribe A left off and B began.) In copying texts scribes were free to follow the spelling of their exemplar or to adapt the spelling to their own habitual practice as they liked. The two scribes of *Beowulf* show different spelling habits in some respects (see below, l. 1939 note), but they are not very different. It is important to note that their spelling habits change from text to text. Thus scribe B's habit of writing *io* for *eo* is characteristic only of his copying of *Beowulf*; in *Judith* he writes *eo*. This suggests that the *io* spellings were characteristic of his exemplar of *Beowulf* but not of his exemplar of *Judith*. Similarly scribes A and B both frequently use the abbreviation *þôn* for *þonne*, but this abbreviation never occurs in the first two texts copied by A and it occurs only once each in *Alexander's Letter* and *Judith*. From this we can surmise with some confidence that the exemplar of *Beowulf* from which the scribes copied made frequent use of *þôn*. Sometimes metre tells us that the two scribes' way of writing the text of *Beowulf* could not have been the way the original text read. The contracted forms throughout the poem often suggest that our manuscript is a late copy of an earlier text (see l. 16 note and ll. 3176–7 note), and the scribes' occasional tendency to substitute synonyms for original words which must be restored to provide alliteration (e.g. *hand gripe* 965, *hild plegan* 1073, *side reced* 1981) is a typical copyist's error, as are the instances where the scribes simply confuse similarly formed letters (e.g. *hetlic* 780, *mid* 976, *að* 1107, *speop* 2854, *wræce* 3060).

§5 Correcting scribal errors and trying to recover the reading of the poet's original text is the task of every editor of an Old English text, but the editor of *Beowulf* faces yet another challenge. In consequence of the fire that swept through Sir Robert Bruce Cotton's library in 1731, the pages of Cotton Vitellius A. xv containing *Beowulf* were badly scorched, as we have said in §3 above. Some letters of the text were burned away, and over succeeding years more crumbling of the charred edges of the pages and further loss have taken place. Lines 1–19 and 53–73 were copied down and published by Humfrey Wanley in 1705 before the fire took place,[4] and so we have these lines intact (except for *le* of *aldorlease* in l. 15, which was apparently missing before the fire). Another valuable witness to original manuscript readings now lost is the Thorkelin transcripts. Grímur Jónsson Thorkelin (1752–1829), an Icelander living in Copenhagen, began a research trip to England in 1786, and while there he hired a professional copyist to make a complete transcription of the poem *Beowulf* for him. Later Thorkelin himself made a second copy of the manuscript text of the poem. These two transcriptions survive and are of primary importance

---

[4] *Antiquæ Literaturæ Septentrionalis Liber Alter . . . seu Humphredi Wanleii . . . Catalogus Historico-Criticus* in George Hickes, *Linguarum Vett. Septentrionalium Thesaurus*, vol. 3 (Oxford, 1705), pp. 218–19.

because at the time Thorkelin's copies were made the charred manuscript pages had not deteriorated as far as they have today. In 1815 Thorkelin published the first edition of *Beowulf*, using his transcripts as his source for the text. His *editio princeps* is a crude edition with many inaccuracies, but other early scholars (such as N. S. F. Grundtvig, J. M. Kemble, Frederic Madden, and Benjamin Thorpe) made careful collations of Thorkelin's edition with the manuscript, and these often provide further witnesses to the manuscript in an earlier state of preservation.[5] Eventually the progressive deterioration of the manuscript leaves was arrested in August 1845 when Sir Frederic Madden, Keeper of Manuscripts in the British Museum, had the codex rebound and the separate folios inlaid in such a way as to stop the chipping of vellum edges.[6]

§6 *Beowulf* is divided into numbered sections, which the Anglo-Saxons seem to have called *fitts*.[7] (See p. 152 below for an example of a fitt-division.) After the first fifty-two lines, which some consider a prologue, the fitt-divisions begin. The beginning of a fitt is normally marked by a capital letter and a prominent roman numeral indicating the number of the fitt.[8] *Beowulf* has forty-three fitts, but in the case of three of the fitts the beginning of the fitt is marked by a capital letter alone, the roman numeral having been omitted. These are fitts XXVIIII, XXX, and XXXVIIII. In our text we supply these fitt-numbers within brackets. Who divided the poem up into these numbered sections? Most scholars have thought that the fitts represent the poet's conception of how the narrative is segmented, and if this is the case, then they are important structural markers. But some have wondered whether fitt-divisions are not arbitrary breaks introduced by scribes, in which case they should play no role in our assessment of the narrative structure of the poem in which they occur. Although the fitt-divisions do not always occur at points in the poem where modern readers would expect a narrative break, there seems to be sufficient pattern and system in their use to suggest that the poet and not a mechanical copyist broke the narrative up into these divisions. For example, ten of the fitts

---

[5] J. R. Hall of the University of Mississippi is currently gathering and evaluating all the early witnesses to the manuscript, and he has kindly made many of his findings available for our use in preparing this edition.

[6] Kevin Kiernan, *Beowulf and the Beowulf Manuscript* (New Brunswick, NJ, 1981), p. 69, n. 7.

[7] The word *fitt* meaning 'poem, song' occurs repeatedly in Old English prose and verse. In the Latin preface to the Old Saxon *Heliand* the term is explained precisely as a section of a poem or a segment suitable for a reading (*lectio*). See Otto Behaghel, *Heliand und Genesis*, 10th edn rev. by Burkhard Taeger (Halle, 1996), p. 2. The authenticity of this preface has been questioned, but the meaning indicated seems confirmed by the gloss *una lectio . fiit* attested both in the glossary called *Erfurt III* and in the recently published Düsseldorf fragment: see Bernhard Bischoff et al., *The Épinal, Erfurt, Werden, and Corpus Glossaries*, Early English Manuscripts in Facsimile, vol. 22 (Copenhagen, 1988), Erfurt, fol. 35, and Düsseldorf, fol. 2.

[8] Scribe A also leaves a space between fitts as a rule, but scribe B does so only once. Both scribes usually end the preceding fitt with punctuation marks.

begin with a *maðelode* formula introducing a speech (VI, VII, VIII, XIIII, XX, XXI, XXII, XXIIII, XXVI, [XXVIIII]), and three of them begin with the narrator speaking in his own voice (*mīne gefrǣge*, *ic gefrægn* – XIII, XXXVII, XXXVIII). Such systematic correlation between fitt-divisions and narrative content may bespeak authorial origin of the segmentation.[9]

§7 Old English poets did not provide their poems with titles, but modern editors invariably compose titles for them. Readers should always remember that the title *Beowulf* has no authority whatever, and we could equally well call the poem *Deeds of Germanic Heroes* or *Men and Monsters in the Ancient North*. (Careful study of the first of the facsimile pages reproduced below should impress on readers' memory the fact that the poem they are reading is untitled in its original state.) The longstanding title *Beowulf* is reasonable enough for practical purposes, since the poem does centre on the hero's life, and it would be pointless for each new editor of the poem to contrive a new title for it. But we should never forget that we have no idea what the poet would have called the poem if asked to name it.

---

[9] On the other hand signs of some confusion in the assigning of fitt-numbers may point rather to scribal origin of the sectional divisions. Besides the omission of three fitt numbers, several of them have been altered in the course of numeration. The last four digits of fitt XXIIII are clearly a later correction (by scribe B?) of the original number, and a digit has been erased from fitts XXVIII and XLI. If the fitts had been marked and the numerals assigned by the poet, then why this scribal confusion in the writing of the numbers? One possible answer: the poet could have marked the divisions, but later scribes could have renumbered the fitts in order to keep serial numbering throughout a manuscript (such as we see in the Junius manuscript, where the sectional divisions of the three separate poems *Genesis*, *Exodus*, and *Daniel* are numbered I through LV seriatim, although with many of the numerals omitted). When scribes A and B were copying *Beowulf*, their exemplar could have been in a manuscript where the fitt numbers started not at I but rather at some advanced number (continuing the numeration of sections from preceding poems in the manuscript), and in that case the scribes would naturally renumber the fitts, and in the course of doing so, they might well blunder occasionally. All in all it seems quite possible that as a rule the structural divisions in poems were authorial while the numeration of the divisions was scribal.

B   Date and Place of Composition

§1 We have seen that the manuscript in which *Beowulf* survives has been dated to around the year 1000. (The first decade in the eleventh century has recently been persuasively proposed.) We have also seen that this manuscript is clearly a copy of an earlier copy of the poem, not an author's holograph. It is quite possible (and was long assumed) that there were many earlier copies of the poem, and that it could have been originally composed centuries before our one surviving manuscript was made. Throughout most of this century there was widespread scholarly agreement that the poem was most likely composed between 650 and 800, some scholars strongly favouring an early date within this period, some a later.

§2 In April 1980 a group of Old English scholars gathered at the University of Toronto to discuss the problem of dating *Beowulf*, and when the conference was over and the proceedings published, it was clear that we know far less about the date of the poem than we had thought.[1] Drawing on linguistic, stylistic, historical, metrical, codicological, and archaeological evidence, participants suggested dates ranging from the eighth century to the eleventh century. The main reason for the collapse of the scholarly consensus which had previously prevailed is the undermining of confidence in linguistic means of determining dates for Old English texts.[2] During the nineteenth and early twentieth centuries scholars had developed a series of phonological and syntactic tests for the dating of Old English verse, and the combined results seemed to indicate that some of the longer narrative poems (e.g. *Beowulf*, *Genesis A*, and *Exodus*) were from the eighth century or earlier while others were later. Consider, for example, ll. 16b and 25b of *Beowulf* as they are preserved in the manuscript:

---

[1] Colin Chase, ed., *The Dating of Beowulf* (Toronto, 1981), reissued with a valuable new introduction by Nicholas P. Howe in 1997. For a judicious summary of the arguments presented in the original volume and a persuasive response to them, see the review article by Theodore M. Andersson in *University of Toronto Quarterly*, 52 (1983), 288–301.

[2] Ashley Crandell Amos, *Linguistic Means of Determining the Dates of Old English Literary Texts*, Medieval Academy Books 90 (Cambridge, MA, 1980), made a definitive and damaging critique of the linguistic criteria in her Yale dissertation completed in 1976 and published in 1980. See further §6 and n. 8 below.

him þæs līffrēa
man geþēon

Neither of these verses will scan. We know, however, that at an earlier
period of Old English *līffrēa* would have had the form *līffrēgea* and *geþēon*
would have had the form *geþēohan*. If we restore these forms to the text,
then the lines scan perfectly. This would seem to indicate that *Beowulf* was
composed long before the copy preserved in MS Cotton Vitellius A. xv was
made, and if we can determine the date at which words like these
underwent the phonological changes we have noted, then we should have
a good reference-point for assigning a period of origin to *Beowulf*. Again,
initial *g-* in Old English was originally pronounced the same no matter what
vowel followed it, but at a later period initial *g-* was sometimes palatalized,
that is pronounced like modern *y-*, and sometimes remained velar, that is
pronounced like modern hard *g-*. Accordingly, later poems alliterate palatal
g- only with palatal *g-* and velar *g-* only with velar *g-*. Since *Beowulf*
alliterates palatal *g-* and velar *g-* indiscriminately, it must be an earlier
composition – at least earlier than the late tenth century, when the change
in metrical practice seems to have occurred. Another phonological development in the course of the Old English period is the simplification of
initial consonant clusters like *hr-*, *hl-*, *hn-*, the *h-* disappearing toward the
end of the period. If words beginning with these clusters alliterate with
other words beginning with *h-*, then obviously the poem in which that
happens is earlier than a poem in which these words alliterate with other
words beginning with *r-*, *l-*, or *n-*. Finally, an example of a syntactic test: in
Beowulf there is an unusually high incidence of weak adjectives modifying
nouns without the expected demonstrative pronoun preceding the adjective. A series of scholars argued that this is a sign of the poem's antiquity
and tried to establish systematic chronological tests based on presence or
absence of definite articles.

§3 Most of these presumed linguistic measures of the dates of texts have
not stood up to close scrutiny. While it is true that numerous verses in
Beowulf become metrical only when contracted forms like *-frēa* and *geþēon*
are decontracted and restored to their earlier form, there are other verses (as
is pointed out below, l. 16 note) which are metrical only if contracted forms
are left contracted, and so this criterion becomes problematic. As for the
handling of initial *hr-*, *hl-*, and *hn-* it has been noted below that the *Beowulf*
poet sometimes alliterates *hraþe* with *r-* and sometimes with *h-*, thus
rendering this test questionable. While the high incidence of weak
adjectives without preceding demonstrative remains an interesting characteristic of *Beowulf*, attempts to establish that there is a steady increase in
the use of demonstratives throughout the history of Old English have
failed, and the usage in *Beowulf* could be attributed to the poet's individual
style or to other factors. Also, this and the other linguistic tests are subject

always to the vagaries of scribal transmission: scribes delete or add demonstratives, respell words, and even decontract contracted forms through analogy. Furthermore, the kinds of linguistic change exemplified here occur at different times and at different rates in different dialect areas, and we cannot be sure where many of the poems (including *Beowulf*) were composed. And even within specific dialect areas it is not always possible to date linguistic changes precisely. For all of these reasons many scholars recently have been persuaded to reject linguistic tests, and the chronology of Old English poetry which had been built on the basis of linguistic features has been set aside.

§4 Without linguistic dating, we are left with more subjective criteria such as style, appeals to archaeology, supposed historical allusions, and the searching out of proper names from *Beowulf* in royal genealogies and attempting to deduce dating (and localization) from them. One historical fact that has received a great deal of attention and interpretation from *Beowulf* scholars is the Scandinavian invasion and colonization of Anglo-Saxon England, which gets seriously under way in the early ninth century. Conybeare in 1826 says that because of its subject matter *Beowulf* 'must in all probability be referred to the Dano-Saxon period',[3] and in recent years several scholars have returned to this view; but other scholars, and most notably Dorothy Whitelock,[4] have argued the precise opposite: because of its subject, they say, *Beowulf* could *not* have been composed after the Scandinavian invasions, because no Anglo-Saxon audience would have tolerated the celebration of a heroic Danish past while Danes 'are burning their homes, pillaging their churches, ravaging their cattle and crops, killing their countrymen or carrying them off into slavery'.[5] The force of this argument has diminished as historians have attained a fuller sense of the variety and subtlety of Anglo-Scandinavian relations in England over the long period that the two cultures were in contact there.[6] But it is fair to ask whether the Scandinavian subject matter of *Beowulf* is of the same kind and style as the Scandinavian literature produced at the time of the Viking settlements in England and whether the forms of proper names in *Beowulf* reflect the forms they had in the Scandinavian areas. Some have thought that the tales of the Danes and Geatas and Swedes in *Beowulf* have rather the character of lore preserved in the unforgotten legends which Angles, Saxons, and Jutes would have brought with them during the prolonged period when they were migrating to England from southern Scandinavia and northern Germany.

[3] John Josias Conybeare, *Illustrations of Anglo-Saxon Poetry*, ed. William Daniel Conybeare (London, 1826), p. 184.

[4] Dorothy Whitelock, *The Audience of Beowulf* (Oxford, 1951), pp. 24–5.

[5] Whitelock, *Audience*, p. 25.

[6] Whitelock's argument is not without historical precedent, however. In the sixth century BC Cleisthenes, tyrant of Sicyon, suppressed the Homeric rhapsodists who sang the exploits of Argos and the Argives because he was then at war with Argos (Herodotus V. 67).

§5 This derivative quality of *Beowulf* and other Old English poetry might lead us to question the wisdom of the whole enterprise of seeking a precise date for the composition of *Beowulf*. The poem is in part constructed from pre-existing materials – the Finnesburh episode, the Sigemund lay, possibly some of the accounts of Geatish–Swedish wars – and phrasing as well as matter may have been grafted onto the *Beowulf*ian narrative. The thoroughly traditional diction of the poem contains verses and perhaps even clusters of verses which could have been recited in primitive Old English by pagan scops on the Jutland peninsula during the reign of King Hrethel in Skandia. The moving account of Scyld's obsequies could be a purple passage which the poet lifted from an old poem he knew, just as Anglo-Saxon homilists borrowed exempla or rhetorical flourishes from each other or as the *Genesis* poet adopted for his own poem another poet's account of the Fall.[7] How does one assign a precise date to composite art of this kind?

§6 What we usually mean by 'date of composition' is the approximate date when the tradition-bound, accretive process we call *Beowulf* assumed more or less the shape it has in the copy we have in Cotton Vitellius A. xv. Broad designations of time like 'the age of Bede' or 'the reign of Offa' (two periods which have been suggested for the poem's composition) are more appropriate than precise dates to describe the time when *Beowulf* took something like the form it has today, and in these broad terms it should be possible to give some indication of when the poem assumed its present dimensions. Despite the widespread despair over linguistic dating, there is substantial agreement that the alliteration of palatal and velar *g* in *Beowulf* rules out the late Old English period as a probable time of composition. And the cumulative evidence of some of the other linguistic tests (such as a significant number of contracted forms which must be decontracted for metre's sake or of disyllables like *wǣpen* and *tācen* which must be restored to their originally monosyllabic forms *wǣpn* and *tācn* for metricality) can probably be taken as symptoms of earliness. Several studies since the Toronto conference argue persuasively that linguistic evidence points to an earlier rather than a later time of origin,[8] and several other recent studies have argued for an early date from other kinds of evidence.[9] We believe

---

[7] Of course it could be a scribe or compiler who united *Genesis A* and *B*.

[8] E.g. Claus-Dieter Wetzel, 'Die Datierung des *Beowulf*: Bemerkungen zur jüngsten Forschungsentwicklung', *Anglia*, 103 (1985), 371–400; Janet Bately, 'Linguistic Evidence as a Guide to the Authorship of Old English Verse: A Reappraisal, with Special Reference to *Beowulf*', in *Learning and Literature in Anglo-Saxon England*, eds Michael Lapidge and Helmut Gneuss (Cambridge, 1985), pp. 409–31; and R. D. Fulk, *A History of Old English Meter* (Philadelphia, 1992), *passim*.

[9] E.g. Sam Newton, *The Origins of Beowulf and the Pre-Viking Kingdom of East Anglia* (Cambridge, 1993); Peter Clemoes, *Interactions of Thought and Language in Old English Poetry* (Cambridge, 1995), pp. xii, 30–72 *passim*; and, somewhat earlier, Michael Lapidge, '*Beowulf*, Aldhelm, the *Liber Monstrorum* and Wessex', *Studi Medievali*, 3rd ser. 23 (1982), 151–92, and Michael J. Swanton, *Crisis and Development in Germanic Society 700–800: Beowulf and the Burden of Kingship*, Göppinger Arbeiten zur Germanistik 333 (Göppingen, 1982).

that the balance of linguistic and non-linguistic evidence gives some credence to a broad date for the composition of *Beowulf* which was urged as long ago as 1968: 680–800.[10] If readers of the poem imagine *Beowulf* to come down to us from a world such as existed in this era, we believe they will be closer to envisioning an appropriate cultural context for the poem than they will if they assume that the poem was composed at the same time as our surviving manuscript of it was written – or if they join the despairing scholars who think that since we don't know everything we don't know anything and therefore decline to conceive any date at all for the composition of the poem.[11]

§7 No less difficult than finding a date for the time of the poem's composition is trying to determine where in Anglo-Saxon England the poem was put into approximately its present form. *Beowulf*, like most Old English poems, is not composed in a single, pure Old English dialect which would enable us to trace its place of birth through its language. The poem is predominantly West Saxon, like the other texts in the manuscript, which, like the majority of surviving manuscripts, was most likely copied in a West Saxon scriptorium. But there is an admixture of other dialectal forms, most notably Anglian. The dialectal mixture which characterizes most Old English poems has been explained as the result of a deliberate development of a trans-dialectal poetic diction which would have made poems intelligible in all dialect areas and would have given them a distinctive poetic language.[12] If this theory is true, then discerning place of origin through scrutinizing the language would be impossible. But many scholars over the years have seen *Beowulf* as most likely an originally Anglian poem surviving in a West Saxon copy. Anglian could mean either Northumbrian or Mercian, and both of these have had their proponents. As with assigning a date, perhaps it is best to seek the broadest possible characterization and say that the language of the poem suggests that it is quite possibly an originally Anglian text preserved in a West Saxon copy. Efforts to be more specific than this based on non-linguistic evidence are highly interesting, but none seems to have found general acceptance.

§8 As important to our understanding of the poem as its geographical place of origin is the cultural setting in which it was composed and

---

[10] *Beowulf*, trans. Kevin Crossley-Holland and intro. Bruce Mitchell (Cambridge and New York, 1968), p. 5. In view of the habitual scribal infidelities alluded to above (IA4), we would not claim that the text composed in this time-period would be identical with the text preserved in Cotton Vitellius A. xv, however; rather the two texts might bear about the same degree of similarity to each other as the text of the late tenth-century Exeter Book riddle no. 35 (Anglo-Saxon Poetic Records numeration) bears to the early ninth-century copy of the same riddle, the *Leiden Riddle*.

[11] For an excellent meditation on both the difficulty and the importance of finding a date for *Beowulf* see Roy Michael Liuzza, 'On the Dating of *Beowulf*', in Peter S. Baker, ed., *Beowulf: Basic Readings* (New York and London, 1995), pp. 281–302.

[12] Kenneth Sisam, 'Dialect Origins of the Earlier Old English Verse', in *Studies in the History of Old English Literature* (Oxford, 1953), pp. 119–39, esp. pp. 138–9.

performed. Dorothy Whitelock did a great deal to characterize the presumed audience of the poem,[13] and subsequently Patrick Wormald has approached the question with thoughtful reasoning.[14] He envisions the poem's milieu as an English Christian community which had retained many of its Germanic cultural traditions. The English warrior nobility in the eighth century was such a community, and any of the secularized monasteries in which aristocrats gathered and which had close ties with royal courts would provide the kind of setting where *Beowulf* could be produced and appreciated. The Mercian royal house is cited as an example of such integration of Germanic aristocratic ideals and patronage of religious foundations. Many things about *Beowulf*'s concerns and attitudes would make sense in the context of Wormald's proposed audience for the poem.[15]

[13] Whitelock, *Audience, passim*.

[14] Patrick Wormald, 'Bede, *Beowulf* and the Conversion of the Anglo-Saxon Aristocracy', in Robert T. Farrell, ed., *Bede and Anglo-Saxon England* (Oxford, 1978), pp. 32–95.

[15] Newton, *Origins*, supports with further evidence the kind of setting Wormald presents (see especially pp. 19–20, 135), but he argues specifically for an eighth-century East Anglian place of origin.

C   The Language

§1 The language of *Beowulf* is in most respects like that of other Old English poems that students may have read and requires that they attend to the same stylistic and linguistic features of the text. As in other poetry, the word-order is relatively free, thus requiring students to remain alert to grammatical endings, which show us how the words relate to each other and how the sentences may be rephrased into modern English word-order. Parallelism (see the discussion of 'variation' below, IE8–9) is ubiquitous, and again grammatical endings enable us to identify which elements are parallel with which other elements. Nouns usually have no definite or indefinite article preceding them, and these must be supplied in translating if modern idiom is to be observed. Thus in reading the first sentence in the poem –

> Wē Gār-Dena   in geārdagum
> þēodcyninga   þrym gefrūnon,
> hū ðā æþelingas   ellen fremedon –

we see first the nominative plural pronoun *Wē*, and our eye scans the ensuing words to find a verb with plural ending to go with the pronoun. On doing so, we encounter *gefrūnon*, and we translate 'we learned about' or 'we have learned about'. (A past tense verb may be translated 'we learned about', 'we have learned about', or 'we did learn about' depending on which gives smoothest sense in modern English.) Now we need a direct object for the verb *gefrūnon*, and the accusative noun *þrym* 'glory' standing directly next to it is the logical candidate. We did not select *Gār-Dena*, because the *-a* of *Dena* tells us that it is a genitive plural noun, and *gefrūnon* requires an accusative object. But now we do have a place for *Gār-Dena* as a genitive plural qualifying *þrym* – 'glory of spear-Danes' – and we note that *þēodcyninga* also ends with the genitive plural sign *-a*, indicating that it is parallel with *Gār-Dena*. (For an alternative explanation, see ll. 1–2 note.) Supplying the definite articles required by modern idiom, we translate 'We have learned about the glory of the spear-Danes, of the kings of the people' and adding the prepositional phrase *in geārdagum*, we translate 'We have learned about the glory of the spear-Danes, of the kings of the people, in days of yore.' Next comes a characteristic example of parallelism in Old English verse: the entire subordinate clause *hū ðā æþelingas ellen fremedon* is parallel with the accusative noun *þrym* and provides a second direct object of the verb *gefrūnon*: 'We have learned about the glory of the spear-Danes, of the kings of the people, in days of yore (we have learned about) how those noblemen performed valour.' (When we encountered the nominative plural *æþelingas*, the nominative plural ending *-as* led us to repeat the step of seeking a plural verb to go with it, and *fremedon* proved to be the only candidate.) The word *ðā* is actually ambiguous: it could be the nominative plural demonstrative pronoun, as we have translated it here, or it could be the adverb *ðā* and the clause could be translated 'how noblemen then performed valour'. The meaning difference is trivial, and so the ambiguity need not detain us. To some modern ears 'performed valour' may sound a little odd; 'performed deeds of valour' would perhaps be more natural. In Old English poets sometimes used abstract nouns in concrete senses, and therefore we are at liberty to translate *ellen* as 'deeds of valour'.

§2 Talking readers through the translation of a sentence in this detailed way may seem to be making a relatively simple procedure appear complicated, but in fact we could continue the analysis further by scrutinizing suffixes. The verb *gefrūnon* in l. 2 consists of the preterite plural *-frūnon* 'asked' with the prefix *ge-* affixed to it. In this instance the *ge-* carries perfective force and changes the sense of the verb to 'asked to completion' – i.e. 'asked and received an answer' or 'learned'. The suffix *-ing* in the words *-cyninga* and *æþelingas* means 'son of' or 'descendant of', and the literal meaning of these two words would be 'descendants of the kin [i.e. the royal kindred]' and 'descendants of the noble'. Thus we see that in this sentence the original language of the poem had an emphasis on heredity which is lost in our renderings 'kings' and 'noblemen'.

§3 In preparing to read *Beowulf* we may find it useful to review some other features of the Old English language that we have encountered in past readings of poetry and that we shall be encountering as we proceed through our text:

1 Adjectives are frequently used as nouns (as in modern English expressions like 'the good die young' or 'the poor you will always have with you'): thus *sigehrēþig* 'victorious' in *gesette sigehrēþig sunnan ond mōnan* (94) 'the victorious [one] established the sun and the moon' or *gomela* 'old' in *Āhlēop ðā se gomela* (1397) 'then the old [one] leapt up'.

2 As in modern English locutions such as 'I want [to go] out of here' and '[I] Thank you' and '[You] Be good!' there are sometimes unexpressed elements in Old English sentences: *wolde ūt þanon* (1292) '[She] wanted [to go] out of there'; *Cōm þā tō Heorote* (1279) '[She] Came then to Heorot'; *lēton holm beran, / gēafon on gārsecg* (48–9) '[they] let the sea bear [him], gave [him] to the ocean'; *þǣr mæg nihta gehwǣm nīðwundor*

sēon (1365) 'There [one] can see a fearful wonder every night'; *swā hyt nō sceolde* (2585) 'as it should not [do]'.

3 While singular subjects usually have singular verbs and plural subjects plural verbs, there are exceptions. For example, when the verb precedes a plural subject, it is usually singular: *Gehwearf þā in Francna fæþm feorh cyninges, / brēostgewǣdu ond se bēah somod* (1210–11) 'the king's life, his armour, and the necklace all together passed [sg.] into the possession of the Franks'.

4 Very often a *þæt* clause is introduced by a preceding *þæt* in a way that seems pleonastic to modern speakers: *Ic þæt gehȳre, þæt þis is hold weorod* (290) 'I hear *that*, [namely,] *that* this is a loyal troop'; *Hwæt, þæt secgan mæg / efne swā hwylc mægþa swā ðone magan cende . . . þæt hyre ealdmetod ēste wǣre* (942–5) 'Lo, whatever woman gave birth to that man can say *that*, [namely,] *that* the ancient measurer was gracious to her.'

5 Plurals are sometimes used with singular meaning: *Ðǣm eafera wæs æfter cenned / geong in geardum* (12–13) 'To that one afterward an heir was born, young in the dwelling [lit., dwellings]'; *þanon eft gewāt / . . . wīca nēosan* (123–5) 'thence he went back to seek out his dwelling-place [lit., dwelling-places]'; *Ðā wæs on burgum Bēowulf Scyldinga* (53) 'Then Beowulf of the Scyldings was in the stronghold [lit., strongholds]'; *wē þē þās sǣlāc . . . lustum brōhton* (1652–3) 'we have brought these sea-trophies to you with pleasure [lit., pleasures]'.

6 The dative plural of nouns sometimes signals adverbial function: *slāt unwearnum* (741) 'tore unrestrainedly'; *ond his ellenweorc / duguðum dēmdon* (3173–4) 'and they praised his valiant deeds highly'.

7 The possessive dative is used in many contexts where modern English uses the genitive: *Him on bearme læg / mādma mænigo* (40–1) 'many treasures lay on his bosom'; *him wæs geōmor sefa* (49) 'his mind was sad'; *Dyde him of healse hring gyldenne* (2809) 'he removed the golden necklace from his neck'; *þǣr wæs Æschere, frōdan fyrnwitan feorh ūðgenge* (2122–3) 'then the life of Æschere, of the wise counsellor, was departing'.

§4 The foregoing comments call attention to some of the features of the Old English language which students must bear in mind as they translate *Beowulf*. We should also address the more scholarly question of what is distinctive about the language of *Beowulf*. Can the language of the poem tell us anything about the origin and history of *Beowulf*? A detailed analysis of the language of the poem is available elsewhere.[1] Here we shall comment briefly on its general character.

§5 Basically the language of the poem is late West Saxon, which we

---

[1] Angus Cameron, Ashley Crandell Amos, and Gregory Waite with the assistance of Sharon Butler and Antonette diPaolo Healey, 'A Reconsideration of the Language of *Beowulf*', in Colin Chase, ed., *The Dating of Beowulf*, reprinted with an introduction by Nicholas P. Howe (Toronto, 1997), pp. 33–75.

assume was the dialect of the two scribes who produced our copy of *Beowulf* in Cotton Vitellius A. xv. It was normal for scribes to alter texts they were copying to conform more or less with their own dialects. But *Beowulf* also has early West Saxon features and non-West Saxon (mainly Anglian) features. Words like *gēn, gēna, symbel, þrēat, bront, gerysne, hægsteald, tīd, wīsfæst, ācweþan, gefēon, sceþþan,* and others give a strongly Anglian flavour to the poet's diction, but it must be mentioned that these words also occur in other poetry preserved in basically late West Saxon form and seem to have been typical of poetic language generally. Spellings like *nīðhēdig* for *nīðhȳdig,* many of the *īo* and *io* spellings, and spellings like *geomor* for *Ēomēr* and *gende* for *gengde,* however, look like Kentish symptoms. And spelling variations like *dryhten, drihten; dēore, dīore, dȳre; Eafores, Eofores; ealdor, aldor; eahtian, æhtian, ehtian; giest, gist, gyst, gæst, gest; gifan, gyfan, giofan; lifað, lyfað, leofað; seoððan, siððan, syððan* suggest a kind of random variation that justifies Klaeber's conclusion 'that the text was copied a number of times, and that scribes of heterogeneous dialectal habits and different individual peculiarities had a share in that work'.[2] This seems especially likely when we recall that the other texts copied by the two scribes of Cotton Vitellius A. xv do not show the same kind of variation. We believe that Klaeber's hypothesis is more credible than the view that this orthographic and dictional melange was concocted by one person late in the Anglo-Saxon period.

---

[2] Klaeber, *Beowulf,* pp. lxxxviii–lxxxix. Other poems which also show such variation could have had similar transmissional histories.

D   Structure

§1   The narration of events in the poem is reasonably clear, and readers should have little difficulty following the story of Beowulf's life. But the narrative is at times embellished and interrupted with ornaments and devices that some readers have found disconcerting. There are sudden flash-forwards like ll. 81–5, where the poet pauses in his narration to tell us of a future event bearing on the matter at hand. Or a chronological lurch to the past may interrupt the flow of events, as in ll. 2610–25. Characters unrelated to the immediate context may be introduced simply for the purpose of pointing a contrast or comparison (e.g. ll. 1931–62 and 1197–1201). Narrative repetitions take place, as when Beowulf, having returned home from his exploits in Denmark, retells the events which the poet has just narrated in the preceding 1700 lines. Most arresting, perhaps, is the way the poem breaks into two narrative units: Beowulf's youth (ll. 1–2199) and Beowulf's old age (ll. 2200–3182), with a fifty-year gap between the two time-periods. *Beowulf* might be described (as Dr Johnson described Milton's *Samson Agonistes*) as having a beginning and end with no middle, echoing Aristotle's dictum that every plot should have a beginning, middle, and end. But at this point we must remind ourselves that Aristotle and the entire classical tradition which we tend to think of as a cultural universal have nothing to do with *Beowulf*, which stands outside the orbit of western classical culture. *Beowulf* was composed not according to a classical western aesthetic but rather according to a barbaric aesthetic, in which plot and decorum and linear narrative do not have the same meaning as they do in our aesthetic derived from the ancient Greeks. In order to appreciate *Beowulf* we must examine some of the principles and devices peculiar to it and to other Germanic poems and try to understand their purpose and effect.

Anticipation of Future Events

§2   Early in the poem, as the poet narrates how King Hrothgar gives orders for men to construct a splendid royal hall and with what happy results they do so (ll. 64–82), he pauses suddenly and announces that in future years this monument to Danish power, splendour, and prosperity will be destroyed by fire when feuding breaks out in the royal family. Again, at the celebration of Beowulf's victory over the monster Grendel, Queen Wealhtheow bestows upon the hero a magnificent golden neck-ring of legendary beauty (ll. 1192–1201), but at this joyous moment the poet leaps forward in time and says that the golden neck-ring will on a future occasion be involved in one of the greatest disasters ever to befall Beowulf's nation (ll. 1202–14). In describing how the Danes were faring when he left them, Beowulf depicts an almost idyllic scene of harmony and joy (ll. 2014–16), but then he predicts a disastrous breakdown in Danish affairs in the future, which will bathe the nation in blood (ll. 2016–69). Near the end of the poem when Wiglaf and Beowulf have succeeded in slaying the dragon and gaining an enormous treasure-trove for the nation, the scene is repeatedly darkened with predictions of the doom of the nation in the near future. The function and significance of these glances to the future throughout *Beowulf* will be apparent from this summary of them. The anticipations are part of the poet's pattern of undercutting moments of success and happiness by pointing to disasters to come. The anticipation of future events is a device for showing that in the ancient heroic world no triumph is lasting and even men's greatest accomplishments cannot escape the doom that overhangs all.

Recollections of Past Events

§3 The poet also leaves the poem's present time occasionally to invoke some past event or personage. Sometimes this seems to be for the purpose of exalting the persons and events of the narrative by suggesting that they partake of a rich, legendary past and are comparable with immemorial heroes and deeds. The splendid gold ring that Wealhtheow presents to Beowulf is compared to a fabulous necklace which is said to have played a part in fourth-century exploits of the Gothic King Eormenric (ll. 1197–1201). Hrothgar's scop recalls the legendary dragon-slayer – Sigemund or his son Siegfried; see ll. 875–97 note – in celebrating Beowulf's victory over Grendel (ll. 874–97), implying that Beowulf has earned a place among the most revered of Germanic heroes. At the beginning of the poem Hrothgar's lofty status is established by a retrospective account of his illustrious forebears and especially of the eponymous King Scyld. But allusions to the past can also be for the purpose of citing negative examples. The violent King Heremod (whose banishment left the Danes in the leaderless state which was remedied by Scyld's mysterious arrival) is cited repeatedly as an example of what a hero and king should avoid becoming. And Queen Hygd of the Geats calls to mind the evil conduct of the fourth-century Angle

Queen Thryth as a reminder of what she herself does not want to become (ll. 1931–62).

§4 Of extraordinary interest is the recitation by Hrothgar's scop of an episode in Danish history involving the Frisian King Finn. A group of Danes who are visiting Finn (who is married to the Danish princess Hildeburh) are treacherously attacked by the Frisians. The ensuing fight in which their leader Hnæf is slain ends in stalemate, and an uneasy truce is patched up between the Danes and the slayer of their lord. The Danes endure this intolerable situation only until an opportunity for vengeance presents itself, at which point they kill King Finn and other Frisians and restore Hildeburh to her homeland. Why does the *Beowulf* poet introduce this episode from the Danish past into his narrative? Presumably the scop and his audience would have seen an appropriate parallel between their deliverance from the longstanding depredations of Grendel and this earlier occasion when the Danes, after being forced to suffer humiliation at the hands of an aggressor, finally prevail and take fitting vengeance. Some readers have seen tragic irony in the recounting of the tale of Finnesburh as well. While to the Danes in Heorot the episode mirrors their deliverance from Grendel, the audience of *Beowulf*, presumably knowledgeable about events in later Danish history to which the poet alludes, may have seen a parallel between the sad fate of Hildeburh, who sees brother, son, and husband die in internecine conflict, and Wealhtheow, who, some believe, will in future years see her sons slain by their cousin Hrothulf following the death of her husband. This would explain the curious emphasis on Hildeburh, with whom the episode begins and ends, and the introduction of Wealhtheow immediately after the recitation of the Finnesburh story (ll. 1162ff). But those who do not believe that Hrothulf was a traitor find this second level of allusion improbable; see ll. 1017b–19 note.

§5 What is most interesting about the Finnesburh narrative, however, is that we have an independent poem (unfortunately fragmentary) recounting the tale of the Danes at Finnesburh. This is a dramatic example of the *Beowulf* poet drawing on pre-existing material for his own narrative. There are some uncertainties as to just how the details of the Finnesburh episode in *Beowulf* relate to the details in the Finnesburh fragment (which is included in IVD4 below with translation provided), but there can be no doubt that the fragment is an independent telling of the same story that the Danish scop tells in *Beowulf*. This has led some scholars to wonder what other material in *Beowulf* could have been the subject of earlier poems in Old English – the story of Sigemund (or Siegfried) and the dragon, the wars of Onela and Ongentheow, the contention between Hama and Eormenric, the saga of Ingeld and Freawaru? (The last is a particularly likely candidate since Alcuin alludes to songs about Ingeld in his often-quoted letter of AD 797; see IVE4.) The possibility that the *Beowulf* poet was drawing on a range of pre-existing poems raises the question whether

Beowulf, rather than being a randomly surviving tale about one hero's life and exploits, is not perhaps a kind of poetic summa of the Germanic heroic age, one which seeks to preserve and take the measure of a whole era and many nations. The poems *Widsith* and *Deor* (included and translated in IVD1 and 2) also draw together allusions to a broad range of Germanic personages, and so it is not unprecedented for Anglo-Saxon poets to see their past not as simply English but as pan-Germanic and to incorporate an encyclopedic component into their narrative structure.

Repetition

§6 Repetition is an important structural device in *Beowulf*. The poet's placing funeral scenes at the beginning and end of his narrative not only frames the poem while emphasizing the theme of how heroes die, but it also places the events firmly in the pre-Christian past since the funerals are both distinctly pagan. The repetition of the motif of the fifty-year reign in ll. 1770–1 and 2208–9 emphasizes the parallel drawn between old Hrothgar at the beginning of the poem and old Beowulf at the end, and this parallel is reinforced by the poet's occasionally using the same formulaic phrases to refer to the aged Beowulf as he had formerly used to refer to the aged king Hrothgar. (Similarly phrases used of young Beowulf are repeated late in the poem in reference to young Wiglaf, thus suggesting another parallel of characters.) Other uses of repetition are more extensive. In ll. 106–14 the poet spells out carefully Grendel's descent from Cain. In ll. 1261–7, as Grendel's mother is introduced, the poet repeats the Grendelkin's descent from Cain. The repetition is understandable, for it is the biblical explanation for the Grendelkin's origins that makes the pagan hero Beowulf an unwitting ally of the Christian forces arrayed against evil as embodied in Cain, and this is an important part of the poet's strategy in giving Beowulf dignity and status in the eyes of a Christian audience. Each time the hero does battle with the Grendelkin the poet wants to remind us of the theological significance of his combat.

§7 The most remarkable example of repetition in *Beowulf* is the hero's report to Hygelac in ll. 2000–151, where Beowulf narrates again everything we have just been told took place in Denmark. Is any use served by this odd narrative structure? One suggestion that has been made is that the poem may have been read aloud in three sittings in Anglo-Saxon times and that the repetition both of the Grendelkin's descent from Cain and of Beowulf's exploits in Denmark may have been reminders to the audience of what had been narrated in the preceding reading. But if the repetitions served this very practical function (and we do not know that they did), we would expect a skilful poet to find a way for them to serve some artistic purpose as well. And in fact, Beowulf's long report to Hygelac does contribute to the telling of the story. First, a careful comparison of the two accounts of the Danish excursion (the poet's and Beowulf's) will show that their content is not identical. Beowulf's account includes a number of details not found in the poet's narration, most notably the entire Ingeld–Freawaru story. Beowulf also omits things told in the first account, such as the contention with Unferth. This omission could be part of the poet's characterization of Beowulf as so magnanimous in spirit that he leaves unmentioned a detail that could put the Danes in a poor light, even though he had been victorious in the debate. In fact the greatest contribution which the repetition makes to our understanding of the poem is precisely the insight it gives us into Beowulf's character. We get to see events through his eyes and to see something of his mental capacities. In his account of the Ingeld–Freawaru episode, for example, we learn how shrewd a judge of people and policy Beowulf is, for the predictions he makes about the breakdown of the marriage and the alliance are all borne out by the surviving analogues, which indicate that things happened just as Beowulf had surmised they would. The repetition may not have been what Aristotle would have approved, but in its barbaric way it helps get the story told.

Macrostructure

§8 The foregoing discussion has suggested that structurally *Beowulf* is composed of static comparisons and contrasts as much as it is of linear narration. Even the repetitions induce us to compare one account with another. This fondness for diptych-like structures probably explains why the poet structures *Beowulf* itself like a diptych, with the account of Beowulf's youth standing in stark contrast with the account of Beowulf's old age, the two being separated by a fifty-year gap announced in a single remarkable sentence in ll. 2200–14. J. R. R. Tolkien describes this structure in his lecture '*Beowulf:* The Monsters and the Critics':

> It is essentially a balance, an opposition of ends and beginnings. In its simplest terms it is a contrasted description of two moments in a great life, rising and setting; an elaboration of the ancient and intensely moving contrast between youth and age, first achievement and final death. . . . This simple and *static* structure, solid and strong, is in each part much diversified, and capable of enduring this treatment.

The diversification consists of the devices described in the foregoing parts of this discussion of structure. Some of them – the allusions to past and future events, the elements introduced for the sake of contrast – supply a good deal of information about the events of Beowulf's life during the fifty-year period which separates Beowulf's youth from his age. The fact that the poet had access to this information but preferred to communicate it through allusions and reminiscences (especially the long descriptions of past wars in the latter part of the poem) rather than in direct sequential narration shows how deliberate and artful is his concern to present his story as a bipartite contrast of youth and age.

§9 But concurrent with this bipartite structure is a tripartite organization of events. The poem unfolds as an account of three great encounters between the hero and his monstrous adversaries. The poet is at some pains to emphasize this three-stage movement in the poem by repetitive patterning and dramatic development. Each of the hero's battles is preceded by a speech in which Beowulf declares his intentions. The poet is careful to inform the audience of the outcome of each battle before it takes place (ll. 696–700, 1553–6, 2419–24), cliff-hanging suspense being no part of his design. Each battle is more difficult than the preceding one. The adversaries struggle mightily in Beowulf's encounter with Grendel, but the hero decisively defeats his foe fairly quickly. The fight with Grendel's mother in her cave proves more difficult and the hero nearly dies, being saved only by the lucky discovery of a supernatural sword that enables him to dispatch the ogress. The last monster is so powerful that the hero cannot defeat him without help from a comrade, and he is himself killed.

§10 The poet deliberately highlights the ascending challenges presented by Beowulf's adversaries by providing each battle with a dramatic audience whose reaction measures the formidability of the monsters. In the fight with Grendel, Beowulf is surrounded by loyal comrades who attempt (although ineffectually) to assist him. In the fight with Grendel's mother the Geats and Danes who accompany Beowulf to the battle site despair when they see blood come to the surface of the water, and the Danes actually abandon the watch for the hero, being convinced he is dead. In the fight with the dragon Beowulf's companions all flee in terror when the monster breathes fire on the hero. (One, Wiglaf, then has second thoughts and returns to aid his leader.) The hero's reliance on weaponry also emphasizes the tripartite progression. Before the Grendel-fight Beowulf forswears the use of any weapon at all, vowing to grapple with Grendel bare-handed. In the fight with Grendel's mother he is persuaded to take Unferth's sword, and when it fails him, he uses the sword he finds in the cave to kill his foe. And in the fight with the dragon he is fully armed and orders a special iron shield forged for his protection, apologizing in effect for needing so much help in the battle (ll. 2518–24).

§11 Although quite different from the ordering principles in most western narratives, these interlocking structural patterns – a bipartite chronological structure together with a tripartite narrative development – give the poem a coherence that leaves no doubt of the poet's artistic control over his matter.

E   Style, Tone, and Metre

Style

§1 The language of poetry is different from the language of prose. Besides freer word-order, the vocabulary of poetry is distinctive. Many words occur exclusively in poetry, e.g. *beorn* 'warrior', *brego* 'lord', *brenting* 'ship', *byre* 'son', *cringan* 'fall [in battle]', *cumbol* 'banner', *dēor*, 'brave', *eafoð* 'strength', *gād* 'lack', *ōretta* 'warrior', *ræswa* 'prince', *reced* 'hall', *rōf* 'strong'. Sometimes a word has one meaning in poetry and another in prose. Thus *swātig* means 'bloody' in verse but 'sweaty' in prose. Of course not all words in poetry are exclusively poetic words; many words occur freely in both prose and verse. (And another large group is restricted to prose.) But the poetic words are common enough in verse so that if an Anglo-Saxon began reading a text aloud, his audience would know immediately if he were reading poetry or prose.

§2 Besides the distinctive vocabulary, there is a great deal distinctive about the way words are used in poetry. Over the centuries of oral and then written verse composition poets evolved a vast number of set expressions which are used again and again in Old English verse; e.g. *gomban gyldan* 'pay tribute', *gēong in geardum* 'young in the courtyards', *folce tō frōfre* 'as a comfort to the people', *tō wīdan fēore* 'ever', *ofer ganotes bæð* 'over the gannet's bathing place (i.e. over the ocean)' all occur in *Beowulf*, but they also occur in other poems as well. This does not indicate that one poet has borrowed phrases from another poet's work. These set expressions were part of a common poetic diction shared by all poets. They all fit the metrical requirements of a single verse or half-line, and many of them alliterate. These metrical properties of the phrases are a major reason why they are so useful for poets: they provide the way to express many concepts in units of speech which are already prepared to fit metrically into a line of verse. The technical term for these phrases is 'formulas', and formulas permeate the diction of *Beowulf*, giving it a lofty and highly traditional character. Around the middle of the twentieth century a school of scholars devoted intensive study to the formulas of Old English poetry, and some drew the conclusion that since formulas have their origin in oral composition, then any poem containing formulas must be an orally improvised composition. Few people hold this simplistic view now. While we all recognize that the ancient Germanic tradition of oral poetry lies behind the surviving corpus of Old English (and Old Saxon, Old High German, and Old Norse) verse, and that many of the distinctive features of that verse result from the oral tradition, few if any of these poems preserved in carefully lettered manuscripts were oral compositions. *Beowulf*, with its artfully conceived structure, polished style, and occasionally complex syntax, is certainly not the product of oral improvisation.

§3 The formulas are actually just one element in the highly patterned diction and syntax of *Beowulf*. There are also formulaic systems – families of phrases which all have a common underlying metrical and syntactical pattern but which can be varied by substitution of words. Thus a formulaic system for expressing the idea 'over the ocean' in a type C verse (see 'Metre' below) and with a vivid image is *ofer —— rāde*. Depending upon what kind of image the poet wants to introduce and depending on what alliterative sound is required, he will choose any one of a number of words to complete the formulaic system: *ofer hronrāde* 'over the whale's path', *ofer swanrāde* 'over the swan's path', *ofer seglrāde* 'over the sail's path'; it should be noted that the last two formulas both alliterate on *s-*. The poet was evidently free to choose the formula that projected the image he judged to be most suitable to the context; the selection of formulas was not determined purely by metrical exigency, as some formulaic scholars once claimed.

§4 Another prominent formulaic system is the verse which often introduces a speech: the loquitur, *—— maþelode*. The poet could fill the blank with any disyllabic name of appropriate syllable length and have a ready-to-hand verse: *Bēowulf maþelode*, *Hrōðgār maðelode*, *Unferð maþelode*, *Wealhðēo maþelode*, *Wīglāf maðelode*, *Wulfgār maðelode*. These formulas always occur in the first half-line (in other Old English poems as well as *Beowulf*). This is a good example of the highly patterned, almost schematized quality of the language of *Beowulf*, and one will become increasingly aware of this quality as one proceeds through the poem for the first time.

§5 And yet within these patterns and conventions there was a good deal of leeway for poetic originality. Seven hundred of the words in *Beowulf* are unique to this poem, and while some of these terms may well have been used in other poems which have not survived, others are very likely of the poet's own coinage. In l. 1606, for example, the poet says that the swordblade with which Beowulf decapitated Grendel melted in the monster's poisonous blood *hildegicelum* 'in battle-icicles'. It is hard to imagine that such a peculiar circumstance existed in many other narratives, and so *hildegicel* is very likely to be a coinage of the poet's. We may suspect that *mūðbona* 'mouth-slayer' (l. 2079) used of the cannibalistic Grendel and *ūhtfloga* 'dawn-flyer' (l. 2760) used of the dragon may also be original coinages. Again, there are tricks of style in *Beowulf* which strike one as characteristic of this particular poet rather than being simply conventional. When he introduces Grendel into the narrative and later when he introduces the dragon the poet uses the same ominous phrasing: *oð ðæt ān ongan . . . fēond* 'until a certain one began, an enemy' (ll. 100–1), *oð ðæt ān ongan . . . draca* 'until a certain one began, a dragon' (ll. 2210–11). Now the verb form *ongan* occurs exactly one hundred times, the variant *ongon* twenty-eight times, and *ongann* eighteen times in Old English poetry, but the verse *oð ðæt ān ongan* is unique to *Beowulf*. As in many other passages in the poem, we seem here to be hearing the distinctive voice of the *Beowulf* poet.

§6 One of the hallmarks of Old English poetic diction is the abundance of compounds. There is poetic power in the compression of such words, as Shakespeare sensed when writing verses like 'vaunt-couriers of oak-cleaving thunderbolts' (*King Lear*, III, ii, 5). A peculiarly Germanic feature, compounds interact particularly well with the verse-patterns of Old Germanic and seem to be intimately cooperative with the metre. Often they have figurative force: *brēostwylm* 'breast-welling (i.e. tear, emotion)', *sceadugenga* 'walker in shade (i.e. nocturnal visitant)', *hringedstefna* 'ship with a curved prow', *feorhsēoc* 'life-sick (i.e. mortally wounded)', *gomen-wudu* 'mirth-wood (i.e. lyre)'. Another characteristic type of two-part construction is the noun linked with another noun in the genitive case: *hringa fengel* 'lord of the rings', *sinces brytta* 'distributor of treasure (i.e. prince)', *heofones wyn* 'heaven's joy (i.e. the sun)'. This type of construction is closely related to the compound, and sometimes the two are used interchangeably: in *Beowulf* we find both *eorlgestrēon* and *eorla gestrēon*, *gumdryhten* and *gumena dryhten*, *ȳðgewinn* and *ȳða gewinn*.

§7 These bipartite constructions sometimes form what are known as kennings. When the base word (i.e. the second element of a compound or the noun qualified by a genitive noun) is wholly metaphorical, that is when it literally refers to something different from the referent, then the construction is a kenning. Examples are *bānhūs* 'house of bone (i.e. human body)', *beadolēoma* 'battle-light (i.e. sword)', *gūðwine* 'war-friend (i.e. sword)', *heofones gim* 'heaven's jewel (i.e. sun)', *merehrægl* 'sea-garment (i.e. sail)', *rodores candel* 'sky's candle (i.e. sun)'. These are all kennings because the human body is not literally a house, a sword is not literally a light or a friend, the sun is not literally a jewel or a candle, and a sail is not literally a garment. But the modifying element combined with context leads the reader to understand that the base word is a metaphor, a comparison of the referent with something different from itself but which the poet has perceived as being in some sense similar to it. These highly characteristic Germanic expressions should not be confused with expressions like *bēaga brytta* 'dispenser of treasure (i.e. king)', *bēahgyfa* 'giver of treasure (i.e. king)', *homera lāf* 'leaving of the hammers (i.e. sword)', *lyftfloga* 'flyer through the air (i.e. dragon)', *mægenwudu* 'wood of power (i.e. spear)', *wegflota* 'floater on the wave (i.e. ship)'. These are not kennings because kings literally did give and dispense treasure, a sword literally was what was left after the blacksmith's hammers had done their job, a dragon was really thought to fly through the air, a spear really was a strong piece of wood, and a ship literally did float on the waves. These terms are vivid, and some are metonymical, but they are not kennings because they do not compare the referent with something it is not.

§8 In IC we saw that apposition and parallelism are prominent features of the *Beowulf*ian poetic style, and in our reading of the first sentence in the poem we saw an example of apposition. Germanic poets used appositions pervasively; modern scholars call this stylistic device 'variation'. Following are examples of variation:

Oferēode þā   æþelinga bearn
stēap stānhliðo   stīge nearwe
1410 enge ānpaðas   uncūð gelād
neowle næssas   nicorhūsa fela;
hē fēara sum   beforan gengde
wīsra monna   wong scēawian
oþ þæt hē færinga   fyrgenbēamas
1415 ofer hārne stān   hleonian funde
wynlēasne wudu;   wæter under stōd
drēorig ond gedrēfed.   Denum eallum wæs
winum Scyldinga   weorce on mōde
tō geþolianne,   ðegne monegum
1420 oncȳð eorla gehwæm   syðþan Æscheres
on þām holmclife   hafelan mētton.

The son of noblemen then traversed the steep stony cliffs, the narrow ascending trails, constricted single-file paths, an unknown way, precipitous promontories, many water-monsters' abodes; one of a few wise men, he walked ahead to examine the area until he suddenly found mountain trees, a joyless wood, leaning over a grey stone; the blood-stained agitated water stood beneath. It was distressing for all the Danes, for the lords of the Scyldings, for many a thane, to endure – distress for each of the noblemen – when they encountered on the sea-cliff Æschere's head.

In ll. 1409–11 solid and broken underlining is used to keep the variations separate from one another. The first variation (*stēap stānhliðo: neowle næssas*) is perfectly symmetrical, the adjective *neowle* 'precipitous, steep' varying the parallel adjective *stēap* 'steep', and the noun *næssas* 'cliffs' varying the parallel noun *stānhliðo* 'stony cliffs'. The next variation is similar: the adjective *nearwe* 'narrow' is varied by the adjective *enge* 'constricted, narrow' and the noun *stīge* 'ascending paths' is varied by the noun *ānpaðas* 'single-file paths'. The third element of the variation, however, more loosely refers to the route as *uncūð gelād* 'an unknown way'. It is none the less a part of the variation because it is parallel with the other two half-lines and has the same referent. The other variations follow the same pattern of having a common referent and of having the same function within the sentence (i.e. they are parallel) and thus are in the same case.

§9 Although repetitive in structure, the variations are not merely otiose. Each restatement of the referent brings out a different aspect of it. Thus *fyrgenbēamas* refers to the trees and identifies what kind they are, whereas *wynlēasne wudu* tells us the atmosphere that pervades the trees. If one scrutinizes the other variations, one will find similar increments of meaning increasing our understanding of the referent with each successive restatement. The variations also add drama to the syntactic unfolding of the sentences. The steady series of interlocking variations in ll. 1409–11 gives us a sense of the passing landscape as the hero makes his way through the mountainous terrain. The variations in ll. 1417–20 work differently. Their primary function (apart from developing our sense of the Danes as numerous, united, and of various degrees of nobility) is to retard the progress of the sentence so that the shocking, climactic half-line revealing what it was that causes the Danes so much distress has maximum effect. We discover the grisly, severed head of Æschere at the end of the sentence in somewhat the same way as the Danes make the same horrible discovery at the end of their excursion to the promontory.

§10 Another Germanic rhetorical device which is prominent in *Beowulf* is what modern scholars call 'the envelope pattern'. This is a means of bracketing a segment of the narrative by repeating words or images at the beginning and end of the segment. The description of Grendel's first attack on Heorot, for example, begins *Gewāt ðā nēosian* (l. 115) and ends *wīca nēosan* (l. 125). The description of Beowulf preparing himself for the battle with Grendel's mother is similarly marked off, beginning with *Gyrede hine Bēowulf* (l. 1441) and closing with *hē hine tō gūðe gegyred hæfde* (l. 1472). Another example is ll. 767–70, framed by *Dryhtsele dynede* and *Reced hlynsode*. A dramatic use of the device is in Beowulf's first speech to Hrothgar (ll. 405–55), which is introduced by

> Bēowulf maðelode   – on him byrne scān
> searonet seowed   smiþes orþancum –:

One might at first wonder why the poet inserts between the loquitur and the speech this odd detail about Beowulf's splendid corselet shining, but then at the end of the speech Beowulf directs the king's attention to that very corselet (ll. 452–5) as the climactic element in his vow to triumph over Grendel or die.

Just as the poet uses repetition as a structural device, he also makes stylistic use of it. Repetitive parallel constructions like those in ll. 1763–7 and ll. 2262–5 are notable examples, but the most memorable, perhaps, is the series of *cōm* clauses that announce the stages of Grendel's approach to Heorot, where Beowulf awaits him: ll. 702, 710, and 720. This effect is echoed briefly in the description of Grendel's mother advancing on Heorot in l. 1279. And the rhetoric of the majestic close of the poem (ll. 3156–82) is heightened by the repetition of clauses introduced by *ðā/þā* and *swā*.

Tone

§11 An eloquent poem narrating the extraordinary accomplishments of its hero cannot fail to leave its readers with a sense of exhilaration, and the hero's exemplary life can only be inspiring. This being so, it is remarkable that the dominant tone most often sensed by readers is one of melancholy. Despite the noble intentions and great feats of the poem's characters, in the end their heroic world seems somehow unavailing. A major reason for the sombre tone of the poem is of course its conclusion, where the prolonged funeral rites and recurrent prophecies of the nation's imminent doom leave us with the impression that all the hero's triumphs and achievements could not avert his nation's nemesis. The poet emphasizes this impression when he says that the great treasure which has been bought with the hero's suffering and death and which he had hoped would be a boon to his nation is in fact returned despairingly to the earth, where it lies 'as useless to men as it was before' (l. 3168). But it is not just at the end that a solemn note is struck. Throughout the poem there have been hints and whispers of sorrow to come and open declarations of the omnipotence of fate and the inevitability of death.

§12 Near the beginning of *Beowulf* we are presented with a paradigm of the hero's life in Scyld's illustrious career, but what the poet emphasizes most is his death and obsequies, and the episode ends with a melancholy uncertainty: no one knows the destination of the hero after his death. Some have seen this as a question that hangs over the entire poem, which deals precisely with a great Germanic hero whose fate after death remains uncertain. Whether this is true or not, there is much in the poem to suggest that the future in general holds more to fear than relish. We noticed in the discussion of structure that the poet's interruptions of present-time narration to tell of future events typically point to tragic reversals of fortune. Notable instances are the allusions to Hygelac's ill-fated raid on the Frisian coast, where he and his army are slain. This disaster so weakened the Geatish nation that only the presence of mighty Beowulf on the throne could keep surrounding enemies at bay, and so when he dies the nation (we are told repeatedly) is doomed. This being the case, each of the four times that the Frisian raid is recounted (ll. 1202–14, 2354–66, 2501–8, 2913–21) is a reminder of the baleful future awaiting the Geats.

§13 Hrothgar's solemn pronouncement that death comes for all and that sorrow can extinguish joy at any time adds to a sense of foreboding in the poem, and all that is prophesied at the poem's end seems to be the fulfilment of that foreboding. The accounts of the Geatish–Swedish wars in the same section of the poem include thrilling deeds like Hygelac's rescue of the besieged Geats (ll 2941–98) and the vengeance exacted on Onela (ll. 2395–6), but they are narrated in a way that does not emphasize Geatish triumphs over evil adversaries. The Swedish king is praised (ll. 2381–4), while the Geats are declared arrogant (ll.2926–7). The Geatish slayers of Ongentheow bear the curious names Eofor ('wild boar') and Wulf ('wolf') and are the offspring of Wonred ('unreason'). All the slaughter of the wars seems only to lead to more wars later on and to further slaughter, so that rather than being narratives of Geatish military glory, the accounts seem to depict what Virgil called *scelerata insania belli* ('the criminal madness of war' – *Aeneid* VII, 461). And this, we are told, is what awaits the Geatish nation at the poem's end.

§14 Nevertheless, despite the recurrent notes of melancholy in *Beowulf* we may well feel a certain exultation in reading of the hero's indomitable spirit and heroic efforts. But if we do, it is not because his achievements have left his nation secure and pre-eminent (for they have not), but solely because his courage and exemplary character have demonstrated what personal greatness man is capable of achieving in this life. That alone is sufficient to ensure that the tone of the poem is not gloomy but complex, as we are left marvelling that while fate may have been invincible in Beowulf's world, yet a man could achieve greatness in defiance of that fate.

Metre

§15 Although scholars discuss and debate the details of the Old English metrical system, there is a fairly broad consensus as to its major features, and that consensus is based upon the work of the German scholar Eduard Sievers in the late nineteenth century. Sievers observed that all the intact verses of *Beowulf* and of other Old English poetry fall into some variation of five basic patterns of stressed and unstressed syllables, and that the verses are bound into pairs by alliteration, the first (and only the first) accented syllable of the second verse in the pair alliterating with one or both of the accented syllables in the first verse of the pair. The five patterns or types are

A: / × / × þrym gefrūnon *or* / × × / × lēode gelǣsten
B: × / × / þurh mīne hand *or* × × / × × / hē þæs frōfre gebād
C: × / / × in geārdagum *or* × × / / × ofer hronrāde
D: / / \ × þēodcyninga *or* / / × \ wēold wīdeferhð
E: / \ × / weorðmyndum þāh *or* / \ × × / meodosetla oftēah

These are merely illustrative. There are many other variations of each basic pattern. For a fuller introduction to the essentials of Old English metre, see *Guide*, pp. 161–7. Here attention is called to the fact that while virtually all Old English poetry adheres to the five types of Sievers, there is a small minority of verses which add an extra foot to half-lines, making them have three major accents instead of two. These are called 'hypermetric lines', and they almost always appear in clusters. In *Beowulf* we encounter three groups of hypermetric lines; see ll. 1163–8, 1705–7, and 2995–6. We do not know what the purpose or effect of these lines was.

F   Subject Matter

§1   As the extract from Ker's description of the manuscript printed on the half-title page reveals, the title *Beowulf* is modern; it was first used by John Mitchell Kemble in his edition *The Anglo-Saxon Poems of Beowulf, The Traveller's Song, and The Battle of Finnes-burh* (London, 1833). The traditional division of the poem which we adopt is also modern:

> *Part One Beowulf the Young Hero* (ll. 1–2199)
> The fight with Grendel (ll. 1-1250)
> The fight with Grendel's mother (ll. 1251–887)
> Beowulf's return to Geatland (ll. 1888–2199)
>
> *Part Two Beowulf the King* (ll. 2200–3182)
> The fight with the dragon (ll. 2200–751)
> Beowulf's death (ll. 2752–3182)

So too are the brief summaries of the contents of the fitts which we present unobtrusively in square brackets before each fitt number, thereby providing the argument of the poem. Some of those we consulted in the planning stages of the edition expressed opposition to these as editorial interruptions likely to influence readers' interpretation of the poem. Such a complaint can of course be levelled against practically everything we have done. Our decision to persist with these summaries was taken in the hope and belief that readers will find them helpful, not only in themselves, but also because they break the poem into a series of manageable portions the completion of each of which will give a sense of accomplishment not easily achieved when confronted by a formidably unbroken stretch of 3182 lines of alliterative verse. We have tried to avoid interpretative comments and to restrict the summaries to factual statements of the contents of the fitts.

§2   That the narrative elements in *Beowulf* are varied in nature can be seen from ll. 99–114, 194–201, and 379b–80a, presented here in the Old English prose paraphrase composed by Henry Sweet for his *First Steps in Anglo-Saxon* (Oxford, 1897):

> On þisse blisse þurhwunode Hrōþgār cyning and his menn lange tīd, oþþæt him fēond onsǣge wearþ. þæt wæs unfǣlu wiht, Grendel

hātte. Sē būde on þǣm mearclande, and hæfde him fæsten geworht
on fennum, on middan þǣm sweartum mōrum.

Sume menn cwǣdon þæt Grendel wǣre of Cāines cynne. Forþǣm,
þā Cāin ofslōg Ābēl his brōþor, þā wearþ him se ælmihtiga gram, and
hine on wræcsīþ āsende, and hēt hine on wēstenne wunian, feorr
mancynne. þanon onwōcon ealle unfǣle wihta, dweorgas, and ielfe,
and eotenas, þe wiþ God wunnon. . . .

þā wæs þǣr sum þēod on Swēolande þe man hǣtt Gēatas; Hygelāc
wæs gehāten hira cyning. Sē hæfde þegn, þæs nama wæs Bēowulf; sē
wæs þæs cyninges nefa. And se Bēowulf wæs ealra manna cēnost and
strengest. Is þæt gesægd þæt hē hæfde þrītigra manna mægen on his
handgripe.

þā wurdon Grendles undǣda ēac on Gēatum cūþe. And hraþe þæs
þe Bēowulf þæt gehīerde, swā hēt hē him scip gierwan: cwæþ þæt hē
wolde Hrōþgār sēcan, þā him wæs manna þearf.

Previous editors have tried to distinguish between the historical and the
fabulous or supernatural, or between history, heroic legend, and folklore.
There are historical elements, e.g. the stories of Hygelac and of the
Geatish–Swedish Wars; see IVB and IVE5. But beyond these, the
historical and the legendary merge. The distinction is a valid one for
modern scholars, though the lines are often hard to draw, but it is by no
means certain that Beowulf, Grendel and his kin, and the dragon, were any
less real to the poet and his audience than was the historical Hygelac. For
what is known about the characters variously classified as historical, heroic,
fabulous, or supernatural, see IVA, the glossary of proper names and the
references given therein, and the relevant portions of IVD and IVE.

§3 As we turn to the Christian elements, we must note that there is no
mention of any of the great dogmas of Christianity – the Incarnation, the
Crucifixion, the Resurrection, or the Ascension – or of the name of Christ
himself. Of the possible references to the Bible, there is not one which
cannot be traced to the Old Testament: Cain and Abel (§2 above), 'the
slayer . . . who shoots from his bow with evil intent' (ll. 1743b–44 and note),
and the *sōðfæstra dōm* (l. 2820b; see Psalm 98.9 and Ecclesiastes 3.17) are
typical examples. Good reasons can of course be adduced to explain why a
Christian poet might have felt that Christ the Redeemer would be out of
place in the pagan world he was portraying and we can easily see from *The
Wanderer* and *The Seafarer* how a situation expressed in pagan terms could
lead to Christian moralizing. But the absence of specific Christian
references has led to great differences of opinion about what Klaeber
called 'the Christian coloring' of *Beowulf*.

§4 The significance of the Christian elements is a topic on which the
authors do not see eye to eye. This is made clear by the fact that where, in
the first sentence of our foreword, we speak of '*Beowulf* with its complex

blend of heroic and Christian', the word 'complex' is a compromise between FCR's 'subtle' and BM's 'baffling'. Their differing opinions can be illustrated by their respective views on ll. 90b–8 and 175–88.

§5 For FCR the creation which the poet sings in ll. 90b–8 is not the Christian creation of Genesis but a creation ascribed by the pagan Danes to whatever god they knew. In ll. 175–88, the pagan Danes are described *hwīlum* 'sometimes, now and again' worshipping pagan idols, by a Christian poet who, speaking, as it were, over the heads of his pagan characters to his Christian contemporaries, comments on the sadness of the fact that, as the Danes in their ignorance prayed for salvation, they were assuring their own destruction, since the pagan idols were really devils in disguise. The implication of these comments would have been understood, as FCR is careful to say, by at least a portion of the poet's audience and was likely to be a conscious element in the poet's design, available to that part of his audience which was knowledgeable and attentive enough to perceive it. This of course implies that the poet was also speaking over the heads of at least a part of his audience and that therefore the audience was not a homogeneous one the members of which had all heard – or not heard – the poem before and who shared the same knowledge, intuitions, and reactions. We are in agreement on this point.

§6 BM, however, finds it hard to believe that the poet was always in such firm control of his material and maintained throughout the poem such a clear understanding of the strategy FCR detects. The phrase 'a conscious element in the poet's design' worries BM simply because so many different conscious designs have been detected in the poem; see G4 below. BM is prepared to concede that most if not all of these theories may have been detected and accepted by some Anglo-Saxon readers or hearers of the poem. But he still does not believe that there is one meaning to *Beowulf* and therefore does not hope or wish to succeed in making sense of the poem in any particular way. He agrees with Sisam that 'in this work the poet was not much concerned with Christianity and paganism'. To some, the lack of references to the great Christian doctrines is part of the design: a Christian poet is celebrating the pagan heroes and warriors of old by portraying their best side without shocking or repelling the devout. To this end, he deliberately blurs such questions as damnation and the fate of the righteous heathen on the death of Beowulf, shirking these issues in the interests of Christian propaganda. As BM sees it, the poet avoids these questions, deliberately or unconsciously, because he is not much concerned with them: if he had been, he would have met them head on.

§7 For BM then it is the creation told in Genesis which the poet sings in ll. 90b–8 and it is a series of momentary relapses to paganism (*Hwīlum* l. 175) which are described in ll. 175–88. The poet is not an antiquarian relating or imagining happenings in the distant past but a man reflecting the position in the England of the seventh and early eighth centuries portrayed by Bede, an England which had not been effectively converted in the sense that all non-Christian beliefs and practices had been eradicated. Æthelbert, king of Kent 560–616, the patron of St Augustine, was succeeded by his son Eadbald (died 640), who was still a heathen at his succession and never became a man intent on imposing Christianity on his people. King Rædwald of East Anglia (died 625/6) was converted to Christianity but subsequently relapsed, attempting to get the best of both worlds by setting up altars to Christ and to the devil in the same temple. In the mid-seventh century, the associate kings of the East Saxons behaved very differently in time of plague: Sighere abandoned Christianity and reverted to paganism; Sebbe zealously kept the faith of Christ. Bede tells us that in the time of Wilfrid (died 709) all the South Saxons were completely ignorant of Christianity apart from their queen Æbbe, who came from another tribe, and in 734 writes of local aristocratic families controlling monasteries for their own ends. The *Dialogue* of Egbert, Archbishop of York (died 766), declares that men who worshipped idols or gave themselves to the devil in other ways should never be appointed to the priesthood. In 797 Alcuin posed his famous question *Quid Hinieldus cum Christo?* 'What has Ingeld to do with Christ?'; see IVE4. And Alcuin, like Gildas before him and Wulfstan after him, saw the invasions of his time as God's retribution on a Christian people who were not living out their faith.

§8 None of this implies that there was a continual see-sawing between pagan and Christian beliefs right up to the Norman Conquest. The Christian faith and the Christian culture were preserved and strengthened by the faithful and were not submerged by the new brand of paganism introduced by the Scandinavian invaders. Yet the use by historians of phrases like 'a Christian nation' and 'the Christian English' must not delude modern readers into accepting the notion of a uniformly converted people. We have already agreed in §5 that the audience of *Beowulf* was not homogeneous. As in any period of English history, their society was one in which attitudes to Christianity varied from the fervent to the lukewarm to the hostile. To this uncertainty must be added others. We cannot be sure of the literary conventions within which *Beowulf* was composed. We do not know who made it or by whom, when, or where, it was first heard. We cannot be certain what the author took for granted in his audience. The result of such ignorance about the poem is inevitable: *Quot homines, tot sententiae.* In the sections which follow, the editors present their differing views on *Beowulf*.

G   Two Views of *Beowulf*

First, that of BM.

§1   *Beowulf* is a poem, not a museum for the antiquarian, a sourcebook for the historian, or a gymnasium for the philologist. Written in the Germanic alliterative verse form, it is the longest and, in my opinion, the best of the surviving Old English poems. It is remarkable for its variety of mood and tone: it contains passages which can variously be described as narrative, dramatic (speeches occupy over thirteen hundred lines), epic, didactic, homiletic, gnomic, descriptive, lyric, and elegiac.

§2   It can be said to resemble a great river as it ebbs and flows in the verse paragraphs which are the unit of Old English poetry – now swift-moving with swirling currents and breath-taking rapids, now calm and leisurely, now slow-moving and majestic. But, in common with other Old English poems, it has also been described (by Adeline Courtney Bartlett) as 'a poetic tapestry, filled with essential but greatly elaborated pictorial groups, and, in addition, heavily encrusted with superimposed (or interposed) ornament'.

§3   E. M. Forster regretfully observed: 'Yes – o dear yes – the novel tells a story.' So, in its way, does *Beowulf*. But, as the comparison with a tapestry suggests, we must not expect logical structure in the modern sense or look for what Klaeber called 'steady advance'. The poem moves forward, sideways, and backward, in time, but also in a circle, for it begins with a leaderless people who have found a leader and ends with a people who, having lost a leader, face a perilous future. Its repetitive syntax (IIIB2) is mirrored in the larger narrative structure; thus Beowulf's three fights are all told three times. It is allusive: a catalogue of so-called digressions and apparent inconsistencies would fill pages. (Some of the latter at any rate are, I believe, the result of the poet's concern with the effect of the moment rather than significant features in an overall strategic development.) Yet it was gripping entertainment for heroic warriors, and remains so for modern admirers.

§4   However, as we must regretfully observe, 'Yes – o dear yes – *Beowulf* has a meaning.' Or rather meanings. Over the years its critics, often reflecting current enthusiasms and aberrations, have given it many labels: it is a wild folk-tale, not a properly conducted epic. It is a Christian reworking of a pagan poem. It is a soldering-together of three independent orally composed lays. It is a poem composed for recitation in three parts to warriors in their hall. An ivory-towered poet of the eighth century wrote it for a 'fit audience . . . though few'. It is a Christian allegory for a monastic audience – with various meanings. It is a Christian evaluation of the heroic code. It symbolizes the as-yet-unended struggle between heaven and hell. And so on in what J. R. R. Tolkien characterized as 'a conflicting babel'.

§5 I must now add my own voice to this babel. For me *Beowulf* is a poetic exploration of life in this world, of the blind forces of nature and the dark passions of humans against 'our little systems [which] have their day and cease to be'. This contest is seen in terms of the system within which the poet lived but of whose inevitable weaknesses he makes us aware through both the story and his own comments. But I believe that the poet meant us to admire, not to condemn, Beowulf and that the poem ends on a note of hope not of despair. Today, in this nuclear age, with man's inhumanity to man daily more apparent on all levels and the powers of darkness in seeming ascendancy throughout the world, we may see *Beowulf* as a triumphant affirmation of the value of a good life: as the poet himself says *Brūc ealles well* 'Make good use of everything.' But I make no claim to be 'right'. To vary a sentence of Dr Johnson in the preface to his *Dictionary*: 'To enchain poetry, and to lash the wind, are equally the undertakings of pride, unwilling to measure its desires by its strength.'[1]

Now the view of FCR.

§6 The best brief description of the subject of *Beowulf*, I believe, appears in an article by the distinguished scholar with whom I have been privileged to collaborate in the preparation of this edition. He is not stating his own view but is summarizing that of Tolkien, who (in BM's words) sees the poem as 'the work of a Christian poet deliberately portraying ancient pre-Christian days and emphasizing the nobility of the pagan Germanic world. . . . [W]e have to do with the Christian interpretation of pagan myths expressed in a very special way, namely, through the evocation of the pagan world at its best: hence the world of *Beowulf* remains pagan, though viewed by a Christian poet.'[2] This perspective of the narrator's gives to the stirring events and impressive characters he depicts a complex and poignant quality which, in my view, makes *Beowulf* unique among heroic poems.

§7 That the poet is Christian is clear from the beginning. He alludes to biblical events like Cain's slaying of Abel and the Deluge; he speaks repeatedly of how the Christian God moves through history, ordering events in the pagan Germanic world (which had no knowledge of Him) as surely as He orders events now; and he laments in ll. 183–6 the damnation

---

[1] For fuller developments of these ideas see Bruce Mitchell, *On Old English* (Oxford, 1988), pp. 3–15, 24–9, and 41–54.

[2] Bruce Mitchell, '"Until the Dragon Comes . . . "': Some Thoughts on *Beowulf*', *Neophilologus*, 47 (1963), 126–38, reprinted in Mitchell, *On Old English*, pp. 3–15.

of Germanic pagans who, in their pathetic ignorance, turned to pagan gods for salvation. That the poet's heroic characters are pagan is equally clear, although he must avoid too prominent dramatization of this fact (e.g. by naming the pagan gods or portraying revolting practices like human sacrifice or exposing children) lest he alienate his Christian audience and the ecclesiastical establishment upon which he depended for propagation of his poem and, most likely, for his livelihood. But no attentive audience of the poem could have missed the fact that the characters are pagans. The poem begins and ends with prominently pagan funerals including ship-burial, cremation, and lavish grave goods, all strictly prohibited by the church. The reading of omens, belief in animal totems' power to protect human life, repeated references to the omnipotence of fate, the extolling of vengeance – these and other distinctly non-Christian behaviour character-ize the world of *Beowulf* as pagan, as does the brief glimpse of Danish warriors worshipping pagan gods in ll. 175–88. There is no confusion between the pagan Germanic heroes and the English of Christian Anglo-Saxon England. The action of the poem is rooted firmly in *Wedermearc*, *Swīorīce, Scedenīg, land Dena, Frēslond*, and other continental lands, and the actors are clearly denominated as *Scyldingas, Gēatas, Wendlas, Francan*, and their neighbours. And the time of the poem's action is emphatically *in geārdagum* 'in ancient days'. The poet and his audience are looking back through time to the places whence the founders of England had come, admiring their deeds, learning from their example, and, perhaps, mourning their crippling paganism.

§8 According to the strictest clerical spokesmen of the day, there was no room in the Anglo-Saxon Christian world for pagan ancestors, but a nation needs a past and pride of ancestry. This is what the *Beowulf* poet gives to his people. Through deep thought and high art he finds a place in his countrymen's collective memory where their ancestors can reside with dignity even as the Anglo-Saxons acknowledge that those ancestors were pagan and lost. It is this accomplishment of the poet that gives to his narration of warrior courage, exultant triumph, and honour in defeat its tinge of sadness and conflicted nostalgia. It also gives the poem its unforgettable gravity and makes it more than an exuberant telling of mighty exploits in bygone days.

PART TWO

Text and Notes

The Text

The authorities on which we base the text of the poem printed here are the manuscript, the Thorkelin transcripts, and other testimonial evidence supplied by J. R. Hall. When a word is damaged or lost but the testimonial evidence is in substantial agreement as to the original reading, and metre, grammar, and sense all fit with this reading, we simply supply the reconstructed form in our text and do not report the various forms of confirming evidence, e.g. *þā* in l. 229 and *þū* in l. 445. Where, however, the manuscript today is incomplete and there is no consensus of testimonial evidence as to what the manuscript originally had, or if there is some other difficulty or uncertainty with a reading not present today in the MS, then we print in our text what seems to us to be the likeliest original reading of the manuscript and supply in our textual note only the evidence present in the manuscript today, using three dots to indicate illegible or missing text of any length, e.g. *aldorlēase* in l. 15 and *bearme* in l. 21. For the testimonial evidence we refer readers to the compilation of J. R. Hall, now in preparation, to which he gave us early, pre-publication access; for a painstaking report on what can be seen in the MS today with the aid of special lighting, we refer readers to Kevin Kiernan, 'The State of the *Beowulf* Manuscript 1882–1983', *Anglo-Saxon England*, 13 (1984), 23–42, reprinted in *Beowulf and the Beowulf Manuscript*, rev. edn (Ann Arbor, Michigan, 1996). We give the manuscript reading in textual notes at the foot of the page when we depart from it, as in ll. 6 and 51, but do not cite the readings and emendations of other scholars and do not normally discuss other possible interpretations of the text. We do not report the inconsistencies in spacing discussed in IIIA6.

Although we have both expressed misgivings in print about the suitability of modern punctuation for Old English texts, we use it in this edition to help those approaching *Beowulf* for the first time. A specimen of a possible alternative punctuation appears in the appendix. We also use modern diacritics. The sign ˆ over a vowel or diphthong, as in l. 1116 *dôn* and l. 16 *lîffreâ*, indicates that the metre requires the original uncontracted dissyllabic form. As in the edition in the Anglo-Saxon Poetic Records, capitalization is restricted to the beginning of sentences and to the initial letter of names of tribes, persons, personified swords, and places. The abbreviations of grammatical terms used in the notes are explained at the beginning of the glossary (p. 238).

Our emendations and interpretations are not necessarily original. Rather we have tried to select what seemed to us the best scholarly view on each point, and usually this has been the view that enjoys a consensus among editors and scholars. We have made no effort to name the scholars who originated and have subscribed to the interpretations selected, for this, it seemed to us, would have cluttered the commentary without serving the student's needs. We make wholesale and grateful acknowledgement here to the Old English scholarly tradition on which we have drawn in preparing this book.

PART ONE

Beowulf the Young Hero
(*lines 1–2199*)

ÞÆT ÞE GARDE

na ingear dagum· þeod cyninga
þrym ge frunon huða æþelingas elle
fremedon· oft scyld sceþing sceaþe
þreatum monegū mægþum meodo setl
ofteah egsode eorl syððan ærest pear
feasceaft funden he þæs frofre geba
peox under polcnum peorð myndum þah
oð þ him æghpylc þara ymb sittendra
ofer hron rade hyran scolde gomban
gyldan þþæs god cyning· ðæm eafera pæs
æfter cenned geong ingeardum þone god
sende folce tofrofre fyren ðearfe on
geat þhie ær drugon aldor ease· lange
hpile him þæs lif frea puldres pealdend
porold are forgeaf beopulf pæs bren
blæd pide sprang scyldes eafera scede
landum in· ·Spa sceal
ge pyrcean fromum feoh giftum on

[Scyld Scefing]

HWÆT!
  WĒ GĀR-DEna   in geārdagum
þēodcyninga   þrym gefrūnon,
hū ðā æþelingas   ellen fremedon.
  Oft Scyld Scēfing   sceaþena þrēatum
5 monegum mǣgþum   meodosetla oftēah,
egsode eorlas   syððan ǣrest wearð
fēasceaft funden.   Hē þæs frōfre gebād,
wēox under wolcnum,   weorðmyndum þāh
oð þæt him æghwylc   þāra ymbsittendra
10 ofer hronrāde   hȳran scolde,
gomban gyldan.   þæt wæs gōd cyning.
  Ðǣm eafera wæs   æfter cenned
geong in geardum   þone god sende

6 eorlas] eorl

1–21 A facsimile of the manuscript containing these lines appears on p. 44.

1 **Hwæt** Many scholars see this word as part of the metrical dip of l. 1 and give it no more accent than a word like 'Now' at the beginning of a modern narrative 'Now we have heard . . .'. However, *Hwæt* is found at the beginning of some OE poems and sermons, and if we consider the present instance as extra-metrical, then we could regard it as a call to attention. We could even imagine it being accompanied by a chord on a harp or lyre; **Gār-Dena** 'Spear-Danes'. Elsewhere the Danes are called *Beorht-Dene* l. 427, *Hring-Dene* l. 116, *Ēast-Dene* l. 392, *Norð-Dene* l. 783, *Sūð-Dene* l. 463, and *West-Dene* l. 383. The first element in these compounds alliterates.

1–2 In prose the order would be *Wē gefrūnon þrym þēodcyninga Gār-Dena in geādagum*. *Gār-Dena* may be parallel with *þēodcyninga* or dependent on it.

2–3 **gefrūnon** has two objects – *þrym* and the *hū* clause. See *Guide* §159. The statement that poet and audience share a knowledge of old heroic stories is to be noted. In this poem we shall find many allusions to this material.

4 **Scyld Scēfing** The eponymous king of the Scyldings or Danes. See l. 30 note. The appellation *Scēfing* is usually taken as a patronymic 'son of Sceaf'; compare *Widsith* l. 32 *Scēafa* [*wēold*] *Longbeardum* 'Sceafa [ruled the] Langobards.' Since, however, Scyld's parentage was presumably unknown, some have explained it as 'with a sheaf', seeing in it a reference to a legend in which a child arrives mysteriously by sea with a sheaf of corn at his head.

5 **meodosetla** 'mead-benches', a metonymy for 'the hall'. The royal hall was an institution of great importance in Anglo-Saxon society and symbolic of a king's prestige and power; see *Beowulf* ll. 67b–81a and *The Wanderer* ll. 22–9a. Its loss or destruction implied subjection. See IVC3.

6 **syððan** conj. 'after'; **wearð** The subject is *hē*, understood from *Scyld Scēfing* l. 4. Such non-expression of a pronoun subject is common in OE; see *Guide* §193.7 and compare ll. 8 and 14. In ll. 6 and 8 (in both of which we have two unexpressed subjects) and in l. 14, the subject is the same as that of the preceding clause.

7 **þæs** gen sg of the neut dem *þæt* referring to the previous sentence 'for that'.

9 **þāra** is often omitted for metrical reasons but it is clear in the manuscript and is syntactically acceptable.

10–11 **scolde** governs the two infs *hȳran* (with its object *him* l. 9) and *gyldan*.

12 **Ðǣm** dat sg masc of dem *se* 'that (one)' referring back to *cyning* l. 11.

...me þ hine onylde oft geþuniȝen ...
gesiþas þonne wiȝ cume · leode ȝelæston
of dædū sceal inmaȝþa ȝehpære mange...
...on· him da scyld ȝepat toȝe scæp hpile
...la hpon peran onrrean þære hi hyne
þa ætbæron tobrumes raroðe spæse ȝesiþas
...pa he selra bæð þenden poïdum peold
...ne scyldinȝa leor land rruma lanȝe
...ahte þær æt hyðe stod hpinȝeð srerna isiȝ
...ut rus æþelinȝes rær· aledon þa leorne
þeoden beaȝa bryttan onbearm scipes
mærne be mæste þær pas madma rela
orpeor pegum rrætpa ȝeleded· Ne hyrde
...he cymlicor ceolȝe syïpan hilde papnum
...þearde pædum billum ȝbyrnum him onbearm
...ne læȝ madma mænȝo þalim mið scol...
...on rlod or æht reor ȝepitan· Nalas
...þ.. lassan lacum teodan þeod ȝesrieo...
...þa h... þon he hine æt rruma scearte
...on...sidon þenne ocei yðe umbor pe...

Lines 21–46

folce tō frōfre;   fyrenðearfe ongeat,
15 þæt hīe ǣr drugon   aldorlēase
    lange hwīle. Him þæs līffreâ
    wuldres wealdend   woroldāre forgeaf:
    Bēowulf wæs brēme   – blǣd wīde sprang –
    Scyldes eafera   Scedelandum in.
20 Swā sceal geong guma   gōde gewyrcean
    fromum feohgiftum   on fæder bearme
    þæt hine on ylde   eft gewunigen
    wilgesīþas   þonne wīg cume,
    lēode gelǣsten: lofdǣdum sceal
25 in mǣgþa gehwǣre   man geþeôn.
    Him ðā Scyld gewāt   tō gescæphwīle
    felahrōr fēran   on frēan wǣre.
    Hī hyne þā ætbǣron   tō brimes faroðe
    swǣse gesīþas   swā hē selfa bæd
30 þenden wordum wēold   wine Scyldinga,
    lēof land fruma   lange āhte.
    þǣr æt hyðe stōd   hringedstefna
    īsig ond ūtfūs   æþelinges fær;

---

15 aldorlease] aldor . . . ase   20 geong guma] . . . uma   21 bearme . . . rme

14 **fyrenðearfe** 'painful need, cruel distress'. Some have seen in it a specific reference to the unsuccessful rule of Scyld's predecessor Heremod, whom *fyren onwōd* (l. 915b).

14–15 **ongeat** has two objects – *fyrenðearfe* and the *þæt* clause; cf. ll. 2–3.

16 **lange hwīle** acc of duration of time (*Guide* §189.2); **Him** dat sg masc referring back to *eafera* l. 12 and forward to *Bēowulf* l. 18; **þæs** cf. *þæs* l. 7; **Him þæs līffreâ** will not scan as it stands, nor will *man geþeôn* in l. 25 and many other half-lines in the poem. But if we restore a more archaic form of these contracted words (**līffrēgea, *geþeohan*) then the verses scan perfectly. This suggests that the poem was composed long before the time of this manuscript copy of it with its scribally modernized forms. But complicating the picture is the fact that at times the later, contracted forms are needed for scansion; e.g. l. 27 *on frēan wǣre* will not scan if we restore *on *frēgean wǣre*. See IB2–3.

18 This Dane named Beowulf is not the hero of the poem. The latter is introduced as *Higelāces þegn* in l. 194 and by name in l. 343.

20 **gōde** instr sg neut 'by good'; **gewyrcean** has as object the *þæt* clause in ll. 22–3a.

21–46 A facsimile of the manuscript page containing these lines appears on p. 46.

23 **þonne** 'whenever'. On the difference between *þonne* and *þā* 'when', as in l. 140, see *Guide* §168 s.v. *þonne*.

24 **lēode** dat sg masc 'man, prince', governed by *gelǣsten*.

26 **Him** refl. Need not be translated.

28–9 **Hī** anticipates the appositional *swǣse gesīþas*. See *Guide* §148.

30 **wordum wēold** 'controlled with his words (dat pl)', i.e. 'still held sway'. Cf. l. 79 *his wordes geweald . . . hæfde* 'had power of his word'; **Scyldinga** gen pl 'of the Scyldings'. Apparently meaning 'the followers of (King) Scyld', the name *Scylding* sometimes refers to the Danes generally (as here) and sometimes to the Danish royal dynasty. The Danes are called Scyldings only in poetry.

31 Previous editions read l. 31a *lēof landfruma*, possibly by analogy with l. 54. Metrical support for our reading will be found in ll. 90a, 376a, and 570a. Translate l. 31 'long had the leader ruled the beloved land'.

32–50a See IVC9 (ships), IVC1 and 2 (treasures), and IVC1, 2, and 10 (burials).

ende þagyf hie hum asetton segen
denne heah ofer heafod leton holm ber
geæfon on garsecg hum þæs geomor sefa
murnende mod men ne cunnon. secgan
soðe sele rædenne hæleð under heofenum
hwa þæm hlæste onfeng.

D· A þæs on burgum beowulf scyldinga leod
leod cyning longe þrage folcum gefrǣge
ge fæder ellor hwearf aldor of earde
oþ þ him eft onwoc heah healf dene heold
þenden lifde gamol ⁊ guð reouw glæde scyl
dingas ðæm feower bearn forð gerimed in
worold wocum weoroda ræswa heoro gar ⁊
hroð gar ⁊ halga til hyrde ic þ elan cwen
heaðo scilfingas healf gebedda þa wæs hroð
gar here sped gyfen wiges weorð myn þ
him his wine magas georne hyr don oðð þ
seo geo guð gewoex mago driht micel him
on mod bearn þ heall reced hatan wolde

Lines 46–68

āledon þā   lēofne þēoden
35 bēaga bryttan   on bearm scipes
mǣrne be mǣste.   þǣr wæs māðma fela
of feorwegum   frætwa gelǣded;
ne hȳrde ic cȳmlīcor   cēol gegyrwan
hildewǣpnum   ond heaðowǣdum
40 billum ond byrnum.   Him on bearme læg
māðma mænigo   þā him mid scoldon
on flōdes ǣht   feor gewītan.
Nalæs hī hine lǣssan   lācum tēodan
þēodgestrēonum   þon þā dydon
45 þe hine æt frumsceafte   forð onsendon
ǣnne ofer ȳðe   umborwesende.
þā gȳt hīe him āsetton   segen gyldenne
hēah ofer hēafod,   lēton holm beran,
gēafon on gārsecg;   him wæs geōmor sefa
50 murnende mōd.   Men ne cunnon
secgan tō sōðe   selerǣdende
hæleð under heofenum   hwā þǣm hlæste onfēng.

[The Danish royal family and the building of Heorot]

I   Ðā wæs on burgum   Bēowulf Scyldinga
lēof lēodcyning   longe þrāge
55 folcum gefrǣge   – fæder ellor hwearf

---

47 gyldenne] g . . . denne   51 selerǣdende] sele rædenne

36–7 **māðma . . . frætwa** Parallel gen pls on *fela*.

38 **ne hȳrde ic** The narrator here speaks in the first person singular to comment on the action of the poem: cf. ll. 74–6a and 1197–201. The only time he uses the plural *wē* is in l. 1, where *Wē* embraces both the poet and his audience; **cȳmlīcor** comparative adv 'more becomingly'.

40 **Him** (poss dat) refers to Scyld, as do *him* l. 41 and *hine* l. 43.

43 **lǣssan** dat pl of comparative of adj *lȳtel* 'smaller, lesser'; **tēodan** *-an* for *-on*. So also in ll. 650, 1945, 2116, and elsewhere.

44 **þon** 'than'.

44–5 **þā . . . þe** 'those who'. See *Guide* §162.1.

46 **umborwesende** uninflected pres ptc referring to acc sg masc *hine* l. 45 and *ǣnne* l. 46; cf. adj *hēah* l. 48, which refers to acc sg masc *segen gyldenne* l. 47.

46–68 A facsimile of the manuscript page containing these lines appears on p. 48.

48 **hēah** See note to l. 46.

48–9 The object of *beran* and *gēafon* is *hine*, understood from *him* l. 47; *him* l. 49 is dat pl referring to *hīe* l. 47.

53 Like most longer poems in OE, *Beowulf* is divided into sections called 'fitts'. These are not numbered in all the poems. But they are in *Beowulf*, where the Roman numeral I marks that the first fitt begins at l. 53. So ll. 1–52 may be taken as a prologue or prelude. There is, however, some uncertainty whether the poet or the scribe assigned these numbers. See IA6.

53–63 On the family tree of the Danes see IVA1.

aldor of earde –   oþ þæt him eft onwōc
hēah Healfdene,   hēold þenden lifde
gamol ond gūðrēouw   glæde Scyldingas.
Ðǣm fēower bearn   forðgerīmed
60 in worold wōcun   weoroda rǣswan:
Heorogār ond Hrōðgār   ond Hālga til;
hȳrde ic þæt * * *   elan cwēn
Heaðo-Scilfingas   healsgebedda.
þā wæs Hrōðgāre   herespēd gyfen
65 wīges weorðmynd   þæt him his winemāgas
georne hȳrdon   oðð þæt sēo geogoð gewēox
magodriht micel.   Him on mōd bearn
þæt healreced   hātan wolde
medoærn micel   men gewyrcean
70 þone yldo bearn   ǣfre gefrūnon,
ond þǣr on innan   eall gedǣlan
geongum ond ealdum   swylc him god sealde
būton folcscare   ond feorum gumena.
Ðā ic wīde gefrægn   weorc gebannan
75 manigre mǣgþe   geond þisne middangeard
folcstede frætwan.   Him on fyrste gelomp
ǣdre mid yldum   þæt hit wearð ealgearo
healærna mǣst;   scōp him Heort naman

---

60 ræswan] ræswa   62 hyrde ic þ elan cwen

58 **glæde Scyldingas** acc pl.

59–60 **Ðǣm** anticipates the appositional *weoroda rǣswan*. See ll. 28–9 note.

62 Absence of alliteration, as well as defective sense and metre, indicates that text has been lost here. Drawing on Scandinavian sources, previous editors have reconstructed l. 62 as *hȳrde ic þæt Yrse wæs Onelan cwēn* 'I heard that Yrse (Hrothgar's sister) was Onela's queen.' King Onela appears in the latter part of the poem (ll. 2616 and 2932).

63 **Heaðo-Scilfingas** Here we have *-as* for gen sg masc *-es*. So also in ll. 2453 and 2921. The reverse spelling *-es* for acc pl masc *-as* occurs in l. 519. On these late spellings, presumably introduced by a tenth-century scribe, see *Guide* §231.

67b–85 See IVC2 and 3 (halls).

67b **bearn** This is not the noun, as in l. 59, but the verb *be-arn*.

70 **þone** acc sg masc of *se* used as a relative 'which' referring to *healreced* l. 68. See *Guide* §162.3; **gefrūnon** can be either pret ind pl 'have always heard of' or pret subj pl 'should hear of forever'. See *Guide* §113.3.

71–2 **eall . . . swylc** are best taken as independent parallel objects of *gedǣlan* 'all . . . such as, whatever'.

74 **wīde** modifies *gebannan* and in prose would follow *weorc*. Such displacement is not uncommon in the poetry.

74–6a I heard, says the narrator, that Hrothgar ordered work to adorn a hall. The subject of the inf *gebannan* is *Hrōðgār*; its object is *weorc*. Contrast l. 69, where the subject of *gewyrcean* is *men* and see *Guide* §161. The inf *frætwan* explains the nature or purpose of the work.

78 **Heort** elsewhere *Heorot* 'Hart'. The name has been explained as coming from horns or antlers fastened to the gables or as symbolic of royalty. The Sutton Hoo sceptre as at present conceived is topped by a hart, possibly a totemic animal among the Danes. See IVC3.

se þe his wordes geweald   wīde hæfde,
80 hē bēot ne ālēh,   bēagas dǣlde
sinc æt symle.   Sele hlīfade
hēah ond horngēap,   heaðowylma bād
lāðan līges;   ne wæs hit lenge þā gēn
þæt se ecghete   āþumswēorum
85 æfter wælnīðe   wæcnan scolde.
Ðā se ellengǣst   earfoðlīce
þrāge geþolode   se þe in þȳstrum bād
þæt hē dōgora gehwām   drēam gehȳrde
hlūdne in healle;   þǣr wæs hearpan swēg
90 swutol sang scopes.   Sǣgde se þe cūþe
frumsceaft fīra   feorran reccan,
cwæð þæt se ælmihtiga   eorðan worhte
wlitebeorhtne wang   swā wæter bebūgeð,
gesette sigehrēþig   sunnan ond mōnan
95 lēoman tō lēohte   landbūendum
ond gefrætwade   foldan scēatas
leomum ond lēafum,   līf ēac gesceōp
cynna gehwylcum   þāra ðe cwice hwyrfaþ.
Swā ðā drihtguman   drēamum lifdon
100 ēadiglīce   oð ðæt ān ongan
fyrene fremman   fēond on helle;
wæs se grimma gǣst   Grendel hāten
mǣre mearcstapa   se þe mōras hēold

---

84 ecghete] secg hete   aþumsweorum] aþum swerian   92 worhte] wo . . .   101 fremman] fre . . . man

79 **se þe** 'he who'. So also in l. 90.

81b–5 On the burning of Heorot see ID1–2.

82 **horngēap** 'wide-gabled' seems to be derived from horn-shaped projections on the gable-ends. But see IVC3.

83 **lenge** is best taken as an adjective 'belonging, related', hence 'near (in time)'.

84 **āþumswēorum** 'son-in-law and father-in-law', an otherwise unrecorded copulative (or 'dvandva') compound. Another such compound *suhtergefæderan* 'nephew (brother's son) and (paternal) uncle' appears in l. 1164 and in *Widsith* l. 46. See IVB. The manuscript reading is probably the result of a misunderstanding of the archaic compound by the scribe.

87 Here *se þe* 'who' has an antecedent *se ellengǣst*. This is the *seþe* relative; see *Guide* §162.4.

90b–8 On the scop's song, see IF4–7.

90 **Sǣgde** 'spoke', parallel to *cwæð* l. 92; **se þe** see note to l. 79.

93 **swā** 'as far as'.

93–114 On Grendel and his kin see ID6 and 9–10, F2, and ll. 1687b–98a note.

98 **þāra ðe** 'of those who'. The most common form in *Beowulf* of the *se'þe* relative (*Guide* §163.1). It can be followed by a pl verb, as here and in l. 785, or by a sg verb, as in ll. 843 and 996. Its antecedent is gen pl *cynna*, which is dependent on *gehwylcum*.

100 **ān** 'one, a certain one'.

101 **fēond on helle** 'a hellish fiend', in apposition with *ān*. It is the narrator of the poem, not the characters in it, who associates Grendel with hell.

103 **se þe** See note to l. 87.

fen ond fæsten,   fīfelcynnes eard
105 wonsǣli wer   weardode hwīle
siþðan him scyppend   forscrifen hæfde
in Cāines cynne;   þone cwealm gewræc
ēce drihten   þæs þe hē Ābel slōg;
ne gefeah hē þǣre fǣhðe   ac hē hine feor forwræc,
110 metod for þȳ māne   mancynne fram.
þanon untȳdras   ealle onwōcon
eotenas ond ylfe   ond orcnêas
swylce gīgantas   þā wið gode wunnon
lange þrāge;   hē him ðæs lēan forgeald.

[Grendel's attacks on Heorot]

II 115   Gewāt ðā nēosian,   syþðan niht becōm,
hêan hūses,   hū hit Hring-Dene
æfter bēorþege   gebūn hæfdon.
Fand þā ðǣr inne   æþelinga gedriht
swefan æfter symble,   sorge ne cūðon
120 wonsceaft wera.   Wiht unhǣlo
grim ond grǣdig   gearo sōna wæs
rēoc ond rēþe   ond on ræste genam
þrītig þegna,   þanon eft gewāt
hūðe hrēmig   tō hām faran
125 mid þǣre wælfylle   wīca nēosan.
Ðā wæs on ūhtan   mid ǣrdæge
Grendles gūðcræft   gumum undyrne,
þā wæs æfter wiste   wōp up āhafen
micel morgenswēg.   Mǣre þēoden
130 æþeling ǣrgōd   unblīðe sæt,
þolode ðrȳðswȳð   þegnsorge drēah
syðþan hīe þæs lāðan   lāst scēawedon,
wergan gāstes;   wæs þæt gewin tō strang

107] Caines *altered from* Cames

106–8 See Genesis 4. 1–16, a version of which appears in IVE2.

108 þæs þe rel pron referring to *þone cwealm* l. 107 'in which' or conj 'because'.

109 ne adv 'not' (*Guide* §184.4); hē . . . hē hine Cain (l. 107) . . . *ēce drihten* (l. 108) Cain.

114 hē him *metod* (l. 110) 'them' = *untȳdras* (l. 111); ðæs See l. 7 note.

115–17 This construction is similar to that explained in the note on ll. 2–3. But here *nēosian* takes the gen *hêan hūses*.

120 Wiht unhǣlo '[The] creature of evil'.

122b–3a In prose the order would be *ond genam þrītig þegna on ræste*.

131 þolode 'suffered' may be used without an object. Or both it and *drēah* 'experienced, endured' may govern *þegnsorge*.

             lāð ond longsum.   Næs hit lengra fyrst

135   ac ymb āne niht   eft gefremede

      morðbeala māre   ond nō mearn fore,

      fǣhðe ond fyrene,   wæs tō fæst on þām.

      þā wæs ēaðfynde   þe him elles hwǣr

      gerūmlīcor   ræste sōhte

140   bed æfter būrum   ðā him gebēacnod wæs

      gesægd sōðlīce   sweotolan tācne

      healðegnes hete,   hēold hyne syðþan

      fyr ond fæstor   se þǣm fēonde ætwand.

      Swā rīxode   ond wið rihte wan

145   āna wið eallum   oð þæt īdel stōd

      hūsa sēlest.   Wæs sēo hwīl micel,

      twelf wintra tīd   torn geþolode

      wine Scyldinga,   wēana gehwelcne

      sīdra sorga;   forðām secgum wearð

150   ylda bearnum   undyrne cūð

      gyddum geōmore   þætte Grendel wan

      hwīle wið Hrōþgār,   hetenīðas wæg

      fyrene ond fǣhðe   fela missēra,

      singāle sæce,   sibbe ne wolde

155   wið manna hwone   mægenes Deniga,

      feorhbealo feorran,   fēa þingian

      ne þǣr nǣnig witena   wēnan þorfte

      beorhtre bōte   tō banan folmum

      ac se ǣglǣca   ēhtende wæs,

160   deorc dēaþscua   duguþe ond geogoþe

      seomade ond syrede,   sinnihte hēold

      mistige mōras;   men ne cunnon

      hwyder helrūnan   hwyrftum scrīþað.

---

139 sohte] *not in MS*   148 Scyldinga] scyldenda   149 secgum] *not in MS*   158 banan]
banū   159 ac se] *gap at edge of MS*

136 **fore** adv 'there-for, for it'.

137 **on þām** d pl 'on them' referring back to the deeds described in ll. 135–7a.

138 **þe** 'he who', with general reference.

142 **healðegnes** g s 'of [the] hall-retainer'. Like *renweardas* 'hall-guardians' l. 770, this is a *hapax legomenon* (a word recorded only once). Both words are used ironically and may have been coined by the poet for the occasion.

143 **se** 'he who'. Cf. *þe* l. 138.

151 **geōmore** adv 'sadly'.

154b–8 According to Anglo-Saxon (and Germanic) law the household of a murdered person was entitled to monetary compensation ('wergild') from the murderer. This system saved society from the endless bloodletting of reciprocal vengeance. Grendel's not paying wergild confirms his utter disdain for human decency, just as Hrothgar's generous wergild payment (ll. 459–72) confirms his civilized status.

159 **ǣglǣca** See glossary; **ēhtende wæs** 'was a persecutor'. See *Guide* §204.1.

Swā fela fyrena   fēond mancynnes
165 atol āngengea   oft gefremede,
heardra hȳnða,   Heorot eardode
sincfāge sel   sweartum nihtum,
nō hē þone gifstōl   grētan mōste,
māþðum for metode   ne his myne wisse.
170 þæt wæs wrǣc micel   wine Scyldinga,
mōdes brecða.   Monig oft gesæt
rīce tō rūne,   rǣd eahtedon
hwæt swīðferhðum   sēlest wǣre
wið færgryrum   tō gefremmanne.
175 Hwīlum hīe gehēton   æt hærgtrafum
wīgweorþunga,   wordum bǣdon
þæt him gāstbona   gēoce gefremede
wið þēodþrēaum   – swylc wæs þēaw hyra
hǣþenra hyht   – helle gemundon
180 in mōdsefan,   metod hīe ne cūþon,
dǣda dēmend,   ne wiston hīe drihten god
ne hīe hūru heofena helm   herian ne cūþon
wuldres waldend.   Wā bið þǣm ðe sceal
þurh slīðne nīð   sāwle bescūfan
185 in fȳres fæþm,   frōfre ne wēnan,
wihte gewendan.   Wēl bið þǣm þe mōt
æfter dēaðdæge   drihten sēcean
ond tō fæder fæþmum   freoðo wilnian.

[Beowulf's arrival in Denmark]

III
Swā ðā mǣlceare   maga Healfdenes
190 singāla sēað,   ne mihte snotor hæleð
wēan onwendan;   wæs þæt gewin tō swȳð
lāþ ond longsum   þe on ðā lēode becōm,
nȳdwracu nīþgrim   nihtbealwa mǣst.

175 hærgtrafum] hrærg trafum

164 Swā adv 'Thus'.
168–9 A much-discussed passage. We suggest this translation: 'By no means was he [Grendel] compelled by God to show respect for the throne, that precious thing, nor did he feel love for it.'
171b–2 Note the change of number in the verbs. See *Guide* §187.3(b).
175–88 On the significance of this passage, see IF4–7.
183 þǣm ðe 'to that [one] who'. Here the relative is ðe and the antecedent þǣm; see *Guide* §162.1.
185b–6a The inf *wēnan*, which depends on *sceal* l. 183, governs both *frōfre* and *wihte gewendan*.
186 wihte d s used as adv 'at all'; þǣm ðe see l. 183 note.

þæt fram hām gefrægn   Higelāces þegn
gōd mid Gēatum,   Grendles dǣda,
se wæs moncynnes   mægenes strengest
195 on þǣm dæge   þysses līfes
æþele ond ēacen.   Hēt him ȳðlidan
gōdne gegyrwan,   cwæð, hē gūðcyning
ofer swanrāde   sēcean wolde
200 mǣrne þēoden   þā him wæs manna þearf.
Ðone sīðfæt him   snotere ceorlas
lȳthwōn lōgon   þēah hē him lēof wǣre,
hwetton higerōfne,   hǣl scēawedon.
205 Hæfde se gōda   Gēata lēoda
cempan gecorone   þāra þe hē cēnoste
findan mihte,   fīftȳna sum
sundwudu sōhte,   secg wīsade
lagucræftig mon   landgemyrcu.
210 Fyrst forð gewāt;   flota wæs on ȳðum
bāt under beorge.   Beornas gearwe
on stefn stigon   — strēamas wundon,
sund wið sande   — secgas bǣron
on bearm nacan   beorhte frætwe
215 gūðsearo geatolīc,   guman ūt scufon
weras on wilsīð   wudu bundenne.
Gewāt þā ofer wǣgholm   winde gefȳsed
flota fāmīheals   fugle gelīcost
oð þæt ymb āntīd   ōþres dōgores
220 wundenstefna   gewaden hæfde
þæt ðā līðende   land gesāwon,
brimclifu blīcan,   beorgas stēape
sīde sǣnæssas;   þā wæs sund liden
eoletes æt ende.   þanon up hraðe

204 higerofne] hige . . .

194 **Higelāces þegn** The first reference to the hero of the poem. We are not told his name until l. 343.

194–5 **þæt** anticipates *Grendles dǣda*.

197 Unusually the dems *þǣm* and *þysses* carry alliteration and stress, thus emphasizing both the contrasting periods and the simultaneous continuity of Anglo-Saxon history.

205–7a Translate: 'The good man had chosen from the people of the Geats the boldest warriors he could find.'

206 **cempan gecorone** are both acc pl masc.

207 **fīftȳna sum** 'one of fifteen', i.e. 'with fourteen others'. Cf. MnE 'foursome'.

208 **secg** probably Beowulf rather than another warrior.

210–26a See IVC9 (ships).

212b–13a Translate: 'the currents eddied, sea against sand'.

223b–4a 'Then had the sea been crossed at the end of the voyage.'

225　Wedera lēode　　on wang stigon,
　　　sǣwudu sǣldon,　　syrcan hrysedon
　　　gūðgewǣdo,　　gode þancedon
　　　þæs þe him ȳþlāde　　ēaðe wurdon.
　　　þā of wealle geseah　　weard Scildinga
230　se þe holmclifu　　healdan scolde
　　　beran ofer bolcan　　beorhte randas
　　　fyrdsearu fūslīcu,　　hine fyrwyt bræc
　　　mōdgehygdum　　hwæt þā men wǣron.
　　　Gewāt him þā tō waroðe　　wicge rīdan
235　þegn Hrōðgāres,　　þrymmum cwehte
　　　mægenwudu mundum,　　meþelwordum frægn:
　　　'Hwæt syndon gē　　searohæbbendra
　　　byrnum werede　　þe þus brontne cēol
　　　ofer lagustrǣte　　lǣdan cwōmon
240　hider ofer holmas?　　Hwæt, ic hwīle wæs
　　　endesǣta,　　ǣgwearde hēold
　　　þē on land Dena　　lāðra nǣnig
　　　mid scipherge　　sceðþan ne meahte.
　　　Nō hēr cūðlīcor　　cuman ongunnon
245　lindhæbbende　　ne gē lēafnesword
　　　gūðfremmendra　　gearwe ne wisson,
　　　māga gemēdu.　　Nǣfre ic māran geseah
　　　eorla ofer eorþan　　ðonne is ēower sum,
　　　secg on searwum,　　nis þæt seldguma
250　wǣpnum geweorðad.　　Nǣfre him his wlite lēoge,
　　　ǣnlic ansȳn!　　Nū ic ēower sceal
　　　frumcyn witan　　ǣr gē fyr heonan
　　　lēasscēaweras　　on land Dena
　　　furþur fēran.　　Nū gē feorbūend
255　mereliðende　　mīnne gehȳrað
　　　ānfealdne geþōht:　　ofost is sēlest
　　　tō gecȳðanne　　hwanan ēowre cyme syndon.'

240b] le wæs　　　255 minne] mine

226　**syrcan hrysedon** 'they shook out their coats of mail'. The same idea is expressed in *Exodus*
176b, where Moses *wælhlencan scēoc*.
228　**þæs þe** 'because'.
231　**beran** The acc subject of this infinitive is the unexpressed *Wedera lēode* l. 225. See *Guide*
§161.
240b–3 Since *ǣgweard* is fem, *þē* cannot refer directly to it. It is best taken as inst sg neut
referring to the whole principal clause 'by that' or 'by which', expressing purpose or result.
244　**cuman ongunnon** Perhaps 'have begun to come' rather than 'have come'. See *OES* §678.
248　**ēower sum** 'one of you' or possibly 'a notable one among you', i.e. Beowulf.

[Beowulf's purpose explained]

IIII   Him se yldesta   andswarode,
            werodes wīsa   wordhord onlēac:
260   'Wē synt gumcynnes   Gēata lēode
            ond Higelāces   heorðgenēatas.
            Wæs mīn fæder   folcum gecȳþed
            æþele ordfruma   Ecgþēow hāten,
            gebād wintra worn   ǣr hē on weg hwurfe
265   gamol of geardum;   hine gearwe geman
            witena wēlhwylc   wīde geond eorþan.
            Wē þurh holdne hige   hlāford þīnne
            sunu Healfdenes   sēcean cwōmon
            lēodgebyrgean;   wes þū ūs lārena gōd.
270   Habbað wē tō þǣm mǣran   micel ǣrende
            Deniga frêan;   ne sceal þǣr dyrne sum
            wesan þæs ic wēne.   þū wāst, gif hit is
            swā wē sōþlīce   secgan hȳrdon,
            þæt mid Scyldingum   sceaðona ic nāt hwylc,
275   dēogol dǣdhata   deorcum nihtum
            ēaweð þurh egsan   uncūðne nīð
            hȳnðu ond hrāfyl.   Ic þæs Hrōðgār mæg
            þurh rūmne sefan   rǣd gelǣran
            hū hē frōd ond gōd   fēond oferswȳðeþ –
280   gyf him edwenden   ǣfre scolde
            bealuwa bisigu   bōt eft cuman –
            ond þā cearwylmas   cōlran wurðaþ
            oððe ā syþðan   earfoðþrāge
            þrēanȳd þolað   þenden þǣr wunað
285   on hēahstede   hūsa sēlest.'
            Weard maþelode   ðǣr on wicge sæt,
            ombeht unforht: 'Ǣghwæþres sceal

280 edwenden] edwend

260 **gumcynnes** can be taken as adv gen 'as to race' or as dependent on *lēode* 'people of the race of the Geats'.
271 **sum** 'anything' or 'anything important'. Cf. *sum* l. 248.
272 **þæs ic wēne** 'from what I expect', i.e. 'if my expectation is fulfilled'; **gif** This conj probably introduces a conditional clause 'if' rather than a noun clause 'if, whether'.
277 **þæs** 'about that'.
278 **þurh rūmne sefan**, i.e. 'without demanding anything in return'.
280–1 The nouns *edwenden* and *bot* are appositional nom sgs governing the gen *bisigu* 'if a change, a remedy, for the torment of afflictions should ever come'.
284b–5 **þǣr** bearing alliteration shows special emphasis, suggesting that Beowulf gestures towards the high hall.
287b–9 'A keen-witted shieldbearer who thinks well must know the meaning of every word and deed.'

scearp scyldwiga   gescād witan
worda ond worca   se þe wēl þenceð.

290 Ic þæt gehȳre,   þæt þis is hold weorod
frēan Scyldinga.   Gewītaþ forð beran
wǣpen ond gewǣdu;   ic ēow wīsige;
swylce ic maguþegnas   mīne hāte
wið fēonda gehwone   flotan ēowerne

295 nīwtyrwydne   nacan on sande
ārum healdan   oþ ðæt eft byreð
ofer lagustrēamas   lēofne mannan
wudu wundenhals   tō Wedermearce;
gōdfremmendra   swylcum gifeþe bið

300 þæt þone hilderǣs   hāl gedīgeð.'
Gewiton him þā fēran;   flota stille bād,
seomode on sāle   sīdfæþmed scip
on ancre fæst.   Eoforlīc scionon
ofer hlēorbergan   gehroden golde;

305 fāh ond fȳrheard   ferhwearde hēold.
Gūþmōd grummon,   guman ōnetton,
sigon ætsomne   oþ þæt hȳ sæl timbred
geatolīc ond goldfāh   ongyton mihton;
þæt wæs foremǣrost   foldbūendum

310 receda under roderum   on þǣm se rīca bād;
līxte se lēoma   ofer landa fela.

---

302 on sale] onsole   304 hleorbergan] hleor beran   307 sæl timbred] æltimbred

299 'to such a doer of noble deeds it will be granted'.

303b For boar-figures see Tacitus, *Germania* §45, where he describes Germanic tribes wearing 'the device of the wild boar, which . . . gives the worshipper a sense of security even among his enemies'. Cf. ll. 299–300. The totemic image of the boar (which was sacred to the Norse god Freyr (Old English Frēa)) was felt to provide protection over the warriors' lives. The Anglo-Saxons did in early days wear helmets with images of boars atop them. One such helmet was found at Benty Grange in 1861, and another was discovered in Northamptonshire in 1997. See IVC5 and, for illustrations, the half-title page and figures 9, 10, and 12.

303b–7a The main difficulty in this much-discussed passage is that the pl vb *scionon* l. 303b is followed by the sg vb *hēold* l. 305b. This change of number can be explained by the fact that the three words which qualify the nom pl neut *eoforlīc* – *gehroden, fāh, fȳrheard* – can be nom pl neut or nom sg neut (see *OES* §77 fn. 11): 'Boar images adorned with gold shone atop the helmets; the gleaming and fire-hardened one held guard over life.' With this interpretation MS *grummon* l. 306b is retained: 'The war-minded ones clamoured, the men hastened, moved together . . .'. An alternative solution is to emend to *grimmon* = *grimmum* dat pl (cf. *scypon* l. 1154), to read

305 fāh ond fȳrheard;   ferhwearde hēold
gūþmōd grimmon.   Guman ōnetton,
sigon ætsomne . . .,

and to translate 'the war-minded one held life-guard over the grim ones'. This transfers the change of number from the verbs to the nouns.

308 **ongyton** inf with *-on* for *-an*; cf. ll. 2167 *bregdon*, 2842 *būon*.

Him þā hildedēor   hof mōdigra
torht getǣhte   þæt hīe him tō mihton
gegnum gangan;   gūðbeorna sum
315 wicg gewende,   word æfter cwæð:
'Mǣl is mē tō fēran.   Fæder alwalda
mid ārstafum   ēowic gehealde
sīða gesunde!   Ic tō sǣ wille
wið wrāð werod   wearde healdan.'

[Beowulf's arrival at Heorot]

V 320   Strǣt wæs stānfāh,   stīg wīsode
gumum ætgædere.   Gūðbyrne scān
heard hondlocen,   hringīren scīr
song in searwum.   þā hīe tō sele furðum
in hyra gryregeatwum   gangan cwōmon,
325 setton sǣmēþe   sīde scyldas
rondas regnhearde   wið þæs recedes weal,
bugon þā tō bence.   Byrnan hringdon,
gūðsearo gumena,   gāras stōdon
sǣmanna searo   samod ætgædere,
330 æscholt ufan grǣg;   wæs se īrenþrēat
wǣpnum gewurþad   þā ðǣr wlonc hæleð
ōretmecgas   æfter æþelum frægn:
'Hwanon ferigeað gē   fætte scyldas
grǣge syrcan   ond grīmhelmas,
335 heresceafta hēap?   Ic eom Hrōðgāres
ār ond ombiht.   Ne seah ic elþēodige
þus manige men   mōdiglīcran.
Wēn' ic þæt gē for wlenco   nalles for wræcsīðum
ac for higeþrymmum   Hrōðgār sōhton.'
340 Him þā ellenrōf   andswarode
wlanc Wedera lēod,   word æfter spræc
heard under helme: 'Wē synt Higelāces
bēodgenēatas;   Bēowulf is mīn nama.
Wille ic āsecgan   sunu Healfdenes
345 mǣrum þēodne   mīn ǣrende,
aldre þīnum   gif hē ūs geunnan wile

312 hof] of   332 æþelum] hæleþum

312 **Him þā** 'To them then'; **hildedēor** 'the one brave in battle' and *gūðbeorna sum* l. 314 'an important warrior' both refer to Hrothgar's coastguard.

þæt wē hine swā gōdne   grētan mōton.'
Wulfgār maþelode   – þæt wæs Wendla lēod,
wæs his mōdsefa   manegum gecȳðed,

350   wīg ond wīsdōm –:   'Ic þæs wine Deniga
frēan Scildinga   frīnan wille,
bēaga bryttan,   swā þū bēna eart,
þēoden mǣrne   ymb þīnne sīð
ond þē þā andsware   ǣdre gecȳðan

355   ðe mē se gōda   āgifan þenceð.'
Hwearf þā hrædlīce   þǣr Hrōðgār sæt
eald ond anhār   mid his eorla gedriht;
ēode ellenrōf   þæt hē for eaxlum gestōd
Deniga frēan;   cūþe hē duguðe þēaw.

360   Wulfgār maðelode   tō his winedrihtne:
'Hēr syndon geferede,   feorran cumene
ofer geofenes begang   Gēata lēode;
þone yldestan   ōretmecgas
Bēowulf nemnað.   Hȳ bēnan synt

365   þæt hīe, þēoden mīn,   wið þē mōton
wordum wrixlan;   nō ðū him wearne getēoh
ðīnra gegncwida,   glædman Hrōðgār.
Hȳ on wīggetāwum   wyrðe þinceað
eorla geæhtlan;   hūru se aldor dēah

370   se þǣm heaðorincum   hider wīsade.'

[Beowulf's offer to Hrothgar]

VI   Hrōðgār maþelode,   helm Scyldinga:
'Ic hine cūðe   cnihtwesende;
wæs his ealdfæder   Ecgþēo hāten
ðǣm tō hām forgeaf   Hrēþel Gēata

375   āngan dohtor;   is his eafora nū
heard hēr cumen,   sōhte holdne wine.
Ðonne sægdon þæt   sǣlīþende,
þā ðe gifsceattas   Gēata fyredon
þyder tō þance,   þæt hē þrītiges

357 anhar] un har   375 eafora] eaforan

358 **þæt** conj 'so that' shading into 'until'.
359b See IVC2.
372 **cnihtwesende** uninflected pres ptc agreeing with *hine*. See l. 46 note.
374 **tō hām** 'in marriage'.
378 **Gēata** g pl 'for the Geats'.
379 **tō þance** 'for a gift'.

380 manna mægencræft   on his mundgripe
     heaþorōf hæbbe.   Hine hālig god
     for ārstafum   ūs onsende
     tō West-Denum,   þæs ic wēn hæbbe,
     wið Grendles gryre.   Ic þǣm gōdan sceal
385 for his mōdþræce   mādmas bēodan.
     Bēo ðū on ofeste,   hāt in gân
     sēon sibbegedriht   samod ætgædere,
     gesaga him ēac wordum   þæt hīe sint wilcuman
     Deniga lēodum.'
390   Word inne ābēad:
     'Ēow hēt secgan   sigedrihten mīn
     aldor Ēast-Dena   þæt hē ēower æþelu can
     ond gē him syndon   ofer sǣwylmas
     heardhicgende   hider wilcuman.
395 Nū gē mōton gangan   in ēowrum gūðgetāwum
     under heregrīman   Hrōðgār gesēon;
     lǣtað hildebord   hēr onbīdan
     wudu wælsceaftas   worda geþinges.'
     Ārās þā se rīca,   ymb hine rinc manig
400 þrȳðlic þegna hēap;   sume þǣr bidon,
     heaðorēaf hēoldon   swā him se hearda bebēad.
     Snyredon ætsomne   þā secg wīsode
     under Heorotes hrōf;
     heard under helme   þæt hē on hēoðe gestōd.
405 Bēowulf maðelode   – on him byrne scān
     searonet sēowed   smiþes orþancum –:
     'Wæs þū, Hrōðgār, hāl.   Ic eom Higelāces
     mæg ond magoðegn;   hæbbe ic mǣrða fela
     ongunnen on geogoþe.   Mē wearð Grendles þing
410 on mīnre eþeltyrf   undyrne cūð;
     secgað sǣlīðend   þæt þæs sele stande
     reced sēlesta   rinca gehwylcum

389b–90a] *no gap in MS. See note*   395 guðgetawum] guð geata wum   403b] *no gap in MS. See note*

383 þæs ic wēn hæbbe Cf. l. 272 and note.
386b–7 OE idiom and the element order combine to suggest that *sibbegedriht* is the object, not the subject, of *sēon*: 'bid [them, the Geats] come in to see the band of kinsmen [the Danes]'. See *Guide* §161 and cf. ll. 395–6.
390 There is no gap in the manuscript and the two half-lines do not alliterate. Either something is lost or *lēodum* was miswritten for an alliterating word like *we(o)rode*. See IIIA7.
391 As in ll. 386b–7 the subject acc of the inf is unexpressed: 'bids [me] tell you'.
398 The parallel nouns *wudu wælsceaftas* combine to mean 'wooden battlespears' or 'deadly wooden spears'.
402 þā can be taken either as conj 'when' or pron 'those whom'.
403 A half-line is missing. There is no gap in the manuscript. Klaeber proposes *herewīsa gēong*.
407 Wæs = *Wes* Cf. *þæs* for *þes* l. 411. These are Northumbrian dialect forms.

<blockquote>

īdel ond unnyt   siððan æfenlēoht
under heofenes haðor   beholen weorþeð.

415 þā mē þæt gelærdon   lēode mīne,
þā sēlestan   snotere ceorlas,
þēoden Hrōðgār,   þæt ic þē sōhte
forþan hīe mægenes cræft   mīnne cūþon;
selfe ofersāwon   ðā ic of searwum cwōm

420 fāh from fēondum   þær ic fīfe geband,
ȳðe eotena cyn   ond on ȳðum slōg
niceras nihtes,   nearoþearfe drēah,
wræc Wedera nīð   – wēan āhsodon –
forgrand gramum;   ond nū wið Grendel sceal

425 wið þām āglæcan   āna gehēgan
ðing wið þyrse.   Ic þē nū ðā,
brego Beorht-Dena,   biddan wille,
eodor Scyldinga,   ānre bēne:
þæt ðū mē ne forwyrne,   wīgendra hlēo

430 frēowine folca,   nū ic þus feorran cōm,
þæt ic mōte āna,   mīnra eorla gedryht
ond þes hearda hēap,   Heorot fælsian.
Hæbbe ic ēac geāhsod   þæt se æglæca
for his wonhȳdum   wæpna ne recceð.

435 Ic þæt þonne forhicge   – swā mē Higelāc sīe
mīn mondrihten   mōdes blīðe –
þæt ic sweord bere   oþðe sīdne scyld,
geolorand tō gūþe   ac ic mid grāpe sceal
fōn wið fēonde   ond ymb feorh sacan,

440 lāð wið lāþum;   ðær gelȳfan sceal
dryhtnes dōme   se þe hine dēað nimeð.
Wēn' ic þæt hē wille   gif hē wealdan mōt
in þæm gūðsele   Gēotena lēode
etan unforhte,   swā hē oft dyde,

445 mægen hrēðmanna.   Nā þū mīnne þearft

</blockquote>

---

414 haðor] hador   418 minne] mine

423b 'They (the monsters) asked for trouble.'

431b–2a This, the reading of the manuscript, is to be taken as a vocative: Beowulf tells the assembled warriors – Geats and Danes in turn – that he will fight alone *āna* ll. 425 and 431. Translate ll. 431–2 '. . . that I, O my band of warriors (the Geats) and this brave company (the Danes), may be permitted to cleanse Heorot alone.'

435 **swā** asseverative 'so may my lord Higelac be gracious in mind to me'.

441 **se** 'he' þe hine 'whom'.

445a **mægen hrēðmanna** is in apposition with *Gēotena lēode* l. 443.

445b–6a **mīnne . . . hafalan hȳdan** 'to cover my head'. Covering the head was part of Germanic burial practice. Beowulf is grimly observing that, if Grendel prevails, there will be no body left to bury.

hafalan hȳdan   ac hē mē habban wile
drēore fāhne   gif mec dēað nimeð,
byreð blōdig wæl,   byrgean þenceð,
eteð āngenga   unmurnlīce,
450 mearcað mōrhopu;   nō ðū ymb mīnes ne þearft
līces feorme   leng sorgian.
Onsend Higelāce,   gif mec hild nime,
beaduscrūda betst   þæt mīne brēost wereð,
hrægla sēlest;   þæt is Hrǣdlan lāf
455 Wēlandes geweorc.   Gǣð ā wyrd swā hīo scel.'

[Hrothgar's account of Grendel]

VII   Hrōðgār maþelode,   helm Scyldinga:
'For werefyhtum þū,   wine mīn Bēowulf,
ond for ārstafum   ūsic sōhtest.
Geslōh þīn fæder   fǣhðe mǣste,
460 wearþ hē Heaþolāfe   tō handbonan
mid Wilfingum;   ðā hine Wedera cyn
for herebrōgan   habban ne mihte.
þanon hē gesōhte   Sūð-Dena folc
ofer ȳða gewealc,   Ār-Scyldinga
465 ðā ic furþum wēold   folce Deniga
ond on geogoðe hēold   gimme rīce
hordburh hæleþa;   ðā wæs Heregār dēad,
mīn yldra mǣg   unlifigende
bearn Healfdenes;   se wæs betera ðonne ic.
470 Siððan þā fǣhðe   fēo þingode,
sende ic Wylfingum   ofer wæteres hrycg
ealde mādmas;   hē mē āþas swōr.
Sorh is mē tō secganne   on sefan mīnum
gumena ǣngum   hwæt mē Grendel hafað
475 hȳnðo on Heorote   mid his heteþancum
fǣrnīða gefremed;   is mīn fletwerod
wīghēap gewanod;   hīe wyrd forswēop

---

457 For werefyhtum] fere fyhtum   461 Wedera] gara   465 Deniga] deninga

452–5a See IVC6 (coats of mail).
454 **Hrǣdlan** gen sg 'of Hrethel', father of Hygelac and grandfather of Beowulf. The gen sg also occurs as *Hrǣdles* l. 1485 and *Hrēþles* l. 1847.
466b–7a **gimme rīce** 'realm of jewels', parallel to *hordburh* 'treasure city'. For gen pl in -*e*, cf. *fyrene* l. 811, *sorge* l. 2004, etc.
470 **Siððan** adv 'after that'.
474b–6a The gen pls *hȳnðo* and *fǣrnīða* depend on *hwæt* 'what sort of' shading into 'how much'.

on Grendles gryre.   God ēaþe mæg
þone dolsceaðan   dǣda getwǣfán.
480 Ful oft gebēotedon   bēore druncne
ofer ealowǣge   ōretmecgas
þæt hīe in bēorsele   bīdan woldon
Grendles gūþe   mid gryrum ecga.
Ðonne wæs þēos medoheal   on morgentīd
485 drihtsele drēorfāh   þonne dæg līxte,
eal bencþelu   blōde bestȳmed
heall heorudrēore;   āhte ic holdra þȳ lǣs,
dēorre duguðe   þē þā dēað fornam.
Site nū tō symle   ond onsǣl meoto
490 sigehrēð secgum   swā þīn sefa hwette.'
þā wæs Gēatmæcgum   geador ætsomne
on bēorsele   benc gerȳmed;
þǣr swīðferhþe   sittan ēodon
þrȳðum dealle.   þegn nytte behēold
495 se þe on handa bær   hroden ealowǣge,
scencte scīr wered.   Scop hwīlum sang
hādor on Heorote.   þǣr wæs hæleða drēam,
duguð unlȳtel   Dena ond Wedera.

[Unferth's taunts: Beowulf's contest with Breca]

VIII   Unferð maþelode,   Ecglāfes bearn
500 þe æt fōtum sæt   frēan Scyldinga,
onband beadurūne –   wæs him Bēowulfes sīð
mōdges merefaran   micel æfþunca
forþon þe hē ne ūþe   þæt ǣnig ōðer man
ǣfre mǣrða þon mā   middangeardes
505 gehēdde under heofenum   þonne hē sylfa –:
'Eart þū se Bēowulf   se þe wið Brecan wunne,

499 Unferð] HVN ferð

487b–8 Translate either 'I had fewer loyal men . . . for that reason *or* than before (*þȳ*) because
(*þē*) death carried them off' or 'I had the (*þȳ*) fewer loyal men . . . in proportion as (*þē*) death
carried them off.'

489–90 **Site nū . . . hwette** 'Sit now to the feast and unbind [your] thoughts, the glory of
victory, to men, as your mind moves you.' The meaning 'thought' assigned here to the nonce-word
meoto is conjectural.

499 **Unferð** Hrothgar's *þyle* 'court spokesman' (ll. 1165, 1456). See ll. 506–86 note.

501 **onband beadurūne** 'unleashed his hostile thought'.

504–5a **ǣfre mǣrða . . . gehēdde** 'should ever care the more about glorious deeds on earth'.

506–86 While Unferth suggests that the adventure was a swimming contest (l. 507b 'competed
at swimming') which Beowulf lost, Beowulf emphasizes that the two men were contending with the
creatures and force of the sea (l. 507b 'competed around the running current'), not with one
another, and that he, Beowulf, had the upper hand throughout the contest (ll. 541b–3 and 583b–6).

on sīdne sǣ   ymb sund flite?
Ðǣr git for wlence   wada cunnedon
ond for dolgilpe   on dēop wæter
510 aldrum nēþdon   ne inc ǣnig mon
ne lēof ne lāð   belēan mihte
sorhfullne sīð   þā git on sund reôn.
þǣr git ēagorstrēam   earmum þehton,
mǣton merestrǣta,   mundum brugdon,
515 glidon ofer gārsecg;   geofon ȳþum wēol
wintrys wylme.   Git on wæteres æht
seofon niht swuncon;   hē þē æt sunde oferflāt,
hæfde māre mægen.   þā hine on morgentīd
on Heaþo-Rǣmes   holm up ætbær,
520 ðonon hē gesōhte   swǣsne ēþel,
lēof his lēodum,   lond Brondinga
freoðoburh fægere   þǣr hē folc āhte
burh ond bēagas.   Bēot eal wið þē
sunu Bēanstānes   sōðe gelǣste.
525 Ðonne wēne ic tō þē   wyrsan geþingea
ðēah þū heaðorǣsa   gehwǣr dohte
grimre gūðe   gif þū Grendles dearst
nihtlongne fyrst   neân bīdan.'
Bēowulf maþelode,   bearn Ecgþēowes:
530 'Hwæt, þū worn fela,   wine mīn Unferð,
bēore druncen   ymb Brecan sprǣce,
sægdest from his sīðe.   Sōð ic talige
þæt ic merestrengo   māran āhte
earfeþo on ȳþum   ðonne ǣnig ōþer man.
535 Wit þæt gecwǣdon   cnihtwesende
ond gebēotedon   – wǣron bēgen þā gīt
on geogoðfēore –   þæt wit on gārsecg ūt

---

516 wylme] wylm   520 eþel] ⋊   530 Unferð] hun ferð

508 **git** 'you two, the two of you'. Dual forms of the second (*git, incer, inc*) and first (*wit, unc*) person pronouns occur often in this exchange between Beowulf and Unferth. See *Guide* §21.

511 **ne lēof ne lāð** 'neither friend nor foe'.

514 **mǣton merestrǣta** 'measured the sea paths', i.e. traversed the water.

518 **þā** adv 'Then'.

519 **Heaþo-Rǣmes** The ending *-es* is a late spelling of acc pl *-as* (see l. 63 note), and *on Heaþo-Rǣmes* means 'onto [the land of the] Heaþo-Rǣmas'. See *Widsith* l. 63 and l. 580 note below.

520–3a *Widsith* l. 25 states that Breca was king of the Brondings, and the statement in *Beowulf* ll. 522b–3a that he possessed the people, the treasure, and the stronghold suggests that Breca held the throne already in the time of his youthful adventure with Beowulf.

525 **tō þē** 'from you'; **wyrsan geþingea** 'the worse of outcomes'; *wyrsan* is gen sg object of *wēne*.

526–7a **ðēah þū . . . gūðe** 'although you may always have been good at fierce attacks, at grim battle'.

aldrum neðdon   ond þæt geæfndon swā.

Hæfdon swurd nacod   þā wit on sund reôn

540 heard on handa: wit unc wið hronfixas

werian þōhton.   Nō hē wiht fram mē

flōdȳþum feor   flēotan meahte

hraþor on holme,   nō ic fram him wolde.

Đā wit ætsomne   on sǣ wǣron

545 fīf nihta fyrst   oþ þæt unc flōd tōdrāf

wado weallende   wedera cealdost

nīpende niht,   ond norþanwind

heaðogrim ondhwearf;   hrēo wǣron ȳþa.

Wæs merefixa   mōd onhrēred;

550 þǣr mē wið lāðum   līcsyrce mīn

heard hondlocen   helpe gefremede,

beadohrægl brōden   on brēostum læg

golde gegyrwed.   Mē tō grunde tēah

fāh fēondscaða,   fæste hæfde

555 grim on grāpe;   hwæþre mē gyfeþe wearð

þæt ic āglǣcan   orde gerǣhte

hildebille;   heaþorǣs fornam

mihtig meredēor   þurh mīne hand.

[The contest with Breca continued. The feast]

VIIII   Swā mec gelōme   lāðgetēonan

560 þrēatedon þearle.   Ic him þēnode

dēoran sweorde   swā hit gedēfe wæs.

Næs hīe ðǣre fylle   gefēan hæfdon

mānfordǣdlan   þæt hīe mē þēgon,

symbel ymbsǣton   sǣgrunde nēah

565 ac on mergenne   mēcum wunde

be ȳðlāfe   uppe lǣgon

sweordum āswefede   þæt syðþan nā

ymb brontne ford   brimlīðende

---

567 sweordum] sweo *at edge of MS*

543 **wolde** Construe with the understood inf *flēotan*. Note the rhetorical emphasis on *him* signalled by accent and alliteration.

562 **Næs** = *Nealles* 'By no means'.

563 **mē** (like *mīnne* l. 445 and *mīnes* l. 450) is a word normally unstressed, but here it is given exceptional rhetorical emphasis by the poet, who places it in a position where it receives accent and alliterates.

565b–7a **mēcum, sweordum** are plural in form but with singular meaning: 'by the swordblade, by the sword'. Similar is *hiltum* l. 1574 'by the hilt'.

lāde ne letton.   Lēoht ēastan cōm
570 beorht bēacen godes,   brimu swaþredon
þæt ic sǣnæssas   gesēon mihte
windige weallas.   Wyrd oft nereð
unfǣgne eorl   þonne his ellen dēah.
Hwæþere mē gesǣlde   þæt ic mid sweorde ofslōh
575 niceras nigene.   Nō ic on niht gefrægn
under heofones hwealf   heardran feohtan
ne on ēgstrēamum   earmran mannon,
hwæþere ic fāra feng   fēore gedīgde
sīþes wērig.   Ðā mec sǣ oþbær
580 flōd æfter faroðe   on Finna land
wudu weallendu.   Nō ic wiht fram þē
swylcra searonīða   secgan hȳrde
billa brōgan.   Breca nǣfre gīt
æt heaðolāce   ne gehwæþer incer
585 swā dēorlīce   dǣd gefremede
fāgum sweordum   – nō ic þæs swīðe gylpe –
þēah ðū þīnum brōðrum   tō banan wurde
hēafodmǣgum;   þæs þū in helle scealt
werhðo drēogan   þēah þīn wit duge.
590 Secge ic þē tō sōðe,   sunu Ecglāfes,
þæt nǣfre Grendel swā fela   gryra gefremede
atol ǣglǣca   ealdre þīnum,
hȳnðo on Heorote   gif þīn hige wǣre
sefa swā searogrim   swā þū self talast
595 ac hē hafað onfunden   þæt hē þā fǣhðe ne þearf

---

578 hwæþere] hwaþere   586 swiðe] *not in MS*   588 helle] *see note*   591 Grendel] gre del

574b The fourth accented syllable (*-slōh*) alliterates, thus violating a cardinal rule of OE metre. To eliminate the alliteration some editors emend *ofslōh* to *ābrēat*. See l. 1151 note.

577 **mannon** is a late spelling of wk acc sg masc *mannan*. Note the same spelling in *hæfton* l. 788 and *hāton* l. 849.

580 **Finna land** Several locations have been proposed, one argument suggesting that *Finna land* and *Heaþo-Rǣmes* l. 519 could have been places around the Kattegat not far apart. There is no reason to think there is a reference to modern Finland, which would be preposterously remote.

579b–81a **Ðā mec sǣ . . . weallendu** 'Then the sea, the wave along the current, the tossing ship, bore me up onto the land.' The *-u* of *weallendu* is a late spelling of *-e* (cf. l. 546, where *weallende* is a late spelling for *weallendu*). Some editors have emended MS *wudu* to *wadu*, thus removing the ship (*wudu*) from the passage.

583 **billa brōgan** 'with frightful swords' (lit. 'with frightfulness of swords').

584 **gehwæþer incer** 'either of you two' i.e. Breca and Unferth.

586 **nō ic . . . gylpe** 'not that I boast a great deal of that'. The word *swīðe*, which is needed for sense and metre, is missing from the MS; cf. *Daniel* l. 711.

588 **helle** Not in the MS. Only traces of *-e* can be descried beneath the paper border protecting the charred edge of the folio. The word *helle* is attested only by the copyist hired by the poem's first editor, Thorkelin, to copy the MS in 1787, and this copyist, who knew no OE, confuses *e*, *æ*, and *ea*. The word here may well have been *healle*, and ll. 588b–9 may have meant 'for that you must endure condemnation in the hall, clever though you may be'.

atole ecgþræce   ēower lēode
swīðe onsittan   Sige-Scyldinga,
nymeð nȳdbāde,   nǣnegum ārað
lēode Deniga   ac hē lust wigeð,
600 swefeð ond sǣndeþ,   secce ne wēneþ
tō Gār-Denum.   Ac ic him Gēata sceal
eafoð ond ellen   ungeāra nū
gūþe gebēodan.   Gǣþ eft se þe mōt
tō medo mōdig   siþþan morgenlēoht
605 ofer ylda bearn   ōþres dōgores
sunne sweglwered   sūþan scīneð.'
þā wæs on sālum   sinces brytta
gamolfeax ond gūðrōf,   gēoce gelȳfde
brego Beorht-Dena,   gehȳrde on Bēowulfe
610 folces hyrde   fæstrǣdne geþōht.
⁕ Ðǣr wæs hæleþa hleahtor,   hlyn swynsode,
word wǣron wynsume.   Ēode Wealhþēow forð
cwēn Hrōðgāres   cynna gemyndig,
grētte goldhroden   guman on healle
615 ond þā frēolīc wīf   ful gesealde
ǣrest Ēast-Dena   eþelwearde,
bæd hine blīðne   æt þǣre bēorþege
lēodum lēofne;   hē on lust geþeah
symbel ond seleful   sigerōf kyning.
620 Ymbēode þā   ides Helminga
duguþe ond geogoþe   dǣl ǣghwylcne,
sincfato sealde   oþ þæt sǣl ālamp
þæt hīo Bēowulfe   bēaghroden cwēn
mōde geþungen   medoful ætbær,

---

600 sǣndeþ] sendeþ

599 **hē lust wigeð** 'he carries out his desire'.

600 **sǣndeþ** Context suggests strongly that this verb means 'devours'. We propose *sǣndeþ* as a metathesized form of OE *snǣdeþ*, which means 'eats, takes a meal'. It is cognate with a more fully documented ON word *snæða* 'to eat, take a meal', and the root appears in the OE noun *snǣding* 'meal, snack', as well as in *snǣd*, which describes Grendel's devouring a corpse in l. 743. The scribe, confused by the metathesis, mistook the word for the familiar verb *sendeþ* 'sends' (which is sometimes spelled *sǣndeð*).

601b–3a **Ac ic . . . gūþe gebēodan** 'But now I must soon proffer to him the force and valour of the Geats in battle' with ironic understatement in 'proffer'. There is no evidence that *gebēodan* can mean 'show', as is often assumed.

603 **se þe** 'whoever' (*Guide* §164).

605 **ōþres dōgores** adv gen 'the next day' (*Guide* §190.5). Cf. l. 219.

612 **Wealhþēow.** See ID2–4 and notes to ll. 1169–87 and 2018.

613 **cynna gemyndig** 'mindful of court usage'. Cf. l. 359b.

617–18 **bæd hine** 'asked him [to be]'. See *Guide* §205.1; **lēofne** 'pleasant' is in apposition with *blīðne*.

623–4 **mōde geþungen** 'virtuous in spirit' is in apposition with *bēaghroden* 'ring-adorned'.

625 grētte Gēata lēod,   gode þancode
     wīsfæst wordum   þæs ðe hire se willa gelamp
     þæt hēo on ænigne   eorl gelȳfde
  � fyrena frōfre.   Hē þæt ful geþeah
     wælrēow wiga   æt Wealhþēôn
630 ond þā gyddode   gūþe gefȳsed,
     Bēowulf maþelode,   bearn Ecgþēowes:
     'Ic þæt hogode,   þā ic on holm gestāh,
     sǣbāt gesæt   mid mīnra secga gedriht,
     þæt ic ānunga   ēowra lēoda
635 willan geworhte   oþðe on wæl crunge
     fēondgrāpum fæst.   Ic gefremman sceal
     eorlīc ellen   oþðe endedæg
     on þisse meoduhealle   mīnne gebīdan.'
     Ðām wīfe þā word   wēl līcodon
640 gilpcwide Gēates;   ēode goldhroden
     frēolīcu folccwēn   tō hire frēan sittan.
     þā wæs eft swā ǣr   inne on healle
     þrȳðword sprecen,   ðēod on sǣlum,
     sigefolca swēg   oþ þæt semninga
645 sunu Healfdenes   sēcean wolde
     æfenræste;   wiste þǣm āhlǣcan
     tō þǣm hēahsele   hilde geþinged
     siððan hīe sunnan lēoht   gesēon meahton
     oþðe nīpende   niht ofer ealle
650 scaduhelma gesceapu   scrīðan cwōman
     wan under wolcnum.   Werod eall ārās.
     Gegrētte þā   guma ōþerne
     Hrōðgār Bēowulf   ond him hæl ābēad
     wīnærnes geweald   ond þæt word ācwæð:
655 'Nǣfre ic ænegum men   ǣr ālȳfde,
     siþðan ic hond ond rond   hebban mihte,
     ðrȳþærn Dena   būton þē nū ðā.
     Hafa nū ond geheald   hūsa sēlest,
     gemyne mǣrþo,   mægenellen cȳð,
660 waca wið wrāþum.   Ne bið þē wilna gād
     gif þū þæt ellenweorc   aldre gedīgest.'

652 Gegrette] grette

626 þæs ðe conj 'because'.
646b–8a wiste þǣm āhlǣcan . . . geþinged siððan hīe 'he (Hrothgar) had known an attack
[to be] planned by the foe (Grendel) against the high hall from the time that they'.
649 oþðe conj 'until'.
655 ænegum men Hrothgar means 'to any man' other than his Danish subjects, who have
obviously been given regular use of the hall.

[The watch for Grendel]

X   Ðā him Hrōðgār gewāt   mid his hæleþa gedryht
   eodur Scyldinga   ūt of healle,
   wolde wīgfruma   Wealhþēo sēcan
665   cwēn tō gebeddan,   hæfde kyningwuldor
   Grendle tōgēanes,   swā guman gefrungon,
   seleweard āseted: sundornytte behēold
   ymb aldor Dena,   eotonweard' ābēad.
   Hūru Gēata lēod   georne truwode
670   mōdgan mægnes,   metodes hyldo,
   ðā hē him of dyde   īsernbyrnan
   helm of hafelan,   sealde his hyrsted sweord
   īrena cyst   ombihtþegne
   ond gehealdan hēt   hildegeatwe.
675   Gespræc þā se gōda   gylpworda sum
   Bēowulf Gēata   ǣr hē on bed stige:
   'Nō ic mē an herewæsmun   hnāgran talige
   gūþgeweorca   þonne Grendel hine;
   forþan ic hine sweorde   swebban nelle,
680   aldre benēotan   þēah ic eal mæge;
   nāt hē þāra gōda   þæt hē mē ongēan sleâ,
   rand gehēawe   þēah ðe hē rōf sîe
   nīþgeweorca;   ac wit on niht sculon
   secge ofersittan   gif hē gesēcean dear
685   wīg ofer wǣpen   ond siþðan wītig god
   on swā hwæþere hond   hālig dryhten
   mǣrðo dēme   swā him gemet þince.'

---

684 he] het

665 **kyningwuldor** 'glorious king' [i.e. Hrothgar]. The normal order of compound elements would seem to be *wuldurcyning* as in l. 2795, but *kyningwuldor* is one of a small number of OE noun–noun compounds in which the reverse order is used. Cf. *eardlufu* l. 692 as well as *eðelwyn* ll. 2493, 2885, *hordwynn* l. 2270, *lyftwynn* l. 3043, and *wæteregesa* l. 1260.

667b–8 The subject of *behēold* and *ābēad* is Beowulf; **eotonweard** 'watch against the monster' is acc sg fem with final *-e* elided before the following vowel. Cf. ll. 338, 442, 1932, 2600. Less likely is the possibility that *eotonweard* is the masc noun 'guardian against the monster' (cf. *seleweard* l. 667): 'the guardian against the monster (i.e. Beowulf) offered, performed, a special service to the lord of the Danes'. For two verbs with one subject see l. 131.

677 **an herewæsmun** 'in martial skills'. The late spelling *-un* for *-um* occurs also in *wīcun* l. 1304; *wæsmun* for *wæstmun* shows simplification of a consonant cluster attested elsewhere sporadically in OE. Translate ll. 677–8 'I do not count myself poorer in martial skills of battle deeds than Grendel [counts] himself.'

680 **þēah . . . eal** 'although'.

681 **nāt hē þāra gōda** 'he knows not of those good practices' (i.e. swordsmanship, as defined in ll. 681b–2a).

Hylde hine þā heaþodēor   – hlēorbolster onfēng
eorles andwlitan–   ond hine ymb monig
690 snellīc sǣrinc   selereste gebēah.
Nǣnig heora þōhte   þæt hē þanon scolde
eft eardlufan   ǣfre gesēcean
folc oþðe frēoburh   þǣr hē āfēded wæs;
ac hīe hæfdon gefrūnen   þæt hīe ǣr tō fela micles
695 in þǣm wīnsele   wældēað fornam
Denigea lēode.   Ac him dryhten forgeaf
wīgspēda gewiofu   Wedera lēodum
frōfor ond fultum   þæt hīe fēond heora
ðurh ānes cræft   ealle ofercōmon
700 selfes mihtum.   Sōð is gecȳþed
þæt mihtig god   manna cynnes
wēold wīdeferhð.
             ✗ Cōm on wanre niht
scrīðan sceadugenga.   Scēotend swǣfon
þā þæt hornreced   healdan scoldon
705 ealle būton ānum   – þæt wæs yldum cūþ
þæt hīe ne mōste,   þā metod nolde,
se scynscaþa   under sceadu bregdan –
ac hē wæccende   wrāþum on andan
bād bolgenmōd   beadwa geþinges.

[Grendel's attack]

XI   710   Ðā cōm of mōre   under misthleoþum
Grendel gongan,   godes yrre bær,

---

702 wideferhð] . . . ferhð   707 scyncaþa] syn scaþa

694b–5 **þæt hīe ǣr . . . fornam** 'that murderous death had taken to destruction much too many [of] them in the wine-hall'.

697 **wīgspēda gewiofu** 'a woven destiny of battle-victories'. Destiny described as a web refers apparently to the ancient Germanic belief that men's fates were woven at looms by supernatural women.

703 **Scēotend swǣfon** 'the warriors slept'. Ll. 705b–7 explain how it is that Beowulf's warriors can fall asleep when in such peril: the Germanic maxim that 'no man will die before the fates will it' (a commonplace in the Old Icelandic sagas) enables the warriors to show manly indifference in the face of danger.

704 **hornreced** See l. 82 note.

707 **scynscaþa** 'spectral foe'. The MS reading *synscaþa* 'evil foe' makes perfect sense and, indeed, is used of Grendel in l. 801, while *scynscaþa* is documented nowhere else. But the second element in a compound (*-scaþa*) never alliterates alone in *Beowulf*, and the emendation provides the needed alliteration in the first element of the compound. Grendel is described as a *scinna* 'demon' in l. 939; **under sceadu bregdan** 'pull down into the shadows', i.e. send to the next world, kill. In Germanic belief, as in classical and Christian, the underworld is a place of darkness.

708 **wrāþum on andan** 'in anger at the evil one'.

mynte se mānscaða   manna cynnes
sumne besyrwan   in sele þām hēan.
Wōd under wolcnum   tō þæs þe hē wīnreced
715   goldsele gumena   gearwost wisse
fǣttum fāhne.   Ne wæs þæt forma sīð
þæt hē Hrōðgāres   hām gesōhte;
næfre hē on aldordagum   ǣr nē siþðan
heardran hæle   healðegnas fand.
720   Cōm þā tō recede   rinc sīðian
drēamum bedæled.   Duru sōna onarn
fȳrbendum fæst   syþðan hē hire folmum onhrān;
onbræd þā bealohȳdig,   ðā hē gebolgen wæs,
recedes mūþan.   Raþe æfter þon
725   on fāgne flōr   fēond treddode,
ēode yrremōd;   him of ēagum stōd
ligge gelīcost   lēoht unfæger.
Geseah hē in recede   rinca manige
swefan sibbegedriht   samod ætgædere
730   magorinca hēap.   þā his mōd āhlōg:
mynte þæt hē gedælde,   ǣr þon dæg cwōme,
atol āglæca   ānra gehwylces
līf wið līce   þā him ālumpen wæs
wistfylle wēn.   Ne wæs þæt wyrd þā gēn
735   þæt hē mā mōste   manna cynnes
ðicgean ofer þā niht.   þrȳðswȳð behēold
mǣg Higelāces   hū se mānscaða
under færgripum   gefaran wolde.
Nē þæt se āglæca   yldan þōhte
740   ac hē gefēng hraðe   forman sīðe
slǣpendne rinc,   slāt unwearnum,
bāt bānlocan,   blōd ēdrum dranc,
synsnǣdum swealh,   sōna hæfde
unlyfigendes   eal gefeormod,
745   fēt ond folma.   Forð nēar ætstōp,

---

722 onhran] . . . ran   723 he ge] *MS very faded and not legible*

714 tō þæs þe conj 'to the point where, until'.

719 heardran hæle 'with sterner greeting' or 'with harder fortune'.

734 Ne wæs . . . gēn 'by no means was it [Grendel's] fortune'.

742b–3a blōd ēdrum . . . swealh 'drank blood from the veins, swallowed sinful morsels'. Swallowing blood (the seat of the soul) was an abomination according to Christian writings before and during OE times.

745b–9 Forð nēar . . . wið earm gesæt Perhaps 'forward [and] nearer he (Grendel) approached; he grasped then with his hand at the strong-hearted warrior in his resting place; the foe (Grendel) reached toward him (Beowulf) with his palm; with hostile intent he (Beowulf) quickly took (Grendel's) arm and pressed against it.' The stated actions are clear, but it is not

      nam þā mid handa   higeþīhtigne
      rinc on ræste,   him ræhte ongēan
      fēond mid folme;   hē onfēng hraþe
      inwitþancum   ond wið earm gesæt.
750 Sōna þæt onfunde   fyrena hyrde
      þæt hē ne mētte   middangeardes
      eorþan scēata   on elran men
      mundgripe māran,   hē on mōde wearð
      forht on ferhðe,   nō þȳ ǣr fram meahte.
755 Hyge wæs him hinfūs,   wolde on heolster flēon,
      sēcan dēofla gedræg;   ne wæs his drohtoð þǣr
      swylce hē on ealderdagum   ǣr gemētte.
      Gemunde þā se gōda   mǣg Higelāces
      ǣfensprǣce,   uplang āstōd
760 ond him fæste wiðfēng;   fingras burston,
      eoten wæs ūtweard,   eorl furþur stōp.
      Mynte se mǣra,   þǣr hē meahte swā,
      wīdre gewindan   ond on weg þanon
      flēon on fenhopu,   wiste his fingra geweald
765 on grames grāpum.   þæt wæs gēocor sīð
      þæt se hearmscaþa   tō Heorute ātēah.
      Dryhtsele dynede.   Denum eallum wearð
      ceasterbūendum   cēnra gehwylcum
      eorlum ealuscerwen.   Yrre wǣron bēgen
770 rēþe renweardas.   Reced hlynsode.
      þā wæs wundor micel   þæt se wīnsele
      wiðhæfde heaþodēorum,   þæt hē on hrūsan ne fēol

---

747 him] h . . .   752 sceata] sceatta   762 þær] *MS illegible at edge*   765 þæt] þæt
he

always clear which of the two combatants is the actor. The confusion in the dark hall is mirrored in the language of the narrative.

750–4a **Sōna þæt . . . ferhðe** 'As soon as the master of crimes became aware that he had never met on earth in the world's compass a greater grip in another man, he became terrified in spirit.' Previous editors have placed a semicolon or full stop after *māran*, thus showing that they take this as two main clauses, but, as our comma after *māran* indicates, we read it as a dependent clause followed by a main clause, with *Sōna* acting as a subordinating conjunction 'as soon as, immediately'.

753b–4 The expression *nō þȳ ǣr* occurs six times in *Beowulf* – here and in ll. 1502, 2081, 2160, 2373, and 2466. It has as yet not been found elsewhere in OE. Its meaning is 'no sooner for/because of that' and so 'yet . . . not'. The inst sg neut *þȳ* refers back to what we have just been told. So here we learn that Grendel's fear did not enable him to get away faster. The verb of motion is unexpressed (*Guide* §205.1).

756 **sēcan dēofla gedræg** 'to return to the hubbub of devils', i.e. the company consisting of Grendel himself and his mother.

760 **burston** In view of ll. 764b–5a it is presumably Grendel's fingers that are breaking.

767–90 See IVC2 and 3 (halls).

769 **eorlum ealuscerwen** 'terror among the warriors'. See IIIA12.

770 **renweardas** See note to l. 142.

       fæger foldbold;   ac hē þæs fæste wæs
       innan ond ūtan   īrenbendum
775   searoþoncum besmiþod.   þǣr fram sylle ābēag
       medubenc monig   mīne gefrǣge
       golde geregnad   þǣr þā graman wunnon.
       þæs ne wēndon ǣr   witan Scyldinga,
       þæt hit ā mid gemete   manna ǣnig
780   betlīc ond bānfāg   tōbrecan meahte,
       listum tōlūcan   nymþe līges fæþm
       swulge on swaþule.   Swēg up āstāg
       nīwe geneahhe;   Norð-Denum stōd
       atelīc egesa   ānra gehwylcum
785   þāra þe of wealle   wōp gehȳrdon,
       gryrelēoð galan   godes andsacan
       sigelēasne sang,   sār wānigean
       helle hæfton.   Hēold hine fæste
       se þe manna wæs   mægene strengest
790   on þǣm dæge   þysses līfes.

[Beowulf's victory]

XII   Nolde eorla hlēo   ǣnige þinga
       þone cwealmcuman   cwicne forlǣtan
       ne his līfdagas   lēoda ǣnigum
       nytte tealde.   þǣr genehost brægd
795   eorl Bēowulfes   ealde lāfe,
       wolde frēadrihtnes   feorh ealgian
       mǣres þēodnes   ðǣr hīe meahton swā.
       Hīe þæt ne wiston   þā hīe gewin drugon

---

780 betlic] hetlic

773b–5a See IVC3.

776 **mīne gefrǣge** inst 'according to my information'. Cf. ll. 837, 1955, etc.

778 **þæs** gen sg neut of dem governed by *wēndon*, anticipates the *þæt* clause in ll. 779–81a.

779 **hit** neut nom sg referring to the hall – cf. l. 771 *se wīnsele* . . . l. 772 *hē* . . . l. 773 *hē* – with lack of concord; see *Guide* §187.2(b).

780 **bānfāg** See IVC3.

783 **nīwe geneahhe** lit. 'new enough', i.e. 'very strange, uncanny'.

785 **þāra þe** See l. 98 note; **of wealle** 'from the wall' of the mead-hall (which is all the Danes could see of the battle).

788 **hæfton** = *hæftan* (wk acc sg masc). Grendel is destined for captivity in hell.

794b–5 **þǣr genehost . . . lāfe** 'Most frequently there a warrior of Beowulf's brandished his sword', i.e. 'Many a warrior brandished his sword' (cf. *hīe* l. 798). Old swords (*ealde lāfe*) were valued more than new since the durability of a blade could be known only if it had stood the test of heavy use in the past. See *īren ǣrgōd* ll. 989, 2586.

798 **þæt** acc sg neut of dem, obj of *wiston*, anticipates the noun clause without conj *þæt* which begins in l. 801b.

heardhicgende   hildemecgas

800 ond on healfa gehwone   hēawan þōhton,
sāwle sēcan: þone synscaðan
ǣnig ofer eorþan   īrenna cyst
gūðbilla nān   grētan nolde
ac hē sigewǣpnum   forsworen hæfde

805 ecga gehwylcre.   Scolde his aldorgedāl
on ðǣm dæge   þysses līfes
earmlīc wurðan   ond se ellorgāst
on fēonda geweald   feor sīðian.
Ðā þæt onfunde   se þe fela ǣror

810 mōdes myrðe   manna cynne,
fyrene gefremede   – hē, fāg wið god –
þæt him se līchoma   lǣstan nolde
ac hine se mōdega   mǣg Hygelāces
hæfde be honda;   wæs gehwæþer ōðrum

815 lifigende lāð.   Līcsār gebād
atol ǣglǣca;   him on eaxle wearð
syndolh sweotol,   seonowe onsprungon,
burston bānlocan.   Bēowulfe wearð
gūðhrēð gyfeþe;   scolde Grendel þonan

820 feorhsēoc flēon   under fenhleoðu,
sēcean wynlēas wīc,   wiste þē geornor
þæt his aldres wæs   ende gegongen
dōgera dægrīm.   Denum eallum wearð
æfter þām wælrǣse   willa gelumpen.

825 Hæfde þā gefǣlsod   se þe ǣr feorran cōm
snotor ond swȳðferhð   sele Hrōðgāres,
genered wið nīðe.   Nihtweorce gefeh
ellenmǣrþum.   Hæfde Ēast-Denum
Gēatmecga lēod   gilp gelǣsted;

830 swylce oncȳþðe   ealle gebētte
inwidsorge   þē hīe ǣr drugon
ond for þrēanȳdum   þolian scoldon

---

812 nolde] . . . olde

804b–5a **forsworen . . . gehwylcre** *Forswerian* means 'to swear falsely' and, in a gloss *forsuor* to Latin *de*[*v*]*otabat*, 'bewitch, cast a spell on'. On the strength of the latter most interpret *forsworen* as 'bewitched, rendered useless through a spell', with *hē* meaning Grendel. Others, pointing to ll. 679–80b, have argued that *hē* (with an abrupt shift in reference) refers to Beowulf and that *forsworen* meant 'renounced', a meaning which is, however, poorly documented in OE. The main problem with this interpretation is that Beowulf has not renounced 'every blade' (*ecga gehwylcre*): in his next monster-fight he uses two swords.

809b–11a **se þe fela . . . gefremede** 'he who had previously done to the race of men much injury of spirit [and much] violence'.

torn unlȳtel.　　þæt wæs tācen sweotol
syþðan hildedēor　　hond ālegde
835　earm ond eaxle　　– þær wæs eal geador
◁ Grendles grāpe –　　under gēapne hrōf.

[Rejoicing at Heorot]

XIII　　　　Đā wæs on morgen　　mīne gefrǣge
ymb þā gifhealle　　gūðrinc monig,
fērdon folctogan　　feorran ond neân
840　geond wīdwegas　　wundor scēawian
lāþes lāstas.　　Nō his līfgedāl
sārlīc þūhte　　secga ǣnegum
þāra þe tīrlēases　　trode scēawode,
hū hē wērigmōd　　on weg þanon
845　nīða ofercumen　　on nicera mere
fǣge ond geflȳmed　　feorhlāstas bær.
Đǣr wæs on blōde　　brim weallende,
atol ȳða geswing　　eal gemenged
hāton heolfre　　heorodrēore wēol;
850　dēaðfǣge dēog　　siððan drēama lēas
in fenfreoðo　　feorh ālegde
hǣþene sāwle;　　þǣr him hel onfēng.
þanon eft gewiton　　ealdgesīðas,
swylce geong manig,　　of gomenwāþe
855　fram mere mōdge　　mēarum rīdan
beornas on blancum.　　Đǣr wæs Bēowulfes
mǣrðo mǣned;　　monig oft gecwæð,
þætte sūð ne norð　　be sǣm twēonum
ofer eormengrund　　ōþer nǣnig
860　under swegles begong　　sēlra nǣre
rondhæbbendra,　　rīces wyrðra.
Ne hīe hūru winedrihten　　wiht ne lōgon

---

836 hrof] h *at edge of MS*

833b–6 Beowulf displays Grendel's severed arm on high (l. 983) beneath the hall's roof as a trophy. Or, alternatively, *hildedēor* (l. 834) refers to Grendel, and the sentence is saying that the monster left his arm and shoulder behind in the hall (*under . . . hrōf*). But in that case we must assume that the poet neglects to tell us who displayed the gruesome trophy on the hall roof (ll. 982–4a) and when it was done.

843 þāra þe See l. 98 note.

845 nīða instrumental gen 'by hostile deeds'.

850 dēog occurs only here. It has been conjectured that this is the preterite of an otherwise unattested OE verb meaning either 'hide' or 'die'. Translate 'doomed to death, he (Grendel) hid himself (or died) when, joyless, he gave up his life, his heathen soul, in the fen-refuge'.

glædne Hróðgār ac þæt wæs gód cyning.
Hwīlum heaþorófe hléapan léton
865 on geflit faran fealwe mēaras
ðǣr him foldwegas fægere þūhton
cystum cūðe. Hwīlum cyninges þegn
guma gilphlæden gidda gemyndig
se ðe ealfela ealdgesegena
870 worn gemunde, word ōþer fand
sōðe gebunden; secg eft ongan
sīð Bēowulfes snyttrum styrian
ond on spēd wrecan spel gerāde,
wordum wrixlan; wēlhwylc gecwæð
875 þæt hē fram Sigemundes secgan hȳrde
ellendǣdum: uncūþes fela
Wælsinges gewin wīde sīðas
þāra þe gumena bearn gearwe ne wiston
fǣhðe ond fyrena būton Fitela mid hine
880 þonne hē swulces hwæt secgan wolde
eâm his nefan swā hīe ā wǣron
æt nīða gehwām nȳdgesteallan;
hæfdon ealfela eotena cynnes
sweordum gesǣged. Sigemunde gesprong
885 æfter dēaðdæge dōm unlȳtel
syþðan wīges heard wyrm ācwealde

875 Sigemundes] sige munde

868–70a **guma gilphlæden . . . gemunde** 'a man gifted with magniloquence [and] with a good memory for narratives, who remembered a great many ancient legends' – i.e. an ideal court poet, one with a silver tongue and a mind well stocked with traditional tales.

870b–1a **word ōþer fand sōðe gebunden** 'found other words rightly linked', i.e. he found words other than those of the *ealdgesegena* to celebrate the new story of Beowulf's victory, words correctly linked by alliteration.

872 **sīð Bēowulfes . . . styrian** 'to treat of Beowulf's exploit skilfully'.

874 **wordum wrixlan** 'to change his words'. Like *word ōþer* this refers to the poet's adapting his stories to the subject at hand – celebrating Beowulf's victory. Elsewhere (e.g. l. 366) *wordum wrixlan* means 'exchange words'. An allusion to the poetic device of variation seems strained and less pertinent to this context.

875–97 By telling the story of Sigemund and the dragon-slaying, Hrothgar's court poet places Beowulf's monster-fight alongside one of the most famous monster-fights in Germanic legend, an exploit celebrated in later works like the Old Icelandic *Volsungasaga* and the Middle High German *Nibelungenlied*. (The former has the fullest account.) Sigemund's early adventures with his son (by his twin sister according to the saga, but the *Beowulf* poet calls him only a nephew – l. 881) are followed by the dragon-slaying. A major discrepancy between *Beowulf* and other tellings of the story is that Sigemund seems to slay the dragon in *Beowulf*, whereas in all other versions his son Siegfried is the dragon-slayer. But if we take *wīges heard* (l. 886) and *æþelinges bearn* (l. 888) as referring to Sigemund's (unnamed) son, then there is no discrepancy. Such a cryptic reference would not be unusual, since the story is not so much narrated as summarized by the *Beowulf* poet, who seems to assume that his audience knows the details of the story.

878 **þāra þe** 'of which'.

hordes hyrde;   hē under hārne stān
æþelinges bearn   āna geneðde
frēcne dǣde   ne wæs him Fitela mid;
890 hwæþre him gesælde   ðæt þæt swurd þurhwōd
wrǣtlīcne wyrm   þæt hit on wealle ætstōd
dryhtlīc īren;   draca morðre swealt.
Hæfde āglǣca   elne gegongen
þæt hē bēahhordes   brūcan mōste
895 selfes dōme: sǣbāt gehleōd,
bær on bearm scipes   beorhte frætwa
Wælses eafera;   wyrm hāt gemealt.
Se wæs wreccena   wīde mǣrost
ofer werþēode   wīgendra hlēo
900 ellendǣdum   – hē þæs ǣr onðāh –
siððan Heremōdes   hild sweðrode,
eafoð ond ellen.   Hē mid Ēotenum wearð
on fēonda geweald   forð forlācen
snūde forsended;   hine sorhwylmas
905 lemede tō lange;   hē his lēodum wearð
eallum æþellingum   tō aldorceare;
swylce oft bemearn   ǣrran mǣlum
swīðferhþes sīð   snotor ceorl monig
se þe him bealwa tō   bōte gelȳfde,
910 þæt þæt ðēodnes bearn   geþēon scolde,
fæderæþelum onfōn,   folc gehealdan
hord ond hlēoburh   hæleþa rīce
ēþel Scyldinga.   Hē þǣr eallum wearð

---

902 eafoð] earfoð   913 eþel] ⚔

892 **draca** . . . **swealt** 'the dragon died from the violent assault'.

895 **selfes dōme** 'according to his own judgement', i.e. 'as much as he wished'.

897 **wyrm hāt gemealt** 'the fiery dragon perished [was consumed by fire]'.

900 **hē þæs ǣr onðāh** 'he had thriven thereby'.

901–15 This abrupt transition from the positive example of the dragon-slaying to the negative example of Heremod (whose bad qualities contrast tellingly with Beowulf's exemplary demeanour) is characteristic of the poet's manner. Cf. ll. 1709b ff and (for another example) ll. 1931b ff.

902b–3 **Hē mid Ēotenum** . . . **forlācen** 'He was given over into the power of his enemies among the Jutes.' The generally held assumption that the cruel King Heremod was deposed and dispatched to the Danes' enemies the Jutes is based upon a somewhat questionable reading of MS *eotenum*, which looks like the dat pl of the common noun *eoten* 'giant', not the dat pl of the name of the Jutes, which would be *Ēotum*. But if we read *eotenum*, then we must assume for the common noun an extended sense such as 'foes' or 'evil people', and for this there is little evidence. Probably the scribe mistook the proper name for the word for 'giants', both here and in l. 1145.

904b–5a **hine sorhwylmas lemede** 'surges of sorrow afflicted him'. What looks like a sg *lemede* must be a late spelling of the pl. See *OES* §19.

909 **him** . . . **tō** 'to him'.

913b–15 **Hē þǣr eallum** . . . **onwōd** 'The kinsman of Hygelac became dearer to all mankind [and] to his friends (than did Heremod); vice pervaded him (Heremod).' With this comparison Hrothgar's poet points the moral of his tale. See l. 14 note.

mæg Higelāces   manna cynne
915 frēondum gefægra;   hine fyren onwōd.
Hwīlum flītende   fealwe strǣte
mēarum mǣton.   Ðā wæs morgenlēoht
scofen ond scynded.   Ēode scealc monig
swīðhicgende   tō sele þām hēan
920 searowundor sēon;   swylce self cyning
of brȳdbūre   bēahhorda weard
tryddode tīrfæst   getrume micle
cystum gecȳþed   ond his cwēn mid him
medostigge mæt   mægþa hōse.

[Hrothgar's congratulations and Beowulf's reply]

XIIII 925   Hrōðgār maþelode   – hē tō healle gēong,
stōd on stapole,   geseah stēapne hrōf
golde fāhne   ond Grendles hond –:
'Ðisse ansȳne   alwealdan þanc
lungre gelimpe!   Fela ic lāþes gebād,
930 grynna æt Grendle;   ā mæg god wyrcan
wunder æfter wundre,   wuldres hyrde.
Ðæt wæs ungeāra   þæt ic ǣnigra mē
wēana ne wēnde   tō wīdan feore
bōte gebīdan   þonne blōde fāh
935 hūsa sēlest   heorodrēorig stōd –
wēa wīdscofen   witena gehwylcum
ðāra þe ne wēndon   þæt hīe wīdeferhð
lēoda landgeweorc   lāþum beweredon
scuccum ond scinnum.   Nū scealc hafað
940 þurh drihtnes miht   dǣd gefremede
ðe wē ealle   ǣr ne meahton
snyttrum besyrwan.   Hwæt, þæt secgan mæg
efne swā hwylc mægþa   swā ðone magan cende
æfter gumcynnum,   gyf hēo gȳt lyfað,
945 þæt hyre ealdmetod   ēste wǣre
bearngebyrdo.   Nū ic, Bēowulf, þec,
secg betsta,   mē for sunu wylle

936 gehwylcum] gehwylcne

926 **stapole** See IVC3.
932b–3a **mē . . . ne wēnde** 'did not expect for myself'.
946b–9a The 'new relationship' (*nīwe sibbe*) in which Hrothgar will cherish Beowulf as a son does not constitute literal adoption but was merely a king's way of affirming a close alliance and firm bonds of fealty; 947a. See p. 80.

frēogan on ferhþe;   heald forð tela
nīwe sibbe.   Ne bið þē nǣnigre gād
950 worolde wilna   þe ic geweald hæbbe.
Ful oft ic for lǣssan   lēan teohhode
hordweorþunge   hnāhran rince
sǣmran æt sæcce.   þū þē self hafast
dǣdum gefremed   þæt þīn dōm lyfað
955 āwa tō aldre.   Alwalda þec
gōde forgylde   swā hē nū gȳt dyde!’
Bēowulf maþelode,   bearn Ecgþēowes:
‘Wē þæt ellenweorc   ēstum miclum,
feohtan fremedon,   frēcne genēðdon
960 eafoð uncūþes.   Ūþe ic swīþor
þæt ðū hine selfne   gesēon mōste
fēond on frætewum   fylwērigne.
Ic hine hrædlīce   heardan clammum
on wælbedde   wrīþan þohte
965 þæt hē for mundgripe   mīnum scolde
licgean līfbysig   būtan his līc swice;
ic hine ne mihte,   þā metod nolde,
ganges getwǣman,   nō ic him þæs georne ætfealh
feorhgenīðlan;   wæs tō foremihtig
970 fēond on fēþe.   Hwæþere hē his folme forlēt
tō līfwraþe   lāst weardian,
earm ond eaxle,   nō þǣr ænige swā þēah
fēasceaft guma   frōfre gebohte,
nō þȳ leng leofað   lāðgetēona
975 synnum geswenced   ac hyne sār hafað
in nīdgripe   nearwe befongen
balwon bendum;   ðǣr ābīdan sceal
maga māne fāh   miclan dōmes,
hū him scīr metod   scrīfan wille.’

949 nænigre] ænigre   954 dom] *not in MS*   957 Ecgþeowes] ec þeo wes   963 hine]
him   965 mundgripe] hand gripe   976 nidgripe] mid gripe

947a **secg betsta** has only three syllables and so will not scan. The original MS probably had
secga betsta or *secg betesta*.

949 **nǣnigre** gen pl masc agreeing with *wilna* l. 950. See IIIA8.

954 **dōm** The scribe omitted this word, but sense and metre leave little doubt that *dōm* was
intended here. Cf. *Andreas* l. 541 and *Elene* l. 450.

958 **Wē** i.e. Beowulf and his Geatish comrades, to whom he generously gives credit. The *Oxford
English Dictionary* s.v. *we* 2.a. mistakes this for the royal *we*.

960b–70 By making Beowulf emphasize that he was not strong enough to prevent Grendel's
escaping, the poet makes clear the hero's human limitations: he is a man, not a demigod. On the
syntax of ll. 960b–2 see *Guide* §198.

965 **mundgripe** dat sg 'handgrip'. See IIIA7.

968 **nō ic . . . ætfealh** 'by no means did I hold him firmly enough'.

980   Ðā wæs swīgra secg   sunu Ecglāfes
     on gylpsprǣce   gūðgeweorca
     siþðan æþelingas   eorles cræfte
     ofer hēanne hrōf   hand scēawedon
     fēondes fingras;   foran æghwǣr wæs
985   stedenægla gehwylc   stȳle gelīcost
     hæþenes handsporu   hilderinces
     eglu unhēoru;   æghwylc gecwæð
     þæt him heardra nān   hrīnan wolde
     īren ǣrgōd   þæt ðæs āhlǣcan
990   blōdge beadufolme   onberan wolde.

[The banquet and giftgiving]

XV   Ðā wæs hāten hreþe   Heort innanweard
     folmum gefrætwod;   fela þǣra wæs
     wera ond wīfa   þe þæt wīnreced
     gestsele gyredon.   Goldfāg scinon
995   web æfter wāgum   wundorsīona fela
     secga gehwylcum   þāra þe on swylc starað.
     Wæs þæt beorhte bold   tōbrocen swīðe
     eal inneweard   īrenbendum fæst,
     heorras tōhlidene;   hrōf āna genæs
1000   ealles ansund   þē se āglǣca
     fyrendǣdum fāg   on flēam gewand
     aldres orwēna.   Nō þæt ȳðe byð
     tō beflēonne   – fremme se þe wille –
     ac gesēcan sceal   sāwlberendra
1005   nȳde genȳdde,   niþða bearna
     grundbūendra,   gearwe stōwe

---

980 Ecglafes] eclafes   984 æghwǣr] æghwylc   985 stedenægla] steda nægla   986 hilde-rinces] hild . . . de rinces   987 eglu] egl   1004 gesecan] ge sacan

984b–5a **æghwǣr** 'everywhere'. The emendation of MS *æghwylc* removes the troublesome repetition *æghwylc . . . gehwylc*; **stedenægla** gen pl 'of the firm nails', an otherwise unrecorded word, is supported by *stedewong* 'plain, firm ground'.

987a **eglu unhēoru** 'horrible, monstrous'. For two adjectives without *and* cf. l. 1641a.

989 **īren ǣrgōd** '[no] proven sword' is parallel to *heardra nān* l. 988; *þæt* conj '[in such a way] that'.

991–2a **Ðā wæs . . . gefrætwod** 'Then forthwith Heorot was ordered adorned with hands' i.e. orders were given for men to adorn Heorot.

992 **fela þǣra wæs** 'it was many a one of them'.

998–9 See IVC3.

1000 **þē** here seems to mean 'when'; see *OES* §2595.

1004–6 'but [each one] (*se þe* l. 1003b) must go to that prepared place ordained (*genȳdde* l. 1005a acc sg fem) by fate for those who have souls, children of men dwelling on earth, [that place] where . . .'.

þǣr his līchoma   legerbedde fæst
swefeþ æfter symle.   þā wæs sǣl ond mǣl
þæt tō healle gang   Healfdenes sunu,
1010   wolde self cyning   symbel þicgan.
Ne gefrægen ic þā mǣgþe   māran weorode
ymb hyra sincgyfan   sēl gebǣran.
Bugon þā tō bence   blǣdāgande,
fylle gefægon;   fægere geþǣgon
1015   medoful manig   māgas þāra
swīðhicgende   on sele þām hēan
Hrōðgār ond Hrōþulf.   Heorot innan wæs
frēondum āfylled;   nalles fācenstafas
þēod-Scyldingas   þenden fremedon.
1020   Forgeaf þā Bēowulfe   brand Healfdenes,
segen gyldenne   sigores tō lēane
hroden hildecumbor,   helm ond byrnan;
mǣre māðþumsweord   manige gesāwon
beforan beorn beran.   Bēowulf geþah
1025   ful on flette,   nō hē þǣre feohgyfte
for scēotendum   scamigan þorfte;
ne gefrægn ic frēondlīcor   fēower mādmas
golde gegyrede   gummanna fela
in ealobence   ōðrum gesellan.
1030   Ymb þæs helmes hrōf   hēafodbeorge
wīrum bewunden   wala ūtan hēold
þæt him fēla lāf   frēcne ne meahte
scūrheard sceþðan   þonne scyldfreca
ongēan gramum   gangan scolde.
1035   Heht ðā eorla hlēo   eahta mēaras
fǣtedhlēore   on flet teôn
in under eoderas;   þāra ānum stōd
sadol searwum fāh   since gewurþad;
þæt wæs hildesetl   hēahcyninges

1022 hildecumbor] hilte cumbor   1026 sceotendum] scotenum   1031 wala] walan

1017b–19 It is generally accepted that these lines, in conjunction with ll. 1162b–5a, imply subsequent treachery on the part of Hrothulf. See ll. 1169–87 note and 1228–31 note. A contrary view is held by Sisam, Morgan, Mitchell, and others, who argue that, as Hrothulf was already co-ruler of the Danes with Hrothgar and as direct succession from father to son was not automatic, Hrothulf had nothing to gain by treachery; see *RES*, 43 (1992), 10–14.

1019 þenden adv.

1020 The unexpressed subject (*Guide* §193.7) of *Forgeaf* is Hrothgar; *brand* 'sword' is its object. For other examples of royal fathers giving their own father's sword to someone other than their sons see ll. 2152–62 and 2190–6a.

1030–4 See IVC5.

1035–42 See IVC9 (horses).

1036 fǣtedhlēore See IVC9.

1040 ðonne sweorda gelāc   sunu Healfdenes
efnan wolde;   nǣfre on ōre læg
wīdcūþes wīg   ðonne walu fēollon.
Ond ðā Bēowulfe   bēga gehwæþres
eodor Ingwina   onweald getēah
1045 wicga ond wǣpna,   hēt hine wēl brūcan.
Swā manlīce   mǣre þēoden
hordweard hæleþa   heaþorǣsas geald
mēarum ond mādmum   swā hȳ nǣfre man lȳhð
se þe secgan wile   sōð æfter rihte.

[The scop's song about Finnesburh]

XVI 1050   Ðā gȳt ǣghwylcum   eorla drihten
þāra þe mid Bēowulfe   brimlāde tēah
on þǣre medubence   māþðum gesealde
yrfelāfe   ond þone ǣnne heht
golde forgyldan   þone ðe Grendel ǣr
1055 māne ācwealde   swā hē hyra mā wolde
nefne him wītig god   wyrd forstōde
ond ðæs mannes mōd.   Metod eallum wēold
gumena cynnes   swā hē nū gīt dêð.
Forþan bið andgit   ǣghwǣr sēlest
1060 ferhðes foreþanc.   Fela sceal gebīdan
lēofes ond lāþes   se þe longe hēr
on ðyssum windagum   worolde brūceð.
þǣr wæs sang ond swēg   samod ætgædere
fore Healfdenes   hildewīsan,
1065 gomenwudu grēted,   gid oft wrecen
ðonne healgamen   Hrōþgāres scop
æfter medobence   mǣnan scolde:
Finnes eaferum   ðā hīe se fǣr begeat
hæleð Healf-Dena,   Hnæf Scyldinga
1070 in Frēswæle   feallan scolde.
Ne hūru Hildeburh   herian þorfte

1051 brimlade] brim leade

1046–8 **Swā manlīce . . . swā** 'So nobly . . . that' (*OES* §2870).

1055–6 **wolde . . . forstōde** pret subjs expressing unrealized condition (*Guide* §179). The subjects of *forstōde* are *god* and *mōd*.

1061 **lēofes and lāþes** 'of good and of bad'.

1066–159a The Finn Episode. See ID4 and D5, and IVD4.

1068 **Finnes eaferum** 'in company with the sons of Finn'. The syntax of this half-line is dubious and something may be missing between ll. 1067 and 1068.

1068b–9 **hīe . . . Healf-Dena** acc pl objects of *begeat*. *Hnæf* is the subject of *scolde* l. 1070.

Ēotena trēowe;   unsynnum wearð
beloren lēofum   æt þām lindplegan
bearnum ond brōðrum;   hīe on gebyrd hruron
1075 gāre wunde.   þæt wæs geōmuru ides.
Nalles hōlinga   Hōces dohtor
meotodsceaft bemearn   syþðan morgen cōm
ðā hēo under swegle   gesēon meahte
morþorbealo māga   þær hēo ær mæste hēold
1080 worolde wynne.   Wīg ealle fornam
Finnes þegnas   nemne fēaum ānum
þæt hē ne mehte   on þæm meðelstede
wīg Hengeste   wiht gefeohtan
ne þā wēalāfe   wīge forþringan
1085 þēodnes ðegne;   ac hig him geþingo budon
þæt hīe him ōðer flet   eal gerȳmdon
healle ond hēahsetl,   þæt hīe healfre geweald
wið Ēotena bearn   āgan mōston
ond æt feohgyftum   Folcwaldan sunu
1090 dōgra gehwylce   Dene weorþode,
Hengestes hēap   hringum wenede
efne swā swīðe   sincgestrēonum
fættan goldes   swā hē Frēsena cyn
on bēorsele   byldan wolde.
1095 Ðā hīe getruwedon   on twā healfa
fæste frioðuwære.   Fin Hengeste
elne unflitme   āðum benemde
þæt hē þā wēalāfe   weotena dōme
ārum hēolde,   þæt ðær ænig mon
1100 wordum ne worcum   wære ne bræce
ne þurh inwitsearo   æfre gemænden
ðēah hīe hira bēaggyfan   banan folgedon

1073 lindplegan] hild plegan   1079 heo] he

1072 **Ēotena** gen pl 'of the Jutes'. The comment here seems to imply that there were Jutes among Finn's warriors; cf. *Ēotena* l. 1141. But see l. 1088a note. On the Jutes see note to ll. 902b–3.

1073–4a **lēofum** pl 'dear ones' . . . **bearnum ond brōðrum** pl with sg reference 'son and brother'. See ll. 565b–7a note; **lindplegan** see IIIA7.

1076 **Hōces dohtor** Hildeburh.

1080b–5a The battle ended in stalemate.

1085 **þēodnes ðegne** dat sg = *Hengeste* l. 1083a, thane of Hnæf.

1085b–8 **hīe** l. 1086a refers to the Frisians, who were the only ones who could provide a second hall; **hīe** l. 1087b refers to the Danes. Who offered terms to whom is uncertain; convincing arguments that it was the Frisians have been met by equally convincing arguments that it was the Danes.

1088a This half-line suggests that there were also Jutes among the Danish warriors; cf. l. 1072 note.

1097 **elne unflitme** 'with undisputed zeal'. The form *unflitme* is unexplained.

1099 **þæt** The sense here seems to be the unusual one 'provided that' (*OES* §3660).

1100–1 The number changes from sg *bræce* to pl *gemænden*.

ðēodenlēase   þā him swā geþearfod wæs;
gyf þonne Frȳsna hwylc   frēcnan spræce
1105 ðæs morþorhetes   myndgiend wære
þonne hit sweordes ecg   syððan scolde . . .
Ād wæs geæfned   ond icge gold
āhæfen of horde.   Here-Scyldinga
betst beadorinca   wæs on bæl gearu.
1110 Æt þæm āde wæs   ēþgesȳne
swātfāh syrce   swȳn ealgylden
eofer īrenheard   æþeling manig
wundum āwyrded;   sume on wæle crungon.
Hēt ðā Hildeburh   æt Hnæfes āde
1115 hire selfre sunu   sweoloðe befæstan,
bānfatu bærnan   ond on bæl dôn
ēame on eaxle.   Ides gnornode,
geōmrode giddum.   Gūðrinc āstāh.
Wand tō wolcnum   wælfȳra mæst,
1120 hlynode for hlāwe;   hafelan multon,
bengeato burston   ðonne blōd ætspranc,
lāðbite līces.   Līg ealle forswealg,
gæsta gīfrost,   þāra ðe þær gūð fornam
bēga folces;   wæs hira blæd scacen.

[The scop's song about Finnesburh continued]

XVII 1125   Gewiton him ðā wīgend   wīca nēosian
frēondum befeallen,   Frȳsland gesēon
hāmas ond hēaburh.   Hengest ðā gȳt
wælfāgne winter   wunode mid Finne

1104 frecnan] frecnen   1107 Ad] að   1117 eame] earme

1106 'then afterwards it must be the sword's edge' or 'then afterwards it must be left to the edge of the sword'.
1107–24 See IVC10 (burials).
1107 'The funeral pyre was made ready.' This seems to give better sense than MS *að* 'The oath was performed'; **icge** The etymology of *icge* (and of the equally puzzling *incge* in l. 2577) is unknown. From context we assume a meaning like 'mighty' or 'splendid'.
1113 **sume** 'some men', possibly an understatement 'many men'.
1117 **ēame on eaxle** lit. 'to the uncle at the shoulder', with *ēame* dat of possession; cf. l. 40 *him on bearme*. Translate 'by his uncle's side'. See IIIA7.
1121 **ðonne** conj 'whenever'.
1123 **þāra ðe** the *se'þe* relative (*Guide* §163.1), with *þāra* dependent on *ealle* l. 1122.
1125–31a The Frisian warriors returned to their homes while the Danes remained with Finn.
1126 **befeallen** uninflected nom pl masc. Cf. l. 46 note.

> eal unhlitme,   eard gemunde
> 1130 þēah þe hē ne meahte   on mere drīfan
> hringedstefnan: holm storme wēol,
> won wið winde,   winter ȳþe belēac
> īsgebinde   oþ ðæt ōþer cōm
> gēar in geardas   swā nū gȳt dêð,
> 1135 þā ðe syngāles   sēle bewitiað
> wuldortorhtan weder.   Ðā wæs winter scacen,
> fæger foldan bearm;   fundode wrecca
> gist of geardum;   hē tō gyrnwræce
> swīðor þōhte   þonne tō sǣlāde,
> 1140 gif hē torngemōt   þurhtēon mihte
> þæt hē Ēotena bearn   inne gemunde.
> Swā hē ne forwyrnde   woroldrǣdenne
> þonne him Hūnlāfing   hildelēoman
> billa sēlest   on bearm dyde;
> 1145 þæs wǣron mid Ēotenum   ecge cūðe.
> Swylce ferhðfrecan   Fin eft begeat
> sweordbealo slīðen   æt his selfes hām
> siþðan grimne gripe   Gūðlāf ond Ōslāf
> æfter sǣsīðe   sorge mǣndon,
> 1150 ætwiton wēana dǣl;   ne meahte wǣfre mōd
> forhabban in hreþre.   Ðā wæs heal roden
> fēonda fēorum,   swilce Fin slægen
> cyning on corþre   ond sēo cwēn numen.
> Scēotend Scyldinga   tō scypon feredon
> 1155 eal ingesteald   eorðcyninges

1129 eal unhlitme] *l* unhlitme   1130 ne] *not in MS*   1151 roden] hroden

1129a MS *l unhlitme* an unexplained half-line, sometimes translated 'without [casting of] lots'. This has been taken to mean 'involuntarily' – he was not given the opportunity to cast lots – or 'voluntarily' – he chose not to, depending on whether one reads *hĕ* or *hĕ ne* in l. 1130.

1130 ne not in MS. We add *ne*, which the scribe could easily have omitted in the sequence *þe he ne meahte* – and so translate l. 1129a as 'involuntarily' – because ll. 1131b–3a seem to explain why Hengest could not sail home.

1135–6a These lines are an appositional variant of *gēar* l. 1134. The nom pl rel pron *þā ðe* 'those which' anticipates, and is explained by, l. 1136a.

1140 The *gif* clause is governed by *þōhte* l. 1139. Translate: 'wondering whether . . . .'.

1141 *þæt* conj 'so that' introducing a clause of purpose; *inne* adv 'therein'.

1142 *Swā* adv.

1143 *þonne* conj with pret 'whenever' (*Guide* §168 s.v. *þonne*).

1142–4 A difficult and much-discussed passage. We translate 'He did not refuse the universal rule [of vengeance] (*woroldrǣdenne*) whenever Hunlafing placed the battle-gleamer, the best of swords, in his lap.' Some, however, take *Hūnlāfing* as the name of the sword.

1145 *þæs* dem pron gen sg dependent on *ecge*; *mid Ēotenum* See note to ll. 902b–3.

1151 roden 'reddened'. MS *hroden* 'adorned' would give grim sense but the four-fold alliteration argues against it. See l. 574b note.

swylce hīe æt Finnes hām   findan meahton
sigla searogimma.   Hīe on sǣlāde
drihtlīce wīf   tō Denum feredon,
lǣddon tō lēodum.
            Lēoð wæs āsungen
1160 glēomannes gyd.   Gamen eft āstāh,
beorhtode bencswēg,   byrelas sealdon
wīn of wunderfatum.   þā cwōm Wealhþēo forð
gān under gyldnum bēage   þǣr þā gōdan twēgen
sǣton suhtergefæderan;   þā gӯt wæs hiera sib ætgædere,
ǣghwylc ōðrum trӯwe.   Swylce þǣr Unferþ þyle
æt fōtum sæt frēan Scyldinga;   gehwylc hiora his ferhþe trēowde
þæt hē hæfde mōd micel   þēah þe hē his māgum nǣre
ārfæst æt ecga gelācum.   Spræc ðā ides Scyldinga:
'Onfōh þissum fulle,   frēodrihten mīn,
1170 sinces brytta.   þū on sǣlum wes,
goldwine gumena,   ond tō Gēatum spræc
mildum wordum   swā sceal man dôn.
Bēo wið Gēatas glæd,   geofena gemyndig
nēan ond feorran   þe þū nū hafast.
1175 Mē man sægde   þæt þū ðē for sunu wolde
hererinc habban.   Heorot is gefælsod,
bēahsele beorhta;   brūc þenden þū mōte
manigra mēdo   ond þīnum māgum lǣf
folc ond rīce   þonne ðū forð scyle
1180 metodsceaft seôn.   Ic mīnne can
glædne Hrōþulf,   þæt hē þā geogoðe wile
ārum healdan   gyf þū ǣr þonne hē,
wine Scildinga,   worold oflǣtest;
wēne ic þæt hē mid gōde   gyldan wille
1185 uncran eaferan   gif hē þæt eal gemon,
hwæt wit tō willan   ond tō worðmyndum
umborwesendum ǣr   ārna gefremedon.'

1165 Unferþ] hun ferþ   1174 þe] *not in MS*   1176 hererinc] here ric

1156 **swylce** acc pl 'such [things] as'. The *swylce* clause is a second object of *feredon* l. 1154. 1162b–5a See ll. 1017b–19 note.
1164 **suhtergefæderan** Hrothgar and Hrothulf. See l. 84 note.
1169–87 Scholars have usually assumed that Wealhtheow's speech is ironical, implying that Hrothulf did not remain loyal to Hrethric and Hrothmund and that there was treachery. But some believe that she was sincere. See ll. 1017b–19 note.
1177 **þenden** conj.
1180b–2a **can** has two objects – a noun and a clause; cf. ll. 2–3 note. Here we could translate 'I know that my gracious Hrothgar . . .'.
1185 **þæt eal** anticipates the noun clause introduced by *hwæt* in l. 1186, which governs gen pl *ārna* l. 1187.

Hwearf þā bī bence   þær hyre byre wǣron
Hrēðrīc ond Hrōðmund   ond hæleþa bearn
1190 giogoð ætgædere;   þær se gōda sæt
Bēowulf Gēata   be þǣm gebrōðrum twǣm.

[The warriors at rest]

XVIII   Him wæs ful boren   ond frēondlaþu
wordum bewægned   ond wunden gold
ēstum geēawed;   earmhrēade twā
1195 hrægl ond hringas,   healsbēaga mǣst
þāra þe ic on foldan   gefrægen hæbbe.
Nǣnigne ic under swegle   sēlran hȳrde
hordmāðum hæleþa   syþðan Hāma ætwæg
tō þǣre byrhtan byrig   Brōsinga mene,
1200 sigle ond sincfæt;   searonīðas fealh
Eormenrīces,   gecēas ēcne rǣd.
þone hring hæfde   Higelāc Gēata
nefa Swertinges   nȳhstan sīðe
siðþan hē under segne   sinc ealgode,
1205 wælrēaf werede;   hyne wyrd fornam
syþðan hē for wlenco   wēan āhsode
fǣhðe tō Frȳsum.   Hē þā frætwe wæg
eorclanstānas   ofer ȳða ful
rīce þēoden;   hē under rande gecranc.
1210 Gehwearf þā in Francna fæþm   feorh cyninges,
brēostgewǣdu   ond se bēah somod;
wyrsan wīgfrecan   wæl rēafeden
æfter gūðsceare,   Gēata lēode
hrēawīc hēoldon.   Heal swēge onfēng.
1215 Wealhðēo maþelode,   hēo fore þǣm werede spræc:
'Brūc ðisses bēages,   Bēowulf lēofa,
hyse, mid hǣle   ond þisses hrægles nēot
þēodgestrēona   ond geþēoh tela,

1194 earmhreade] earm reade   1198 hordmaðum] hord mad mum   1199 þære] here
1218 þeodgestreona] þeo ge streona

1199 **Brōsinga mene** 'the necklace of the Brosings'. The reference is uncertain.
1201 **gecēas ēcne rǣd** '[he] chose long-lasting (i.e. temporal) benefits' or '[he] chose eternal (i.e. spiritual) benefits'.
1202–14a Hygelac died in a raid on the Frisian territory of the Franks. See IVB.
1202 **þone hring** 'That ring', i.e. *healsbēaga mǣst* l. 1195 'the greatest of neck-rings', and *ðisses bēages* l. 1216 'this ring'. In ll. 2172–4a we learn that Beowulf gave to Hygd, Hygelac's wife, *ðone healsbēah* which Wealhtheow gave him.
1214b 'The hall received noise', i.e. it echoed with applause or cheering.

cen þec mid cræfte,   ond þyssum cnyhtum wes
1220 lára líðe.   Ic þē þæs lēan geman.
Hafast þū gefēred   þæt ðē feor ond nēah
ealne wīdeferhþ   weras ehtigað
efne swā sīde   swā sǣ bebūgeð,
windgeard weallas.   Wes þenden þū lifige,
1225 æþeling, ēadig.   Ic þē an tela
sincgestrēona.   Bēo þū suna mīnum
dǣdum gedēfe,   drēamhealdende.
Hēr is ǣghwylc eorl   ōþrum getrȳwe
mōdes milde   mandrihtne hold,
1230 þegnas syndon geþwǣre,   þēod ealgearo,
druncne dryhtguman   dōð swā ic bidde.'
Ēode þā tō setle.   þǣr wæs symbla cyst,
druncon wīn weras.   Wyrd ne cūþon
geōsceaft grimne   swā hit āgangen wearð
1235 eorla manegum   syþðan ǣfen cwōm
ond him Hrōþgār gewāt   tō hofe sīnum
rīce tō ræste.   Reced weardode
unrīm eorla   swā hīe oft ǣr dydon.
Bencþelu beredon;   hit geondbrǣded wearð
1240 beddum ond bolstrum.   Bēorscealca sum
fūs ond fǣge   fletræste gebēag.
Setton him tō hēafdon   hilderandas
bordwudu beorhtan;   þǣr on bence wæs
ofer æþelinge   ȳþgesēne
1245 heaþostēapa helm   hringed byrne
þrecwudu þrymlīc.   Wæs þēaw hyra
þæt hīe oft wǣron   an wīg gearwe,
ge æt hām gē on herge   ge gehwæþer þāra
efne swylce mǣla   swylce hira mandryhtne
1250 þearf gesǣlde;   wæs sēo þēod tilu.

1229 hold] hol

1219 **þyssum cnyhtum** Hrethric and Hrothmund. See ll. 1169–87 note and cf. ll. 1226b–7.
1224 **þenden** conj 'while'.
1228–31 Here too irony has been assumed. See ll. 1169–87 note.
1231 **druncne** 'having drunk'. Cf. l. 1233a.
1238 **unrīm eorla** 'a countless number of warriors'. *Næs Bēowulf ðǣr* . . . l. 1299!
1246b–8a 'It was their custom that they were regularly ready for combat, both on the defensive and on the offensive . . .'. For *an wīg gearwe* cf. *on bæl gearu* l. 1109 and *an = on* l. 677.
1248 **ge gehwæþer þāra** 'and [in] each of those [situations]'.
1249 **efne swylce mǣla swylce** 'just at such times as'.

THE FIGHT WITH GRENDEL'S MOTHER (*lines 1251–1887*)

[The attack by Grendel's mother]

XVIIII   Sigon þā tō slǣpe.   Sum sāre angeald
                æfenrǣste   swā him ful oft gelamp
                siþðan goldsele   Grendel warode,
                unriht æfnde   oþ þæt ende becwōm,
     1255   swylt æfter synnum.   þæt gesȳne wearþ
                wīdcūþ werum   þætte wrecend þā gȳt
                lifde æfter lāþum   lange þrāge
                æfter gūðceare;   Grendles mōdor
                ides āglǣcwīf   yrmþe gemunde
     1260   se þe wæteregesan   wunian scolde
                cealde strēamas   siþðan Cāin wearð
                tō ecgbanan   āngan brēþer
                fæderenmǣge;   hē þā fāg gewāt
                morþre gemearcod   mandrēam flêon,
     1265   wēsten warode.   þanon wōc fela
                geōsceaftgāsta;   wæs þǣra Grendel sum,
                heorowearh hetelīc   se æt Heorote fand
                wæccendne wer   wīges bīdan;
                þǣr him āglǣca   ætgrǣpe wearð;
     1270   hwæþre hē gemunde   mægenes strenge
                gimfæste gife   ðe him god sealde
                ond him tō anwaldan   āre gelȳfde
                frōfre ond fultum;   ðȳ hē þone fēond ofercwōm,
                gehnǣgde helle gāst.   þā hē hēan gewāt
     1275   drēame bedǣled   dēaþwīc sêon,
                mancynnes fēond.   Ond his mōdor þā gȳt
                gīfre ond galgmōd   gegān wolde
                sorhfulne sīð,   sunu dēoð wrecan.
                Cōm þā tō Heorote   ðǣr Hring-Dene
     1280   geond þæt sæld swǣfun.   þā ðǣr sōna wearð

1261 Cain] camp   1278 deoð] þeod

1257 **lange þrāge** 'for a long time' satisfies the demands of alliteration rather than of context. Its position between two *æfter* phrases in the subordinate clause makes it difficult to take it with *wīdcūþ* l. 1256.

1260 This is one of the five examples in the poem in which the rel pron *se þe* or *se* refers to a feminine antecedent. There are similar examples in other OE texts. See *OES* §2358.

1273 **ðȳ** 'by that'. Cf. ll. 240b–3 note.

1278 **sunu** gen sg.

edhwyrft eorlum siþðan inne fealh
Grendles mōdor. Wæs se gryre læssa
efne swā micle swā bið mægþa cræft
wīggryre wīfes, be wæpnedmen,
1285 þonne heoru bunden, hamere geþrūen,
sweord swāte fāh, swīn ofer helme
ecgum dyhtig andweard scireð.
Đā wæs on healle heardecg togen
sweord ofer setlum, sīdrand manig
1290 hafen handa fæst; helm ne gemunde
byrnan sīde þā hine se brōga angeat.
Hēo wæs on ofste, wolde ūt þanon,
feore beorgan þā hēo onfunden wæs;
hraðe hēo æþelinga ānne hæfde
1295 fæste befangen, þā hēo tō fenne gang.
Se wæs Hrōþgāre hæleþa lēofost
on gesīðes hād be sǣm twēonum
rīce randwiga þone ðe hēo on ræste ābrēat
blǣdfæstne beorn. Næs Bēowulf ðǣr
1300 ac wæs ōþer in ǣr geteohhod
æfter māþðumgife mǣrum Gēate.
Hrēam wearð in Heorote; hēo under heolfre genam
cūþe folme; cearu wæs genīwod,
geworden in wīcun. Ne wæs þæt gewrixle til
1305 þæt hīe on bā healfa bicgan scoldon
frēonda fēorum. þā wæs frōd cyning
hār hilderinc on hrēon mōde
syðþan hē aldorþegn unlyfigendne
þone dēorestan dēadne wisse.
1310 Hraþe wæs tō būre Bēowulf fetod
sigorēadig secg. Samod ǣrdæge
ēode eorla sum æþele cempa

1285 geþruen] geþuren

1282b–4 The narrator's account of the fight against Grendel's mother does not bear out this statement, unless it is taken to refer to the fact that the female kills only one thane whereas the male kills thirty.

1284 be wǣpnedmen 'in comparison with a man'. Strict grammar would require *be wǣpnedmannes* 'in comparison with a man's'.

1286–7 andweard adj 'opposing' i.e. enemy, qualifies *swīn* 'boar [image]'. Both can be either neut sg or neut pl; see *Guide* §§34 and 67.

1290b Unexpressed subject; cf. l. 1020 note and translate 'No one remembered the helmet . . .'.

1292 Hēo . . . wolde ūt 'She . . . wanted out'!

1298 þone ðe 'whom', an example of the *'seþe* rel pron (*Guide* §163). So also *se þe* l. 1342.

1300 in not a prep but a noun = *inn* (nom) 'dwelling'.

1305 þæt rel pron.

self mid gesīðum   þǣr se snotera bād
hwæþer him alwalda   ǣfre wille
1315 æfter wēaspelle   wyrpe gefremman.
Gang ðā æfter flōre   fyrdwyrðe man
mid his handscale   – healwudu dynede –
þæt hē þone wīsan   wordum nǣgde
frēan Ingwina,   frægn gif him wǣre
1320 æfter nēodlaðu   niht getǣse.

[Hrothgar's description of the haunted mere]

XX   Hrōðgār maþelode,   helm Scyldinga:
'Ne frīn þū æfter sǣlum.   Sorh is genīwod
Denigea lēodum.   Dēad is Æschere,
Yrmenlāfes   yldra brōþor
1325 mīn rūnwita   ond mīn rǣdbora
eaxlgestealla   ðonne wē on orlege
hafelan weredon   þonne hniton fēþan,
eoferas cnysedan.   Swylc scolde eorl wesan
æþeling ǣrgōd   swylc Æschere wæs.
1330 Wearð him on Heorote   tō handbanan
wælgǣst wǣfre;   ic ne wāt hwæþer
atol ǣse wlanc   eftsīðas tēah
fylle gefægnod.   Hēo þā fǣhðe wræc
þe þū gystran niht   Grendel cwealdest
1335 þurh hǣstne hād   heardum clammum
forþan hē tō lange   lēode mīne
wanode ond wyrde.   Hē æt wīge gecrang
ealdres scyldig   ond nū ōþer cwōm
mihtig mānscaða,   wolde hyre mǣge wrecan
1340 ge feor hafað   fǣhðe gestǣled
þæs þe þincean mæg   þegne monegum
se þe æfter sincgyfan   on sefan grēoteþ –
hreþerbealo hearde: nū sēo hand ligeð
se þe ēow wēlhwylcra   wilna dohte.

1314 hwæþer] hwæþre   alwalda] alf walda   1318 nǣgde] hnæg *at edge of MS*   1329 æþeling]
not in MS   1333 gefægnod] ge frægnod

1314 **wille** 3rd sing pres subj where the pret *wolde* might have been expected.
1328 **eoferas** See IVC5.
1334 **þe** indeclinable rel pron 'in which'.
1340 **feor** 'far', i.e. 'a long way, grievously'.
1344 **se þe** masc refers to fem *sēo hand* l. 1343; see l. 1260 note. It might be explained by the fact
that *sēo hand* is a synecdoche for masc *Æschere*.

1345 Ic þæt londbūend   lēode mīne
      selerǣdende   secgan hȳrde
      þæt hīe gesāwon   swylce twēgen
      micle mearcstapan   mōras healdan,
      ellorgǣstas.   Ðǣra ōðer wæs,
1350 þæs þe hīe gewislīcost   gewitan meahton,
      idese onlīcnæs,   ōðer earmsceapen
      on weres wæstmum   wræclāstas træd
      næfne hē wæs māra   þonne ǣnig man ōðer;
      þone on geārdagum   Grendel nemdon
1355 foldbūende;   nō hīe fæder cunnon
      hwæþer him ǣnig wæs   ǣr ācenned
      dyrnra gāsta.   Hīe dȳgel lond
      warigeað wulfhleoþu   windige næssas
      frēcne fengelād   ðǣr fyrgenstrēam
1360 under næssa genipu   niþer gewīteð
      flōd under foldan.   Nis þæt feor heonon
      mīlgemearces   þæt se mere standeð;
      ofer þǣm hongiað   hrinde bearwas,
      wudu wyrtum fæst   wæter oferhelmað.
1365 þǣr mæg nihta gehwǣm   nīðwundor sēon
      fȳr on flōde.   Nō þæs frōd leofað
      gumena bearna   þæt þone grund wite.
      Ðēah þe hǣðstapa   hundum geswenced
      heorot hornum trum   holtwudu sēce
1370 feorran geflȳmed,   ǣr hē feorh seleð
      aldor on ōfre   ǣr hē in wille
      hafelan hȳdan;   nis þæt hēoru stōw.
      þonon ȳðgeblond   up āstīgeð
      won tō wolcnum   þonne wind styreþ
1375 lāð gewidru   oð þæt lyft drysmaþ,
      roderas rēotað.   Nū is se rǣd gelang

1354 nemdon] nem . . .   1362 standeð] standeð   1372 hydan] *not in MS*

1349b–51 oðer . . . oðer 'one . . . the other'; þæs þe conj 'as'.
1353 næfne conj 'except that'.
1355b–7a Lit. 'They did not know of a father, whether any had been begotten of mysterious spirits for them.' Translate 'They did not know whether any father . . .'. Cf. ll. 1180b–2a note.
1357b–76a The description of Grendel's mere will repay careful analysis.
1362 mīlgemearces adv gen (*Guide* §190.5) 'in the measure of miles'.
1365 The absence of a subject for mæg . . . sēon is unexplained but occurs elsewhere. Translate 'There one can see . . .'.
1366 fȳr on flōde 'fire in the water'. See ll. 1512b–17.
1366b–7 A difficult and disputed idiom. We take þæs . . . þæt as a conj and translate 'Not at all lives among the sons of men [one] so wise that [he] may know the bottom.' See *OES* §§2878 and 2993.
1370–1 ǣr . . . ǣr adv . . . conj 'before'.

eft æt þē ānum.   Eard gīt ne const
frēcne stōwe   ðǣr þū findan miht
felasinnigne secg;   sēc gif þū dyrre.
1380 Ic þē þā fǣhðe   fēo lēanige
ealdgestrēonum   swā ic ǣr dyde
wundnum golde   gyf þū on weg cymest.'

[The expedition to the mere]

XXI   Bēowulf maþelode,   bearn Ecgþēowes:
            'Ne sorga, snotor guma.   Sēlre bið ǣghwǣm
1385 þæt hē his frēond wrece   þonne hē fela murne.
            Ūre ǣghwylc sceal   ende gebīdan
            worolde līfes;   wyrce se þe mōte
            dōmes ǣr dēaþe;   þæt bið drihtguman
            unlifgendum   æfter sēlest.
1390 Ārīs, rīces weard,   uton hraþe fēran
            Grendles māgan   gang scēawigan.
            Ic hit þē gehāte: nō hē on helm losaþ
            ne on foldan fæþm   ne on fyrgenholt
            ne on gyfenes grund,   gā þǣr hē wille.
1395 Ðȳs dōgor þū   geþyld hafa
            wēana gehwylces   swā ic þē wēne tō.'
            Āhlēop ðā se gomela,   gode þancode
            mihtigan drihtne   þæs se man gespræc.
            þā wæs Hrōðgāre   hors gebǣted
1400 wicg wundenfeax.   Wīsa fengel
            geatolīc gende;   gumfēþa stōp
            lindhæbbendra.   Lāstas wǣron
            æfter waldswaþum   wīde gesȳne,
            gang ofer grundas   þǣr gegnum fōr
1405 ofer myrcan mōr,   magoþegna bǣr
            þone sēlestan   sāwollēasne
            þāra þe mid Hrōðgāre   hām eahtode.
            Oferēode þā   æþelinga bearn
            stēap stānhliðo   stīge nearwe

1382 wundnum] wundini   1404 þær] *not in MS*

1390 The alliteration here is on *r-*, the *h-* of *hraþe* apparently being unpronounced. Cf. the spelling *rape* in l. 724. (Elsewhere *hraþe* can alliterate on *h*, e.g. ll. 1576, 1937, etc.)

1392–4 **hē** . . . **hē** masc pron, referring to Grendel's mother, takes the grammatical gender of *magan* l. 1391.

1398 **þæs** 'for what' (*Guide* §163.5).

1408–21 See IE8.

1408 **bearn** nom sg Beowulf.

1410 enge ānpaðas   uncūð gelād
neowle næssas   nicorhūsa fela;
hē fēara sum   beforan gengde
wīsra monna   wong scēawian
oþ þæt hē fǣringa   fyrgenbēamas
1415 ofer hārne stān   hleonian funde
wynlēasne wudu;   wæter under stōd
drēorig ond gedrēfed.   Denum eallum wæs
winum Scyldinga   weorce on mōde
tō geþolianne,   ðegne monegum
1420 oncȳð eorla gehwǣm   syðþan Æscheres
on þām holmclife   hafelan mētton.
Flōd blōde wēol   – folc tō sǣgon –
hātan heolfre.   Horn stundum song
fūslīc fyrdlēoð.   Fēþa eal gesæt.
1425 Gesāwon ðā æfter wætere   wyrmcynnes fela
sellīce sǣdracan   sund cunnian,
swylce on næshleoðum   nicras licgean
ðā on undernmǣl   oft bewitigað
sorhfulne sīð   on seglrāde,
1430 wyrmas ond wildēor.   Hīe on weg hruron
bitere ond gebolgne;   bearhtm ongēaton,
gūðhorn galan.   Sumne Gēata lēod
of flānbogan   fēores getwǣfde
ȳðgewinnes   þæt him on aldre stōd
1435 herestrǣl hearda;   hē on holme wæs
sundes þē sǣnra   ðē hyne swylt fornam.
Hræþe wearð on ȳðum   mid eofersprēotum
heorohōcyhtum   hearde genearwod,
nīða genǣged   ond on næs togen,
1440 wundorlīc wǣgbora;   weras scēawedon
gryrelīcne gist.   Gyrede hine Bēowulf
eorlgewǣdum,   nalles for ealdre mearn;
scolde herebyrne   hondum gebrōden
sīd ond searofāh   sund cunnian,
1445 sēo ðe bāncofan   beorgan cūþe

1424 fyrdleoð] . . . leoð

1418 **weorce** dat sg used adverbially, lit. 'as a distress', in combination with *wæs* l. 1417. Translate 'It was distressing . . .'.

1428 **ðā** rel pron nom pl 'who'.

1434 **þæt** conj 'so that/in such a way that'.

1435b–6 Several explanations for the *þē* . . . *ðē* sequence are possible; see *OES* §§2106 and 3138. We detect grim humour here and translate 'He was slower at swimming in the sea because death had destroyed him.'

1443–7 See IVC6 (coats of mail).

<blockquote>

þæt him hildegrāp   hreþre ne mihte
eorres inwitfeng   aldre gesceþðan
ac se hwīta helm   hafelan werede,
se þe meregrundas   mengan scolde

1450 sēcan sundgebland   since geweorðad
befongen frēawrāsnum;   swā hine fyrndagum
worhte wǣpna smið,   wundrum tēode,
besette swīnlīcum   þæt hine syðþan nō
brond ne beadomēcas   bītan ne meahton.

1455 Næs þæt þonne mǣtost   mægenfultuma
þæt him on ðearfe lāh   ðyle Hrōðgāres
– wæs þǣm hæftmēce   Hrunting nama –
þæt wæs ān foran   ealdgestrēona;
ecg wæs īren   ātertānum fāh

1460 āhyrded heaþoswāte;   nǣfre hit æt hilde ne swāc
manna ǣngum   þāra þe hit mid mundum bewand
se ðe gryresīðas   gegān dorste
folcstede fāra;   næs þæt forma sīð
þæt hit ellenweorc   æfnan scolde.

1465 Hūru ne gemunde   mago Ecglāfes
eafoþes cræftig   þæt hē ǣr gespræc
wīne druncen,   þā hē þæs wǣpnes onlāh
sēlran sweordfrecan,   selfa ne dorste
under ȳða gewin   aldre genēþan,

1470 drihtscype drēogan;   þǣr hē dōme forlēas
ellenmǣrðum.   Ne wæs þǣm ōðrum swā
syðþan hē hine tō gūðe   gegyred hæfde.

</blockquote>

[Beowulf's attack on Grendel's mother]

XXII   Bēowulf maþelode,   bearn Ecgþēowes:
            'Geþenc nū, se mǣra   maga Healfdenes,

1446–7 **hreþre . . . aldre** parallel dat sgs governed by the inf *gesceþðan*.
1448–54 See IVC5.
1451b–3 **swā . . . þæt** 'in such a way . . . that'.
1454 **brond ne beadomēcas** 'searing sword nor blades of war'.
1455–64 See IVC8 (swords).
1455–8 **þæt . . . þæt . . . þæt** dem 'that [thing]' . . . rel pron 'which' . . . dem 'that [thing]'.
1456 **ðyle Hrōðgāres** Unferth.
1459 **ātertānum fāh** See IVC8.
1461 **mid mundum** dat pl. See IVC8.
1465 **mago Ecglāfes** Unferth.
1471 **þǣm ōðrum** Beowulf.
1474 **Geþenc nū, se mǣra** Ignore *se*. The idiom by which the demonstrative is used with the vocative occurs in other OE poems but cannot be translated naturally into MnE.

1475   snottra fengel,   nū ic eom sīðes fūs,
      goldwine gumena,   hwæt wit geō spræcon:
      gif ic æt þearfe   þīnre scolde
      aldre linnan,   þæt ðū mē ā wære
      forðgewitenum   on fæder stæle.

1480   Wes þū mundbora   mīnum magoþegnum
      hondgesellum   gif mec hild nime;
      swylce þū ðā mādmas   þe þū mē sealdest,
      Hrōðgār lēofa,   Higelāce onsend.
      Mæg þonne on þæm golde ongitan   Gēata dryhten,

1485   gesēon sunu Hrædles,   þonne hē on þæt sinc starað,
      þæt ic gumcystum   gōdne funde
      bēaga bryttan,   brēac þonne mōste.
      Ond þū Unferð læt   ealde lāfe
      wrætlīc wægsweord   wīdcūðne man

1490   heardecg habban;   ic mē mid Hruntinge
      dōm gewyrce   oþðe mec dēað nimeð.'
      Æfter þæm wordum   Weder-Gēata lēod
      efste mid elne,   nalas andsware
      bīdan wolde;   brimwylm onfēng

1495   hilderince.   Ðā wæs hwīl dæges
      ær hē þone grundwong   ongytan mehte,
      sōna þæt onfunde   se ðe flōda begong
      heorogīfre behēold   hund missēra
      grim ond grædig   þæt þær gumena sum

1500   ælwihta eard   ufan cunnode.
      Grāp þā tōgēanes,   gūðrinc gefēng
      atolan clommum;   nō þȳ ær in gescōd
      hālan līce;   hring ūtan ymbbearh
      þæt hēo þone fyrdhom   ðurhfōn ne mihte

1488 Unferð] hunferð

1476 **hwæt wit geō spræcon** i.e. in ll. 946b–50.

1485 **Hrædles** See l. 454 note.

1487 **brēac** 'enjoyed [them]', the antecedent being *beaga* in l. 1487a. For unexpressed objects see *Guide* §193.7.

1488–91 Beowulf tells Hrothgar that if he, Beowulf, does not survive the monster-fight, then Hrothgar should give to Unferth his (Beowulf's) sword. Beowulf hopes to win glory with the sword Hrunting that Unferth has lent him.

1495b–1500 **Ðā wæs hwīl dæges . . . cunnode** 'As it was daytime before he (Beowulf) could discover the bottom, the grim and ravenous one who, furiously greedy, had guarded the watery region for fifty years immediately perceived that some man was exploring the alien creatures' domain from above.' The fact that it was now daytime explains why the ogress detected Beowulf's presence so quickly.

1497 **se ðe** rel pron 'that [one] who' is masc even though it refers to Grendel's mother. See l. 1260 note.

1502 **nō þȳ ær** 'no sooner for that'. Grendel's mother seized Beowulf, but that did not make it easier for her to wound him. See ll. 753b–4 note.

1505 locene leoðosyrcan   lāþan fingrum.
Bær þā sēo brimwylf,   þā hēo tō botme cōm,
hringa þengel   tō hofe sīnum
swā hē ne mihte   – nō hē þæs mōdig wæs –
wǣpna gewealdan   ac hine wundra þæs fela
1510 swencte on sunde,   sǣdēor monig
hildetūxum   heresyrcan bræc,
ēhton āglǣcan.   Đā se eorl ongeat
þæt hē in nīðsele   nāthwylcum wæs
þǣr him nǣnig wæter   wihte ne sceþede
1515 ne him for hrōfsele   hrīnan ne mehte
fǣrgripe flōdes;   fȳrlēoht geseah,
blācne lēoman   beorhte scīnan.
Ongeat þā se gōda   grundwyrgenne
merewīf mihtig,   mægenrǣs forgeaf
1520 hildebille,   hond sweng ne oftēah
þæt hire on hafelan   hringmǣl āgōl
grǣdig gūðlēoð.   Đā se gist onfand
þæt se beadolēoma   bītan nolde,
aldre sceþðan   ac sēo ecg geswāc
1525 ðēodne æt þearfe;   ðolode ǣr fela
hondgemōta,   helm oft gescær
fǣges fyrdhrægl;   ðā wæs forma sīð
dēorum mādme   þæt his dōm ālæg.
Eft wæs anrǣd,   nalas elnes læt,
1530 mǣrða gemyndig   mæg Hȳlāces
wearp ðā wundenmǣl   wrǣttum gebunden
yrre ōretta   þæt hit on eorðan læg

1506 brimwylf] brim wyl   1508 þæs] þæm   1510 swencte] swecte   1513 in] *not in*
MS   1520 hond sweng] hord swenge   1531 wundenmǣl] wundel mæl

1508 **nō hē . . . wæs** 'no matter how brave he was'. See *OES* §§3473–5.

1512 **ēhton āglǣcan** '[the sea-beasts] vexed [their] adversary'; *āglǣcan* is gen sg obj of *ēhton* and refers to Beowulf. For the change in number, see *Guide* §187.3(b).

1512b–17 Beowulf's fight with the ogress takes place in a dry interior where no water can penetrate and there is ample air to sustain both animal life and fire. In a close analogue to this episode in the *Grettissaga* the locale of the battle is markedly similar, and the saga makes clearer what the setting is: the hero dives into the mere and swims down beneath the turbulence of a waterfall, emerging behind the waterfall, where he discovers a cave above the waterline of the mere. It is in this cave that the monster dwells and it is here that the battle takes place. See IVE6.

1519b–22a **mægenrǣs . . . grǣdig gūðlēoð** 'he (Beowulf) gave a powerful impetus to his sword, his hand did not shrink from the blow, so that the ring-patterned [blade] sang a greedy war-song on her head'.

1521 **hringmǣl** See IVC8 and figures 15, and 9 and 17b.

1522b **gist** 'visitor, intruder' (i.e. Beowulf).

1522b–8 Other monsters in Germanic lore are invulnerable to all weapons except their own. Cf. ll. 1557ff.

1529–30 **Eft wæs . . . Hȳlāces** 'the kinsman of Hygelac, mindful of glorious deeds, was yet again resolute, not at all slack in valour'.

stīð ond stȳlecg;   strenge getruwode,
mundgripe mægenes.   Swā sceal man dôn
1535 þonne hē æt gūðe   gegān þenceð
longsumne lof;   nā ymb his līf cearað.
Gefēng þā be eaxle   – nalas for fæhðe mearn –
Gūð-Gēata lēod   Grendles mōdor,
brægd þā beadwe heard,   þā hē gebolgen wæs,
1540 feorhgenīðlan   þæt hēo on flet gebēah.
Hēo him eft hraþe   handlēan forgeald
grimman grāpum   ond him tōgēanes fēng;
oferwearp þā wērigmōd   wigena strengest
fēþecempa   þæt hē on fylle wearð.
1545 Ofsæt þā þone selegyst   ond hyre seaxe getēah
brād ond brūnecg,   wolde hire bearn wrecan
āngan eaferan.   Him on eaxle læg
brēostnet brōden,   þæt gebearh fēore,
wið ord ond wið ecge   ingang forstōd.
1550 Hæfde ðā forsīðod   sunu Ecgþēowes
under gynne grund   Gēata cempa
nemne him heaðobyrne   helpe gefremede
herenet hearde –   ond hālig god
gewēold wīgsigor,   wītig drihten
1555 rodera rædend   hit on ryht gescēd
ȳðelīce   syþðan hē eft āstōd.

[Beowulf's victory and return to Heorot]

XXIII   Geseah ðā on searwum   sigeēadig bil
ealdsweord eotenisc   ecgum þȳhtig
wigena weorðmynd;   þæt wæs wæpna cyst
1560 būton hit wæs māre   ðonne ænig mon ōðer

1546 ond] *not in MS*   1559 wæs] *not in MS*

1537 **Gefēng þā be eaxle** '[Beowulf] grasped by the shoulder then'. As in l. 758, a verb in the first accented syllable of an a-line alliterates instead of the following substantive, which would usually take the alliteration rather than the verb. Though not numerous, such half-lines occur throughout OE poetry and may signal special emphasis on the verb.

1541 **Hēo him . . . forgeald** 'She swiftly gave him requital with her hand', i.e. requital for his having grasped her by the shoulder and thrown her to the ground.

1545–6a. **Ofsæt þā . . . brūnecg** '[Grendel's mother] then set upon (i.e. charged) the intruder in her hall and drew her broad and bright-edged sword.' The fact that *brād* and *brūnecg* do not agree with dat sg *seaxe* is not surprising; cf. ll. 2703b–4a and l. 46 note. See IVC8.

1550–2 **Hæfde** and **gefremede** are pret subj expressing an unfulfilled condition: 'would have . . . had performed'. See *Guide* §179.1 and 179.4, and *OES* §3654.

1553 **ond** 'but'. See *OES* §§1737 and 3654.

1557–69 See IVC8 (swords).

1560 **būton** conj 'except that'.

　　　tō beadulāce　　ætberan meahte
　　　gōd ond geatolīc　　gīganta geweorc.
　　　Hē gefēng þā fetelhilt,　　freca Scyldinga
　　　hrēoh ond heorogrim　　hringmǣl gebrægd
1565　aldres orwēna,　　yrringa slōh
　　　þæt hire wið halse　　heard grāpode,
　　　bānhringas bræc,　　bil eal ðurhwōd
　　　fǣgne flǣschoman;　　hēo on flet gecrong;
　　　sweord wæs swātig;　　secg weorce gefeh.
1570　Līxte se lēoma,　　lēoht inne stōd
　　　efne swā of hefene　　hādre scīneð
　　　rodores candel.　　Hē æfter recede wlāt,
　　　hwearf þā be wealle,　　wǣpen hafenade
　　　heard be hiltum　　Higelāces ðegn
1575　yrre ond anrǣd;　　næs sēo ecg fracod
　　　hilderince　　ac hē hraþe wolde
　　　Grendle forgyldan　　gūðrǣsa fela
　　　ðāra þe hē geworhte　　tō West-Denum
　　　oftor micle　　ðonne on ænne sīð
1580　þonne hē Hrōðgāres　　heorðgenēatas
　　　slōh on sweofote,　　slǣpende frǣt
　　　folces Denigea　　fȳftȳne men
　　　ond ōðer swylc　　ūt offerede
　　　lāðlīcu lāc.　　Hē him þæs lēan forgeald
1585　rēþe cempa　　tō ðæs þe hē on ræste geseah
　　　gūðwērigne　　Grendel licgan
　　　aldorlēasne　　swā him ǣr gescōd
　　　hild æt Heorote　　– hrā wīde sprong
　　　syþðan hē æfter dēaðe　　drepe þrōwade
1590　heorosweng heardne –　　ond hine þā hēafde becearf.
　　　Sōna þæt gesāwon　　snottre ceorlas
　　　þā ðe mid Hrōðgāre　　on holm wliton
　　　þæt wæs ȳðgeblond　　eal gemenged,
　　　brim blōde fāh.　　Blondenfeaxe
1595　gomele ymb gōdne　　ongeador sprǣcon
　　　þæt hig þæs æðelinges　　eft ne wēndon,

1563 **þā fetelhilt** The gender of OE *hilt* is unstable. Here and in l. 1614b it appears to be acc sg fem. See IVC8.

1574 **be hiltum** See ll. 565b–7a note.

1583 **ōðer swylc** 'another such' i.e. 'another fifteen'. Cf. ll. 122b–3a.

1584 **him þæs lēan forgeald** 'had given him requital for that'.

1585 **tō ðæs þe** 'to the extent that'.

1588b–90 **hrā . . . hēafde becearf** 'the corpse gaped widely when after death it (*hē*) received the blow, the hard sword-stroke – and he (Beowulf) then cut it (*hine*) from the head'.

1596–8a **þæt hig þæs . . . þēoden** 'that they did not expect of the prince that he would again come rejoicing in victory to seek their renowned king'. For the syntax cf. ll. 115–17 note.

þæt hē sigehrēðig   sēcean cōme
mǣrne þēoden;   þā ðæs monige gewearð
þæt hine sēo brimwylf   ābroten hæfde.
1600 Ðā cōm nōn dæges.   Næs ofgēafon
hwate Scyldingas;   gewāt him hām þonon
goldwine gumena.   Gistas sǣtan
mōdes sēoce   ond on mere staredon,
wīston ond ne wēndon   þæt hīe heora winedrihten
1605 selfne gesāwon.   þā þæt sweord ongan
æfter heaþoswāte   hildegicelum
wīgbil wanian;   þæt wæs wundra sum
þæt hit eal gemealt   īse gelīcost
ðonne forstes bend   fæder onlǣteð,
1610 onwindeð wǣlrāpas   se geweald hafað
sǣla ond mǣla;   þæt is sōð metod.
Ne nōm hē in þǣm wīcum   Weder-Gēata lēod
māðmǣhta mā,   þēh hē þǣr monige geseah,
būton þone hafelan   ond þā hilt somod
1615 since fāge;   sweord ǣr gemealt,
forbarn brōdenmǣl;   wæs þæt blōd tō þæs hāt,
ǣttren ellorgǣst   se þǣr inne swealt.
Sōna wæs on sunde   se þe ǣr æt sæcce gebād
wīghryre wrāðra,   wæter up þurhdēaf;
1620 wǣron ȳðgebland   eal gefǣlsod
ēacne eardas   þā se ellorgāst
oflēt līfdagas   ond þās lǣnan gesceaft.
Cōm þā tō lande   lidmanna helm
swīðmōd swymman,   sǣlāce gefeah
1625 mægenbyrþenne   þāra þe hē him mid hæfde.
Ēodon him þā tōgēanes,   gode þancodon,
ðrȳðlīc þegna hēap   þēodnes gefēgon
þæs þe hī hyne gesundne   gesēon mōston.
Ðā wæs of þǣm hrōran   helm ond byrne

1599 abroten] abreoten   1602 sætan] secan

1598b–9a **þā ðæs ... gewearð þæt** 'concerning that (*ðæs*) it occurred to many that . . .'; *monige* is the obj. of impersonal *gewearð*. Cf. ll. 2026–9a.

1600b–5a Hrothgar and his Danish retainers despair of Beowulf's life and go home, but his loyal Geats (*Gistas*) continue the watch for his return.

1604 **wīston ond ne wēndon** 'they wished but did not expect'.

1605 **gesāwon** = *gesāwen* 'might see'.

1606 **hildegicelum** 'in battle-icicles' describes how the metal blade of the sword turned molten and dripped away.

1617 **ǣttren ellorgǣst** 'poisonous alien spirit' is in apposition with *blōd* l. 1616 and refers to the identification of the spirit or soul with blood.

1625 **mægenbyrþenne ... mid hæfde** 'the mighty burden of those things he had with him'.

1628 **þæs þe** conj 'because'.

1630 lungre ālȳsed.   Lagu drūsade,
        wæter under wolcnum   wældrēore fāg.
        Fērdon forð þonon   fēþelāstum
        ferhþum fægne,   foldweg mǣton
        cūþe strǣte,   cyningbalde men
1635 from þǣm holmclife   hafelan bǣron
        earfoðlīce   heora ǣghwæþrum
        felamōdigra   – fēower scoldon
        on þǣm wælstenge   weorcum geferian
        tō þǣm goldsele   Grendles hēafod –
1640 oþ ðæt semninga   tō sele cōmon
        frome fyrdhwate   fēowertȳne
        Gēata gongan   gumdryhten mid;
        mōdig on gemonge   meodowongas trǣd.
        Ðā cōm in gân   ealdor ðegna
1645 dǣdcēne mon   dōme gewurþad
        hæle hildedēor   Hrōðgār grētan.
        þā wæs be feaxe   on flet boren
        Grendles hēafod   þǣr guman druncon,
        egeslīc for eorlum   ond þǣre idese mid,
1650 wlitesēon wrǣtlīc;   weras on sāwon.

[Beowulf's report and Hrothgar's advice]

XXIIII   Bēowulf maþelode,   bearn Ecgþēowes:
        'Hwæt, wē þē þās sǣlāc,   sunu Healfdenes
        lēod Scyldinga,   lustum brōhton
        tīres tō tācne,   þe þū hēr tō lōcast.
1655 Ic þæt unsōfte   ealdre gedīgde
        wigge under wætere,   weorc geneþde
        earfoðlīce;   ætrihte wæs
        gūð getwǣfed   nymðe mec god scylde. Gods Protection
        Ne meahte ic æt hilde   mid Hruntinge
1660 wiht gewyrcan   þēah þæt wǣpen duge,
        ac mē geūðe   ylda waldend

1636–7a **earfoðlīce . . . felamōdigra** 'with difficulty for each pair of very bold men'. Two men
at each end of the *wælsteng* l. 1638 carried the head.

1649 **ond þǣre idese mid** 'and before the woman (Wealhtheow) too'.

1650b Only the men can bring themselves to look at it.

1654 **tīres tō tācne** 'as evidence of our victory'; **þe** rel pron 'which' referring to *þās sǣlāc*
l. 1652.

1655–6a **þæt** 'that [encounter]'; **ealdre gedīgde wigge** 'survived with my life through
warfare'.

1657b–8a **ætrihte wæs gūð getwǣfed** 'the battle was almost ended'.

þæt ic on wāge geseah   wlitig hangian
ealdsweord ēacen   – oftost wīsode
winigea lēasum–   þæt ic ðȳ wǣpne gebrǣd.
1665 Ofslōh ðā æt þǣre sæcce,   þā mē sǣl āgeald,
hūses hyrdas.   þā þæt hildebil
forbarn brogdenmǣl   swā þæt blōd gesprang
hātost heaþoswāta.   Ic þæt hilt þanan
fēondum ætferede,   fyrendǣda wræc
1670 dēaðcwealm Denigea   swā hit gedēfe wæs.
Ic hit þē þonne gehāte   þæt þū on Heorote mōst
sorhlēas swefan   mid þīnra secga gedryht,
ond þegna gehwylc   þīnra lēoda
duguðe ond iogoþe,   þæt þū him ondrǣdan ne þearft,
1675 þēoden Scyldinga,   on þā healfe
aldorbealu eorlum   swā þū ǣr dydest.'
Ðā wæs gylden hilt   gamelum rince
hārum hildfruman   on hand gyfen
enta ǣrgeweorc;   hit on ǣht gehwearf
1680 æfter dēofla hryre   Denigea frēan,
wundorsmiþa geweorc   ond, þā þās worold ofgeaf
gromheort guma   godes andsaca
morðres scyldig   ond his mōdor ēac,
on geweald gehwearf   woroldcyninga
1685 ðǣm sēlestan   be sǣm twēonum
ðāra þe on Scedenigge   sceattas dǣlde.
Hrōðgār maðelode,   hylt scēawode
ealde lāfe   on ðǣm wæs ōr writen
fyrngewinnes   syðþan flōd ofslōh
1690 gifen gēotende   gīganta cyn;
frēcne geferdon;   þæt wæs fremde þēod
ēcean dryhtne;   him þæs endelēan
þurh wæteres wylm   waldend sealde.
Swā wæs on ðǣm scennum   scīran goldes

1666 **hūses hyrdas** 'inhabitants of the dwelling-place'. The pl has been questioned, since Beowulf killed only one monster in the cave. But *ofslōh* l. 1665 has a more general meaning than 'killed'; it means 'struck down, cut off, destroyed' and so could refer to both the slaying of the ogress and the decapitation of Grendel's corpse.

1673 **gehwylc** Being nom, it must be parallel with *þū* (l. 1674).

1674b–6a **þæt þū him . . . eorlum** *him* and *eorlum* are in apposition; **on þā healfe** 'on that account' i.e. because of the Grendelkin.

1681 **ond** introduces an explanatory clause and can be translated 'for'. See *OES* §1735; **þā** conj 'when'.

1687b–98a Carved on the sword-hilt in pictures or in runic characters or in both is the biblical story of the Deluge, in which God destroyed the race of giants and Cain's descendants (Wisdom 14.6, Genesis 6–7). The Grendelkin appear to have escaped God's punishment and lived on amid the waters of the mere. See IVC8.

1691 **frēcne geferdon** 'they fared terribly'.

1695 þurh rūnstafas   rihte gemearcod

geseted ond gesǣd   hwām þæt sweord geworht

īrena cyst   ǣrest wǣre,

wreoþenhilt ond wyrmfāh.   Đā se wīsa sprǣc

sunu Healfdenes   swīgedon ealle:

1700 'þæt, lā, mæg secgan   se þe sōð ond riht

fremeð on folce,   feor eal gemon,

eald eþelweard,   þæt ðes eorl wǣre

geboren betera.   Blǣd is ārǣred

1704 geond wīdwegas,   wine mīn Bēowulf,

ðīn ofer þēoda gehwylce.   Eal þū hit geþyldum healdest,

mægen mid mōdes snyttrum.   Ic þē sceal mīne gelǣstan

frēode swā wit furðum sprǣcon.   Đū scealt tō frōfre weorþan

eal langtwīdig   lēodum þīnum

hæleðum tō helpe.   Ne wearð Heremōd swā

1710 eaforum Ecgwelan   Ār-Scyldingum;

ne gewēox hē him tō willan   ac tō wælfealle

ond tō dēaðcwalum   Deniga lēodum,

brēat bolgenmōd   bēodgenēatas

eaxlgesteallan   oþ þæt hē āna hwearf

1715 mǣre þēoden   mondrēamum from,

ðēah þe hine mihtig god   mægenes wynnum

eafeþum stēpte,   ofer ealle men

forð gefremede;   hwæþere him on ferhþe grēow

brēosthord blōdrēow;   nallas bēagas geaf

1720 Denum æfter dōme,   drēamlēas gebād

1702 eþelweard] ♀weard

1696 **hwām** 'for whom'. The runic characters on the sword-hilt indicate who ordered the sword forged and became its first owner. Alternatively the name could be that of the artificer 'by whom' the sword was made, since archaeologists have recovered Anglo-Saxon swords with the names of their makers as well as of their owners carved on them. See IVC8.

1700–2a **þæt, lā, . . . eþelweard** 'Lo, he who furthers truth and right among his people, an old guardian of the homeland who remembers everything from far [back in time], can say . . .'.

1703 **betera** 'better [than all others]'.

1705 **Eal . . . hit** anticipates *mægen* 'all this power' l. 1706; **geþyldum** 'with equanimity'. (OE *geþyld* usually means 'patience', but Hrothgar seems to be praising Beowulf for not letting his fame and greatness go to his head. In *Gifts of Men* ll. 79–80 *geþyld* is equated with *fæstgongel ferð* 'a steadfast mind', and so here.)

1706b–7a **Ic . . . gelǣstan frēode** 'I shall fulfil my friendship with you.' See ll. 946b–50.

1709b–22a Heremod is again contrasted with Beowulf. Cf. ll. 901–15 note and ll. 913b–15 note.

1710 **eaforum Ecgwelan** 'for the scions of Ecgwela' i.e. 'the Danes'. Ecgwela was evidently a Danish king of yore. Nothing more is known of him.

1711 **him tō willan** 'according to their desire', 'as they would have liked'; **ac tō wælfealle** 'but as [a source of] slaughter'.

1714b–15 **oþ þæt . . . from** This refers to Heremod's exile and death. Cf. ll. 902b–4a.

1720 **æfter dōme** 'according to custom' or 'according to honour'.

1720b–2a **drēamlēas gebād . . . longsum** 'he (Heremod) remained joyless, he suffered misery, lasting harm from his people, because of that strife'. This is a cryptic reference to his exile and ultimate death among the Jutes. That there was a period of suffering before his death is indicated in ll. 904b–5a.

þæt hē þæs gewinnes   weorc þrōwade
lēodbealo longsum.   Đū þē lǣr be þon,
gumcyste ongit.   Ic þis gid be þē
āwrǣc wintrum frōd.   Wundor is tō secganne

1725   hū mihtig god   manna cynne
þurh sīdne sefan   snyttru bryttað
eard ond eorlscipe;   hē āh ealra geweald.
Hwīlum hē on lufan   lǣteð hworfan
monnes mōdgeþonc   mǣran cynnes,

1730   seleð him on ēþle   eorþan wynne
tō healdanne   hlēoburh wera,
gedēð him swā gewealdene   worolde dǣlas
sīde rīce   þæt hē his selfa ne mæg
for his unsnyttrum   ende geþencean.

1735   Wunað hē on wiste;   nō hine wiht dweleð
ādl ne yldo   ne him inwitsorh
on sefan sweorceð   ne gesacu ōhwǣr
ecghete ēoweð   ac him eal worold
wendeð on willan;   hē þæt wyrse ne con.

[Hrothgar's advice continued]

XXV 1740   Oð þæt him on innan   oferhygda dǣl
weaxeð ond wrīdað,   þonne se weard swefeð,
sāwele hyrde;   bið se slǣp tō fæst,

1734 for] *missing at edge of MS but reported by Thorkelin A and in Thorkelin's edition*   1737 sefan] sefa *at edge of MS*

1728–9 **Hwīlum . . . mǣran cynnes** 'At times he allows the thought of a man of noble race to turn toward his desires.' The identity and meaning of *lufan* has been much discussed. We take it to be the common noun *lufu* (with weak inflection, as frequently elsewhere) carrying the attested meaning 'strong liking, object of desire'. The highborn man is allowed first to review in his mind all the things he would like to have, and then these things are given to him.

1732 **gedēð . . . gewealdene** 'makes subject to him in this way'.

1733b–4 **þæt hē . . . geþencean** 'so that, because of his unwisdom, he cannot himself imagine an end to it'.

1737b–8a **ne gesacu . . . ēoweð** 'nor does strife eventuate in warfare anywhere'.

1739b–41a Most editions construe l. 1739b as a main clause followed by a dependent clause beginning with the conjunction *oðþæt*: 'He knows no worse [fortune], until a measure of arrogant thoughts grows and flourishes within him.' But this construction would have a fitt-division (XXV) falling in the middle of a sentence, which is most improbable. It is more likely that 1739b is a complete sentence and that *Oð þæt* functions adverbially and begins a new sentence. See *OES* §2754 and translate ll. 1740–1a 'And then a measure of arrogant thoughts grows and flourishes within him'. (Cf. l. 2039.)

1740–57 Hrothgar's arresting allegory depicting the process by which an unwary man allows pride and avarice to corrupt his character has been widely discussed, and many supposed sources have been adduced. But the meaning is self-evident: the soul's guardian (reason or conscience) falls asleep, and the sharp arrows of vice penetrate the man's unwary soul, leaving him arrogant, stingy – and doomed. (If a Germanic ruler ceases to be generous with his retinue, his days are numbered.)

bisgum gebunden,   bona swīðe nēah,
se þe of flānbogan   fyrenum scēoteð.
1745 þonne bið on hreþre   under helm drepen
biteran strǣle   – him bebeorgan ne con –
wōm wundorbebodum   wergan gāstes;
þinceð him tō lȳtel   þæt hē lange hēold,
gȳtsað gromhȳdig,   nallas on gylp seleð
1750 fætte bēagas   ond hē þā forðgesceaft
forgyteð ond forgȳmeð   þæs þe him ǣr god sealde,
wuldres waldend,   weorðmynda dǣl.
Hit on endestæf   eft gelimpeð
þæt se līchoma   lǣne gedrēoseð,
1755 fǣge gefealleð;   fēhð ōþer tō
se þe unmurnlīce   mādmas dǣleþ
eorles ǣrgestrēon,   egesan ne gȳmeð.
Bebeorh þē ðone bealonīð,   Bēowulf lēofa,
secg betsta,   ond þē þæt sēlre gecēos,
1760 ēce rǣdas,   oferhȳda ne gȳm,
mǣre cempa.   Nū is þīnes mægnes blǣd
āne hwīle;   eft sōna bið
þæt þec ādl oððe ecg   eafoþes getwǣfeð
oððe fȳres feng   oððe flōdes wylm
1765 oððe gripe mēces   oððe gāres fliht
oððe atol yldo,   oððe ēagena bearhtm
forsiteð ond forsworceð;   semninga bið
þæt ðec, dryhtguma,   dēað oferswȳðeð.
Swā ic Hring-Dena   hund missēra
1770 wēold under wolcnum   ond hig wigge belēac

1750 fætte] fædde

1743a **bisgum gebunden** 'oppressed with cares' refers to the man's slumber.

1743b–4 **bona . . . fyrenum scēoteð** 'the slayer exceedingly near who shoots from his bow with evil intent' could be reminiscent of Psalm 11.2 or of Ephesians 6.16 or of the preternatural archers (elves, witches, or pagan gods) who in the OE charms afflict their victims with debilitating elf-shot.

1747 **wōm wundorbebodum** 'perverse mysterious promptings' is parallel with *biteran strǣle* l. 1746.

1750b–2 **ond hē þā forðgesceaft . . . dǣl** 'and he forgets his future destiny and disregards the portion of wordly honours, of that which had been divinely granted to him', i.e. he is overcome by hybris. The gen *þæs þe* l. 1751 may be here because this clause was perceived as being parallel with *weorðmynda* and thus dependent upon *dǣl* ('a portion of that which the deity had given him, of worldly honours').

1755b 'another takes over', i.e. succeeds him.

1757 **egesan ne gȳmeð** 'he has no regard for timorousness [over dispensing wealth]'.

1759 **secg betsta** See l. 947a note.

1760 **ēce rǣdas** 'lasting gains', 'enduring benefit' (in contrast with the short-term satisfaction of arrogance and miserliness); **ne gȳm** 'have no regard for' i.e. 'avoid'.

1761b–2a **Nū is . . . hwīle** 'The flowering of your strength is [only] for a little while now.'

1770b–1a **ond hig . . . mǣgþa** 'and by warfare protected them from many tribes'.

        manigum mǣgþa   geond þysne middangeard,
        æscum ond ecgum,   þæt ic mē ǣnigne
        under swegles begong   gesacan ne tealde.
        Hwæt, mē þæs on ēþle   edwenden cwōm,
1775   gyrn æfter gomene,   seoþðan Grendel wearð
        ealdgewinna   ingenga mīn;
        ic þǣre sōcne   singāles wæg
        mōdceare micle.   þæs sig metode þanc
        ēcean dryhtne   þæs ðe ic on aldre gebād
1780   þæt ic on þone hafelan   heorodrēorigne
        ofer eald gewin   ēagum starige!
        Gā nū tō setle,   symbelwynne drēoh
        wīggeweorþad;   unc sceal worn fela
        māþma gemǣnra   siþðan morgen bið.'
1785   Gēat wæs glædmōd,   gēong sōna tō
        setles nēosan   swā se snottra heht.
        þā wæs eft swā ǣr   ellenrōfum
        fletsittendum   fægere gereorded
        nīowan stefne.   Nihthelm geswearc
1790   deorc ofer dryhtgumum.   Duguð eal ārās;
        wolde blondenfeax   beddes nēosan,
        gamela Scylding.   Gēat unigmetes wēl
        rōfne randwigan   restan lyste;
        sōna him seleþegn   sīðes wērgum
1795   feorrancundum   forð wīsade
        se for andrysnum   ealle beweotede
        þegnes þearfe   swylce þȳ dōgore
        heaþolīðende   habban scoldon.
        Reste hine þā rūmheort,   reced hlīuade
1800   gēap ond goldfāh,   gǣst inne swæf
        oþ þæt hrefn blaca   heofones wynne
        blīðheort bodode.   Ðā cōm beorht scacan
                            Scaþan ōnetton,
        wǣron æþelingas   eft tō lēodum

1774 edwenden] ed wendan   1796 beweotede] be weotene   1803a] *no gap in MS. See note*

1772b–3 **þæt ic . . . tealde** 'so that I did not consider [there to be] any enemy to me beneath the heavens' expanse'.

1778b–9 **þæs . . . þæs ðe** Either 'Therefore . . . because' or 'For that . . . for that which/what'.

1781 **ofer eald gewin** 'after the age-long trouble'.

1797 **þȳ dōgore** 'in that day' i.e. 'in those times' seems more significant than 'on that particular day', and the unusual stress and alliteration on *þȳ* is like that on *þæm* in the similar statement made in ll. 197, 790, and 806.

1803a There is no gap in the MS, but metre and sense leave no doubt that a half-line is missing; *scīma ofer sceadwa* and *scīma æfter sceadwa* 'light after darkness' have been suggested as plausible reconstructions.

1805 fūse tō farenne,   wolde feor þanon
cuma collenferhð   cēoles nēosan.
Heht þā se hearda   Hrunting beran
sunu Ecglāfes,   heht his sweord niman
lēoflīc īren,   sægde him þæs lēanes þanc,
1810 cwæð, hē þone gūðwine   gōdne tealde
wīgcræftigne,   nales wordum lōg
mēces ecge;   þæt wæs mōdig secg.
Ond þā sīðfrome   searwum gearwe
wīgend wǣron,   ēode weorð Denum
1815 æþeling tō yppan   þǣr se ōþer wæs,
hæle hildedēor   Hrōðgār grētte.

[The departure of the Geats]

XXVI   Bēowulf maþelode,   bearn Ecgþēowes:
'Nū wē sǣlīðend   secgan wyllað
feorran cumene   þæt wē fundiaþ
1820 Higelāc sēcan.   Wǣron hēr tela
willum bewenede;   þū ūs wēl dohtest.
Gif ic þonne on eorþan   ōwihte mæg
þīnre mōdlufan   māran tilian,
gumena dryhten,   ðonne ic gȳt dyde,
1825 gūðgeweorca,   ic bēo gearo sōna.
Gif ic þæt gefricge   ofer flōda begang
þæt þec ymbsittend   egesan þȳwað,
swā þec hetende   hwīlum dydon,
ic ðē þūsenda   þegna bringe
1830 hæleþa tō helpe.   Ic on Higelāce wāt,
Gēata dryhten,   þēah ðe hē geong sȳ
folces hyrde,   þæt hē mec fremman wile

1805 farenne] . . . ene ne *at edge of MS*   1816 hæle] helle

1807–9 **Heht þā . . . þanc** 'The brave one (Beowulf) then ordered Hrunting to be brought to the son of Ecglaf (Unferth), commanded him (Unferth) to take his sword, the precious blade, said thanks to him for the [temporary] gift.' Some emend *lēanes* 'gift' to *lǣnes* 'loan', which makes much better sense. But *lǣn* in OE is normally fem (although the cognates in other Germanic languages are usually neut – ON *lán*, OFris *lén*, OHG *lehan*). Some interpret the passage as saying that Unferth gave Hrunting to Beowulf, but this requires an unsignalled shift of subject in l. 1809b and the assumption that the poet forgot to say that Beowulf had returned Hrunting to Unferth.
1813 **þā** conj 'when'.
1820b–1a **Wǣron hēr . . . bewenede** 'We were entertained well here, according to our desires.'
1825 **gūðgeweorca** goes with *ōwihte* l. 1822 'by aught [further] of warlike deeds' and, by implication, with *gearo* 'I shall immediately be prepared [for such deeds]'.
1830b–1a If *dryhten* were parallel with *Hygelāce*, we would expect it to be dat sg (*dryhtne*); so construe *dryhten* with the following *hē*: 'As for Hygelac, I know that the lord of the Geats, the people's protector, although he is young, will want to support me with words and deeds.'

wordum ond weorcum þæt ic þē wēl herige
ond þē tō gēoce gārholt bere
1835 mægenes fultum þǣr ðē bið manna þearf.
Gif him þonne Hrēþrīc tō hofum Gēata
geþingeð þēodnes bearn, hē mæg þǣr fela
frēonda findan; feorcȳþðe bēoð
sēlran gesōhte þǣm þe him selfa dēah.'
1840 Hrōðgār maþelode him on andsware:
'þē þā wordcwydas wigtig drihten
on sefan sende; ne hȳrde ic snotorlīcor
on swā geongum feore guman þingian.
þū eart mægenes strang ond on mōde frōd,
1845 wīs wordcwida. Wēn ic talige,
gif þæt gegangeð þæt ðe gār nymeð
hild heorugrimme Hrēþles eaferan,
ādl oþðe īren ealdor ðīnne
folces hyrde, ond þū þīn feorh hafast,
1850 þæt þe Sǣ-Gēatas sēlran næbben
tō gecēosenne cyning ǣnigne
hordweard hæleþa gyf þū healdan wylt
māga rīce. Mē þīn mōdsefa
līcað leng swā wēl, lēofa Bēowulf.
1855 Hafast þū gefēred þæt þām folcum sceal
Gēata lēodum ond Gār-Denum
sib gemǣne ond sacu restan,

1833 wordum ond weorcum] weordum ond worcum   1836 Hreþric] hreþrinc   1837 geþingeð]
geþinged   1857 gemæne] ge mænum

1834 **gārholt** 'a forest of spears' i.e. a large army.
1836–7a **Gif him . . . bearn** 'If Hrethric, the king's son, lodges a plea for himself at the Geats'
court'. Responding to Wealhtheow's appeal to him to support her son and heir to the throne
(ll. 1226b–7), Beowulf assures his Danish hosts that Hrethric will receive help in Geatland if he
needs it. In l. 1837a *geþingeð* (MS *geþinged*) is a late spelling of *geþingað*, 3rd sg pres ind of *geþingian*.
1839 **þǣm þe . . . dēah** 'by the one who will do well for himself', i.e. by the one who wants to
succeed or prevail.
1842b–3 **ne hȳrde ic . . . þingian** 'I have never heard a man so young make diplomatic
arrangements more wisely.' The verb *þingian* 'intercede, arrange a settlement' refers specifically to
Beowulf's concern to negotiate with his people on Hrethric's behalf.
1846 **þæt ðe** (also in l. 1850) is usually taken as a form of conj *þætte* 'that', which is a reduced
form of *þæt þe*. But these would be the only places in *Beowulf* where *þætte* is spelled this way, and
one must wonder whether *þe* is not the pronoun *þē* 'from you' l. 1846, 'than you' l. 1850.
1847 **Hrēþles eaferan** Hygelac, Beowulf's king.
1853b–4a **Mē þīn . . . wēl** 'Your character pleases me well the longer [I know you].' Probably
wēl is a scribal error for *sēl* 'better', the intended sense being '. . . pleases me better the longer [I
know you]'.
1857b–8 **ond sacu . . . drugon** 'and the conflict, the hostile acts that they (i.e. Danes and Geats)
formerly practised, will cease'. The former 'hostile acts' between the Danes and Geats probably
refers to the events described in Saxo Grammaticus's *Gesta Danorum*, where we read that the son of
Scyld (Skiold) vanquished the Geats (Götar). See *Saxo Grammaticus: The History of the Danes*
trans. Peter Fisher (Exeter, 1979), p. 20.

inwitnīþas   þe hīe ǣr drugon;
wesan, þenden ic wealde   wīdan rīces,
1860 māþmas gemǣne,   manig ōþerne
gōdum gegrēttan   ofer ganotes bæð,
sceal hringnaca   ofer heaþu bringan
lāc ond luftācen.   Ic þā lēode wāt
ge wið fēond ge wið frēond   fæste geworhte,
1865 ǣghwæs untǣle   ealde wīsan.'
Ðā gīt him eorla hlēo   inne gesealde
mago Healfdenes   māþmas twelfe,
hēt hine mid þǣm lācum   lēode swǣse
sēcean on gesyntum,   snūde eft cuman.
1870 Gecyste þā   cyning æþelum gōd,
þēoden Scyldinga   ðegn betstan
ond be healse genam;   hruron him tēaras
blondenfeaxum.   Him wæs bēga wēn
ealdum infrōdum,   ōþres swīðor,
1875 þæt hīe seoððan nō   gesēon mōston
mōdige on meþle.   Wæs him se man tō þon lēof
þæt hē þone brēostwylm   forberan ne mehte
ac him on hreþre   hygebendum fæst
æfter dēorum men   dyrne langað
1880 beorn wið blōde.   Him Bēowulf þanan
gūðrinc goldwlanc   græsmoldan træd
since hrēmig;   sægenga bād
āgendfrean   se þe on ancre rād.
þā wæs on gange   gifu Hrōðgāres
1885 oft geæhted;   þæt wæs ān cyning
ǣghwæs orleahtre   oþ þæt hine yldo benam
mægenes wynnum   se þe oft manegum scōd.

1868 hine] inne   1875 hie seoððan no] he seoðða . . . geseon   1883 agendfrean] agedfrean

1859 **wesan** Supply *sculon* from *sceal* l. 1855. Similarly supply *sceal* with *gegrēttan* l. 1861.
1862 **ofer heaþu** 'after the war' (cf. l. 1781). The reference is to the conflict alluded to in ll. 1857–8. For *ofer* 'after' see ll. 736 and 1781.
1863b–5 **Ic þā lēode . . . wīsan** 'I know those people (i.e. Danes and Geats) to be firmly disposed toward both friend and foe, altogether blameless in the ancient way.'
1866b **inne** i.e. 'within the hall'.
1871 **ðegn betstan** will not scan because it has only three syllables. The original MS probably had *ðegna betstan* or *ðegn betestan*. Cf. l. 947a.
1873b–6a **Him wæs . . . meþle** 'There was in the old, venerable one expectation of two [possible] things, but more especially of one: that they, courageous ones, would never be allowed to see each other [again] in council.'
1878b **on hreþre . . . fæst** 'in his bosom, firm in the bonds of his heart'.
1886b–7 **oþ þæt . . . scōd** 'until old age, which has always done injury to many, deprived him of the joys of strength'. The pronoun *se* l. 1887 does not agree with the fem antecedent *yldo*, and some editors emend to *sēo*. But the personification of age as an injurer of men probably shifted in the poet's mind to a masculine figure. The understatement *oft* for 'always' is common.

BEOWULF'S RETURN TO GEATLAND (*lines 1888–2199*)

[The arrival at Hygelac's court. The story of Thryth]

XXVII   Cwōm þā tō flōde   felamōdigra
           hægstealdra hēap,   hringnet bǣron
1890   locene leoðosyrcan.   Landweard onfand
           eftsīð eorla   swā hē ǣr dyde,
           nō hē mid hearme   of hlīðes nōsan
           gǣstas grētte   ac him tōgēanes rād,
           cwæð þæt wilcuman   Wedera lēodum
1895   scaþan scīrhame   tō scipe fōron.
           þā wæs on sande   sǣgēap naca
           hladen herewǣdum   hringedstefna
           mēarum ond māðmum,   mǣst hlīfade
           ofer Hrōðgāres   hordgestrēonum.
1900   Hē þǣm bātwearde   bunden golde
           swurd gesealde   þæt hē syðþan wæs
           on meodubence   māþme þȳ weorþra
           yrfelāfe.   Gewāt him on naca
           drēfan dēop wæter,   Dena land ofgeaf.
1905   þā wæs be mǣste   merehrægla sum
           segl sāle fæst,   sundwudu þunede,
           nō þǣr wēgflotan   wind ofer ȳðum
           sīðes getwǣfde,   sǣgenga fōr,
           flēat fāmigheals   forð ofer ȳðe
1910   bundenstefna   ofer brimstrēamas
           þæt hīe Gēata clifu   ongitan meahton
           cūþe næssas,   cēol up geþrang
           lyftgeswenced,   on lande stōd.
           Hraþe wæs æt holme   hȳðweard geara
1915   se þe ǣr lange tīd   lēofra manna

1889 heap] *not in MS*   1893 gæstas] *lost at edge of MS*   1902 maþme þy weorþra] maþma þy weorþre   1903 naca] nacan

1894–5 **cwæð þæt . . . fōron** '[the shore guard] said that the bright-mailed warriors [who] were going to their ship [would be] welcome to the people of the Weders'.

1900 **Hē** Beowulf.

1903b **Gewāt him . . . naca** 'The ship went on.' MS *nacan* makes acceptable sense ('[He] departed in the ship') but impossible metre: the preposition *on* could never carry stress and alliteration. The emendation converts *on* into an adverb, which can easily bear stress and alliteration. The sense is also improved slightly: it is the ship that sets out to stir the deep water, not Beowulf. For *him* see l. 26 note.

1907–8a **nō þǣr . . . getwǣfde** 'by no means did the wind over the waves hinder the ship from its journey'. Litotes: the wind drove the ship on its way.

1915–16 **se þe . . . wlātode** 'who, eager at the shore, had watched from afar for the dear men for a long time'.

fūs æt faroðe   feor wlātode,
sælde tō sande   sīdfæþme scip
oncerbendum fæst   þȳ læs hym ȳþa ðrym
wudu wynsuman   forwrecan meahte.

1920 Hēt þā up beran   æþelinga gestrēon
frætwe ond fǣtgold;   næs him feor þanon
tō gesēcanne   sinces bryttan
Higelāc Hrēþling   þǣr æt hām wunað
selfa mid gesīðum   sǣwealle nēah.

1925 Bold wæs betlīc,   bregorōf cyning
hēah in healle,   Hygd swīðe geong
wīs wēlþungen   þēah ðe wintra lȳt
under burhlocan   gebiden hæbbe
Hæreþes dohtor,   næs hīo hnāh swā þēah

1930 ne tō gnēað gifa   Gēata lēodum
māþmgestrēona.   Mōd þrȳðo wæg
fremu folces cwēn,   firen' ondrysne;
nǣnig þæt dorste   dēor genēþan
swǣsra gesīða,   nefne sinfreâ,

1935 þæt hire an dæges   ēagum starede
ac him wælbende   weotode tealde
handgewriþene;   hraþe seoþðan wæs
æfter mundgripe   mēce geþinged
þæt hit sceādenmǣl   scȳran mōste,

1940 cwealmbealu cȳðan.   Ne bið swylc cwēnlīc þēaw

1918 oncer] oncear   1926 heah in healle] hea healle

1923b–4a **þǣr æt . . . gesīðum** 'where [the king] himself lives with his retainers'. The shift to present tense may be an attempt to increase vividness. The historic present is rare in OE.

1931b–2a **Mōd þrȳðo . . . cwēn** 'The excellent queen of the people (Hygd) weighed the arrogance of Thryth.' In recalling the nefarious Queen Thryth as a model to avoid, Hygd is doing what Hrothgar bade Beowulf do when he proposed to him Heremod as an example to avoid following (ll. 1709b–24a). Besides this obvious function of the narrative contrast between Hygd and Thryth, some scholars have suspected that the poet is concerned to mention King Offa (Thryth's husband) because he is an ancestor of the historical King Offa of the Mercians (who ruled AD 757–96), as the genealogy in the Anglo-Saxon Chronicle suggests. The poet's praise of the earlier Offa (ll. 1955–60a) would then be an indirect compliment to his later namesake (and the one allusion in *Beowulf* to an Englishman); **wæg** 'weighed'. Cf. *DOE* s.v. *āwegan* 2.C. 'to consider, ponder'.

1933–7a **nǣnig þæt . . . handgewriþene** 'not any brave man of her own retinue dared to risk that he should look upon her with his eyes openly (lit., during the day) – except as her husband – but [if he did] he might count on mortal bonds twisted by hand [being] ordained for him'; 1935 **an** 'upon': being placed after its dat obj, *an* assumes stress and thus can carry metrical accent and alliteration.

1936–57 A facsimile of the manuscript containing these lines appears on p. 113.

1937b–40a **hraþe seoþðan . . . cȳðan** 'soon afterward, after his seizure, the swordblade was invoked so that the damascened sword might settle it, exercise mortal punishment'.

1939 **scȳran** This is the last word copied by the first scribe. The rest of the poem is in the hand of the second scribe. See the facsimile page on p. 113 (end of third line) and notice the contrast in the handwriting of the two scribes. You will also begin to notice differences in spelling, the second scribe using, for example, *io* for *eo* much more often than did the first scribe (*hīo* for *hēo*, *Bīowulf* for *Bēowulf*, *hīold* for *hēold*, etc.).

ceulde hund ʒeþʃupene hƿaþ
dan paʃ æʃteꞃ mund ʒꞃupe mæce
hnʒeð þ hꞃe ʃceaden mæl ʃcyꞃian
ʃce cƿealm bealu coꞃ dan neꞃd ʃpꞃle
lic þaꞃƿ ideʃe to ʒenanne hꞃuh de
ænlicu ʃy þ te ꞃꞃꞃ du pelde ꞃꞃꞃes
ꞃꞃce æꞃcꞃꞃ liʒe coꞃne læꞃꞃne mannan
uꞃu þ on holʃnod hꞃꞃ nꞃnʒes mꞃtʒ
dꞃꞃncdꞃ de oðcꞃ ꞃædan þ hꞃo læd
lepa lꞃ ʒeꞃꞃemede inꞃꞃc nꞃda
ddan chꞃeʃc paꞃꞃd ʒꞃꞃcꞃ ʒold hꞃo
ꞃꞃ ʒꞃꞃ ʒu canpan adelum dꞃoꞃꞃe
ddan lꞃo oꞃꞃan ꞃꞃc oꞃcꞃ ꞃꞃlone
ꞃod beꞃꞃcꞃ laꞃꞃ ꞃꞃde ʒeʃohce
dꞃ lꞃo ꞃꞃddaꞃpell ꞃnꞃum ꞃcole
ʒode mꞃꞃꞃe lꞃꞃ ʒe ꞃcauꞃca lꞃꞃʒꞃde
bꞃeac lꞃoco hꞃul luꞃun pꞃd hæle
ꞃa bꞃꞃʒo æallꞃ mon cꞃnneʃ mꞃne
ʒeꞃꞃꞃ þaʃꞃe leʃcan bꞃ ꞃꞃn ꞃpꞃo
nꞃ coꞃꞃcꞃ cꞃꞃcꞃ ꞃon dam oꞃꞃ

Lines 1936–57

idese tō efnanne,　　þēah ðe hīo ænlīcu sȳ,
þætte freoðuwebbe　　fēores onsǣce
æfter ligetorne　　lēofne mannan.
Hūru þæt onhōhsnode　　Hemminges mǣg;
1945　ealodrincende　　ōðer sǣdan,
þæt hīo lēodbealewa　　lǣs gefremede
inwitnīða　　syððan ǣrest wearð
gyfen goldhroden　　geongum cempan
æðelum dīore　　syððan hīo Offan flet
1950　ofer fealone flōd　　be fæder lāre
sīðe gesōhte,　　ðǣr hīo syððan well
in gumstōle　　gōde mǣre
līfgesceafta　　lifigende brēac,
hīold hēahlufan　　wið hæleþa brego,
1955　ealles moncynnes　　mīne gefrǣge
þæs sēlestan　　bī sǣm twēonum
eormencynnes;　　forðām Offa wæs
geofum ond gūðum　　gārcēne man
wīde geweorðod,　　wīsdōme hēold
1960　ēðel sīnne,　　þonon Ēomēr wōc
hæleðum tō helpe,　　Hemminges mǣg
nefa Gārmundes　　nīða cræftig.

[Hygelac's welcome]

XXVIII　　　　Gewāt him ðā se hearda　　mid his hondscole
sylf æfter sande　　sǣwong tredan
1965　wīde waroðas.　　Woruldcandel scān
sigel sūðan fūs.　　Hī sīð drugon,
elne geēodon　　tō ðæs ðe eorla hlēo,

1944 onhohsnode] on hohsnod　　Hemminges] hem ninges　　　　1960 Eomer] geomor
1961 Hemminges] hem inges

1944 **Hemminges mǣg** Offa.
1945 **ealodrincende ōðer sǣdan** 'men drinking ale told another [story]' i.e. that Thryth reformed after her marriage to Offa.
1946 **lǣs** meiosis 'nothing'.
1948 **geongum cempan** Offa.
1952 **gōde** dat sg 'for [her] goodness'.
1954–6 **hīold . . . sǣm twēonum** 'she maintained deep affection towards the lord of men, the best between the seas of all mankind, as I have heard tell'; *brego* and *þæs sēlestan* are parallel gen objects of *wið*.
1961 **Hemminges mǣg** Eomer.
1963 **se hearda** Beowulf.
1967 **tō ðæs ðe** 'to where'. Having been told that the king is at that very moment holding court in the mead-hall, Beowulf and his men proceed directly there.

bonan Ongenþēoes   burgum in innan,
geongne gūðcyning   gōdne gefrūnon
1970   hringas dǣlan.   Higelāce wæs
sīð Bēowulfes   snūde gecȳðed
þæt ðǣr on worðig   wīgendra hlēo
lindgestealla   lifigende cwōm
heaðolāces hāl   tō hofe gongan.
1975   Hraðe wæs gerȳmed,   swā se rīca bebēad,
fēðegestum   flet innanweard.
Gesæt þā wið sylfne   se ðā sæcce genæs,
mǣg wið mǣge,   syððan mandryhten
þurh hlēoðorcwyde   holdne gegrētte
1980   mēaglum wordum.   Meoduscencum hwearf
geond þæt hēahreced   Hæreðes dohtor,
lufode ðā lēode,   līðwǣge bær
hǣðnum tō handa.   Higelāc ongan
sīnne geseldan   in sele þām hēan
1985   fægre fricgcean;   hyne fyrwet bræc
hwylce Sǣ-Gēata   sīðas wǣron:
'Hū lomp ēow on lāde,   lēofa Bīowulf,
þā ðū fǣringa   feorr gehogodest
sæcce sēcean   ofer sealt wæter
1990   hilde tō Hiorote?   Ac ðū Hrōðgāre
wīdcūðne wēan   wihte gebēttest
mǣrum ðēodne?   Ic ðæs mōdceare
sorhwylmum sēað,   sīðe ne truwode
lēofes mannes,   ic ðē lange bæd
1995   þæt ðū þone wælgǣst   wihte ne grētte,
lēte Sūð-Dene   sylfe geweorðan
gūðe wið Grendel.   Gode ic þanc secge
þæs ðe ic ðē gesundne   gesēon mōste.'

1981 heahreced] side reced   1983 hæðnum] hæðnū *with* ð *partially erased*   1991 wid] wið

1968 **bonan Ongenþēoes** Hygelac. We learn in ll. 2961–4a that it was Eofor's hand that actually killed Ongentheow, but he was acting on Hygelac's orders, and so the king is properly designated as the author of Ongentheow's death.

1977 **Gesæt þā . . . sylfne** '[Beowulf] sat opposite [the king] himself'.

1978 **mandryhten** nom sg. The king greets his loyal retainer, inviting him to take the seat of honour.

1980b–2a **Meoduscencum hwearf . . . lēode** 'Hæreth's daughter (Hygd) passed throughout the lofty hall with cups of mead; she cherished the people'; **heahreced** see IIIA9.

1992b–8 Hygelac's caution and circumspection in his first speech in the poem contrast dramatically with his reckless and ill-starred attack on the Franks, which the poet alludes to repeatedly. See ll. 1202–14a note.

[Beowulf's account of his victories and the tale of Freawaru]

[XXVIIII]   Bīowulf maðelode,   bearn Ecgðīoes:
2000   'þæt is undyrne,   dryhten Higelāc,
             mǣru gemēting   monegum fīra,
             hwylc orleghwīl   uncer Grendles
             wearð on ðām wange   þær hē worna fela
             Sige-Scyldingum   sorge gefremede
2005   yrmðe tō aldre;   ic ðæt eall gewræc
             swā begylpan ne þearf   Grendeles māga
             ænig ofer eorðan   ūhthlem þone,
             se ðe lengest leofað   lāðan cynnes
             fācne bifongen.   Ic ðǣr furðum cwōm
2010   tō ðām hringsele   Hrōðgār grētan;
             sōna mē se mǣra   mago Healfdenes,
             syððan hē mōdsefan   mīnne cūðe,
             wið his sylfes sunu   setl getǣhte.
             Weorod wæs on wynne;   ne seah ic wīdan feorh
2015   under heofones hwealf   healsittendra
             medudrēam māran.   Hwīlum mǣru cwēn
             friðusibb folca   flet eall geondhwearf,
             bǣdde byre geonge,   oft hīo bēahwriðan
             secge sealde   ǣr hīe tō setle gēong.
2020   Hwīlum for duguðe   dohtor Hrōðgāres
             eorlum on ende   ealuwǣge bær
             þā ic Frēaware   fletsittende
             nemnan hȳrde   þær hīo nægled sinc
             hæleðum sealde.   Sīo gehāten is,

2000 Higelac] hige . . . *at edge of MS*   2001 mæru] *word lost at edge of MS*   2002 orleghwil] . . .
hwil   2006 swa begylpan ne þearf] swa . . . gylpan þearf   2007 ænig] *word lost at edge of MS*
2009 facne] f . . .   2019 sealde] *word lost at edge of MS*   2020 duguðe] . . . e   2023 nægled]
. . . ed   2024 is] *word lost at edge of MS*

2002 **uncer Grendles** 'of us two, of Grendel [and of me]'. The dual *uncer* expresses the second of the pair.

2004b–5a **sorge . . . yrmðe** = *sorga . . . yrmða* Late spellings of the gen pl (dependent on *worna* l. 2003).

2006–9a 'so that not any of Grendel's kinsmen on earth who live longest of that hateful race enveloped in crime need to boast of that tumult in the night'. Beowulf assumes that the monster race lives on; he has not eliminated all evil creatures.

2015b–16a **healsittendra medudrēam māran** 'greater conviviality of courtiers'.

2018 **bǣdde byre geonge** 'she exhorted her young sons [to partake of the banquet]'. Previous editors have proposed the unique sense 'youths, boys' for *byre* in this passage, but everywhere else in *Beowulf* and in OE at large *byre* means 'son, descendant'. That Wealhtheow should single out her sons (rather than singling out all the young among her guests) is in character. In each of her speeches in the poem her subject is her sons.

2025   geong goldhroden,   gladum suna Frōdan;
hafað þæs geworden   wine Scyldinga,
rīces hyrde,   ond þæt rǣd talað
þæt hē mid ðȳ wīfe   wælfǣhða dǣl
sæcca gesette.   Oft seldan hwǣr
2030   æfter lēodhryre   lȳtle hwīle
bongār būgeð   þēah sēo brȳd duge.
Mæg þæs þonne ofþyncan   ðēodne Heaðo-Beardna
ond þegna gehwām   þāra lēoda
þonne hē mid fǣmnan   on flett gǣð:
2035   dryhtbearn Dena   duguða biwenede,
on him gladiað   gomelra lāfe,
heard ond hringmǣl   Heaða-Beardna gestrēon
þenden hīe ðām wǣpnum   wealdan mōston.

[The tale of Freawaru continued]

[XXX]   Oð ðæt hīe forlǣddan   tō ðām lindplegan
2040   swǣse gesīðas   ond hyra sylfra feorh.
þonne cwið æt bēore   se ðe bēah gesyhð,
eald æscwiga   se ðe eall geman

2026 hafað] . . . fað   2032 ðeodne] ðeoden   2037 Heaða-Beardna] heaðabearna
2042 geman] g . . .

2026–9a **hafað þæs . . . gesette** 'concerning that one (i.e. Froda's son Ingeld) it has occurred to the lord of the Scyldings, the guardian of the realm, and he considers it a [good] plan, that with the woman (Freawaru) he may settle a number of deadly feuds [and] conflicts'. Hrothgar's plan to settle a feud with the Heathobards by arranging a marriage between his daughter and a Heathobard prince is typical royal strategy in the early Middle Ages. Beowulf's speculation (ll. 2032–69a) that the plan will not succeed is borne out by the Scandinavian analogues of this story: despite the marriage, Ingeld's warriors, who had witnessed Freawaru's people killing their comrades in the earlier battles, remain aggrieved and seek blood vengeance.

2029b–31 **Oft seldan . . . duge** 'It is always rare everywhere that the murderous spear will remain idle for [even] a little while after a nation's defeat [on the battlefield], even though the bride be excellent.' *Oft* is the usual understatement for 'always'.

2032–8 Our proposed translation below involves taking *þæs* l. 2032 as a neut dem governed in the gen by the impersonal verb *ofþyncan* anticipating the noun clause (see *Guide* §148) in ll. 2035–8 in which the conj *þæt* is not expressed (see ll. 2200–8a note); *hē mid fǣmnan* l. 2034 as Ingeld with Freawaru; and *dryhtbearn* l. 2035a as nom pl. *Duguða* (l. 2035), the gen pl of the noun *duguð* 'excellence, wealth, magnificence', is used here adverbially. We translate: 'It can give offence to the prince of the Heatho-Bards (Ingeld), and to each of the thanes of those peoples, when he walks into the hall with his bride: the well-born sons of the Danes [are] lavishly entertained; on them gleam the heirlooms of ancestors, the strong and ring-adorned treasures which had belonged to the Heathobards while they might wield their weapons.'

2039 **Oð ðæt** adv 'And then'. See ll. 1739b–41a note; *hīe* nom pl the Heathobards.

2040 Both phrases are acc pl.

2041 **bēah** 'ring', one of the *gomelra lāfe*; cf. l. 2036 and the *mēce* 'sword' of l. 2047. The word may refer to the hilt-ring of the sword (see l. 1563 and figures 9 and 17b) or may be used in a general sense 'precious thing'.

gārcwealm gumena   – him bið grim sefa –
onginneð geōmormōd   geongum cempan
2045 þurh hreðra gehygd   higes cunnian,
wīgbealu weccean   ond þæt word ācwyð:
"Meaht ðū, mīn wine,   mēce gecnāwan
þone þīn fæder   tō gefeohte bær
under heregrīman   hindeman sīðe,
2050 dȳre īren,   þær hyne Dene slōgon,
wēoldon wælstōwe,   syððan Wiðergyld læg,
æfter hæleþa hryre   hwate Scyldungas?
Nū hēr þāra banena   byre nāthwylces
frætwum hrēmig   on flet gǣð,
2055 morðres gylpeð   ond þone māðþum byreð
þone þe ðū mid rihte   rǣdan sceoldest."
Manað swā ond myndgað   mǣla gehwylce
sārum wordum   oð ðæt sǣl cymeð
þæt se fǣmnan þegn   fore fæder dǣdum
2060 æfter billes bite   blōdfāg swefeð
ealdres scyldig;   him se ōðer þonan
losað lifigende,   con him land geare.
þonne bīoð gebrocene   on bā healfe
āðsweord eorla;   syððan Ingelde
2065 weallað wælnīðas   ond him wīflufan
æfter cearwælmum   cōlran weorðað.
þȳ ic Heaðo-Beardna   hyldo ne telge,
dryhtsibbe dǣl   Denum unfǣcne,
frēondscipe fæstne.

2043 sefa] fa   2044 geongum] geon . . .   2055 gylpeð] gylp . . .   2062 lifigende] . . . e
. . .   2063 gebrocene] . . . ocene   2064 aðsweord] að sweorð   syððan] . . . ðan
2067 Heaðo-Beardna] heaðobearna

2052 **hwate Scyldungas** nom pl.
2053 **Nū** adv; **byre** a young Dane whom we identify with *se fǣmnan þegn* 'the servant of Freawaru' l. 2059.
2056 **þone þe** rel pron agreeing with its antecedent *þone māðþum* l. 2055. Since *rǣdan* governs the dat *dǣdum* in l. 2858, *þone þe* here is an example of the *se 'þe* rel pron (*Guide* §163.1).
2059 **se fǣmnan** (gen sg) **þegn** is the Danish warrior who was wearing the Heathobard *mēce* l. 2047. See l. 2053 note.
2061 **se ōðer** is the *geong cempa* l. 2044.
2063–4a Fighting is renewed.
2064 **syððan** adv 'thereafter'.
2067 **þȳ** 'for that [reason]'.
2069b–117a Beowulf tells of the fight with Grendel, adding new details.

[Beowulf's account continued]

Ic sceal forð sprecan

2070 gēn ymbe Grendel   þæt ðū geare cunne,
      sinces brytta,   tō hwan syððan wearð
      hondrǣs hæleða.   Syððan heofones gim
      glād ofer grundas,   gǣst yrre cwōm
      eatol ǣfengrom   ūser nēosan
2075 ðǣr wē gesunde   sǣl weardodon.
      þǣr wæs Hondsciô   hild onsǣge
      feorhbealu fǣgum,   hē fyrmest læg,
      gyrded cempa,   him Grendel wearð
      mǣrum maguþegne   tō mūðbonan,
2080 lēofes mannes   līc eall forswealg;
      nō ðȳ ǣr ūt ðā gēn   īdelhende
      bona blōdigtōð   bealewa gemyndig
      of ðām goldsele   gongan wolde
      ac hē mægnes rōf   mīn costode,
2085 grāpode gearofolm.   Glōf hangode
      sīd ond syllīc,   searobendum fæst,
      sīo wæs orðoncum   eall gegyrwed
      dēofles cræftum   ond dracan fellum.
      Hē mec þǣr on innan   unsynnigne
2090 dīor dǣdfruma   gedōn wolde
      manigra sumne;   hyt ne mihte swā
      syððan ic on yrre   uppriht āstōd.
      Tō lang ys tō reccenne   hū ic ðām lēodsceaðan
      yfla gehwylces   hondlēan forgeald,
2095 þǣr ic, þēoden mīn,   þīne lēode
      weorðode weorcum.   Hē on weg losade,
      lȳtle hwīle   līfwynna brēac;
      hwæþre him sīo swīðre   swaðe weardade

2076 hild] hilde   2079 magu] magū   2085 gearofolm] geareofolm   2093 hu ic ðam leodsceaðan] hui . . . leod sceaðan   2094 hondlean] hon . . .   2097 breac] br . . .

2070 **þæt** conj 'so that'.

2071 **tō hwan** interrog introducing a dependent question 'to what [result]'.

2072 **Syððan** conj.

2074 **ūser** gen pl 'us' governed by *nēosan*.

2076 **Hondsciô** dat sg.

2081 **nō ðȳ ǣr** 'no sooner for that'. His killing of Hondscioh did not make Grendel readier to leave the hall. See ll. 753b–4 note.

2084 **mīn** gen sg 'me' governed by *costode*.

2085 **Glōf** This seems to have been part of the equipment of a troll in Old Norse story. It may have been a large glove or possibly a bag.

2091b The inf *wesan* is to be understood here.

2098 **swaðe weardade** 'guarded the track' i.e. 'remained behind'.

hand on Hiorte   ond hē hēan ðonan
2100   mōdes geōmor   meregrund gefēoll.
    Mē þone wælrǣs   wine Scildunga
    fǣttan golde   fela lēanode
    manegum māðmum   syððan mergen cōm
    ond wē tō symble   geseten hæfdon.
2105   þǣr wæs gidd ond glēo: gomela Scilding
    felafricgende   feorran rehte,
    hwīlum hildedēor   hearpan wynne
    gomenwudu grētte,   hwīlum gyd āwræc
    sōð ond sārlīc,   hwīlum syllīc spell
2110   rehte æfter rihte   rūmheort cyning,
    hwīlum eft ongan   eldo gebunden
    gomel gūðwiga   gioguðe cwīðan
    hildestrengo;   hreðer inne wēoll
    þonne hē wintrum frōd   worn gemunde.
2115   Swā wē þǣr inne   andlangne dæg
    nīode nāman   oð ðæt niht becwōm
    ōðer tō yldum.   þā wæs eft hraðe
    gearo gyrnwræce   Grendeles mōdor,
    sīðode sorhfull;   sunu dēað fornam,
2120   wīghete Wedra.   Wīf unhȳre
    hyre bearn gewræc,   beorn ācwealde
    ellenlīce;   þǣr wæs Æschere,
    frōdan fyrnwitan   feorh ūðgenge.
    Nōðer hȳ hine ne mōston,   syððan mergen cwōm,
2125   dēaðwērigne   Denia lēode
    bronde forbærnan   nē on bēl hladan
    lēofne mannan;   hīo þæt līc ætbær
    fēondes fæðmum   under firgenstrēam.
    þæt wæs Hrōðgāre   hrēowa tornost
2130   þāra þe lēodfruman   lange begēate.
    þā se ðēoden mec   ðīne līfe
    healsode hrēohmōd   þæt ic on holma geþring
    eorlscipe efnde,   ealdre genēðde,
    mǣrðo fremede;   hē mē mēde gehēt.
2135   Ic ðā ðæs wælmes,   þē is wīde cūð,
    grimne gryrelīcne   grundhyrde fond.

2108 gomen] go . . .   2128 fæðmum under] fæð . . . der   2136 grimne] grimme

2105 **gomela Scilding** Hrothgar (l. 2110) or *cyninges þegn* (l. 867)?
2117b–43 Beowulf tells of the fight with Grendel's mother.
2119b The element order is object, subject, verb.
2131 **ðīne līfe** instr sg 'by thy life'.
2135–6 **ðæs wælmes** depends on *grundhyrde*; **þē** conj 'as'.

þǣr unc hwīle wæs   hand gemǣne,
holm heolfre wēoll   ond ic hēafde becearf
in ðām grundsele   Grendeles mōdor
2140   ēacnum ecgum,   unsōfte þonan
feorh oðferede;   næs ic fǣge þā gȳt
ac mē eorla hlēo   eft gesealde
māðma menigeo,   maga Healfdenes.

[An exchange of gifts]

XXXI   Swā se ðēodkyning   þēawum lyfde;
2145   nealles ic ðām lēanum   forloren hæfde
mægnes mēde   ac hē mē māðmas geaf,
sunu Healfdenes,   on mīnne sylfes dōm
ðā ic ðē, beorncyning,   bringan wylle,
ēstum geȳwan.   Gēn is eall æt ðē
2150   lissa gelong;   ic lȳt hafo
hēafodmāga   nefne, Hygelāc, ðec.'
Hēt ðā in beran   eafor hēafodsegn
heaðostēapne helm   hāre byrnan
gūðsweord geatolīc,   gyd æfter wræc:
2155   'Mē ðis hildesceorp   Hrōðgār sealde,
snotra fengel;   sume worde hēt
þæt ic his ǣrest ðē   ēst gesægde,
cwæð þæt hyt hæfde   Hiorogār cyning
lēod Scyldunga   lange hwīle,
2160   nō ðȳ ǣr suna sīnum   syllan wolde

2139 grund] *not in MS*   2146 māðmas] *word lost at edge of MS*   2147 minne] . . . ne

2137 'There for a while it was hand to hand for the two of us', lit. 'our hands were in common'. See ll. 1563–8a.

2138b–40a **ond** here shades into meaning 'when' or 'because'.

2139 **grundsele** MS *sele*. We supply *grund*. The region of the Grendelkin is described as *grundwong* (l. 1496) and *under gynne grund* (l. 1551). Grendel's mother is called a *grundwyrgenne* (l. 1518) and a *grundhyrde* (l. 2136).

2141 **næs** = *ne wæs*.

2144–54 Beowulf received many gifts while he was in Denmark. After his victory over Grendel, Hrothgar gave him a sword, banner, helmet, and coat of mail (ll. 1020–4a) and eight horses and a saddle (ll. 1035–9), and Wealhtheow gave him gold, two armlets, a corslet, and rings, one rivalling the *Brōsinga mene* (ll. 1192–1200a). After he had killed Grendel's mother, he received twelve gifts from Hrothgar (ll. 1866–7). The gifts specified in ll. 2152–4a coincide with those described in ll. 1020–4a.

2147 **on mīnne sylfes dōm** 'according to my own judgement', i.e. 'as much as I wished'. This is a piece of new information.

2151 **nefne** conj 'except'.

2152 **hēafodsegn** 'a sign of special importance'. See IVC5.

2157 **his** gen sg 'of it', referring to *ðis hildesceorp* l. 2155.

2160 **nō ðȳ ǣr** 'no sooner for that'. The fact that Heoroweard was his son did not make Hiorogar readier to give him his sword. See ll. 753b–4 note.

hwatum Heorowearde,   þēah hē him hold wǣre,
brēostgewǣdu.   Brūc ealles well.'
Hȳrde ic þæt þām frætwum   fēower mēaras
lungre gelīce   lāst weardode,
2165 æppelfealuwe;   hē him ēst getēah
mēara ond māðma.   Swā sceal mǣg dôn,
nealles inwitnet   ōðrum bregdon
dyrnum cræfte,   dēað rēnian
hondgesteallan.   Hygelāce wæs
2170 nīða heardum   nefa swȳðe hold
ond gehwæðer ōðrum   hrōþra gemyndig.
Hȳrde ic þæt hē ðone healsbēah   Hygde gesealde
wrǣtlīcne wundurmāððum   ðone þe him Wealhðēo geaf,
ðēodnes dohtor,   þrīo wicg somod
2175 swancor ond sadolbeorht;   hyre syððan wæs
æfter bēahðege   brēost geweorðod.
Swā bealdode   bearn Ecgðēowes
guma gūðum cūð   gōdum dǣdum,
drēah æfter dōme,   nealles druncne slōg
2180 heorðgenēatas;   næs him hrēoh sefa
ac hē mancynnes   mǣste cræfte
ginfæstan gife   þe him god sealde,
hēold hildedēor.   Hēan wæs lange
swā hyne Gēata bearn   gōdne ne tealdon
2185 ne hyne on medobence   micles wyrðne
drihten wereda   gedōn wolde;
swȳðe wēndon   þæt hē slēac wǣre,
æðeling unfrom.   Edwenden cwōm
tīrēadigum menn   torna gehwylces.
2190 Hēt ðā eorla hlēo   in gefetian,
heaðorōf cyning,   Hrēðles lāfe
golde gegyrede;   næs mid Gēatum ðā
sincmāððum sēlra   on sweordes hād;
þæt hē on Bīowulfes   bearm ālegde

2168 renian] re . . .   2174 ðeodnes] ðeo . . .   2176 breost] brost   2187 wendon] . . .
don

2164 **lāst weardode** 'followed', lit. 'occupied the track of'. The combination governs the dat *þām frætwum* l. 2163 and *weardode*, despite its form, is to be taken as pl.
2167 **bregdon** See l. 308 note.
2172–4a See l. 1202 note.
2173 **ðone þe** acc sg of *sepe* relative (*Guide* §162.4) 'which'.
2174a **dohtor** is more probably dat sg, referring to *Hygde* l. 2172, than nom sg referring to *Wealhðēo* l. 2173.
2174b–5a See IVC9 (horses).
2181 **mǣste cræfte** (inst sg) 'with the greatest power'.
2184 **swā** conj 'so that'.

2195 ond him gesealde   seofan þūsendo,
      bold ond bregostōl.   Him wæs bām samod
      on ðām lēodscipe   lond gecynde
      eard ēðelriht,   ōðrum swīðor
      sīde rīce   þām ðær sēlra wæs.

2195 **seofan þūsendo** 'seven thousand [hides of land]'. The size of a *hīd* varied greatly.

2199b 'to the one [who] was of higher rank there'. The principal clause requires the dative case, the adjective clause the nominative. Such examples are rare; see *OES* §2313. The temptation to read *þām þe* is strong. For another example see l. 2779.

PART TWO

Beowulf the King
(*lines 2200–3182*)

THE FIGHT WITH THE DRAGON (*lines 2200–2751*)

[The accession of Beowulf. The plundering of the dragon's hoard]

2200   Eft þæt geīode   ufaran dōgrum
        hildehlæmmum   syððan Hygelāc læg
        ond Heardrēde   hildemēceas
        under bordhrēoðan   tō bonan wurdon
        ðā hyne gesōhtan   on sigeþēode
2205   hearde hildfrecan   Heaðo-Scilfingas,
        nīða genǣgdan   nefan Hererīces,
        syððan Bēowulfe   brāde rīce
        on hand gehwearf;   hē gehēold tela
        fīftig wintra   – wæs ðā frōd cyning
2210   eald ēþelweard –   oð ðæt ān ongan
        deorcum nihtum   draca ricsian
        sē ðe on hēaum hope   hord beweotode
        stānbeorh stēapne;   stīg under læg
        eldum uncūð.   þǣr on innan gīong
2215   niðða nāthwylc   se þe nīde gefēng
        hǣðnum horde,   hond wǣge nam,

2202 Heardrede] hearede   2205 hildfrecan] hildefrecan   2207 brade] brǣde (*or* brade?)
2211 ricsian] *lost at edge of MS*   2212 heaum] hea   hope] he . . . e   2215 niðða] nið . . .   se
þe nide gefeng] . . . g . . . f . . . g   2216 wæge nam] *MS illegible*

2200–6 On these incidents see IVB.
2200–8a þæt dem anticipates the passage of dependent speech which begins at *syððan* conj
'after' l. 2201b (correlative with *syððan* adv 'then' l. 2207a) and ends at *gehwearf* l. 2208a. The conj
þæt would normally have preceded *syððan* l. 2207a in prose and in poetry (*OES* §1978) but must be
understood before *syððan* l. 2201b to give an idiomatic translation. For the sequence *þæt* dem . . .
þæt conj see ll. 2219b–20.
2206 **nefan Hererīces** Heardred.
2208 **hē** Beowulf.
2210 **ān** stressed and emphatic: someone in particular. Translate 'a certain one'.
2212–20 Folio 182ʳ (179ʳ), which contains these lines, is damaged.
2216 **wǣge** Cf. *fǣted wǣge* l. 2282.

smǣte, since fāh;   ne hē syððan þāh
þēah ðe hē slǣpende   besyred wurde
þēofes cræfte;   þæt sīe ðīod onfand
2220 būfolc beorna   þæt hē gebolgen wæs.

XXXII   Nealles mid gewealdum   wyrmhord ātrǣd
sylfes willum   se ðe him sāre gescēod
ac for þrēanēdlan   þēow nāthwylces
hæleða bearna   heteswengeas flēah
2225 ærnes þearfa   ond ðǣr inne fealh
secg synbysig.   Sōna him þā tīde
þæt grim ðām gyste   gryrebrōga stōd;
hwæðre . . . . sceapen . . . .
. . . . sceapen
2230 . . . . se fǣr begeat,
sincfæt sōhte.   þǣr wæs swylcra fela
in ðām eorðhūse   ǣrgestrēona
swā hȳ on geārdagum   gumena nāthwylc
eormenlāfe   æþelan cynnes
2235 þanchycgende   þǣr gehȳdde
dēore māðmas.   Ealle hīe dēað fornam
ǣrran mǣlum   ond se ān ðā gēn
lēoda duguðe   se ðǣr lengest hwearf
weard winegēomor   wēnde þæs ylcan
2240 þæt hē lȳtel fæc   longgestrēona
brūcan mōste.   Beorh eallgearo
wunode on wonge   wæterȳðum nēah
nīwe be næsse   nearocræftum fæst;
þǣr on innan bær   eorlgestrēona

2217 smæte] *MS illegible*   þah] *MS illegible*   2218 þeah ðe he] þ . . . ð . . .   besyred] besyre . . .
wurde] . . . de   2219 onfand] *MS illegible*   2220 gebolgen] gebolge . . .   2221 wyrmhord atræd]
wyrmhorda cræft   2223 þeow] þ   2225 ærnes] *MS illegible*   fealh] weall   2226 him þa
tide] mwatide   2227 grim] *MS illegible*   gyste] gyst . . .   gryrebroga] br . . . g . . .
2230 fær] fæs   2231 sohte] *word lost at edge of MS*   2232 eorðhuse] eorð . . .   2237 se] si

2217a **smǣte** Cf. *smǣte gold Elene* 1309 and *smǣtes goldes Widsith* 91 and *Solomon and Saturn* 15.
2217b–19a 'Nor did he (the thief) prosper thereafter, though in his sleep he (the dragon) was
deceived by the skill of the thief.' Before *syððan*, Thorkelin A has *þ*, Thorkelin B *þæt*. But this
would make no sense, and so we have not given it a place in our text. (There is no surviving trace of
a word here, the manuscript having crumbled away at this point.)
2222 **se ðe** 'who' the intruder; **him** the dragon.
2223 **þēow** 'servant, slave' for MS *þ*. The word does not occur elsewhere in *Beowulf* except as
the second element of names, e.g. *Wealhþēow*. Other proposed readings are *þegn* 'retainer, warrior'
or *þēof* 'thief' (cf. l. 2219).
2226 **Sōna him þā tīde** 'Immediately it befell him then'. The MS reading *sona mwatide* gives
no sense. We emend *mwa* to *him þā*, and take *tide* for *tīdde* 'it befell, it happened'.
2227–31 Another damaged passage.
2233 **hȳ** acc pl object of *gehȳdde* l. 2235 anticipating *eormenlāfe* l. 2234 and *dēore māðmas* l. 2236.
2237–8 **se ān** . . . **se** 'that one . . . who'.
2239 **þæs ylcan** 'the same [fate]'.

2245   hringa hyrde   hordwyrðne dæl
       fættan goldes,   fēa worda cwæð:
       'Heald þū nū, hrūse,   nū hæleð ne mōstan,
       eorla æhte.   Hwæt, hyt ær on ðē
       gōde begēaton;   guðdēað fornam
2250   feorhbealo frēcne   fȳra gehwylcne
       lēoda mīnra   þāra ðe þis līf ofgeaf:
       gesāwon seledrēam.   Nāh hwā sweord wege
       oððe forð bere   fǣted wǣge
       dryncfæt dēore;   duguð ellor scōc.
2255   Sceal se hearda helm   hyrstedgolde
       fǣtum befeallen;   feormynd swefað
       þā ðe beadogrīman   bȳwan sceoldon;
       ge swylce sēo herepād   sīo æt hilde gebād
       ofer borda gebræc   bite īrena
2260   brosnað æfter beorne.   Ne mæg byrnan hring
       æfter wīgfruman   wīde fēran
       hæleðum be healfe.   Næs hearpan wyn
       gomen glēobēames   ne gōd hafoc
       geond sæl swingeð   ne se swifta mearh
2265   burhstede bēateð.   Bealocwealm hafað
       fela feorhcynna   forð onsended.'
       Swā giōmormōd   giohðo mænde
       ān æfter eallum,   unblīðe hwearf
       dæges ond nihtes   oð ðæt dēaðes wylm
2270   hrān æt heortan.   Hordwynne fond
       eald ūhtsceaða   opene standan
       se ðe byrnende   biorgas sēceð
       nacod nīðdraca,   nihtes flēogeð
       fȳre befangen;   hyne foldbūend
2275   swīðe ondrǣdað.   Hē gesēcean sceall
       hord on hrūsan   þǣr hē hǣðen gold

2245 hordwyrðne] hard wyrðne   2247 mostan] mæstan   2250 fyra] fyrena   2251 þara]
þana   lif] *not in MS*   2253 forð bere] f . . .   2254 duguð] dug . . .   scoc] seoc
2255 hyrsted] . . . sted   2268 hwearf] hwe . . .   2275 swiðe ondrædað] . . . da . . .
2276 hord on hrusan] . . . r . . . rusan

2247 **nū** adv 'now' . . . **nū** conj 'since'.
2252a A summarizing comment: 'they had seen the [last of] hall joy'.
2252b **hwā** 'whoever, anyone who' interr introducing a dependent question.
2255–6a The inf *wesan* must be supplied here.
2256b–7a **feormynd, swefað**, and **þā ðe** are all plural.
2260b–2a 'The ringed corslet cannot travel far alongside the heroes after [the death of] the warrior.'
2262b **Næs** = Ne wæs Cf. ll. 2141 and 2432.
2268 **ān æfter eallum** the last survivor of ll. 2237b–8.

waraðˣ wintrum frōd;   ne byðˣ him wihte ðȳ sēl.
Swā se ðēodsceaðˣa   þrēo hund wintra
hēold on hrūsan   hordærna sum
2280 ēacencræftig   oðˣ ðˣæt hyne ān ābealch
mon on mōde: mandryhtne bær
fǣted wǣge,   frioðˣowǣre bæd
hlāford sīnne.   Ðā wæs hord rāsod,
onboren bēaga hord,   bēne getīðˣad
2285 fēasceaftum men;   frēa scēawode
fīra fyrngeweorc   forman sīðˣe.
þā se wyrm onwōc   – wrōht wæs genīwad –
stonc ðˣā æfter stāne,   stearcheort onfand
fēondes fōtlāst;   hē tō forðˣ gestōp
2290 dyrnan cræfte   dracan hēafde nēah.
Swā mæg unfǣge   ēaðˣe gedīgan
wēan ond wrǣcsīðˣ   se ðˣe waldendes
hyldo gehealdeþ.   Hordweard sōhte
georne æfter grunde,   wolde guman findan
2295 þone þe him on sweofote   sāre getēode;
hāt ond hrēohmōd   hlǣw oft ymbehwearf
ealne ūtanweardne   – ne ðˣǣr ǣnig mon
on þām wēstenne   hwæðˣre wīges gefeh
beaduwe weorces   – hwīlum on beorh æthwearf,
2300 sincfæt sōhte;   hē þæt sōna onfand
ðˣæt hæfde gumena sum   goldes gefandod,
hēahgestrēona.   Hordweard onbād
earfoðˣlīce   oðˣ ðˣæt ǣfen cwōm,
wæs ðˣā gebolgen   beorges hyrde,
2305 wolde se lāðˣa   līge forgyldan
drincfæt dȳre.   þā wæs dæg sceacen

2279 hrusan] hrusam   2296 hlæw] hlæwū (= hlæwum)   2298 þam] þ . . .   wiges]
hilde   2299 beaduwe] bea   2305 se laðˣa] fela ðˣa

2277 **wihte** acc sg used as adv 'at all'; **ðȳ** instr of comparison 'than that' or 'than before' (*OES* §3245). The half-line means that it will not be at all better for the dragon than it was before he had the gold. Translate 'and not be at all better for it'.

2280–1 **ān . . . mon** cf l. 2210 note.

2289 **hē** 'the intruder'; **tō forðˣ** advs of direction '(thither) forward'; **gestōp** pluperfect 'had stepped'.

2291–3a If *hyldo* fem is the subject of *gehealdeþ*, *ðˣe* is acc 'So may an undoomed man whom the favour of the Almighty protects easily survive both woe and banishment' (the *se 'þe* relative). If *hyldo* is acc, *se ðˣe* is nom 'So may an undoomed man who retains the favour of the Almighty' (the *seþe* relative). See *Guide* §163.1, note 1. On the sentiment cf. ll. 572a–3.

2295 **þone þe** The *se 'þe* relative; see *Guide* §163.1.

2297b–9a Translate ' – yet no man in that wasteland was eager for conflict, for the toil of battle – '.

2298 **wīges** See IIIA7.

wyrme on willan;   nō on wealle læng
bīdan wolde   ac mid bǣle fōr
fȳre gefȳsed.   Wæs se fruma egeslīc
2310 lēodum on lande   swā hyt lungre wearð
on hyra sincgifan   sāre geendod.

[The dragon's attacks. Beowulf's decision to fight]

XXXIII   Ðā se gæst ongan   glēdum spīwan,
beorht hofu bærnan,   brynelēoma stōd
eldum on andan,   nō ðǣr āht cwices
2315 lāð lyftfloga   lǣfan wolde.
Wæs þæs wyrmes wīg   wīde gesȳne
nearofāges nīð   nēan ond feorran,
hū se gūðsceaða   Gēata lēode
hatode ond hȳnde.   Hord eft gescēat
2320 dryhtsele dyrnne   ǣr dæges hwīle,
hæfde landwara   līge befangen
bǣle ond bronde,   beorges getruwode,
wīges ond wealles;   him sēo wēn gelēah.
þā wæs Bīowulfe   brōga gecȳðed
2325 snūde tō sōðe   þæt his sylfes hām,
bolda sēlest   brynewylmum mealt
gifstōl Gēata.   þæt ðām gōdan wæs
hrēow on hreðre   hygesorga mǣst;
wēnde se wīsa   þæt hē wealdende
2330 ofer ealde riht   ēcean dryhtne
bitre gebulge;   brēost innan wēoll
þēostrum geþoncum   swā him geþȳwe ne wæs.
Hæfde līgdraca   lēoda fæsten
eal ond ūtan   eorðweard ðone
2335 glēdum forgrunden;   him ðæs gūðkyning
Wedera þīoden   wræce leornode.
Heht him þā gewyrcean   wīgendra hlēo
eallīrenne,   eorla dryhten,

2307 læng] læg   2325 ham] him

2307 **wyrme** dat of possession; **on** prep 'in accordance with'; **on wealle** 'on the wall'.
2312 **Ðā** adv 'Then'.
2324–7a Cf. ll. 81b–3a and 778–82a.
2329–31a Beowulf learns the true reason in ll. 2403–5.
2335 **ðæs** gen sg of dem 'for that'.
2338 **eallīrenne** adj acc sg neut wk agreeing with *wīgbord* l. 2339 'all of iron'.

wisse ingearde phi holt wudu s[...]

ne meahte lind wið lige r[...]ld[...] *182*

þsnd daga æþeling an god ærd[...]

bidan worulde lifes ⁊ re þynm [...]

mod þauh ðe hond welan h[...]lde l[...]

of su hozode ða hiunza ængel þhe

þone wið flozan weorwode zesoh[...]

siðan hen ze no he li[...] þa wæcce un

drued . nehim þæt wynnes wiz [...]

wihte dyde . æuwod ⁊ ellen worðon li[...]

æn wela nauro nedænde niða zedyh[...]

lnlde hlæm ma wyðwan helmod zu

sizon æidiz sæz wele wælwode . Iuiz

forznaw gnærdeles mæzu laðan

cynnes no þæt læfest wæs hond za

þæt mon hyzelac wloh. wyððan zau[...]

crninz zuðe wesum wnæwine wola

fwes londum on hwed les æurowa

hiowo dwyncum swealt bille zebæ[...]

þonan biowulf com wylwes cwæwe

wund nytte dweah hæfde hi on æwm[...]

NRIÐ

      wīgbord wrǣtlīc;   wisse hē gearwe
2340 þæt him holtwudu   helpan ne meahte
      lind wið līge.   Sceolde līþenddaga
      æþeling ǣrgōd   ende gebīdan
      worulde līfes   ond se wyrm somod
      þēah ðe hordwelan   hēolde lange.
2345 Oferhogode ðā   hringa fengel
      þæt hē þone wīdflogan   weorode gesōhte
      sīdan herge;   nō hē him þā sæcce ondrēd
      ne him þæs wyrmes wīg   for wiht dyde
      eafoð ond ellen   forðon hē ǣr fela
2350 nearo nēðende   nīða gedīgde
      hildehlemma   syððan hē Hrōðgāres
      sigorēadig secg   sele fǣlsode
      ond æt gūðe forgrāp   Grendeles mǣgum
      lāðan cynnes.   Nō þæt lǣsest wæs
2355 hondgemōta   þǣr mon Hygelāc slōh
      syððan Gēata cyning   gūðe rǣsum
      frēawine folca   Frēslondum on
      Hrēðles eafora   hiorodryncum swealt
      bille gebēaten.   þonan Bīowulf cōm
2360 sylfes cræfte,   sundnytte drēah,
      hæfde him on earme   eorla þrītig
      hildegeatwa   þā hē tō holme stāg.
      Nealles Hetware   hrēmge þorfton
      fēðewīges   þe him foran ongēan
2365 linde bǣron;   lȳt eft becwōm
      fram þām hildfrecan   hāmes nīosan.
      Oferswam ðā sioleða bigong   sunu Ecgðēowes
      earm ānhaga   eft tō lēodum

2340 helpan] he . . .   2341 liþenddaga] . . . þend daga   2347 þa] þā (= þam)
2355 gemota] ge . . .   2361 eorla] *for word lost at corner of page*   2362 stag] . . . g
2363 þorfton] þorf *at end of line*

2339–61 A facsimile of the manuscript containing these lines appears on p. 130.
2344 The unexpressed subject of *hēolde* is *se wyrm* l. 2343.
2349 **fela** governs the gen pls *nīða* l. 2350 and *hildehlemma* l. 2351.
2353 **Grendeles mǣgum** Grendel and his mother.
2354 **lāðan cynnes** descriptive gen (*Guide* §190.3) 'of hateful race'.
2354b–9a On the death of Hygelac see IVB.
2356 **syððan** conj 'when'.
2358 **hiorodryncum swealt** 'died by sword drinks'.
2360 **sundnytte drēah** 'undertook a sea-journey'.
2362 **hildegeatwa** acc pl; **stāg** 'embarked'.
2363 An infinitive is to be understood with *þorfton*. It could be *wesan* or *gangan* or *becuman* from *becwōm* l. 2365.
2367 **Oferswam** 'crossed'.

þær him Hygd gebēad   hord ond rīce
2370 bēagas ond bregostōl: bearne ne truwode
þæt hē wið ælfylcum   ēþelstōlas
healdan cūðe   ðā wæs Hygelāc dēad;
nō ðȳ ǣr fēasceafte   findan meahton
æt ðām æðelinge   ænige ðinga
2375 þæt hē Heardrēde   hlāford wǣre
oððe þone cynedōm   cīosan wolde.
Hwæðre hē him on folce   frēondlārum hēold
ēstum mid āre   oð ðæt hē yldra wearð,
Weder-Gēatum wēold.   Hyne wrǣcmǣcgas
2380 ofer sǣ sōhtan   suna Ōhteres,
hæfdon hȳ forhealden   helm Scylfinga
þone sēlestan   sǣcyninga
þāra ðe in Swīorīce   sinc brytnade,
mǣrne þēoden.   Him þæt tō mearce wearð;
2385 hē þǣr for feorme   feorhwunde hlēat
sweordes swengum   sunu Hygelāces
ond him eft gewāt   Ongenðīoes bearn
hāmes nīosan   syððan Heardrēd læg,
lēt ðone bregostōl   Bīowulf healdan,
2390 Gēatum wealdan.   þæt wæs gōd cyning.

[Beowulf's reconnaissance and speech]

XXXIIII   Se ðæs lēodhryres   lēan gemunde
                 uferan dōgrum,   Ēadgilse wearð

2385 for] or

2369–70a **þǣr** conj 'where'. On Hygd's offer of the kingdom to Beowulf, cf. ll. 1017b–19 note.
2370b–2a **bearne** dat sg (referring to Heardred) governed by *truwode*, on which the *þæt* clause also depends. For the construction cf. ll. 1180b–2a note.
2372 **ðā** conj 'when, now that'.
2373 **nō ðȳ ǣr** 'no sooner for that'. Hygd's offer did not make Beowulf more willing to become Heardred's king. See ll. 753b–4 note; **fēasceafte** nom pl the Geats, who had lost their king and supported Hygd's offer.
2377–8a Here *healdan* has the meaning 'to perform for someone (dat sg *him*) the action suggested by the nouns (dat pl *frēondlārum . . . ēstum*)'. Translate: 'Indeed, he (Beowulf) honourably (*mid āre*) gave him (Heardred) friendly advice and showed good will towards him.'
2379b–96 On the Geatish–Swedish wars see IVB.
2379 **Hyne** Heardred.
2380 **suna Ōhteres** Eanmund and Eadgils.
2381 **helm Scylfinga** Onela, who succeeded his brother Ohthere as king of the Swedes.
2384 **Him** Heardred = *sunu Hygelāces* l. 2386.
2387 **him** reflexive dat with *gewāt*; **Ongenðīoes bearn** Onela.
2391 **Se** Beowulf.
2392 **Ēadgilse** dat sg Eadgils, younger son of Ohthere l. 2394.

     fēasceaftum frēond;   folce gestēpte
     ofer sǣ sīde   sunu Ōhteres
2395 wigum ond wǣpnum;   hē gewrǣc syððan
     cealdum cearsīðum,   cyning ealdre binēat.
     Swā hē nīða gehwane   genesen hæfde
     slīðra geslyhta,   sunu Ecgðīowes,
     ellenweorca   oð ðone ānne dæg
2400 þe hē wið þām wyrme   gewegan sceolde.
     Gewāt þā twelfa sum   torne gebolgen
     dryhten Gēata   dracan scēawian,
     hæfde þā gefrūnen   hwanan sīo fǣhð ārās
     bealonīð biorna: him tō bearme cwōm
2405 māðþumfæt mǣre   þurh ðæs meldan hond.
     Se wæs on ðām ðrēate   þreottēoða secg
     se ðæs orleges   ōr onstealde
     hæft hygegiōmor,   sceolde hēan ðonon
     wong wīsian.   Hē ofer willan gīong
2410 tō ðæs ðe hē eorðsele   ānne wisse
     hlǣw under hrūsan   holmwylme nēh
     ȳðgewinne;   se wæs innan full
     wrǣtta ond wīra.   Weard unhīore
     gearo gūðfreca   goldmāðmas hēold
2415 eald under eorðan;   næs þæt ȳðe cēap
     tō gegangenne   gumena ǣnigum.
     Gesæt ðā on næsse   nīðheard cyning,
     þenden hǣlo ābēad   heorðgenēatum
     goldwine Gēata.   Him wæs geōmor sefa
2420 wǣfre ond wælfūs,   wyrd ungemete nēah
     se ðone gomelan   grētan sceolde,
     sēcean sāwle hord,   sundur gedǣlan
     līf wið līce;   nō þon lange wæs
     feorh æþelinges   flǣsce bewunden.

2395 **hē** Eadgils.

2396 **cyning** Onela.

2397 **hē** Beowulf; **gehwane** acc sg masc 'each' governs three gen pls *nīða* l. 2397, *slīðra geslyhta* l. 2398, and *ellenweorca* l. 2399.

2401 **twelfa sum** 'one of twelve', i.e. 'with eleven others'; cf. l. 207 note. The eleven are Wiglaf l. 2602 and the *tȳne* who deserted Beowulf in his need l. 2847. The one who plundered the dragon's treasure is the thirteenth l. 2406–9a.

2405 **ðæs meldan** gen sg 'of the informer', the thirteenth man of ll. 2406–9a.

2406–7 **Se ... se** 'That one ... who'.

2410 **tō ðæs ðe** conj lit 'to that [point] at which' and so 'until'.

2418 **þenden** adv 'meanwhile, then'.

2420 **wǣfre ond wælfūs** 'enraged and eager for slaughter'.

2421 **se** nom sg masc rel pron referring to *wyrd* (fem) l. 2420. See l. 1260 note.

2423 **nō þon lange** An unexplained combination. It might mean 'not for long after that'; *þon* is inst sg neut.

2425 Bīowulf maþelade   bearn Ecgðēowes:
'Fela ic on giogoðe   gūðrǣsa genæs
orleghwīla;   ic þæt eall gemon.
Ic wæs syfanwintre   þā mec sinca baldor
frēawine folca   æt mīnum fæder genam,
2430 hēold mec ond hæfde   Hrēðel cyning,
geaf mē sinc ond symbel,   sibbe gemunde;
næs ic him tō līfe   lāðra ōwihte
beorn in burgum   þonne his bearna hwylc
Herebeald ond Hæðcyn   oððe Hygelāc mīn.
2435 Wæs þām yldestan   ungedēfelīce
mǣges dǣdum   morþorbed strēd
syððan hyne Hæðcyn   of hornbogan
his frēawine   flāne geswencte,
miste mercelses   ond his mǣg ofscēt
2440 brōðor ōðerne   blōdigan gāre.
þæt wæs feohlēas gefeoht   fyrenum gesyngad,
hreðre hygemēðe;   sceolde hwæðre swā þēah
æðeling unwrecen   ealdres linnan.
Swā bið geōmorlīc   gomelum ceorle
2445 tō gebīdanne   þæt his byre rīde
giong on galgan: þonne hē gyd wrece,
sārigne sang   þonne his sunu hangað
hrefne tō hrōðre   ond hē him helpe ne mæg
eald ond infrōd   ǣnige gefremman;
2450 symble bið gemyndgad   morna gehwylce
eaforan ellorsīð.   Ōðres ne gȳmeð

     tō gebīdanne   burgum in innan
     yrfeweardas   þonne se ān hafað
     þurh dēaðes nȳd   dǣda gefondad;
2455   gesyhð sorhcearig   on his suna būre
     wīnsele wēstne   windge reste
     rēōte berofene.   Rīdend swefað
     hæleð in hoðman;   nis þǣr hearpan swēg
     gomen in geardum   swylce ðǣr iū wǣron.

[The conclusion of Beowulf's speech.
The beginning of the fight]

XXXV 2460   Gewīteð þonne on sealman,   sorhlēoð gǣleð
     ān æfter ānum;   þūhte him eall tō rūm,
     wongas ond wīcstede.   Swā Wedra helm
     æfter Herebealde   heortan sorge
     weallende wæg: wihte ne meahte
2465   on ðām feorhbonan   fǣghðe gebētan;
     nō ðȳ ǣr hē þone heaðorinc   hatian ne meahte
     lāðum dǣdum   þēah him lēof ne wæs.
     He ðā mid þǣre sorhge   þe him sīo sār belamp
     gumdrēam ofgeaf,   godes lēoht gecēas,
2470   eaferum lǣfde,   swā dēð ēadig mon,
     lond ond lēodbyrig   þā hē of līfe gewāt.
     þā wæs synn ond sacu   Swēona ond Gēata
     ofer wīd wæter   wrōht gemǣne
     herenīð hearda   syððan Hrēðel swealt

2473 wid] *lost at edge of MS*

2453 **yrfeweardas** gen sg with *ōðres* l. 2451; see l. 63 note. Both are governed by *tō gebīdanne* l. 2452 'to live to see'.

2454 **dǣda** gen pl. The verb *gefondian*, here 'to have one's portion of', takes the gen.

2457b–8a **Ridend, swefað**, and **hæleð** are all plural; cf. l. 2256.

2459 **wǣron** 3rd pl pret. The number suggests that *swylce* may be a pl rel pron 'such [things] as'. It may in the poet's mind have embraced the riders of l. 2457.

2460 The unexpressed subject of *Gewīteð* is the grieving father; cf. ll. 2451b–7a note.

2461 **ān æfter ānum** Either 'one (one song of sorrow) after another' or 'one (the father) for the other (the son)'. Comparison with *ān æfter eallum* l. 2268 may tilt the balance in favour of the latter; the translation 'the lone one for the lost one' has been suggested.

2462b–7 By taking ll. 2464b–5 as defining Hrethel's sorrow, we can explain *nō ðȳ ǣr* l. 2466 as 'no sooner for that', the sense assigned to it in its five other occurrences in *Beowulf*; see ll. 753b–4 note. Hrethel's sorrow did not make it less impossible for him to avenge his son.

2465 **ðām feorhbonan** and **þone heaðorinc** l. 2466 both refer to Hæthcyn.

2466 **hatian ne meahte** Here *ne* is an example of double negation and can be disregarded in translation.

2468 **Hē . . . þe him** 'He . . . to whom'. For this form of rel pron see *Guide* §162.2; **sīo sār** 'that grief'. The word is usually neut but here we have evidence that it was sometimes fem.

2469 **godes lēoht gecēas** i.e. 'he died'.

2472–89 The Geatish–Swedish wars. See IVB.

2475 oððe him Ongenðeowes   eaferan wæran
    frome fyrdhwate,   freode ne woldon
    ofer heafo healdan   ac ymb Hreosnabeorh
    eatolne inwitscear   oft gefremedon.
    þæt mægwine   mīne gewræcan,
2480 fæhðe ond fyrene   swā hyt gefræge wæs
    þeah ðe ōðer his   ealdre gebohte
    heardan cēape;   Hæðcynne wearð
    Gēata dryhtne   gūð onsæge.
    þā ic on morgne gefrægn   mæg ōðerne
2485 billes ecgum   on bonan stælan
    þær Ongenþeow   Eofores nīosað;
    gūðhelm tōglād,   gomela Scylfing
    hrēas heoroblāc;   hond gemunde
    fæhðo genōge,   feorhsweng ne oftēah.
2490 Ic him þā māðmas   þe hē mē sealde
    geald æt gūðe,   swā mē gifeðe wæs,
    lēohtan sweorde;   hē mē lond forgeaf
    eard ēðelwyn.   Næs him ænig þearf
    þæt hē tō Gifðum   oððe tō Gār-Denum
2495 oððe in Swīorīce   sēcean þurfe
    wyrsan wīgfrecan,   weorðe gecȳpan:
    symle ic him on fēðan   beforan wolde
    āna on orde   ond swā tō aldre sceall
    sæcce fremman   þenden þis sweord þolað
2500 þæt mec ær ond sīð   oft gelæste
    syððan ic for dugeðum   Dæghrefne wearð
    tō handbonan,   Hūga cempan;
    nalles hē ðā frætwe   Frēscyninge
    brēostweorðunge   bringan mōste

2478 gefremedon] ge gefremedon   2488 heoro] *not in MS*   2503 Frescyninge] fres cyning

2475 **oððe** conj usually means 'or' or 'until'. Here, since there is no exclusion of what precedes, it seems to mean 'and'; **him** dat pl probably refers to the Geats (l. 2472) 'to them'; **Ongenðeowes eaferan** Ohthere and Onela.

2476a The juxtaposition of parallel adjs without a conj occurs elsewhere; see ll. 1641a and 1874a.

2479 **þæt** anticipates the acc pl nouns in l. 2480a; **mægwine mīne** Hæthcyn (*ōðer* l. 2481 and *ōðerne* l. 2484) and Hygelac (*mæg* l. 2484).

2486 **Ongenþeow** = *gomela Scylfing* l. 2487; **Eofores** gen sg governed by *nīosað*. Eofor, a Geatish warrior under Hygelac, actually struck the fatal blow.

2490 **Ic** Beowulf; **him** Hygelac, king of the Geats.

2496 **weorðe gecȳpan** 'to buy for a price' and so 'to hire as mercenaries'.

2501–9 This seems to be another reference to Hygelac's fatal expedition; see IVB. Beowulf describes how he slew Dæghrefn, a warrior of the *Hugas* Franks (cf. l. 2914), and took from him a sword (ll. 2499b–502) which has been identified as Nægling (l. 2680).

2503 **Frēscyninge** dat sg 'to the king of the Frisians'. Cf. ll. 2914b–15.

2504 **brēostweorðunge** This seems to be a reference to the neck-ring or collar which Wealhtheow gave to Beowulf; see l. 1202 note.

2505　ac in campe gecrong　　cumbles hyrde
　　　　æþeling on elne;　　ne wæs ecg bona
　　　　ac him hildegrāp　　heortan wylmas
　　　　bānhūs gebræc.　　Nū sceall billes ecg
　　　　hond ond heard sweord　　ymb hord wīgan.'
2510　Bēowulf maðelode,　　bēotwordum spræc
　　　　nīehstan sīðe:　'Ic genēðde fela
　　　　gūða on geogoðe;　　gȳt ic wylle
　　　　frōd folces weard　　fæhðe sēcan,
　　　　mærðum fremman,　　gif mec se mānsceaða
2515　of eorðsele　　ūt gesēceð.'
　　　　Gegrētte ðā　　gumena gehwylcne,
　　　　hwate helmberend　　hindeman sīðe
　　　　swǣse gesīðas:　'Nolde ic sweord beran
　　　　wǣpen tō wyrme　　gif ic wiste hū
2520　wið ðām āglǣcean　　elles meahte
　　　　gylpe wiðgrīpan　　swā ic giō wið Grendle dyde
　　　　ac ic ðǣr heaðufȳres　　hātes wēne
　　　　oreðes ond attres;　　forðon ic mē on hafu
　　　　bord ond byrnan.　　Nelle ic beorges weard
2525　oferfleôn fōtes trem　　ac unc furður sceal
　　　　weorðan æt wealle　　swā unc wyrd getēoð
　　　　metod manna gehwæs.　　Ic eom on mōde from
　　　　þæt ic wið þone gūðflogan　　gylp ofersitte.
　　　　Gebīde gē on beorge　　byrnum werede
2530　secgas on searwum　　hwæðer sēl mæge
　　　　æfter wælrǣse　　wunde gedȳgan
　　　　uncer twēga.　　Nis þæt ēower sīð
　　　　ne gemet mannes　　nefne mīn ānes
　　　　þæt hē wið āglǣcean　　eofoðo dǣle,
2535　eorlscype efne.　　Ic mid elne sceall
　　　　gold gegangan　　oððe gūð nimeð
　　　　feorhbealu frēcne　　frēan ēowerne.'
　　　　Ārās ðā bī ronde　　rōf ōretta,
　　　　heard under helme,　　hiorosercean bær
2540　under stāncleofu,　　strengo getruwode
　　　　ānes mannes;　　ne bið swylc earges sīð.

2505 in campe] incempan　　　2523 oreðes ond attres] reðes 7 hattres　　　2525 furður] *not in*
MS　　2533 nefne] nef . . .　　　2534 þæt] wat

2514 **mærðum** dat pl used adverbially 'gloriously'.
2521 **gylpe** dat sg used adverbially 'with glory, gloriously'.
2522–3a The verb *wēnan* 'to expect' governs the gen.
2526 **wyrd** (fem) can be nom sg (cf. l. 2574) or acc sg (cf. l. 1056).
2529–32a **Gebīde** . . . **hwæðer** . . . **uncer twēga** 'Wait [to see] which of us two . . .'.

Geseah ðā be wealle   se ðe worna fela
gumcystum gōd   gūða gedīgde
hildehlemma,   þonne hnitan fēðan,
2545　stondan stānbogan,   strēam ūt þonan
brecan of beorge,   wæs þǣre burnan wælm
heaðofȳrum hāt;   ne meahte horde nēah
unbyrnende   ǣnige hwīle
dēop gedȳgan   for dracan lēge.
2550　Lēt ðā of brēostum,   ðā hē gebolgen wæs,
Weder-Gēata lēod   word ūt faran,
stearcheort styrmde;   stefn in becōm
heaðotorht hlynnan   under hārne stān.
Hete wæs onhrēred,   hordweard oncnīow
2555　mannes reorde,   næs ðǣr māra fyrst
frēode tō friclan.   From ǣrest cwōm
oruð āglǣcean   ūt of stāne
hāt hildeswāt;   hrūse dynede.
Biorn under beorge   bordrand onswāf
2560　wið ðām gryregieste   Gēata dryhten;
ðā wæs hringbogan   heorte gefȳsed
sæcce tō sēceanne.   Sweord ǣr gebrǣd
gōd gūðcyning   gomele lāfe
ecgum unglēaw;   ǣghwæðrum wæs
2565　bealohycgendra   brōga fram ōðrum.
Stīðmōd gestōd   wið stēapne rond
winia bealdor   ðā se wyrm gebēah
snūde tōsomne;   hē on searwum bād.
Gewāt ðā byrnende   gebogen scrīðan,
2570　tō gescipe scyndan.   Scyld wēl gebearg
līfe ond līce   lǣssan hwīle
mǣrum þēodne   þonne his myne sōhte;
ðǣr hē þȳ fyrste   forman dōgore
wealdan mōste   swā him wyrd ne gescrāf
2575　hrēð æt hilde.   Hond up ābrǣd
Gēata dryhten,   gryrefāhne slōh

2545 stondan] stodan   2564 ungleaw] un gl . . . aw

2547 **meahte** The unexpressed subject is *se ðe* 'that one who' (l. 2542).
2549 **dēop** adj used as noun 'hollow passage'.
2556 **From** adv 'forth'.
2564 **ecgum unglēaw** 'dull of edge, ineffective'. Compare ll. 2575b–80a.
2564b–5 **ǣghwæðrum . . . fram ōðrum** 'to each . . . from the other'.
2573–5a **ðǣr** adv 'there'; **forman dōgore** 'for the first time'; **swā . . . ne** 'without' (*Guide* §168 under *swā* 2(d)). Translate 'there on that occasion for the first time he had to manage without fate having granted him triumph in battle'.

incge lāfe   þæt sīo ecg gewāc
brūn on bāne,   bāt unswīðor
þonne his ðīodcyning   þearfe hæfde
2580 bysigum gebæded.   þā wæs beorges weard
æfter heaðuswenge   on hrēoum mōde,
wearp wælfȳre,   wīde sprungon
hildelēoman.   Hrēðsigora ne gealp
goldwine Gēata;   gūðbill geswāc
2585 nacod æt nīðe   swā hyt nō sceolde
īren ærgōd.   Ne wæs þæt ēðe sīð
þæt se mæra   maga Ecgðēowes
grundwong þone   ofgyfan wolde;
sceolde ofer willan   wīc eardian
2590 elles hwergen   swā sceal æghwylc mon
ālætan lændagas.   Næs ðā long tō ðon
þæt ðā āglæcean   hȳ eft gemētton.
Hyrte hyne hordweard,   hreðer æðme wēoll
nīwan stefne;   nearo ðrōwode
2595 fȳre befongen   se ðe ær folce wēold.
Nealles him on hēape   handgesteallan
æðelinga bearn   ymbe gestōdon
hildecystum   ac hȳ on holt bugon,
ealdre burgan.   Hiora in ānum wēoll
2600 sefa wið sorgum;   sibb' æfre ne mæg
wiht onwendan   þām ðe wēl þenceð.

[Despite Wiglaf's aid, Beowulf is mortally wounded]

XXXVI   Wīglāf wæs hāten,   Wēoxstānes sunu
lēoflīc lindwiga   lēod Scylfinga
mæg Ælfheres,   geseah his mondryhten
2605 under heregrīman   hāt þrōwian.

2589 ofer] *not in MS*   2596 hand] heand

2577 **incge lāfe** See l. 1107 note.
2579 **his** 'of it'.
2586b–91a 'It was no easy thing for the famous son of Ecgtheow to agree to leave that position. He was compelled against his will to occupy ground elsewhere just as every man is compelled to leave the world at life's end.' Beowulf feels chagrin at having to retreat when he had boasted that he would not (ll. 2524b–7a). In what may seem a surprising comparison, the poet says that his retreat was unavoidable.
2591b–2 **tō ðon þæt** 'until'; **ðā āglæcean** Beowulf and the dragon.
2599 **Hiora in ānum** 'in one of them', i.e. in Wiglaf l. 2602.
2600b–1 **sibb'** acc sg . . . **wiht** nom sg; **þām ðe** 'for him who'. See l. 183 note.
2602 On **Wēoxstān**, also spelled **Wīhstān** and **Wēohstān**, see glossary, proper names.
2604–6 **his mondryhten** . . . **hē** Beowulf; **his** Wiglaf's.

Gemunde ðā ðā āre   þe hē him ǣr forgeaf
wīcstede weligne   Wǣgmundinga,
folcrihta gehwylc   swā his fæder āhte;
ne mihte ðā forhabban,   hond rond gefēng
2610 geolwe linde,   gomel swyrd getēah;
þæt wæs mid eldum   Ēanmundes lāf
suna Ōhtheres;   þām æt sæcce wearð
wræccan winelēasum   Wēohstān bana
mēces ecgum   ond his māgum ætbær
2615 brūnfāgne helm   hringde byrnan
ealdsweord etonisc;   þæt him Onela forgeaf
his gædelinges   gūðgewǣdu
fyrdsearo fūslīc;   nō ymbe ðā fǣhðe spræc
þēah ðe hē his brōðor bearn   ābredwade.
2620 Hē ðā frætwe gehēold   fela missēra
bill ond byrnan   oð ðæt his byre mihte
eorlscipe efnan   swā his ǣrfæder,
geaf him ðā mid Gēatum   gūðgewǣda,
ǣghwæs unrīm   þā hē of ealdre gewāt
2625 frōd on forðweg.   þā wæs forma sīð
geongan cempan   þæt hē gūðe ræs
mid his frēodryhtne   fremman sceolde.
Ne gemealt him se mōdsefa   nē his mægenes lāf
gewāc æt wīge;   þæt se wyrm onfand
2630 syððan hīe tōgædre   gegān hæfdon.
Wīglāf maðelode,   wordrihta fela
sægde gesīðum   – him wæs sefa geōmor –:
'Ic ðæt mǣl geman   þær wē medu þēgun,
þonne wē gehēton   ūssum hlāforde
2635 in bīorsele   ðe ūs ðās bēagas geaf
þæt wē him ðā gūðgetāwa   gyldan woldon

2612 Ohtheres] ohtere   2613 wræccan] wr . . .   Weohstan] weohstanes   2620 ða] *not in MS*   2629 þæt] þa

2607 **Wǣgmundinga** gen pl. Beowulf also belongs to this family; see ll. 2813–16.
2608 **swā** 'as far as'. Cf. l. 93; **his** Wiglaf's.
2611–25a Another reference to the Geatish–Swedish wars; see IVB.
2612b–13a **þām . . . wræccan winelēasum** dat sg Eanmund.
2614 **his** Weohstan's.
2616–17 **þæt** dem . . . **his gædelinges gūðgewǣdu** the war-gear of Onela's nephew Eanmund.
2618b–19 The subject of *spræc* is Onela (l. 2616); **his brōðor bearn** Eanmund. Onela did not seek vengeance against Weohstan because he had been fighting on Onela's side against his nephews, whereas Onela did fight and kill Heardred (ll. 2202–6) because he had given refuge to Eanmund and Eadgils (ll. 2379–88). Onela allowed Beowulf to rule the Geats on the death of Heardred (ll. 2389–90).
2623 **gūðgewǣda** acc pl.
2624 **ǣghwæs unrīm** acc sg 'countless number of everything'. Cf. l. 3135.
2635 **ðe** rel pron 'who'.

gif him þyslīcu   þearf gelumpe,
helmas ond heard sweord.   Ðē hē ūsic on herge gecēas
tō ðyssum sīðfate   sylfes willum,
2640 onmunde ūsic mǣrða   ond mē þās māðmas geaf,
þē hē ūsic gārwīgend   gōde tealde
hwate helmberend   þēah ðe hlāford ūs
þis ellenweorc   āna āðōhte
tō gefremmanne,   folces hyrde,
2645 forðām hē manna mǣst   mǣrða gefremede
dǣda dollīcra.   Nū is se dǣg cumen
þæt ūre mandryhten   mægenes behōfað
gōdra gūðrinca;   wutun gongan tō,
helpan hildfruman   þenden hyt sȳ
2650 glēdegesa grim.   God wāt on mec
þæt mē is micle lēofre   þæt mīnne līchaman
mid mīnne goldgyfan   glēd fæðmie.
Ne þynceð mē gerysne   þæt wē rondas beren
eft tō earde   nemne we ǣror mægen
2655 fāne gefyllan,   feorh ealgian
Wedra ðēodnes.   Ic wāt geare
þæt nǣron ealdgewyrht   þæt hē āna scyle
Gēata duguðe   gnorn þrōwian,
gesīgan æt sæcce;   ūrum sceal sweord ond helm
2660 byrne ond beaduscrūd   bām gemǣne.'
Wōd þā þurh þone wælrēc,   wīgheafolan bær
frēan on fultum,   fēa worda cwæð:
'Lēofa Bīowulf,   lǣst eall tela
swā ðū on geoguðfēore   geāra gecwǣde
2665 þæt ðū ne ālǣte   be ðē lifigendum
dōm gedrēosan;   scealt nū dǣdum rōf,
æðeling anhȳdig,   ealle mægene

2660 beaduscrud] byrdu scrud

2638b–42a **Ðē** . . . **þē** inst sg neuts serving as adv 'for this reason' . . . conj 'because'.
2647 **behōfað** is preceded and followed by a gen object.
2648b–50a 'let us go forth, give help to our battle-leader while there (*hyt*) is grim fire-terror'.
2650b–2 Wiglaf is saying that he would rather die with Beowulf [than fail him in battle]. The 'than' clause is implied in ll. 2653–6a.
2654–5 **mægen . . . gefyllan** 'can fell the dragon'; *mægen* is pres subj 1p of *magan*.
2656b–9a **þæt** l. 2657a conj 'that' introducing a noun clause object of *wāt*; **nǣron** pret as perfect 'have not been' (*Guide* §197.3); **ealdgewyrht** nom pl either (a) '[Beowulf's] deserts for past deeds' or (b) '[Beowulf's] past deeds'. If (a), *þæt* l. 2657b introduces a noun clause complement of *nǣron*, with the subj *scyle* expressing desire or doubt (*Guide* §156): 'that he alone of the warrior-band of the Geats ought to suffer affliction . . .'. If (b), *þæt* l. 2657b introduces a clause with the subj expressing hypothetical result (*Guide* §175.2): 'so that he alone ought to suffer affliction . . .'.
2659b–60 **ūrum . . . bām** 'to both of us'.
2665 **be ðē lifigendum** 'with you [still] living', i.e. 'as long as you were alive'.

feorh ealgian;   ic ðē fullæstu.'

Æfter ðām wordum   wyrm yrre cwōm,
2670 atol inwitgæst   ōðre sīðe
fȳrwylmum fāh   fīonda nīosian
lāðra manna.   Līg ȳðum fōr,
born bord wið rond,   byrne ne meahte
geongum gārwigan   gēoce gefremman
2675 ac se maga geonga   under his mǣges scyld
elne geēode   þā his āgen wæs
glēdum forgrunden.   þā gēn gūðcyning
mǣrða gemunde,   mægenstrengo slōh
hildebille   þæt hyt on heafolan stōd
2680 nīþe genȳded;   Nægling forbærst,
geswāc æt sæcce   sweord Bīowulfes
gomol ond grǣgmǣl.   Him þæt gifeðe ne wæs
þæt him īrenna   ecge mihton
helpan æt hilde;   wæs sīo hond tō strong
2685 se ðe mēca gehwane   mīne gefrǣge
swenge ofersōhte;   þonne hē tō sæcce bær
wǣpen wundum heard,   næs him wihte ðē sēl.
þā wæs þēodsceaða   þriddan sīðe
frēcne fȳrdraca   fǣhða gemyndig,
2690 rǣsde on ðone rōfan   þā him rūm āgeald,
hāt ond heaðogrim   heals ealne ymbefēng
biteran bānum;   hē geblōdegod wearð
sāwuldrīore,   swāt ȳðum wēoll.

[The dragon's death]

XXXVII   Ðā ic æt þearfe gefrægn   þēodcyninges
2695 andlongne eorl   ellen cȳðan
cræft ond cēnðu   swā him gecynde wæs.
Ne hēdde hē þæs heafolan   ac sīo hand gebarn

2671 niosian] nio . . .   2676 wæs] *for word lost at edge of page*   2678 mǣrða] m . . .
2694 gefrægn] *not in MS*

2668 **ic ðē fullæstu** 'I will help/assist you'. With the artful contrast of *læst* (l. 2663) and *fullæstu* here, Wiglaf emphasizes his subordinate status.

2671b–2a **nīosian** is preceded and followed by a gen object.

2684b–5 **sīo hond . . . se ðe** See l. 1344 note.

2687 **wundum** For the idea of swords hardened in battle cf. l. 1460a; **ðē** inst sg neut 'for that' i.e. for having the weapon.

2692 **hē** Beowulf.

2694 **æt þearfe** is to be construed with *þēodcyninges*.

2697–9 **Ne hēdde hē . . . hwēne slōh** 'He disregarded the [dragon's] head, for the hand of the brave man was burned where he helped his kinsman so that he struck the hostile creature somewhat lower down.' (See *OES* §1770 on *ac* 'for'.) Since his hand was burned striking at the head, Wiglaf

mōdiges mannes   þǣr hē his mǣges healp
þæt hē þone nīðgǣst   nioðor hwēne slōh,
2700 secg on searwum,   þæt ðæt sweord gedēaf
fāh ond fǣted   þæt ðæt fȳr ongon
sweðrian syððan.   þā gēn sylf cyning
gewēold his gewitte,   wællseaxe gebrǣd
biter ond beaduscearp   þæt hē on byrnan wæg,
2705 forwrāt Wedra helm   wyrm on middan.
Fēond gefyldan   – ferh ellen wræc –
ond hī hyne þā bēgen   ābroten hæfdon,
sibæðelingas;   swylc sceolde secg wesan
þegn æt ðearfe.   þæt ðām þēodne wæs
2710 sīðast sigehwīle   sylfes dǣdum,
worlde geweorces.   Ðā sīo wund ongon,
þe him se eorðdraca   ǣr geworhte,
swelan ond swellan;   hē þæt sōna onfand
þæt him on brēostum   bealonīðe wēoll
2715 attor on innan.   Ðā se æðeling gīong
þæt hē bī wealle   wīshycgende
gesæt on sesse,   seah on enta geweorc,
hū ðā stānbogan   stapulum fæste
ēce eorðreced   innan healde.
2720 Hyne þā mid handa   heorodrēorigne
þēoden mǣrne   þegn ungemete till
winedryhten his   wætere gelafede
hilde sædne   ond his helm onspēon.
Bīowulf maþelode –   hē ofer benne spræc,
2725 wunde wælblēate,   wisse hē gearwe
þæt hē dæghwīla   gedrogen hæfde
eorðan wynne;   ðā wæs eall sceacen

2698 mæges] mægenes   2710 siðast] siðas   2714 bealoniðe] beal   2723 helm] he . . .
2727 wynne] wyn . . .

stabs the dragon lower down, where, in fact, it is most vulnerable. This completes the pattern of a fortuitous event aiding the hero(es) to victory in each monster-fight (ll. 679–80 [in the light of ll. 801b–5a], 1557). This pattern is important because it is a confirmation of the poet's theme repeated throughout the poem that 'God ruled over the events of men's lives then in pagan times even as he still does now'.

2703a **gewēold his gewitte** 'controlled his wit(s)' i.e. regained his senses.

2703b–4 **biter ond beaduscearp** modify *wællseaxe*. For the absence of dative inflexion, see l. 46 note. See IVC8.

2706 **ferh ellen wræc** '[their] valour had driven out [its] life'.

2715b **gīong** 'went'.

2717b–19 **seah on . . . healde** *enta geweorc* and the *hū* clause are parallel objects of *seah on*: 'he looked at the work of giants (i.e. the dragon's barrow), [looked at] how the age-old earth-hall upholds firmly with pillars the rocky arches within'. On the subj *healde* see *OES* §626.

2724 **ofer benne** 'over [his] wound', i.e. wounded as he was.

dōgorgerīmes,   dēað ungemete nēah –:

'Nū ic suna mīnum   syllan wolde

2730 gūðgewǣdu   þǣr mē gifeðe swā

ǣnig yrfeweard   æfter wurde

līce gelenge.   Ic ðās lēode hēold

fīftig wintra;   næs sē folccyning

ymbesittendra   ǣnig ðāra

2735 þe mec gūðwinum   grētan dorste,

egesan ðeôn.   Ic on earde bād

mǣlgesceafta,   hēold mīn tela,

ne sōhte searonīðas   ne mē swōr fela

āða on unriht.   Ic ðæs ealles mæg

2740 feorhbennum sēoc   gefēan habban

forðām mē wītan ne ðearf   waldend fīra

morðorbealo māga   þonne mīn sceaceð

līf of līce.   Nū ðū lungre geong

hord scēawian   under hārne stān,

2745 Wīglāf lēofa,   nū se wyrm ligeð,

swefeð sāre wund   since berēafod.

Bīo nū on ofoste   þæt ic ǣrwelan,

goldǣht ongite,   gearo scēawige

swegle searogimmas   þæt ic ðȳ sēft mæge

2750 æfter māððumwelan   mīn ālǣtan

līf ond lēodscipe   þone ic longe hēold.'

BEOWULF'S DEATH AND FUNERAL (*lines 2752–3182*)

[Beowulf's last words and death]

XXXVIII   Ðā ic snūde gefrægn   sunu Wīhstānes

æfter wordcwydum   wundum dryhtne

hȳran heaðosīocum,   hringnet beran

2755 brogdne beadusercean   under beorges hrōf.

2755 under] urder

2730b–2a þǣr mē . . . gelenge 'if any heir related to my person had been so granted to me then'.

2735 mec . . . grētan 'to attack me with swords'.

2736b–7a bād mǣlgesceafta 'awaited the events destined [for me]'.

2737b hēold mīn tela 'held my own well'.

2738b–9a ne mē swōr . . . unriht Typical Germanic understatement (cf. ll. 3029b–30a). The meaning is that Beowulf swore *no* false oaths.

2747–51 As Beowulf makes clear in ll. 2797–8 and 2800b–1a, he takes comfort in the treasure because he thinks it will serve his people's needs after his death. His interest in it is selfless, not avaricious.

2752 snūde modifies *hȳran* in l. 2754.

Geseah ðā sigehrēðig, þā hē bī sesse gēong,
magoþegn mōdig māððumsigla fealo,
gold glitinian grunde getenge
wundur on wealle ond þæs wyrmes denn
2760 ealdes ūhtflogan, orcas stondan
fyrnmanna fatu feormendlēase
hyrstum behrorene; þǣr wæs helm monig
eald ond ōmig, earmbēaga fela
searwum gesǣled. Sinc ēaðe mæg
2765 gold on grunde gumcynnes gehwone
oferhīgian hȳde se ðe wylle.
Swylce hē siomian geseah segn eallgylden
hēah ofer horde, hondwundra mǣst
gelocen leoðocræftum; of ðām lēoma stōd
2770 þæt hē þone grundwong ongitan meahte,
wrǣte giondwlītan. Næs ðæs wyrmes þǣr
onsȳn ǣnig ac hyne ecg fornam.
Đā ic on hlǣwe gefrægn hord rēafian
eald enta geweorc ānne mannan,
2775 him on bearm hladan bunan ond discas
sylfes dōme, segn ēac genōm,
bēacna beorhtost. Bill ǣr gescōd
– ecg wæs īren – ealdhlāfordes
þām ðāra māðma mundbora wæs
2780 longe hwīle, līgegesan wæg
hātne for horde hioroweallende
middelnihtum oð þæt hē morðre swealt.
Ār wæs on ofoste eftsīðes georn
frætwum gefyrðred, hyne fyrwet bræc
2785 hwæðer collenferð cwicne gemētte

2765 grunde] gru . . . 2769 leoma] leoman 2771 wræte] wræce 2775 hladan] hlodon

2756–62a The verb *Geseah* takes as its objects a series of parallel words and phrases: *māððumsigla fealo, gold glitinian, wundur, þæs wyrmes denn*, and *orcas stondan*.

2764b–6 This generalization about the nature of gold has proved puzzling because the meaning of the verb *oferhīgian*, which occurs only here, is uncertain. Since the preceding lines emphasize the perishability of material treasure (*hyrstum behrorene* l. 2762, *ōmig* l. 2763) and the brevity of its owner's tenure of it, we suggest that *oferhīgian* is a derivative of *hīgian* 'hye, hasten' and means 'pass away from, escape from'. Cf. *ofergān* 'pass away, end'. (Just as *on-* makes *onhīgian* 'to attack, despoil' transitive, so *ofer-* transitivizes *oferhīgian*.); **hȳde se ðe wylle** 'hide it who will', 'no matter how carefully he hides it'. 'Treasure, gold in the ground, can easily escape from any man, no matter how carefully he hides it.'

2771b–2a In prose the order would be *Næs ǣnig onsȳn ðæs wyrmes þǣr*.

2777b–9 **ealdhlāfordes** goes with *Bill, mundbora* with *ðāra māðma*; **þām** = 'the one who'. See l. 2199b note.

2783b–4a **eftsīðes georn** . . . **gefyrðred** 'desirous of return and made eager by the treasures [which he wanted to show the king]'.

in ðām wongstede   Wedra þēoden
ellensīocne   þær hē hine ǣr forlēt.
Hē ðā mid þām māðmum   mǣrne þīoden
dryhten sīnne   drīorigne fand
2790 ealdres æt ende,   hē hine eft ongon
wæteres weorpan   oð þaet wordes ord
brēosthord þurhbræc.
gomel on giohðe,   gold scēawode:
'Ic ðāra frætwa   frēan ealles ðanc
2795 wuldurcyninge   wordum secge
ēcum dryhtne,   þe ic hēr on starie,
þæs ðe ic mōste   mīnum lēodum
ǣr swyltdæge   swylc gestrȳnan.
Nū ic on māðma hord   mīne bebohte
2800 frōde feorhlege,   fremmað gēna
lēoda þearfe;   ne mæg ic hēr leng wesan.
Hātað heaðomǣre   hlǣw gewyrcean
beorhtne æfter bǣle   æt brimes nōsan,
se scel tō gemyndum   mīnum lēodum
2805 hēah hlīfian   on Hronesnæsse
þæt hit sǣlīðend   syððan hātan
Bīowulfes biorh,   ðā ðe brentingas
ofer flōda genipu   feorran drīfað.'
Dyde him of healse   hring gyldenne
2810 þīoden þrīsthȳdig,   þegne gesealde
geongum gārwigan   goldfāhne helm
bēah ond byrnan,   hēt hyne brūcan well:
'þū eart endelāf   ūsses cynnes
Wǣgmundinga;   ealle wyrd forswēop
2815 mīne māgas   tō metodsceafte
eorlas on elne;   ic him æfter sceal.'

2792b] *no gap in MS. See note*   2793 giohðe] giogoðe   2799 mine] minne   2814 for-
sweop] for speof.

2792b There is no gap in the MS but metre and meaning leave no doubt that a half-line is
missing. We suggest supplying *Bregorōf gespræc*, which resembles the preceding half-line at both
beginning and end and so could have been skipped easily in copying. Compare *Bregorōf gespræc /
gomel on giohðe* here with *worn eall gespræc / gomol on gehðo* (ll. 3094b–5a).

2796 The antecedent of *þe* is *ðāra frætwa* l. 2794.

2799–801a Nū ic . . . þearfe 'Now that I have exchanged my old life for the hoard of treasures,
they will accomplish the needs of the people'. The plural *fremmað* agrees with *māðma*.

2802 Hātað heaðomǣre . . . gewyrcean 'The battle-famed ones will order a barrow to be
made'.

2806 hit The masculine gender of the antecedents (*hlǣw, se*) is forgotten, and natural gender
prevails. See *Guide* §187.2(b).

2809 Dyde . . . of 'doffed, removed'.

2814 Wǣgmundinga See note to l. 2607.

þæt wæs þām gomelan   gingæste word
brēostgehygdum   ǣr hē bǣl cure
hāte heaðowylmas;   him of hræðre gewāt
2820   sāwol sēcean   sōðfæstra dōm.

[Wiglaf's rebuke to the cowards]

[XXXVIIII]   Ðā wæs gegongen   guman unfrōdum
earfoðlīce   þæt hē on eorðan geseah
þone lēofestan   līfes æt ende
blēate gebǣran.   Bona swylce læg
2825   egeslīc eorðdraca   ealdre berēafod
bealwe gebǣded.   Bēahhordum leng
wyrm wōhbogen   wealdan ne mōste
ac him īrenna   ecga fornāmon,
hearde heaðoscearde   homera lāfe
2830   þæt se wīdfloga   wundum stille
hrēas on hrūsan   hordærne nēah.
Nalles æfter lyfte   lācende hwearf
middelnihtum,   māðmǣhta wlonc
ansȳn ȳwde   ac hē eorðan gefēoll
2835   for ðæs hildfruman   hondgeweorce.
Hūru þæt on lande   lȳt manna ðāh
mægenāgendra   mīne gefrǣge,
þēah ðe hē dǣda gehwæs   dyrstig wǣre,
þæt hē wið attorsceaðan   oreðe gerǣsde
2840   oððe hringsele   hondum styrede
gif hē wæccende   weard onfunde
būon on beorge.   Bīowulfe wearð
dryhtmāðma dǣl   dēaðe forgolden;
hæfde ǣghwæðer   ende gefēred

2819 hræðre] hwæðre   2821 guman] gumū (= gumum)   2844 æghwæðer] æghwæðre

2820 **sōðfæstra dōm** The syntax is ambiguous: *sōðfæstra* could be either subjective genitive 'judgement by those speaking the truth' or objective genitive 'judgement passed on those who are firm in truth'.

2821–2a **Ðā wæs . . . earfoðlīce** 'Then it came to pass painfully for the young man.'

2829 **heaðoscearde** 'notched in battle' confirms the sword's hardness; it is the hardest swords that survive many battles.

2830 **wundum stille** 'still (i.e. dead) as a result of his wounds'.

2834 **eorðan gefēoll** 'fell to the earth'.

2836 **Hūru þæt . . . ðāh** 'Indeed, it has prospered with few men on earth'. 'It' (*þæt*) refers to the clause introduced by *þæt* in l. 2839. See *Guide* §148 second paragraph.

2839 **þæt hē . . . gerǣsde** 'that he should charge into the breath of a venomous foe'.

2841b–2a **weard onfunde būon** (= *būan*) 'found a guard (i.e. the dragon) dwelling'.

2845   lænan līfes.   Næs ðā lang tō ðon
   þæt ðā hildlatan   holt ofgēfan
   tȳdre trēowlogan   tȳne ætsomne
   ðā ne dorston ǣr   dareðum lācan
   on hyra mandryhtnes   miclan þearfe
2850   ac hȳ scamiende   scyldas bǣran
   gūðgewǣdu   þǣr se gomela læg,
   wlitan on Wīlāf.   Hē gewērgad sæt
   fēðecempa   frēan eaxlum nēah,
   wehte hyne wætre;   him wiht ne spēow.
2855   Ne meahte hē on eorðan,   ðēah hē ūðe wēl,
   on ðām frumgāre   feorh gehealdan
   ne ðæs wealdendes   wiht oncirran:
   wolde dōm godes   dǣdum rǣdan
   gumena gehwylcum   swā hē nū gēn dêð.
2860   þā wæs æt ðām geongan   grim andswaru
   ēðbegēte   þām ðe ǣr his elne forlēas.
   Wīglāf maðelode   Wēohstānes sunu
   secg sārigferð,   seah on unlēofe:
   'þæt, lā, mæg secgan   se ðe wyle sōð specan,
2865   þæt se mondryhten   se ēow ðā māðmas geaf
   ēoredgeatwe   þe gē þǣr on standað –
   þonne hē on ealubence   oft gesealde
   healsittendum   helm ond byrnan,
   þēoden his þegnum   swylce hē þrȳdlīcost
2870   ōwer feor oððe nēah   findan meahte –
   þæt hē gēnunga   gūðgewǣdu
   wrāðe forwurpe   ðā hyne wīg beget.
   Nealles folccyning   fyrdgesteallum
   gylpan þorfte;   hwæðre him god ūðe,
2875   sigora waldend,   þæt hē hyne sylfne gewræc
   āna mid ecge   þā him wæs elnes þearf.
   Ic him līfwraðe   lȳtle meahte
   ætgifan æt gūðe   ond ongan swā þēah

2854 speow] speop   2860 geongan] geongū (= geongum)   2863 secg] sec

2848 **dareðum lācan** 'wield their spears'.

2850 **bǣran** *-an* for *-on* (as with *wlitan* l. 2852).

2854 **wehte** normally means 'roused, awakened' but here apparently 'sought to rouse'. But see *Anglo-Saxon England*, 4 (1975), 16.

2857 **ne ðæs . . . oncirran** 'nor change aught [ordained] of God'.

2858–9 **wolde dōm . . . dêð** 'God's authority would hold sway over the deeds [performed] by each one of men, as it now still does.'

2860 **æt ðām geongan** 'from the young man'.

2869b–70 **swylce hē . . . meahte** 'the finest such as he was able to find anywhere, far or near'.

2878a **ætgifan** Since a verb *ætgifan* occurs nowhere else in OE, the prefix *æt-* here may be an unintentional dittograph and the correct reading *gifan æt gūðe*.

      ofer mīn gemet   mǣges helpan;
2880 symle wæs þȳ sǣmra   þonne ic sweorde drep
      ferhðgenīðlan,   fȳr unswīðor
      wēoll of gewitte.   Wergendra tō lȳt
      þrong ymbe þēoden   þā hyne sīo þrāg becwōm.
      Hū sceal sincþego   ond swyrdgifu,
2885 eall ēðelwyn   ēowrum cynne,
      lufen ālicgean!   Londrihtes mōt
      þǣre mǣgburge   monna ǣghwylc
      īdel hweorfan   syððan æðelingas
      feorran gefricgean   flēam ēowerne
2890 dōmlēasan dǣd.   Dēað bið sēlla
      eorla gehwylcum   þonne edwītlīf.'

[The messenger's forebodings]

XL   Heht ðā þæt heaðoweorc   tō hagan bīodan
      up ofer ecgclif   þǣr þæt eorlweorod
      morgenlongne dæg   mōdgiōmor sæt
2895 bordhæbbende,   bēga on wēnum
      endedōgores   ond eftcymes
      lēofes monnes.   Lȳt swīgode
      nīwra spella   se ðe næs gerād
      ac hē sōðlīce   sægde ofer ealle:
2900 'Nū is wilgeofa   Wedra lēoda
      dryhten Gēata   dēaðbedde fæst,
      wunað wælreste   wyrmes dǣdum;
      him on efn ligeð   ealdorgewinna

2882 Wergendra] fergendra

2879 **ofer mīn gemet** 'beyond my measure [of strength]'.

2884–6a **Hū sceal . . . ālicgean** 'How must come to an end for your people all joy of the nation – sword-giving, treasure-receiving, beloved things!' *Hū* is clear in the manuscript but is often emended to *Nū*. However, an exclamation seems to fit logically. Cf. *Wanderer* l. 95 and see *OES* §§1671–3 for buttressing examples.

2886b–88a **Londrihtes . . . īdel hweorfan** 'each man of the nation must go without his land-right', i.e. must be deprived of his native land.

2890b–1 Since Tacitus, *Germania* VI, says that Germanic warriors who show cowardice on the battlefield often 'end their disgrace by hanging themselves', some scholars have thought that Wiglaf is here suggesting that the twelve shirkers should take their own lives.

2892 **Heht ðā . . . bīodan** 'He then commanded the outcome of the battle to be announced at the encampment.'

2898 **se ðe næs gerād** 'he who rode up to the headland (where the encampment was)'. This mounted warrior is not one of the twelve cowards but an official messenger and spokesman for the nation. His predictions of disaster receive authorial confirmation at both beginning and end of his speech (l. 2899 *sōðlīce*, ll. 3029b–30a).

2899 **sægde ofer ealle** 'spoke to everyone', i.e. spoke within the hearing of all.

sexbennum sēoc: sweorde ne meahte
2905 on ðām āglǣcean   ǣnige þinga
wunde gewyrcean.   Wīglāf siteð
ofer Bīowulfe,   byre Wīhstānes
eorl ofer ōðrum   unlifigendum,
healdeð higemǣðum   hēafodwearde
2910 lēofes ond lāðes.   Nū ys lēodum wēn
orleghwīle   syððan underne
Froncum ond Frȳsum   fyll cyninges
wīde weorðeð.   Wæs sīo wrōht scepen
heard wið Hūgas   syððan Higelāc cwōm
2915 faran flotherge   on Frēsna land
þǣr hyne Hetware   hilde genǣgdon,
elne gēeodon   mid ofermægene
þæt se byrnwiga   būgan sceolde,
fēoll on fēðan;   nalles frætwe geaf
2920 ealdor dugoðe.   Ūs wæs ā syððan
Merewīoingas   milts ungyfeðe.
Ne ic te Swēoðēode   sibbe oððe trēowe
wihte ne wēne   ac wæs wīde cūð
þætte Ongenðīo   ealdre besnyðede
2925 Hæðcen Hrēþling   wið Hrefnawudu
þā for onmēdlan   ǣrest gesōhton
Gēata lēode   Gūð-Scilfingas.
Sōna him se frōda   fæder Ōhtheres,
eald ond egesfull   ondslyht āgeaf,

2904 sexbennum] siexbennum   2911 underne] under   2916 genægdon] ge hnægdon
2929 ondslyht] hond slyht

2904 **sweorde ne meahte** Beowulf is the subject of *meahte*. The messenger is alluding to the fact that the *sweord* failed (ll. 2680b–2a) and it was Beowulf's *seax* that killed the dragon (ll. 2702b–5).

2908 **eorl . . . unlifigendum** 'one nobleman over the other dead one'.

2909–10a **healdeð higemǣðum . . . lāðes** 'holds guard with weariness of heart over the head of [both] friend and foe (i.e. Beowulf and the dragon)'. For the adverbial use of the dat pl *higemǣðum* see *Guide* §191.3.

2910b–20a On the death of Hygelac see IVB.

2913b–14a **Wæs sīo . . . Hūgas** 'That intense hostility with the Franks was created.'

2919b **frætwe** This is the golden torque which Wealhtheow gave to Beowulf (ll. 1195b–6) and which the poet says Hygelac lost to the Franks on this expedition (ll. 1202–11). Beowulf retrieved the torque, which Dæghrefn was carrying (ll. 2503–4).

2920b–1 **Ūs wæs . . . ungyfeðe** 'The good will of the Merovingian (king) has been denied to us ever since.' *Merewīoingas* shows a late spelling of the gen sg ending *-es*. See l. 63 note.

2922–98 On the Geatish–Swedish wars see IVB.

2922 **te Swēoðēode** 'from the Swedes'. *te* is an unaccented form of *tō*.

2924–5 **þætte Ongenðīo . . . Hrefnawudu** 'that Ongentheow deprived Hæthcyn, son of Hrethel, of his life near Raven's Wood'.

2927 **Gēata lēode** is the subject, *Gūð-Scilfingas* the object.

2928 **him** = Hæthcyn; **fæder Ōhtheres** = Ongentheow.

2930 ābrēot brimwīsan,   brȳd āhredde,
      gomela iōmēowlan   golde berofene
      Onelan mōdor   ond Ōhtheres
      ond ðā folgode   feorhgenīðlan
      oð ðæt hī oðēodon   earfoðlīce
2935 in Hrefnesholt   hlāfordlēase.
      Besæt ðā sinherge   sweorda lāfe
      wundum wērge,   wēan oft gehēt
      earmre teohhe   ondlonge niht,
      cwæð, hē on mergenne   mēces ecgum
2940 gētan wolde,   sume on galgtrēowum
      fuglum tō gamene.   Frōfor eft gelamp
      sārigmōdum   somod ærdæge
      syððan hīe Hygelāces   horn ond bȳman
      gealdor ongēaton   þā se gōda cōm
2945 lēoda dugoðe   on lāst faran.

[The messenger's conclusion.
The Geats visit the scene of conflict]

XLI   Wæs sīo swātswaðu   Swēona ond Gēata
         wælrǣs weora   wīde gesȳne,
         hū ðā folc mid him   fǣhðe tōwehton.
         Gewāt him ðā se gōda   mid his gædelingum
2950 frōd felageōmor   fæsten sēcean,
      eorl Ongenþīo   ufor oncirde,
      hæfde Higelāces   hilde gefrūnen

2930 bryd ahredde] bryda heorde   2940 sume on galgtreowum] sum on galg treowu
2941 fuglum] *not in MS*   2946 Sweona] swona

2930b–1 **brȳd āhredde . . . berofene** 'the old one (i.e. Ongentheow) rescued his wife, the woman of old deprived of her gold [adornments]'.

2936 **sinherge** 'with his standing retinue'. The *sinhere* or 'permanent force' of the king would be his personal retinue of warriors (as opposed to a large levy raised for a special military action).

2937–64 A facsimile of the manuscript containing these lines appears on p. 152.

2939b–41a **mēces ecgum . . . gamene** 'would spill the blood of some of them with the blades of swords, [would hang] some on the gallows as sport for the birds'. Apparently Ongentheow is telling the besieged Geats that after he has defeated them the next day he will sacrifice them to the war god. There are numerous reports of pagan Germanic troops sacrificing some or all of their vanquished enemies to Woden or Tiw following a battle. See for example H. R. Ellis Davidson, *Gods and Myths of Northern Europe* (Harmondsworth, 1964), pp. 54–7.

2941b–5 After hearing Ongentheow's threats all night, the Geatish raiding party is relieved to hear the arrival of the main force of the Geats under Hygelac, who rescues them; **þā se gōda . . . faran** 'when the good one (Hygelac) followed the track of the retinue of (Swedish) people'.

2948 **hū ðā . . . tōwehton** 'how those nations stirred up hostility among themselves'.

2949 **se gōda** = Ongentheow.

2951 **ufor oncirde** 'moved farther away'.

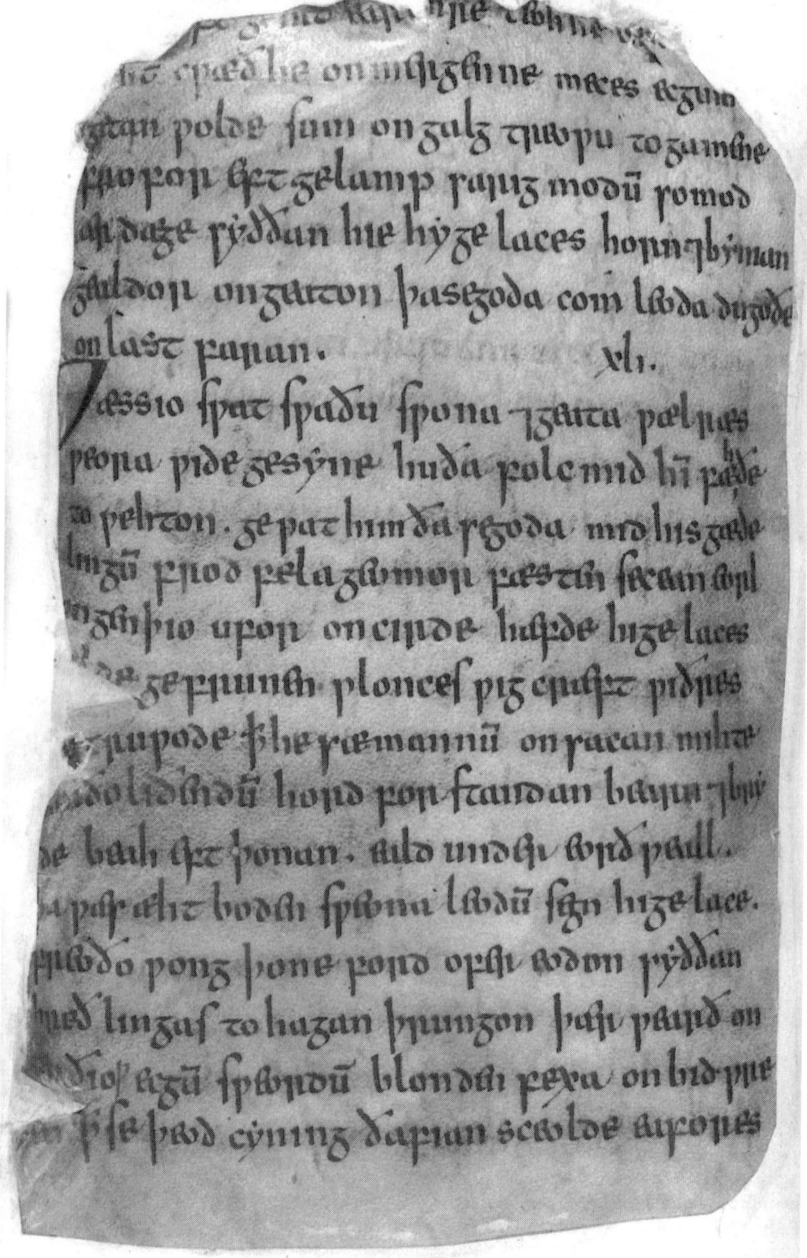

Lines 2937–64

wlonces wīgcræft,   wiðres ne truwode,
þæt hē sǣmannum   onsacan mihte,
2955 heaðolīðendum   hord forstandan
bearn ond brȳde,   bēah eft þonan
eald under eorðweall.   þā wæs æht boden
Swēona lēodum,   segn Higelāces
freoðowong þone   forð oferēodon
2960 syððan Hrēðlingas   tō hagan þrungon.
þǣr wearð Ongenðīow   ecgum sweorda
blondenfexa   on bid wrecen
þæt se þēodcyning   ðafian sceolde
Eafores ānne dōm.   Hyne yrringa
2965 Wulf Wonrēding   wǣpne geræhte
þæt him for swenge   swāt ædrum sprong
forð under fexe.   Næs hē forht swā ðēh
gomela Scilfing   ac forgeald hraðe
wyrsan wrixle   wælhlem þone
2970 syððan ðēodcyning   þyder oncirde.
Ne meahte se snella   sunu Wonrēdes
ealdum ceorle   ondslyht giofan
ac hē him on hēafde   helm ǣr gescer
þæt hē blōde fāh   būgan sceolde,
2975 fēoll on foldan;   næs hē fǣge þā gīt
ac hē hyne gewyrpte   þēah ðe him wund hrine.
Lēt se hearda   Higelāces þegn
brādne mēce,   þā his brōðor læg,
ealdsweord eotonisc   entiscne helm
2980 brecan ofer bordweal;   ðā gebēah cyning
folces hyrde,   wæs in feorh dropen.
Ðā wǣron monige   þe his mǣg wriðon,
ricone ārǣrdon   ðā him gerȳmed wearð

2958 Higelaces] hige lace   2959 forð] ford   2961 sweorda] sweordū (= sweordum)
2972 ondslyht] hond slyht   2978 bradne] brade

2953 **wiðres ne truwode** 'did not have confidence in his ability to resist (Hygelac)'; *wiðres* and the *þæt* clause l. 2954 are parallel objects of *truwode*.
2956 **bēah** 'he retreated'.
2962 **on bid wrecen** 'brought to bay'.
2964–5 **Eafores ānne dōm** 'Eafor's judgement alone' (i.e. he was at Eafor's mercy); **Hyne . . . geræhte** 'Wulf Wonreding struck him (Ongentheow) with his weapon angrily'.
2973 **hē** = Ongentheow; **him** = Wulf.
2974–6 The three *hē*s all refer to Wulf, as do *hyne* (refl) and *him* l. 2976.
2977 **se hearda Higelāces þegn** Eofor.
2981 **in feorh dropen** 'mortally stricken'.
2982 **his mǣg** Eofor's brother, Wulf.
2983b–4 **ðā him . . . mōston** 'when it was granted to them that they might have control of the battlefield'.

    þæt hīe wælstōwe   wealdan mōston.
2985 þenden rēafode   rinc ōðerne,
    nam on Ongenðīo   īrenbyrnan
    heard swyrd hilted   ond his helm somod,
    hāres hyrste   Higelāce bǣr.
    Hē ðām frætwum fēng   ond him fǣgre gehēt
2990 lēana mid lēodum   ond gelǣste swā,
    geald þone gūðrǣs   Gēata dryhten
    Hrēðles eafora,   þā hē tō hām becōm,
    Iofore ond Wulfe   mid ofermāðmum,
    sealde hiora gehwæðrum   hund þūsenda
landes ond locenra bēaga   – ne ðorfte him ðā lēan oðwītan
mon on middangearde   syððan hīe ðā mǣrða geslōgon –
    ond ðā Iofore forgeaf   āngan dohtor
    hāmweorðunge,   hyldo tō wedde.
    þæt ys sīo fæhðo   ond se fēondscipe
3000 wælnīð wera,   ðæs ðe ic wēn hafo,
    þe ūs sēceað tō   Swēona lēoda
    syððan hīe gefricgeað   frēan ūserne
    ealdorlēasne   þone ðe ǣr gehēold
    wið hettendum   hord ond rīce

2989 ðam] *lost at edge of MS*   2990 mid] *lost at edge of MS*   gelǣste] gelǣsta   2996 syððan]
syðða   3000 wen] *not in MS*

2985 **rinc** Eofor; **ōðerne** Ongentheow.

2986 **nam on Ongenðīo** '(Eofor) took from Ongentheow'.

2989–90a **Hē** = Hygelac; **him** = Eofor and Wulf; **him fǣgre . . . lēodum** 'he fittingly promised them rewards among the people'; **gehēt** takes a gen object here.

2994–5a **sealde hiora . . . bēaga** '(Hygelac) gave each of them land and linked rings worth a hundred thousand (*sceattas*)'. That the unit of value is the *sceatt*, a common Anglo-Saxon coin, is a plausible conjecture.

2995b–6a **ne ðorfte . . . middangearde** 'nor need anyone on earth reproach them (or him?) for the reward'. Wulf and Eofor are beyond reproach in accepting the reward since they had successfully carried out their mission; Hygelac is beyond reproach in conferring it since it is fitting for a king to reward loyal service by his subjects. It is not clear which meaning the poet intends.

2998 **hāmweorðunge**, in apposition with *dohtor* l. 2997, means 'ennobler of his estate'. Having a royal bride obviously enhances Eofor's status in the world; **hyldo tō wedde** 'as a pledge of his (Hygelac's) favour'.

2999–3003a On the Geatish–Swedish wars see IVB.

3000 **ðæs ðe** 'of which'.

3001 **þe** 'for which'.

3003b–7a **ðe ǣr gehēold . . . efnde** 'who protected our treasure and realm against enemies after the heroes' fall, (protected) the valiant Danes, advanced the people's welfare or otherwise carried out noble deeds'. This summation of high points in Beowulf's career – his defence of the Geats after the fall of Hygelac's army in Frisia, his saving the Danes from the Grendelkin, his long and beneficent rule – seems perfectly appropriate, and the excision by some editors of the reference to the hero's Danish exploit is misguided. Elsewhere in the last part of the poem there are fleeting references to Beowulf's earlier triumph in Denmark, e.g. ll. 2351b–4a, 2521b, and perhaps 2511b–12a.

3005 æfter hæleða hryre,   hwate Scildingas,
folcrēd fremede   oððe furður gēn
eorlscipe efnde.   Nū is ofost betost
þæt wē þēodcyning   þær scēawian
ond þone gebringan,   þe ūs bēagas geaf,
3010 on ādfære.   Ne scel ānes hwæt
meltan mid þām mōdigan   ac þær is māðma hord
gold unrīme   grimme geceapod
ond nū æt sīðestan   sylfes fēore
bēagas gebohte: þā sceall brond fretan,
3015 æled þeccean,   nalles eorl wegan
māððum tō gemyndum   ne mægð scȳne
habban on healse   hringweorðunge
ac sceal geōmormōd   golde berēafod
oft nalles æne   elland tredan
3020 nū se herewīsa   hleahtor ālegde
gamen ond glēodrēam.   Forðon sceall gār wesan
monig morgenceald   mundum bewunden
hæfen on handa,   nalles hearpan swēg
wīgend weccean   ac se wonna hrefn
3025 fūs ofer fǣgum   fela reordian,
earne secgan   hū him æt ǣte spēow
þenden hē wið wulf   wæl rēafode.'
Swā se secg hwata   secggende wæs
lāðra spella,   hē ne lēag fela
3030 wyrda ne worda.   Weorod eall ārās,

3007 Nu] me   3012 geceapod] gecea . . .   3014 gebohte] . . . te

3007b–182 See IVC1, 2, and 10 (burials).

3007b–8 **Nū is ofost . . . scēawian** 'Now it is best that we make haste to see the people's king there'.

3010 **ānes hwæt** 'one part only'.

3010b–21a The messenger's saying that the entire hoard should all be burned with the king since the Geats are doomed and will therefore have no use for it is an emphatic way of expressing his despair over the nation's future. In the event, some trappings are burned with the king while the remainder is buried with his ashes.

3013–14a **ond nū æt . . . gebohte** 'and now at the end he has purchased the rings with his own life'.

3021b–2 **monig** modifies *gār* 'many a spear'; **sceall** is to be construed with the infinitives *weccean* l. 3024, *reordian* l. 3025, and *secgan* l. 3026, as well as with *wesan* l. 3021; **morgenceald** morning is the time traditionally associated with misery by the Anglo-Saxons.

3024b–7 The beasts of battle scavenging the dead are a recurrent motif in OE poetry, but this is the only place where they are personified and endowed with speech.

3028–9a the genitives *lāðra spella* suggest that *secggende* is a verbal noun: 'the bold man was the teller of grim tales'.

3029 **hē ne lēag fela** Litotes meaning that everything he said is true.

3030 **wyrda ne worda** 'concerning destined events or words'. Apparently *worda* refers to his narration of past events, *wyrda* to his predictions of future events.

ēodon unblīðe   under Earnanæs
wollentēare   wundur scēawian.
Fundon ðā on sande   sāwullēasne
hlimbed healdan   þone þe him hringas geaf
3035   ǣrran mǣlum;   þā wæs endedæg
gōdum gegongen   þæt se gūðcyning
Wedra þēoden   wundordēaðe swealt.
Ǣr hī þǣr gesēgan   syllīcran wiht
wyrm on wonge   wiðerræhtes þǣr
3040   lāðne licgean: wæs se lēgdraca
grimlīc gryrefāh   glēdum beswǣled,
se wæs fīftiges   fōtgemearces
lang on legere,   lyftwynne hēold
nihtes hwīlum,   nyðer eft gewāt
3045   dennes nīosian;   wæs ðā dēaðe fæst,
hæfde eorðscrafa   ende genyttod.
Him big stōdan   bunan ond orcas,
discas lāgon   ond dȳre swyrd
ōmige þurhetone   swā hīe wið eorðan fæðm
3050   þūsend wintra   þǣr eardodon;
þonne wæs þæt yrfe   ēacencræftig,
iūmonna gold   galdre bewunden
þæt ðām hringsele   hrīnan ne mōste
gumena ænig   nefne god sylfa
3055   sigora sōðcyning   sealde þām ðe hē wolde
– hē is manna gehyld –   hord openian,
efne swā hwylcum manna   swā him gemet ðūhte.

3041 gryrefah] gry . . .

3034 **hlimbed healdan** 'occupying his bed of rest'.
3035b–6a **þā wæs . . . gegongen** 'then his final day had come to pass for the good one'.
3038 **Ǣr hī . . . wiht** 'They had previously seen a stranger creature there.' The dragon's bulk was sighted first because it is so much larger than Beowulf.
3046 **hæfde . . . genyttod** 'He had made his last use of earth-caves.'
3049b–50 **swā hīe . . . eardodon** 'as if they had lain there in the earth's embrace a thousand years'; **eardodon** is subj.
3051 **þonne** 'furthermore'.
3052–7 **galdre bewunden** 'encompassed with a spell'. The pagan spell has power only if the true God of Christendom chooses not to overrule it and allow someone of his own choosing to open the hoard.

[Preparations for the funeral]

XLII
þā wæs gesȳne   þæt se sīð ne ðāh
þām ðe unrihte   inne gehȳdde
3060 wræte under wealle.   Weard ǣr ofslōh
fēara sumne;   þā sīo fǣhð gewearð
gewrecen wrāðlīce.   Wundur hwār þonne
eorl ellenrōf   ende gefēre
līfgesceafta   þonne leng ne mæg
3065 mon mid his māgum   meduseld būan.
Swā wæs Bīowulfe   þā hē biorges weard
sōhte searonīðas,   seolfa ne cūðe
þurh hwæt his worulde gedāl   weorðan sceolde.
Swā hit oð dōmes dæg   dīope benemdon
3070 þēodnas mǣre,   þā ðæt þǣr dydon,
þæt se secg wǣre   synnum scildig
hergum geheaðerod   hellbendum fæst
wommum gewītnad   se ðone wong strude;
næs he goldhwæte   gearwor hæfde
3075 āgendes ēst   ǣr gescēawod.
Wīglāf maðelode   Wīhstānes sunu:
'Oft sceall eorl monig   ānes willan
wrǣc ādrēogan   swā ūs geworden is.
Ne meahton wē gelǣran   lēofne þēoden

3060 wræte] wræce   3065 magum] . . . ū (= um)   3073 strude] strade   3078 adreogan] adreogeð

3058b–60a **þæt se sīð . . . wealle** 'that the undertaking was not profitable for the one (i.e. the dragon) who wrongly kept the treasure hidden below the wall'.

3061 **fēara sumne** 'one of a few' perhaps understatement for 'a unique man' or 'a very great man'.

3062b–4a **Wundur hwār . . . līfgesceafta** 'It is a mystery then where a brave man may reach the fated end of his life.'

3066b–7a **weard** and **searonīðas** are parallel objects of *sōhte*.

3069–75 **Swā hit . . . gescēawod** A difficult passage whose meaning has been widely disputed and in which further emendations have been proposed. A possible translation of the text as printed here: 'Thus the famous lords who put that [treasure] there solemnly declared that until the day of doom the man who should plunder that place would be guilty of crimes, imprisoned in pagan temples, firm in hell's bonds, punished with misfortunes. Previously he (Beowulf) had not at all seen the gold-bestowing favour of God more clearly (i.e. God had never given Beowulf a greater treasure than this one).'

3077 **ānes willan** 'through the will of one'. 'One' could refer to Beowulf, the dragon (cf. l. 2210), the man who first plundered the hoard (ll. 2214b–17a and ll. 2404b–8a), or wyrd.

3079–83 **Ne meahton . . . woruldende** This has been taken to mean that the Geats tried to persuade Beowulf not to fight the dragon (but that he obstinately persisted in doing so). It could as well mean 'We could not advise our dear lord, the king of the realm, that he should not engage the dragon (because we had no other defence against the dragon but him).' They could not tell him 'to let him (the dragon) lie where he long was, to remain in his dwelling until the world's end' because the dragon was determined to exterminate the Geats rather than remain in his den (ll. 2314b–15). The only other occurrence of *rǣd gelǣran* in *Beowulf* (l. 278) means 'advise', not 'persuade'.

3080 rīces hyrde   rǣd ǣnigne,
þæt hē ne grētte   goldweard þone,
lēte hyne licgean   þǣr hē longe wæs,
wīcum wunian   oð woruldende.
Hēold on hēahgesceap;   hord ys gescēawod,
3085 grimme gegongen;   wæs þæt gifeðe tō swīð
þe ðone þēodcyning   þyder ontyhte.
Ic wæs þǣr inne   ond þæt eall geondseh
recedes geatwa   þā mē gerȳmed wæs,
nealles swǣslīce   sīð ālȳfed
3090 inn under eorðweall.   Ic on ofoste gefēng
micle mid mundum   mægenbyrðenne
hordgestrēona,   hider ūt ætbær
cyninge mīnum.   Cwico wæs þā gēna
wīs ond gewittig,   worn eall gespræc
3095 gomol on gehðo   ond ēowic grētan hēt,
bæd þæt gē geworhton   æfter wines dǣdum
in bǣlstede   beorh þone hēan
micelne ond mǣrne   swā hē manna wæs
wīgend weorðfullost   wīde geond eorðan
3100 þenden hē burhwelan   brūcan mōste.
Uton nū efstan   ōðre sīðe
sēon ond sēcean   searogimma geþræc
wundur under wealle,   ic ēow wīsige
þæt gē genōge   nēon scēawiað
3105 bēagas ond brād gold.   Sīe sīo bǣr gearo
ǣdre geæfned   þonne wē ūt cymen,
ond þonne geferian   frēan ūserne
lēofne mannan   þǣr hē longe sceal
on ðæs waldendes   wǣre geþolian.'
3110 Hēt ðā gebēodan   byre Wīhstānes
hæle hildedīor   hæleða monegum

3084 **Hēold on hēahgesceap** 'He held to his high destiny.'
3089–90a **nealles swǣslīce . . . eorðweall** 'by no means was passage under the earth-wall pleasantly allowed to me'.
3091 **micle** qualifies *mægenbyrðenne*.
3094 **wīs ond gewittig** 'sound of mind and conscious'; **worn eall** 'a great many things'.
3096 **geworhton** subj 'should build'; **æfter** 'in memory of'.
3098b–9 **swā hē . . . eorðan** 'since he was of [all] men the most glorious warrior far and wide throughout the earth'.
3104b **nēon** = *nēan* 'from nearby'; **scēawiað** ind 'you will see', not 'you may see'. The meaning of conj *þæt* l. 3104a is 'so that', here shading into 'until'.
3107 **geferian** subj 'let us carry'.
3110–12a **Hēt ðā . . . boldāgendra** 'The son of Wihstan, a valiant man, had orders given to many men of rank'.

> boldāgendra   þæt hīe bælwudu
> feorran feredon,   folcāgende,
> gōdum tōgēnes: 'Nū sceal glēd fretan,
> 3115 weaxan wonna lēg   wigena strengel
> þone ðe oft gebād   īsernscūre
> þonne strǣla storm   strengum gebǣded
> scōc ofer scildweall,   sceft nytte hēold
> fæðergearwum fūs,   flāne fullēode.'
> 3120 Hūru se snotra   sunu Wīhstānes
> ācīgde of corðre   cyniges þegnas
> syfone ætsomne   þā sēlestan,
> ēode eahta sum   under inwithrōf
> hilderinca;   sum on handa bær
> 3125 æledlēoman   se ðe on orde gēong.
> Næs ðā on hlytme   hwā þæt hord strude
> syððan orwearde   ænigne dæl
> secgas gesēgon   on sele wunian
> lǣne licgan;   lȳt ænig mearn
> 3130 þæt hī ofostlīce   ūt geferedon
> dȳre māðmas;   dracan ēc scufun,
> wyrm ofer weallclif,   lēton wēg niman,
> flōd fæðmian   frætwa hyrde.
> þā wæs wunden gold   on wǣn hladen
> 3135 æghwæs unrīm,   æþeling boren,
> hār hilderinc   tō Hronesnæsse.

[Beowulf's funeral]

> XLIII   Him ðā gegiredan   Gēata lēode
> ād on eorðan   unwāclīcne

3119 fæðergearwum] fæðergearwū (= um)   3122 syfone] *only partially legible around tear in MS*
ætsomne] somne *partially legible around tear in MS*   3124 hilderinca] hilde rinc   3130 ofostlice]
ofostli . . .   3134 þa] þ (= þæt)   3135 æþeling] æþelinge   3136 hilderinc] hilde *followed
by an empty space with room for three or four letters*

3113 **feredon** subj 'should bring'.
3114 **gōdum tōgēnes** 'to the good one (Beowulf)', i.e. to where Beowulf lay.
3115 **weaxan wonna lēg** This half-line is usually taken as a parenthesis, with *weaxan* translated
'grow' – 'the dark flame must grow'. But this is a singularly awkward and unlikely parenthesis. We
prefer to take *weaxan* as a form of the infinitive *wæscan, waxan* meaning 'wash, bathe' standing
parallel with *fretan* l. 3114: 'Now the fire must consume, the dark flame engulf the ruler of men.'
3117–19 **þonne strǣla . . . fullēode** 'when a storm of arrows propelled by the bowstrings
passed over the wall of shields, the arrow-shaft hastening with its feather-gear performed its task,
assisted the arrow-head'.
3126 **Næs ðā . . . strude** 'It was not [decided] by lot who should take from the hoard.' That is,
all eight participated in the plundering of the hoard.
3129 **lǣne licgan** 'lie perishing' (referring to the hoard, l. 3126).

              helmum behongen   hildebordum

3140   beorhtum byrnum   swā hē bēna wæs;

              ālegdon ðā tōmiddes   mǣrne þēoden

              hæleð hīofende   hlāford lēofne.

              Ongunnon þā on beorge   bǣlfȳra mǣst

              wīgend weccan;   wudurēc āstāh

3145   sweart ofer swioðole,   swōgende lēg

              wōpe bewunden   – windblond gelæg –

              oð þæt hē ðā bānhūs   gebrocen hæfde

              hāt on hreðre.   Higum unrōte

              mōdceare mǣndon   mondryhtnes cwealm;

3150   swylce giōmorgyd   Gēatisc mēowle

              æfter Bīowulfe   bundenheorde

              song sorgcearig,   sǣde geneahhe

              þæt hīo hyre hēofungdagas   hearde ondrēde

              wælfylla worn   werudes egesan

3155   hȳnðo ond hæftnȳd.   Heofon rēce swealg.

              Geworhton ðā   Wedra lēode

              hlǣw on hlīðe   se wæs hēah ond brād

              wēglīðendum   wīde gesȳne

              ond betimbredon   on tȳn dagum

3160   beadurōfes bēcn,   bronda lāfe

              wealle beworhton   swā hyt weorðlīcost

              foresnotre men   findan mihton.

              Hī on beorg dydon   bēg ond siglu,

              eall swylce hyrsta   swylce on horde ǣr

3165   nīðhēdige men   genumen hæfdon,

3139 helmum] helm   3144 wudurec] w . . . ec   3145 swioðole] swicðole   leg] let
3149 cwealm] . . . lm   3150 Geatisc] . . . iat . . .   3151 æfter Biowulfe   bundenheorde] . . .
unden heord . . .   3152 song] *MS illegible*   sæde] sælðe   3153 heofungdagas] . . . gas   ondrede]
. . . de   3154 worn] wonn   werudes] . . . udes   3155 hynðo] hyðo   ond hæftnyd] . . . h . . .
d   swealg] swe . . . lg   3157 hlæw] hl . . .   hliðe] liðe (*or* lide)   3158 wegliðendum] . . .
gliðendū (= um)   gesyne] g . . . syne   3159 betimbredon] beti . . . bredon

3140 **swā hē bēna wæs** i.e. 'as he had requested' (ll. 2799–808).

3147 **hē** The antecedent is *swōgende lēg* 'the soughing flame' (l. 3145).

3148 **hāt on hreðre** 'hot to its innermost part' refers to the fire, not to Beowulf's body.

3149 **mōdceare** and **cwealm** are parallel objects of *mǣndon*.

3150–5a Another reference to the Geatish–Swedish wars; see IVB.

3151 **bundenheorde** modifies *mēowle* l. 3150 and indicates that she is an older woman.
(Germanic women wore hair loose and flowing when young.) The woman's lament has been
compared to Andromache's lament for Hector (*Iliad* xxiv), where she too fears that nothing but
captivity awaits the people now that the nation's hero is dead.

3152 **song** 'sang' (object: *giōmorgyd* in l. 3150); **geneahhe** 'frequently, repeatedly'.

3154 **werudes egesan** 'the host's terror', i.e. the horror of invading warriors.

3158 **wēglīðendum** The first three letters of this word are unclear in the manuscript but in
view of *wēg* 'wave' in l. 3132 we read *wēg*.

3160b–2 '[they] surrounded the residue of the flames (i.e. the ashes) with a wall as splendid as
very wise people could possibly devise it'.

forlēton eorla gestrēon   eorðan healdan
gold on grēote   þǣr hit nū gēn lifað
eldum swā unnyt   swā hyt ǣror wæs.
þā ymbe hlǣw riodan   hildedēore
3170 æþelinga bearn   ealra twelfe,
woldon care cwīðan   ond cyning mǣnan,
wordgyd wrecan   ond ymb wer sprecan,
eahtodan eorlscipe   ond his ellenweorc
duguðum dēmdon.   Swā hit gedēfe bið
3175 þæt mon his winedryhten   wordum herge,
ferhðum frēoge   þonne hē forð scile
of līchaman   lǣded weorðan,
swā begnornodon   Gēata lēode
hlāfordes hryre,   heorðgenēatas:
3180 cwǣdon þæt hē wǣre   wyruldcyninga
mannum mildust   ond monðwǣrust,
lēodum līðost   ond lofgeornost.

3168 hyt æror] hy . . . or   3170 twelfe] twelfa   3171 care] *for word unclear at beginning of line*
ond cyning] scyning   3172 wer] w . . .   3174 gedefe] ḡd . . . (ḡ = ge)
3177 lichaman] lachaman   lǣded] *MS illegible*   3179 hryre] . . . re   3180 wyruldcyninga]
wyruldcyning   3181 mannum] . . . annū (= um)   monðwærust] mon . . . ust

3167 **lifað** 'exists, remains'.
3168 **eldum swā unnyt** 'as useless to men'.
3170 **ealra twelfe** 'twelve in all'.
3174 **duguðum** adverbial dat: '(praised his courageous deeds) highly'.
3176–7 **ferhðum frēoge** 'cherish in his heart'; **þonne hē . . . weorðan** 'when he must be led forth from the body'. The word *lǣded* 'led' is supplied where the MS is illegible. Note that *of līchaman lǣded wǣre* is documented in both MSS of the poem *Soul and Body*, l. 21. Actually there is not room in the *Beowulf* MS for the full form *lǣded*, although that must be what the poet intended, since a dissyllable is needed for the metre. No doubt the scribe used the contracted form *lǣd* to save space, for he crowds and abbreviates his words toward the end of the poem so as to finish copying it without having to start a new page. There is ample space in the MS for *lǣd*.

PART THREE

How We Arrived at our Text

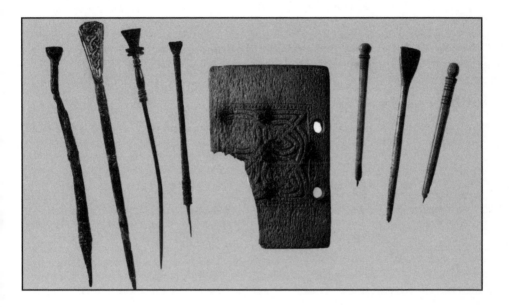

Anglo-Saxon writing implements. The largest stylus is about $5^1/_2$ inches
long. The carved bone tablet in the middle of
the picture is hollowed on the other side to receive a wax writing surface.
The styli to its left are made of bronze, those to the right of bone. The
object on the extreme right is a miniature whetstone, used for sharpening
a small knife. With the exception of the tablet, which was found at
Blythburgh, all these objects were discovered during excavations at
Whitby in the 1920s.
(*British Museum, Department of Medieval and Later Antiquities*).

A   Problems in Editing the Text

§1 The general principles on which we base our printed text are set out in the note which immediately precedes the text (pp. 41–2). Our editorial approach can be described as conservative in that we prefer to retain the manuscript reading where possible. In this we differ from the bold, who are prepared to emend readily even when the manuscript can be defended, and the zealots, who are willing to rewrite Old English poetry in the light of their own metrical or syntactical theories. But we do not seek to indulge in what Sisam called 'tenacious defence of the manuscript'. When we judge that emendation is necessary, we regard it as our obligation to ensure that what we print is palaeographically, philologically, and metrically, acceptable.

§2 For discussion of the manuscript, its relation to the Thorkelin transcripts, the fitt divisions and numbering, and the capitals and accent marks in the manuscript, the reader is referred to I and to the editions of Klaeber and Dobbie.

§3 In establishing the text, editors have to decide first which words to print, taking due account of the available authorities, the scribal practices including abbreviations, and the corrections in the manuscript, most of which are in the original hands; and second how to arrange and punctuate these words. Line and half-line divisions in *Beowulf* present few problems. On punctuation, see IIIB.

§4 There are some long stretches in the manuscript where we find no difficulty in establishing the reading and no need of emendation, e.g. ll. 600b–51, 780b–812a, 813–36a, 1425–87, 1603–1733, and 2385b–448a. But there are places where the manuscript is damaged. Sometimes (most of) a word has been lost as a result of the crumbling of the scorched edges, e.g. l. 588, where only the *e* of *helle* attested by Thorkelin A is now visible; see the note on this line. In other places, the damage is more extensive; in some indeed the full text is irrecoverable, e.g. ll. 2212–31a and 3150–8. Even where the manuscript is clear, there can be difficulty, e.g. l. 810 (is *myrðe* a noun or an adjective?); l. 1320 (the meaning of each of the elements of the compound *nēodlaðu* is disputed); l. 2820 (is *sōðfæstra dōm* the judgement by the righteous (subjective genitive) or on them (objective genitive)?); and ll. 3074–5 (described by Bugge as a *locus desperatus*, where there has been much discussion but little agreement). It is, however, certain that the scribes did make mistakes. This is not surprising: cold, bad light, fatigue, carelessness – all are factors which could have led to misreading and misunderstanding. So emendation is sometimes essential. But it is usually easier to decide to emend than to do so satisfactorily.

§5 Scribal errors take many forms. The different varieties of errors and the different explanations discussed below overlap, and readers will find that some examples will belong to more categories than the one to which they are, for the sake of illustration, assigned. We find letters omitted, e.g. *n* at the beginning of *nǣnigre* in l. 949 (see §8) and *n* at the end of *rǣswan* in l. 60; single words omitted in l. 586 (where we prefer to supply *swīðe* rather than *fela*), ll. 954, 1513, and 2941; and words and/or elements of words omitted in l. 62 (see note) and l. 457. Such examples could be multiplied. Even half-lines are sometimes omitted, e.g. ll. 389b and 390a, 403b, and 1803a. Scribes often add letters; typical examples are l. 684 *het* for *he* and l. 902 *earfoð* for *eafoð* (wrong word) and l. 375 (*eaforan* for *eafora* and l. 3135 *æþelinge* for *æþeling* (wrong form of word). Errors involving abbreviations occur, e.g. l. 2377 *hī* (= *him*) for *hine* and l. 2961 *sweordū* (= *sweordum*) for *sweorda*. However, editors who resolve *þ* in l. 15 as *þe* should indicate that it is an emendation: the abbreviation means *þæt*.

§6 Inconsistencies in spacing – endemic in the manuscripts of prose and poetry – give rise to problems. The reading *hat on* for *haton* in l. 849 can scarcely be called a problem and in l. 84 the scribe replaces the unusual compound *aþumsweorum* with two familiar words *aþum swerian*. But in l. 445 *mægen hreð manna* and l. 490 *sige hreð secg* (with letter(s) lost from crumbling), disagreement about how to link the three separate elements persists. We do not report these inconsistencies in the textual notes.

§7 Examples in which the addition of a letter produced the wrong (form of a) word have been given in §5. But substitution of other kinds produces *gehwylcne* for *gehwylcum* in l. 936 and *þæm* for *þæs* in l. 1508 (wrong form) and *hæleþum* for *æþelum* (l. 332), *æghwylc* for *æghwær* (l. 984), and *þeod* for *deoð* (l. 1278) – all wrong words. In l. 1117a, we believe with many other editors, the natural association of 'arm' and 'shoulder' led the scribe to write *earme on eaxle* for *eame on eaxle*. Occasionally one (near-)synonym replaces another and so the alliteration is lost, e.g. l. 965 *hand gripe* for *mundgripe*, l. 1073 *hild plegan* for *lindplegan*, l. 2298 *hilde* for *wiges*, and l. 1981 (see §9). In l. 1151 some at any rate regret that the fourfold alliteration which MS *hroden* 'adorned' produces demands the emendation *roden* 'reddened'.

§8 The scribe also upset the alliteration when he wrote *ænigre* in l. 949. The emendation to *nǣnigre* (§5) seems inevitable to restore the alliteration. But syntactically one would expect *ænigre*; there is no parallel in *Beowulf* to support the emendation though it would of course be quite acceptable in prose; see BM's article in *Poetica* (Tokyo), 15–16 (1983), 9–12. We may say that the scribe's 'error' reflects his feeling that *ænigre* was to be expected in *Beowulf*. That the poet used a variant acceptable in prose suggests that he – like Chaucer, who used both *toos* and *toon* 'toes' in rhyme, and like Byron, who wrote 'whate'er she loveth, so she loves thee not' – was willing to choose without regard to strict linguistic propriety that alternative which suited him better.

§9 Sometimes we accept the need for emendation but adopt a new reading; examples will be found in ll. 586 (§5), 1404, 1981, and 2341. The scribe's *side reced* in l. 1981 loses the alliteration. It is usually emended to *healreced*. We prefer to view it as another example of the near-synonym substitution discussed in §7 and, replacing one adjective by another, read *hēahreced*.

§10 But problems are not always the fault of the scribes. We believe that editors have not infrequently emended unnecessarily; places where we retain the manuscript reading include ll. 250 (*næfre*), 432 (the position of *ond*), 811 (we do not insert *wæs* after *he*), 1020 (*brand*), 2186 (*wereda*), 2468 (see below), and 2884 (*hu*). Those who emend l. 2468 do so because the noun *sār* is attested only as neuter, not feminine. Since we do not accept the argument that 'because there are no examples, this cannot be one' and since many OE nouns have more than one gender, we retain the manuscript as evidence that *sār* was feminine as well as neuter.

§11 Problems can arise as the result of the context. Thus in l. 1130 the manuscript clearly has *he*. Most editors, including us, are reluctant to believe that it would have been possible for Hengest to sail back home in the wintry conditions described, and so substitute *ne* for *he* or (as we prefer) read *hē ne*. A few retain the manuscript reading, though they can hardly argue that it was a mild winter.

§12 In l. 769, where the manuscript *ealuscerwen* is clear beyond dispute, the difficulty is of another kind. BM expounded it thus in *RES*, 43 (1992), 4–7:

> It seems like twenty years – so I suppose it is forty – since I read somewhere in the literature of the subject that the word *ealuscerwen* in *Beowulf* 769a was becoming a philological joke. If this was true then, it must have become one by now. But it remains a fascinating problem for philologists.
>
> The word is of course a *hapax legomenon* and is used by the poet during the description of the fight in Heorot between Grendel and Beowulf in an excellent example of the so-called 'envelope pattern':

> Dryhtsele dynede: Denum eallum wearð,
> ceasterbuendum, cenra gehwylcum,
> eorlum ealuscerwen. Yrre wæron begen,
> 770 reþe renweardas. Reced hlynsode.

As Dobbie wrote: 'More has been written about this word than any other in *Beowulf.* The one certain thing about it is that, like *meoduscerwen* in *Andreas* 1526, it has the figurative meaning of "terror, distress".'[1] The relevant *Andreas* passage reads in Anglo-Saxon Poetic Records II:

Andreas   Næs þa wordlatu   wihte þon mare
            þæt se stan togan.   Stream ut aweoll,
            fleow ofer foldan.   Famige walcan
  1525 mid ærdæge   eorðan þehton,
            myclade mereflod.   Meoduscerwen wearð
            æfter symbeldæge,   slæpe tobrugdon
            searuhæbbende.   Sund grunde onfeng,
            deope gedrefed.   Duguð wearð afyrhted
  1530 þurh þæs flodes fær.   Fæge swulton,
            geonge on geofene   guðræs fornam
            þurh sealtne weg.   þæt wæs sorgbyrþen,
            biter beorþegu.   Byrlas ne gældon,
            ombehtþegnas.   þær wæs ælcum genog
  1535 fram dæges orde   drync sona gearu.
            Weox wæteres þrym.

There is almost universal agreement that *ealuscerwen* carries the general meaning 'terror, distress, panic'. I myself like to think that *ealuscerwen* was felt by both the Danes and the Geats so that the envelope pattern of lines 767–70 presents the whole fight in microcosm – the noise in the hall, the terror of *cenra gehwylcum* Dane and Geat, and the fury of the combatants. But if anyone wished to argue that the four dative expressions were in apposition and only the Danes were affected by what was happening, I would not press my point. However, two voices which disturb the almost universal agreement must receive attention.

The first, which has been described as offering 'a less serious suggestion'[2] and is mentioned here only because what it said deserves a place in any article entitled 'Literary Lapses', although its relevance to moments of extreme fear cannot be questioned, is the voice of Roy Peter Clark suggesting that *ealuscerwen* is a kenning for urination, at once a 'deprivation' and a 'pouring out of ale'.[3] (In the general context of fear associated with *ealuscerwen*, it is interesting to note that, as far as I know, no one has yet been tempted to link *ealu-* with *ellor* 'elsewhere'; even the formidable Grendel *wolde on heolster fleon*

---

[1] E. v. K. Dobbie, Anglo-Saxon Poetic Records, IV, p. 154
[2] *Old English Newsletter*, 12/1 (1978), 60 is my authority. I have not myself seen this article.
[3] *Scholia Satyrica*, 2 (1976), 35–6.

(line 755b) and his mother later shared the same feeling when she *wolde ut þanon* (line 1292b).)

The second voice is that of Stephen O. Glosecki, suggesting that *ealuscerwen* is a drink of death for Grendel.[4] 'This reading', P. S. B[aker] wrote, 'requires reinterpreting *Denum* (767) and its variants as "benefactive" datives – a term not found, as far as I know, in Mitchell['s *Old English Syntax*].'[5] Glosecki's own words are:

> Here we need to recognize a particular use of the benefactive dative, too, in *Beowulf* ll. 767b–769a: the ale-share, the *poculum mortis*, is not given *to* the Danish warriors. Rather, the drink of death is given to Grendel by Beowulf *for* (on behalf of) the Danish warriors. Grendel is the one who receives *ealuscerwen* or, in modern terms, gets his wagon fixed.[6]

The term 'benefactive dative' is indeed not found in *OES* but it could be subsumed under the dative of interest expressing advantage, whereas if we take *Denum* and its variants as the recipients of *ealuscerwen*, they are datives of interest expressing disadvantage; see *OES*, §§1350 and 1355. But the dative of advantage or 'benefactive' dative and the dative of disadvantage or (dare I say?) 'malefactive' dative are not syntactic concepts. They are purely contextual or semantic; contrast 'joy for the Danes' but 'terror for the Danes'. Hence I have to say that I should have expected the dative *Grendle* if the poet had intended to say what Glosecki claims he said. The traditional interpretation of the datives in question as datives of interest expressing disadvantage seems to me both natural and inescapable.

But the problem which has made *ealuscerwen* famous or notorious is how one arrives at the general meaning of 'terror, distress, panic', given the facts that *ealu-* has been explained as OE *ealu* 'ale' or as a nonce-occurrence of a word meaning 'good luck' which occurs in the form *ǫl* in Old Norse and that *-scerwen* has been explained as 'deprivation, taking away' or as 'giving, dispensing'; for details see the standard editions. This gives four possible meanings: 'taking away of ale', the ironic 'dispensing of ale', 'taking away of good luck', or 'giving of good luck'. Only the first three can be made to fit the context. All three are plausible. None can be proved either right or wrong.

The problem is complicated by the existence of the word *meoduscerwen* in *Andreas* 1526. Is it a borrowing from *Beowulf*, with a change in the first element to provide alliteration? Or is it an independent variation of a poetic formula? Does it mean 'taking away

---

[4] *English Language Notes*, 25 (1987), 1–9.
[5] *Old English Newsletter*, 22/1 (1988), 73.
[6] *English Language Notes*, 25 (1987), 9.

of mead' or is it also ironic 'dispensing of mead'? If it is a borrowing from *Beowulf*, did the *Andreas* poet fail to understand that *ealu* meant 'good luck', not 'ale'? The process could have been similar to that which, according to Wrenn,[7] produced *scurheard* in *Beowulf* 1033 in the mistaken belief that the first element in *Beowulf* 326 *regnheard* meant 'rain', whereas (he argued) it is etymologically related to the Gothic *raginon* 'to rule', and to that process which led to the First Folio correction of 'listed' to 'lusted' in *Richard III*, III.v.83 (First Quarto):

> Euen where his lustfull eye, or sauage heart
> Without controll listed to make his prey.

We cannot deny the possibility that the *Andreas* poet borrowed from *Beowulf* and made a mistake in so doing. If he did, the following equations are possible:

		Mistakes by
ealuscerwen	*meoduscerwen*	*Andreas* poet
pouring out of ale	pouring out of mead	0
taking away of ale	taking away of mead	0
taking away of ale	pouring out of mead	1
pouring out of ale	taking away of mead	1
taking away of good luck	taking away of mead	1
taking away of good luck	pouring out of mead	2

I have no means of solving this problem and no intention of trying to do so. But I conclude by drawing attention to what seems to me a remarkable volte-face by Klaeber. In his original note to *Beowulf* 769, he wrote: 'It is to be noted that the author of *Andreas* (a better judge than modern scholars) understood the corresponding formation *meoduscerwen* (1526) in a sense which precludes the rendering "taking away of (strong) drink"; to him it was "plenty of (fateful) drink."' But in the Second Supplement we read:

> 769. Holthausen (L 5.26.27) refers to names like OHG. *Alu-berht*, OE. *Alu-*, *Ealu-berht*, *-burg*, *-wine*, ON. *Ǫl-bjǫrn*, *-valdr*, and runic *alu*, frequently met with in runic inscriptions and apparently meaning 'good luck', 'safety.' Thus *ealuscerwen* 'taking away of good luck.' (Cf. note on p. 455.) Thus the annoying riddle of *ealuscerwen* (*meoduscerwen*) seems to be happily solved by a twofold misunderstanding: 1) (taking away of) good luck: ale; 2) taking away: dispensing (of ale,

---

[7] Wrenn, *Beowulf with the Finnesburg Fragment* (London, 1953), p. 81.

mead). The actual meaning of the noun in l. 769 is, most likely, 'disaster,' with a subaudition of 'terror.'

I must confess that I find myself more in sympathy with his earlier proposition that the *Andreas* poet was 'a better judge than modern scholars'.

§13 Reading through these sections should have given you some idea of the hidden currents, whirlpools, reefs, and shipwrecked theories, which are to be found beneath the surface of the river of poetry we present to you. In conclusion we repeat that our editorial policy is conservative and add the hope that you will not find us guilty of what Edwin Guest in 1844 described as 'those miserable "corrections" of which our editors are so proud and their readers, for the most part, so impatient'.

B   Punctuation

The Manuscript

§1 Apart from the ten exceptions described below, the only mark of punctuation in the manuscript is the point, of which there are something less than seven hundred, scattered sporadically throughout the poem. They demarcate verses, about 2 per cent of them being erroneously marked. Examples which can be seen in the facsimile pages which accompany the text of the poem include BM folio 132v EETS 129v (ll. 21–46) – after *cume* l. 2, [*þ*]*eon* l. 4, and *fær* l. 10 – and BM folio 133r EETS 130r (ll. 46–68) – after *cunnon* l. 4, in and after *on.feng* l. 6, and after *Heoro gar* l. 14.

The ten exceptions are: the combination of two raised points followed by a comma after *reccan* l. 91b; the colons in the text after *hafelan* l. 1372a and after *gemunde* l. 2488b; and seven examples in the work of scribe B of a colon followed by a curved dash, one after the fitt number XL and six at the end of a fitt, viz, fitts XXVII, XXXII, XXXV, XXXVII, XLI, and XLII.

There are large capitals at the beginning of each of the forty-three fitts and sixty-five small capitals, fifty-three of them in ll. 1–1939, the work of the first scribe. Most of these occur at the beginning of an important syntactical sub-division.

This Edition

§2 As we have explained in the preliminary note to the text, we have decided, despite our reservations, to use modern punctuation. (A possible alternative is discussed in the appendix.) We aim to punctuate or not to punctuate in accordance with the simple, minimal system set out below, trying to preserve the flow of the verse paragraph which we see as the unit of Old English poetry.

This flow results from the constantly repetitive syntactical structure of the poetry, with its parallelisms and ubiquitous apposition. These repetitions do advance the poem because they are not only syntactical but also semantic. However, they are strange to most people and initially can be very confusing. Readers are therefore urged to study with particular care the remarks on apposition in §4 (a) and (b) below.

§3 The use of modern punctuation sometimes causes problems. Thus in

126 Ðā wæs on ūhtan   mid ærdæge
Grendles gūðcræft   gumum undyrne
þā wæs æfter wiste   wōp up āhafen
micel morgenswēg

there are no linguistic criteria by which editors can decide whether *Ðā* in l. 126 is a conjunction meaning 'When' or an adverb meaning 'Then'. So the decision whether to put a comma or a semicolon or stop after *undyrne* at the end of l. 127 can only be based on editorial preference or prejudice. A similar situation arises in

194 þæt fram hām gefrægn   Higelāces þegn
gōd mid Gēatum   Grendles dæda
se wæs moncynnes   mægenes strengest
on þǣm dæge   þysses līfes
æþele ond ēacen

Here *se* is ambiguously either a demonstrative 'that one, he' or a relative 'who' and there are no linguistic grounds for deciding whether to put a comma or a semicolon or stop after *dæda* in l. 195. A third example is

4 Oft Scyld Scēfing   sceaþena þrēatum
monegum mægþum   meodosetla oftēah
egsode eorlas   syððan ærest wearð
fēasceaft funden   hē þæs frōfre gebād
wēox under wolcnum   weorðmyndum þāh . . .

Here the *syððan* clause in ll. 6a–7 can quite logically be connected with both the principal clause which precedes it and the one which follows it. In other words, the *syððan* clause can be used *apo koinou* (in common) or as a *koinon* (a common element). Again an editorial decision to put a full stop after *eorlas* in l. 6 or, as is usual, after *funden* in l. 7 must be arbitrary; to compromise by putting a comma after *funden* in l. 7 would evoke the accusation 'comma splice'. The cumulative effect of such arbitrary decisions and a possible way out are discussed in the appendix.

We have tried to avoid using a mark of punctuation where the sense is clear without one. Here it may be timely to observe that, as half-lines tend to be syntactic as well as metrical entities, half-line and end-line divisions are in themselves a form of punctuation. Details of our system follow. The marks of punctuation are numbered for convenience of reference.

1   The paragraph inset marks major changes of theme or argument, particularly at the beginning of a fitt. Klaeber's over-frequent use of

the inset tends in our view to confuse the reader and to break the narrative flow unnecessarily.

2 We restrict capitalization to the beginning of sentences and to the initial letter of names of tribes, persons, personified swords, or places.

3 The full stop or point marks the end of a major sense unit or sentence.

4 The colon is used to introduce speeches or, in the words of H. W. Fowler, for 'delivering the goods that have been invoiced in the preceding words'.

5 The semicolon marks the end of a sense unit where a full stop would be too strong and a comma would produce a 'comma splice'.

6 The comma is discussed in §§4–6.

7 Dashes mark off the parentheses which play an important part in Old English, especially in the poetry.

8 The question mark is used at the end of non-dependent questions.

9 The exclamation mark is used after exclamations (ll. 1, 2886) and wishes proper (ll. 251, 318, 929, 956, and 1781) but not after statements (l. 11), commands (l. 660), or greetings (l. 407). Klaeber, who could be described as an hysterical punctuator, used fifty-five exclamation marks in his *Beowulf*. We retain four of these (ll. 318, 929, 956, and 1781) and add that after the *Hwæt* which introduces the poem and those in ll. 251 and 2886, where we retain the manuscript readings.

10 Single inverted commas, with double inverted commas inside when needed, mark off quotations.

§4 §§4–6 discuss the comma, which is used more sparingly than in Modern English. Within clauses we use it as follows:

1 Parts of speech in apposition are not marked off when contiguous (ll. 32b–3 and ll. 53b–4a) or when they are separated by an adverb or adverbial element (ll. 252b–3a and 34–6a) or by a verb or verbal element (ll. 43–4a, 20–1, and 128b–9a) UNLESS a comma is needed to prevent confusion, e.g. ll. 194–6 where *Grendles dæda* is a second object of *gefrægn* parallel to *þæt* but is not the antecedent of *se*; ll. 250b–1a where *ænlīc ansȳn* is not the object of *lēoge*; and ll. 212–13 where we take *sund* in apposition with *strēamas* and not as object of *wundon*.

2 Vocatives are marked off, e.g. ll. 365a, 416b–17a, and 456.

§5 §§5 and 6 set out the principles adopted between clauses.

1 There is no comma before syndetic coordinate clauses (those beginning with conjunctions such as *ond* l. 96, *ac* l. 109, *oþþe* l. 283, and the like). On such clauses beginning with the negative conjunction *ne* see §6.

2 (a) Parallel asyndetic coordinate clauses (those with no introductory

conjunction) with the same subject are preceded by a comma, whether the subject is repeated (l. 80 *hē*) or not (ll. 7b–8). On such clauses beginning with a negative adverb see §6.

(b) When the subject changes, appropriate heavier stopping is used, e.g. ll. 59–63 (semicolon), ll. 16a–19 (colon), and ll. 26–31 (full stop).

3 Elements with no finite verb expressed are preceded by a comma, e.g. ll. 484–7a.

4 Noun clauses in apposition with an anticipatory noun or pronoun are preceded by a comma (ll. 1–3, 115–17, and 290–1a).

5 Apart from this, subordinate clauses are not marked off from preceding principal clauses (end of ll. 21 and 29a) even when the immediately preceding clause is in asyndetic coordination (end of ll. 6a and 8b–9).

6 Subordinate clauses which occur in the middle of their governing clause are marked off by commas (ll. 115b and 352b) UNLESS no ambiguity or confusion can arise (l. 57b).

§6 Clauses which begin with one of the negatives *ne*, *nā*, or *nō*, are punctuated according to the principles enunciated here.

1 When unambiguously a conjunction, i.e. when not immediately followed by a verb, *ne* is not preceded by a comma (end of ll. 156, 169a, and 245a).

2 The adverb *nā* or *nō* is preceded by the appropriate mark of punctuation, which may be a comma (end of l. 167), a semicolon (end of l. 366a), or a full stop (end of l. 445a).

3 When *ne* is immediately followed by a verb in mid-sentence, as in l. 50 *Men ne cunnon . . .*, it is an adverb. But it must be regarded as an ambiguous adverb/conjunction in sequences like ll. 36b–40a, where *ne hȳrde ic* might mean 'I did not hear' or 'Nor did I hear'. As the former seems to us more likely, we treat initial *ne* followed by a verb as an adverb and accordingly precede it by a comma when there is no change of subject (end of ll. 180a and 190a) and by a semicolon (end of ll. 37 and 83a) or full stop (end of ll. 660a and 716a) when the subject changes. But this 'rule', like the others, can be broken when sense requires, as in l. 336, where we read *Ne seah* when the subject is repeated but does not change.

PART FOUR

The Background

Gold pommel with interlacing decoration,
East Yorkshire, sixth century

Burial of warrior with horse, sword, and shield,
Lakenheath, Suffolk, mid-sixth century.

A   Genealogical Tables

1 *The Danes*

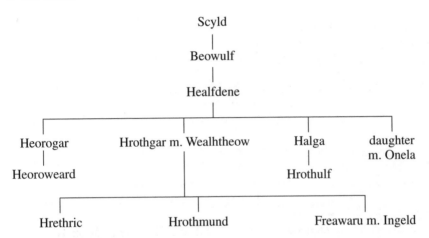

Scyld
|
Beowulf
|
Healfdene

Heorogar   Hrothgar m. Wealhtheow   Halga   daughter m. Onela
| |
Heoroweard   Hrothulf

Hrethric   Hrothmund   Freawaru m. Ingeld

2 *The Geats*

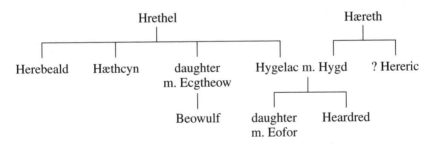

Hrethel   Hæreth

Herebeald   Hæthcyn   daughter m. Ecgtheow   Hygelac m. Hygd   ? Hereric
|
Beowulf   daughter m. Eofor   Heardred

3   *The Half-Danes and the Frisians*

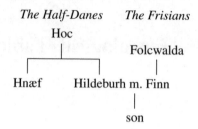

4   *The Heathobards*

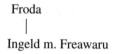

5   *The Swedes*

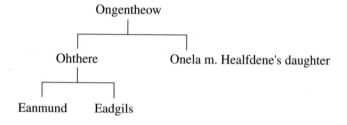

B   The Geatish–Swedish Wars

For the relevant genealogical tables see IVA.

The struggles between the Geats and the Swedes are referred to only once in part one (ll. 1–2199): in l. 1968 Hygelac is described as *bonan Ongenþēoes* 'the slayer of Ongentheow'. Part two (ll. 2200–3182), which tells only of Beowulf's fight with the dragon and of the Geatish–Swedish wars, opens with this reference to them:

> Afterwards, in later days, through the tumult of battles, things happened thus: when Hygelac lay dead and battle blades were the death of Heardred despite the protecting shield and when the warlike Swedes, hardy warriors, hunted him down among his glorious people, attacked the nephew of Hereric [Heardred] in force, then the great kingdom [of the Geats] passed into Beowulf's hands.

The main stages of these wars can be set out thus:

1   After the death of Herebeald and Hrethel, war breaks out between the Swedes and the Geats – perhaps started by the Swedes (ll. 2472–8).
2   The Geats make an expedition of revenge against the Swedes (ll. 2479–80). A battle near Ravenswood falls into three stages (ll. 2481–9 and 2922–98):
   (*a*)   The Geats under Hæthcyn are at first successful; Ongentheow's queen is captured.
   (*b*)   Ongentheow slays Hæthcyn and rescues his queen.
   (*c*)   Hygelac's forces kill Ongentheow.

[Hygelac raids the Frisian territory of the Franks. He is routed and slain. Beowulf, after prodigies of valour, escapes by sea. For line references, see the table below.]

3   Heardred as King of the Geats gives refuge to Eanmund and Eadgils, the nephews of Onela, who has seized the Swedish throne. Onela slays Heardred and, through Weohstan (ll. 2611–25), Eanmund. Beowulf becomes King. Eadgils, assisted by the Geats, slays Onela and presumably becomes King of the Swedes (ll. 2379–96).

4 The messenger fears further Geatish–Swedish wars on the death of Beowulf (ll. 2999–3005):

> That is the [story of] feud and enmity, deadly hatred among men [and] because of it, according to my expectation, the people of the Swedes will attack us as soon as they learn that our lord is dead.

And a Geatish woman, mourning at Beowulf's funeral pyre (ll. 3150–5),

> with hair bound up, sad at heart, sang a dirge in memory of Beowulf, repeatedly said that she greatly feared days of mourning for herself, much carnage, the terror of the foe, humiliation and captivity.

The poet nowhere gives a connected chronological account of these events. The table which follows contains line references to all the passages where he refers to them.

		Death of Hygelac	*Geatish–Swedish wars*
Part one	1	1202–14	
	2		1968
Part two	3	2200–6	
	4	2354–79	2379–96
	5	2490–509[1]	2472–89
	6		2611–25
	7	2910–21	2922–98
	8		2999–3005
	9		3150–5

[1] Presumably this is relevant. Swedes (*Hugas*) are mentioned at ll. 2502 and 2914.

C   Archaeology and *Beowulf*

by Leslie Webster

Introduction

§1 In his introduction to the 1925 Wyatt and Chambers edition of *Beowulf*, Chambers wrote eloquently of the subtle pitfalls of translating Old English, especially of being led astray by our knowledge of the modern language.[1] Any study of the archaeological background to *Beowulf* must be aware that this is even more true of attempts to relate academic knowledge of the archaeology of early medieval north-western Europe to the poem. Marrying the specialized intentions of poetic description and the complex history of the text with the archaeological record as it survives, with the intentions of those who created it, and with our own contemporary perceptions, presents multiple opportunities for misunderstanding.[2] To take burials, for example: the poetic description of Beowulf's burial and the great Sutton Hoo ship burial are both carefully constructed messages for their respective contemporary audiences, in which conceptions of the past play a significant part; but they may not necessarily have had identical aims in view.[3] Moreover, archaeology is a fragile and incomplete witness; what

---

[1] A. J. Wyatt, ed., rev. R. W. Chambers, *Beowulf and the Finnsburg Fragment* (Cambridge, 1925), p. xxiv.

[2] The most useful and comprehensive archaeological studies of *Beowulf* are K. Stjerna, *Essays on Questions Connected with the Old English Poem of Beowulf*, Viking Society Extra Series 3 (Coventry, 1912); R. J. Cramp, 'Beowulf and Archaeology', *Medieval Archaeology*, 1 (1957), 57–77; Rosemary Cramp, 'The Hall in *Beowulf* and in Archaeology', in *Heroic Poetry in the Anglo-Saxon Period: Studies in Honor of Jess B. Bessinger, Jr.*, eds Helen Damico and John Leyerle (*Studies in Medieval Culture* XXXII; Medieval Institute, Kalamazoo, 1993), 331–46; and C. M. Hills, 'Beowulf and Archaeology', in *A Beowulf Handbook*, eds R. E. Bjork and J. D. Niles (Lincoln, 1997), pp. 291–310. The first, though now very outdated in both contents and its use of evidence, remains a remarkable survey. Cramp's excellent 1957 study, though again to some extent overtaken by new discoveries and research, is still essential reading, as is her more recent discussion of halls (1993). Hill's survey article gives a thoroughgoing review of past and current archaeological approaches to the poem.

[3] Indeed M. O. H. Carver, 'Ideology and Allegiance in East Anglia', in *Sutton Hoo: Fifty Years After*, eds R. Farrell and C. Neuman de Vegvar (Oxford, Ohio, 1992), pp. 173–82, esp. 181, has

survives in a burial is only a small part of what was involved in the process, including rituals and organic offerings which we can only guess at. In making sense of that partial evidence, we bring our own contemporary preconceptions, just as nineteenth-century archaeologists and editors interpreted the sources very differently from their twentieth-century successors. How we relate these differing forms of evidence therefore needs delicacy and care. What follows aims to avoid too literal and dogmatic an approach, in the hope of respecting the subtleties of both the poem and archaeology.

How the past was looked at is an important factor in this. Its own past was certainly important to the audience of *Beowulf*. The poem is, of course, set in the past; it reverberates not only with ancestral legend, but also with repeated reference to heirlooms, to the mighty works of forebears, long-dead smiths and giants, and to ancient treasure, *ealde lāfe* (ll. 795, 1488, 1688) of all kinds; indeed, mention of *gēardagum* (l. 1) sets the scene in the opening line. Significantly, however, descriptions of past treasures – the dragon's hoard, for example – though sometimes characterized as decayed (ll. 2255–62, ll. 2756–64), differ little from those of the possessions of Beowulf and his contemporaries in the surviving text, which would themselves have been archaic in the late tenth century when it was written down. So for Anglo-Saxons, the past was, in a sense, the present, and this too colours the way in which things are represented in the poem, and hence the way in which we need to look at them – there is little point, for example, in using archaeological evidence for attempting any sophisticated chrono-logical analysis of the text,[4] or in speculating why relevant practices known from the archaeological record – votive offerings of weapons and gold, for example – find no reference in *Beowulf*. It is a poem, not an archaeological textbook.

Warrior Culture

§2 Before going on to examine specific topics in a little more detail, a general word on the archaeology of aristocratic warrior culture and its place in the understanding of *Beowulf* is appropriate. Much stress is laid in the poem on the integrity and loyalty of the fighting troop, the virtues of the warrior hero on whom they depend, and the almost chivalric bonds

argued that, in a sense, the Sutton Hoo Mound 1 burial is itself a form of poem. See also L. Webster, 'Death's Diplomacy: Sutton Hoo in the Light of Other Male Princely Burials', in Farrell and Neuman de Vegvar, *Sutton Hoo*, pp. 75–82, esp. 75–81; and L. Webster and M. P. Brown, eds, *The Transformation of the Roman World AD 400–900* (London and Los Angeles, 1997), pp. 222–3.

[4] Though it seems that the most detailed and concrete descriptions – those of swords and helmets especially – probably reached their present form no later than the eighth century.

between the two. Wiglaf's rallying speech to Beowulf's *comitatus* (warrior band, ll. 2633–60) is one of several such statements of *duguðe þēaw* (l. 359) in the poem. We know from many documentary sources of the importance of warrior culture in the Germanic world; and how the opportunistic getting and ritual dispensing of treasure, made easier in the fluid circumstances of post-Roman Europe, underpinned and sustained this powerbase.[5] Archaeology also reflects this, not only in the migration-period treasure-hoards of gold coins and neck-rings from Scandinavia and the Netherlands (figure 19),[6] but also nearer home, in the great seventh-century burials at Sutton Hoo and Taplow.[7] In both, the dead man was accompanied by a symbolic array of vessels for the provisioning of a troop, buckets, hanging cauldrons, and great tubs for the feasts in hall, as well as many drinking vessels of every kind – from elaborately mounted aurochs horns to tiny burr-wood cups for stronger stuff than ale (figure 5).[8] Horns, like the equally unstable glass claw beakers from Taplow, were designed to be passed from hand to hand, perhaps by women, in formal drinking ceremonies of the kind described at Heorot and in Hygelac's hall, where Wealhtheow and Hygd served the warriors in courtly ritual. Other symbols of the joys and ceremonies of life in hall are to be seen in the lyres which occur in both burials; this instrument is the *glēobēam* (l. 2263), *hearpe* (l. 89), *gomenwudu* (l. 1065) of the poem, the essential accompaniment to the deeds of heroes sung in hall. Multiple weapon sets too are a feature of both burials, symbolizing the arming of the warrior band; and so too, is treasure *nēan ond feorran* (l. 1174). At Sutton Hoo, for instance, treasure took the shape of Frankish gold, Byzantine silver, Swedish armour, and Celtic precious vessels. It is in this context that we can see something of the leader of the war-band as gainer and giver of gold, provider of battle-gear, and of the joys of life in hall. It is time to turn to that centre of lordly activity, the hall itself.

[5] For a general survey of the historical context, see Webster and Brown, *Transformation of the Roman World, passim.*

[6] M. Alkemade and A. Pol, 'Elite Lifestyle and the Transformation of the Roman World in Northern Gaul' and 'The Lifestyle of the Elite', in Webster and Brown, *Transformation of the Roman World,* pp. 180–4, 185–93, esp. pls 50–1; J. P. Lamm, 'The Great Ring-Gold Hoards' and 'The Gold Collars', in *The Magic of Gold in Life and Legend,* ed. A. Knape (Stockholm, 1994), pp. 33–51, esp. 37–51.

[7] A. C. Evans, *The Sutton Hoo Ship Burial* (London, 1986); R. A. Smith, 'Anglo-Saxon Remains', *Victoria County History of Buckinghamshire,* 1 (1905), pp. 199–204; L. Webster, 'The Taplow Barrow', in *A Companion to Anglo-Saxon England,* eds M. Lapidge with J. Blair, S. Keynes and D. Scragg (Oxford, forthcoming); K. East and L. E. Webster, *The Anglo-Saxon High-Status Burials at Taplow (Bucks.), Broomfield (Essex) and Caenby (Lincs.)* (London, forthcoming).

[8] C. Fell, 'Old English *beor*', *Leeds Studies in English,* n.s. 8 (1975), 76–95.

Figure 1 Viking ships at sea

Figure 2 Reconstruction of hall from the late tenth-century Viking fortress at Trelleborg, Denmark

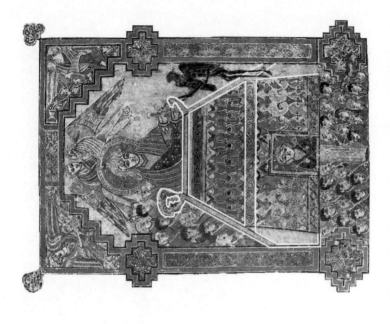

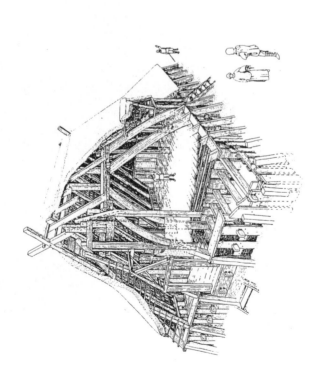

Figure 4 The Temple of Jerusalem from the Book of Kells (f. 202ᵛ), showing horned gables. Insular, *c.*800

Figure 3 Reconstruction of an eighth-century Anglo-Saxon hall from Cowdery's Down, Hampshire

Figure 5 Anglo-Saxon drinking-horns and glassware

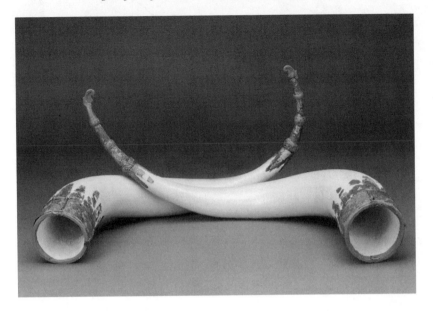

The Sutton Hoo drinking-horns

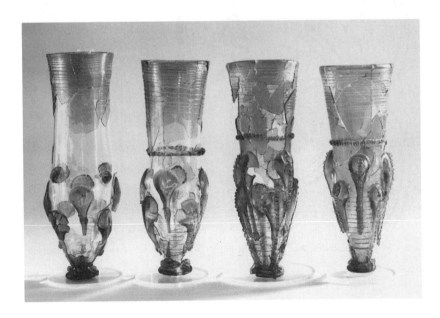

The Taplow claw beakers

Figure 7 Reconstruction of a sixth-century Anglo-Saxon shield

Figure 6 Goliath depicted as an Anglo-Saxon warrior from the Tiberius Psalter (f. 9). Anglo-Saxon, *c.*1050

Figure 8 Shields, spears, and battleaxes, depicted in late Anglo-Saxon manuscripts

Figure 9 Bronze die with warriors, from Tor-slunda, Öland, Sweden, late sixth or seventh century

Figure 11 Iron helmet with ribbed crest from grave 5, Vals-gärde, Uppland, Sweden, mid-seventh century

Figure 10 Detail from iron helmet with bronze fittings and warrior friezes, from boat-grave 14, Vendel, Uppland, Sweden, late sixth or seventh century. The decoration can clearly be seen in this early engraving of an old reconstruction, now superseded.

Figure 14 Bronze die from Torslunda, Öland, Sweden, showing warrior with a seax, late sixth or seventh century

Figure 13 The helmet from the Anglo-Saxon royal ship burial at Sutton Hoo, Suffolk, late sixth or early seventh century

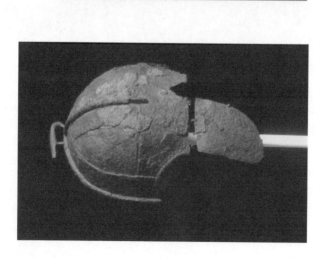

Figure 12 Boar-crested iron helmet from an Anglo-Saxon warrior grave, Wollaston, Northants., seventh century

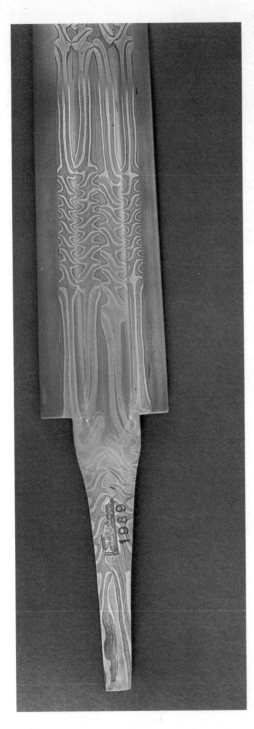

Figure 15 Copy (made by Scott Lankton and Robert Engström) of the sword blade from the Sutton Hoo ship burial, showing the pattern-welded effect

Figure 16 Seax with inlaid runic *fuþorc*, from the River Thames at Battersea. Anglo-Saxon, tenth century

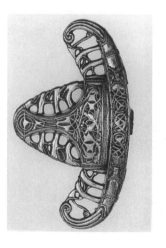

(c)

(b)

Figure 17 Anglo-Saxon sword fittings:

(a) Silver-gilt pommel with interlacing animal decoration, Beckley, Oxon, eighth century

(b) Ring-hilt with silver mounts, from Gilton, Kent, sixth century

(c) Gold and garnet-inlaid mounts from the Sutton Hoo sword and its harness, early seventh century

(d) Silver-gilt sword hilt from Fetter Lane, London, eighth century

(a)

(d)

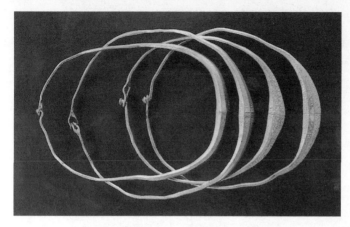

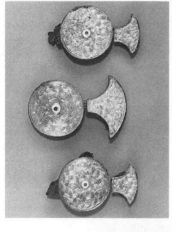

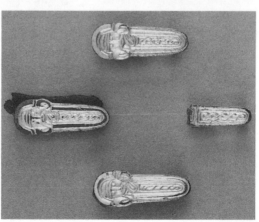

Figure 19 Gold neck-rings from Olst, Netherlands, *c.*400

Figure 18 Trappings from a bridle and other horse equipment from the Anglo-Saxon prince's grave (mound 17), Sutton Hoo, Suffolk, early seventh century

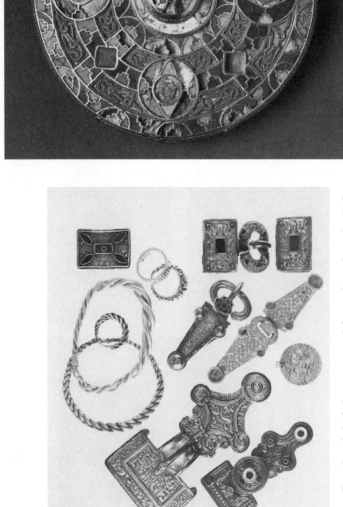

Figure 21 Anglo-Saxon gold and garnet brooch from grave 205, Kingston, Kent, early seventh century

Figure 20 Brooches, belt fittings, arm- and finger-rings, from Anglo-Saxon England, fifth to tenth century

Figure 22 The princely barrow at Taplow, Bucks., looking westwards, early seventh century

Halls

§3 The idea of the hall – as a place of joy and security until threatened by external forces of evil – plays a major part in the poem. Heorot, above all, symbolizes this; and recent work has now shown that its lofty splendour can be paralleled by archaeological examples. Edwin's Northumbrian seventh-century royal palace at Yeavering provided an excavated Anglo-Saxon example of the kind of massive wooden hall described in the poem, while even grander halls are known from Danish and other Germanic early medieval contexts (figure 2).[9] The recent discovery of an Anglo-Saxon high-status hall complex at Cowdery's Down, Hampshire, has given a much more concrete idea of how Heorot might have looked, in the form of building C12, which is dated to the seventh to eighth century.[10] The excavators have suggested various superstructures which could have fitted on the excavated ground-plan (figure 3). But common to all is the evidence for a raised wooden floor, which would have echoed to any step – *healwudu dynede* (l. 1317) – and an elaborate scheme of external supporting timber braces. Could this latter be what is implied by the well-known crux of *stapol* (l. 926), elsewhere in the poem unambiguously a pillar or support (l. 2718)? In this interpretation, Hrothgar would have had to stand at, not on, the *stapol* to look up at Grendel's hand hanging from the gable. This may stretch the grammar too far. Fortunately, the Cowdery's Down building also provides support for the usual explanation of *stapol* as a step of some kind. The archaeological evidence confirms that the raised floor of that elaborate structure had timber supports for steps to the entrance at its gable end. The excavators have also deduced from the complex and massive ground-plan that the building must have had a steeply pitched roof of gabled construction. Heorot's *steapne hrof* (l. 926) certainly finds a parallel here. The descriptions of Heorot as *horngeap* (l. 82) and *hornreced* (l. 704) have also more usually been interpreted as references to gables, rather than to decoration with antlers or horns. From another perspective, however, *horn* could imply an architectural element invisible in excavation, but well known from manuscripts, and from the evidence of certain house-shaped shrines and oratories. Some manuscript depictions of Insular gabled wooden structures – and their occasional stone and metal imitations – have projecting cross members at the peak of the gable, rather like a pair of horns (figure 4).[11] Could this be an explanation both of *horngeap* and even

[9] Cramp, 'Beowulf and Archaeology', pp. 68–77; B. Hope-Taylor, *Yeavering: An Anglo-British Centre of Early Northumbria*, Department of the Environment Archaeological Report 7 (London, 1977), p. 315; Cramp, 'The Hall in *Beowulf* and in Archaeology'; Hills, 'Beowulf and Archaeology', pp. 302–3.

[10] M. Millett and S. James, 'Excavations at Cowdery's Down, Basingstoke, Hampshire, 1978–81', *Archaeological Journal*, 140 (1983), 151–279, esp. 215–17, 233–46.

[11] P. Harbison, 'How Old is Gallarus Oratory?', *Medieval Archaeology*, 14 (1970), 34–59,

of that term opaque to archaeological scrutiny, *bānfāg* (l. 780)? This is probably to stray too far into unsubstantiated speculation; but there are possible explanations for other descriptions of Heorot's external appearance, notably terms such as *goldfāh* (l. 308) and *fǣttum fāhne* (l. 716). There is no archaeological evidence for the embellishment of Anglo-Saxon or any other Germanic halls with gold; but if the description is not simply pure hyperbole, it would not seem unreasonable to read in the description of the golden, shining-plated exterior a poetic image of thatch or of gleaming shingles, both attested in the archaeological record.

Among other constructional details, the references to iron fittings and door-hinges (ll. 998–9) can now find clear archaeological parallels; the *īrenbendum searoponcum besmiþod* which secured the hall *innan ond ūtan* (ll. 774–5) are well represented in the numerous clench-bolts from sites such as York and Flixborough, where they were clearly used in the construction of planked timber buildings.[12]

Inside the hall, the evidence for hangings and fittings is inevitably less good. Benches are known from excavated Scandinavian and continental timber buildings;[13] more ephemeral details such as wall-hangings (ll. 994–5) hardly at all, though the presence of what seem to have been coloured hangings in the burial chamber at Sutton Hoo Mound I clearly hints at the splendours of earthly halls.[14]

Arms and Armour

§4 Essential to the conduct of warrior culture was the weapon set, more rarely accompanied in the archaeological record by armour (figures 6–8). In the poem, it too is presented as a kit (e.g. ll. 1242–50), though the elements are different: the possession of swords, not uncommon in archaeological contexts, seems confined to those of the highest status in the poem, while helmets and chain mail, still exceptionally rare survivals, are depicted in the poem as the regular equipment of the warrior troop. It is impossible to say whether this apparent discrepancy arises from an artificial poetic convention, or from the practice of handing on such

esp. 54–5; F. Henry, *The Book of Kells: Representations from the Manuscript in Trinity College Dublin* (London, 1974), pl. 68; J. D. Alexander, *A Survey of Manuscripts Illuminated in the British Isles*, vol. 1: *Insular Manuscripts, Sixth-Century to Ninth-Century* (London, 1978), fig. 255; L. Webster and J. Backhouse, eds, *The Making of England: Anglo-Saxon Art and Culture AD 600–900* (London, 1991), p. 176.

[12] P. Ottaway, *Anglo-Scandinavian Ironwork from 16–22 Coppergate, The Archaeology of York: The Small Finds*, 17/8 (London, 1992), pp. 615–18.

[13] E. Roesdahl, *The Vikings* (Harmondsworth, 1987), p. 45.

[14] R. L. S. Bruce-Mitford, *The Sutton Hoo Ship Burial*, vol. 1: *Excavations, Background, the Ship, Dating and Inventory* (London, 1975), p. 480; Roesdahl, *Vikings*, pp. 44–5.

expensive prestige items, rather than discarding them in graves. However, recent discoveries of complete Anglo-Saxon helmets (see below) and the identification of fragments from others suggest that these were in more widespread use than was formerly apparent; the poem may indeed reflect the realities of *comitatus* equipment more accurately than had been imagined.

Helmets

§5 The image *par excellence* of the Germanic warrior, the helmet is one of the dominant images of the poem. Like a number of late sixth- to seventh-century Scandinavian helmets,[15] it is explicitly a crested or combed helmet of the kind known from the seventh- and eighth-century Anglo-Saxon examples at Sutton Hoo, Wollaston, and York:[16]

> Ymb þæs helmes hrōf   hēafodbeorge
> wīrum bewunden   wala ūtan hēold. (ll. 1030–1)

These three complete helmets have particularly prominent crests or combs (the *wala*) which pass across the crown to reinforce the iron cap, in the case of the York (front cover) and Wollaston (figure 12) examples, two such crests pass over the crown crosswise. The Sutton Hoo single iron comb (figure 13) is inlaid with twisted wires, *wīrum bewunden* (l. 1031), while the York helmet, like some of the Swedish examples (figure 11) copies twisted wire in bronze. Another passage (l.1451) describes Beowulf's helmet as *befongen frēawrāsnum*, set about with chains; Professor Cramp's perceptive identification of this as a description of a mail curtain is now reinforced by the York helmet, with its neck-guard of mail. These three Anglo-Saxon helmets, and their Swedish counterparts, all have face masks (*heregrīman* l. 396, *grīmhelm* l. 334), cheek-guards (*hlēorbergan* l. 304), and neck protection, which also derive from late antique parade models.[17] The descent from this particular helmet type is also significant, in that the archaeological evidence suggests that its use is confined to the peripheral areas of north-western Europe – Anglo-Saxon England and Scandinavia. In the Frankish territories and beyond, a different kind of helmet was current. The archaeological evidence here thus corresponds directly to the cultural milieu of the poem. These late antique prototypes were often gilded, and

---

[15] D. Tweddle, *The Anglian Helmet from 16–22 Coppergate, The Archaeology of York: The Small Finds*, 17/8 (London, 1992), pp. 1104–25.

[16] Cramp, 'Beowulf and Archaeology', pp. 60–3; Evans, *Sutton Hoo Ship Burial*, pp. 46–9; I. Meadows, 'The Pioneer Helmet', *Current Archaeology*, 154 (1997), 391–5; Tweddle, *Anglian Helmet*.

[17] Tweddle, *Anglian Helmet*, pp. 1087–90; Webster and Brown, *Transformation of the Roman World*, p. 222.

the Sutton Hoo and York helmets emulate this in being decorated with bronze, silvered or gilded elements – *brūnfāgne* (l. 2615), *hwīta* (l. 1448), and *goldfāhne* (l.2811). *Beowulf* interestingly refers to the stripping of precious fittings from helmets (ll. 2255–6), a practice now visible in a number of bronze fittings from helmets which have been recognized in recent years.[18] The new helmet find from a seventh-century warrior grave at Wollaston, Northamptonshire, at first appeared as if it might have been stripped of precious metal fittings, but close examination now suggests that it is simply a very sturdy all-iron construction – not a ceremonial item, but a highly functional piece of regular fighting equipment.

The most spectacular aspect of this helmet is, however, the presence of a three-dimensional boar figure on its crown (figure 12). Such images resonate throughout the poem – the *swȳn ealgylden eofer īrenheard* of Hnæf's funeral pyre (ll. 1111–12), the *swīn ofer helme* (l. 1286) – to the extent that the boar image even comes to represent the warriors themselves (l. 1328). The Wollaston helmet is, moreover, not the only surviving example of this potent tradition: the Benty Grange, Derbyshire, helmet also bears a fine boar figure on its crown (p. i),[19] and an unmounted boar helmet crest comes from an old grave find at Guilden Morden in Cambridge-shire.[20] Depictions of warriors wearing helmets of this kind are also known from Swedish contexts (figure 10); one of the best known occurs on a die for making repoussé panels from a seventh-century site at Torslunda, Gotland (figure 9). A very late representation of a boar or similar animal on a helmet crest can be seen in an eighth-century Anglo-Saxon manuscript now in St Petersburg, where it adorns the defeated Goliath's helmet.[21] Perhaps in such a context, and by this time, it was only possible to depict such a pagan image of courage and strength on the headgear of the unrighteous. In the poem the motif is certainly one of strength and protection; it also appears (ll. 303–6, 1451–4) in contexts where it seems to be not a crest but an image on a helmet, protecting the wearer in a manner similar to the amuletic boar and beast heads which shield the brows of the Sutton Hoo and York helmets. A more ambiguous image is presented by the *eafor hēafodsegn* (l. 2152) on the list of Beowulf's gifts to Hygelac (ll. 2152–4a), which match those given by Hrothgar to Beowulf (ll. 1020–4a). If the reading of this as a boar ensign, a standard with a boar image, is

[18] E.g. Tweddle, *Anglian Helmet*, p. 1083.

[19] R. L. S. Bruce-Mitford and M. R. Luscombe, 'The Benty Grange Helmet and Some Other Supposed Anglo-Saxon Helmets', in *Aspects of Anglo-Saxon Archaeology*, R. L. S. Bruce-Mitford (London, 1974), pp. 223–52.

[20] J. Foster, 'A Boar Figurine from Guilden Morden, Cambs.', *Medieval Archaeology*, 21 (1977), 166–7.

[21] M. J. Swanton, 'The Manuscript Illustration of a Helmet of Benty Grange Type', *Journal of the Arms and Armour Society*, 10 (1980), 1–5; Tweddle, *Anglian Helmet*, fig. 534.

correct, it serves to remind us that archaeological evidence has its own limitations.

Mail-coats

§6 Like the helmet, the mail-coat is a rarity in archaeological contexts, though, as we have already seen, this probably reflects burial practice rather than actual usage. The latter wills and the evidence of the Bayeux Tapestry suggest that mail-coats were in widespread military use by the later tenth century.[22] The mail-coat from the Sutton Hoo ship burial is an elaborate construction consisting of rows of riveted rings apparently alternating with rows of butt-welded ones;[23] a similar technique is seen in the chain-mail neck-guard on the York helmet in the later eighth century, where lapped and riveted rings are combined in alternate rows with welded ones. The poetic accounts of these garments accord very precisely with the archaeological evidence. They are of grey steel (l. 334), skilfully formed of rings in an intricate mesh (ll. 321–3, 406, 550–3), and they clink and jingle on the move (l. 226).

Shields

§7 Shields are a much more standard item of warrior equipment as represented in Anglo-Saxon and other Germanic burials; they form, with the spear, the basic fighting kit of the member of a war-band.[24] The poetic vocabulary highlights elements of the shield which have a certain archaeological reality (figures 7 and 8). They are characteristically described as broad, probably with a rim of some kind, e.g. *rondas regnhearde* (l. 326), *sīdrand* (l. 1289), *bordrand* (l. 2559), and they may possess a tall central boss (*stēapne rond* l. 2566). Each of these elements can be matched in archaeological material from the early Anglo-Saxon period, though metal edge bindings are rare; Sutton Hoo again provides the best surviving example of this, and interestingly, a rare instance of the use of lime-wood in a shield.[25] The regular use of *lind* and its compounds to denote shields or warriors in *Beowulf* may therefore depend upon a notion of high-class rather than everyday shields, but it would be unwise to press the meaning of this trope too far.

---

[22] S. A. O'Connor, 'Technology and Dating of the Mail', in Tweddle, *Anglian Helmet*, pp. 1052–87, esp.1052–9.

[23] Evans, *Sutton Hoo Ship Burial, p. 41.*

[24] T. M. Dickinson and H. Härke, *Early Anglo-Saxon Shields*, *Archaeologia*, 110 (1992).

[25] Ibid., p. 48.

Swords and Seaxes

§8 The defining heroic weapon, swords (figures 15–17) play a large part in the poem, and are described in considerable detail. They are archetypally the *ealde lāfe* (§1), powerful heirlooms to be prized for their power and might; some are the work of marvellous smiths (l. 1681), or *eotenisc* (l. 1558), the work of giants long ago; they may have names, or carry owner inscriptions and images which tell of the mythic past (ll. 1688–98). They have richly decorated hilts (l. 1698) and bear twisting and branching patterns (*wyrmfāh* l. 1698, *ātertānum fāh* l. 1459); their iron blades are fearsome double-edged weapons, which need two hands to swing them (l. 1461). Supporting archaeological evidence for much of this has long been recognized.[26] The descriptions of snaking (l. 1698) and poisonous branching patterns (l. 1459) suggest the intricate twisted patterns produced by the pattern welding technique used to make the best and strongest of blades in the pre-Viking period[27] (figure 15). The word *hringmǣl*, which occurs more than once as a description of swords (ll. 1521, 1564, 2037), may also refer to the twisted coiling patterns sometimes seen in pattern-welded blades (figure 15). An alternative explanation has been that this signifies the attached rings seen on certain Anglo-Saxon and other Germanic swords (figures 9 and 17b), which possibly denote a bond between lord and retainer.[28] The reference to *fetelhilt* (l. 1563) has also sometimes been taken to refer to this phenomenon, but the more probable and simpler explanation is that this term, 'belted hilt', denotes a sword harness such as one sees in very grand form in the Sutton Hoo burial, as well as in more modest Anglo-Saxon and other Germanic examples (figure 17c).

A number of sixth-century sword-hilts from Anglo-Saxon graves carry runic inscriptions which seem to include personal names,[29] like the hilt of the mighty sword which despatched Grendel's mother (ll. 1694–8); and while no surviving sword carries anything resembling the story of the downfall of the giants (ll. 1687–93), there are a number of elaborately decorated hilts dating from the sixth to the eighth century in both England and Scandinavia where the complex motifs may carry special meaning.

[26] H. R. Ellis Davidson, *The Sword in Anglo-Saxon England: Its Archaeology and Literature* (Oxford, 1962), *passim*.

[27] Cramp, 'Beowulf and Archaeology', p. 65; J. Lang and B. Ager, 'Swords of the Anglo-Saxon and Viking Periods in the British Museum: A Radiographic Study', in *Weapons and Warfare in Anglo-Saxon England*, ed. S. C. Hawkes, Oxford University Committee for Archaeology Monograph 21, pp. 85–122; R. Engstrom, S. M. Lankton and A. Lesher Engstrom, *A Modern Replication Based on the Pattern-Welded Sword of Sutton Hoo*, Medieval Institute Publications (Kalamazoo, 1989).

[28] Cramp, 'Beowulf and Archaeology', p. 64; V. I. Evison, 'The Dover Ring-Sword and Other Sword-Rings and Beads', *Archaeologia*, 101 (1967), 63–118.

[29] S. C. Hawkes and R. I. Page, 'Swords and Runes in South-East England', *Antiquaries Journal*, 47 (1967), 11–18.

Professor Cramp has drawn attention to the images on the gold-sheeted hilt of the early sixth-century sword from Snartemo, Norway,[30] while from Anglo-Saxon contexts, the eloquent and complex animal decorations on the eighth-century Fetter Lane hilt and the Beckley pommel present other examples of swords which may carry a visual message[31] (figures 17d and 17a). There is even a certain amount of archaeological as well as documentary evidence for swords as heirlooms: some from graves show extreme wear, or have had their fittings removed, sometimes only the pommel is buried, the sword apparently kept for another generation.[32] These potent weapons were as significant in real life as in poetry.

The sword was a double-edged, two-handed weapon; but the seax (figure 16), its single-edged counterpart, though a slighter weapon, was just as effective. The broad and bright-edged knife that Grendel's mother draws on Beowulf (l. 1545) and the *wællseax* with which Beowulf despatched the dragon (l. 2703) were as deadly as swords. Seaxes grew in popularity throughout the Anglo-Saxon period; a fine example, seemingly drawn, like Beowulf's from the mail-coat, is shown on one of the Torslunda plates (figure 14), and by the eighth century, they appear on Insular figural sculpture as equipment proper to the highest rank; the Repton warrior king bears one alongside his sword, and so does the mighty figure of King David on the great Pictish St Andrews Sarcophagus.[33]

Ships and Other Transport

§9 The ship (figure 1) plays a prominent part in the poem, in the rituals of death, which we shall turn to shortly, as well as in the life of these North Sea fighting bands. It is of tarred clinker-built construction (l. 295), like the Sutton Hoo Mound I ship and other migration-period boats, broad-beamed to accommodate the warriors and their fighting gear. Unlike the Sutton Hoo ship, however, it goes under sail (ll. 217–24 and 1905–10), rather than propelled by oarsmen; Viking ships certainly used sail, and it was certainly in use during the later Saxon period, as the evidence of the tenth-century Graveney boat shows.[34] The ship is variously described as *hringedstefna*

[30] Cramp, 'Beowulf and Archaeology', pl. XIb.

[31] Webster and Brown, *Transformation of the Roman Empire*, pp. 211, 236–7.

[32] Ellis Davidson, *Sword in Anglo-Saxon England*, p. 13; and e.g. the Sarre Anglo-Saxon cemetery contained at least two graves where pommels only seem to have been buried with the dead (J. Brent, 'Account of the Society's Researches in the Anglo-Saxon Cemetery at Sarre', *Archaeologia Cantiana*, 6 (1866), 157–85, esp. 173).

[33] Webster and Brown, *Transformation of the Roman World*, p. 227, fig. 100.

[34] V. H. Fenwick, ed., The Graveney Boat: A Tenth-Century Find from Kent, National Maritime Museum Archaeological Series 3, British Archaeological Reports, British Series 53 (Oxford, 1978).

(l. 32), *hringnaca* (l. 1862), *bundenstefna* (l. 1910), and *wundenstefna* (l. 220), all of them terms which have given rise to suggestions that it had ring-decorated or twisted prows. More prosaically, these terms may rather describe a prow like the ship's stem post dredged from the River Scheldt at Moerzeke-Mariekerke,[35] which is radio-carbon-dated to the mid-fourth century ± 70 years. The curving neck of this open-jawed creature is encircled by a series of carved collars, a feature which can also be seen on some of the English ships' prows on the Bayeux Tapestry.

Land-based transport, when not on foot, was by horse; and though the references in the poem are few, it is worth noting in passing that the equipment of these splendid creatures finds echoes in the archaeological record. The *fǣtedhlēore* (l. 1036), decorated bridle plates, now have a close parallel in the gilded bridle and other horse trappings from the new prince's burial at Sutton Hoo Mound 17 (figure 18).[36] The horses are also equipped with gleaming saddles, described as *searwum fāh since gewurþad* (l. 1038). These recall the sixth-century Germanic saddle fittings from burials at Krefeld Gellep in the Rhineland and from Ravenna, which are lavishly decorated with gold and garnet inlays.[37] Richly adorned saddles must also have existed in Anglo-Saxon England, as the Anglo-Saxon ninth-century saddle fragment from York suggests; it is worthily embellished with animal ornament and silver studs.[38]

Death and Burial

§10　This is a powerful theme in the poem; *Beowulf* begins and ends with a hero's funeral, and other burials – Hnæf's cremation, and the ancient barrow burial guarded by the dragon – play a significant part in the narrative. Each of these contexts recalls elements which can be matched with archaeological evidence, but in doing so, we should be aware that each is a literary construction, with its own purpose within the text, rather than any kind of documentary account. The burial of Scyld Scefing, with which the poem opens, has often attracted comparison with the great Sutton Hoo ship-burial, and other boat-burials from East Anglian and Swedish contexts;[39] here too, the dead man is buried amidships surrounded by treasures and battle-gear of all kinds. But Scyld's boat is consigned to the

[35] R. L. S. Bruce-Mitford, 'A New Ship's Figure-Head Found in the Scheldt, Moerzeke-Mariekerke', *Acta Archaeologica*, 38 (1967), 199–209.

[36] A. C. Evans, 'The Pony-Bridle in Mound 17: Problems and Challenges', *Saxon*, 25 (1997), 1–3; and see, for a fine Frankish example, R. Pirling, 'Ein Frankisches Fürstengrab aus Krefeld Gellep', *Germania*, 42 (1964), 188–216, esp. pls 47 and 52.

[37] Pirling, 'Ein Frankisches Fürstengrab', pl. 46, 2.

[38] Webster and Backhouse, *Making of England*, pp. 278–9.

[39] R. L. S. Bruce-Mitford, *The Sutton Hoo Ship Burial: A Handbook*, 3rd edn (London, 1979), pp. 81–3.

sea, not buried under a mound like the others. We cannot know whether this is a genuine or garbled tradition of the past, or a literary invention. It is striking, however, that each of the burials in the poem exemplifies a different theme, which suggests a conscious literary intention. Beowulf's own burial, with which the poem ends, is by contrast a barrow on the headland, visible for miles:

> hlæw on hlīðe   se wæs hēah ond brād
> wēglīðendum   wīde gesyne; (ll. 3157–8)

exactly the kind of sentinel burial we see in the Taplow barrow (figure 22), and again at Sutton Hoo;[40] this is an expression of fame and a territorial claim that is equally familiar from the archaeological evidence. But first, Beowulf is cremated, like Hnæf (ll. 1107–24), with full battle equipment. This recalls the unusual case of the Asthall barrow, where a rich cremation was buried in the mound,[41] but the placing of the unburnt treasure with the cremated remains in Beowulf's barrow finds no real archaeological parallel, and suggests that the narrative is led by the need to consign the ill-gotten treasure back to the earth.

The account of the fated ancient barrow which became the dragon's lair is a particularly fascinating blend of archaeological verisimilitude and moral fable. The Anglo-Saxons certainly were not averse to robbing the graves of their own contemporaries;[42] they were equally aware of the ancient past about them, often choosing prehistoric burial sites for their own cemeteries in the pagan period. So the description of the stone barrow, *stānbeorh stēapne* (l. 2213), with its chambers and elaborate masonry (ll. 2542–5, 2717–19) could certainly represent a contemporary awareness of the inside of a neolithic tomb, such as Weland's Smithy. The treasure it contains, with its goblets, helmets, swords, and mail-coats, its jewelled gold artefacts and golden standard, is, however, an image of Anglo-Saxon not prehistoric riches (e.g. ll. 2756–71, 3047–50; figures 20–1); these are earthly treasures intended to be recognizable to the audience, gold which, in the end, brought grief.

As this final example shows, the poem's adaptation here of archaeological evidence demonstrates that subtlety and invention in marrying past to present which makes this such a remarkable and densely textured poetic achievement.

---

[40] E. O'Brien, 'Post-Roman Britain to Anglo-Saxon England: The Burial Evidence Reviewed', vol. 1, unpublished D.Phil. thesis, Oxford, 1996.

[41] T. M. Dickinson and G. Speake, 'The Seventh-Century Cremation Burial in Asthall Barrow, Oxfordshire: A Reassessment', in *The Age of Sutton Hoo*, ed. M. O. H. Carver (Woodbridge, 1992), pp. 95–130, esp. 95–127.

[42] Unequivocal instances of persistent contemporary grave-robbing were observed at the St Peter's Tip cemetery, Broadstairs, Kent (C. Hogarth, pers. comm.; C. Haith, *The Anglo-Saxon Cemetery at St Peter's Tip, Broadstairs, Kent* (London, forthcoming)).

D Some Related Poems in Old English

The text is that of the Anglo–Saxon Poetic Records: Volume III for *Widsith*, *Deor* and the extract from *Maxims I*, and Volume VI for *Waldere* and *The Battle of Finnesburh*. The punctuation is ours and follows the principles laid down in IIIB. Names which occur in *Beowulf* are printed in bold type.

Editions

Collections

Runic and Heroic Poems of the Old Teutonic Peoples, ed. Bruce Dickins (Cambridge: Cambridge University Press, 1915) prints *Deor*, *Waldere*, and *The Battle of Finnesburh*.

Old English Minor Heroic Poems, ed. Joyce Hill (Durham and St Andrews Medieval Texts: Durham, 1983).

and

Leoð: Six Old English Poems, ed. Bernard James Muir (New York, etc.: Gordon and Breach, 1989)

both print *Widsith*, *Deor*, *Waldere*, and *The Battle of Finnesburh*.

Individual Editions

Widsith, ed. Kemp Malone (Copenhagen: Rosenkilde and Bagger, 1962)

R. W. Chambers, *Widsith: A Study in Old English Heroic Legend* (New York: Russell and Russell, 1965)

Deor, ed. Kemp Malone (London: Methuen, 3rd edn, 1961)

Waldere, ed. F. Norman (London: Methuen, 1933)

Waldere, ed. Arne Zettersten (Manchester: Manchester University Press, 1979)

Finnesburh Fragment and Episode, ed. Donald K. Fry (London: Methuen, 1974)

Blanche Colton Williams, *Gnomic Poetry in Anglo–Saxon* (New York: Columbia University Press, 1914)

A Critical Edition of the Old English Gnomic Poems in the Exeter Book and MS Cotton Tiberius B. I, ed. J. M. Kirk, Jr (privately printed, 1976 [after the author's untimely death])

[Copies of Kirk's edition were deposited in the libraries of the Australian National University, Brown University, the Dictionary of Old English University of Toronto, the University of Edinburgh, the English Faculty University of Oxford, Institut für Englische Philologie der Universität München, Princeton University, and St Edmund Hall Oxford, and can be obtained from Mrs J. M. Kirk, Jr, PO Box 541, Middlebury, VT 05753, USA.]

1 Widsith*

Exeter Book ff. 84b–87a

Widsið maðolade,   wordhord onleac,
se þe monna mæst   mægþa ofer eorþan
folca geondferde;   oft he on flette geþah
mynelicne maþþum.   Him from Myrgingum
5 æþele onwocon.   He mid Ealhhilde
fælre freoþuwebban   forman siþe
Hreðcyninges   ham gesohte
eastan of Ongle,   **Eormanrices**
wraþes wærlogan.   Ongon þa worn sprecan:
10 'Fela ic monna gefrægn   mægþum wealdan.
Sceal þeodna gehwylc   þeawum lifgan
eorl æfter oþrum   eðle rædan
se þe his þeodenstol   geþeon wile.
þara wæs Hwala   hwile selast
15 ond Alexandreas   ealra ricost
monna cynnes   ond he mæst geþah
þara þe ic ofer foldan   gefrægen hæbbe.
Ætla weold Hunum,   **Eormanric** Gotum,
Becca Baningum,   Burgendum Gifica.
20 Casere weold Creacum   ond Cælic Finnum,
Hagena Holmrygum   ond Heoden Glommum.
Witta weold Swæfum,   Wada Hælsingum,
Meaca Myrgingum,   Mearchealf Hundingum.
þeodric weold **Froncum**,   þyle Rondingum,
25 **Breoca Brondingum**,   Billing Wernum.
Oswine weold Eowum   ond Ytum Gefwulf,
Fin Folcwalding   **Fresna** cynne.
Sigehere lengest   Sædenum weold,
Hnæf Hocingum,   Helm Wulfingum,
30 Wald Woingum,   Wod þyringum,
Sæferð Sycgum,   **Sweom Ongendþeow**,
Sceafthere Ymbrum,   Sceafa Longbeardum,
Hun Hætwerum   ond Holen Wrosnum.
Hringweald wæs haten   herefarena cyning.

---

2 monna] *Not in MS.*   mægþa] mærþa   3 on] *Not in MS.*   4 Him] hine
11 þeodna] þeoda   14 Hwala] wala   20 Cælic] cęlic   21 Holmrygum] holm rycum
Heoden] henden

* The name *Widsith* means 'far journey', but since in other Germanic languages a nickname 'far traveller' occurs (e.g. the Old Norse epithet *inn víðförli* 'the far traveller' affixed to various men's names), *Widsith* is usually taken to mean 'far traveller'. Cf. *Withergield* 'revenge', i.e. 'revenger'.

According to his own account, Widsith was not only a much-travelled man but also a man who lived to a very ripe old age and had a remarkable gift for languages. Passages of relevance to *Beowulf* will be found in ll. 5b–9a, 27, 29a, 31b, 32b, 35–44, 45–9, 88–92, 109–11, and 124b–30. See the notes below, which discuss only the persons mentioned in *Beowulf*.

> Widsith spoke, unlocked his word-hoard, he who of men travelled through most races and peoples over the earth; often he had received in hall desirable treasure. His ancestors sprang from the Myrgings. He with Ealhhild, gracious weaver of peace, first, from Angel in the east, sought the home of the Gothic king Eormanric, the savage breaker of his promises. He began then to speak many things: 'I have heard of many men ruling over the peoples; every prince must live fittingly; one man after another must rule the land, a man who wishes his throne to prosper. Of these Hwala was for a time the best and Alexander mightiest of all the race of men, and he prospered most of those of whom I have heard tell throughout the earth. Ætla ruled the Huns, Eormanric the Goths, Becca the Banings, Gifica the Burgundians. Caesar ruled the Greeks and Cælic the Finns, Hagena the Island-Rugians and Heoden the Glommas. Witta ruled the Swabians, Wade the Hælsings, Meaca the Myrgings, Mearchealf the Hundings. Theodric ruled the Franks, Thyle the Rondings, Breoca the Brondings, Billing the Wærnas. Oswine ruled the Eowan, and Gefwulf the Jutes, Fin Folcwalding the race of the Frisians. Sigehere ruled the Sea-Danes for a very long time, Hnæf the Hocings, Helm the Wulfings, Wald the Woingas, Wod the Thuringians, Sæferth the Secgan, Ongendtheow the Swedes, Sceafthere the Ymbras, Sceafa the Longobards, Hun the Hætwere, and Holen the Wrosnas. Hringweald was called king of the pirates.

5b–9a   See *Beowulf* 1200b–1a.
27   *See Beowulf* 1068–124.
29a   See *Beowulf* 1068–124.
31b   See IVA5, IVB, and the references given in Proper Names s.v. *Ongenþēow*.
32b   See *Beowulf* 4 note.

35 **Offa** weold Ongle,　　Alewih **Denum;**
se wæs þara manna　　modgast ealra,
no hwæþre he ofer **Offan**　　eorlscype fremede
ac **Offa** geslog　　ærest monna
cnihtwesende　　cynerica mæst;
40 nænig efeneald him　　eorlscipe maran
on orette;　　ane sweorde
merce gemærde　　wið Myrgingum
bi Fifeldore.　　Heoldon forð siþþan
Engle ond Swæfe　　swa hit **Offa** geslog.
45 **Hroþwulf** ond **Hroðgar**　　heoldon lengest
sibbe ætsomne　　suhtorfædran,
siþþan hy forwræcon　　wicinga cynn
ond **Ingeldes**　　ord forbigdan,
forheowan æt **Heorote**　　**Heaðobeardna** þrym.
50 Swa ic geondferde fela　　fremdra londa
geond ginne grund.　　Godes ond yfles
þær ic cunnade,　　cnosle bidæled
freomægum feor　　folgade wide.
Forþon ic mæg singan　　ond secgan spell,
55 mænan fore mengo　　in meoduhealle
hu me cynegode　　cystum dohten.
Ic wæs mid Hunum　　ond mid Hreðgotum,
mid **Sweom** ond mid **Geatum**　　ond mid **Suþdenum**.
Mid Wenlum ic wæs ond mid Wærnum　　ond mid Wicingum.
60 Mid Gefþum ic wæs ond mid Winedum　　ond mid Gefflegum.
Mid Englum ic wæs ond mid Swæfum　　ond mid Ænenum.
Mid Seaxum ic wæs ond Sycgum　　ond mid Sweordwerum.
Mid Hronum ic wæs ond mid Deanum　　ond mid **Heaþoreamum**.
Mid þyringum ic wæs　　ond mid þrowendum,
65 ond mid Burgendum,　　þær ic beag geþah;
me þær Guðhere forgeaf　　glædlicne maþþum
songes to leane.　　Næs þæt sæne cyning.
Mid **Froncum** ic wæs ond mid **Frysum**　　ond mid Frumtingum.
Mid Rugum ic wæs ond mid Glommum　　ond mid Rumwalum.
70 Swylce ic wæs on Eatule　　mid Ælfwine;
se hæfde moncynnes,　　mine gefræge,
leohteste hond　　lofes to wyrcenne,
heortan unhneaweste　　hringa gedales
beorhtra beaga,　　bearn Eadwines.

49 Heaðobeardna] heaðo bear,ᵈna　　65 geþah] geþęah

Offa ruled Angel, Alewih the Danes: he was bravest of all these men, yet he did not surpass Offa in deeds of courage, for Offa, first of men, while still a youth, gained the greatest of kingdoms; no one of the same age achieved greater deeds of valour in battle than he: with his single sword he fixed the boundary against the Myrgings at Fifeldor. Afterwards the Angles and Swabians held it as Offa had won it. Hrothwulf and Hrothgar kept peace together for a very long time, uncle and nephew, when they had driven away the race of the Vikings and crushed the army of Ingeld, destroyed at Heorot the host of the Heathobards. Thus I traversed many foreign lands through this wide world; good and evil I suffered there; cut off from family, far from noble kinsmen, I served far and wide. Therefore I may sing and tell my story, recite before the company in the mead-hall how the noble ones were liberal to me in their generosity. I was with the Huns and with the Ostrogoths, with the Swedes and with the Geats and with the South-Danes. With the Wendlas I was and with the Wærnas and with the Vikings. With the Gefthas I was and with the Wends and with the Gefflegas. With the Angles I was and with the Swabians and with the Ænenas. With the Saxons I was and with the Secgan and with the Sweordweras. With the Hronas I was and with the Danes and with the Heathoreamas. With the Thuringians I was and with the Throwendas and with the Burgundians, where I received an armlet; Guthhere gave me there a shining jewel in reward for my song; that was no sluggard king. With the Franks I was and with the Frisians and with the Frumtings. With the Rugas I was and with the Glommas and with the Romans. Likewise I was in Italy with Ælfwine; he had, I have heard, the quickest hand among mankind to gain praise, a heart most generous in giving of rings, gleaming armlets, the son of Eadwine.

35–44 See *Beowulf* 1944–62.
45–9 See *Beowulf* 1011–19, 1180b–7, and 2032–69a.

75 Mid Sercingum ic wæs   ond mid Seringum.
Mid Creacum ic wæs ond mid **Finnum**   ond mid Casere
se þe winburga   geweald ahte
wiolena ond wilna   ond Wala rices.
Mid Scottum ic wæs ond mid Peohtum   ond mid Scridefinnum.
80 Mid Lidwicingum ic wæs ond mid Leonum   ond mid Longbeardum,
mid hæðnum ond mid hæleþum   ond mid Hundingum.
Mid Israhelum ic wæs   ond mid Exsyringum,
mid Ebreum ond mid Indeum   ond mid Egypturn.
Mid Moidum ic wæs ond mid Persum   ond mid Myrgingum
85 ond Mofdingum   ond ongend Myrgingum
ond mid Amothingum.   Mid Eastþyringum ic wæs
ond mid Eolum ond mid Istum   ond Idumingum.
Ond ic wæs mid **Eormanrice**   ealle þrage;
þær me Gotena cyning   gode dohte;
90 se me beag forgeaf   burgwarena fruma
on þam siex hund wæs   smætes goldes
gescyred sceatta   scillingrime;
þone ic **Eadgilse**   on æht sealde
minum hleodryhtne   þa ic to ham bicwom,
95 leofum to leane   þæs þe he me lond forgeaf,
mines fæder eþel,   frea Myrginga.
Ond me þa Ealhhild   oþerne forgeaf
dryhtcwen duguþe   dohtor Eadwines.
Hyre lof lengde   geond londa fela
100 þonne ic be songe   segan sceolde
hwær ic under swegle   selast wisse
goldhrodene cwen   giefe bryttian.
Ðonne wit Scilling   sciran reorde
for uncrum sigedryhtne   song ahofan
105 – hlude bi hearpan   hleoþor swinsade –
þonne monige men   modum wlonce
wordum sprecan   þa þe wel cuþan
þæt hi næfre song   sellan ne hyrdon.
Ðonan ic ealne geondhwearf   eþel Gotena,
110 sohte ic a gesiþa   þa selestan;
þæt wæs innweorud   **Earmanrices**.
Heðcan sohte ic ond Beadecan   ond Herelingas.
Emercan sohte ic ond Fridlan   ond Eastgotan
frodne ond godne   fæder Unwenes.

---

78 wiolena] wiolane   101 swegle] swegl   103 Ðonne] dōn   110 gesiþa] siþa

I was with the Saracens and with the Serings. With the Greeks I was and with the Finns and with Caesar who had festive cities in his power, riches and desirable things, and the kingdom of the Welsh. With the Scots I was and with the Picts and with the Scride-Finns. With the Lidwicings I was and with the Leonas and with the Longobards, with heathens and with brave men and with the Hundings. With the Israelites I was and with the Assyrians, with the Hebrews and with the Jews and with the Egyptians. With the Medes I was and with the Persians and with the Myrgings and the Mofdings and against the Myrgings and with the Amothingas. With the East Thuringians I was and with the Eolas and with the Iste and with the Idumingas. And I was with Eormanric all the time; then the king of the Goths treated me well; he, prince of the city-dwellers, gave me a ring in which there was reckoned to be six hundred pieces of pure gold counted by shillings; I gave it into the keeping of Eadgils, my protecting lord, when I came home, as reward to the dear one because he, the prince of the Myrgings, gave me land, my father's dwelling-place; and then Ealhhild, the daughter of Eadwine, a queen noble in majesty, gave me another. Her praise was spread through many lands, whenever it fell to me to tell in song where under the sky I best knew a gold-adorned queen bestowing gifts. When Scilling and I with clear voice raised the song before our victorious lord – loud to the harp the sound echoed harmoniously – then many men proud in mind who were well skilled said they had never heard a better song. Thence I passed through all the land of the Goths, I sought ever the best of companions; that was the household of Eormanric. Hethca I sought and Beadeca and the Harlungs. Emerca and Fridla I sought, and Ostrogotha wise and good, father of Unwen.

88–92 See *Beowulf* 1200b–1a.
109–11 See *Beowulf* 1200b–1a.

115 Seccan sohte ic ond Beccan,   Seafolan ond þeodric,
Heaþoric ond Sifecan,   Hliþe ond **Incgenþeow**.
Eadwine sohte ic ond Elsan,   Ægelmund ond Hungar
ond þa wloncan gedryht   Wiþmyrginga.
Wulfhere sohte ic ond Wyrmhere;   ful oft þær wig ne alæg
120 þonne Hræda here   heardum sweordum
ymb Wistlawudu   wergan sceoldon
ealdne eþelstol   Ætlan leodum.
Rædhere sohte ic ond Rondhere,   Rumstan ond Gislhere,
Wiþergield ond Freoþeric,   Wudgan ond **Haman**;
125 ne wæran þæt gesiþa   þa sæmestan,
þeah þe ic hy anihst   nemnan sceolde.
Ful oft of þam heape   hwinende fleag
giellende gar   on grome þeode;
wræccan þær weoldan   wundnan golde
130 werum ond wifum,   Wudga ond **Hama**.
Swa ic þæt symle onfond   on þære feringe
þæt se biþ leofast   londbuendum
se þe him god syleð   gumena rice
to gehealdenne   þenden he her leofað.'
135   Swa scriþende   gesceapum hweorfað
gleomen gumena   geond grunda fela,
þearfe secgað,   þoncword sprecaþ,
simle suð oþþe norð   sumne gemetað
gydda gleawne   geofum unhneawne
140 se þe fore duguþe wile   dom aræran,
eorlscipe æfnan   oþþæt eal scæceð
leoht ond lif somod;   lof se gewyrceð,
hafað under heofonum   heahfæstne dom.

Secca I sought and Becca, Seafola and Theodric, Heathoric and Sifeca, Hlithe and Incgentheow. Eadwine I sought and Elsa, Ægelmund and Hungar and the proud band of the Withmyrgings. Wulfhere I sought and Wyrmhere; very often there war did not cease when the army of the Goths with their strong swords had to defend their ancient domain against the people of Ætla by the Vistula wood. Rædhere I sought and Rondhere, Rumstan and Gislhere, Withergield and Frederick, Wudga and Hama; those were not the worst companions though I have had to name them last. Very often from that band the yelling spear flew whizzing against the hostile people; Wudga and Hama, wanderers, held sway there over men and women with twisted gold. So I ever found it in my journeying, that he is most dear to dwellers in a land to whom God gives power over men to hold while he lives here.'

Thus the minstrels of men go wandering, as fate directs, through many lands; they utter their need, speak the word of thanks; south or north, they always meet one wise in measures, liberal in gifts, who wishes to exalt his glory before the warriors, to perform deeds of valour, until everything passes away, light and life together; he who does what is worthy of praise has everlasting glory under the heavens.

124a Whether Wiþergield is the Wiðergyld of _Beowulf_ 2051b–2 is a matter of dispute.
124b–30 See _Beowulf_ 1198b–201.

2 Deor

Exeter Book ff. 100a–100b

Welund him be wurman   wræces cunnade
anhydig eorl,   earfoþa dreag,
hæfde him to gesiþþe   sorge ond longaþ,
wintercealde wræce,   wean oft onfond
5   siþþan hine Niðhad on   nede legde
swoncre seonobende   on syllan monn.
    þæs ofereode,   þisses swa mæg.

Beadohilde ne wæs   hyre broþra deaþ
on sefan swa sar   swa hyre sylfre þing,
10   þæt heo gearolice   ongieten hæfde
þæt heo eacen wæs;   æfre ne meahte
þriste geþencan   hu ymb þæt sceolde.
    þæs ofereode,   þisses swa mæg.

We þæt Mæðhilde   monge gefrugnon
15   wurdon grundlease   Geates frige,
þæt hi seo sorglufu   slæp ealle binom.
    þæs ofereode,   þisses swa mæg.

Ðeodric ahte   þritig wintra
Mæringa burg;   þæt wæs monegum cuþ.
20   þæs ofereode,   þisses swa mæg.

We geascodan   **Eormanrices**
wylfenne geþoht;   ahte wide folc
Gotena rices.   þæt wæs grim cyning.
Sæt secg monig   sorgum gebunden
25   wean on wenan,   wyscte geneahhe
þæt þæs cynerices   ofercumen wære.
    þæs ofereode,   þisses swa mæg.

Siteð sorgcearig   sælum bidæled,
on sefan sweorceð,   sylfum þinceð
30   þæt sy endeleas   earfoða dæl.
Mæg þonne geþencan   þæt geond þas woruld
witig dryhten   wendeþ geneahhe,
eorle monegum   are gesceawað
wislicne blæd,   sumum weana dæl.

30 earfoða] earfoda

In this lament of a scop supplanted by a rival, the poet recalls tales from heroic legend of past troubles suffered by men and women and in the refrain states that, as those past troubles and his own happiness passed over, so can his own present unhappiness. The references to Weland (ll. 1–13) and to Eormanric (ll. 21–7) are relevant to *Beowulf;* see below.

> Weland, the resolute warrior, experienced misery through the sword; he suffered hardships; sorrow and longing he had for companions, wintry cold exile; often he found woes after Nithhad put compulsion upon him, supple bonds of sinew upon a better man.
>   That passed over, so can this.
> Her brothers' death was not so grievous to Beadohild's mind as her own state, when she had clearly seen that she was with child. She could never think resolutely of what must come of that.
>   That passed over, so can this.
> Many of us have heard that the Geat's love for Mæthhild grew boundless, that his grievous passion completely deprived him of sleep.
>   That passed over, so can this.
> Theodric ruled for thirty years the stronghold of the Visigoths; that was known to many.
>   That passed over, so can this.
> We have heard of the wolfish mind of Eormanric; he held wide sway in the kingdom of the Goths. He was a savage king. Many a warrior sat, bound by sorrows, expecting woe, often wishing his kingdom would be overcome.
>   That passed over, so can this.
> The sad-minded man sits bereft of joys; there is gloom in his mind; it seems to him that his portion of sufferings is endless. Then he may think that throughout this world the wise Lord brings many changes; to many a man He grants honour, certain fame, to some a sorrowful portion.

1 **Weland**, the famous maker of weapons, is mentioned in *Beowulf* 455, *Waldere* I, 2 and II, 9, and *Metres of Boethius* 10.33. See further the notes on ll. 5 and 8 below; **wurman** lit. 'serpent', metaphorically (we assume) 'sword'.

5 **Niðhad**, the king who captured Weland and, in order to prevent his escape and so retain his services, had him hamstrung.

7 Lit. 'It passed over as regards that; so it can as regards this.'

8 **Beadohild**, Niðhad's daughter. In revenge for his hamstringing and captivity, Weland killed her brothers and ravished her. As a result she gave birth to Widia or Wudga; see *Waldere* II 4–10 and note, and *Widsith* 124b–30. The front panel of the Franks Casket depicts a scene from this story.

21 **Eormanric**, king of the East Goths; see *Beowulf* 1201.

35 þæt ic bi me sylfum   secgan wille
  þæt ic hwile wæs   Heodeninga scop
  dryhtne dyre.   Me wæs Deor noma;
  ahte ic fela wintra   folgað tilne,
  holdne hlaford   oþþæt Heorrenda nu
40 leoðcræftig monn   londryht geþah
  þæt me eorla hleo   ær gesealde.
    þæs ofereode,   þisses swa mæg.

I will say this of myself, that once I was a minstrel of the Heodeningas, dear to my lord. Deor was my name. For many years I had a good office, a gracious lord, until now Heorrenda, a man skilled in song, has received the land that the protector of warriors formerly gave me.

That passed over, so can this.

3 Waldere

MS Ny kgl. saml. 167b, Royal Library, Copenhagen

I

         . . . hyrde hyne georne:
'Huru **Welande**[.]   worc ne geswiceð
monna ænigum   ðara ðe Mimming can
heardne gehealdan.   Oft æt hilde gedreas
5 swatfag and sweordwund   secg æfter oðrum.
Ætlan ordwyga,   ne læt ðin ellen nu gy[.]
gedreosan to dæge,   dryhtscipe * * *
[..] is se dæg cumen
þæt ðu scealt aninga   oðer twega:
10 lif forleosan   oððe l[..]gne dom
agan mid eldum,   Ælfheres sunu.
Nalles ic ðe, wine min,   wordum cide
ðy ic ðe gesawe   æt ðam sweordplegan
ðurh edwitscype   æniges monnes
15 wig forbugan   oððe on weal fleon
lice beorgan   ðeah þe laðra fela
ðinne byrnhomon   billum heowun.
Ac ðu symle furðor   feohtan sohtest,
mæl ofer mearce;   ðy ic ðe metod ondred
20 þæt ðu to fyrenlice   feohtan sohtest
æt ðam ætstealle   oðres monnes,
wigrædenne.   Weorða ðe selfne
godum dædum   ðenden ðin god recce.
Ne murn ðu for ði mece;   ðe wearð maðma cyst
25 gifeðe to geoce;   mid ðy ðu Guðhere scealt
beot forbigan   ðæs ðe he ðas beaduwe ongan
[..]d unryhte   ærest secan:
forsoc he ðam swurde   and ðam syncfatum
beaga mænigo;   nu sceal bega leas
30 hworfan from ðisse hilde,   hlafurd secan
ealdne ⚲   oððe her ær swefan
gif he ða . . .'

I,4 heardne] hearne *with a dot below* n   5 secg] sec   10 l[..]gne] l[..]ge   13 sweordple-
gan] sweord wlegan   25 gifeðe] gifede   geoce] eoce   29 bega] beaga   30 from]
fró

We are told this story in a Latin chronicle written in the early tenth century by a monk of St. Gall. Walther of Aquitaine (Waldere, son of Ælfhere), his betrothed Hildegunde of the Burgundians (Hildegyth), and Hagen of the Franks (Hagena), were taken hostage by Attila, king of the Huns (Ætla). Hagen escaped and rejoined the Franks. Later, Walther and Hildegunde also escaped, with much treasure, and were attacked by the Frankish king Gunther (Guðhere), who was accompanied by twelve warriors, including a reluctant Hagen. Walther slew eleven of the warriors including Hagen's sister's son (*swustersunu*). The next day, Gunther and Hagen again attacked Walther. After a fierce fight, in which Walther lost his right hand, Hagen an eye, and Gunther a leg, the combatants made peace and jested while Hildegunde served them with wine. The two fragments printed here are all that survive of an Anglo-Saxon version of the story. In the first, the speaker, Hildegyth, encourages Waldere to further deeds of valour. On the second see the introductory note to II below.

The specific references of relevance to *Beowulf* are discussed in the notes. Perhaps of more interest is the content and tone of the three speeches, which contain many echoes of sentiments expressed in *Beowulf* and in other poems including *The Battle of Maldon*.

I

. . . [she] encouraged him eagerly: 'Surely the work of Weland will fail not any of those men who can hold strong Mimming. Often in the battle one warrior after another has fallen blood-stained and stricken with the sword. Best warrior of Attila, let not your courage now perish today, your valour fail. Now the day has come when you, son of Ælfhere, must do one of two things – lose your life or achieve lasting glory among men. Never shall I blame you in words, my friend, that I saw you at the sword-play flee from any man's onset in disgrace or escape to the wall to save your life, though many foes cut your corslet with swords. But you were always eager to pursue the fight rashly; therefore I feared for your fate, that you would seek the fight too keenly, battle with another man on the field. Bring honour on yourself by brave deeds and may God guard you the while. Do not be anxious about your sword; the choicest of treasures was given to you as an aid; with it you shall humble the boast of Guthhere, since he first sought the battle wrongly: he refused the sword and the treasures, the many rings; now must he needs depart from this battle bare of rings; the lord must seek his old domain or here die before, if he then . . .'

2 **Weland** See *Deor* 1–8 and the notes thereto.

3 **Mimming**, a famous sword said to have been made by Weland and owned by Widia; see *Deor* 8 note. It may be the sword of ll. 24–6a below.

6 **Ætla**, Attila, king of the Huns, d. 453.

18–19a This difficult passage seems to mean that Waldere pressed the fight too far by going outside the natural protection of the defile in which the first contest took place.

31 The rune signifies *eþel* 'country, native land, ancestral home'.

II

'. . . ce bæteran
buton ðam anum   ðe ic eac hafa
on stanfate   stille gehided.
Ic wat þæt hit ðohte   Ðeodric Widian
5 selfum onsendon   and eac sinc micel
maðma mid ði mece,   monig oðres mid him
golde gegirwan;   iulean genam
þæs ðe hine of nearwum   Niðhades mæg
Welandes bearn.   Widia ut forlet;
10 ðurh fifela gewe[.]ld   forð onette.'
Waldere mað[.]lode,   wiga ellenrof,
hæfde him on handa   hildefrofre
guðbilla gripe,   gyddode wordum:
'Hwæt, ðu huru wendest,   wine Burgenda,
15 þæt me Hagenan hand   hilde gefremede
and getwæmde [..]ðewigges;   feta, gyf ðu dyrre,
æt ðus heaðuwerigan   hare byrnan.
Standeð me her on eaxelum   Ælfheres laf
god and geapneb   golde geweorðod
20 ealles unscende   æðelinges reaf
to habbanne   þonne hand wereð
feorhhord feondum;   ne bið fah wið me
þonne [..] unmægas   eft ongynnað,
mecum gemetað   swa ge me dydon.
25 Ðeah mæg sige syllan   se ðe symle byð
recon and rædfest   ryh[.]a gehwilces;
se ðe him to ðam halgan   helpe gelifeð
to gode gioce   he þær gearo findeð

* * *

gif ða earnunga   ær geðenceð.
30 þonne moten wlance   welan britnian,
æhtum wealdan,   þæt is . . .'

II,4 hit] ic   10 gewe[.]ld] ge fe[.]ld   12 hildefrofre] hilde frore   15 Hagenan] *With the* e *added above the line*   16 [..]ðewigges] *It is impossible to tell whether the first letter preserved is* d *or* ð
18 Standeð] standeð   19 geweorðod] *With the* ð *added above the line*   21 hand] had
22 ne] he   30 moten] mtoten

II

The identity of the first speaker in this fragment is in dispute. He has been identified as Guðhere, Hagen, or Waldere himself; what would be the repetition of Waldere's name in l. 11 can be paralleled in OE poetry and is therefore no argument against this last view. It is not possible to rehearse the arguments here.

'. . . a better sword except the one which I also have quietly concealed in a scabbard set with jewels. I know that Theodric thought of sending it to Widia himself and also great treasure with the sword, and of adorning much beside it with gold. The kinsman of Nithhad, Widia, son of Weland, received a reward for past deeds because he had delivered him from captivity; through the domain of the monsters he hastened forth.'

Waldere spoke, daring warrior; he had in his hand the help in battle, the cutting war-sword; he spoke in measured words: 'Lo, surely, you did think, friend of the Burgundians, that Hagen's hand would prevail against me and remove me from combat; come and take, if you dare, the grey corslet from me, who am thus weary of battle. The heirloom of Ælfhere lies here on my shoulders good and broadly woven, adorned with gold, no mean dress for a prince to bear when his hand protects his life against foes; it will not turn against me when evil kinsmen launch a new attack, beset me with swords, as you did to me. Yet He can give victory who is ever prompt and wise in every matter of right; he who trusts to the Holy One for help, to God for aid, finds it ready there, if he takes thought before how to deserve it. Then may the proud give wealth, rule over possessions; that is . . .'

1–3 Much has been written about these two swords and who owned them. There is no agreement.

4–10 **Ðeodric**, king of the Ostrogoths, 454–526. He may be the Ðeodric of *Deor* 18–20; **Widia**, son of Weland (see *Deor* 1–8 and notes) and owner of Mimming (see I, 3 and note above), who went into the service of Ðeodric. But the circumstances of the escape described here in ll. 8–10 are obscure.

4 The Battle of Finnesburh

This fragment survives only in the transcript by George Hickes printed, from a now-lost single leaf in a codex in Lambeth Palace Library, in his *Thesaurus. Linguarum vett. septentrionalium thesaurus grammatico-criticus et archaeologicus* (Oxford, 1705)

 '. . .   nas byrnað?'
Hnæf hleoþrode ða heaþogeong cyning:
'Ne ðis ne dagað eastan ne her draca ne fleogeð
ne her ðisse healle hornas ne byrnað.
5 Ac her forþ berað, fugelas singað,
gylleð græghama, guðwudu hlynneð,
scyld scefte oncwyð. Nu scyneð þes mona
waðol under wolcnum; nu arisað weadæda
ðe ðisne folces nið fremman willað.
10 Ac onwacnigeað nu, wigend mine,
habbað eowre linda, hicgeaþ on ellen,
winnað on orde, wesað onmode.'
Ða aras mænig goldhladen ðegn, gyrde hine his swurde;
ða to dura eodon drihtlice cempan
15 Sigeferð and Eaha hyra sword getugon
and æt oþrum durum Ordlaf and **Guþlaf**
and **Hengest** sylf hwearf him on laste.
Ða gyt Garulf Guðere styrde
ðæt he swa freolic feorh forman siþe
20 to ðære healle durum hyrsta ne bære
nu hyt niþa heard anyman wolde
ac he frægn ofer eal undearninga
deormod hæleþ hwa ða duru heolde.

---

2 Hnæf] Næfre heaþogeong] hearo geong 3 eastan] Eastun 11 linda] landa hicgeaþ]
Hie geaþ 12 winnað] Windað 18 styrde] styrode 20 bære] bæran

16 **Guþlaf** It is not clear whether this Guþlaf, who must be with the Danes, is to be identified with the Guðlaf of l. 33, the father of Garulf ll. 18a and 31b, who, with Guðere l. 18b, seems to be with the Frisians, since one of them asks a defender inside the hall who holds the door. It is not necessary to make this identification but, if it is made, we have another tragic situation: father and son fighting on opposite sides.

How we reconstruct the story of Finnesburh depends on whether we think that the Fragment tells of the first fight, which resulted in the death of Hnæf and his *swustersunu*, as most scholars today seem to, or of the second fight after the truce. The *Beowulf* poet (*Beowulf* 1068–159a) uses the story allusively by portraying the tragic plight of Hildeburh after the death of her brother and her son; the frustration of Hengest, unable to take revenge but forced to follow the slayer of his lord; the funeral pyre; the slaughter-stained winter; and the second outbreak of violent carnage in which Hildeburh's brother is avenged and her husband slain. The ravages of time allow the Fragment to tell us only a small part of the story. But what remains is related with brief and graphic starkness by an author skilled in compressed description and rapid conversation. He portrays the dawn attack – compare ll. 1–7a with *Beowulf* 3021b–7 – and the warriors' eagerness for action and readiness for death as, fulfilling their thanely obligations (unlike the warriors reprimanded by Wiglaf in *Beowulf* 2864–72), they fight to defend their living lord or to avenge his slaying.

In ll. 1068–159a the *Beowulf* poet tells in a Danish hall the story of a Danish victory and stresses, as he does again in ll. 2020–69a, the hopelessness of compromise in the face of tribal enmity. However, those who believe that Hrothulf is a traitor buttress their case by suggesting that a parallel is implied between Hildeburh and Wealhtheow: just as Hildeburh was the victim of the treachery of the Jutes, so Wealhtheow is to be the victim of the (assumed) treachery of Hrothulf.

The reader may wish to tease out other possible parallels between *Beowulf* and the Fragment and to consider further the stylistic differences between the two.

'. . . [gab]les burning?' Then the king young in war spoke:
'This is not the dawn from the east nor is a dragon flying here nor are the gables of this hall here burning. But they are launching a sudden attack, the birds are singing, the grey corslet rings, the spear clashes, shield answers to shaft. Now shines the wandering moon beneath the clouds; now dire deeds come to pass which will fulfil the hatred of this people. But awake now, my warriors, grasp your shields, be mindful of courage, strive in the front of the fight, be resolute.'

Then rose up many a gold-decked thane, girded on his sword; then to the door went the excellent warriors, Sigeferth and Eaha, drew their swords; and Ordlaf and Guthlaf at the other door, and Hengest himself came behind them. Then Guthere exhorted Garulf that he in his armour should not risk so noble a life at the first onslaught on the doors of the hall, since one bold in attack was minded to take it away; but he, the daring-minded hero, openly asked over all who held the door.

'Sigeferþ is min nama,' cweþ he,　　'ic eom Secgena leod,
25 wreccea wide cuð,　　fæla ic weana gebad
heardra hilda.　　Ðe is gyt her witod
swæþer ðu sylf to me　　secean wylle.'
Ða wæs on healle　　wælslihta gehlyn,
sceolde cellod bord　　cenum on handa,
30 banhelm berstan　　– buruhðelu dynede –
oð æt ðære guðe　　Garulf gecrang
ealra ærest　　eorðbuendra
Guðlafes sunu,　　ymbe hyne godra fæla
hwearflicra hræw.　　Hræfen wandrode
35 sweart and sealobrun.　　Swurdleoma stod
swylce eal Finnisburuh　　fyrenu wære.
Ne gefrægn ic næfre wurþlicor　　æt wera hilde
sixtig sigebeorna　　sel gebæran
ne nefre swetne medo　　sel forgyldan
40 ðonne **Hnæfe** guldan　　his hægstealdas.
Hig fuhton fif dagas　　swa hyra nan ne feol
drihtgesiða　　ac hig ða duru heoldon.
Ða gewat him wund hæleð　　on wæg gangan,
sæde þæt his byrne　　abrocen wære
45 heresceorp unhror　　and eac wæs his helm ðyrel.
Ða hine sona frægn　　folces hyrde
hu ða wigend hyra　　wunda genæson
oððe hwæþer ðæra hyssa . . .

---

25 wreccea] Wrecten　　weana] weuna　　26 heardra] Heordra　　29 cellod bord] Celæs borð
cenum on] Genumon　　34 hwearflicra hræw] Hwearflacra hrær　　36 Finnisburuh] Finnsburuh　　38 gebæran] gebærann　　39 swetne] swa noc hwitne　　45 heresceorp
unhror] Here sceorpum hror　　ðyrel] ðyrl

'Sigeferth is my name', said he, 'I am a warrior of the Secgan, a hero widely known; many trials have I undergone, stern conflicts. Now is decreed for you here which [of victory or defeat, life or death] you will attain to for yourself from me.'

Then by the wall there was the tumult of carnage; the round shield must be in the hands of bold men, the helmet was destined to shatter – the floor of the fortress rang – until Garulf, son of Guthlaf, fell in the fight, first of all the dwellers in the land; round him the corpses of many valiant mortals. The raven circled, dusky and dark brown. There was gleaming of swords as if all Finnesburh was in flames. Never have I heard of sixty triumphant warriors bearing themselves better, more worthily, in the battle of men nor ever making better requital for sweet mead than his retainers yielded to Hnæf.

Five days they fought without any of the warriors falling; but they held the doors. Then the hero departed wounded; he said that his corslet was broken, his battle-dress useless, and his helmet also was pierced. Then the protector of the people straightway asked him how their warriors had survived their wounds, or which of the young men . . .

---

36 **Finnisburuh** Hickes' reading *Finnsburuh* is accepted by Dobbie in ASPR. But as the one-syllabled *Finns-* is not an OE gen sg and as Hickes made eighteen transcriptional errors in forty-eight lines of text, we follow the more reliable Wanley and print *Finnisburuh* on the assumption that Hickes overlooked a minim when transcribing.

5 Maxims I

Exeter Book ff. 88b–92b

. . .   . . .

Cyning sceal mid ceape   cwene gebicgan,
bunum ond beagum;   bu sceolon ærest
geofum god wesan.   Guð sceal in eorle
wig geweaxan   ond wif geþeon
85 leof mid hyre leodum,   leohtmod wesan,
rune healdan,   rumheort beon
mearum ond maþmum,   meodorædenne
for gesiðmægen   symle æghwær,
eodor æþelinga   ærest gegretan,
90 forman fulle   to frean hond
ricene geræcan   ond him ræd witan
boldagendum   bæm ætsomne.

. . .   . . .

85 leof] lof   89 æþelinga] æþelinge

This passage is of particular relevance to the descriptions of feasting in Heorot; see especially *Beowulf*, ll. 611–46a, 991–1070, and 1159b–1233a.

> A king must buy/win a queen with a property, with drinking-vessels and bracelets; both must above all be generous in gifts. Valour in war must increase in the man and the woman must prosper and be cheerful among her people, keep secrets, be generous with horses and treasures, always at the banquet be everywhere among the band of companions, greet first of all the protector of nobles, quickly put the first cup into her lord's hand, and give good advice for both of them as they live together in the hall.

81 **gebicgan** On the status of women in Anglo-Saxon society, see Christine Fell, *Women in Anglo-Saxon England and the Impact of 1066* (London, 1984). This and other relevant passages from the poetry are discussed at pp. 34–8.

85 **leohtmod** 'cheerful'. The noun *leohtmodness* sometimes carries the sense 'frivolity' or 'inconstancy'. But such an idea is inappropriate here.

E   Documents bearing on *Beowulf*

There is so much (possibly) relevant material that we can offer here only a small selection of what seem to us key documents – and even those in translation unaccompanied by the original text. Our omissions, for which we apologize, can be rectified from *'Beowulf' and its Analogues*, translated by G. N. Garmonsway and Jacqueline Simpson including 'Archaeology and *Beowulf*' by Hilda Ellis Davidson (London and New York, 1968). This book opens with a translation of *Beowulf*, accompanied by genealogies; then provides 'Analogues and Related Documents' referring to I The Geats, II The Danes, III The Swedes, IV The Angles, V The Heathobards, VI The Frisians and their Foes, VII The Volsungs, VIII The Goths, IX The Fight against Manlike Monsters, X The Dragon Fight, and XI Funerary Customs; and concludes with 'Archaeology and *Beowulf*' and an Index of Sources. It is referred to in this section under the short title *Analogues*. The documents we have chosen appear in the following order:

1 Genealogies
2 Cain and Abel
3 The Flood
4 Letter of Alcuin to a Mercian Bishop, 797
5 Hygelac
6 The Fight behind the Waterfall
7 The Dragon Fight

Names which occur in *Beowulf* are printed in bold type.

1 Genealogies
(*Analogues*, pp. 118–19, 222, and 248)

(a) *The Anglo-Saxon Chronicle* (MSS B and C), for the year 855

[A genealogy of King Æthelwulf of Wessex, traced back through twelve generations to Cerdic, then through nine generations from Cerdic to Woden, then continuing:]

... Woden, [Ā adds: the son of Frithuwald], the son of Freawine, the son of Frealaf, [Ā adds: the son of Frithuwulf], the son of Finn, the son of Godwulf, the son of Geata [Ā, D: Geat; C: Geatt], the son of Tætwa, the son of Beaw, the son of **Scyldwa** [Ā: Sceldwea; C: Scealdwa], the son of **Heremod**, the son of Itermon, the son of Hathra, the son of Hwala, the son of Bedwig [D: Beowi], the son of **Sceaf**, who is the son of Noah and was born in Noah's Ark. . . .

[The genealogy then continues from Noah to Adam.]

(b) Asser, *Life of King Alfred* (893), ch. 1

[The same genealogy of Æthelwulf as far as Woden, then:]

... Woden, who was the son of Frithowald, who was the son of Frealaf, who was the son of Frithuwulf, who was the son of Finn, who was the son of Godwulf, who was the son of Geata, and this Geata the heathens long ago worshipped as a god. This Geata was the son of Tætwa, who was the son of Beaw, who was the son of **Sceldwea**, who was the son of **Heremod**, who was the son of Hathra, who was the son of Hwala, who was the son of Bedwig, who was the son of Seth [i.e. Scef?], who was the son of Noah . . . Adam.

(c) Æthelweard (d. *c.*1000), *Chronicle* III 3

[The same genealogy as Asser gives, as far as Godwulf, then:]

... Godwulf, the son of Geat, the son of Tetwa, the son of Beo, the son of **Scyld**, the son of **Scef**. This **Scef** was driven ashore in a warship on an island in the ocean which is called Scani, and was surrounded by weapons; he was indeed a very young child, and unknown to the inhabitants of that country. However, he was adopted by them, and they willingly looked after him as one of their own household, and later chose him as their king; and from his stock King Athulf [i.e. Æthelwulf] traces his descent.

(d) William of Malmesbury (d. 1143), *De Gestis Regum Anglorum* II
   § 116

[The same genealogy, ending:]

... Godulfus, the son of Getius, the son of Tetius, the son of Boewius, the son of **Sceldius**, the son of **Sceaf**. He, so they say, as a small child, was driven ashore in a boat without oars on a certain island of Germany called Scandza, of which Jordanes, the historian of the Goths, speaks. He was asleep, and at his head was laid a sheaf of corn; for this reason he was given the name **Sceaf**, and was received as a miracle by the men of that region, and carefully reared. As an adult he reigned in the town which was then called Sleswic, but is now in fact called Hedeby. That region is called 'Old Anglia'; from there the Angles came to Britain, and it lay between the Saxons and the Goths. **Sceaf** was the son of **Heremodius**. . . .

(e) *The Anglo-Saxon Chronicle* (MSS Ā, B, C) for AD 755

In this same year Offa succeeded to the kingdom [of Mercia], and ruled for thirty-nine years; and his son Ecgfrith ruled one hundred and forty-one days. That Offa was the son of Thingfrith, the son of Eanwulf, the son of Osmond, the son of Eawa, the son of Pybba, the son of Creoda, the son of Cynewald, the son of Cnebba, the son of Icel, the son of Eomer, the son of Angeltheow, the son of **Offa**, the son of Wermund, the son of Wihtlæg, the son of Woden.

(f) Nennius, *History of the Britons* (*c.*800), § 31

Meanwhile there arrived three ships driven into exile from Germany, on board which were Hors and **Hengest**; these were brothers, the sons of Guictgils, the son of Guitta, the son of Guectha, the son of Woden, the son of Frealaf, the son of Fredulf, the son of **Finn**, the son of **Folcwald**, the son of Geta, who was, so they say, the son of a god.

2 Cain and Abel
(Genesis 4.1–16)
(The Revised Version of the Holy Bible, 1912)

4 1 And the man knew Eve his wife; and she conceived, and bare **Cain** and said, I have gotten a man with the help of the Lord. 2 And again she bare his brother **Abel**. And **Abel** was a keeper of sheep, but **Cain** was a tiller of the ground. 3 And in process of time it came to pass, that **Cain** brought of the fruit of the ground an offering unto the Lord. 4 And **Abel** he also brought of the firstlings of his flock and of the fat thereof. And the Lord had respect unto **Abel** and to his offering: 5 but unto **Cain** and to his offering he had not respect. And **Cain** was very wroth, and his countenance fell. 6 And the Lord said unto Cain, Why art thou wroth? and why is thy countenance fallen? 7 If thou doest well, shalt thou not be accepted? and if thou doest not well, sin coucheth at the door: and unto thee shall be his desire, and thou shalt rule over him. 8 And **Cain** told **Abel** his brother. And it came to pass, when they were in the field, that **Cain** rose up against **Abel** his brother, and slew him. 9 And the Lord said unto

Cain, Where is **Abel** thy brother? And he said, I know not: am I my brother's keeper?   10 And he said, What hast thou done? the voice of thy brother's blood crieth unto me from the ground.   11 And now cursed art thou from the ground, which hath opened her mouth to receive thy brother's blood from thy hand;   12 when thou tillest the ground, it shall not henceforth yield unto thee her strength; a fugitive and a wanderer shalt thou be in the earth.   13 And **Cain** said unto the Lord, My punishment is greater than I can bear.   14 Behold, thou hast driven me out this day from the face of the ground; and from thy face shall I be hid; and I shall be a fugitive and a wanderer in the earth; and it shall come to pass, that whosoever findeth me shall slay me.   15 And the Lord said unto him, Therefore whosoever slayeth **Cain,** vengeance shall be taken on him sevenfold. And the Lord appointed a sign for **Cain,** lest any finding him should smite him.

16 And **Cain** went out from the presence of the Lord, and dwelt in the land of Nod, on the east of Eden.

3 The Flood

(Genesis 6.1–9.17

(The Revised Version of the Holy Bible, 1912)

6   1 And it came to pass, when men began to multiply on the face of the ground, and daughters were born unto them,   2 that the sons of God saw the daughters of men that they were fair: and they took them wives of all that they chose.   3 And the Lord said, My spirit shall not strive with man for ever, for that he also is flesh: yet shall his days be an hundred and twenty years.   4 The Nephilim were in the earth in those days, and also after that, when the sons of God came in unto the daughters of men, and they bare children to them: the same were the mighty men which were of old, the men of renown.   5 And the Lord saw that the wickedness of man was great in the earth, and that every imagination of the thoughts of his heart was only evil continually.   6 And it repented the Lord that he had made man on the earth, and it grieved him at his heart.   7 And the Lord said, I will destroy man whom I have created from the face of the ground; both man, and beast, and creeping thing, and fowl of the air; for it repenteth me that I have made them.   8 But Noah found grace in the eyes of the Lord.

9 These are the generations of Noah. Noah was a righteous man, and perfect in his generations: Noah walked with God.   10 And Noah begat three sons, Shem, Ham, and Japheth.   11 And the earth was corrupt before God, and the earth was filled with violence.   12 And God saw the

earth, and, behold, it was corrupt; for all flesh had corrupted his way upon the earth.

13 And God said unto Noah, The end of all flesh is come before me; for the earth is filled with violence through them; and, behold, I will destroy them with the earth. 14 Make thee an ark of gopher wood; rooms shalt thou make in the ark, and shalt pitch it within and without with pitch. 15 And this is how thou shalt make it: the length of the ark three hundred cubits, the breadth of it fifty cubits, and the height of it thirty cubits. 16 A light shalt thou make to the ark, and to a cubit shalt thou finish it upward; and the door of the ark shalt thou set in the side thereof; with lower, second, and third stories shalt thou make it. 17 And I, behold, I do bring the flood of waters upon the earth, to destroy all flesh, wherein is the breath of life, from under heaven; everything that is in the earth shall die. 18 But I will establish my covenant with thee; and thou shalt come into the ark, thou, and thy sons, and thy wife, and thy sons' wives with thee. 19 And of every living thing of all flesh, two of every sort shalt thou bring into the ark, to keep them alive with thee; they shall be male and female. 20 Of the fowl after their kind, and of the cattle after their kind, of every creeping thing of the ground after its kind, two of every sort shall come unto thee, to keep them alive. 21 And take thou unto thee of all food that is eaten, and gather it to thee; and it shall be for food for thee, and for them. 22 Thus did Noah; according to all that God commanded him, so did he.

7 1 And the Lord said unto Noah, Come thou, and all thy house into the ark; for thee have I seen righteous before me in this generation. 2 Of every clean beast thou shalt take to thee seven and seven, the male and his female; and of the beasts that are not clean two, the male and his female; 3 of the fowl also of the air, seven and seven, male and female: to keep seed alive upon the face of all the earth. 4 For yet seven days, and I will cause it to rain upon the earth forty days and forty nights; and every living thing that I have made will I destroy from off the face of the ground. 5 And Noah did according unto all that the Lord commanded him.

6 And Noah was six hundred years old when the flood of waters was upon the earth. 7 And Noah went in, and his sons, and his wife, and his sons' wives with him, into the ark, because of the waters of the flood. 8 Of clean beasts, and of beasts that are not clean, and of fowls, and of every thing that creepeth upon the ground, 9 there went in two and two unto Noah into the ark, male and female, as God commanded Noah. 10 And it came to pass after the seven days, that the waters of the flood were upon the earth. 11 In the six hundredth year of Noah's life, in the second month, on the seventeenth day of the month, on the same day were all the fountains of the great deep broken up, and the windows of

heaven were opened. 12 And the rain was upon the earth forty days and forty nights. 13 In the selfsame day entered Noah, and Shem, and Ham, and Japheth, the sons of Noah, and Noah's wife, and the three wives of his sons with them, into the ark; 14 they, and every beast after its kind, and all the cattle after their kind, and every creeping thing that creepeth upon the earth after its kind, and every fowl after its kind, every bird of every sort. 15 And they went in unto Noah into the ark, two and two of all flesh wherein is the breath of life. 16 And they that went in, went in male and female of all flesh, as God commanded him; and the Lord shut him in. 17 And the flood was forty days upon the earth; and the waters increased, and bare up the ark, and it was lift up above the earth. 18 And the waters prevailed, and increased greatly upon the earth; and the ark went upon the face of the waters. 19 And the waters prevailed exceedingly upon the earth; and all the high mountains that were under the whole heaven were covered. 20 Fifteen cubits upward did the waters prevail; and the mountains were covered. 21 And all flesh died that moved upon the earth, both fowl, and cattle, and beast, and every creeping thing that creepeth upon the earth, and every man: 22 all in whose nostrils was the breath of the spirit of life, of all that was in the dry land, died. 23 And every living thing was destroyed which was upon the face of the ground, both man, and cattle, and creeping thing, and fowl of the heaven; and they were destroyed from the earth: and Noah only was left, and they that were with him in the ark. 24 And the waters prevailed upon the earth an hundred and fifty days.

8 1 And God remembered Noah, and every living thing, and all the cattle that were with him in the ark: and God made a wind to pass over the earth, and the waters assuaged; 2 the fountains also of the deep and the windows of heaven were stopped, and the rain from heaven was restrained; 3 and the waters returned from off the earth continually: and after the end of an hundred and fifty days the waters decreased. 4 And the ark rested in the seventh month, on the seventeenth day of the month, upon the mountains of Ararat. 5 And the waters decreased continually until the tenth month: in the tenth month, on the first day of the month, were the tops of the mountains seen. 6 And it came to pass at the end of forty days, that Noah opened the window of the ark which he had made: 7 and he sent forth a raven, and it went forth to and fro, until the waters were dried up from off the earth. 8 And he sent forth a dove from him, to see if the waters were abated from off the face of the ground; 9 but the dove found no rest for the sole of her foot, and she returned unto him to the ark, for the waters were on the face of the whole earth: and he put forth his hand, and took her, and brought her in unto him into the ark. 10 And he stayed yet other seven days; and again he sent forth the dove out of the ark: 11 and the dove came in to him at eventide; and, lo, in her mouth an

olive leaf pluckt off: so Noah knew that the waters were abated from off the earth.   12 And he stayed yet other seven days; and sent forth the dove; and she returned not again unto him any more.   13 And it came to pass in the six hundred and first year; in the first month, the first day of the month, the waters were dried up from off the earth; and Noah removed the covering of the ark, and looked, and, behold, the face of the ground was dried.   14 And in the second month, on the seven and twentieth day of the month, was the earth dry.

15 And God spake unto Noah, saying,   16 Go forth of the ark, thou, and thy wife, and thy sons, and thy sons' wives with thee.   17 Bring forth with thee every living thing that is with thee of all flesh, both fowl, and cattle, and every creeping thing that creepeth upon the earth; that they may breed abundantly in the earth, and be fruitful, and multiply upon the earth.   18 And Noah went forth, and his sons, and his wife, and his sons' wives with him: 19 every beast, every creeping thing, and every fowl, whatsoever moveth upon the earth, after their families, went forth out of the ark.   20 And Noah builded an altar unto the Lord; and took of every clean beast, and of every clean fowl, and offered burnt offerings on the altar.   21 And the Lord smelled the sweet savour; and the Lord said in his heart, I will not again curse the ground any more for man's sake, for that the imagination of man's heart is evil from his youth; neither will I again smite any more every thing living, as I have done.   22 While the earth remaineth, seedtime and harvest, and cold and heat, and summer and winter, and day and night shall not cease.

9   1 And God blessed Noah and his sons, and said unto them, Be fruitful, and multiply, and replenish the earth.   2 And the fear of you and the dread of you shall be upon every beast of the earth, and upon every fowl of the air; with all wherewith the ground teemeth, and all the fishes of the sea, into your hand are they delivered.   3 Every moving thing that liveth shall be food for you; as the green herb have I given you all.   4 But flesh with the life thereof, which is the blood thereof, shall ye not eat.   5 And surely your blood, the blood of your lives, will I require; at the hand of every beast will I require it: and at the hand of man, even at the hand of every man's brother, will I require the life of man.   6 Whoso sheddeth man's blood, by man shall his blood be shed: for in the image of God made he man.   7 And you, be ye fruitful, and multiply; bring forth abundantly in the earth, and multiply therein.

8 And God spake unto Noah, and to his sons with him, saying,   9 And I, behold, I establish my covenant with you, and with your seed after you;   10 and with every living creature that is with you, the fowl, the cattle, and every beast of the earth with you; of all that go out of the ark, even every beast of the earth.   11 And I will establish my covenant with you; neither shall all flesh be cut off any more by the waters of the flood;

neither shall there any more be a flood to destroy the earth.   12 And God said, This is the token of the covenant which I make between me and you and every living creature that is with you, for perpetual generations;   13 I do set my bow in the cloud, and it shall be for a token of a covenant between me and the earth.   14 And it shall come to pass, when I bring a cloud over the earth, that the bow shall be seen in the cloud,   15 and I will remember my covenant, which is between me and you and every living creature of all flesh; and the waters shall no more become a flood to destroy all flesh.   16 And the bow shall be in the cloud; and I will look upon it, that I may remember the everlasting covenant between God and every living creature of all flesh that is upon the earth.   17 And God said unto Noah, This is the token of the covenant which I have established between me and all flesh that is upon the earth.

4 Letter of Alcuin to a Mercian Bishop, 797
(*Analogues*, p. 242)

. . . Let the Word of God be read when the clergy are at their meal. It is seemly to hear a reader there, not a harper; to hear the sermons of the Fathers of the Church, not the lays of the heathen. For what has **Hinieldus** to do with Christ? The house is narrow; it cannot contain them both; the King of Heaven will have no part with so-called kings who are heathen and damned, for the One King reigns eternally in Heaven, while the other, the heathen, is damned and groans in Hell. In your houses the voices of readers should be heard, not a rabble of men making merry in the streets.

5 Hygelac
(*Analogues*, pp. 112–15)

I B   HYGELĀC – ON Hugleikr –
Lat. Huiglaucus/Higlacus/Hyglacus/Hugletus/
Chochilaicus/Chlochilaichus

1 Gregory of Tours (d. 594), *History of the Franks*, III, ch. 3

After all this had happened, the **Danes**, together with their king, whose name was **Chlochilaichus**, attacked the Frankish lands by sea in a ship-borne raid. Having gone up on shore, they laid waste one district of the kingdom of Theuderic [King of the **Franks**], and carried off captives; then, having loaded their ships with these captives as well as with the rest of their booty, they set out to return to their own land. But their king remained on shore while the ships were taking to the deep sea, for he was to follow in due course. Now when the news had been brought to Theudericus that a region belonging to him had actually been laid waste by foreigners, he sent his son Theudebertus to those parts with a strong army and a great store of arms. And he, having first killed the king, fell upon the enemy in a naval battle, overwhelmed them, and restored all the plunder to his own land.

2 *The Book of Monsters* (*Liber Monstrorum*) (eighth century?) Part I, ch. 2

Concerning King **Huiglaucus** of the **Getae**, and his amazing hugeness.

Now there are also these monsters of amazing hugeness, namely King **Huiglaucus**, who ruled the **Getae** and was slain by the **Franks**. Even when he was twelve years old, no horse could carry him. His bones are preserved on an island in the Rhine, where it flows into the sea, and are shown as a prodigy to people who come from afar.

3 *The Book of the History of the Franks* (*Gesta Francorum*) *(c.*727), ch. 19

In those days the **Danes**, together with their king, whose name was **Chochilaicus**, attacked the Frankish lands over the deep sea with a ship-borne host. They laid waste a district belonging to Theuderic, that of the Atuarii or others, and carried off captives; then they went aboard their ships, which were full of captives, setting out for the deep sea, with their king remaining on the sea shore. When this news had been brought to Theudericus, he sent his son Theudobert to those parts with a large army. And he, pursuing them, fought against them and routed them with great slaughter, killed their king, seized the booty, and restored it to his own land.

4 Saxo Grammaticus, *Danish History* (*c.*1200), IV § 117

After this **Hugletus** was king [of Denmark], who is said to have defeated in battle at sea Hömothus and Högrimus, the despots of Sweden.

5 Saxo Grammaticus, *Danish History*, VI §§ 185–6

Therefore [Starkatherus] took his fleet into Ireland with Haco [King of Denmark], in order that even the farthest kingdoms of the world might not be untouched by the Danish arms. The king of the island at this time was **Hugletus**, who, though he had a well-filled treasury, was yet so prone to avarice that once, when he gave a pair of shoes which had been adorned by the hand of a careful craftsman, he took off the ties, and thus by removing the latchets turned his present into a slight. This unhandsome act blemished his gift so much that he seemed to reap hatred for it instead of thanks. Thus he used never to be generous to any respectable man, but to spend all his bounty upon mimes and jugglers. For so base a fellow was bound to keep company with the base, and such a slough of vices to wheedle his partners in sin with pandering endearments. Still he had Gegathus and Suipdagerus, nobles of tried valour, who by the singular lustre of their warlike deeds shone out among their unmanly companions like jewels embedded in ordure; these alone were found to defend the riches of the king. When a battle began between Hugletus and Haco, the hordes of mimes, whose lightmindedness unsteadied their bodies, broke their ranks and scurried off in a panic; and this shameful flight was their sole requital for all their king's benefits. Then Gegathus and Suipdagerus faced all those thousands of the enemy single-handed, and fought with such incredible courage that they seemed to do the part not merely of two warriors, but of a whole army. Gegathus, moreover, dealt Haco, who pressed him hard, such a wound in the breast that he exposed the upper part of his liver. It was here that Starkatherus, while he was attacking Gegathus with his sword, received a very sore wound on the head; wherefore he afterwards related in a certain song that a ghastlier wound had never befallen him at any time; for, though the divisions of his gashed head were bound up by the surrounding outer skin, yet the livid unseen wound concealed a foul gangrene below. Starkatherus conquered, killing **Hugletus** and also routing the Irish; and he had any of the actors beaten whom chance made prisoner, thinking it better to order a pack of buffoons to be ludicrously punished by the loss of their skins than to command a more deadly punishment and take their lives.

6 Snorri Sturluson, *Heimskringla* (*c*.1223–35), *Ynglinga saga*, ch. 22

Hugleikr was the name of Álfr's son, who took the kingship over the Swedes after those brothers, since Yngvi's sons were children at the time. King **Hugleikr** was no warrior, but sat at home quietly in his own lands; he was a rich man, but was miserly over his wealth. He used to have all sorts of entertainers at his court, harpers and fiddlers; he also kept wizards about him, and all kinds of folk learned in magic lore.

There were two brothers named Haki and Hagbarðr, very excellent men; they were sea-kings and had a great following, and sometimes they sallied out together, and sometimes each on his own. There were many champions with them. King Haki went to Sweden with his host to attack King **Hugleikr**, and King **Hugleikr** gathered a host to meet him. Two brothers named Svipdagr and Geigaðr joined his host, most excellent men and great champions. King Haki had twelve champions with him, and Starkaðr the Old was also with him; King Haki was also a very great champion himself.

They met at Fyrisvellir, and there was a very great battle, and **Hugleikr**'s host soon fell. The two champions Svipdagr and Geigaðr made an attack, but six of King Haki's champions opposed them, and they were captured. Then King Haki broke through the shield-wall and reached King **Hugleikr**, and killed him and his two sons there; after this the Swedes fled, and King Haki subdued the country and made himself king of the Swedes.

6 The Fight behind the Waterfall

(The *Grettissaga* (*c.*1300–20). *Analogues*, pp. 312–16)

[A farmstead called Sandhaugar has twice been raided at Yule by some supernatural being, and each time a man has disappeared, leaving only traces of blood. Grettir comes to offer his help to the mistress of the household, but as he is by now an outlaw he comes in disguise, calling himself Gestr.]

When he had eaten his fill, he told the servants to go to the far end of the hall. Then he took some boards and loose timbers and flung them down across the middle of the hall, and built a large barricade, so that none of the servants could get past it; none of them dared contradict him or grumble about anything. The entrance was in the side wall of the hall near the gable end, and near by was the cross-dais at the end of the room; Gestr lay down there, and did not take off his clothes. There was a light burning in the hall, opposite the door. So Gestr lay, until far into the night. . . .

As it drew near midnight he heard a great din outside. The next thing was that a great she-troll strode into the hall; she had a trough in one hand and in the other a knife, a rather big one. She looked round her as she came in, and saw where Gestr was lying, and rushed at him; but he jumped up to face her, and they attacked each other fiercely, and fought for a long time in the hall. She was the stronger, but he avoided her cleverly. They broke everything that came in their way, even the partition of the hall. She dragged him out through the doorway and into the entrance porch, and there he grappled grimly with her. She wanted to drag him out of the farmhouse but before that could be done they had torn down all the framework of the outer door and carried it off on their shoulders. Then she went lumbering down to the river, and on towards the ravine. By then Gestr was very weary, but there were only two things to be done: either he must summon up his strength or else she would fling him down into the ravine.

They fought all night. He thought he had never grappled with so horrible a creature, as far as sheer strength was concerned. She held him so tightly clasped that he could make no use of either arm, except to keep a hold on her waist; but when they came to the river ravine he swung the hag right round. In this way he got his right arm free; then he quickly grasped the short-sword which he wore at his belt, drew it, and then struck at the hag's shoulder so that he cut her right arm off; and so he got free, but she hurtled down into the ravine, and so into the waterfall. Gestr was very stiff and weary by then, and he lay there for a long time among the rocks. Then he went home when daylight came, and lay down in bed; he was swollen and black and blue.

And when the mistress of the house came home from Mass, she thought her home had been pretty well turned upside-down; so then she went to Gestr and asked what had been going on, that everything should be broken and smashed to bits. He told her everything that had happened. She thought it a most noteworthy affair, and asked him who he was; then he told her the truth, and bade her fetch the priest, saying he wanted to meet him, and this was done.

And when Steinn the priest came to Sandhaugar, he soon realized that it was Grettir Ásmundarson who had come there, calling himself Gestr. The priest asked him what he thought had become of the men who had disappeared, and Grettir said he thought they must have disappeared into the ravine. The priest said he could not put any faith in his stories if he did not see some token to prove them. Grettir said that they would know the truth of the matter later. The priest went home.

Grettir lay in bed for many days. The mistress of the house looked after him well, and so Yuletide passed by. It is Grettir's own account that the she-troll hurtled down into the ravine when she got that wound; but the men of Bárðardalr say that the light of dawn turned her to stone while they were wrestling, so that her heart burst just as he cut her arm off, and that she is still standing there on the cliff, in the shape of a woman. The men of the valley hid Grettir there all winter.

One day after Yule, Grettir went to Eyjardalsár, and when he and the priest met, Grettir said: 'I can see, priest', said he, 'that you don't put much faith in my stories. Now I want you to go to that river with me, and see how much likelihood you think there is in them.'

The priest did so. When they came to the waterfall they saw a cave high up under the overhanging cliff; the cliff-face was so sheer that there was no place to climb it, and it was almost sixty feet from the top to the pool below. They had a rope with them.

The priest said: 'It seems to me utterly impossible to reach that place, so you won't be able to get down.'

Grettir answered: 'Of course it's possible to reach it, but it is men who have some pluck in them who will come off best there. I will go and find out what there is in that waterfall, but you are to keep watch over the rope.'

The priest told him he could have his own way, and he drove a stake into the cliff, piled stones round it and sat down beside it. As for Grettir, he tied a stone in a loop at the end of the rope, and lowered it down to the pool.

'Now how do you mean to get down there yourself?' said the priest.

'I don't want to be tied up when I get to the waterfall,' said Grettir. 'I have a feeling it would be a bad thing.'

After this he prepared himself for the expedition; he had few clothes on, and wore a short-sword at his belt but had no other weapons. Then he leaped down from the cliff, down into the waterfall. The priest got a glimpse of the soles of his feet, but after that had no idea what had become of him.

Grettir dived down under the fall, which was very difficult because there was a great whirlpool there, and he had to dive right down to the bottom before he came up again behind the fall, where there was a jutting-out rock, and he got round to the far side of it and climbed up on to it. There was a large cave behind the fall, and the water poured down in front of it from the top of the cliff. Then he went into the cave, where a great fire of logs was burning; Grettir saw that a fearsome giant was sitting beside it, and he was terrible to look at. And when Grettir came towards him the giant jumped up and seized a pike and swung it at the man who had come in – for one could either swing or thrust with this weapon. There was a wooden shaft to it; men called a weapon made in this way a 'hafted short-sword'. Grettir struck back with his short-sword, and it struck the shaft and cut it in two. Then the giant tried to stretch his arm behind him for a sword that was hanging there in the cave. At this very moment Grettir struck him on the breast in such a way as to cut open almost all his ribcage and belly, so that his guts came tumbling out and fell in the river and were swept away downstream.

And as the priest was sitting beside the rope, he saw some shreds sweeping down the current, all covered with blood. Then he was seized by panic, feeling certain that Grettir must be dead; instead of holding the rope he ran away and went home. By then evening had come, and the priest said it was certain that Grettir was dead, and he said that such a man was a great loss.

Now to speak of Grettir – he did not leave much pause between his blows until the giant died. Then Grettir went farther into the cave; he kindled a light and explored the cave. It is not said how much wealth he found in the cave, but men think that there was some; he stayed there till late in the night. He found the bones of two men there, and put them in a bag. Then he made his way out of the cave, and swam to the rope and shook it, thinking that the priest would be there; but when he realized that the priest had gone home he was forced to go hand over hand up the rope, and so he reached the top of the cliff. Then he went back to Eyjardalsár, and brought the bag in which the bones were to the church porch, together with a wooden rod inscribed with runes, on which these verses were extremely well carved:

Into a dark gulf I went;
The rolling rock-filled torrent
Gaped its wet and icy mouth
To swallow up this swordsman.
The flowing current smote my breast
In the ogress' dwelling;
The whirlpool's hostile fury
Beat about my shoulders.

And also these:

The she-troll's ugly husband
Left his cave to meet me;
Long he fought against me,
And hard, if truth be told.
The hard-edged hafted short-sword
I hewed from off its shaft;
The giant's breast and belly
I clove with my bright blade.

7 The Dragon Fight
(*Analogues*, pp. 335–7)

Saxo Grammaticus, *Danish History* (*c.*1200) II §§ 38–9

Hadingus [King of Denmark] was succeeded by Frotho, his son, whose fortunes were many and changeful. When he had passed the years of a stripling he displayed the fullness of a warrior's prowess; and being loath that this should be spoilt by slothfulness, he sequestered his mind from delights, and perseveringly constrained it to arms. Warfare having drained his father's treasury, he lacked a stock of pay to maintain his troops, and cast about diligently for the supplies that he required; and while thus employed, a man of the country met him, and roused his hopes by the following strain:

'Not far off is an island rising in delicate slopes, hiding treasure in its hills and ware of its rich booty. Here a noble pile is kept by the occupant of the mount, who is a snake wreathed in coils, doubled in many a fold, with tail drawn out in winding whorls, shaking his manifold spirals and shedding venom. If thou wouldst conquer him, thou must use thy shield and stretch thereon bulls' hides, and cover thy body with the skins of kine, nor let thy limbs lie bare to the sharp poison; his slaver burns up what it bespatters. Though the three-forked tongue flicker and leap out of the gaping mouth, and with awful yawn menace ghastly wounds, remember to keep the dauntless temper of thy mind; nor let the point of the jagged tooth trouble thee, nor the starkness of the beast, nor the venom spat from the swift throat. Though the force of his scales spurn thy spears, yet know that there is a place under his lowest belly whither thou mayst plunge the blade; aim at this with thy sword, and thou shalt probe the snake to his centre. Thence go fearless up to the hill, drive the mattock, dig and ransack the holes; soon fill thy pouch with treasure and bring back to the shore thy craft laden.'

Frotho believed, and crossed alone to the island, loath to attack the beast with any stronger escort than that wherewith it was the custom for champions to attack. When it had drunk water and was repairing to its cave, its rough and sharp hide spurned the blow of Frotho's steel. Also the darts that he flung against it rebounded idly, foiling the effort of the thrower. But when the hard back yielded not a whit, he noted the belly heedfully, and its softness gave entrance to the steel. The beast tried to retaliate by biting, but only struck the sharp point of its mouth upon the shield. Then it shot out its flickering tongue again and again, and gasped away life and venom together.

The money which the king found made him rich.

Bibliography

A Short Titles

Analogues
G. N. Garmonsway and Jacqueline Simpson, *Beowulf and its Analogues*,
   including 'Archaeology and *Beowulf*' by Hilda Ellis Davidson (London
   and New York: Dent and Dutton, 1968)

DOE
Dictionary of Old English (published for the *Dictionary of Old English*
Project, Centre for Medieval Studies, University of Toronto, by the
Pontifical Institute of Mediaeval Studies, 1986–)

Guide
Bruce Mitchell and Fred C. Robinson, *A Guide to Old English* (Oxford:
   Blackwell, 5th edn 1992, reprinted 1992, 1994, 1995, 1996, 1997)

Klaeber, *Beowulf*
Klaeber, Fr., ed., *Beowulf and the Fight at Finnsburg*, 3rd edn with 1st and
   2nd supplements (Boston: D. C. Heath, 1950)

OES
Bruce Mitchell, *Old English Syntax* (Oxford: Clarendon Press, 1985), 2 vols

RES
The Review of English Studies (Oxford: Clarendon Press)

B Suggestions for Further Reading

The student's first resort in finding out what has been published about
Beowulf are the following two volumes, which include excellent brief
summaries of the contents of all items listed:

Douglas D. Short, *Beowulf Scholarship: An Annotated Bibliography* (New
   York and London: Garland, 1980)
Robert J. Hasenfratz, *Beowulf Scholarship: An Annotated Bibliography,
   1979–1990* (New York and London: Garland, 1993)

For exhaustive bibliography through 1972 see

Stanley B. Greenfield and Fred C. Robinson, *A Bibliography of Publications on Old English Literature to the End of 1972* (Toronto: University of Toronto Press, 1980)

For recent years these two serials provide exhaustive annual bibliographies:

Old English Newsletter (The Medieval Institute, Western Michigan University Press)
Anglo-Saxon England (Cambridge: Cambridge University Press)

Language

Beginning students are the intended audience of

Bruce Mitchell and Fred C. Robinson, *A Guide to Old English* (Oxford: Blackwell, 5th edn 1992, reprinted 1992, with corrections and revisions, 1994, reprinted 1995, 1996, 1997, 1998, 1999)

Also for students but connecting the study of language with the study of literature and culture at large:

Bruce Mitchell, *An Invitation to Old English and Anglo-Saxon England* (Oxford: Blackwell, 1995, reprinted 1996, 1997, 1998)

Comprehensive scholarly treatments of grammar, syntax, and vocabulary are

Alistair Campbell, *Old English Grammar* (Oxford: Clarendon Press, 1959)
Richard M. Hogg, ed., *The Cambridge History of the English Language*, vol. 1: *The Beginnings to 1066* (Cambridge: Cambridge University Press, 1992) [Essays by several specialists on grammar, dialects, literary language, etc.]
Bruce Mitchell, *Old English Syntax* (Oxford: Clarendon Press, 1985), 2 vols
Joseph Bosworth and T. Northcote Toller, *An Anglo-Saxon Dictionary* (London: Oxford University Press, 1898); *Supplement* by T. Northcote Toller (1921); *Enlarged Addenda and Corrigenda* by Alistair Campbell (1972)
John R. Clark Hall, *A Concise Anglo-Saxon Dictionary*, 4th edn with a supplement by Herbert Dean Meritt (Cambridge: Cambridge University Press, 1960), reprinted in paperback by University of Toronto Press, 1984.
Antonette diPaolo Healey et al., *Dictionary of Old English* [in microfiche], published for the *Dictionary of Old English* Project, University of Toronto, by the Pontifical Institute of Mediaeval Studies, 1986– [The most detailed and authoritative treatment of the vocabulary but complete only through the letter *E*]

Manuscript Facsimiles

Norman Davis, ed., *Beowulf Reproduced in Facsimile*, with a transliteration and notes by Julius Zupitza, Early English Text Society o.s. 245 (London: Oxford University Press, 2nd edn 1959) [Handy facsimile of the manuscript of the poem *Beowulf* alone]

Kemp Malone, ed., *The Nowell Codex*, Early English Manuscripts in Facsimile, vol. 12 (Copenhagen: Rosenkilde & Bagger, 1963) [Facsimile of all the texts in the *Beowulf* manuscript, but without a transcription]

Translations

We list here only prose translations since it is these that students translating the poem for the first time will find most helpful.

John R. Clark Hall, *Beowulf and the Fight at Finnsburg*, rev. edn by C. L. Wrenn, with preface by J. R. R. Tolkien (London: Allen and Unwin, 1940)

E. Talbot Donaldson, *Beowulf: A New Prose Translation* (New York: W. W. Norton, 1966)

G. N. Garmonsway and Jacqueline Simpson, *Beowulf and its Analogues*, including 'Archaeology and *Beowulf*' by Hilda Ellis Davidson (London and New York: Dent and Dutton, 1968). [Following the translation of *Beowulf* are valuable translations of the most important analogues to the poem.]

General Introductions to Beowulf

Peter S. Baker, ed., *Beowulf: Basic Readings* (New York and London: Garland, 1995) [A selection of essays by several specialists on various aspects of the poem.]

Robert E. Bjork and John D. Niles, eds, *A Beowulf Handbook* (Lincoln: University of Nebraska Press, 1997)

Jess B. Bessinger, Jr, and Robert F. Yeager, *Approaches to Teaching Beowulf* (New York: Modern Language Association of America, 1984)

R. W. Chambers, *Beowulf: An Introduction to the Study of the Poem*, with a supplement by C. L. Wrenn (Cambridge: Cambridge University Press, 3rd edn, 1959) [Scholarly, detailed, voluminous. To be used cautiously for reference only by beginners, who should avoid becoming bogged down in controversies of secondary importance.]

Marijane Osborn, *Beowulf: A Guide to Study* (Los Angeles: Pentangle Press, 1986)

One Essential Essay

J. R. R. Tolkien, '*Beowulf*: The Monsters and the Critics', *Proceedings of the*

British Academy, 22 (1936), 245–95. [The most influential literary criticism of the poem ever published. Reprinted in numerous collections of *Beowulf* criticism, including Donald K. Fry, ed., *The Beowulf Poet: A Collection of Critical Essays* (Englewood Cliffs, NJ: Prentice Hall, 1968), pp. 8–56, and Lewis Nicholson, ed., *An Anthology of Beowulf Criticism* (Notre Dame, IN: University of Notre Dame Press, 1963), pp. 51–103, and further developed in, *inter alia*, Bruce Mitchell, '"Until the Dragon Comes . . .": Some Thoughts on *Beowulf*', *Neophilologus*, 47 (1963), 126–38, reprinted in Bruce Mitchell, *On Old English* (Oxford: Blackwell, 1988), pp. 3–15.]

Some Recent Books on Beowulf[1]

Colin Chase, *The Dating of Beowulf* [reprint] with an afterword by Nicholas Howe (Toronto: University of Toronto Press, 1997)

James W. Earl, *Thinking about Beowulf* (Stanford: Stanford University Press, 1994)

John M. Hill, *The Cultural World of Beowulf* (Toronto: University of Toronto Press, 1995)

Edward B. Irving, *Rereading Beowulf* (Philadelphia: University of Pennsylvania Press, 1989)

Bruce Mitchell, *On Old English* (Oxford: Blackwell, 1988) [Especially part 1, pp. 3–62]

Sam Newton, *The Origins of Beowulf and the Pre-Viking Kingdom of East Anglia* (Cambridge: D. S. Brewer, 1993)

Andy Orchard, *Pride and Prodigies: Studies in the Monsters of the Beowulf Manuscript* (Cambridge: D. S. Brewer, 1995)

Gillian R. Overing, *Language, Sign, and Gender in Beowulf* (Carbondale and Edwardsville: Southern Illinois University Press, 1990)

Fred C. Robinson, *Beowulf and the Appositive Style* (Knoxville: University of Tennessee Press, 1985)

Fred C. Robinson, *The Tomb of Beowulf and Other Essays on Old English* (Oxford: Blackwell, 1993)

E. G. Stanley, *In the Foreground: Beowulf* (Cambridge: D. S. Brewer, 1994)

Raymond P. Tripp, Jr, *Literary Essays on Language and Meaning in the Poem called Beowulf* (Lampeter: Edwin Mellen Press, 1992)

Metre

The best introduction for students beginning the study of Old English poetry is

---

[1] Among older works that still have value is Kenneth Sisam, *The Structure of Beowulf* (Oxford: Clarendon Press, 1965).

C. S. Lewis, 'The Alliterative Metre', in *Rehabilitations and Other Essays* (London: Oxford University Press, 1939), pp. 117–32

Advanced scholarly studies including references to earlier works on metre:
Geoffrey Russom, *Old English Metre and Linguistic Theory* (Cambridge: Cambridge University Press, 1987)
Calvin B. Kendall, *The Metrical Grammar of Beowulf* (Cambridge: Cambridge University Press, 1991)

Glossary

Abbreviations and Symbols

Languages and dialects

Gmc.	Germanic	nWS	non-West-Saxon
IE	Indo-European	OE	Old English
Lat.	Latin	OHG	Old High German
ME	Middle English	WS	West-Saxon
MnE	Modern English		

Before the name of a language or dialect

e = Early   l = Late   Pr = Primitive

Grammatical terms

a, acc	accusative	interr	interrogative
adj	adjective, adjectival	intr	intransitive
adv	adverb, adverbial	irreg	irregular
anom	anomalous	m, masc	masculine
art	article	n, neut	neuter
aux	auxiliary	n, nom	nominative
comp, compar	comparative	num	numeral
conj	conjunction	p ptc	past participle
contr	contracted	p, pl	plural
correl	correlative	part	partitive
d, dat	dative	pass	passive
decl	declinable	perf	perfect
def	definite	p, pers	person
dem	demonstrative	pers n	personal name
f, fem	feminine	poss	possessive
fut	future	prep	preposition
g, gen	genitive	pres	present
i, inst	instrumental	pret	preterite
imp	imperative	pret-pres	preterite-present
impers	impersonal	pron	pronoun
ind	indicative	ptc	participle
indecl	indeclinable	refl	reflexive
indef	indefinite	rel	relative
inf	infinitive	s, sg	singular
infl	inflected	st	strong
interj	interjection	subj	subjunctive

superl	superlative	wd	with dative object
tr	transitive	wg	with genitive object
v, vb	verb	wi	with instrumental object
w	with	w refl	with reflexive object
wa	with accusative object	wk	weak

's' may be added where appropriate to form a plural

Symbols

>	gives, has given
<	derived from
*	a reconstructed form
I, ‖	(in verse) the medial and end caesura respectively
. . .	(in quotations) word or words omitted
/	(in phrases like *burg* 'city/walled town') alternative translations
/	(in citation of forms) alternatives.
( )	(in citation of forms) optional elements
[ ]	enclose phonetic symbols

Notes on the Glossary

The letter *æ* follows *a*, *þ/ð* follows *t*. The prefix *ge-* is ignored in alphabetizing words, so that *ge*met (noun), *ge*myndig (adj), and *ge*myndgian (verb), all appear under *m*.

With the exception of some very common words, e.g. *hē*, *hit*, *is*, and *wæs*, all occurrences are cited. Reference is by line.

Abbreviations are the same as those above except that within entries case, number, and gender are indicated with a single initial letter (nsm = nominative singular masculine, gpf = genitive plural feminine, isn = instrumental singular neuter, etc.) and verb classes are identified with a simple numeral, Roman for strong verbs and Arabic for weak, or else with *anom* for anomalous verbs and *pret pres* for preterite present verbs. Thus if an entry word is followed by m or f, this means it is a masculine noun or a feminine noun. If it is followed by II, this means it is a second-class strong verb, while a 2 would mean it was a second-class weak verb.

In analysing verb forms we use an Arabic numeral to indicate person and s or p to indicate singular or plural (3p = third person plural). When verb forms are indicative, no mood is specified, but subjunctives and imperatives are marked subj and imp respectively.

The information set out below about the vocabulary of *Beowulf* may prove useful.

1 Some Very Common Words
(Both as Independent Words and as Elements of Compounds)

atol 'terrible, horrid'
gilp(-), *gylp*(-) 'boast, exultation'
ellen(-) 'valour'
byrne 'byrnie, coat of mail'
bēag, *bēah* 'ring, treasure'
sīð 'voyage, venture, time, occasion'
guð(-) 'battle'
bēado- 'battle'

hēaðo- 'battle'
heoru- 'battle'
hild(e-) 'battle'
wæl 'slaughter, the slain'
sige- 'victory'
ȳð(-) 'wave, ocean-wave'
maððum 'treasure'
brim(-) 'sea'

Klaeber, *Beowulf*, p. lxiii, fn. 3, lists synonyms for 'hall', 'man', 'mind', etc.

2 *Some Varying Forms of Words*

beorht, byrht 'bright'
bregdan, brægd, bregdon, brugdon, broden 'move, weave, draw (a sword)'
gamol, gomel 'old'
eald, yldra, yldesta 'old, older, oldest'
ēaðe, ȳðe 'easy'
sweord, swurd, swyrd 'sword'
æfnan, efnde, efnanne 'perform, do'
āglǣca, ǣglǣca, āhlǣca 'adversary, combatant'

Note the *kinds* of variation of spelling as well as the particular words here: *-eorht* often alternates with *-yrht*, *-am-* and *-an-* often alternate with *-om-* and *-on-*, *-weor-* often alternates with *-wur-* and *-wyr-*, *ag-* often alternates with *ah-*, etc.

3 *Some Pairs of Words Which Look Alike and Are Sometimes Easily Confused*

gāst, gǣst 'spirit, demon, ghost'
gist, gyst, gǣst 'stranger, visitor, guest' } Note the wide variety of spellings!

ealdor, aldor 'life' (very common in compounds with meaning 'mortal, lifelong')
ealdor, aldor 'leader, lord'

bearn 'child, son' (cf. the Scots dialect word 'bairn' meaning 'child')
beorn 'man, hero, warrior'

dēor, dīor 'brave, bold'
dēore, dīorre, dȳre 'dear, precious'

fāg, fāh 'variegated, shining'
fāg, fāh 'hostile, guilty'

lēod 'people, nation, man'
þēod 'people, nation, troop'
þēoden 'people's leader, prince'

mǣg, māga, 'kinsman'
maga, mago 'son'

nīð 'violence, affliction'
nȳd 'necessity, compulsion'

symbel, symle 'banquet'
symble, symle 'always, forever'

Glossary of *Beowulf*

ā adv *always* 455, 881, 930, 1478, 2920; *ever* 779; ā syþðan *forever afterward* 283

ābelgan III *enrage* pret 3s ābealch 2280

ābēodan II, *address, speak (words)* pret 3s ābēad 390; *offer, provide* 668; *wish (success, luck)* 653, 2418

ābīdan I wg *await* 977 [MnE abide]

ābredwian 2 *strike down, kill* pret subj 3s ābredwade 2619

ābregdan III *raise* pret 3s ābrǣd 2575

ābrēotan II *kill* pret 3s ābrēat 1298, ābrēot 2930; p ptc ābroten 1599, 2707

ābūgan II *be overturned, be torn loose* pret 3s ābēag 775

ac conj *but* 109, 135, 159, 339, 438, 446, 565, 595, 599, 601, 683, 694, 696, 708, 740, 773, 804, 813, 863, 975, 1004, 1085, 1300, 1448, 1509, 1524, 1576, 1661, 1711, 1738, 1878, 1893, 1936, 1990, 2084, 2142, 2146, 2181, 2223, 2308, 2477, 2505, 2507, 2522, 2525, 2598, 2675, 2772, 2828, 2834, 2850, 2899, 2923, 2968, 2973, 2976, 3011, 3018, 3024, *for* 2697

ācennan 1 *beget* p ptc ācenned 1356

ācīgan 1 *summon* pret 3s ācīgde 3121

ācwellan 1 *kill* pret 3s ācwealde 886, 1055, 2121

ācweðan V *say* pres 3s ācwyð 2046; pret 3s ācwæð 654

ād m *funeral pyre* ns 1107; as 3138; ds āde 1110, 1114

ādfaru f *way to the funeral pyre* ds ādfære 3010

ādl f *illness* ns 1736, 1763, 1848

ādrēogan II *suffer, endure* inf 3078

āfēdan 1 *bring up, rear, nourish* p ptc āfēded 693

āfyllan 1 *fill* p ptc āfylled 1018

āgalan VI *sing* pret 3s āgōl 1521

āgan pret pres *have, possess* inf 1088; pres 3s āh 1727; pret 1s āhte 487, 533; 3s 2608; *rule* 31, 522. With negative: **nāh** *does not have* pres 1s 2252

āgangan VII *happen, befall* p ptc āgangen 1234

āgen adj (p ptc of āgan) nsm *own* 2676

āgend m *god, owner* gs āgendes 3075

āgendfrēa m *lord, owner* gs āgendfrēan 1883

āgifan V *give back* inf 355; pret 3s āgeaf 2929

āglǣca m *fierce combatant, adversary* ns æglǣca 159, 433, 592, 816, āglǣca 732, 739, 893, 1000, 1269; as āglǣcan 556, āglǣcean 2534; gs āhglǣcan 989, āglǣcan 1512, āglǣcean 2557; ds āglǣcan 425, āhlǣcan 646, āglǣcean 2520, 2905; np āglǣcean 2592

āglǣcwīf n *warrior-woman, female combatant* ns 1259

āgyldan III *allow, permit* pret 3s āgeald (þā mē sǣl / rūm āgeald *when opportunity permitted me*) 1665, 2690

āh see āgan

āhebban VI *raise, take* p ptc āhafen 128, āhæfen 1108

āhlǣca see āglǣca

āhlēapan VII *leap up* pret 3s āhlēop 1397

āhliehhan VI *laugh, exult* pret 3s āhlōg 730

āhreddan 1 *rescue* pret 3s āhredde 2930

āhsian 2 *ask* pret 3s āhsode 1206; pret 3p āhsodon 423

geāhsian 2 *learn, hear through inquiry* p ptc geāhsod 433

āht n *aught, anything* as 2314

āhte see āgan

āhyrdan 1 *harden* p ptc āhyrded 1460

ālǣtan VI *give up, let go of* inf 2591, 2750; *allow* pret subj 2s ālǣte 2665

aldor, aldor- see ealdor, ealdor-

ālecgan 1 *lay down* pret 3s ālegde 834, 2194; pret 3p ālēdon 34, ālegdon 3141; *give up, lay aside* pret 3s ālegde 851, 3020

ālēdon see ālecgan

ālēh see ālēogan

ālēogan II *fail to perform, belie* pret 3s ālēh 80

ālicgan V *fail, fall short, come to an end* inf ālicgean 2886; pret 3s ālæg 1528

ālimpan III *occur, befall* pret 3s ālamp 622; p ptc ālumpen 733

alwalda adj *all-ruling, omnipotent* nsm 316; m *all-ruling (one)* ns 955, 1314; ds alwealdan 928

ālȳfan 1 *entrust, grant* pret 1s ālȳfde 655; p ptc ālȳfed 3089

ālȳsan 1 *loosen, remove* p ptc 1630

an, an- see on, on-

an pret pres see unnan

ān adj *one* asm ǣnne 2399; gsm ānes 2541; asf āne 135, 1762; *alone* nsm āna 425, 431, 888, 999, 1714, 2498, 2643, 2657, 2876; asm ǣnne

ān (*cont.*)

2964, ǣnne 46, 1579; gsm ānes 2533; dsm ānum 1377; dpm 1081; *one* as a noun (with or without dem pron) nsm ān 2268, 2453, 2461, āna 145; asm ǣnne 1053; gsm ānes 699, 3077; dsm ānum 705, 2461; gsf ānre 428; gpm ānra 732, 784; (w part gen) nsm ān 2237; asm ānne 1294; dsm ānum 1037, 2599; nsn 1458; *a certain (one)* nsm ān 100, 2210, 2280; asm ānne 2410, 2774; *an exceptional (one), peerless* nsm 1885; nsn ān 1458; (*a part*) *only* gsn ānes (hwæt) 3010

ancor m *anchor* ds ancre 303, 1883

ancorbend f *anchor-rope* dp oncerbendum 1918

and, and- see ond, ond-

anda m *anger* ds andan 708; *vexation* (eldum on andan *as a vexation to men*) as 2314

andgit n *understanding* ns 1059

andlēan n *requital* as 1541

andlong adj *standing at full height, upright* asm andlongne 2695; *entire, continuous* asm andlangne 2115; asf ondlonge 2938

andrysnu f *courtesy, respect* dp andrysnum 1796

andsaca m *adversary, foe* ns 1682; as andsacan 786

andswarian 2 *answer* pret 3s andswarode 258, 340

andswaru f *answer* ns 2860; as andsware 354, 1840; gs 1493

andweard adj *standing opposite, opposing* asn 1287

andwlita m *face* ds andwlitan 689

ānfeald adj *simple, straightforward, onefold* asm ānfealdne 256

ānga adj *only* asm āngan 1547; dsm 1262; asf 375, 2997

angeat see ongitan

āngenga m *solitary strider, lone walker* ns 449, āngengea 165 or **angenga** *attacker*

angyldan III wg *pay (the penalty) for* pret 3s angeald 1251

ānhaga m *solitary one* ns (earm ānhaga *wretched lone survivor*) 2368

anhār adj *very hoary, grizzled* nsm 357

ānhȳdig adj *resolute, single-minded* nsm 2667

ānpæð m *narrow (single-file) path* ap ānpaðas 1410

ānrǣd adj *resolute* ns 1529, 1575

ansund adj *sound, uninjured* ns 1000

ansȳn f *appearance* ns 251 *sight, presence* ns onsȳn 2772; as ansȳn 2834; gs ansȳne 928

āntīd f *appropriate time* as 219

ānunga adv *altogether, completely* 634

anwalda m *ruler* ds anwaldan 1272

ār m *messenger* ns 336, 2783

ār f *help* as āre 1272; ds 2378; *benefit, property* as 2606; gp ārna 1187; *kindness* dp ārum 1182; *honour* dp (*honourably*) 296, 1099

ārǣran 1 *raise, lift up, establish* pret 3p ārǣrdon 2983; p ptc ārǣred 1703

ārfæst adj *kind* nsm 1168

ārian 2 wd *spare* pres 3s āraþ 598

ārīsan I *arise* imp s ārīs 1390; pret 3s ārās 399, 651, 1790, 2403, 2538, 3030

ārna see **ār** f

ārstafas m p *kindness, favour* dp ārstafum 317, 382, 458

āsecgan 3 *tell* inf 344

āsettan 1 *place* pret 3p āsetton 47; *appoint* p ptc āseted 667

āsingan III *sing* p ptc āsungen 1159

āstandan VI *stand up* pret 1s āstōd 2092; 3s 759, 1556

āstīgan I *arise, ascend* pres 3s āstīgeð 1373; pret 3s āstāg 782, āstāh 1118, 3144; *start, start up* 1160

āswebban 1 *kill* (lit. *put to sleep*) p ptc npm āswefede 567

atelic see **atollīc**

ātēon II *take (a journey)* pret 3s ātēah 766

ātertān m *poison twig* dp ātertānum fāh *gleaming with poison twigs* (referring to ornamental damascening on a swordblade) 1459

atol adj *terrible* nsm atol 165, 592, 732, 816, 1332, 2670, eatol 2074; asm eatolne 2478; nsf atol 848; nsf 1766; asf atole 596; dpm atolan (= -um) 1502

atollīc adj *terrible* nsm atelīc 784

ātredan V *tread upon, violate* pret 3s ātræd 2221

attor n *venom* ns 2715; gs attres 2523

attorsceaða m *venomous assailant* gs attorsceaðan 2839

āð m *oath* ap āþas 472; gp āða 2739; dp āðum 1097

āðencan 1 *intend* pret 3s āðōhte 2643

āðsweord n *oath* np 2064

āþumswēoras m p *son-in-law and father-in-law* dp āþumswēorum 84

āwa adv *ever* āwa tō aldre *for ever and ever* 955

āwrecan V *tell* pret 1s āwræc 1724; *recite* 3s 2108

āwyrdan 1 *kill* p ptc āwyrded 1113

ǣdr f *vein* dp ǣdrum 2966, ēdrum 742

ǣdre adv *swiftly* 77, 354, 3106

æfen m, n *evening* ns 1235, 2303

æfengrom adj *hostile in the evening* nsm 2074

æfenlēoht n *evening light* ns 413

æfenrest f *evening rest* as æfenreste 646; gs 1252

æfensprǣc f *evening speech* as æfensprǣce 759

æfnan I *perform, carry out* inf 1464, efnan 1041, 2622; infl inf (tō) efnanne 1941; pres subj 3s efne 2535; pret subj 1s efnde 2133; 3s æfnde 1254, efnde 3007; *prepare, make ready* p ptc geæfned 1107, 3106

geæfnan I *carry out* pret 1p geæfndon 538

ǣfre adv *ever* 70, 280, 504, 692, 1101, 1314, 2600

æfter I. adv *afterwards* 12, 1389, 2731; *thereupon* 315, 341, 2154. II. prep *after, as a result of* 85, 117, 119, 128, 187, 724, 824, 885, 931, 1008, 1149, 1213, 1255, 1258, 1301, 1315, 1492, 1589, 1606, 1680, 1775, 1938, 1943, 2030, 2052, 2060, 2066, 2176, 2531, 2581, 2669, 2753, 2803, 3005; *after (the death of)* 1257, 2260, 2261, 3151; *in memory of* 3096; *after (seeing)* 2750; *along* 580, 995, 1067, 1316, 1403, 1572, 1964, 2288, 2294; *among* 140, 944; *about* 332, 1322; *through* 2832; *on* 1425; *for* 1342, 1879, 2268, 2461, 2463; *according to* 1049, 2110; *after, in view of* 1320; *(follow) after* 2816; *(striving) after* 1720, 2179

æfþunca m *cause of displeasure, vexation* ns 502

ǣghwā pron m *everyone* ds ǣghwǣm 1384

ǣghwǣm see ǣghwā

ǣghwǣr adv *everywhere, in every respect* 984, 1059

ǣghwæs see ǣghwæt

ǣghwæt n *everything* gs ǣghwæs 2624, 3135; adv g *altogether* 1865, 1886

ǣghwæðer pron *each, each (of two)* nsm 2844; dsm ǣghwæðrum 1636, 2564; gsn ǣghwæþres 287

ǣghwylc pron *each* nsm 1228, 2590; asm ǣghwylcne 621; *each (one)* nsm ǣghwylc 9, 987, 1165, 1386, 2887; dsm ǣghwylcum 1050

ǣglǣca see āglǣca

ǣgweard f *watch by the sea* as ǣgwearde 241

ǣht f *possession, domain* as 42, 516, 1679; ap ǣhte 2248

ǣht f *pursuit* ns 2957

æhtian see eahtian

geæhtle f *respect* gs geæhtlan 369

ǣled m *fire* ns 3015

ǣledlēoma m *fire-brand, torch* as ǣledlēoman 3125

ælfylce n *foreign army* dp ælfylcum 2371

ælmihtig adj *almighty, all-powerful* ns (se) ælmihtiga *(the) all-powerful (one)* 92

ælwiht f *alien creature, monster* gp ælwihta 1500

ǣne adv *once* 3019

ǣnig adj *any* nsm 503, 510, 534, 1099, 1353, 1560, 2297, 2731; asm ǣnigne 627, 1772, 1851, 3080, 3127; dsm ǣnegum 655; gpm ǣnigra 932; nsf ǣnig 802, 2493, 2772; asf ǣnige 972, 2449, 2548; pron *any(one)* nsm ǣnig 3129; (w part gen) nsm 779, 1356, 2007, 2734, 3054; dsm ǣngum 474, 1461, ǣnigum 793, 2416, ǣnegum 842; isn ǣnige þinga *for anything, in any way* 791, 2374, 2905

ǣnlīc adj *peerless, beautiful* nsf 251, ǣnlīcu 1941

ǣnne see ān

æppelfealu adj *apple-fallow, bay* (i.e. *reddish brown*) npm æppelfealuwe 2165

ǣr I. adv *before, previously* w pret vb (to which ǣr often gives pluperfect sense) 15, 655, 694, 757, 778, 825, 831, 941, 1054, 1079, 1187, 1238, 1300, 1356, 1381, 1466, 1525, 1587, 1615, 1618, 1676, 1751, 1858, 1891, 1915, 2248, 2349, 2562, 2595, 2606, 2712, 2777, 2787, 2848, 2861, 2973, 3003, 3060, 3075, 3164; *first* 3038; *always* (ǣr ond sīð) 2500; *at any time* (ǣr ne siþðan) 718; *yet . . . not* (nō þȳ ǣr) 754, 2160, *no sooner (for that)* 1502, 2081, 2373, 2466; w pres vb *sooner* 1182; *sooner . . . before , rather . . . than* ǣr . . . ǣr) 1370–1. II. conj *before* 252, 264, 676, 1496, 2019, 2818; ǣrþon 731. III. prep wd *before* 1388, 2320, 2798 [MnE ere]

ǣrdæg m *before day, earliest dawn* ds ǣrdæge 126, 1311, 2942

ǣrende n *message* as 270, 345

ǣrest adv *first* 6, 616, 1697, 1947, 2157, 2556, 2926

ǣrfæder m *old father, late father* ns 2622

ǣrgestrēon n *ancient treasure* as 1757; gp ǣrgestrēona 2232

ǣrgeweorc n *ancient work* ns 1679

ǣrgōd adj *good from olden times* nsm 130, 1329, 2342; nsn 989, 2586

ærn n *house, dwelling* gs ærnes 2225

ǣror adv *previously* 809, 3168; *first* 2654

ǣrra adj *earlier* dp ǣrran 907, 2237, 3035

ǣrwela m *ancient wealth* as ǣrwelan 2747

ǣs n *carrion* ds ǣse 1332

æsc m *(ash-wood) spear* dp æscum 1772

æscholt n *ash forest, stack of ash-wood spears* ns 330

æscwiga m *warrior, (ash-wood) spear-warrior*
ns 2042

æt prep wd *at* 32, 45, 81, 175, 224, 500, 517,
584, 617, 882, 953, 1073, 1089, 1110, 1114,
1147, 1156, 1166, 1168, 1248, 1267, 1337,
1460, 1477, 1525, 1535, 1588, 1618, 1659,
1665, 1914, 1916, 1923, 2041, 2258, 2270,
2353, 2491, 2526, 2575, 2585, 2612, 2629,
2659, 2681, 2684, 2694, 2709, 2790, 2803,
2823, 2878, 3013, 3026; *from* (with verbs of
taking or receiving) 629, 930, 2374, 2429,
2860

ǣt m *meal* ds ǣte 3026

ætberan IV *carry off, bear* inf 1561; pret ætbær
1s 3092; 3s 519, 624, 2127, 2614; 3p ætbǣron
28

ætfēolan III wd *hold onto* pret 1s ætfealh 968

ætferian 1 wd *carry away from* pret 1s ætferede
1669

ætgædere adv *together* 321, 1164, 1190; samod
ætgædere *all together* 329, 387, 729, 1063

ætgifan V *give* inf 2878

ætgrǣpe adj *at grips with, seizing* nsm 1269

æthweorfan III *return* pret 3s æthwearf 2299

ætrihte adv *almost* 1657

ætsomne adv *together* 307, 402, 544, 2847,
3122; geador ætsomne *all together* 491

ætspringan III *gush out, stream forth* pret 3s
ætspranc 1121

ætstandan VI *stand fixed, stick* pret 3s ætstōd
891

ætsteppan VI *step, advance* pret 3s ætstōp 745

ættren adj *poisonous* nsm 1617

ætwegan V *carry off* pret 3s ætwǣg 1198

ætwindan III wd *escape* pret 3s ætwand 143

ætwītan 1 wa *assign blame for* pret 3p ætwiton
1150 [MnE twit]

æþele adj *noble* nsm 198, 263, 1312; gsn æþelan
2234

æþeling m *atheling, nobleman* ns 130, 1112,
1225, 1329, 1815, 2342, 2506, 3135, æðeling
2188, 2443, 2667, 2715; gs æþelinges 33, 888,
æðelinges 1596, 2424; ds æþelinge 1244,
æðelinge 2374; np æþelingas 3, 982, 1804,
æðelingas 2888; gp æþelinga 118, 1294, 1408,
1920, 3170, æðelinga 2597; dp æþellingum
906

æþelu n p *(noble) lineage* ap 392; dp æþelum
332, 1870, 1949

ǣðm m *breath, breathing* ds ǣðme 2593

bā see bēgen

baldor see bealdor

baluon see bealo

bām see bēgen

bān n *bone* ds bāne 2578; *fang* dp bānum 2692

bana m *slayer, murderer* ns 2613, bona 1743,
2082, 2506, 2824; as bonan 1968, 2485; gs
banan 158; ds 1102, tō banan weorðan *become
the slayer of, kill* 587, bonan 2203; gp banena
2053 [MnE bane]

bāncofa m *bone chamber* (i.e. *body*) ds bāncofan
1445

bānfāg adj *decorated with bone* asn 780

bānfæt n *bone vessel* (i.e. *body*) ap bānfatu 1116

bānhring m *bone-ring* (i.e. *vertebra*) ap bānhringas 1567

bānhūs n *bone-house* (i.e. *body*) as 2508; ap
3147

bānloca m. *bone-lock* (i.e. *joint*) np bānlocan
818; ap 742

gebannan VII wd of person and a of thing
command, order inf 74 [MnE ban 'summon']

gebarn see gebyrnan

bāt m *ship, boat* ns 211

bātweard m *ship-guard, boat-warden* ds bātwearde 1900

bǣdan 1 *exhort, encourage* pret 3s bǣdde 2018;
oppress p ptc gebǣded 2580, 2826; *impel* 3117

bǣl n *funeral pyre* as 1109, 1116, bēl 2126, bǣl
2818; ds bǣle 2803; *fire* ds 2308, 2322

bǣlfȳr n *funeral fire* gp bǣlfȳra 3143

bǣlstede m *place for the funeral pyre* ds 3097
[MnE -stead]

bǣlwudu m *wood for the funeral pyre* as 3112

bǣr f *bier* ns 3105

gebǣran 1 *bear oneself* inf 1012; *fare, endure*
2824

bærnan 1 *burn* inf 1116, 2313

gebǣtan 1 *bridle, equip with a bit* p ptc gebǣted
1399

bæð n *bath* as 1861

be, bī prep wd *by, beside* 36, 566, 814, 1191,
1537, 1574, 1647, 1872, 1905, 2243, bī 1188,
2438, 2716, 2756, big 3047; be (bī) . . .
twēonum *between* 858, 1297, 1685, 1956;
about, concerning 1723; *along* 1573, 2542; *in
comparison to* 1284; *according to* 1950; *from*
1722; be healfe *alongside* 2262; be ðē lifigendum *during your lifetime* 2665

bēacen n *beacon, monument* ns 570; as bēcn
3160; gp bēacna 2777

gebēacnian 2 *indicate, show* p ptc gebēacnod
140 [MnE beckon]

beado f *battle* gs beadwe 1539, beaduwe 2299;
gp beadwa 709

beadogrīma m *battle-mask, helmet* as beado-
grīman 2257

beadohrægl n *battle garment, mail-coat* ns 552
[MnE -rail]

beadolēoma m *battle-gleam, sword* ns 1523

beadomēce m *battle-sword* np beadomēcas
1454

beadorinc m *warrior* gp beadorinca 1109

beadufolm f *battle-hand* as beadufolme 990

beadulāc n *war-sport, battle* ds beadulāce 1561

beadurōf adj *battle-strong* gsm beadurōfes 3160

beadurūn f *hostile utterance (battle-rune)* as
beadurūne 501

beaduscearp adj *battle-sharp* asn 2704

beaduscrūd n *battle-garment, corslet* ns 2660;
gp beaduscrūda 453 [MnE -shroud]

beaduserce f *mail-coat, battle-sark* as beadusercean 2755

bēag m *ring (of gold used as ornaments or as
treasure which leaders distributed to their followers)* np bēagas 3014; ap 80, 523, 1719,
1750, 2370, 2635, 3009, 3105; gp bēaga 35,
352, 1487, 2284, 2995; *necklace, gold torque* ns
bēah 1211; as 2812, bēg 3163; gs bēages 1216;
crown (or necklace) ds bēage 1163; *hilt-ring
(on a sword)* as bēah 2041

bēaggyfa m *ring-giver, lord* gs bēaggyfan 1102

bēaghroden adj (p ptc) *ring-adorned* ns 623

bēah see **bēag, būgan**

bēahhord n *ring-hoard* gs bēahhordes 894; gp
bēahhorda 921; dp bēahhordum 2826

bēahsele m *hall (in which a lord distributes
rings)* ns 1177

bēahðegu f *receiving of rings* ds bēahðege 2176

bēahwriða m *ring-band, precious circlet* as
bēahwriðan 2018 [MnE -wreath]

bealdian 2 *be brave, show oneself bold* pret 3s
bealdode 2177

bealdor m *lord* ns 2567, baldor 2428

bealo adj *baleful, deadly* dp balwon 977

bealo n *evil, affliction, bale* ds bealwe 2826; gp
bealuwa 281, bealwa 909, bealewa 2082

bealocwealm m ns *baleful death* 2265

bealohycgende adj (pres ptc) *hostile* gp bealohycgendra 2565

bealohȳdig adj *hostile, intending evil* ns 723

bealonīð m *baleful affliction* ns 2404; as 1758;
ds bealonīðe 2714

bearhtm m *brightness* ns 1766; *bright sound* as
1431

bearm m *bosom* ns 1137; as 35, 214, 896, 2775;
ds bearme 40; *lap* bearm as 1144, 2194;
possession ds bearme 21, 2404

bearn (67) see **beirnan**

bearn n *son, offspring* ns 469, 499, 529, 631,
888, 910, 957, 1383, 1408, 1473, 1651, 1817,
1837, 1999, 2177, 2387, 2425; as 1546, 2121,
2619; ds bearne 2370; np bearn 59, 70, 878,
1189, 2184, 2597, 3170; ap 605, 1088, 1141,
2956; gp bearna 1005, 1367, 2224, 2433; dp
bearnum 150, 1074 [MnE bairn]

bearngebyrdo f *child-bearing* gs 946

bearu m *grove* np bearwas 1363

bēatan VII *beat, tramp, overcome* pres 3s bēateð
2265; p ptc gebēaten 2359

bebēodan II *instruct, command* pret 3s bebēad
401, 1975

bebeorgan III *protect, guard* (w refl d) inf 1746;
imp s bebeorh 1758

bebūgan II *surround* pres 3s bebūgeð 93, 1223

bebycgan I *sell* pret 1s on . . . bebohte *exchange
for* 2799 [MnE buy]

beceorfan III *cut, carve* (wa of pers and d of
thing cut) pret 1s becearf 2138; 3s 1590

bēcn see **bēacen**

becuman IV *come* pret 3s becōm 115, 192,
2552, 2992, becwōm 1254, 2116, 2365; wa
befall pret 3s 2883 [MnE become]

bedǣlan I *deprive* (wd of thing) p ptc bedǣled
721, 1275 [MnE -deal]

bedd n *bed* as bed 140, 676; gs beddes 1791; dp
beddum 1240

*ge*bedda m *bedfellow* ds gebeddan 665

befǣstan *commit, give over* inf 1115 [MnE
-fast(en)]

befeallan VII *deprive (of)* wd p ptc befeallen
1126, 2256 [MnE -fall]

beflēon II *flee from, escape* infl inf tō befléonne
1003

befōn VII *seize, grip, envelop, surround, encompass* p ptc befongen 976, 1451, 2595, bifon-
gen 2009, befangen 1295, 2274, 2321

beforan adv *in front, ahead* 1412

beforan prep wa *before, into the presence of*
1024; wd *before, in front of* 2497

bēg see **bēag**

begang see **begong**

bēgen num *both* nm 536, 769, 2707; gm bēga
1124; dm bām 2196, 2660; gn bēga 1043,
1873, 2895; af bā 1305, 2063

begitan V *get* pret 3p begēaton 2249; *befall* pret
3s begeat 1068, 1146, 2230; beget 2872; subj
3s begēate 2130

begnornian 2 *lament* pret 3p begnornodon
3178

begong m *region, circuit* as begang 362, 1826, begong 860, 1497, 1773, bigong 2367

begylpan III wa *boast* inf 2006 [MnE yelp]

behealdan VII *hold, occupy* pret 3s behēold 1498; *do, perform* 494, 667; *behold, see* 736

behelan IV *hide* p ptc beholen 414

behōfian 2 wg *have need of* pres 3s 2647 [MnE behoove]

behōn VII *hang (something) onto, behang* p ptc behongen 3139

behrēosan II *deprive* p ptc wd behrorene 2762

behrorene see **behrēosan**

beirnan III *occur, come (into one's mind)* pret 3s bearn 67 [MnE be-run]

bēl see **bǣl**

belēan VI *dissuade from* (wd of pers and a of thing) inf 511

belēosan II *deprive of* p ptc wd beloren 1073 [MnE -lose]

*ge*belgan III *enrage* p ptc gebolgen 723, 1539, 2220, 2304, 2401, 2550, np gebolgne 1431; *offend* pret subj 3s gebulge 2331

belimpan III *befall* pret 3s belamp 2468

belūcan II *lock* pret 3s belēac 1132; *protect* 1s 1770

bemurnan III *mourn, deplore* pret 3s bemearn 907, 1077

bēn f *favour, request* gs bēne 428, 2284

bēna m *requester, petitioner* ns 352, swā hē bēna wæs *as he requested* 3140; np bēnan 364

benc f *bench* ns 492; ds bence 327, 1013, 1188, 1243

bencsweg m *bench harmony* (i.e. *conversation in the hall*) ns 1161

bencþel n *bench-board, bench* np bencþelu 486; ap 1239

bend f *fetter, bond* as 1609; dp bendum 977

benemnan I *declare, swear (an oath)* pret 3s benemde 1097; pret 3p benemdon 3069

benēotan II *deprive of* wd inf 680; pret 3s binēat 2396

bengeat n *gash (wound-gate)* np bengeato 1121

beniman IV *deprive of* wd pret 3s benam 1886

benn f *wound* as benne 2724

bēodan II *offer* inf 385; pret 3p budon 1085; *give* p ptc boden 2957; *announce* inf bīodan 2892

*ge*bēodan II *offer, proffer* inf 603; pret 3s gebēad 2369; *command* inf gebēodan 3110

bēodgenēat m *table-companion* np bēodgenēatas 343; ap 1713

bēon anom *be* imp s bēo 386, 1173, 1226, bīo 2747; pres 1s bēo 1825, eom 335, 407, 1475,

2527; 2s eart 352, 506, 1844, 2813; 3s bið 183, 186, 299, 660, 949, 1059, 1283, 1384, 1388, 1742, 1745, 1762, 1767, 1784, 1835, 1940, 2043, 2444, 2450, 2541, 2890, 3174, is 248, 256, 272, 290, 316, 343, 375, 454, 473, 476, 700, 1176, etc., ys 2093, 2910, 2999, 3084; w negative nis 249, 1361, 1372, 2458, 2532; 1p synt 260, 342; 2p syndon 237, 393; 3p bīoð 2063, sint 388, synt 364, syndon 257, 361, 1230; subj 3s sīe 435, 682, 3105, sig 1778, sȳ 1941, 1831, 2649; wes, wæs, wǣron, næs, etc. see **wesan**

bēor n *beer* ds bēore 480, 531, æt bēore *at the beer-drinking* 2041

beorg, beorh m *hill, cliff* ds beorge 2529, 3143; *elevated shore, high beach* ds 211; ap beorgas 222; *grave-mound, (dragon's) barrow* ns beorh 2241; as 2299, 3097, biorh 2807, beorg 3163; gs beorges 2304, 2322, 2524, 2580, 2755, biorges 3066; ds beorge 2546, 2559, 2842; ap biorgas 2272

beorgan III wd *save (one's life)* inf 1293; pret 3p burgan (= -on) 2599; *protect* inf beorgan 1445

*ge*beorgan III wd *protect* pret 3s gebearh 1548, gebearg 2570

beorh see **beorg**

beorht adj *bright, shining, splendid* ns beorht . . . *bright (day? sun? daylight?)* 1802, nsm beorhta 1177; asm beorhtne 2803; apm beorhte 231, beorhtan 1243; nsn beorht 570, beorhte 997; apn beorht 2313; gsf beorhtre 158; dsf byrhtan 1199; apf beorhte 214, 896; dpf beorhtum 3140. Superl asn beorhtost 2777

beorhte adv *brightly* 1517

beorhtian 2 *glitter, resound brightly* pret 3s beorhtode 1161

beorn (1880) see **byrnan**

beorn m *warrior* ns 2433, biorn 2559; as beorn 1024, 1299, 2121; ds beorne 2260; np beornas 211, 856; gp beorna 2220, biorna 2404

beorncyning m *warrior-king* ns 2148

bēorscealc m *beer-drinker, banqueter* gp bēorscealca 1240

bēorsele m *banquet-hall, beer-hall* ds 482, 492, 1094, bīorsele 2635

bēorþegu f *beer-drinking* ds bēorþege 117, 617

bēot n *vow, formal promise* as 80, 523

*ge*bēotian 2 *vow, make a formal promise* pret 1p gebēotedon 536; pret 3p 480

bēotword n *vow, formal promise* dp bēotwordum 2510

bēoð see bēon

beran IV *bear, wear, carry, bring* inf 48, 231, 291, 1024, 1807, 1920, 2152, 2518, 2754; pres 3s byreð 296, 448, 2055; pres subj 1s bere 437, 1834; 3s 2253; 1p beren 2653; pret 3s bær 495, 711, 846, 896, 1405, 1506, 1982, 2021, 2048, 2244, 2281, 2539, 2661, 2686, 2988, 3124; 3p bǣron 213, 1635, 1889, 2365, bǣran (= -on) 2850; p ptc boren 1192, 1647, 3135

*ge*beran IV *bear, give birth to* p ptc geboren 1703

berēafian 2 wd *deprive, despoil* p ptc berēafod 2746, 2825, 3018 [MnE bereave]

berēofan II *deprive* p ptc berofene 2457, 2931

berian 1 *clear, bare* pret 3p beredon 1239

berstan III *crack, burst* pret 3p burston 760, 818, *burst open* 1121

bescūfan II *shove, cast* inf 184

besettan 1 *adorn, beset* pret 3s besette 1453

besittan V *besiege* pret 3s besæt 2936 [MnE besit]

besmiþian 2 *secure by the smith's work, fasten with forged braces* p ptc besmiþod 775

besnyððan 1 *deprive of* (wa of pers and d of thing) pret 3s besnyðede 2924

bestȳman 1 *soak, drench* p ptc bestȳmed 486 [MnE -steam]

beswǣlan 1 *scorch, singe* p ptc beswǣled 3041

besyrwan 1 *ensnare, trick* inf 713; p ptc besyred 2218; *cunningly accomplish* inf besyrwan 942

*ge*bētan 1 *remedy, settle (by compensation [bōt] or retaliation)* inf 2465; pret 2s gebēttest 1991; pret 3s gebētte 830

betera see gōd

betost see gōd

betst see gōd

betimbran 1 *construct, build* pret 3p betimbredon 3159 [MnE betimber]

betlīc *magnificent, stately* nsn 1925; asn 780

bewǣgnan 1 *offer* p ptc bewǣgned 1193

bewennan 1 *entertain* p ptc np bewenede 1821, biwenede 2035

beweotode see bewitian

bewerian 1 *defend* (wa of thing defended and d of those from whom defended) pret subj 3p beweredon (= -en) 938

bewindan III *grasp* pret 3s bewand 1461; p ptc bewunden 3022; *encircle* p ptc 1031; *envelop* 2424; *encompass* 3052; *intertwine* 3146 [MnE bewind]

bewitian 2 *observe* pres 3p bewitiað 1135; *attend to, watch over* pret 3s beweotede 1796, beweotode 2212; *undertake* pres 3p bewitigað 1428

bewyrcan 1 *surround, enclose* pret 3p beworhton 3161

bī see be

bicgan 1 *pay for* inf 1305 [MnE buy]

bid n *halt* as on bid wrecen *brought to bay* 2962

bīdan I *wait for* wg inf 482, 528, 1268, 1494; pret 1s bād 2736; 3s 82, 709, 1882; *wait, dwell, remain* inf bīdan 2308; pret 3s bād 87, 301, 310, 1313, 2568; 3p bidon 400 [MnE bide]

*ge*bīdan I wg *await* imp p gebīde 2529; *experience, live to see* wa inf gebīdan 638, 934, 1060, 1386, 2342; infl inf (tō) gebīdanne 2452; pret 1s gebād 929; 3s 7, 264, 815, 1618, 2258, 3116; p ptc gebiden 1928; w þæt clause pret 1s gebād 1779; *remain* pret 3s 1720; *endure* infl inf (tō) gebīdanne 2445

biddan V *request, ask* inf wg 427; pres 1s bidde 1231; pret 3s bæd 29, 2282, 3096; *urge* wa pret 3s bæd 617, pret 1s 1994; *pray* pret 3p bǣdon 176

bifōngen see befōn

big see be

bigong see begong

bill n *sword* ns 2777, bil 1567; as 1557, bill 2621; gs billes 2060, 2485, 2508; ds bille 2359; gp billa 583, 1144; dp billum 40

bindan III *bind, oppress* p ptc gebunden 1743, 2111, asn 1900; apn 871; p ptc asm *well-braced* bundenne 216; *ornamented* nsm bunden 1285

*ge*bindan III *bind* pret 1s geband 420; p ptc gebunden 1531

binēotan see benēotan

bīor see bēor

biorh see beorh

biorn see beorn

bīoð see bēon

bīodan see bēodan

bisigu see bysigu

bītan I *cut, bite* inf 1454, 1523; pret 3s bāt 742, 2578

bite m *cut* as 2259, ds 2060 [MnE bite]

biter adj *sharp* dsm biteran 1746; dpn 2692; asn biter 2704; *angry* np bitere 1431 [MnE bitter]

bitre adv *grievously* 2331

bið see bēon

biwennan see bewennan

blāc adj *gleaming* asm blācne 1517 [MnE bleak]

blanca m *horse* dp blancum 856

blæc adj *black* nsm blaca 1801

blǣd m *glory, renown* ns 18, 1124, 1703, *flowering* 1761

blǣdāgende pres ptc *glorious ones, possessors of glory* nsm blǣdāgande 1013

blǣdfæst adj *splendid* asm blǣdfæstne 1299

blēate adv *wretchedly* 2824

blīcan I *gleam* inf 222

blīðe adj *gracious, kind* nsm 436; *joyous* asm blīðne 617 [MnE blithe]

blīðheort adj *joyful at heart* nsm 1802 [MnE blitheheart(ed)]

blōd n *blood* ns 1121, 1616, 1667; as 742; ds blōde 486, 934, 1422, 1594, 1880, 2974, on blōde *bloody* 847

geblōdegod see blōdgian

blōdfāg adj *blood-stained* nsm 2060

blōdgian 2 *make bloody, bloody* p ptc geblōdegod 2692

blōdig adj *bloody* dsm blōdigan 2440; asn blōdig 448; asf blōdge 990

blōdigtōð adj *bloody-toothed* nsm 2082

blōdrēow adj *bloodthirsty* nsn 1719

blondenfeax adj *grizzly-haired, grey-haired* nsm 1791, blondenfexa 2962; dsm blondenfeaxum 1873; npm blondenfeaxe 1594

boden see bēodan

bodian 2 *proclaim* pret 3s bodode 1802 [MnE bode]

gebogen see gebūgan

bolca m *deck* as bolcan 231

bold n *hall, building* ns 997, 1925; as 2196; gp bolda 2326

boldāgend m *man of rank, hall owner* gp boldāgendra 3112

gebolgen see gebelgan

bolgenmōd adj *swollen with rage, enraged* nsm 709, 1713

bolster m or n *cushion* dp bolstrum 1240 [MnE bolster]

bona see bana

bongār m *deadly spear* ns 2031 [MnE bane-]

bord n *shield* ns 2673; as 2524; gp borda 2259 [MnE board]

bordhæbbend m *shield-bearer* np bordhæbbende 2895 [MnE board-have(r)]

bordhrēoða m *shield-protection, shield* ds bordhrēoðan 2203

bordrand m *shield* as 2559

bordweal m *shield-wall, phalanx of shields* as 2980 [MnE board-wall]

bordwudu m ap 1243

born see byrnan

bōt f *relief, remedy* ns 281; as bōte 909, 934; *compensation, legal recompense for an injury* gs 158 [MnE boot 'something to equalize a trade']

botm m *bottom* ds botme 1506

brād adj *broad, ample, spacious* nsm 3157; asm brādne 2978; nsn brāde 2207; asn brād 1546, 3105

brand see brond

gebræc n *clash* as 2259

brecan IV *break, tear* inf 2980; pret 3s bræc 1511 (*were tearing*), 1567, hine fyrwyt bræc *he was eager to know* 232, 1985, 2784; pret subj 3s brǣce 1100; *burst forth* inf brecan 2546

gebrecan IV *break, crush* pret 3s gebræc 2508, ptc gebrocene 2063, gebrocen 3147

brecð f *grief, heartbreak* brecða np 171

bregdan III *weave* (metaphorically, *to interlink chainmail*), *move quickly* pret 2p brugdon 514; p ptc brōden 552, 1548, brogdne 2755; *pull* inf bregdan 707, pret 3s brægd 1539; *draw (a sword or knife)* pret 3s 794; *contrive* inf bregdon (= -an) 2167 [MnE braid]

gebregdan III *weave* (metaphorically, *to interlink chainmail*) p pct gebrōden 1443; *draw (a sword or knife)* pret 1s (wi) gebrǣd 1664; pret 3s 2703; (wa) 2562, gebrægd 1564

brego m *lord* ns 427, 609; gs 1954

bregorōf adj *powerful, majestic* ns 1925; cf. 2792 n

bregostōl m *throne, royal power* as 2196, 2370, 2389 [MnE -stool]

brēme adj *famous* ns 18

brenting m *tall ship* ap brentingas 2807

brēost n, f *breast* ns 2176, 2331; as 453; dp (w sg meaning) brēostum 552, 2550, 2714

brēostgehygd n., f *heart's thought* dp brēostgehygdum 2818

brēostgewǣde n *breast-garment, corslet* np (w sg meaning) brēostgewǣdu 1211; ap (w sg meaning) 2162

brēosthord n *mind, thought* (lit. *breast-hoard*) ns 1719; as 2792

brēostnet n *corslet, breast-net* ns 1548

brēostweorðung f *breast adornment, gold collar* as brēostweorðunge 2504

brēostwylm m *tear, weeping* as 1877 [MnE breast-well(ing)]

brēotan II *kill, break* pret 3s brēat 1713 [MnE britt(le)]

brim n *sea* ns 847, 1594; gs brimes 28, 2803; np brimu 570

brimclif n *sea-cliff* ap brimclifu 222

brimlād f *sea-journey* as brimlade 1051

brimliðend m *seafarer* ap brimliðende 568

brimstrēam m *sea-current* ap brimstrēamas 1910

brimwīsa m *sea-king* as brimwīsan 2930

brimwylf f *she-wolf of the sea or mere* ns 1506, 1599

brimwylm m *sea-surge, surging water* ns 1494

bringan I *bring* inf 1862, 2148, 2504; pres 1s bringe 1829; pret 1p brōhton 1653

gebringan I *bring* pres subj 1p gebringan (= -en) 3009

brōden see bregdan

brōdenmǣl see brogdenmǣl

brōga m *terror* ns 1291, 2324, 2565; ds brogan 583

brogdenmǣl n *damascened sword* ns 1667, brōdenmǣl 1616

brond m *fire* ns 3014; ds bronde 2126, 2322; gp bronda 3160; *sword* ns brond 1454; as brand 1020 [MnE brand]

bront adj *tall* asm brontne 238; *deep* asm 568

brosnian 2 *decay, rust away* pres 3s brosnað 2260

brōðor m *brother* ns 1324, 2440, 2978; gs 2619; ds brēþer 1262; dp brōðrum 587, 1074

gebrōðor mp *brothers* dp gebrōðrum 1191

brūcan II wg *enjoy, make use of* inf 894, 1045, 2241, 2812, 3100; pres 3s brūceð 1062; imp s brūc 1177, 1216, 2162; pret 1s brēac 1487; pret 3s 1953, 2097 [MnE brook]

brūn adj *shining, burnished* nsn 2578 [MnE brown]

brūnecg adj *with shining blade* asn 1546 [MnE brown, edge]

brūnfāg adj *shining, burnished* asm brūnfāgne 2615

brȳd f *wife* ns 2031; as 2930; ap brȳde 2956 [MnE bride]

brȳdbūr m *bed-chamber* ds brȳdbūre 921 [MnE bride, bower]

brynelēoma m *firelight* ns 2313 [MnE burn-]

brynewylm m *surge of fire* dp brynewylmum 2326

brytnian 2 *dispense* pret 3s brytnade 2383

brytta m *dispenser, giver* ns 607, 1170, 2071; as bryttan 35, 352, 1487, 1922

bryttian 2 *dispense* pres 3s bryttað 1726

būan VII *occupy, inhabit* inf 3065; būon (= -an) *dwell* 2842

gebūan VII *occupy, lodge in* p ptc gebūn 117

būfolc n *nation* ns 2220

būgan II *fall (in battle)* inf 2918, 2974; *rest, lie idle* pres 3s būgeð 2031; *lower oneself (to a sitting position), sit down* pret 3p bugon 327, 1013; *retreat, flee* pret 3s bēah 2956; pret 3p bugon 2598 [MnE bow]

gebūgan II *fall down, fall (in battle)* pret 3s gebēah 1540, 2980; *coil oneself* pret 3s 2567; p ptc gebogen 2569; *lie down on* pret 3s gebēah 690, gebēag 1241

bundenheord adj *with hair bound up* nsf bundenheorde 3151 [MnE bounden-]

bundenstefna m *ship with bound prow* ns 1910 [MnE bounden, stem]

bune f *drinking vessel, goblet* np bunan 3047; ap 2775

būr m *private chamber* ds būre 1310, 2455; *small dwelling separate from the main hall* dp būrum 140 [MnE bower]

burh f *stronghold, residence of an important personage* as 523; ds byrig 1199; dp (w sg meaning) burgum 53, 1968, 2433, 2452 [MnE borough]

burhloca m *stronghold, royal residence* ds under burhlocan *in the royal residence* 1928 [MnE borough, lock]

burhstede m *stronghold, grounds of a stronghold* as 2265 [MnE borough, stead]

burhwela m *wealth of the royal stronghold* gs burhwelan 3100 [MnE borough, weal]

burne f *stream* gs burnan 2546

būton prep wd *except, but* 73, 705

būton conj w ind *except that, but that* 1560; w subj būtan *unless* 966; after negative, no verb following, būton *except for* 657 (+ dat), 879 (+ nom); ne ... mā ... būton *no ... more ... than* 1614

gebycgan I *obtain, pay for* pret 3s gebohte 973, 2481; p ptc npm gebohte 3014 [MnE buy]

byldan I *encourage, favour* inf 1094

bȳme f *trumpet* as bȳman 2943

gebyrd f *fate* as on gebyrd *to their fate* 1074

byre m *son, youth* ns 2053, 2445, 2621, 2907, 3110; np 1188; ap 2018

byrele m *cupbearer* np byrelas 1161

byreð see beran

byrgean I *taste, eat* inf 448

byrht see beorht

byrig see burh

byrnan III *burn* pres ptc byrnende 2272, 2569; pret 3s beorn 1880, born 2673

gebyrnan III *to be burned* pret 3s gebarn 2697

byrne f *corslet, mail-coat, byrnie* ns 405, 1245, 1629, 2660, 2673; as byrnan 1022, 1291,

byrne (*cont.*)
2153, 2524, 2615, 2621, 2812, 2868; gs 2260; ds 2704; np 327; dp byrnum 40, 238, 2529, 3140

byrnwiga m *mailed warrior* ns 2918

bysigu f *distress, care, affliction* gs bisigu 281; dp bisgum 1743, bysigum 2580 [MnE busi(-ness)]

byð see **bēon**

bȳwan I *polish, burnish* inf 2257

camp m, n *battle* ds campe 2505

can see **cunnan**

candel f *candle* ns rodores candel *sun* 1572

care see **cearu**

ceald adj *cold* apm cealde 1261; dpm cealdum 2396; superl nsn cealdost 546

cēap m *purchase, bargain* ns 2415; ds cēape 2482 [MnE cheap]

gecēapian 2 *purchase, acquire* p ptc gecēapod 3012

cearian 2 *care, be concerned* pres 3s cearað 1536

cearsīð m *expedition fraught with care* dp cearsīðum 2396

cearu f *care, sorrow* ns 1303; as care 3171

cearwylm m *seething sorrow* np cearwylmas 282; dp cearwælmum 2066 [MnE care, well(ing)]

ceasterbūend m *local inhabitant* dp ceasterbūendum 768

cempa m *warrior* ns 1312, 1551, 1585, 1761, 2078; ds cempan 1948, 2044, 2502, 2626; ap 206

cēne adj *brave* gpm cēnra 768; superl apm cēnoste 206 [MnE keen]

cennan I *show, make (oneself) known* imp sg cen 1219

cennan I *give birth to, be born* pret 3s cende 943; p ptc cenned 12

cēnðu f *bravery* as 2696

cēol m *ship* ns 1912; as 38, 238; gs cēoles 1806 [MnE keel 'flat-bottomed barge']

ceorl m *man* ns 908; ds ceorle 2444, 2972; np ceorlas 202, 416, 1591 [MnE churl]

cēosan II *choose* inf cīosan *accept* 2376; pret subj 3s cure 2818

gecēosan II *choose* imp s gecēos 1759; infl inf (tō)gecēosenne 1851; pret 3s gecēas 1201, 2469, 2638; p ptc apm gecorone 206

cīosan see **cēosan**

clamm m *grip* dp clammum 963, 1335, clommum 1502

clif n *cliff* ap clifu 1911

clomm see **clamm**

gecnāwan VII *recognize* inf 2047 [MnE know]

cnihtwesende adj *being a boy, as a youth* as 372; np 535

cnyht m *boy* dp cnyhtum 1219 [MnE knight]

cnyssan I *strike* pret 3p cnysedan 1328

cōl adj *cool* compar np cōlran 282, 2066

collenferhð adj *boldhearted* ns 1806, collenferð 2785

con see **cunnan**

const see **cunnan**

corðer n *warrior troop* ds corþre 1153, corðre 3121

costian 2 wg *test, make trial of* pret 3s costode 2084

gecranc see **gecringan**

cræft m *power, strength* ns 1283; as 418, 699, 2696; ds cræfte 982, 1219, 2181, 2360; *cunning* ds cræfte 2219, 2168, *craftiness* 2290

cræftig adj *powerful* ns 1466, 1962 [MnE crafty]

cringan III *fall (in battle)* pret 3p crungon 1113; pret subj 1s crunge 635 [MnE cringe]

gecringan III *fall (in battle)* pret 3s gecranc 1209, gecrang 1337, gecrong 1568, 2505

gecrong see **gecringan**

cuma m *visitor* ns 1806 [MnE come(r)]

cuman IV *come* inf 244, 281, 1869; pres 2s cymest 1382; 3s cymeð 2058; pres subj 3s cume 23; 1p cymen 3106; pret 1s cwōm 419, 2009, cōm 430; 3s cwōm 1162, 1235, 1338, 1774, 1888, 1973, 2073, 2124, 2188, 2303, 2404, 2556, 2669, 2914, cōm 569, 702, 710, 720, 825, 1077, 1133, 1279, 1506, 1600, 1623, 1644, 1802, 2103, 2359, 2944; 1p cwōmon 268; 2p 239; 3p 324, cwōman 650, cōmon 1640; pret subj 3s cwōme 731, cōme 1597; p ptc cumen 376, 2646, np cumene 361, 1819

cumbol n *battle standard* gs cumbles 2505

cunnan pret-pres *know how to, be able to* w inf pres 3s con 1746; 3p cunnon 50; pret 3s cūþe 90, 1445, 2372; 3p cūþon 182; wa or clause pres 1s can 1180; 2s const 1377; 3s can 392, con 1739, 2062; 3p cunnon 162, 1355; pres subj 2s cunne 2070; pret 1s cūðe 372; 3s 359, 2012, 3067; 3p cūðon 119, 180, 418, 1233 [MnE can]

cunnian 2 wg or a *make trial of, test, explore* inf 1426, 1444, 2045; pret 3s cunnode 1500; 2p cunnedon 508

cure see **cēosan**

cūð adj *known, well known* ns 150, 410, 705,

2135, 2178, 2923; asf cūþe 1303, 1634: npm
867; npf 1145; apm 1912 [MnE (un)couth]
cūðlīce adv *openly, brazenly* compar cūðlīcor
244
cwealm m *murder, death* as 107, 3149 [MnE
qualm (?)]
cwealmbealu n *death-bale, execution* as 1940
cwealmcuma m *murderous visitor* as cwealm-
cuman 792
cweccan I *shake* pret 3s cwehte 235
cwellan I *kill* pret 2s cwealdest 1334 [MnE
quell]
cwēn f *queen* ns 62, 613, 623, 923, 1153, 1932,
2016; as 665
cwēnlīc adj *queenly, befitting a queen* nsf 1940
cweðan V *say, speak* pres 3s cwið 2041; pret 3s
cwæð 92, 199, 315, 1810, 1894, 2158, 2246,
2662, 2939; pret 3p cwædon 3180 [MnE
quoth, (be)queath]
*ge*cweðan V *say* pret 2s gecwæde 2664; 3s
gecwæð 857, 874, 987; 1p gecwædon 535
cwico adj *alive* nsm 3093; asm cwicne 792,
2785; gsn cwices 2314; npn cwice 98 [MnE
quick]
cwīðan I wa *lament, bewail* inf 2112, 3171
cyme m *coming* np 257
cymen see **cuman**
cȳmlīce adv *becomingly* compar cȳmlīcor 38
[MnE comely]
cyn n *courtesy, court usage* gp cynna 613
*ge*cynde adj *natural, inherited in common* nsn
2197, 2696 [MnE kind]
cynedōm m *kingship, kingdom, royal power* as
2376
cyning m *king* ns 11, 863, 920, 1010, 1153,
1306, 1870, 1885, 1925, 2110, 2158, 2191,
2209, 2356, 2390, 2417, 2430, 2702, 2980,
kyning 619; as cyning 1851, 2396, 3171; gs
cyninges 867, 1210, 2912, cyniges 3121; ds
cyninge 3093
cyningbald adj *brave as a king, very brave* npm
cyningbalde 1634 [MnE king, bold]
kyningwuldor n *glorious king* ns 665
cynn n *kin, race* ns cyn 461; as 421, 1093, 1690;
gs cynnes 701, 712, 735, 883, 1058, 1729,
2008, 2234, 2354, 2813; ds cynne, 107, 810,
914, 1725, 2885; gp cynna 98, *usage* 613
*ge*cȳpan I *buy, hire* inf 2496
*ge*cyssan I *kiss* pret 3s gecysste 1870
cyst f *the best* ns 802, 1232, 1559, 1697; as 673;
excellence, good attribute dp cystum 867, 923
cȳðan I *display, exercise* inf 1940, 2695; imp s

cȳð 659; p ptc *manifest* gecȳðed 700, *well
known* 262, 349, 923
gecȳðan I *make known, report* inf 354; infl inf
(tō) gecȳðanne 257; p ptc nsm gecȳðed 1971,
2324
gedāl n *departure* ns 3068

daroð m *spear* dp dareðum 2848
dǣd f *deed, act, exploit* as 585, 940, 2890, dǣde
889; ap dǣda 195; gp 181, 479, 2646, 2838,
hafað . . . dǣda gefondad *has . . . had his
portion of (violent) deeds* 2454; dp dǣdum
954, 1227, 2059, 2178, 2436, 2467, 2666,
2710, 2858, 2902, 3096
dǣdcēne adj *brave in deeds* nsm 1645
dǣdfruma m *doer of deeds* ns 2090
dǣdhata m *one who shows hatred through his
deeds, perpetrator* ns 275
dæg m *day* ns 485, 731, 2306, 2646; as 2115,
2399, 2894, 3069; gs dæges 1495, 1600, 2320,
(adv *by day*) 1935, 2269; ds dæge 197, 790,
806; dp dagum 3159
dæghwīl f *day* ap dæghwīla 2726 [MnE day-
while]
dægrīm n *count of one's days, life span* ns 823
dǣl m *part, portion* ns 2843, oferhygda dǣl *a
(large) measure of arrogance* 1740; as 621,
1150, 1752, 2028, 2068, 2245, 3127; ap
worolde dǣlas *parts* (i.e. *regions*) *of the world*
1732 [MnE deal]
dǣlan I *dispense, distribute* inf 1970; pres 3s
1756; pret 3s dǣlde 80, 1686; pres subj 3s
eofoðo dǣle *fight* 2534 [MnE deal]
gedǣlan I *share out* inf 71; *separate, sever* inf
2422; pret subj 3s gedǣlde 731
dēad adj *dead* nsm 467, 1323, 2372; asm dēadne
1309
gedēaf see **gedūfan**
dēagan VII *hide* (?), *die* (?) pret 3s dēog 850
dēah see **dugan**
deall adj *proud, exulting* npm (þrýðum) dealle
exulting (in [their] strength) 494
dear see **durran**
dearst see **durran**
dēað m *death* ns 441, 447, 488, 1491, 1768,
2119, 2236, 2728, 2890; as 2168, dēoð 1278;
gs dēaðes 2269, 2454; ds dēaþe 1388, dēaðe
1589, 2843, 3045
dēaðbedd n *bed of death* ds dēaðbedde 2901
dēaðcwalu f *death* dp dēaðcwalum 1712
dēaðcwealm m *death, killing* as 1670
dēaðdæg m *death-day* ds dēaðdæge 187, 885
dēaðfǣge adj *death-doomed* ns 850

dēaþscūa m *death-shadow, murderous ogre* ns 160

dēaðwērig adj *death-weary* asm dēaðwērigne 2125

dēaþwīc n *place of death* as 1275

gedēfe adj *fitting* nsn 561, 1670, 3174; *good* nsm 1227

dēman 1 *adjudge, assign* pres subj 3s dēme 687; *judge favourably, praise* pret 3p dēmdon 3174 [MnE deem]

dēmend m *judge* as 181

denn n *den, lair* as 2759; gs dennes 3045

dēofol m, n *devil, demon* gs dēofles 2088; gp dēofla 756, 1680

dēog see **dēagan**

dēogol adj *secret, secluded* nsm 275; asn dȳgel 1357

dēop adj *deep* asn 509, 1904

dēop n *deep place* as 2549

dēope adv *solemnly* dīope 3069 [MnE deep(ly)]

dēor adj *brave, ferocious* nsm 1933, dīor 2090

deorc adj *dark* nsm 160, 1790; dpf deorcum 275, 2211

dēore adj *dear, beloved, costly, noble* asn 2254, dȳre 2050, 2306; dsn dēoran 561; dsm dēorum 1528, 1879; nsf dīore 1949; gsf dēorre 488; npn dȳre 3048; apm dēore 2236, dȳre 3131. **Superl** asm dēorestan 1309

dēorlīc adj *brave* asf dēorlīce 585

dēoð see **dēað**

dēð see **dōn**

gedīgan 1 *survive, endure* inf 2291, gedȳgan 2531, 2549; pres 2s gedīgest 661; 3s gedīgeð 300; pret 1s gedīgde 578, 1655; pret 3s 2350, 2543

dīope see **dēope**

dīor see **dēor**

dīore see **dēore**

disc m *dish* np discas 3048; ap 2775

dōgor n *day* gs dōgores 219, 605; ds dōgor 1395, dōgore 1797, 2573; gp dōgora 88, dōgera 823, dōgra 1090; dp dōgrum 2200, 2392

dōgorgerīm n *count of days, life span* gs dōgorgerīmes 2728

dohte(st) see **dugan**

dohtor f *daughter* ns 1076, 1929, 1981, 2020; as 375, 2997; ds 2174 (or ns)

dolgilp n *foolish boast* ds dolgilpe 509 [MnE dol(tish) yelp]

dollīc adj *foolish* gpf dollīcra 2646

dolsceaða m *rash foe* as dolsceaðan 479

dōm m *judgement, determination* as 2147, 2820,

2964; gs dōmes 978, 3069; ds dōme 441, 895, 1098, 2776; *glory, fame* (i.e. *favourable judgement by others*) ns dōm 885, 954, 1528; as 1491, 2666; gs dōmes 1388; ds dōme 1470, 1645, *custom, honour* 1720, 2179; *decree, authority* ns dōm 2858 [MnE doom]

dōmlēas adj *infamous* as dōmlēasan 2890 [MnE doom, less]

dōn anom *do* inf 1172, dôn 1534, 2166; pres 3s dêð 1058, 1134, 2470, 2859; 3p dōð 1231; pret 1s dyde 1381, 1824, 2521; 2s dydest 1676; 3s dyde 444, 956, 1891, 2809; 3p dydon 44, 1238, 1828; *put, place, take* inf dôn 1116; pret 3s dyde 671, 1144, 2809; 3p dydon 3070, 3163; *consider, regard* pret 3s dyde 2348

gedōn anom *do* inf hyne . . . micles wyrðne . . . gedōn *do him much honour* (i.e. *make him worthy of much*) 2186; *make* pres 3s gedēð 1732; *put, place* inf gedōn 2090

dorste see **durran**

draca m *dragon* ns 892, 2211; as dracan 2402, 3131; gs 2088, 2290, 2549 [MnE drake 'dragon']

gedræg n *clamour, hubbub* as 756

drēam m *joy, revelry* ns 497; as 88; ds drēame 1275; gp drēama 850; dp drēamum 99, 721 [MnE dream]

drēamhealdende adj *possessing joy, joyful* nsm 1227

drēamlēas adj *joyless* nsm 1720

drēfan 1 *stir up* inf 1904; p ptc gedrēfed 1417

drēogan II *strive* pret 3s drēah 2179; sundnytte drēah *swam* 2360; 3p gewin drugon *fought, engaged in conflict* 798; sīð drugon *journeyed, performed a journey* 1966; *perform* inf drēogan 1470; *experience, endure* inf drēogan 589; p ptc gedrogen 2726; imp s drēoh 1782; pret 1s drēah 422; 3s 131; 3p drugon 831, 1858; *suffer* (intr) 3p 15 [archaic MnE dree]

drēor m, n *blood* ds drēore 447

drēorfāh adj *bloodstained* nsm 485

drēorig adj *bloody* nsn 1417; asm drīorigne 2789 [MnE dreary]

gedrēosan II *decline* inf 2666; pres 3s gedrēoseð 1754

drepan V, IV *hit (the mark), strike (home)* pret 1s drep 2880; p ptc drepen 1745, dropen 2981

drepe m *blow* as 1589

drīfan I *drive* inf 1130; pres 3p drīfað 2808

driht- see **dryht-**

drincan III *drink* pret 3s dranc 742; 3p druncon 1233, 1648; p ptc *having drunk* druncen

531, 1467, npm druncne 480, 1231; apm 2179

drincfæt see dryncfæt

drīorig see drēorig

drohtoð m *situation, condition* ns 756

dropen see drepan

drūsian 2 *subside* pret 3s drūsade 1630 [MnE drowse]

gedryht f *troop, band* ns 431; as 662, 1672, gedriht 118, 357, 633

dryhtbearn n *well-born son* np 2035

dryhten m *lord, prince* ns 686, 696, 1484, 1824, 2000, 2338, 2402, 2560, 2576, 2901, 2991, drihten 108, 1050, 1554, 1841, 2186; as 181, 187, dryhten 1831, 2789; gs dryhtnes 441, drihtnes 940; ds dryhtne 1692, 1779, 2330, 2483, 2753, 2796, drihtne 1398

dryhtguma m *retainer, warrior, man* ns 1768; ds drihtguman 1388; np 99, dryhtguman 1231; dp dryhtgumum 1790

dryhtlīc adj *lordly, noble* nsn 892; asn drihtlīce 1158

dryhtmāðum m *lordly treasure* gp dryhtmāðma 2843

dryhtscype m *noble deeds, valour* as drihtscype 1470

dryhtsele m *splendid hall* ns 767, drihtsele 485; as dryhtsele 2320

dryhtsybb f *alliance of nations, peace* gs dryhtsibbe 2068

dryncfæt n *drinking cup* as 2254, drincfæt 2306

drysmian 2 *become gloomy* pres 3s drysmaþ 1375

gedūfan II *penetrate* pret 3s gedēaf 2700 [MnE dive]

dugan pret-pres *be mighty, be good, do well* pres 3s dēah 369, 573, 1839; pres subj 3s duge 589, 1660, 2031; *treat* pret 2s dohtest 1821; 3s se þe ēow wēlhwylcra wilna dohte *which had power with respect to your every desire,* (i.e. *was willing to give you whatever you desired*) 1344; subj 2s dohte 526

duguð f *veteran retainers, proven warriors* (*sometimes contrasted with* geogoþ *young warriors*) ns 498, 1790, 2254; gs duguþe 160, 359, 488, 621, 1674, 2238, 2658; ds duguðe 2020, dugoðe 2920, 2945; dp dugeðum 2501; *lavishly* gp duguða (adv) 2035; dp duguðum dēmdon *praised highly* 3174

durran pret-pres *dare* pres 2s dearst 527; 3s dear 684; pres subj 2s dyrre 1379; pret 3s dorste 1462, 1468, 1933, 2735; 3p dorston 2848

duru f *door* ns 721

dwellan I *impair* pres 3s dweleð 1735

dyde see dōn

dydon see dōn

gedȳgan see gedīgan

dȳgel see dēogol

dyhtig adj *strong* ns 1287 [MnE doughty]

dynnan I *resounded* pret 3s dynede 767, 1317, 2558 [MnE din]

dȳre see dēore

dyrne adj *concealed, secret, furtive, mysterious* nsn 271; nsm 1879; asm dyrnne 2320; dsm dyrnum 2168, dyrnan 2290; gpm dyrnra 1357

dyrre see durran

dyrstig adj *daring* nsm 2838

ēac adv *also* 97, 388, 433, 1683, 2776, ēc 3131 [archaic MnE eke]

ēacen adj *mighty* ns 198, 1663; dsf ēacnum 2140; *vast* npm ēacne 1621

ēacencræftig adj *mighty, exceedingly strong* nsn 3051; asn 2280

ēadig adj *blessed, wealthy* nsm 1225, 2470

ēadiglīce adv *happily* 100

eafor see eofer

eafora m *son, offspring, scion* ns eafera 12, 19, 897, eafora 375, 2358, 2992; as eaferan 1547, 1847; gs eaforan 2451; np eaferan 2475; dp eaferum 1068, 1710, 2470, eaferan 1185

eafoð n *strength* ns 902; as 602, 960, 2349; gs eafoþes 1466, 1763; ap eofoðo 2534; dp eafeþum 1717

ēage n *eye* gp ēagena 1766; dp ēagum 726, 1781, 1935

ēagorstrēam m *sea current* as 513

eahta num *eight* g 3123; a 1035

eahtian 2 *attend to, study* pret 3p eahtedon 172; *watch over* pret 3s eahtode 1407; *esteem, praise* pres 3p ehtigað 1222; pret 3p eahtodan 3173; p ptc geæhted 1885

eald adj *old, ancient* nsm 357, 1702, 2042, 2210, 2271, 2415, 2449, 2763, 2929, 2957; gsm ealdes 2760; dsm ealdum 1874, 2972; apm ealde 472; dpm ealdum 72; asn eald 1781, 2330, 2774; asf ealde 795, 1488, 1688, 1865. Compar yldra *elder, older* nsm 468, 1324, 2378. Superl yldesta *eldest, oldest* nsm *senior man, leader* 258; asm yldestan 363; dsm 2435

ealdfæder m *late father* nsm 373

ealdgesegen f *ancient saga* gp ealdgesegena 869

ealdgesīð m *old retainer* np ealdgesīðas 853

ealdgestrēon n *ancient treasure* gp ealdgestrēona 1458; dp ealdgestrēonum 1381
ealdgewinna m *ancient adversary* ns 1776
ealdgewyrht n *past deeds, deserts for past deeds*
np 2657
ealdhlaford m *aged lord, old lord* gs ealdhla-
fordes 2778
ealdmetod m *ancient measurer, god of old* ns
945
ealdor m *lord, leader* ns 1644, 2920, aldor 56,
369, 392; as 668, ealdor 1848; ds aldre 346,
ealdre 592 [MnE alder(man)]
ealdor n *life* as aldor 1371; gs aldres 822, 1002,
1565, ealdres 1338, 2061, 2443, 2790; ds
aldre 661, 680, 1434 (*vital organs*), 1447,
1469, 1478, 1524, ealdre 1442, 1655, 2133,
2396, 2481, 2599, 2624, 2825, 2924, on aldre
ever, in my life 1779, tō aldre *always, forever*
955, 2005, 2498; dp aldrum 510, 538
ealdorbealu n *death (life-bale)* as aldorbealu
1676
ealdorcearu f (*a cause of*) *anxiety for one's life*
ds aldorceare 906
ealdordagas mp *days of life* dp aldordagum
718, ealderdagum 757
ealdorgedāl n *separation from life, death* ns
aldorgedāl 805
ealdorgewinna m *deadly foe* ns 2903
ealdorlēas adj *lacking a lord* npm aldorlēase 15
ealdorlēas adj *lifeless, dead* asm aldorlēasne
1587, ealdorlēasne 3003
ealdorþegn m *chief thane, leading retainer* as
aldorþegn 1308
ealdsweord n *ancient sword* as 1558, 1663,
2616, 2979
ealfela adj *a great many* wg as 869, 883
ealgian 2 *defend, protect* inf 796, 2655, 2668;
pret 3s ealgode 1204
eall adj, pron *all* nsm eal 1424; asm ealne 1222,
2297, 2691; npm ealle 111, 699, 705, 941,
1699; apm ealle 649, 1080, 1122, 1717, 2236,
2814, 2899; gpm ealra 3170; dpm eallum 145,
767, 823, 906, 1057, 1417, 2268; nsn eal 835,
848, 998, 1567, 1593, 1608, eall 651, 2149,
2461, 2727, 3030; asn eal 523, 744, 1086,
1155, 1185, 1701, 1705, eall 71, 2005, 2017,
2042, 2080, 2427, 2663, 3087, 3094; gsn
ealles 1955, 2162, 2739, 2794, (adv) ealles
entirely 1000; dsn eallum 913; isn ealle 2667;
npn eal 486, 1620; gpn ealra 1727; nsf eal
1738, 1790, eall 2087, 2885; asf ealle 830; apf
ealle 1796
eall adv *entirely, altogether* eal 680 (þeah . . . eal

although) , 1129, 1567, eal 2334, eall 3164,
very eal 1708
eallgearo adj *fully prepared* nsm 2241; nsn
ealgearo 77; nsf 1230
eallgylden adj *all-golden* nsn ealgylden 1111;
asn eallgylden 2767
eallīren adj *all of iron* asn eallīrenne 2338
ealobenc f *ale-bench* ds ealobence 1029, ealubence 2867
ealodrincend m *ale-drinkers* np ealodrincende
1945
ealuscerwen f *ale-shower* (i.e. *terror*) ns 769
ealuwǣge n *ale-cup* as 2021, ealowǣge 481, 495
ēam m *mother's brother, uncle* ns 881; ds ēame
1117
eard m *native region, homeland, land* ns 2198; as
104, 1129, 1377, 1500, 1727, 2493; ds earde
56, 2654, 2736; np (w sg meaning) 1621
eardian 2 *occupy* inf 2589; pret 3s eardode 166;
remain pret 3p eardodon 3050
eardlufu f *dear home* (lit. *home-love*) as eardlufan 692
earfoþe n *hardship* ap earfeþo 534
earfoðlīce adv *with difficulty, painfully* 86,
1636, 1657, 2303, 2822, 2934
earfoðþrāg f *distress, a time of stress* as ear-
foðþrāge 283
earg adj *cowardly* gsm earges 2541
earm m *arm* as 749, 835, 972; ds earme 2361;
dp earmum 513
earm adj *wretched, miserable* nsm 2368; dsf
earmre 2938. Compar asm earmran 577
earmbēag m *arm-ring* gp earmbēaga 2763
earmhrēad f *arm-ring* np earmhrēade 1194
earmlīc adj *wretched* nsm 807
earmsceapen adj *wretchedly shaped, miscreated*
ns 1351
earn m *eagle* ds earne 3026
eart see **bēon**
ēastan adv *from the east* 569
eatol see **atol**
ēaðe adj *easy* nsm ēðe 2586, nsn ȳðe 1002; nsm
2415; npf ēaðe 228
ēaðe adv *easily* 478, 2291, 2764
ēaðfynde adj *easily found* nsm 138
geēawan see **geȳwan**
ēaweð see **ȳwan**
eaxl f *shoulder* as eaxle 835, 972; ds 816, 1117,
1537, 1547; dp eaxlum 358, 2853
eaxlgestealla m *shoulder companion, comrade*
ns 1326; ap eaxlgesteallan 1714
ēc see **ēac**
ēce adj *eternal, lasting* nsm 108; asm ēcne 1201;

dsm ēcum 2796, ēcean 1692, 1779, 2330; apm
  ēce 1760; *age-old* nsn 2719
ecg f *swordblade, sword, edge* ns 1106, 1459,
  1524, 1575, 1763, 2506, 2508, 2577, 2772,
  2778; as ecge 1549; ds 2876; np ecga 2828,
  ecge 1145, 2683; ap ecge 1812; gp ecga 483,
  805, 1168; dp ecgum 1287, 1558, 1772, 2140,
  2485, 2564, 2614, 2939, 2961
ecgbana m *slayer by the sword* ds ecgbanan
  1262 [MnE edge, bane]
ecgclif n *cliff by the water's edge, shoreline cliff*
  as 2893
ecghete m *violent enmity, sword-hate* ns 84; as
  1092, 1223, 1283, 1571, 1738, 3057
ecgþracu f *sword-storm, violent attack* as
  ecgþræce 596
ēdrum see ǣdr
edhwyrft m *reversal (of fortunes)* ns 1281
edwenden f *reversal, change (of fortunes)* ns
  280, 1774, 2188
edwītlīf n *life of shame* ns 2891
efn adj *even* on efn *alongside* 2903
efnan see æfnan
efne adv *even, just* 1092, 1223, 1249, 1283,
  1571, 3057, efne swā hwylc *whosoever* (efne
  swā hwylc mægþa *whatever woman*) 943
efstan 1 *hasten* inf 3101; pret 3s efste 1493
eft adv *afterwards, back, again* 22, 56, 123, 135,
  281, 296, 603, 642, 692, 853, 871, 1146, 1160,
  1377, 1529, 1541, 1556, 1596, 1753, 1762,
  1787, 1804, 1869, 2111, 2117, 2142, 2200,
  2319, 2365, 2368, 2387, 2592, 2654, 2790,
  2941, 2956, 3044
eftcyme m *return* gs eftcymes 2896
eftsīð m *journey back, return* as 1891; gs eftsīðes
  2783; ap eftsīðas tēah *returned* 1332
egesa m *fear, terror* ns 784; as egsan 276, egesan
  3154; gs egesan ne gȳmeð *has no regard for
  timorousness (in dispensing treasure)* 1757; ds
  1827, 2736
egesful adj *terrible* nsm 2929
egeslīc adj *terrible* nsm 2309, 2825; nsn 1649
egle adj *horrible* nsf eglu 987
egsan see egesa
egsian 2 *terrify* pret 3s egsode 6
ēgstrēam m *sea current* dp ēgstrēamum 577
ēhtan 1 wg *pursue* pret 3p ēhton 1512
ēhtend m *persecutor* nsm ēhtende 159
ehtigan see eahtian
elde see ylde
eldo see yldo
elland n *foreign land* as 3019
ellen n *valour, courage* ns 573, 902, 2706; as

602, 2349, 2695; gs elnes 1529, 2876; ds elne
  893, 1493, 1967, 2506, 2535, 2676, 2861; isn
  1097; *deeds of courage* as ellen 3, 637
ellendǣd f *deeds of courage* dp ellendǣdum
  876, 900
ellengǣst m *powerful creature* ns 86
ellenlīce adv *boldly* 2122
ellenmǣrþu f *deed of valour, fame for valour* dp
  ellenmǣrþum 828, 1471
ellenrōf adj *brave, powerful* nsm 340, 358,
  3063; dpm ellenrōfum 1787
ellensīoc adj *with failing strength, strengthless*
  asm ellensīocne 2787 [MnE -sick]
ellenweorc n *valiant deed* as 661, 958, 1464,
  2643; ap 3173; gp ellenweorca 2399 [MnE
  -work]
elles adv *else, otherwise* 138, 2520, 2590
ellor adv *elsewhere* 55, 2254, 2520
ellorgāst m *alien creature* ns 807, 1621, ellorgǣst *alien spirit* 1617; ap ellorgǣstas 1349
ellorsīð m *journey elsewhere, death* ns 2451
elne see ellen
elnes see ellen
elra compar adj *another* dsm elran 752
elþēodig adj *foreign* apm elþēodige 336
ende m *end* ns 822, 1254; as 1386, 1734, 2342,
  2844, 3046, 3063, on ende *in turn* 2021; ds
  224, 2790, 2823
endedæg m *final day, day of death* ns 3035; as
  637
endedōgor *final day, death* gs endedōgores
  2896
endelāf f *last remnant* ns 2813
endelēan n *final retribution* as 1692
endesǣta m *border guard* ns 241
endestæf m *end* as on endestæf *in the end* 1753
geendian 2 *end* pp geendod 2311
enge adj *narrow* apm 1410
ent m *giant* gp enta 1679, 2717, 2774
entisc adj *made by giants* asm entiscne 2979
geēode see gegān
eodor m *enclosure, sheltering building* ap (w sg
  meaning) eoderas 1037; *protector, lord* ns 428,
  1044, eodur 663
eofer m *boar, boar-image (on a helmet)* ns 1112;
  as eafor 2152; ap eoferas 1328
eofersprēot m *boar-spear* dp eofersprēotum
  1437
eoforlīc n *boar-image* np 303
eofoð see eafoð
eolet n *water-course (?), voyage (?)* gs eoletes
  224 [a word of uncertain meaning which
  occurs only here]

eorclanstān m *precious stone* ap eorclanstānas 1208

ēoredgeatwe fp *war-gear* ap 2866

eorl m *warrior, nobleman* ns 761, 795, 1228, 1328, 1512, 1702, 2908, 2951, 3015, 3063, 3077; as 573, 627, 2695; gs eorles 689, 982, 1757; ap eorlas 6, 2816; gp eorla 248, 357, 369, 431, 791, 1035, 1050, 1235, 1238, 1312, 1420, 1866, 1891, 1967, 2064, 2142, 2190, 2248, 2338, 2361, 2891, 3166; dp eorlum 769, 1281, 1649, 1676, 2021 [MnE earl]

eorlgestrēon n *lordly treasure* gp eorlgestrēona 2244

eorlgewǣde n *armour, warrior's trappings* dp eorlgewǣdum 1442

eorlīc adj *noble* asn 637

eorlscipe m *nobility, heroic deed(s)* as 1727, 2133, 2622, 3007, 3173, eorlscype 2535

eorlwerod n *band of retainers* ns 2893

eormencynn n *mighty race*, (i.e. *mankind*) gs eormencynnes 1957 [MnE -kin]

eormengrund m *vast earth, the whole world* as 859 [MnE -ground]

eormenlāf f *immense legacy* as eormenlāfe 2234

eorres see **yrre**

eorðcyning m *king of the land* gs eorðcyninges 1155

eorðdraca m *earth-dragon, dragon that lives in the earth* ns 2712, 2825

eorðe f *earth* as eorðan 92, 248, 266, 802, 2007, 2834, 3099, 3166; gs 752, 1730, 2727, 3049; ds 1532, 1822, 2415, 2822, 2855, 3138

eorðhūs n *earth-house, cave* ds eorðhūse 2232

eorðreced m, n *earth-hall, cave* ns 2719

eorðscræf n *earth-cave, cave* gp eorðscrafa 3046

eorðsele m *earth-hall, cave* as 2410; ds 2515

eorðweall m *earth-wall, earthen chamber* as 2957, 3090

eorðweard m *stronghold* as 2334 [MnE earth, ward]

eoten m *giant* ns 761; np eotenas 112; gp eotena 421, 883

eotenisc adj *made by giants* asn 1558, 2979, etonisc 2616

eotonweard f *watch against a monster* as 668

ēow see **þū**

ēower poss pron *your* nsm 2532; asm ēowerne 294, 2537, 2889; npm ēowre 257, gpm ēowra 634; asn ēower 251; dsn ēowrum 2885; apn ēower 392; dpn ēowrum 395

ēower, ēowic pers pron see **þū**

ēoweð see **ȳwan**

ēst f *gift, favour, good will* as 2165, 3075, *legacy, history* 2157; dp ēstum *with good will, kindly* 958, 1194, 2149, 2378

ēste adj *gracious* nsm 945

etan V *eat* inf 444; pres 3s eteð 449

etonisc see **eotenisc**

ēðbegēte adj *easy to obtain, forthcoming* nsf 2861

ēðe see **ēaðe**

ēþel m *native land* as 520, 913, 1960; ds ēþle 1730, 1774

ēðelriht n *ancestral domain* ns 2198 [MnE -right]

ēþelstōl m *ancestral throne* ap ēþelstōlas 2371

ēþelturf f *native soil* ds ēþeltyrf 410

ēþelweard m *guardian of the homeland* ns 1702, 2210; ds ēþelwearde 616

ēþelwyn f *joy of ancestral land, joy of the nation* ns 2885; as 2493

ēþgesȳne adj *readily seen* nsm 1110, yþgesēne 1244

fācen n *evil, crime* ds fācne 2009

fācenstæf m *treachery (?), wrongful act (?)* (see ll. 1017b–19 note) ap fācenstafas 1018

fāg, fāh adj *stained, decorated, shining* nsm fāh 420, 978, 1038, 2671, 2974, fāg 1001, 1263, 1631; asm fāhne 447, 716, 927, fāgne 725; nsn fāh 934, 1286, 1594, 2701; asn 2217; npn 305; dpn fāgum 586; nsf fāh 1459; asf fāge 1615

fāh, fāg adj *hostile* nsm 420, 554, 811, 2671; asm fāne 2655; gpm fāra 578, 1463

fāmīgheals adj *foamy-necked* nsm 1909, fāmīheals 218

gefandian 2 wg *search out, disturb* p ptc gefandod 2301; *have one's portion of* p ptc gefondad 2454

fāne see **fāh**

fāra see **fāh**

faran VI *go* inf 124, 865, 2551, 2915, 2945; infl inf tō farenne 1805; pret 3s fōr 1404, 1908, 2308, 2672; 3 p fōron 1895 [MnE fare]

gefaran VI *proceed, behave* inf 738

faroð m *current, tide* ds faroðe 28, 580, 1916

fæc n *while, (period of) time* as 2240

fæder m *father* ns 55, 262, 316, 459, 1609, 2048, 2608, 2928; as 1355; gs 21, 188, 1479, 1950, 2059; ds 2429

fæderæþelu n pl *ancestral virtue, father's noble qualities* dp fæderæþelum 911

fæderenmǣg m *father's son* ds fæderenmǣge 1263

ge**fæg** adj *dear, pleasing* comp nsm gefægra 915

fæge adj *doomed, fated to die* nsm 846, 1241, 1755, 2141, 2975; asm fægne 1568; gsm fæges 1527; dsm fægum 2077; *dead* dpm 3025 [MnE fey]

fægen adj *rejoicing* npm fægne 1633 [MnE fain]

fæger adj *beautiful, pleasant* nsm 1137; npm fægere 866; nsn fæger 773; asf fægere 522 [MnE fair]

fægere, fægre adv *courteously, fittingly* 1014, 1788, 1985, 2989

ge**fægnian** 2 *gladden, make glad* p ptc gefægnod 1333

ge**fægon** see ge**fēon**

fǣhð f *enmity, hostility, feud* ns fǣhð 2403, 3061; fǣhðo 2999; as fǣhðe 137, 153, 459, 470, 595, 879, 1207, 1333, 1340, 1380, 2480, 2513, 2618, 2948, fǣghðe 2465; gs fǣhðe 109; ds 1537; ap fǣhðo 2489; gp fǣhða 2689

fælsian 2 *cleanse* inf 432; p ptc gefælsod 825, 1176, 1620; pret 3s fælsode 2352

fǣmne f *bride* gs fǣmnan 2059; ds 2034

fær n *ship* ns 33

fǣr m *sudden attack* ns 1068, 2230 [MnE fear]

fǣrgripe m *sudden grasp, sudden onrush* ns 1516; dp fǣrgripum 738 [MnE fear-grip]

fǣrgryre m *sudden horror* dp fǣrgryrum 174

fǣringa adv *suddenly* 1414, 1988

fǣrnīð m *sudden attack* gp fǣrnīða 476

fæst adj *fast, fixed, firm* nsm 137, 636, 1007, 1290, 1364, 1742, 1878, 1906, 2243, 2901, 3045, 3072; asm fæstne 2069; apm fæste 2718; fæst nsn 303, 998; asn 1918; nsf 722, 2086; asf fæste 1096

fæste adv *fast, firmly* 554, 760, 773, 788, 1295, 1864. Compar fæstor *safer* 143

fæsten n *fastness, stronghold* as 104, 2333, 2950

fæstrǣd adj *steadfast* asm fæstrǣdne 610

fæt n *cup, flagon* ap fatu 2761 [MnE vat]

fǣt n *gold plating* dp fǣttum 716, fǣtum 2256

fǣted adj *gold-plated* apm fǣtte 333, 1750; nsn fǣted 2701; asn 2253, 2282; gsn fǣttan 1093, 2246; dsn 2102

fǣtedhlēor adj *with gold-plated bridle* apm fǣtedhlēore 1036

fǣtgold n *plated gold* as 1921

fǣttan see **fǣted**

fǣtte see **fǣted**

fǣttum see **fǣt**

fæðergearwe fp *feather-gear* dp fæðergearwum 3119

faþm m *embrace* ns 781; as 185; dp faðmum 188, 2128; *bosom* as faþm 1393, 3049; *grasp, possession* as 1210 [MnE fathom]

faðmian 2 *embrace, envelop* inf 3133; pres subj 3s faðmie 2652

fēa adj *few* ap 2246, 2662; gp fēara 1412, 3061; dp fēaum 1081

fēa (156) see **feoh**

ge**fēa** m *joy* as gefēan 562, 2740

ge**feah** see ge**fēon**

fealh see **fēolan**

feallan VII *fall* inf 1070; pret 3s fēol 772, fēoll 2919, 2975; pret 3p fēollon 1042

ge**feallan** VII *fall* pres 3s gefealleð 1755; *fall to* pret 3s gefēoll 2100, 2834

fealo see **fela**

fealu adj *tawny, dusky* asm fealone 1950; apm fealwe 865; asf 916 [MnE fallow]

fēasceaft adj *destitute, wretched* nsm 7, 973; dsm fēasceaftum 2285, 2393; npm fēasceafte 2373

feax n *hair* ds feaxe 1647, fexe 2967

ge**fēgon** see ge**fēon**

ge**feh** see ge**fēon**

fēhð see **fōn**

fēl f *file* gp fēla 1032

fela n (indeclinable) *much, many* (usually w part gen) 36, 153, 164, 311, 408, 530, etc., fealo 2757

felafricgende adj *having learned many things* nsm 2106

felageōmor adj *much saddened* nsm 2950

felahrōr adj *having done much* nsm 27

felamōdig adj *very bold* gpm felamōdigra 1637, 1888 [MnE -moody]

felasinnig adj *very guilty* asm felasinnigne 1379 [MnE -sin]

fell n *hide, skin* dp fellum 2088 [MnE fell]

fenfreoðo f *fen-refuge* as 851

feng m *grip* ns 1764; as 578

fēng see **fōn**

ge**fēng** see ge**fōn**

fengel m *prince, lord* ns 1400, 1475, 2156, 2345

fengelād n *fen-tract, fen-path* as 1359

fenhleoðu np *fen-slopes* ap 820

fenhop n *fen-retreat* ap fenhopu 764

fenn n *fen, marsh* as fen 104; ds fenne 1295

fēo see **feoh**

feoh n *payment, treasure, money* ds fēa 156, fēo 470, 1380 [MnE fee]

feohgift f *gift of treasure, treasure-giving* gs feohgyfte 1025; dp feohgiftum 21, feohgyftum 1089

feohlēas adj *uncompensated, not atoned for with payment* nsn 2441 [MnE feeless]

gefeoht n *assault, battle* ns 2441; ds gefeohte 2048 [MnE fight]

gefeohtan III *fight* inf wig . . . gefeohtan *fight the battle to the finish* 1083

feohte f *fight* as feohtan 576, 959

fēolan III *enter, penetrate* pret 3s fealh 1281, 2225, *endured* 1200

fēoll see **feallan**

gefēon V wg or d *rejoice* pret 3s gefeah 109, 1624, gefeh 827, 1569; 3p gefægon 1014, gefēgon 1627; *be eager for* pret 3s gefeh 2298

fēond m *enemy, foe* ns 101, 164, 725, 748, 970, 1276; as 279, 698, 962, 1273, 1864, 2706; gs fēondes 984, 2128, 2289; ds fēonde 143, 439; gp fēonda 294, 808, 903, 1152, fīonda 2671; dp fēondum 420, 1669 [MnE fiend]

fēondgrāp f *foe's grasp* dp fēondgrāpum 636

fēondscaða m *enemy assailant* ns 554

fēondscipe m *enmity* ns 2999 [MnE fiendship]

feor adv *far* 42, 109, 542, 808, 1221, 1340, 1361, 1805, 1916, 1921, 2870, feorr 1988; feor *from far back, from long ago* 1701. Compar fyr *further off, further* 143, 252

feorbūend m *far dweller, foreigner* np 254

feorcȳþðu f *friendship afar, friends far away* np feorcȳþðe 1838

feorh m, n *life* ns 2123, 2424; as 439, 796, 851, 1370, 1849, 2141, 2655, 2668, 2856, 2981, ferh 2706, wīdan feorh *ever* 2014; gs fēores 1433, 1942; ds fēore 578, 1293, 1548, 3013, feore 1843, tō wīdan feore *ever* 933; ap feorh 2040; dp fēorum 1306, feorum 73; *(living) body* ns feorh 1210; *life's blood* dp fēorum 1152

feorhbealu n *deadly evil, mortal bale* ns 2077, 2537, feorhbealo 2250; as 156

feorhbenn f *mortal wound* dp feorhbennum 2740

feorhbona m *slayer* ds feorhbonan 2465

feorhcynn n *race of mortals, humankind* gp feorhcynna 2266

feorhgenīðla m *deadly foe* as feorhgenīðlan 1540; ds 969; dp 2933

feorhlāst m *mortal step* ap feorhlāstas bær *took his dying steps* 846

feorhlegu f *life span, life* as feorhlege 2800

feorhsēoc adj *sick unto death, mortally wounded* nsm 820

feorhsweng m *mortal blow* as 2489

feorhwund f *mortal wound* ds feorhwunde 2385

feorm f *sustenance* as 451; *hospitality* feorme 2385

feormendlēas adj *without a polisher* apm feormendlēase 2761

gefeormian 2 *eat* p ptc gefeormod 744

feormynd m (pres ptc) *polisher* np 2256

feorr see **feor**

feorran 1 *remove* inf 156

feorran adv *from afar* 361, 430, 825, 839, 1174, 1370, 1819, 2317, 2808, 2889, 3113; *from far back, from long ago* 91, 2106

feorrancund adj *come from afar* dsm feorrancundum 1795

feorweg m *far way* dp feorwegum 37

fēower num *four* np 59, 1637, 2163; ap 1027

fēowertȳne num *fourteen* np 1641

fēran 1 *go* inf 27, 301, 316, 1390, 2261; pres subj 2p 254; pret 3p fērdon 839, 1632 [MnE fare]

gefēran 1 *go to, reach, fare* pres subj 3s gefēre 3063; pret 3p gefērdon 1691; p ptc gefēred 2844; *bring (it) about* 1221, 1855

ferh see **feorh**

ferhð m, n *heart, spirit, mind* gs ferhðes 1060; ds ferhðe 754, 948, 1166, 1718; dp ferhðum 1633, 3176

ferhðfrec adj *boldhearted* asm ferhðfrecan 1146

ferhðgenīðla m *mortal foe* as ferhðgenīðlan 2881

ferhweard f *guard over life, life protection* as ferhwearde 305

ferian 1 *carry, convey, bring* pres 2p ferigeað 333; pret 3p feredon 1154, 1158, fyredon 378; pret subj 3p feredon 3113; p ptc npm geferede 361 [MnE ferry]

geferian 1 *carry* inf 1638; pres subj 1p 3107; pret 3p geferedon 3130

fetelhilt f *sword-hilt* ap (w sg meaning) 1563

fetian 2 *fetch* p ptc fetod 1310

gefetian 2 *bring* inf 2190

fēþa m *foot-troop, warrior band* ns 1424; ds fēðan 2497, 2919; np 1327, 2544

fēþe n *going, departure* ds 970

fēþecempa m *foot-soldier* ns 1544, 2853

fēðegest m *foot-soldier guest* dp fēðegestum 1976

fēþelāst m *footstep* dp fēþelāstum 1632

fēðewīg n *pitched battle* gs fēðewīges 2364

fex see **feax**

fīf num *five* gp 545; ap fīfe 420

fīfelcynn n *monster-race* gs fīfelcynnes 104

fīftig num *fifty* ap 2209, 2733; gs fīftiges 3042

fīftȳne num *fifteen* ap fȳftȳne 1582; gp fīftȳna 207

findan III *find* inf 207, 1156, 1378, 1838, 2294, 2373, 2870; pret 1s fond 2136, funde 1486; pret 3s fand 118, 719, 870, 1267, 2789, fond 2270, funde 1415; pret 3p fundon 3033; p ptc funden 7; *devise* inf findan 3162; findan . . . æt *persuade* 2373

finger m *finger* np fingras 760; ap 984; gp fingra 764; dp fingrum 1505

fīond see fēond

fīras mp *men, human beings* gp fīra 91, 2001, 2286, 2741, fȳra 2250

firen see fyren

firgen- see fyrgen-

flān m *arrow, arrow-head* ds flāne 2438, 3119

flānboga m *(arrow) bow* ds flānbogan 1433, 1744

flǣsc n *flesh* ds flǣsce 2424

flǣschoma m *body, flesh-garment* as flǣschoman 1568

flēah see flēon

flēam m *flight* as 1001, 2889

flēogan II *fly* pres 3s flēogeð 2273

flēon II *flee* inf 755, 764, flēon 820, 1264; pret 3s flēah 2224

flēotan II *float, sail* inf 542; pret 3s flēat 1909

flet n *floor* as 1540, 1568; *hall* ns 1976; as 1036, 1086, 1647, 1949, 2017, 2054, flett 2034; ds flette 1025

fletrǣst f *pallet in the hall* as fletrǣste 1241

fletsittende m *one sitting in the hall* ap 2022; dp fletsittendum 1788

fletwerod n *hall-troop* ns 476

fliht m *flight* ns 1765

geflit n *competition* as 865

flītan I *compete* pres ptc flītende npm 916; pret 2s flite 507

flōd m *flood* ns 545, 580, 1361, 1422, 1689; as 1950, 3133; gs flōdes 42, 1516, 1764; ds flōde 1366,1888; gp flōda 1497, 1826, 2808

flōdȳþ f *flood-wave, ocean wave* dp flōdȳþum 542

flōr m *floor* as 725; ds flōre 1316

flota m *ship* ns 210, 218, 301; as flotan 294 [MnE float(er)]

flothere m *naval attack force* ds flotherge 2915

geflȳman I *put to flight* p ptc geflȳmed 846, 1370

folc n *folk, people, troop* as 463, 522, 693, 911, 1179; gs folces 610, 1124, 1582, 1832, 1849, 1932, 2513, 2644, 2981; ds folce 14, 465, 1701, 2377, 2393, 2595; np folc 1422, 2948; gp folca 430, 2017, 2357, 2429; dp folcum 55, 262, 1855

folcāgende m *ruler of a people, leader* ds 3113

folccwēn f *queen of the people* ns 641

folccyning m *king of the people* ns 2733, 2873

folcrēd m *people's welfare* as 3006

folcriht n *right (among the people), entitlement* gp folcrihta 2608 [MnE folk-right]

folcscaru f *public land* ds folcscare 73 [MnE folk-share]

folcstede m *people's place* as 76; *meeting place* as 1463 [MnE folk-stead]

folctoga m *leader of the people* np folctogan 839

foldbold n *building* ns 773

foldbūend m *dweller in the land* np 2274, foldbūende 1355; dp foldbūendum 309

folde f *earth, ground* as foldan 1361, 2975; gs 96, 1137, 1393; ds 1196

foldweg m *path* as 1633; np foldwegas 866

folgian 2 wd *follow, pursue* pret 3s folgode 2933; pret subj 3p folgedon 1102

folm f *(palm of the) hand* as folme 970, 1303; ds 748; ap folma 745; dp folmum 158, 722, 992

fōn VII *grapple, grasp, take* inf 439; pres 3s fēhð 1755; pret 3s fēng 1542; *accept* pret 3s (wd) 2989

gefōn VII *grasp, seize* pret 1s gefēng 3090; 3s 740, 1501, 1537, 1563, 2215, 2609

gefondad see gefandian

for prep wa *for, as* 947, 1175, 2348; wd *for, because of* 169, 338, 339, 382, 434, 457, 458, 462, 508, 509, 832, 965, 1206, 1442, 1515, 1537, 1734, 1796, 2223, 2549, 2781, 2835, 2926, 2966; wi 110 *before, in front of* 358, 1026, 1120, 1649, 2020, 2501; *in return for* 385, 951, 2385

foran adv *from in front, at the front, at the tip* 984, 2364, þæt wæs ān foran *that was one pre-eminent* 1458

forbærnan I *burn up* (trans) inf 2126

forberan IV *restrain, hold back* 1877 [MnE forbear]

forberstan III *snap, break* pret 3s forbærst 2680 [MnE -burst]

forbyrnan III *burn up* (intrans) pret 3s forbarn 1616, 1667

ford m *sea* as 568 [MnE ford]

fore adv *for it* 136; prep wd *before, in the presence of* 1064, 1215, *because of* 2059

foremǣre adj *famous* superl ns foremǣrost 309

foremihtig adj *powerful* nsm 969

foresnotor adj *exceedingly wise* npm foresnotre 3162

foreþanc m *deliberation* ns 1060

forgifan V *give* pret 3s forgeaf 17, 374, 696, 1020, 1519, 2492, 2606, 2616, 2997 [MnE forgive]

forgrindan III *destroy* pret 1s forgrand 424; p ptc forgrunden 2335, 2677 [MnE -grind]

forgrīpan I *destroy* pret 3s forgrāp 2353

forgyldan III *pay recompense for, requite, reward, pay (for)* inf 1054, 1577, 2305; pres subj 3s forgylde 956; pret 3s forgeald 2968; p ptc forgolden 2843; hondlēan forgeald *gave requital with the hand* pret 1s 2094; pret 3s 1541; lēan forgeald *gave requital* pret 3s 114, 1584

forgȳman 1 *disregard* pres 3s forgȳmeð 1751

forgytan V *forget* pres 3s forgyteð 1751

forhabban 3 *hold itself back, hold oneself back* inf 1151, 2609

forhealdan VII *rebel against* p ptc forhealden 2381

forhicgan 3 *disdain* pres 1s forhicge 435

forht adj *afraid* nsm 754, 2967

forlācan VII *betray, seduce* n p ptc forlācen 903

forlǣdan 1 *lead to destruction* pret 3p forlǣddan 2039

forlǣtan VII *leave, release* inf 792; pret 3s forlēt 970, 2787; pret 3p forlēton 3166

forlēosan II wd *lose* pret 3s forlēas 1470, 2861; p ptc forloren 2145

forma adj *first* nsm 716, 1463, 1527, 2625; ds forman 740, 2286, 2573. Superl fyrmest 2077

forniman IV *take to destruction, destroy* pret 3s fornam 488, 557, 695, 1080, 1123, 1205, 1436, 2119, 2236, 2249, 2772; wd pret 3p fornāmon 2828

forscrīfan I wd *condemn* p ptc forscrifen 106

forsendan 1 *kill* p ptc forsended 904 [MnE -send]

forsittan V *grow weak, fail* pres 3s forsiteð 1767

forsīðian 2 *perish* p ptc forsīðod 1550

forst m *frost* gs forstes 1609

forstandan VI *prevent* pret 3s forstōd 1549; pret subj 3s forstōde 1056; *defend (against)* inf forstandan 2955

forswāpan VII *sweep, sweep to destruction* pret 3s forswēop 477, 2814

forswelgan III *swallow up* pret 3s forswealg 1122, 2080

forsweorcan III *grow dim* pres 3s forsworceð 1767

forswerian VI wd *bewitch, make useless by a spell* p ptc forsworen 804

forsworceð see forsweorcan

forð adv *forth, forward* 45, 210, 291, 612, 745, 903, 1162, 1179, 1632, 1718, 1795, 1909, 2253, 2266, 2959, 2967, 3176, *henceforth* 948, forð sprecan *speak on, continue speaking* 2069; tō forð *(thither) forward* 2289

forðām, forðan, forðon adv *therefore* forðām 149, forþan 679, 1059, forðon 2523, 3021

forðām, forþan, forþon conj *because, for, since* forðām 1957, 2645, 2741, forþan 418, 1336, forðon 2349, forþon þe 503

forðgerīmed (p ptc of forðgerīman 1) *all told* npn 59

forðgesceaft f *future destiny* as 1750

forðgewiten (p ptc of forðgewītan I) *being dead* dsm forðgewitenum 1479

forðon see forðām

forþringan III *force out, dislodge* inf 1084

forðweg m *way forth* as 2625

forweorpan III *throw away* pret subj 3s forwurpe 2872

forwrecan V *dash to pieces (against the rocky shore)* inf 1919; *expel* pret 3s forwrǣc 109

forwrītan I *cut through* pret 3s forwrāt 2705

forwyrnan 1 *refuse* pres subj 2s forwyrne 429; pret 3s forwyrnde 1142

fōt m *foot* gs fōtes 2525; ap fēt 745; dp fōtum 500, 1166

fōtgemearc n *foot-length, foot-measure* gs fōtgemearces 3042

fōtlāst m *track* as 2289

fracod adj *useless* nsf 1575

fram adv *away, forth* 754, 2556

fram, from prep wd *from* 110, 420, 541, 543, 775, 855, 1635, 1715, 2366, 2565, *about, concerning* 532, 581, 875, *at* 194

gefrǣge n *hearsay, information* is mīne gefrǣge *as I have heard say* 776, 837, 1955, 2685, 2837

gefrǣge adj *renowned, well known* nsm 55; nsn 2480

gefrægn see gefrignan

frætwan 1 *adorn* inf 76

frætwe f *treasure, accoutrement* as 2503; ap 214, 1207, 1921, 2620, 2919, frætwa 896; gp 37, 2794, 3133; dp frætwum 2054, 2163, 2784, 2989, frætewum 962

gefrætwian 2 *adorn* pret 3s gefrætwade 96; p ptc gefrætwod 992

frēa m *lord, king* ns 2285; as frēan 351, 1319, 2537, 3002, 3107; gs 27, 2853; ds 291, 500, 641, 1166, 2662, frèan 271, 359, 1680, 2794

frēadrihten m *lord* gs frēadrihtnes 796

frēawine m *lord and friend, dear lord* ns 2357, 2429; as 2438

frēawrāsn f *lordly chain, chain mail (protecting back of neck)* dp frēawrāsnum 1451

freca m *warrior* ns 1563

frēcne adj *daring* asf 889, *perilous, terrible* nsm 2689; nsn 2250, 2537; asn 1359; asf 1378, frēcnan 1104

frēcne adv *daringly, severely, terribly* 959, 1032, 1691

fremde adj *alien* nsf 1691

freme adj *excellent* nsf fremu 1932

fremman 1 *support* inf 1832, *do, perform* inf 101, 2499, 2514, 2627; pres 3p fremmað 2800; pres subj 3s fremme 1003; pret 3s fremede 3006; 1p fremedon 959; 3p 3, 1019, subj 1s fremede 2134; *further* pres 3s fremeð 1701

gefremman 1 *advance* pret subj 3s gefremede 1718; *perform, do* inf gefremman 636, 1315, 2449, 2674; infl inf tō gefremmanne 174, 2644; pret 3s gefremede 135, 165, 551, 585, 811, 1946, 2004, 2645; 1p gefremedon 1187; 3p 2478; subj 3s gefremede 177, 591, 1552; p ptc gefremed 476, 954, asf gefremede 940

frēoburh f *noble city* as 693

frēod f *friendship* as frēode 1707, 2476; gs 2556

frēodrihten m *noble lord* ns 1169; ds frēo-dryhtne 2627

frēogan 2 *love* inf 948; pres subj 3s frēoge 3176

frēolīc adj *noble* nsn 615; nsf frēolīcu 641

frēond m *friend* ns 2393; as 1385, 1864; gp frēonda 1306, 1838; dp frēondum 915, 1018, 1126

frēondlār f *friendly counsel* dp frēondlārum 2377

frēondlaþu f *friendly invitation* ns 1192

frēondlīce adv *in a friendly manner* comp frēondlīcor 1027

frēondscipe m *friendship* as 2069

freoðo f *peace* gs 188

freoðoburh f *stronghold* as 522

freoðowong m *peaceful field* as 2959

freoðuwebbe f *weaver of peace, lady* ns 1942

frēowine m *noble friend* ns 430

fretan V *devour* inf 3014, 3114; pret 3s frǣt 1581

fricgan V *question, interrogate* inf 1985

gefricgan V *learn of* pres 1s gefricge 1826; 3p gefricgeað 3002; subj 3p gefricgean 2889

friclan 1 wg *ask for* inf 2556

frignan III *ask* inf frīnan 351; imp s frīn 1322; pret 3s frægn 236, 332, 1319

gefrignan III *learn by asking, obtain knowledge of, hear of* pret 1s gefrægn 74, 575, 1027, 2484, 2694, 2752, 2773, gefrǣgen 1011; 3s gefrægn 194; 1p gefrūnon 2; 3p 70, 1969, gefrungon 666; p ptc gefrǣgen 1196, gefrūnen 694, 2403, 2952

frioðuwǣr f *peace agreement* as frioðuwǣre 1096; gs frioðowǣre 2282

friðusibb f *pledge of peace* ns 2017

frōd adj *old, wise* nsm 279, 1306, 1366, 1724, 1844, 2114, 2209, 2277, 2513, 2625, 2950, frōda 2928; dsm frōdan 2123; asf frōde 2800

frōfor f *comfort, consolation, relief* ns 2941; as frōfre 7, 628, 973, 1273, frōfor 698; gs frōfre 185; ds 14, 1707

from prep see fram

from adj *bold, resolute* nsm 2527; npm frome 1641, 2476; *splendid* dpf fromum 21

fruma m *beginning* ns 2309; *king, ruler* 31

frumcyn n *origin* as 252

frumgār m *(military) leader* ds frumgāre 2856

frumsceaft f *creation, beginning* as 91; ds frumsceafte 45

gefrūnen, gefrūnon see gefrignan

gefrungon see gefrignan

fugol m *bird* ds fugle 218; dp fuglum 2941 [MnE fowl]

ful adv *full, very* 480, 951, 1252

full n *cup* ns ful 1192; as 615, 628, 1025, 1208; ds fulle 1169

full adj wg *full* nsm 2412

fullǣstan 1 wd *help* pres 1s fullǣstu 2668

fullēode see fullgān

fullgān anom *aid* pret 3s fullēode 3119

fultum m *aid, support* as 698, 1273, 1835, 2662

funden see findan

fundian 2 *be eager to go* pres 1p fundiaþ 1819; pret 3s fundode 1137

furðum adv *first* 323, 465, 2009, *previously* 1707

furþur adv *further, forward* 254, 761, *in time* 2525, furður gēn *still more* 3006

fūs adj *ready, eager, hastening* nsm 1916, 1475, 3025, 3119; npm fūse 1805; nsn fūs 1966; *about to die* nsm 1241

fūslīc adj *ready, eager* asn 1424, 2618; fūslīcu 232

fȳftȳne see fīftȳne

fyll m *fall* ns 2912; ds on fylle wearð *took a fall, fell* 1544

gefyllan 1 *fell, cut down* inf 2655; pret 3p gefyldan 2706

fyllo f *feast* gs fylle 562, 1014; ds 1333 [MnE fill]

fylwērig adj *death-weary, dying* asm fylwērigne 962

fyr see feor

fȳr n *fire* ns 2701, 2881; as fȳr, 1366; gs fȳres 185, 1764; ds fȳre 2274, 2309, 2595

fȳras see fīras

fȳrbend f *fire-forged bar* dp fȳrbendum 722

fyrdgestealla m *comrade in arms* dp fyrdgesteallum 2873

fyrdhom m *army-coat, coat of mail* as 1504

fyrdhrægl n *coat of mail* as 1527

fyrdhwæt adj *martially vigorous, valiant* npm fyrdhwate 1641, 2476

fyrdlēoð n *war-song* as 1424

fȳrdraca m *fire-dragon* ns 2689

fyrdsearo n *war-gear* as 2618; ap fyrdsearu 232

fyrdwyrðe adj *distinguished in war* nsm 1316

fyredon see ferian

fyren f *crime, violence, suffering* ns 915; as fyrene 101, 137, 153, 2480, firen' 1932; gs fyrene 811; ap fyrena 879; gp 164, 628, 750; dp fyrenum 2441, *with evil intent* 1744

fyrendǣd f *violent deed* ap fyrendǣda 1669; dp fyrendǣdum 1001

fyrenðearf f *extreme distress, painful need* as fyrenðearfe 14

fyrgenbēam m *mountain tree* ap fyrgenbēamas 1414

fyrgenholt n *mountain-wood* as 1393

fyrgenstrēam m *mountain-stream, waterfall* ns 1359; as firgenstrēam 2128

fȳrheard adj *fire-hardened* npn 305

fȳrlēoht n *fire-light* as 1516

fyrmest see forma

fyrndæg m *day of yore* dp fyrndagum 1451

fyrngeweorc n *ancient work* as 2286

fyrngewinn n *ancient strife* gs fyrngewinnes 1689

fyrnmann m *man of old* gp fyrnmanna 2761

fyrnwita m *counsellor of old* ds fyrnwitan 2123

fyrst m *space of time, allotted time, time* ns 134, 210, 2555; as 528, 545; ds fyrste 76; is 2573

gefyrðran I *impel, make eager* p ptc gefyrðred 2784 [MnE further]

fyrwet n *curiosity* ns 1985, 2784, fyrwyt 232

fȳrwylm m *surge of fire* dp fȳrwylmum 2671

gefȳsan I *impel, be eager (for)* p ptc gefȳsed 217, 630, 2309, 2561

gād n *lack* ns 660, 949

galan VI *sing, sound out* inf 786, 1432; pres 3s gæleð 2460

galdor see gealdor

galga m *gallows* ds galgan 2446

galgmōd adj *grim-spirited* ns 1277 [MnE gallow(s), mood]

galgtrēow n *gallows-tree* dp galgtrēowum 2940

gamen see gomen

gamol adj *old, ancient* nsm 58, 265, gomol 3095, gomel 2112, 2793, gamela 1792, gomela 1397, 2105, 2487, 2851, 2931, 2968; asm gomelan 2421; dsm gamelum 1677, gomelum 2444, gomelan 2817; npm gomele 1595; gpm gomelra *ancestors* 2036; nsn gomol 2682; asn gomel 2610; asf gomele 2563

gamolfeax adj ns *grey-haired* 608

gān anom *go, walk* inf 1163, gân 386, 1644; pres 3s gǣð 455, 603, gâð 2034, 2054; pres subj 3s gā 1394; imp s 1782; p ptc gegān 2630; pret 3s ēode 358, 389, 403, 612, 640, 726, 918, 1232, 1312, 1814, 3123; 3p ēodon 493, 1626, 3031

gegān anom *go* pret 3s geēode 2676; 3p geēodon 1967; *undertake* inf gegān 1277, 1462; *gain* 1535; *bring about* pret 3p geēodon 2917; *come to pass* pret 3s geīode 2200

gang m *going* gs ganges 968; ds gange 1884; *track, trail* ns gang 1404; as 1391

gangan VII *go, walk* inf 314, 324, 395, 1034, gongan 711, 1642, 1974, 2083, 2648; imp s geong 2743; pret 3s gēong 925, 1785, 2019, 2756, 3125, gīong 2214, 2409, 2715, gang 1009, 1295, 1316

gegangan VII *win, obtain* inf 2536; infl inf tō gegangenne 2416; p ptc gegongen 3085; *bring about* p ptc gegongen 893; *reach* p ptc gegongen; *come to pass* pres 3s gegangeð 1846; p ptc gegongen 822, 2821, 3036

ganot m *gannet* gs ganotes 1861

gār m *spear* ns 1846, 3021; gs gāres 1765; ds gāre 1075; np gāras 328; *arrow* ds gāre 2440

gārcēne adj *martially brave* nsm 1958

gārcwealm m *death by spear* as 2043

gārholt n *forest of spears* as 1834

gārsecg m *ocean* as 49, 515, 537

gārwiga m *spearman, warrior* ds gārwigan 2674, 2811

gārwīgend m *spearman, warrior* ap 2641

gāst m *ghost, creature, demon, spirit* ns gǣst 102, 2073, 2312; as gāst 1274; gs gāstes 133, 1747; gp gāsta 1357, gǣsta 1123

gāstbona m *slayer of souls, devil* ns 177

gǣdeling m *kinsman* gs gǣdelinges 2617; dp gǣdelingum 2949

gǣst see gāst

gǣst see gist

ge conj *and* 1340, 2258; correl ge . . . ge *both* . . . *and* 1248, 1864
gē pron see þū
geador adv *together* 835, geador ætsomne 491
geald see gyldan
gealdor n *sound* as 2944; *spell* ds galdre 3052
gealp see gylpan
gēap adj *broad, spacious* nsm 1800; as gēapne 836
gēar n *year, spring* ns 1134; gp geāra adv *long ago* 2664
geara adj see gearo
geard m *dwelling, precinct* ap geardas 1134; dp geardum 13, 265, 1138, 2459 [MnE yard]
geārdagas mp *days of yore* dp geārdagum 1, 1354, 2233
geare see gearwe
gearo adj *ready* nsm 1825, 2414, gearu 1109, geara 1914; nsf gearo 121, 2118, 3105; asf 1006; npm gearwe 211, 1247, *equipped* 1813
gearo adv see gearwe
gearofolm adj *ready-handed* nsm 2085
gearwe adv *readily, well* 265, 2339, 2725, geare 2062, 2070, 2656, gearo 2748; gearwe ne *not at all* 246, 878. Compar gearwor *more clearly* 3074. Superl gearwost *most clearly* 715
geatolīc adj *splendid* nsn 1562; asn 308, 2154; apn 215; nsm *in fine array* 1401
geatwa f *precious objects* ap 3088
gegncwide m *answer* gp gegncwida 367
gegnum adv *directly, straight* 314, 1404
gehðo see giohðo
gēn adv *still, further, yet* 83, 734, 2070, 2081, 2149, 2237, 2677, 2859, 3006, 3167, *again* 2702
gēna adv *henceforward* 2800, *still* 3093
gende see gengan
gengan 1 *ride, go* pret 3s gengde 1412, gende 1401
gēnunga adv *completely* 2871
geō adv *formerly* 1476, iū 2459, giō 2521
gēoc f *help* as gēoce 177, 608, 2674; ds 1834
gēocor adj *grievous* nsm 765
geofena see gifu
geofon m, n *sea, ocean* ns 515, gifen 1690; gs geofones 362, gyfenes 1394
geofum see gifu
geogoð f *young warriors, youth* ns 66, giogoð 1190; as geogoðe 1181; gs geogoþe 160, 621, iogoþe 1674; *youth, early time of life* as gioguðe 2112; ds geogoþe 409, 466, 2512, giogoðe 2426

geogoðfeorh m, n *youth, youthful time of life* ds geogoðfēore 537, geoguðfēore 2664
geolo adj *yellow* asf geolwe 2610
geolorand m *yellow shield, golden shield* as 438
geōmēowle f *wife of old, woman of a former day* as iōmēowlan 2931
geōmor adj *sad* nsm 49, 2100, 2632; nsf geōmuru 1075; *troubled, grim* nsm geōmor 2419
geōmore adv *sadly* 151
geōmorgyd n *mournful song* as giōmorgyd 3150
geōmorlīc adj *sad* nsn 2444
geōmormōd adj *sad at heart* nsm 2044, giō-mormōd 2267; nsf 3018
geōmrian 2 *lament* pret 3s geōmrode 1118
geōmuru see geōmor
geond prep wa *throughout, through* 75, 266, 840, 1280, 1704, 1771, 1981, 2264, 3099 [MnE (be)yond]
geondbrǣdan 1 *overspread* p ptc geondbrǣded 1239
geondhweorfan III *go throughout* pret 3s geondhwearf 2017
geondsēon V *look over* pret 1s geondseh 3087 [MnE (be)yond, see]
geondwlītan I *look over* inf giondwlītan 2771
geong adj *young* nsm 13, 20, 854, 1831, giong 2446, geonga 2675; asm geongne 1969; dsm geongum 1843, 1948, 2044, 2674, 2811, geongan 2626, 2860; apm geonge 2018; dpm geongum 72; nsf geong 1926, 2025. Superl nsn gingæste *last* 2817
gēong see gangan
geong see gangan
georn adj wg *eager* nsm 2783
georne adv *eagerly, willingly, firmly* 66, 669, 968, 2294. Compar geornor *the more surely* 821
geōsceaft m *fate* as 1234
geōsceaftgāst m *fateful creature* gp geōsceaft-gāsta 1266
gēotan II *rush, overwhelm* pres ptc nsn gēo-tende 1690
gestsele m *guest-hall* as 994
gētan 1 *let blood, bleed (*causative*)* inf 2940
gidd n *song, tale, dirge* ns 2105, gid 1065, gyd 1160; as gid 1723, gyd 2108, 2446; gp gidda 868; dp giddum 1118, gyddum 151; *speech* as gyd 2154
gif conj *if* 272, 346, 442, 447, 452, 527, 593, 661, 684, 1185, 1379, 1477, 1481, 1822, 1826, 1836, 1846, 2514, 2519, 2637, 2841, gyf 280,

gif (*cont.*)

944, 1104, 1182, 1382, 1852; *whether, if* gif 1140, 1319

gifan V *give* inf giofan 2972; pret 3s geaf 1719, 2146, 2173, 2431, 2623, 2635, 2640, 2865, 2919, 3009, 3034; 3p gēafon 49; p ptc gyfen 64, 1678, 1948

gifen see geofon

gifeðe adj *granted (by fate)* nsm 2730; nsn 299, 2491, 2682, gyfeþe 555, 819

gifeðe n. fate ns 3085

gifheall f *gift-hall* as gifhealle 838

gīfre adj *greedy* nsf 1277. Superl nsm gīfrost 1123

gifsceatt m *gift* ap gifsceattas 378

gifstōl m *throne, gift-seat* ns 2327; as 168 [MnE gift, stool]

gifu f *gift* ns 1884; as gife 1271, 2182; gp gifa 1930, geofena 1173; dp geofum 1958

gīgant m *giant* np gīgantas 113; gp gīganta 1562, 1690

gilp n *boast, vow* as 829, gylp 2528, on gylp *high-mindedly, honourably* 1749; ds gylpe (adv) *gloriously* 2521 [MnE yelp]

gilpcwide m *vow, boast* ns 640

gilphlæden adj *gifted with magniloquence, eloquent* nsm 868 [MnE yelp, laden]

gim m *jewel* ns 2072; gp gimme (= a) 466

ginfæst adj *ample, great* asf gimfæste 1271; asf ginfæstan 2182

gingæst see geong

giō see geō

giofan see gifan

giogoð see geogoð

giohðo f *sorrow* as 2267; ds giohðe 2793, gehðo 3095

giōmor see geōmor

giond- see geond-

giong see geong

gīong see gēong

*ge*giredan see *ge*gyrwan

gist m *stranger, guest* ns 1138, 1522, gæst 1800; as gist 1441; np gistas 1602; ap gæstas 1893; ds gyste *intruder* 2227

git see þū

gīt see gȳt

gladian 2 *shine, gleam* pres 3p gladiað 2036

glæd adj *gracious, kind* nsm 1173; asm glædne 863, 1181; dsm gladum 2025; apm glæde 58 [MnE glad]

glædman adj *gracious* ns 367

glædmōd adj *glad in mind* nsm 1785

glēd f *flame, fire* ns 2652, 3114; dp glēdum 2312, 2335, 2677, 3041

glēdegesa m *fiery terror* ns 2650

glēo n *music* ns 2105 [MnE glee]

glēobēam m *harp, lyre* gs glēobēames 2263 [MnE glee, beam]

glēodrēam m *mirth* as 3021 [MnE glee, dream]

glēomann m *minstrel, singer* gs glēomannes 1160 [MnE gleeman]

glīdan I *glide* pret 3s glād 2073; 2p glidon 515

glitinian 2 *glitter* inf 2758

glōf f *glove, sack* ns 2085

gnēað adj *niggardly, frugal* nsf 1930

gnorn m *affliction* as 2658

gnornian 2 *mourn* pret 3s gnornode 1117

god m *god* ns 13, 72, 381, 478, 685, 701, 930, 1056, 1271, 1553, 1658, 1716, 1725, 1751, 2182, 2650, 2874, 3054; as 181, 811; gs godes 570, 711, 786, 1682, 2469, 2858; ds gode 113, 227, 625, 1397, 1626, 1997

gōd adj *good* nsm 11, 195, 279, 863, 1870, 2263, 2390, 2543, 2563, gōda 205, 355, 675, 758, 1190, 1518, 2944, 2949; asm gōdne 199, 347, 1486, 1595, 1810, 1969, 2184; dsm gōdum 3036, 3114, gōdan 384, 2327, npm gōde 2249, gōdan 1163; apm gōde 2641; gpm gōdra 2648; nsn gōd 1562; dpf gōdum 2178; nsm lārena gōd *generous with advice* 269. Compar betera *better* nsm 469, 1703, sēlra 860, 2193, sēlla 2890; asm sēlran 1197, 1850; dsm 1468; nsn sēlra 1384; asn 1759; npf sēlran 1839; nsm sēlra *of higher rank* 2199. Superl bet(o)st *best* nsm betst 1109, betsta 947, 1759, nsm sēlesta 412; asm betstan 1871, sēlestan 1406, 1956, 2382; npm 416; apm 3122; nsn sēlest 146, 173, 285, 935, 1059, 1389, 2326; asn betst 453, sēlest 454, 658, 1144; dsm sēlestan 1685; nsf betost 3007, sēlest 256

gōd n *goodness* ds gōde 956, 1952; *good actions, good deeds* ds gōde 20, 1184; *goods, gifts* dp gōdum 1861; *skill, good practice* gp gōda 681

gōdfremmend m *doer of good* gp gōdfremmendra 299

gold n *gold* ns 1107, 1193, 2765, 3012, 3052, 3134; as 2276, 2536, 2758, 2793, 3105, 3167; gs goldes 1093, 1694, 2246, 2301; ds golde 304, 553, 777, 927, 1028, 1054, 1382,1484, 1900, 2102, 2192, 2931, 3018

goldæht f *gold-hoard* as 2748

gold-fāg adj *adorned with gold* nsm goldfāh

goldfähne 2811; asn goldfäh 308;
npn goldfäg 994
goldgyfa m *lord, gold-giver* as goldgyfan 2652
goldhroden adj *adorned with gold* nsf 614, 640,
1948, 2025
goldhwæt adj *gold-bestowing* asf goldhwæte
3074
goldmāðum m *gold-treasure* ap goldmāðmas
2414
goldsele m *gold-hall* as 715, 1253; ds 1639,
2083
goldweard m *guardian of the gold* as 3081[MnE
gold, ward]
goldwine m *prince, gold-friend* ns 1171, 1602,
1476, 2419, 2584
goldwlanc adj *proud of his gold (rewards)* nsm
1881
gombe f *tribute* as gomban 11
gomol see **gamol**
gomen n *joy, revelry* ns 2263, 2459, gamen
1160; as gamen 3021; ds gomene 1775,
gamene *sport* 2941 [MnE game]
gomenwāþ f *happy journey* ds gomenwāþe 854
gomenwudu m *harp, lyre, mirth-wood* ns 1065;
as 2108
*ge*gongan see *ge*gangan
gram adj *hostile* gsm grames 765; npm graman
777; dpm gramum 424, 1034
grāp f *grip* ds grāpe 438, 555; dp grāpum 765,
1542; gs grāpe *claw* 836
grāpian 2 *strike, grope* pret 3s grāpode 1566,
2085
grǣdig adj *greedy* nsf 121, 1499; asn 1522
grǣg adj *grey* npn 330; apf grǣge 334
grǣgmǣl adj *grey-coloured* nsn 2682
grǣsmolde f *grassy land* as grǣsmoldan 1881
[MnE grass-mould]
grēot n *earth* ds grēote 3167 [MnE grit]
grēotan II *weep* pres 3s grēoteþ 1342
grētan I *salute, greet, pay respect to* inf 168, 347,
1646, 2010, 3095; pret 3s grętte 614, 625,
1816; *attack, touch, approach* inf grētan 803,
2421, 2735; pret 3s grętte 1893, 2108; pret
subj 2s 1995; 3s 3081; p ptc grēted 1065
*ge*grētan I *greet, address* inf gegrēttan 1861;
pret 3s gegrętte 652, 1979, 2516
grīmhelm m *mask-helmet* ap grīmhelmas 334
grimlīc adj *fierce* nsm 3041
grimm adj *grim* nsm grim 555, 2043, 2227,
2650, grimma 102; asm grimne 1148, 1234,
2136; nsf grim 121, 1499, 2860; gsf grimre
527; dpf grimman 1542
grimman III *clamour* pret 3p grummon 306

grimme adv *grimly* 3012, 3085
grīpan I *seek to get hold of, reach (towards)* pret
3s grāp 1501
gripe m *attack* ns 1765; as 1148
gromheort adj *hostile-hearted* nsm 1682
gromhȳdig adj *hostile-minded* nsm 1749
grōwan VII *grow* pret 3s grēow 1718
grund m *ground, earth* as 1551; ap grundas
1404, 2073; *ground, bottom* as grund 1367,
1394; ds grunde 553, 2294, 2758, 2765
grundbūend m *earth-dweller* gp grundbūendra
1006
grundhyrde m *guardian of the deep* as 2136
grundsele m *earth-hall, cave* ds 2139
grundwong m *bottom* as 1496, *earth, ground* as
2588, *floor* as 2770
grundwyrgen f *(female) monster of the deep* as
grundwyrgenne 1518
grynna see **gyrn**
gyre m *terror, horror* ns 1282; as 478; ds 384;
gp gryra 591; dp gryrum ecga *with terrible
swords* 483
gyrebrōga m *horror* ns 2227
gyrefāh adj *gleaming horribly* adj nsm 3041;
asm gryrefāhne 2576
gyregeatwe fp *fearsome equipment* dp gryregeatwum 324
gyregiest m *terrible stranger* ds gryregieste
2560
gyreleōð n *song of terror* as 786
gyrelīc adj *terrible* asm gryrelīcne 1441, 2136
gyresīð m *perilous expedition* ap gryresīðas
1462
guma m *man* ns 20, 652, 868, 973, 1384, 1682,
2178; as guman 1843, 2294; ds 2821; np 215,
306, 666, 1648; ap 614; gp gumena 73, 328,
474, 715, 878, 1058, 1171, 1367, 1476, 1499,
1602, 1824, 2043, 2233, 2301, 2416, 2516,
2859, 3054; dp gumum 127, 321
gumcynn n *race* gs gumcynnes 260, *mankind*
2765; dp æfter gumcynnum *among men* 944
gumcyst f *manly virtue, generosity to men* ap
gumcyste 1723; dp gumcystum 1486, 2543
gumdrēam m *joy of men, life* as 2469
gumdryhten m *lord of men* ns 1642
gumfēþa m *foot-troop* ns 1401
gummann m *man* gp gummanna 1028
gumstōl m *throne* ds gumstōle 1952
gūð f *war, battle* ns 1123, 1658, 2483, 2536; as
gūðe 603; gs 483, 527, 630, 1997, 2356, 2626;
ds 438, 1472, 1535, 2353, 2491, 2878; gp
gūða 2512, 2543; dp gūðum 1958, 2178
gūðbeorn m *warrior* gp gūðbeorna 314

gūðbill n *war-sword* ns 2584; gp gūðbilla 803

gūðbyrne f *battle-corslet* ns 321

gūðcearu f *battle-sorrow* ds gūðceare 1258

gūðcræft m *battle-strength* ns 127

gūðcyning m *war-king* ns 2335, 2563, 2677, 3036; as 199, 1969

gūðdēað m *death in battle* ns 2249

gūðfloga m *winged attacker* as gūðflogan 2528

gūðfreca m *fighter* ns 2414

gūðfremmend m *war-maker* gp gūðfremmendra 246

gūðgetāwa fp *battle-gear* ap 2636; dp gūðgetāwum 395

gūðgewǣde n *war-garments, armour* np gūðgewǣdo 227; ap gūðgewǣdu 2617, 2730, 2851, 2871, gūðgewǣda 2623

gūðgeweorc n *warlike deed* gp gūðgeweorca 678, 981, 1825 [MnE -work]

gūðhelm n *battle-helmet* ns 2487

gūðhorn n *war-horn* as 1432

gūðhreð n *triumph in battle* ns 819

gūðlēoð n *war-song* as 1522

gūþmōd adj *war-minded one* np 306

gūðrǣs m *battle-storm, attack* as 2991; gp gūðrǣsa 1577, 2426

gūðrēouw adj *fierce in battle* nsm 58

gūðrinc m *warrior* ns 838, 1118, 1881; as 1501; gp gūðrinca 2648

gūðrōf adj *brave in battle* nsm 608

gūðscear m *battle-carnage* ds gūðsceare 1213

gūðsceaða m *hostile ravager* ns 2318

gūðsearo n *armour* np 328; ap 215

gūðsele m *hall of warriors* ds 443

gūðsweord n *war-sword* as 2154

gūðwērig adj *exhausted by battle* asm gūðwērigne 1586 [MnE -weary]

gūðwiga m *warrior* ns 2112

gūðwine m *war-friend, sword* as 1810; dp gūðwinum 2735

gyd see gidd

gyddian 2 *speak* pret 3s gyddode 630

gyf see gif

gyfen n see geofon

gyfen p ptc see gifan

gyfeþe see gifeðe

gyldan III *pay, repay* inf 11, 1184, 2636; pret 1s geald 2491; 3s 1047, 2991 [MnE yield]

gylden adj *golden* asm gyldenne 47, 1021, 2809; dsm gyldnum 1163; nsn gylden 1677

gylp see gilp

gylpan III *boast* inf 2874; pres 1s gylpe 586; 3s gylpeð 2055; pret 3s gealp 2583 [MnE yelp]

gylpsprǣc f *boasting speech* ds gylpsprǣce 981

gylpword n *boastful word* gp gylpworda 675

gȳman 1 wg *have regard for, heed, be obsessed with* pres 3s gȳmeð 1757, 2451; imp s gȳm 1760

gynn adj *spacious* asm gynne 1551

gyrdan 1 *gird* p ptc gyrded *girded, belted* 2078

gyrede see gyrwan

gyrn mfn? *affliction* ns 1775; gp grynna 930

gyrnwracu f *revenge for injury* gs gyrnwræce 2118; ds 1138

gyrwan 1 *prepare, arm, equip (oneself), adorn* pret 3s gyrede 1441; 3p gyredon 994; p ptc gegyred 1472, nsf gegyrwed 2087, nsn 553, asf gegyrede 2192, apm 1028

gegyrwan 1 *adorn, prepare* inf 38, 199; pret 3p gegiredan 3137

gyst see gist

gystran adv *yester(day)* adv gystran niht *yesternight, yesterday night* 1334

gȳt adv *yet, still* 944, 956, 1127, 1134, 1164, 1256, 1276, 1824, 2141, 2512, gīt 536, 583, 1058, 1377, 2975, *furthermore* gȳt 47, 1050, gīt 1866

gȳtsian 2 *become covetous* pres 3s gȳtsað 1749

habban 3 *have, hold* inf 446, 1176, 1490, 1798, 2740, 3017, *keep, harbour* 462; pres 1s hæbbe 383, 408, 433, 950 etc., hafu 2523, hafo 2150, 3000; pres 2s hafast 953, 1174, 1221, 1849, 1855; pres 3s hafað 474, 595, 939, etc.; pres 1p habbað 270; pres subj 3s hæbbe 381, 1928; imp s hafa 658, 1395; negative pres 3p næbben 1850; pret 1s hæfde 2145; pret 3s 79, 106, 205, 220, 518, 554, 1625, 2158, 2430, 2579, etc.; pret 1p hæfdon 539, 2104; pret 3p 117, 562; pret subj 3s hæfde 1550

hād m *rank, form, manner* as on gesīðes hād *with the rank of companion* 1297, on sweordes hād *in the form of a sword* 2193; þurh hæstne hād *in violent manner* 1335 [MnE -hood (as in childhood, brotherhood)]

hādor adj *clear-voiced* nsm 497

hādre adv *brightly* 1571

hafa see habban

hafela m *head* as hafelan 1327, 1421, 1448, 1614, 1635, 1780, hafalan 446; gs heafolan 2697; ds 2679, hafelan 672, 1372, 1521; np 1120

hafen see hebban

hafenian 2 *raise* pret 3s hafenade 1573

hafo see habban

hafoc m *hawk* ns 2263

hafu see habban

haga m *enclosure, encampment* ds hagan 2892, 2960

hāl adj *unharmed, hale* nsm 300, 1974; dsn hālan 1503; nsm wes þū . . . hāl *greetings, hail to you* 407 [MnE whole, hale]

hālig adj *holy* nsm 381, 686, 1553

hals see heals

hām m *home* ns 2325; as 717, 1407, 1601 (adv *homewards*); gs hāmes 2366, 2388; ds hām 124, 194, 374, 1147, 1156, 1248, 1923, 2992; ap hāmas 1127

hamer m *hammer* ds hamere 1285; gp homera 2829

hāmweorðung f *ennobler of an estate, exalter of a home* as hāmweorðunge 2998

hand f *hand* ns 1343, 2099, 2137, 2697, hond 1520, 2216, 2488, 2509, 2609, 2684; as hand 558, 983, 1678, 2208, hond 656, 686, 834, 927, 2405, 2575; ds handa 495, 540, 746, 1290, 1983, 2720, 3023, 3124, honda 814; dp hondum 1443, 2840

handbona m *slayer with the hand* ds handbonan 460, handbanan 1330, 2502 [MnE hand, bane]

handgestealla m *comrade* ds hondgesteallan 2169; np handgestealan 2596 [MnE hand-]

handgewrīþen adj *twisted by hand* apf handgewrīþene 1937

handlēan n *requital with the hand, return blow* as 1541, hondlēan 2094

handscolu f *troop of retainers* ds handscale 1317, hondscole 1963 [MnE hand, shoal]

handsporu f *claw* ns 986 [MnE hand, spur]

hangian 2 *hang* inf 1662; pres 3s hangað 2447; pres 3p hongiað 1363; pret 3s hangode 2085

hār adj *hoary* nsm 1307, 3136; gsm hāres 2988; *grey* asm hārne 887, 1415, 2553, 2744; dsm hārum 1678; asf hāre 2153

hāt adj *hot* nsm 897, 2296, 2547, 2558, 2691, 3148; asm hātne 2781; dsm or n hāton 849, hātan 1423; apm hāte 2819; nsn hāt 1616; gsn hātes 2522. Superl hātost 1668

hāt n *heat* as 2605

hātan VII *order, command* inf 68; pres 1s hāte 293; 3p hātað 2802; pret 3s hēt 198, 391, 674, 1045, 1114, 1868, 1920, 2152, 2156, 2190, 2812, 3095, 3110, heht 1035, 1053, 1786, 1807, 1808, 2337, 2892; imp s hāt 386; p ptc hāten 991; *name, call* pres subj 3p hātan 2806; p ptc hāten 102, 263, 373, 2602 [archaic MnE hight]

gehātan VII *promise* pres 1s gehāte 1392, 1671; pret 3s gehēt 2134, 2989; pret 1p gehēton

2634; p ptc nsf gehāten 2024; *threaten* pret 3s gehēt 2937; *vow* pret 3p gehēton 175

hatian 2 *hate, show hatred* inf 2466; pret 3s hatode 2319

haðor n *compass, vault* as 414

hæf n *sea* ap heafo 2477

hæfen see hebban

hæft m *captive* ns 2408; as hæfton 788

hæftmēce m *hilted sword* ds 1457

hæftnȳd f *captivity* as 3155

hægsteald adj *young (man)* gpm hægstealdra 1889

hǣl n *omen* ap 204

hǣl f *success* as 653

hæle m *hero, man* ns 1646, 1816, 3111, hæleð 190, 331; np 52, 2247, 2458, 3142; ap 1069; gp hæleþa 467, 611, 662, 912, 1047, 1189, 1198, 1296, 1830, 1852, 1954, 2052, hæleða 497, 2072, 2224, 3005, 3111; dp hæleðum 1709, 1961, 2024, 2262

hæleð see hæle

hǣlo f *prosperity, fortune, luck* as hæle 719, 2418; ds 1217 [MnE hail]

hærgtræf n *heathen temple* dp hærgtrafum 175

hǣste adj *violent* asm hǣstne 1335

hǣðen adj *heathen* gsm hǣþenes 986; gpm hǣþenra 179; asn hǣðen 2276; dsn hǣðnum 2216; asf hǣþene 852

hǣðen m *heathen* dpm hǣðnum 1983

hǣðstapa m *stag, heath-rover* ns 1368

hē pers pron m *he* ns hē 7, 29, 80, 88, 108, 109, 114, 168, 199, etc. as *him* hine 22, 43, 45, 109, 232, 265, 347, 372, 381, etc., hyne 28, 142, 975, 1205, 1436, 1628, etc.; gs *his* his 65, 79, 169, 250, 349, 357, 360, 373, 375, etc.; ds *him, to him, by him* him 9, 16, 40, 41, 47, 56, 65, 67, 72, 106, etc., *for it* 78, *to it* 313, poss dat 40, 67, 726, 755, 816, 1547, 1718, etc.; refl dat (usually not translated) 26, 234, 662, 1272, 2061, 2062, etc.; n *it hit* ns 77, 83, 134, 272, 561, 891, 1239, 1460, 1532, etc., hyt 2091, 2310, 2649, 2679, etc.; as hit 116, 779, 1461, 1671, etc. hyt 2158, 2248, etc.; gs *of it* his 2157; ds him *for it* 78, *to it* 313; f *she* hēo ns 627, 944, 1215, etc., hīo 623, 1929, 1941, *it* 455, etc., hīe 2019; gs hire 641, 1115, 1546, hyre 1188, 1339, 1545; 2121; ds 626, 1521, 1566, 1935, hyre 945, 2175, 3153; np hīe 15, 47, 132, 175, 180, 2039, etc., hī 28, 43, 1628, 1966, etc., hig 1085, 1596, hȳ 307, 364, 368, 2124, etc.; ap hīe 477, 694, 706, 1068, 2236, hig 1770, hȳ 1048, 2233, 2592; gp heora 691, 698, 1604, 1636, hiora 1166, 2599, 2994,

hē (*cont.*)

hiera 1164, hira 1102, 1124, 1249, hyra 178, 324, 1012, 1055, etc.; dp him 177, 203, 228, 301 (refl), 312, 1127 (refl), 1252, poss dat 47, 49, 1242

hēaburh f *lofty stronghold* as 1127

heafo see **hæf**

hēafod n *head* ns 1648; as 48, 1639; ds hēafde 1590, 2138, 2290, 2973; dp hēafdon 1242

hēafodbeorg f *head-protection* as hēafodbeorge 1030

hēafodmǣg m *close kinsman* gp hēafodmāga 2151; dp hēafodmǣgum 588

hēafodsegn m, n *sign of special importance* as 2152

hēafodweard f *watch at the head* as hēafodwearde 2909

heafola see **hafela**

hēah adj *high, tall, illustrious* nsm 57, 82, 1926, 2805, 3157; asm 48, hēanne 983, hēan 3097; dsm hēaum 2212, hēan 713, 919, 1016, 1984; asn hēah 48, 2768; gsn hēan 116

hēahcyning m *high-king* gs hēahcyninges 1039

hēahgesceap n *high destiny* as 3084

hēahgestrēon n *great treasure* gp hēahgestrēona 2302

hēahlufu f *deep love* as hēahlufan 1954

hēahreced n *lofty building* as 1981

hēahsele m *lofty hall* ds 647

hēahsetl n *throne, high seat* as 1087

hēahstede m *lofty place* ds 285

healdan VII *hold, guard, occupy, possess, rule* inf 230, 296, 319, 704, 1182, 1348, 1852, 2372, 2389, 2477, 3034, 3166; infl inf tō healdanne 1731; pres 2s healdest 1705; 3s healdeð 2909; subj 3s healde 2719; pret 1s hēold 241, 466, 2732, 2737, 2751; 3s 57, 103, 142, 161, 305, 788, 1031, 1079, 1748, 1959, 2183, 2279, 2414, 2430, 3043, 3084, 3118, hīold 1954; 3p hēoldon 401, 1214; subj 3s hēolde 1099, 2344; imp s heald 948, 2247; *perform* pret 3s hēold 2377

*ge*healdan VII *hold, guard, keep, rule* inf 674, 911, 2856; pres 3s gehealdeþ 2293; subj 3s gehealde 317; pret 3s gehēold 2208, 2620, 3003; imp s geheald 658

healf adj *half* gsf healfre 1087

healf f *half* ds healfe 2262; ap 2063, healfa 1095, 1305; gp 800; *account* as healfe 1675

healgamen n *entertainment in the hall* as 1066

heall f *hall* ns 487, heal 1151, 1214; as healle 1087; ds 89, 614, 642, 663, 925, 1009, 1288, 1926

heallǣrn n *hall-building* gp healǣrna 78

healreced n *hall-building* as 68

heals m *neck* as 2691; ds healse 1872, 2809, 3017, halse 1566

healsbēag m *neck-ring, torque* as healsbēah 2172; gp healsbēaga 1195

healsgebedda m *wife, close bedfellow* ns 63

healsian 2 *implore* pret 3s healsode 2132

healsittende m *one sitting in the hall, courtier* gp healsittendra 2015; dp healsittendum 2868

healðegn m *hall-thane* gs healðegnes 142; ap healðegnas 719

healwudu m *hall-wood, floor* ns 1317

hēan adj *humiliated, abject, despised* nsm 1274, 2099, 2183, 2408

hēan, hēanne see **hēah**

hēap m *troop, multitude* ns 400, 432, 1627, 1889; as 335, 730, 1091; ds hēape 2596 [MnE heap]

heard adj *hard, strong, brave, intense, stern, severe* nsm 322, 342, 376, 404, 886, 1539, 2539, hearda 401, 432, 1435, 1807, 1963, 2255, 2474, 2977; asm heardne 1590; dsm heardum 2170, heardan 2482; nsn heard 1566, 2037, 2509, hearde 1343, 1553, asn heard 1574, 2687, 2987; nsf 551, 2914; dpm heardum 1335, heardan 963; apn heard 540, 2638; npf hearde 2829; gpf heardra 166; gpn 988. Compar asf heardran 576, 719

hearde adv *hard, sorely* 1438, 3153

heard-ecg adj *hard-edged* nsn 1288; asn 1490

heardhicgende adj *brave-minded* npm 394, 799

hearm m *harm, insult* ds hearme 1892

hearmscaþa m *terrible ravager* ns 766

hearpe f *harp, lyre* gs hearpan 89, 2107, 2262, 2458, 3023

heaðerian 2 *imprison* p ptc geheaðerod 3072

heaðobyrne f *battle corslet, armour* ns 1552

heaþodēor adj *brave in battle* ns 688; dpm heaþodēorum 772

heaðofȳr n *deadly fire* gs heaðufȳres 2522; dp heaðofȳrum 2547

heaðogrim adj *battle-grim, fierce in battle* ns 548, 2691

heaðolāc n *battle* gs heaðolāces 1974; ds heaðolāce 584

heaþolīðende m *sea-warrior* np 1798; dp heaðolīðendum 2955

heaðomǣre adj *battle-famed (one)* npm 2802

heaþorǣs m *storm of battle, fierce attack* ns 557; ap heaþorǣsas 1047; gp heaðorǣsa 526

heaðorēaf n *war-gear* as 401

heaðorinc m *warrior* as 2466; dp heaðorincum 370

heaþorōf adj *brave in battle* nsm 381, 2191; npm heaþorofe 864

heaðosceard adj *notched in battle* npf heaðoscearde 2829 [MnE shard, sherd]

heaðosīoc adj *sick from battle, wounded* dsm heaðosīocum 2754

heaþostēap adj *towering in battle* nsm heaþostēapa 1245; asm heaðostēapne 2153 [MnE steep]

heaþoswāt m *battle-sweat*, (i.e. *blood*) ds heaþoswāte 1460, 1606; gp heaþoswāta 1668

heaðotorht adj *clear in battle* nsf 2553

heaðowǣd f *battle garments* dp heaðowǣdum 39

heaðoweorc n *outcome of battle* as 2892

heaðowylm m *hostile surge, fire* gp heaðowylma 82; ap heaðowylmas 2819

heaþu m *war* as 1862

heaðusweng m *battle-blow, sword-stroke* ds heaðuswenge 2581

hēawan VII *hew* inf 800

*ge*hēawan VII *hew, cut through* pres subj 3s gehēawe 682

hebban VI *lift* inf 656; p ptc hafen 1290, hæfen 3023 [MnE heave]

hēdan 1 *wg heed, regard* pret 3s hēdde 2697

*ge*hēdan 1 *care about* pret subj 3s gehēdde 505

*ge*hēgan 1 *hold (a meeting)* inf 425

heht see **hātan**

hell f *hell* ns hel 852; as helle 179; gs 788, 1274; ds 101, 588

hellbend f *hell-bond* dp hellbendum 3072

helm m *helmet* ns 1245, 1448, 1629, 2255, 2659, 2762; as 672, 1022, 1290, 1526, 1745, 2153, 2615, 2723, 2811, 2868, 2973, 2979, 2987; gs helmes 1030; ds helme 342, 404, 1286, 2539; ap helmas 2638; dp helmum 3139; *refuge, cover* as helm 1392; *protector, lord* ns 371, 456, 1321, 1623, 2462, 2705; as 182, 2381

helmberend m *helmet-wearer, warrior* ap 2517, 2642

help f *help* as helpe 551, 1552, 2448; ds 1709, 1961, 1830

helpan III *help* wd inf 2340, 2649, 2684, wg 2879; pret 3s healp 2698

helrūne f *demon* (lit. *one skilled in the mysteries of hell*) np helrūnan 163

hēo see **hē**

heofon m *heaven* ns 3155; gs heofenes 414, heofones 576, 1801, 2015, 2072; ds hefene 1571; gp heofena 182; dp heofenum 52, 505

hēofungdæg m *day of lamentation* ap hēofungdagas 3153

heolfor m or n *gore* ds heolfre 849, 1302, 1423, 2138

heolster m *concealment, hiding* as 755

heonan adv *hence* 252, heonon 1361

hēore adj *pleasant* nsf hēoru 1372

heoroblāc adj *pale from the sword, wounded* nsm 2488

heorodrēore see **heorudrēor**

heorodrēorig adj *sword-gory*, (i.e. *blood-stained*) nsn 935; asm heorodrēorigne 1780, 2720 [MnE dreary]

heorogīfre adj *fiercely ravenous* nsm 1498

heorogrim adj *sword-grim*, (i.e. *fierce*) nsm 1564; nsf heorugrimme 1847

heorohōcyhte adj *barbed* dpm heorohōcyhtum 1438

heorosweng m *sword-stroke* as 1590

heorot m *stag* ns 1369 [MnE hart]

heorowearh m *fierce outcast* ns 1267

heorr m *hinge* np heorras 999

heorte f *heart* ns 2561; gs heortan 2463, 2507; ds 2270

heorðgenēat m *hearth-comrade*, (i.e. *retainer*) np heorðgenēatas 261, 3179; ap 1580, 2180; dp heorðgenēatum 2418

heoru m *sword* ns 1285

heorudrēor m or n *blood, sword-gore* ds heorudrēore 487, heorodrēore 849

hēoðo f *hall, interior* ds hēoðe 404

hēr adv *here* 244, 361, 376, 397, 1061, 1228, 1654, 1820, 2053, 2796, 2801

here m *army* ds herge 1248, 2347, 2638

herebrōga m *fear of armies* ds herebrōgan 462

herebyrne f *army-corslet* ns 1443

heregrīma m *army-mask, helmet* ds heregrīman 396, 2049, 2605

herenet n *army-net, coat of mail* ns 1553

herenið m *hostility* ns 2474

herepād f *army-coat, coat of mail* ns 2258

hererinc m *warrior* as 1176

heresceaft m *army-shaft, spear* gp heresceafta 335

herespēd f *military success* ns 64

herestrǣl m *arrow* ns 1435

heresyrce f *coat of mail* as heresyrcan 1511

herewǣd f *armour* dp herewǣdum 1897

herewǣsm m *martial skill* dp herewǣsmum 677

herewīsa m *army leader* ns 3020

herg m *pagan shrine* dp hergum 3072

herge see here, herian

herian I *praise* inf 182, 1071; pres subj 3s herge 3175; *honour, support* pres subj 1s herige 1833

hete m *hatred* ns 142, 2554

hetelīc adj *hateful* ns 1267

hetend see hettend

hetenīð m *deep enmity* ap hetenīðas 152

hetesweng m *hostile blow* ap heteswengeas 2224

heteþanc m *hateful thought* dp heteþancum 475

hettend m *foe* np hetende 1828; dp hettendum 3004

hī see hē

hicgean see hycgan

hider adv *hither* 240, 370, 394, 3092

hīe see hē

hiera see hē

hig see hē

hige f *mind, heart* ns 593, hyge 755; as hige 267; gs higes 2045; dp higum 3148

higemǣðu f *weariness of heart* dp higemǣðum 2909

higerōf adj *brave-hearted* asm higerōfne 204

higeþīhtig adj *strong-hearted* asm higeþīhtigne 746

higeþrymm m *magnanimity* dp higeþrymmum 339

hild f *war, battle, attack* ns 452, 1481, 1588, 1847, 2076; as hilde 647, 1990; gs 2723; ds 1460, 1659, 2258, 2575, 2684, 2916; *prowess in battle* ns hild 901; as hilde 2952

hildebill n *battle-sword* ns hildebil 1666; ds hildebille 557, 1520, 2679

hildebord n *war-shield* ap 397; dp hildebordum 3139 [MnE -board]

hildecumbor n *battle-standard* as 1022

hildecyst f *martial virtue* dp hildecystum 2598

hildedēor adj *brave in battle* nsm 312, 834, 1646, 1816, 2107, 2183, hildedīor 3111; npm hildedēore 3169

hildegeatwe f *battle-gear* ap 674, hildegeatwa 2362

hildegicel m *battle-icicle* dp hildegicelum 1606

hildegrāp f *battle-grip* ns 1446, 2507

hildehlæmm m *clash of battle* gp hildehlemma 2351, 2544; dp hildehlæmmum 2201

hildelēoma m *battle-gleamer, sword* as hildelēoman 1143; np 2583

hildemēce m *battle-sword* np hildemēceas 2202

hildemecg m *warrior* np hildemecgas 799

hilderand m *battle-shield* ap hilderandas 1242

hilderǣs m *storm of battle* as 300

hilderinc m *warrior* ns 1307, 3136; gs hilderinces 986; ds hilderince 1495, 1576; gp hilderinca 3124

hildesceorp n *armour* as 2155

hildesetl n *saddle, war-seat* ns 1039

hildestrengo f *battle-strength* as 2113

hildeswāt m *battle-vapour* ns 2558

hildetūx m *warlike tusk* dp hildetūxum 1511

hildewǣpen n *war-weapon* dp hildewǣpnum 39

hildewīsa m *battle-leader* ds hildewīsan 1064

hildfreca m *warrior* ds hildfrecan 2366; np 2205

hildfruma m *war-leader* gs hildfruman 2649, 2835; ds 1678

hildlata m *coward* np hildlatan 2846 [MnE late]

hilt n f *hilt* ns 1677; as 1614, 1668, hylt 1687; dp hiltum 1574

hilted adj *hilted* asn 2987

hindema adj superl *last* dsm hindeman 2049, 2517

hine see hē

hinfūs adj *eager to escape* nsm 755

hīo see hē

hīofan II *lament* pres ptc npm hīofende 3142

hiora see hē

hiorodrync m *sword-drink* dp hiorodryncum 2358

hioroserce f *coat of mail* as hiorosercean 2539

hioroweallende adj *gushing with destruction* nsm 2781

hira see hē

hire see hē

his see hē

hit see hē

hladan VI *lay, load* inf 2126, 2775; p ptc hladen 1897, nsn 3134 [MnE lade]

gehladan VI *load* pret 3s gehleōd 895

hlāford m *lord* ns 2375, 2642; as 267, 2283, 3142; gs hlāfordes 3179; ds hlāforde 2634

hlāfordlēas adj *without a lord, leaderless* npm hlāfordlēase 2935

hlāw see hlǣw

hlæst m *cargo, freight* ds hlæste 52

hlǣw m *barrow, burial mound* as 2296, 2411, 2802, 3157, 3169; ds hlāwe 1120, hlǣwe 2773

hleahtor m *laughter* ns 611; as 3020

hlēapan VII *gallop* inf 864 [MnE leap]

hlēo m *protector, lord* ns 429, 791, 899, 1035, 1866, 1972, 2142, 2190, 2337; as 1967 [MnE lee] hlēoburh f *stronghold* as 912, 1731 [MnE lee, borough]

gehlēod see gehladan

hleonian 2 *lean* inf 1415

hlēorberg f *cheek-guard* dp hlēorbergan 304 [MnE leer]

hlēorbolster m *pillow* ns 688

hlēotan II *receive* pret 3s hlēat 2385

hlēoðorcwyde m *courtly speech* as 1979

hlīfian 2 *tower* inf 2805; pret 3s hlīfade 81, 1898, hlīuade 1799

hlimbed n *bed of rest* as 3034

hlīðe n *cliff* gs hlīðes 1892; ds hlīðe 3157

hlīuade see hlīfian

hlūd adj *loud* asm hlūdne 89

hlyn m *noise, din* ns 611

hlynnan 1 *roar, reverberate* inf 2553; pret 3s hlynode 1120

hlynsian 2 *resound* pret 3s hlynsode 770

hlytm m *lot* ds hlytme 3126

gehnǣgan 1 *subdue* pret 3s gehnǣgde 1274

hnāh adj *poor, lowly, niggardly* nsf 1929. Compar dsm hnāhran 952, hnāgran 677

hnītan I *clash* pret 3p hniton 1327, hnitan 2544

hof n *dwelling, court* as 312; ds hofe 1236, 1507, 1974; ap hofu 2313; dp hofum 1836

gehogode see gehycgan

hold adj *loyal, well disposed* nsm 1229, 2161, 2170; asm holdne 267, 376, 1979; gpm holdra 487; nsn hold 290

hōlinga adv *without cause* 1076

holm m *water, sea* ns 519, 1131, 2138; as 48, 632, 1592; ds holme 543, 1435, 1914, 2362; ap holmas 240; gp holma 2132

holmclif n *sea-cliff* ds holmclife 1421, 1635; ap holmclifu 230

holmwylm m *surging sea* ds holmwylme 2411

holt n *wood* as 2598, 2846

holtwudu m *wood, forest* ns 2340; as 1369

homer see hamer

hond see hand

hondgemōt n *hand-to-hand battle* gp hondgemōta 1526, 2355

hondgesella m *close comrade* dp hondgesellum 1481

hondgeweorc n *handiwork* ds hondgeweorce 2835

hondlēan see handlēan

hondlocen adj *linked by hand* nsf 322, 551

hondrǣs m *hand-to-hand battle* ns 2072

hondwundor n *hand-made marvel* gp hondwundra 2768

hongian see hangian

hop n *plateau (in a wasteland), hope* ds 2212

hord n *hoard, treasure* ns 2283, 2284, 3011, 3084; as 912, 2212, 2276, 2319, 2369, 2422, 2509, 2744, 2773, 2799, 2955, 3004, 3056, 3126; gs hordes 887; ds horde 1108, 2216, 2547, 2768, 2781, 3164

hordærn n *treasure-cave* ds hordærne 2831; gp hordærna 2279

hordburh f *treasure-city* as 467 [MnE hoard, borough]

hordgestrēon n *hoarded treasure* gp hordgestrēona 3092; dp hordgestrēonum 1899

hordmāðum m *treasure* as 1198

hordweard m *guardian of a hoard*, (i.e. *a dragon*) ns 2293, 2302, 2554, 2593; (i.e. *a king*) ns 1047; as 1852 [MnE hoard, ward]

hordwela m *hoarded wealth* as hordwelan 2344

hordweorþung f *valuable reward* as hordweorþunge 952

hordwynn f *delightful hoard* as hordwynne 2270

hordwyrðe adj *worthy of being hoarded* asm hordwyrðne 2245

horn m *horn* ns 1423; as 2943; dp hornum 1369

hornboga m *bow (decorated with horn?)* ds hornbogan 2437

horngēap adj *wide-gabled* ns 82

hornreced n *gabled building* as 704

hors n *horse* ns 1399

hōs f *group, retinue* ds hōse 924

hoðma m *grave* ds hoðman 2458

hrā n *corpse* ns 1588

hrāfyl m *fall of the slain, slaughter* as 277

hraþe adv *quickly* 224, 740, 748, 1294, 1310, 1390, 1541, 1576, 1914, 1937, 1975, 2117, 2968, hræþe 1437, hreþe 991, raþe 724. Compar hraþor 543 [MnE rather]

hrædlīce adv *quickly* 356, 963

hrægl n *garment, accoutrement* ns 1195; gs hrægles 1217; gp hrægla 454

hræðre see hreðer

hrēam m *outcry* ns 1302

hrēawīc n *place of corpses* as 1214

hrefn m *raven* ns 1801, 3024; ds hrefne 2448

hrēmig adj *exulting* nsm 124, 1882, 2054; npm hrēmge 2363

hrēoh adj *rough, troubled, fierce* nsm 1564, 2180; dsn hrēoum 2581, hrēon 1307; npf hrēo 548

hrēohmōd adj *troubled in mind, angry* nsm 2132, 2296

hrēosan II *fall* pret 3s hrēas 2488, 2831; 3p hruron 1074, 1430, 1872 hrēow f *sorrow* ns 2328; gp hrēowa 2129 [MnE rue]

hrēð n *triumph* as 2575

hreþe see hraþe

hreðer n *breast, heart, core* ns 2113, 2593; ds hreþre 1151, 1446, 1745, 1878, 2328, 2442, 3148, hræðre 2819; gp hreðra 2045

hreþerbealo n *heartache* ns 1343

hrēðmann m *glorious warrior* gp hrēðmanna 445

hrēðsigor m *glorious victory* gp hrēðsigora 2583

hrīnan I *reach* inf 1515, 3053; *touch* pret 3s hrān 2270; *injure* inf 988; pret subj 3s hrine 2976

hrinde adj *frost-covered* npm 1363

hring m *ring (of gold–used as ornaments and money)* as 1202, 2809; np hringas 1195; ap 1970, 3034; gp hringa 2245, 2345; dp hringum 1091; *ring-mail* ns hring 1503, 2260; gp hringa 1507

hringan I *ring, reverberate* pret 3p hringdon 327

hringboga m *coiled serpent* gs hringbogan 2561

hringed adj *made of ring-mail* nsf 1245; asf hringde 2615

hringedstefna m *curve-prowed ship* ns 32, 1897; as hringedstefnan 1131 [MnE ring, stem]

hringīren n *ring-mail* ns 322 [MnE ring, iron]

hringmæl adj *ring-patterned, ring-adorned* nsn 2037; *ring-patterned sword* ns 1521; as 1564

hringnaca m *curve-prowed ship* ns 1862

hringnet n *coat of mail* as 2754; ap 1889 [MnE ring, net]

hringsele m *ring-hall* ds 2010; *ring-cave (dragon's lair)* as 2840; ds 3053

hringweorðung f *ring-adornment* as hringweorðunge 3017

hroden p ptc *adorned* asn 495, 1022

gehroden p ptc *adorned* npn 304

hrōf m *roof* ns 999; as 403, 836, 926, 983, 1030, 2755

hrōfsele m *roofed hall* ds 1515

hronfisc m *whale* ap hronfixas 540

hronrād f *ocean, whale's riding-place* as hronrāde 10 [MnE -raid, -road]

hrōr adj *strong* dsm hrōran 1629

hrōðor n *benefit, joy* ds hrōðre 2448; gp hrōþra 2171

hruron see hrēosan

hrūse f *ground, surface of the earth* ns 2247, 2558; as hrūsan 772, 2831; ds 2276, 2279, 2411

hrycg m *back* as 471[MnE ridge]

hryre m *fall, death* as 3179; ds 1680, 2052, 3005

hryssan I *shake* pret 3p hrysedon 226

hū adv, conj *how* 3, 116, 279, 737, 844, 979, 1725, 1987, 2093, 2318, 2519, 2718, 2884, 2948, 3026

hund m *dog* dp hundum 1368 [MnE hound]

hund num *hundred* ap 1498, 1769, 2278, 2994

hūru adv *indeed* 182, 369, 669, 1071, 1465, 2836, 3120; *however* 862, 1944

hūs n *house* gs hūses 116, 1666; gp hūsa 146, 285, 658, 935

hūð f *booty* ds hūðe 124

hwā pron m, f *who* ns 52, 2252, 3126; asm hwone *anyone* 155; dsm hwām *whom* 1696; isn tō hwan *to what (result)* 2071; *anyone who* ns hwā 2252

gehwā pron (w part g preceding) *each, every* asm gehwone 294, 800, 2765, gehwane 2397, 2685; gsm gehwæs 2527, 2838; dsm gehwæm 1365, 1420, gehwām 882, 2033; dsn 88; dsf in mǣgþa gehwǣre *in each of tribes,* (i.e. *in every tribe*) 25

hwan see hwā

hwanan adv *whence* 257, 2403, hwanon 333

gehwane see gehwā

hwār see hwǣr

hwat- see hwæt

gehwǣm see gehwā

hwǣr adv, conj *where* hwār 3062, hwǣr *anywhere* 2029, elles hwǣr *elsewhere* 138

gehwǣr adv *everywhere, always* 526

gehwǣre see gehwā

gehwǣs see gehwā

hwæt adj *valiant, bold* nsm hwata 3028; dsm hwatum 2161; npm hwate 1601, 2052; apm 2517, 2642, 3005

hwæt pron n *what* nsn 173; asn 1186, 1476, 3068; *who* nsn 233; *what sort of* 237, asn 474; isn to hwan *to what (result)* 2071; nsn ānes hwæt *one part* 3010; asn swulces hwæt *something of such a matter* 880

hwæt interj *lo, ah* 1 (but see note), 240, 530, 942, 1652, 1774, 2248

hwæðer pron *which of two* 2530, asf swā hwæþere . . . swā *whichsoever* 686 [MnE whether]

gehwæþer pron *either, each* nsm 584, 814, 2171; dsm gehwæðrum 2994; nsn gehwæþer 1248; gsn gehwæþres 1043

hwæþer conj *whether* 1314, 1331, 1356, 2785

hwæþre adv *however, yet* 555, 890, 1270, 2098, 2228, 2298, 2377, 2874, hwæþere 574, 578,

970, 1718, hwæðre swā þēah *yet nevertheless* 2442

hwealf n *vault* as 576, 2015

gehwelc see **gehwylc**

hwēne adv *somewhat* 2699

hweorfan III *go, turn, move* inf 2888, hworfan 1728; pret 3s hwearf 55, 356, 1188, 1573, 1714, 1980, 2238, 2268, 2832; pret subj 3s hwurfe 264

gehweorfan III *pass, go* pret 3s gehwearf 1210, 1679, 1684, 2208

hwergen adv *somewhere* elles hwergen *elsewhere* 2590

hwettan I *encourage, urge* pres subj 3s hwette 490; pret 3p hwetton 204 [MnE whet]

hwīl f *while, space of time* ns 146; as hwīle 16, 1762, 2030, 2097, 2137, 2159, 2548, 2571, 2780; *daytime* ns hwīl dæges 1495; ds dæges hwīle 2320; *night-time* dp nihtes hwīlum 3044; *sometimes, at times* dp hwīlum 175, 496, 864, 867, 916, 1728, 1828, 2016, 2020, 2107, 2108, 2109, 2111, 2299; *for a long time* as hwīle 105, 152, 240

hwīt adj *shining* nsm hwīta 1448

hworfan see **hweorfan**

hwyder adv *whither* 163

hwylc adj *what, what kind of* npm hwylce 1986, nsf hwylc 2002

hwylc pron (w part g) *which, what* nsm 274; *any(one)* nsm 1104; nsn hwylc 2433; *whichsoever* swā hwylc . . . swā nsf 943; dsm hwylcum 3057

gehwylc pron (w part g) *each, every* nsm 985, 1166, 1673; asm gehwelcne 148, gehwylcne 2250, 2516; gsm gehwylces 732, 1396; dsm gehwylcum 412, 768, 784, 936, 996, 2859, 2891; ism gehwylce 2450; asn gehwylc 2608; gsn gehwylces 2094, 2189; dsn gehwylcum 98; isn gehwylce 1090, 2057; asf 1705; dsf gehwylcre 805

hwyrfan I *move about* pres 3p hwyrfaþ 98

hwyrft m *roaming, movement* dp hwyrftum 163

hycgan 3 *intend, resolve* pret 1s hogode 632

gehycgan 3 *resolve* pret 2s gehogodest 1988

hȳdan I *hide* inf 446, 1372; pres subj 3s hȳde 2766

gehȳdan I *hide* pret 3s gehȳdde 2235, 3059

gehygd f *thought* as 2045

hyge see **hige**

hygebend f *heart's bond* dp hygebendum 1878

hygegīomor adj *sad in mind* nsm 2408

hygemēðe adj *heartsick, weary of mind* nsn 2442

hygesorh f *sorrow* gp hygesorga 2328

hyht m *hope* ns 179

gehyld n *protector* ns 3056

hyldan I *recline* pret 3s hylde 688

hyldo f *favour* as 2293; gs 670, 2998; *loyalty* as 2067

hyne see **hē**

hȳnan I *afflict* pret 3s hȳnde 2319

hȳnðu f *humiliation, affliction* as 277, hȳnðo 3155; gp hȳnða 166, hȳnðo 475, 593

hyra see **hē**

hȳran I *hear, hear of* pret 1s hȳrde 38, 62, 582, 1197, 1346, 1842, 2023, 2163, 2172; 3s 875; 1p hȳrdon 273; wd *obey* inf hȳran 10, 2754; pret 3p hȳrdon 66

gehȳran I *hear, learn* pres 1s gehȳre 290; pret 3s gehȳrde 88, 609; 3p gehȳrdon 785; imp p gehȳrað 255

hyre see **hē**

hyrde m *guardian, keeper, master* ns 610, 750, 931, 1742, 1832, 2245, 2304, 2505, 2644, 2981; as 887, 1849, 2027, 3080, 3133; ap hyrdas 1666

hyrst f *adornment, accoutrement* ap hyrste 2988, hyrsta 3164; dp hyrstum 2762

hyrstan I *adorn* p ptc asn hyrsted 672

hyrstedgold n *golden adornment* ds hyrstedgolde 2255

hyrtan I *encourage* pret 3s hyrte 2593

hyse m *young man* ns 1217

hyt see **hē**

hȳð f *harbour* ds hȳðe 32

hȳðweard m *harbour-guard* ns 1914

ic pron *I* ns 38, 62, 74, 247, 251, etc.; as mec 447, 452, 559, 579, 1481, etc., mē 415, 446, 553, 563, 677; gs mīn 262, 343, 345, etc.; ds mē 316, 355, 409, 472, 2142, etc.; dual n *wit* we two 535, 537, 539, 540, 544, 683, etc.; a unc 540, 545; g uncer 2002, 2532; d unc 1783, 2137, 2525, 2526; np wē 1, 260, 267, 270, 3106, etc.; ap ūsic 458, 2638, 2640, 2641; gp ūser 2074, ūre 1386; dp ūs 269, 346, 382, 1821, 2635, etc., ūrum 2659

icge adj *splendid, mighty* (i.e. *much*) (?) nsn 1107 [a word of uncertain meaning which occurs only here; cf. *incge* 2577]

īdel adj *empty* nsm 413; nsn 145, *bereft, deprived* 2888 [MnE idle]

īdelhende adj *empty-handed* nsm 2081

ides f *woman* ns 620, 1075, 1117, 1168, 1259; gs idese 1351; ds 1649, 1941

in I adv *in, inside* 386, 1037, 1371, 1502, 1644,

in (*cont.*)
  2152, 2190, 2552, inn 3090. II prep wd
  (usually indicating rest) *in* 1, 13, 25, 87, 89,
  180, 324, 395, etc. (postpositioned and
  stressed) 19; *with, as one of* 107; wa (usually
  indicating motion into) *into* 60, 185, 1134,
  1210, 2935, 2981. The case distinctions do
  not always hold: e.g. *in* wa 851
in (1300) see inn n
inc see þū
incer see þū
incge adj *splendid, mighty* (?) dsf 2577 [a word
  of uncertain meaning which occurs only
  here; cf. *icge* 1107]
infrōd adj *very wise* nsm 2449; dsm infrōdum
  1874
ingang m *entry* as 1549
ingenga m *invader* nsm 1776
ingesteald n *household goods* as 1155
inn n *lodging-place, dwelling* ns 1300 [MnE inn]
inn see in adv
innan adv *within, inside* 71, 774, 1017, 1740,
  1968, 2089, 2214, 2244, 2331, 2412, 2452,
  2715, 2719
innanweard adj *within* nsm 991; nsn 1976
  [MnE inward]
inne adv *within, inside* 390, 642, 1281, 1570,
  1800, 1866, 2113, 3059; *þær inne therein* 118,
  1141, 1617, 2115, 2225, 3087
inneweard adj *within* nsn 998 [MnE inward]
inwidsorg see inwitsorh
inwitfeng m *malicious grasp* ns 1447
inwitgæst m *malicious foe* ns 2670
inwithrōf m *inimical roof* as 3123
inwitnet n *net of malice* as 2167
inwitnīð m *enmity, malicious deed* np inwit-
  nīðas 1858; gp inwitnīða 1947
inwitscear m *murderous attack* as 2478
inwitsearo n *malicious cunning, malice* as 1101
inwitsorh f *dire sorrow* ns 1736; as inwidsorge
  831
inwitþanc m *hostile intention* dp inwitþancum
  749
geīode see gegān
iogoð see geogoð
iōmēowle see geōmēowle
īren n *iron sword* ns 892, 989, 1848, 2586; as
  1809, 2050; gp īrenna 802, 2683, 2828, īrena
  673, 1697, 2259
īren adj *iron* nsf 1459, 2778; npf īrenna 802
īrenbend f *iron band* dp īrenbendum 774, 998
īrenbyrne f *iron corslet* as īrenbyrnan 2986
īrenheard adj *iron-hard* nsm 1112

īrenþrēat m *ironclad troop* ns 330
is see bēon
īs n *ice* ds īse 1608
īsernbyrne f *iron corslet* as īsernbyrnan 671
īsernscūr f *shower of iron (arrows)* as īsernscūre
  3116
īsgebind n *icy bond* ds īsgebinde 1133
īsig adj *icy* nsm 33
iū see geō
iūmonn m *man of old* gp iūmonna 3052

kyning see cyning
kyningwuldor see under cyning-

lā interj. *lo, indeed* 1700, 2864
lāc n *gift* ap 1863; dp lācum 43, 1868; *booty* ap
  lāc 1584
gelāc n *interplay* as 1040; dp gelācum 1168
lācan VII *fly* pres ptc lācende 2832; *wield* inf
  lācan 2848
lād f *passage, voyage* gs lāde 569; ds 1987 [MnE
  load, lode(star)]
gelād n *way* as 1410
lāf f *leavings, what is left over* ns 1032, as lāfe
  2936, 3160; np 2829; *heirloom (usually referring to swords or armour)* ns lāf 454, 2611,
  2628; as lāfe 795, 1488, 1688, 2191, 2563; ds
  2577; np 2036
gelafian 2 *lave, bathe* pret 3s gelafede 2722
lagu m *water, mere* ns 1630
lagucræftig adj *skilled in seamanship* ns 209
  [MnE -crafty]
lagustræt f *seaway* as lagustræte 239 [MnE
  -street]
lagustrēam m *sea-current* ap lagustrēamas 297
  [MnE -stream]
lāh see lēon
land n *land* ns lond 2197; as 521, 1357, 2471,
  2492; land 31, 221, 242, 253, 580, 1904, 2062,
  2915; gs landes 2995; ds lande 1623, 1913,
  2310, 2836; gp landa 311
landbūend m *dwellers on earth, dwellers in the
  land* ap londbūend 1345; dp landbūendum 95
landgemyrce n *shore* ap landgemyrcu 209
landgeweorc n *stronghold* as 938 [MnE land,
  work]
landwaru f *people of the land, inhabitants* ap
  landwara 2321
landweard m *shore-guard* ns 1890 [MnE land,
  ward]
lang see long
gelang adj *dependent* nsm 1376; nsn gelong
  2150

langað m *longing* ns 1879

langtwīdig adj *long-lasting* nsm 1708

lār f *advice, counsel* ds lāre 1950; gp lāra 1220, lārena 269 (wes þū ūs larena gōd *advise us well*) [MnE lore]

lāst m *track, footprint* as 132; np lāstas 1402; ap 841; as on lāst faran *following behind* 2945; lāst weardian *remain behind* 971, *follow* 2164

lāð adj *hateful, hostile* (used as a noun: *foe, hated foe*) nsm 440, 511, 815, 2315, lāða 2305; asm lāðne 3040; gsm lāþes 841, 2910, lāðan 83, 132; dsm lāþum 440, 1257; gpm lāðra 242, 2672; dpm lāðum 550, 938, lāþan 1505; nsn lāð 134, lāþ 192; gsn lāþes 929, 1061, lāðan 2008, 2354; apn lāð 1375; gpn lāðra 3029; dpf lāðum 2467. Compar nsm lāðra 2432 [MnE loath]

lāðbite m *wound* np 1122 [MnE loath, bite]

lāðgetēona m *hostile assailant* ns 974; np lāðgetēonan 559

lāðlīc adj *loathsome* apn lāðlīcu 1584

lǣdan 1 *lead, bring* inf 239; pret 3p lǣddon 1159; p ptc lǣded 3177, gelǣded 37

lǣfan 1 *leave* inf 2315; pret 3s lǣfde 2470; imp s lǣf 1178

lǣndæg m *transitory day* ap lǣndagas 2591

lǣne adj *transitory, fleeting, perishing* nsm 1754; asn 3129; gsn lǣnan 2845; asf 1622 [Cf MnE loan]

lǣng see longe

lǣran 1 *teach* imp s lǣr 1722

gelǣran 1 *teach, advise* inf 278, 3079; pret 3p gelǣrdon 415

lǣs see lȳt

lǣsest see lȳtel

lǣssa see lȳtel

lǣstan 1 *endure, hold out* inf 812; *accomplish, carry out* imp s lǣst 2663 [MnE last]

gelǣstan 1 *stand by, be of service* pres subj 3p gelǣsten 24; pret 3s gelǣste 2500; *fulfil* inf gelǣstan 1706; pret 3s gelǣste 524, 2990; p ptc gelǣsted 829

lǣt adj *slack, negligent* nsm 1529 [MnE late]

lǣtan VII *let, allow* pres 3s lǣteð 1728; pret 3s lēt 2389, 2550, 2977; 3p lēton 48, 864, 3132; subj 2s lēte 1996; 3s 3082; imp s lǣt 1488; imp p lǣtað 397

lēaf n *leaf* dp lēafum 97

lēafnesword n *permission, word of leave* as 245

lēag see lēogan

gelēah see gelēogan

lēan n *requital, reward, gift* as 114, 951, 1220, 1584, 2391; gs lēanes 1809; ds lēane 1021; ap lēan 2995; gp lēana 2990; dp lēanum 2145

lēan VI *find fault with, blame* pres 3s lyhð 1048; pret 3s lōg 1811; 3p lōgon 203, 862

lēanian 2 *requite, recompense* (wd of pers and a of thing) pres 1s lēanige 1380; pret 3s lēanode 2102

lēas adj *deprived, without* (wg) nsm 850; dsm lēasum 1664

lēasscēawere m *spy* np lēasscēaweras 253

lēg see līg

leger n *lying* ds on legere *lying there, where it lay* 3043 [MnE lair]

legerbedd n *grave* ds legerbedde 1007 [MnE lair, bed]

lemman 1 *cripple, oppress* pret 3s lemede 905

leng see long

lenge adj *near (in time), at hand* nsn 83

gelenge adj *related to* nsm 2732

lengest see long

lengra see long

lēod m *man, person* ns 341, 348, 669, 829, 1432, 1492, 1538, 1612, 1653, 2159, 2551, 2603; as 625; ds lēode 24; np 225, 260, 362, 415, 1213, 2125, 2927, 3137, 3156, 3178, lēoda 3001; ap lēode 192, 443, 696, 1336, 1345, 1863, 1868, 1982, 2095, 2318, 2732; gp lēoda 205, 634, 793, 938, 1673, 2033, 2238, 2251, 2333, 2801, 2900, 2945; dp lēodum 389, 521, 618, 697, 905, 1159, 1323, 1708, 1712, 1804, 1856, 1894, 1930, 2310, 2368, 2797, 2804, 2910, 2958, 2990, 3182

lēod f *nation* gs lēode 596, 599

lēodbealo n *punishment by his people* as 1722; *affliction to a people* gp lēodbealewa 1946

lēodburg f *estate* ap lēodbyrig 2471

lēodcyning m *king of a people* ns 54

lēodfruma m *people's ruler* as lēodfruman 2130

lēodgebyrgea m *people's protector, king* as lēodgebyrgean 269

lēodhryre m *fall of a people, nation's defeat* gs lēodhryres 2391; ds lēodhryre 2030

lēodsceaða m *ravager of a people* ds lēodsceaðan 2093

lēodscipe m *nation* as 2751; ds 2197

lēof adj *dear, beloved* nsm 54, 203, 511, 521, 1876, 2467, lēofa 1216, 1483, 1758, 1854, 1987, 2663, 2745; asm lēofne 34, 297, 1943, 2127, 3079, 3108, 3142; gsm lēofes 1061, 1994, 2080, 2897, 2910; gpm lēofra 1915; dp lēofum 1073; asn lēof 31; *pleasant* asm lēofne 618. Compar nsn lēofre 2651. Superl nsm lēofost 1296; asm lēofestan 2823

leofað see **libban**

lēoflīc adj *precious, admirable* nsm 2603; asn 1809

lēogan II *belie* pres subj 3s lēoge 250; *lie, be in error* pret 3s lēag 3029

ge**lēogan** II *deceive* pret 3s gelēah 2323

lēoht n *light* ns 569, 727, 1570; as 648, 2469; ds lēohte 95

lēoht adj *gleaming, bright* dsn lēohtan 2492 [MnE light]

lēoma m *light* ns 311, 1570, 2769; as lēoman 1517; *luminary* ap 95

leomum see **lim**

lēon I *lend* pret 3s lāh 1456

leornian 2 *intend, think about* pret 3s leornode 2336 [MnE learn]

lēoð n *lay, song* ns 1159

leoðocræft m *skill* dp leoðocræftum 2769

leoðosyrce f *coat of mail* as leoðosyrcan 1505; ap 1890

lēton see **lǣtan**

lettan 1 *hinder* pret 3p letton 569

libban 3 *live, exist* pres 3s lifað 3167, leofað 974, 1366, 2008, lyfað 944, 954; subj 2s lifige 1224; pret 3s lifde 57, 1257, lyfde 2144; 3p lifdon 99; pres ptc lifigende 815, 1953, 1973, 2062, dsm lifigendum 2665

līc n *body* ns 966; as 2080, 2127; gs līces 451, 1122; ds līce 733, 1503, 2423, 2571, 2743, *person* 2732

ge**līc** adj *alike* npm gelīce 2164. Superl gelīcost *most like* nsm 218, 985; nsn 727, 1608

licgan V *lie, lie dead, die* inf 1586, 3129, licgean 966, 1427, 3040, 3082; pres 3s ligeð 1343, 2745, 2903; pret 3s læg 40, 552, 1532, 1547, 2051, 2077, 2201, 2213, 2388, 2824, 2851, 2978; pret 3p lǣgon 566, lāgon 3048; *fail* 3s lǣg 1041

ge**licgan** V *subside* pret 3s gelǣg 3146

līchoma m *body* ns 812, 1007, 1754; as līchaman 2651; ds 3177

līcian 2 wd *please* pres 3s līcað 1854; pret 3p līcodon 639 [MnE like]

līcsār n *bodily pain* as 815 [MnE sore]

līcsyrce f *coat of mail* ns 550

liden see **līðan**

lidmann m *seafarer* gp lidmanna 1623

līf n *life* as 97, 733, 1536, 2251, 2423, 2743, 2751; gs līfes 197, 790, 806, 1387, 2343, 2823, 2845, ds līfe 2471, 2571, tō līfe *throughout his life* 2432; is ðīne līfe *by thy life* 2131

līfbysig adj *struggling for life* nsm 966 [MnE life, busy]

līfdæg m *day of life, life* ap līfdagas 793, 1622

līffrēa m *lord of life* ns līffrea 16

līfgedāl n *parting from life, death* ns 841

līfgesceaft f *life (as determined by fate)* gp līfgesceafta 1953, 3064

lifige see **libban**

lifigende see **libban**

līfwraðu f *life-protection* as līfwraðe 2877; ds tō līfwraðe *to save his life* 971

līfwynn f *joy of life* gp līfwynna 2097

līg m *flame, fire* ns 1122, 2672, lēg 3115, 3145; gs līges 83, 781; ds līge 2305, 2321, 2341, ligge 727, lēge 2549

līgdraca m *fire-dragon* ns 2333, lēgdraca 3040

līgegesa m *terrifying fire* as līgegesan 2780

ligetorn n *imagined insult* ds ligetorne 1943 [MnE lie-]

ligge see **līg**

lim n *limb, branch* dp leomum 97

limpan III *happen* pret 3s hū lomp *what happened* 1987

ge**limpan** III *happen* pres 3s gelimpeð 1753; pret 3s gelamp 1252, gelomp 76; *be given* pres subj 3s gelimpe 929; *come about* pret 3s gelamp 626, 2941; *befall* subj 3s gelumpe 2637; *fulfil* p ptc gelumpen 824

lind f *shield (made of lindenwood)* ns 2341; as linde 2610; ap 2365

lindgestealla m *comrade in battle* ns 1973

lindhæbbend m *shield-bearer* np lindhæbbende 245; gp lindhæbbendra 1402

lindplega m *battle, shield-play* ds lindplegan 1073, 2039

lindwiga m *shield-warrior* ns 2603

linnan III *yield, lose* inf 1478, 2443

liss f *happiness* gp lissa 2150

list m *cunning* dp listum 781

līðan I *travel (by water), cross (a body of water)* p ptc liden 223; pres ptc līðende *seafarer* npm 221

līðe adj *kind* nsm 1220. Superl līðost 3182 [MnE lithe]

līþenddæg m *fleeting day, transitory day* gp līþenddaga 2341

līðwǣge n *cup with strong drink* as 1982

līxan 1 *shine* pret 3s līxte 311, 1570 *grow light* 485

locen see **lūcan**

lōcian 2 *look* pres 2s lōcast 1654

lof m *fame* as 1536

lofdǣd f *praiseworthy deed* dp lofdǣdum 24

lofgeorn adj *eager for fame* superl nsm lofgeornost 3182

lōg see lēan VI

lōgon see lēan VI

gelōme adv *frequently* 559

lond see land

londriht n *land-right* gs londrihtes 2886

long adj *long* nsn lang 2093, nsm 3043; long 2591, lang 2845; asf lange 16, 114, 1257, 1915, 2159, longe 54, 2780. Compar lengra 134

gelong see gelang

longe adv *long* 1061, 2751, 3082, 3108, lange 31, 905, 1336, 1748, 1994, 2130, 2183, nō þon lange *not for long after that* 2344, 2423. Compar leng 451, 974, 1854, 2801, 2826, 3064, læng 2307, lenge 83. Superl lengest 2008, 2238

longgestrēon n *ancient treasure* gp longgestrēona 2240

longsum adj *long-lasting* asm longsumne 1536; nsn longsum 134, 192; asn 1722

losian 2 *escape* pres 3s losaþ 1392, 2062; pret 3s losade 2096

lūcan II *interlink, weave* p ptc gpm locenra 2995, asn gelocen 2769, asf locene 1505, apf 1890

lufian 2 *love, care for* pret 3s lufode 1982

luftācen n *token of affection* ap 1863

lufu f *desire, object of desire* as lufan 1728, *beloved thing* lufen 2886

lungor adj *swift* npm lungre 2164

lungre adv *quickly, immediately* 929, 1630, 2310, 2743

lust m *pleasure, desire* as 599, 618; dp lustum *gladly* 1653 [MnE lust]

gelȳfan I *trust (in), count on* inf 440; pret 3s gelȳfde 608, 627, 909, 1272

lyfað see libban

lyfde see libban

lyft f m *air* ns 1375; ds lyfte 2832

lyftfloga m *air-flyer* ns 2315

lyftgeswenced adj *driven by the wind* ns 1913

lyftwynn f *joyous air* as lyftwynne 3043

lyhð see lēan VI

lystan I *want* (impersonal, wa of person) pret 3s randwigan restan lyste *the warrior wanted to rest* 1793

lȳt n *little, few* ns 2365, 2836, 2882; as 1927, 2150; adv *little* 2897, 3129. Compar læs *less* asn 487, 1946, þȳ læs *lest* 1918

lȳtel adj *little, small* nsn 1748; asn 2240; asf lȳtle 2877, 2030, 2097. Compar læssa *less, lesser* 1282; dsn læssan 951; asf 2571; dpn 43. Superl læsest *least* nsn 2354

lȳthwōn adv *little* 203

mā adv *more* 504, 735, 1055, 1613. Superl mæst *most* 2645

mādmas see māð首um

mādmum see māðum

māga see mæg

maga m *son* ns 189, 1474, 2143, 2587; *young man* ns 978, 2675; as magan 943

magan pret-pres *can* pres 1s mæg 277, 1822, 2739, 2801; 2s meaht 2047, miht 1378; 3s mæg 478, 930, 942, 1365, 1484, 1700, 1733, 1837, 2260, 2291, 2448, 2600, 2764, 2864; subj 1s mæge 680, 2749; 3s 2530; pret 1s meahte 1659, 2877, mihte 571, 656, 967; 3s meahte 542, 754, 762, 1032, 1078, 1130, 1150, 1561, 2340, 2464, 2466, 2547, 2673, 2770, 2855, 2870, 2904, 2971, mehte 1082, 1496, 1515, 1877, mihte 190, 207, 462, 511, 1446, 1504, 1508, 2091, 2609, 2621, 2954; 1p meahton 941, 3079; 3p meahton 648, 797, 1156, 1350, 1454, 1911, 2373, mihton 308, 313, 2683, 3162; subj 1s meahte 2520; 3s 243, 780, 1130, 1919, mihte 1140; *may* pres 3s mæg 1341, 2032

māgas see mæg

māge f *kinswoman* gs māgan 1391

mago m *son* ns 1465, 1867, 2011

magodriht f *young retinue* ns 67

magorinc m *young warrior* gp magorinca 730

magoðegn m *young thane* ns 408, 2757; ds maguþegne 2079; ap maguþegnas 293; gp magoþegna 1405; dp magoþegnum 1480

man see monn

mān n *crime, wickedness* ds māne 978, 1055; is 110

mānfordædla m *wicked destroyer* np mānfordædlan 563

manian 2 *urge* pres 3s manað 2057

manig see monig

manlīce adv *nobly* 1046 [MnE manly]

mann see monn

mannan see monn

mannon see monn

mānscaða m *wicked ravager* ns 712, 737, 1339, 2514

māra see micel

maþelian 2 *speak* pret 3s maþelode 286, 348, 360, 371, 405, 456, 499, 529, 631, 925, 957, 1215, 1321, 1383, 1473, 1651, 1687, 1817, 1840, 1999, 2510, 2631, 2724, 2862, 3076, maþelade 2425

māðmæht f *treasure* gp māðmæhta 1613, 2833

māþmgestrēon n *treasure* gp māþmgestrēona 1931

māþðum m *treasure* as 169, 1052, 2055,

māþðum (*cont.*)
māðð̄um 3016; ds māþme 1902, mādme 1528;
np māþmas 1860; ap 1867, 2146, 2236, 2490,
2640, 2865, 3131, mādmas 385, 472, 1027,
1482, 1756; gp māþma 1784, 2143, 2166,
2779, 2799, 3011, mādma 36, 41; dp
māðmum 1898, 2103, 2788, mādmum 1048

māðþumfæt n *precious cup* ns 2405

māþðumgifu f *treasure-giving* ds māþðumgife
1301

māðð̄umsigle n *precious jewel* gp māðð̄umsigla
2757

māðþumsweord n *splendid sword* as 1023

māðð̄umwela m *treasure-hoard* ds māðð̄um-
welan 2750

mæg m *kinsman* ns 408, 468, 737, 758, 813,
914, 1530, 1944, 1961, 1978, 2166, 2604; as
1339, 2439, 2484, 2982; gs mæges 2436,
2675, 2698, 2879; ds mæge 1978; np māgas
1015; ap 2815; gp māga 247, 1079, 1853,
2006, 2742; dp māgum 1167, 1178, 2614,
3065, mægum 2353

mægburg f *nation* gs mægburge 2887

mægen n *strength, power* as 518, 1706; gs
mægenes 196, 418, 1270, 1534, 1716, 1835,
1844, 1887, 2647, mægnes 670, 1761, 2084,
2146, 2628; ds mægene 789, 2667; *army,
military force* as mægen 445; gs mægenes
155 [MnE (might and) main]

mægenāgende pres ptc *mighty (ones)* gpm
mægenāgendra 2837

mægenbyrþenn f *mighty burden* as mægenbyrþenne 3091; ds 1625

mægencræft m *strength* as 380

mægenellen n *great valour* as 659

mægenfultum m *powerful help* gp mægenfultuma 1455

mægenrǣs m *mighty impetus* as 1519

mægenstrengo f *great strength* ds 2678

mǣgum see **mǣg**

mægenwudu m *mighty spear* as 236 [MnE
main, wood]

mægð̄ f *maiden, woman* ns 3016; gp mægþa
924, 943, 1283

mægþ f *nation, people* as mægþe 1011; ds 75; gp
mægþa 25, 1771; dp mægþum 5

mægwine m *dear kinsman* np 2479

mǣl n *time, occasion* ns 316, 1008; as 2633; gp
mǣla 1249, 1611, 2057; dp mǣlum 907,
2237, 3035 [MnE meal]

mǣlcearu f *care of the time* as mǣlceare 189

mǣlgesceaft f *destined event* gp mǣlgesceafta
2737

mǣnan 1 *relate, announce* inf 1067; p ptc
mǣned 857; *bemoan* pret 3s mǣnde 2267;
3p mǣndon 1149, 3149; *mourn for* inf mǣnan
3171 [MnE mean]

gemǣnan 1 *complain* pret subj 3p gemǣnden
1101

gemǣne adj *shared, in common* npm 1860; gpm
gemǣnra 1784; nsf gemǣne 1857, 2137,
2660; *mutual* 2473

mǣnigo see **menigeo**

mǣre adj *renowned, illustrious* nsm 129, 1046,
1715, 1761, mǣra 1474, 2011, 2587; asm
mǣrne 36, 201, 353, 1598, 2384, 2721,
2788, 3098, 3141; gsm mǣres 797; dsm
mǣrum 345, 1301, 1992, 2079, 2572 mǣran
270; npm mǣre 3070; nsn mǣre 2405; asn
1023; gsn mǣran 1729; nsf mǣru 2001, 2016,
mǣre 1952; *well known, notorious* nsm mǣre
103, mǣra 762. Superl nsm mǣrost 898

mǣrð̄o f *glorious deed, glory, fame* ns 857; as
659, 687, 2134; ap 2678, 2996; gp mǣrð̄a 408,
504, 1530, 2640, 2645; dp mǣrð̄um (adv)
gloriously 2514

mǣst m *mast* ns 1898; ds mǣste 36, 1905

mǣst see **micel**

mǣte adj *little* superl *least* mǣtost nsm 1455

mē see **ic**

mēagol adj *forceful, hearty* dp mēaglum 1980

mearc f *mortal end, death* ds mearce 2384
[MnE mark]

mearcian 2 *mark, mark down, stain* pres 3s
mearcað 450; p ptc gemearcod 1264, nsn
1695

mearcstapa m *prowler of the outskirts* ns 103;
ap mearcstapan 1348

mearh m *horse* ns 2264; np mēaras 2163; ap
865, 1035; gp mēara 2166; dp mēarum 855,
917, 1048, 1898 [MnE mare]

mearn see **murnan**

mec see **ic**

mēce m *sword* ns 1938; as 2047, 2978; gs mēces
1765, 1812, 2614, 2939; gp mēca 2685; dp
mēcum 565

mēd f *reward* as mēde 2134; ds 2146; gp mēdo
1178 [MnE meed]

gemēde n *consent, permission* ap gemēdu 247

medoærn n *mead-hall* as 69

medobenc f *mead-bench* ns 776; ds medubence
1052, medobence 1067, 2185, meodubence
1902

medoful f *mead-cup* as 624, 1015

medoheal f *mead-hall* ns 484; ds meoduhealle
638

medostīg f *path to the mead-hall* as medostīgge
924

medu m *mead* as 2633; ds medo 604

medudrēam m *rejoicing with mead* as 2016
[MnE mead, dream]

meduseld n *mead-hall* as 3065

melda m *informer* gs meldan 2405

meltan III *burn up, be consumed (by fire)* inf
3011; pret 3s mealt 2326; 3p multon 1120
[MnE melt]

gemeltan III *burn up* pret 3s gemealt 897; *melt*
pret 3s 1608, 1615; *flag, weaken* pret 3s 2628

mene m *necklace* as 1199

mengan 1 *mix, stir up* inf 1449; p ptc nsn
gemenged 848, 1593

menigeo f *multitude* ns mænigo 41; menigeo
2143

meodosetl n *mead-hall seat* gp meodosetla 5

meodowong m *meadow around the mead-hall*
ap meodowongas 1643

meodubenc see **medobenc**

meoduheal see **medoheal**

meoduscenc m *mead-cup* dp meoduscencum
1980

meoto f *thought* (?) ap 489 [a word of uncertain
meaning which occurs only here]

meotod see **metod**

mēowle f *woman* ns 3150

mercels m *mark, target* gs mercelses 2439

mere m *mere, lake, tarn* ns 1362; as 845, 1130,
1603; ds 855

meredēor m, n. *sea-beast* as 558

merefara m *seafarer* gs merefaran 502

merefisc m *sea-fish* gp merefixa 549

meregrund m *bottom of a mere* as 2100; ap
meregrundas 1449 [MnE mere, ground]

merehrægl n *sea-garment*, (i.e. *sail*) gp merehrægla 1905

merelīðend m *seafarer* np merelīðende 255

merestrǣt f *sea-way* ap merestrǣta 514 [MnE
mere, street]

merestrengo f *strength in swimming* as 533
[MnE mere, streng(th)]

merewīf n *sea-woman* as 1519 [MnE mere,
wife]

mergen see **morgen**

gemet n *power, measure of strength* ns 2533; as
2879; *means* ds mid gemete *by any means* 779

gemet adj *fitting* nsn 687, 3057 [MnE meet]

metan V *measure, traverse* pret 3s mæt 924; 2p
mæton 514; 3p 917, 1633 [MnE mete]

mētan 1 *encounter, come upon* pret 3s mētte
751; 3p mētton 1421 [MnE meet]

gemētan 1 *meet, encounter, find* pret 3s gemētte 757; 3p gemētton 2592; subj 3s gemētte
2785

gemēting f *encounter* ns 2001 [MnE meeting]

metod m *god, ruler* ns 110, 706, 967, 979, 1057,
1611, 2527; as 180; gs metodes 670; ds
metode 169, 1778

metodsceaft f *destined end, destiny* as meotodsceaft 1077, metodsceaft 1180; ds metodsceafte 2815

meþel n *gathering-place* ds meþle 1876

meðelstede m *meeting-place* (i.e. *battlefield*) ds
1082

meþelword n *formal word* dp meþelwordum
236

micel adj *great, large, much* nsm 129, 502; asm
micelne 3098; gsm miclan 978; dsm 2849;
apm micle 1348; nsn 170, 771; asn micel 69,
1167; gsn micles 2185, (adv) *by much, far*
694; isn micle 922, 1283, 1579, 2651; nsf
micel 67, 146; asf micle 1778, 3091; dpf
miclum 958; *important* asn micel 270.
Compar **māra** *more, greater* nsm 1353,
2555; asm māran 247, 753, 2016; nsn māre
1560; asn 136, 518; dsn māran 1011; asf 533;
gsf 1823. Superl **mǣst** *greatest* nsm 1195;
nsn 78, 193, 1119; asn 2768, 3143; isn mǣste
2181; nsf mǣst 2328; asf mǣste 459, 1079

mid I adv *with them, withal, therewith* 1642,
1649. II prep. wa *with, together with* 357, 633,
662, 879, 1672, 2652; wd *with, among* 41, 77,
125, 195, 274, 461, 889, 902, 923, 1051, 1128,
1145, 2948, etc. *with, by means of* 243, 438,
475, 574, 746, 748, 1184, 1437, 1461, 1490,
1659, 2535, etc., mid gewealdum *by his own
volition* 2221; wi *by means of* 2028 [MnE
(a)mid]

middangeard m *world, earth* as 75, 1771; gs
middangeardes 504, 751; ds middangearde
2996 [MnE mid(dle), yard]

midde f *middle* ds on middan *in the middle* 2705

middelniht f *middle of the night* dp middelnihtum 2782, 2833

miht f *might, power* as 940; dp mihtum 700

mihtig adj *mighty* nsm 701, 1716, 1725; dsm
mihtigan 1398; asn mihtig 558, 1519

milde adj *generous, well disposed* nsm 1229; dpn
mildum 1172. Superl nsm mildust 3181
[MnE mild]

mīlgemearc n *measure of miles* gs mīlgemearces 1362 [MnE mile, mark]

milts f *good will, benevolence* ns 2921

mīn (gs of *ic*) see **ic**

mīn poss. pron *my, mine* nsm 262, 343, 365, 391, 436, 457, 468, 530, 1169, 1325, 1704, 1776, 2047, 2095, 2434; asm mīnne 255, 418, 445, 638, 1180, 2012, 2147, 2651, 2652; dsm mīnum 473, 965, 1226, 2429, 2729, 3093; npm mīne 415, 2479; apm 293, 1336, 1345, 2815; gpm mīnra 431, 633, 2251; dpm mīnum 1480, 2797, 2804; nsn mīn 476, 2742; mīn asn 2750; gsn mīnes 450; isn mīne 776, 837, 1955, 2685, 2837; nsf mīn 550; asf mīne 453, 558, 1706, 2799; dsf mīnre 410

missan 1 *miss* wg pret 3s miste 2439

missēre n *half-year* gp missēra 153, 1498, 1769, 2620

misthliþ n *misty slopes* dp misthleoþum 710

mistig adj *misty* apm mistige 162

mōd n *mind, heart, spirit* ns 50, 549, 1150; as 67; gs mōdes 171, 436, 810, 1229, 1603, 1706, 2100; ds mōde 624, 753, 1307, 1418, 1844, 2281, 2527, 2581; *courage* ns mōd 1057; as 1167; *anger* ns 730; *pride, arrogance* as 1931 [MnE mood]

mōdcearu f *grief of mind, grief, anxiety of mind* as mōdceare 1778, 1992, 3149

mōdgehygd f *thought* dp mōdgehygdum 233

mōdgeþonc m, n *mind* as 1729

mōdgiōmor adj *sad at heart* nsn 2894

mōdig adj *courageous, brave* nsm 604, 1508, 1643, 1812, 2757, mōdega 813; gsm mōdges 502, mōdiges 2698, mōdgan 670; dsm mōdigan 3011; npm mōdge 855, mōdige 1876; gpm mōdigra 312 [MnE moody]

mōdiglīc adj *brave-looking* compar apm mōdiglīcran 337

mōdlufu f *deep affection* gs mōdlufan 1823 [MnE mood, love]

mōdor f *mother* ns 1258, 1276, 1282, 1683, 2118; as 1538, 2139, 2932

mōdsefa m *character* ns 349, 1853; *spirit* 2628; *mind* as mōdsefan 2012; ds 180

mōdþracu f *daring* ds mōdþræce 385

mōna m *moon* as mōnan 94

moncynn n *mankind* gs moncynnes 196, 1955, mancynnes 164, 1276, 2181; ds mancynne 110

mondrēam m *joy of (life among) men* as mandrēam 1264; dp mondrēamum 1715 [MnE man, dream]

mondryhten m *liege lord* ns 2865, mandryhten 1978, 2647, mondrihten 436; as mondryhten 2604; gs mondryhtnes 3149, mandryhtnes 2849; ds mandryhtne 1249, 2281, mandrihtne 1229

gemong n *throng* ds gemonge 1643

monig adj *many a* (when qualifying a sg noun), *many* (when qualifying a pl noun) nsm 689, 838, 908, 918, 2762, 3022, 3077, manig 399, 854, 1112, 1289; dsm monegum 1341, 1419; apm manige 337; dpm manegum 2103; nsn monig 1510; asn manig 1015; nsf monig 776; dsf manigre 75; apf monige 1613; gpf manigra 1178; dpf monegum 5; used absolutely: nsm monig 857, 171, manig 1860; dsm manegum 1887; npm monige 2982, manige 1023; apm monige 1598; gpm manigra 2091; dpm manegum 349; used with part g: apm manige 728; dpm monegum 5, 2001, 3111, manegum 1235; dpf manigum 1771

monn m *man* ns mon 209, 510, 1099, 1560, 1645, 2281, 2297, 2355, 2470, 2590, 2996, 3065, 3175, man 503, 534, 1048, 1172, 1175, 1316, 1353, 1398, 1534, 1876, 1958; as man 1489, mannan 297, 1943, 2127, 2774, 3108, mannon 577; gs monnes 1729, 2897, mannes 1057, 1994, 2080, 2533, 2541, 2555, 2698; ds men 655, 752, 1879, 2285, menn 2189; np men 50, 162, 233, 1634, 3162, 3165; gp monna 1413, 2887, manna 155, 201, 380, 701, 712, 735, 779, 789, 810, 914, 1461, 1725, 1835, 1915, 2527, 2645, 2672, 2836, 3056, 3057, 3098; ap men 69, 337, 1582, 1717; dp mannum 3181; man, mon ns used as an indefinite subject *one, a man* 25, 1048, 1172, 1175, 1534, 2355; man ns unexpressed 1365

monðwǣre adj *kind to people* superl nsm monðwǣrust 3181

mōr m *moor* as 1405; ds mōre 710; ap mōras 103, 162, 1348

morgen m *morning* ns 1077, 1784; mergen 2103, 2124; as morgen 837; ds morgne 2484, mergenne 565, 2939; gp morna 2450

morgenceald adj *cold in the morning* ns 3022

morgenlēoht n *morning light* ns 604, 917

morgenlong adj *morning-long* asm morgenlongne 2894

morgenswēg m *morning-cry* ns 129

morgentīd f *morning* as 484, 518 [MnE morn, tide]

mōrhop n *moor-retreat* ap mōrhopu 450

morna see **morgen**

morðbealu n *slaughter* as morðbeala 136

morðor n *murder, slaying* gs morðres 1683, 2055; ds morþre 1264, morðre 2782; *violent assault* ds 892

morþorbealu n *slaughter* as 1079, 2742

morþorbed n *bed of violent death* ns 2436

morþorhete m *deadly hatred* gs morþorhetes 1105

mōtan pret-pres *may, be allowed* pres 2s mōst 1671; 3s mōt 186, 442, 603; 1p mōton 347; 2p 395; subj 1s mōte 431; 2s 1177; 3s 1387; 3p mōton 365; pret 1s mōste 1487, 1998, 2797; 3s 706, 735, 894, 2504, 2574, 2827, 3053, 3100; 3p mōston 1628, 2038, 2124, 2984, mōstan 2247; subj 2s mōste 961; 3s 2241; 3p mōston 1088, 1875; *must, have to* pres 3s mōt 2886; pret 3s mōste 168, 1939, 2574

*ge*munan pret-pres *remember, think of, bear in mind* pres 1s geman 1220, 2633, gemon 2427; 3s geman 265, 2042; gemon 1185, 1701; pret 3s gemunde 758, 870, 1129, 1141, 1259, 1270, 1290, 1465, 2114, 2391, 2431, 2488, 2606, 2678; 3p gemundon 179; subj 3s gemunde 1141; imp s gemyne 659

mund f *hand* dp mundum 236, 514, 1461, 3022, 3091

mundbora m *protector, guardian* ns 1480, 2779

mundgripe m *handgrip* as 753; ds 380, 965, 1534, *seizure* 1938

murnan III *mourn* pres subj 3s murne 1385; pret 3s mearn 3129; pres ptc nsn murnende 50; *feel anxiety* pret 3s mearn 1442, 1537; *feel remorse* pret 3s 136

mūþa m *mouth, opening* as mūþan 724

mūðbona m *slayer with the mouth, devourer* ds mūðbonan 2079 [MnE mouth, bane]

*ge*mynd f *memorial, remembrance* dp gemyndum 2804, 3016

myndgian 2 *remind* pres 3s myndgað 2057; pres ptc myndgiend 1105

*ge*myndgian 2 *call to mind* p ptc gemyndgad 2450

*ge*myndig adj *mindful* nsm 1173, 2171; nsf 613; *intent on* nsm 1530, 2082, 2689; *recalling* nsm 868

myne m *love, respect* as 169; *mind, desire* ns 2572

*ge*myne see *ge*munan

myntan 1 *intend* pret 3s mynte 712, 731, 762

myrce adj *dark* asm myrcan 1405

myrðu f *injury* gs myrðe 810

nā see nō

naca m *ship* ns 1896, 1903; as nacan 295; gs 214

nacod adj *bare, smooth* nsm 2273; nsn 2585; apn 539 [MnE naked]

nāh see āgan

nalas, nalles, etc. see nealles

nam see niman

nama m *name* ns 343, 1457; as naman 78

nāman see niman

nān pron adj *no, not any* nsn 803, 988

nāt see witan

nāthwylc adj *some kind of* dsm nāthwylcum 1513

nāthwylc pron (w part g) *some, some one* nsm 2215, 2233; gsm nāthwylces 2053, 2223

næbben see habban

næfne see nefne

næfre adv *never* 247, 250, 583, 591, 655, 718, 1041, 1048, 1460

nægan 1 *greet, address* pret 3s nægde 1318

*ge*nægan 1 *attack* pret 3p genægdan 2206, genægdon 2916; p ptc genæged 1439

næglan 1 *bejewel* p ptc asn nægled 2023 [MnE nail]

nænig (ne + ænig) adj-pron *no, no one, none* nsm 157, 242, 691, 859, 1933; asm nænigne 1197; dsm nænegum 598; gpm nænigre 949; nsn nænig 1514

nære (ne + wære) see wesan

næron (ne + wæron) see wesan

næs (ne + wæs) see wesan

næs adv see nealles

næshlið n *headland slope* dp næshleoðum 1427

næss m *cliff, headland* as næs 1439, 1600, 2898; ds næsse 2243, 2417; ap næssas 1358, 1411, 1912; gp næssa 1360 [MnE ness]

ne adv *not* 38, 50, 80, 83, 109, 119, etc. Often found fused with following word: nænig, nære, nealles, nolde, etc.

ne conj *nor, not* used alone: 157 ne þær nænig witena . . . þorfte *nor did any of the counsellors need*, 169, 577, 584, 793, etc. used with another negative: ne . . . ne 154–7, 245–6, 511; ne . . . ne . . . ne 1393–4; nō . . . ne 450, 1453–4, 2466; nalles . . . ne 3015–16; with the first negative unexpressed: 858 sūð ne norð *(neither) south nor north*

nēah adv *near* 1221, 2870 [MnE nigh]

nēah prep (always following its object) *near* 564, 1924, 2242, 2290, 2547, 2831, 2853, nēh 2411

nēah adj *near* nsm 1743, 2728; nsf 2420. Compar nēar *nearer* 745. Superl nīehsta *last* dsm nīehstan 2511, nȳhstan 1203

*ge*neahhe adv *repeatedly* 783, 3152. Superl genehost *most frequently* 794

nealles (ne + ealles) adv *not at all, by no means* 2145, 2167, 2179, 2221, 2363, 2596, 2873, 3089, nalles 338, 1018, 1076, 1442, 2503,

nealles (*cont.*)
2832, 2919, 3015, 3019, 3023, nales 1811, nallas 1719, 1749, nalas 1493, 1529, 1537, nalæs 43, næs 562, 2262

nēan adv *from near, near* neân 528, 839, nēan 1174, 2317, nēon 3104

nēar see **nēah**

nearo adj *narrow* ap f nearwe 1409

nearo n *harsh straits* as 2350, 2594

nearocræft m *strategem for inaccessibility* dp nearocræftum 2243

nearofāh adj *cruelly hostile* gsm nearofāges 2317

nearoþearf f *severe distress* as nearoþearfe 422

nearwe adv *tightly* 976

nearwian 2 *press hard* p ptc genearwod 1438

nefa m *nephew* ns 2170, 1203 (or *grandson*); as nefan 2206; ds 881; *grandson* ns nefa 1962

nefne prep wd *except* 1934, nemne 1081

nefne conj w indic. *except that* næfne 1353; *except* nefne 2151, 2533; w subj *unless, if* . . *not* nefne 1056, 3054, nemne 1552, 2654

nēh see **nēah**

*ge*nehost see *ge*neahhe

nelle see **willan**

nemnan 1 *call* inf 2023; pres 3p nemnað 364; pret 3p nemdon 1354 [MnE *name*]

nemne see **nefne**

nēodlaðu f *urgent summons* ds 1320

nēon see **nēan**

nēosan, nēosian 1, 2 wg *seek out, go to* inf nēosan 125, 1786, 1791, 1806, 2074, nīosan 2366, 2388; nēosian 115, 1125, nīosian 2671, 3045; pres 3s nīosað 2486

nēotan II *make use of, enjoy* imp s nēot 1217

neowol adj *precipitous* apm neowle 1411

nerian 1 *save* pres 3s nereð 572; p ptc genered 827

*ge*nesan V *survive* pret 1s genæs 2426; 3s 999, 1977; p ptc genesen 2397

nēðan 1 *risk, venture* pret 2p nēþdon 510; subj 1p nēðdon 538; pres ptc nēðende 2350

*ge*nēþan 1 *risk, venture* inf 1469, 1933; pret subj 1s genēðde 2133; *venture upon, dare* pret 1s 1656, 2511; 3s 888; 1p genēðdon 959

nicor m *water-monster* ap niceras 422, 575, nicras 1427; gp nicera 845

nicorhūs n *water-monster's abode* gp nicorhūsa 1411 [MnE -house]

nīdgripe m *powerful grip* ds 976

nīehsta see **nēah**

nigon num *nine* ap nigene 575

niht f *night* ns 115, 547, 649, 1320, 2116; as 135, 736, 2938; gs nihtes adv *by night* 422, 2269, 2273, 3044; ds niht 575, 683, 702, 1334; ap 517; gp nihta 545, 1365; dp nihtum 167, 275, 2211

nihtbealu n *night-evil* gp nihtbealwa 193

nihthelm m *cover of night* ns 1789 [MnE night, helm(et)]

nihtlong adj *lasting a night* asm nihtlongne 528 [MnE night-long]

nihtweorc n *night's work* ds nihtweorce 827

niman IV *take* inf 1808, 3132; pres 3s nymeð 598; pret 3s nōm 1612, nam 746, 2216, 2986; 1p nāman 2116; p ptc numen 1153; *carry off* pres 3s nimeð 441, 447, 1491, 2536, nymeð 1846; subj 3s nime 452, 1481

*ge*niman IV *take, seize* pret 3s genōm 2776, genam 122, 1302; p ptc genumen 3165; *clasp* pret 3s genam 1872, *receive* 2429

nīod f *pleasure* as nīode 2116

nīosian see **nēosan**

nioðor see **niþer**

nīowe see **nīwe**

*ge*nip n *mist* ap genipu 1360, 2808

nīpan I *darken* pres ptc nīpende 547, 649

nis see **bēon**

nīð m *hostility, persecution* ns 2317; as 276, 423; ds nīþe 2680; *affliction* as nīð 184; ds nīðe 827; *battle, assault* ds 2585; gp nīða 845, 882, 1962, 2170, 2206, 2350, 2397; adv *violently* 1439

nīðdraca m *hostile dragon* ns 2273

niþer adv *down, downwards* 1360, nyðer 3044. Compar nioðor *lower down* 2699 [MnE nether]

nīðgæst m *hostile creature* as 2699 [MnE -ghost]

nīðgeweorc n *vicious deed* gp nīþgeweorca 683 [MnE -work]

nīþgrim adj *oppressively cruel* nsf 193

nīðheard adj *brave in battle* ns 2417 [MnE -hard]

nīðhēdig adj *disposed to strife* npm nīðhēdige 3165

nīðsele m *hostile hall* ds 1513

niþðas mp *men* gp niþða 1005, 2215

nīðwundor n *fearful wonder* as 1365

nīwe adj *new, anew* nsm 2243; dsm nīwan 2594, nīowan 1789; gpn nīwra 2898; asf nīwe 949; *startling* nsm 783

*ge*nīwian 2 *renew* p ptc genīwod 1303, 1322, genīwad 2287

nīwtyrwed adj *newly tarred* asm nīwtyrwydne 295

nō (ne + ā, ō) adv *not at all, by no means, never* 136, 168, 244, 366, 450, 541, 543, 575, 581, 586, 677, 754, 841, 968, 972, 974, 1002, 1025, 1355, 1366, 1392, 1453, 1502, 1508, 1735, 1875, 1892, 1907, 2081, 2160, 2307, 2314, 2347, 2354, 2373, 2423, 2466, 2585, 2618, nā 445, 567, 1536

genōg adj *enough, many* ap genōge 2489, 3104

nolde see willan

nōm see niman

nōn n *ninth hour* (i.e. 3 p.m.) ns 1600

norð adv *north* 858

norþanwind m *north wind* ns 547

nōse f *promontory, ness* ds nōsan 1892, 2803

nōðer conj *nor* 2124

nū adv *now* 251, 254, 375, 395, 424, 489, 602, 658, 939, 946, 1174, etc.

nū conj *now, now that, since* 430, 2799, 3020; correl with nū adv: 1475, 2247, 2745

nȳd f *necessity* as 2454; ds nȳde 1005, nīde 2215

genȳdan 1 *compel* p ptc nsn genȳded 2680, asf genȳdde 1005

nȳdbād f *toll, enforced contribution* as nȳdbāde 598

nȳdgestealla m *close comrade* np nȳdgesteallan 882

nȳdwracu f *dire distress* ns 193

nȳhsta see nēah

nyllan see willan

nyman see niman

nymþe conj *unless* 781; *if . . . not* nymþe mec god scylde *if the lord had not protected me* 1658

nytt f *duty, service* as nytte 494, 3118

nytt adj *useful* apm nytte 794

genyttian 2 *make use of* p ptc genyttod 3046

of prep *from* 37, 56, 229, 265, 419, 672, 710, 726, 785, 854, 921, 1108, etc. Following its object: him of *off from himself* 671

ōfer m *shore* ds ōfre 1371

ofer prep wd (rest) *over, above* 304, 1244, 1286, 1289, 1363, 1790, 1899, 1907, 2768, 2907, 2908, 3025, 3145; wa (motion) *over, across* 10, 46, 48, 200, 217, 231, 239, 240, 248, 297, 311, 362, 393, 464, 481, etc.; *beyond* 1717, 2879; *to* 2899; *against, contrary to* 2330, 2409, 2589; *after* 736, 1781; *without* 685; *throughout* 899; ofer benne *wounded as he was* 2724. The distinction between rest and motion is at times hazy, and where the case of the object is ambiguous, opinions may differ.

ofercuman IV *overcome* pret 3s ofercwōm 1273; 3p ofercōmon 699; p ptc ofercumen 845

oferēode see ofergān

oferfleôn II *flee from* inf 2525

oferflītan I *overcome, defeat* pret 3s oferflāt 517

ofergān anom *walk across, overrun* pret 3s oferēode 1408; 3p oferēoden 2959 [MnE overgo]

oferhelmian 2 *overshadow* pres 3s oferhelmað 1364

oferhīgian 2 *escape from* inf 2766

oferhycgan 3 *disdain* pret 3s oferhogode 2345

oferhygd f *prideful thought* gp oferhygda 1740, oferhȳda 1760

ofermāððum m *exceedingly great treasure* dp ofermāðmum 2993

ofermægen n *superior force* ds ofermægene 2917

ofersēcan 1 *overtax, overstrain* pret 3s ofersōhte 2686

ofersēon V *look on* pret 3p ofersāwon 419 [MnE oversee]

ofersittan V *forgo* inf 684; pres 1s ofersitte 2528

oferswimman III *cross (a body of water)* pret 3s oferswam 2367

oferswȳðan 1 *overcome, overpower* pres 3s oferswȳðeþ 279, 1768

oferweorpan III *stumble* pret 3s oferwearp 1543

offerian 1 *carry off* pret 3s offerede 1583 [MnE off, ferry]

ofgyfan V *give up, leave* inf 2588; pret 3s ofgeaf 1681, 1904, 2251, 2469; 3p ofgēafon 1600, ofgēfan 2846

oflǣtan VII *leave* pres 2s oflǣtest 1183; pret 3s oflēt 1622

ofost f *speed, haste* ns 256, 3007; ds ofoste 2747, 2783, 3090, ofeste 386, ofste 1292

ofostlīce adv *hastily* 3130

ofscēotan II *shoot dead* pret 3s ofscēt 2439

ofsittan V *set upon, charge* pret 3s ofsæt 1545

ofslēan VI *slay, kill, cut off* pret 1s ofslōh 574, 1665; 3s 1689, 3060

oft adv *often* 4, 165, 171, 444, 480, 857, 907, 951, 1065, 1428, etc.; understatement for *as a rule, always* 572, 1247, 2029. Compar oftor 1579. Superl oftost 1663

oftēon I, II *deprive, take away from* pret 3s oftēah 5; *hold back* pret 3s 1520, 2489

ofþyncan 1 *displease, offend* inf 2032

ōhwǣr adv *anywhere* 1737, ōwer 2870

ombeht m *officer* ns 287, ombiht 336

ombihtþegn m *attendant thane* ds ombiht-þegne 673

ōmig adj *rusty* nsm 2763; np ōmige 3049

on prep wd (rest) *on, in* 21, 22, 40, 53, 122, 210, 249, 285, 286, 295, 310, 368, 404, etc.; *from* 101, 609, 2986, 3164, etc.; *by, from* 1484; *at* 126, 303, 575, 3148, etc.; *among* 962, 1557, 1701, 2204, etc.; *with respect to* 1830; in phrases which give adjectival sense: on salum (*happy*) 607, 643, 1170; on wynne (*joyful*) 2014; on hrēon mōde (*troubled, angry*) 1307, 2581; etc.; wa *onto, into* 27, 35, 67, 212, 253, 507, 539, 896, 1393, 1439, 2460, etc.; *according to* 1739; with expressions of time: 484, 837, 1428, etc.; in phrases which give adverbial sense: on ryht (*rightly*) 1555, on unriht (*falsely*) 2739, on gylp (*proudly*) 1749, etc.

onarn see **onirnan**

onberan IV *injure, plunder* inf 990; p ptc nsn onboren 2284

onbīdan I *await, wait* inf 397; pret 3s onbād 2302

onbindan III *unbind, unleash* pret 3s onband 501

onbregdan III *tear open* pret 3s onbrǣd 723 [MnE on, braid]

oncerbendum see **ancorbend**

oncirran I *change* inf 2857; *move, go* pret 3s oncirde 2951, 2970

oncnāwan VII *perceive* pret 3s oncnīow 2554 [MnE on, know]

oncȳðð f *grief* ns oncȳð 1420; as oncȳþðe 830

ond conj *and* 33, 39, 40, 58, 61, 71, 72, 73, etc.; *and, when* 2138; *for* 1681. In the MS *ond* is spelled out four times (600, 1148, 2040, 2334); elsewhere it is always represented by the nota 7.

ondhweorfan III *turn against* pret 3s norþan-wind . . . ondhwearf *the northwind turned against (us)* 548

ondlēan see **andlēan**

ondlong see **andlong**

ondrǣdan VII *dread, fear* inf 1674; pres 3p ondrǣdað 2275; pret 3s ondrēd 2347; subj 3s ondrēde 3153

ondrysne adj *terrible* asf 1932

ondslyht m *counterblow* as 2929, 2972

ōnettan I *hasten* pret 3p ōnetton 306, 1803

onfindan III *discover, find* pret 3s onfand 1522, 2219, 2288, 2300, 2629, onfunde 809; subj 3s 2841; p ptc onfunden 1293; *perceive* pret 3s onfand 2713, onfunde 750, 1497; p ptc onfunden 595; *observe* pret 3s onfand 1890

onfōn VII *receive, take* inf 911; pret 3s onfēng 52, 688, 748, 852, 1214, 1494; imp s onfōh 1169

ongeador adv *together* 1595

ongēan prep wd *against* 681, 747, 1034, 2364

onginnan III *undertake* p ptc ongunnen 409; (w inf) *begin* pres 3s onginneð 2044; pret 1s ongan 2878; 3s 100, 871, 1605, 1983, 2111, 2210, 2312, ongon 2701, 2711, 2790; 3p ongunnon 244, 3143

ongitan V *see, perceive* inf 1484, 1911, 2770, ongyton 308; pres subj 1s ongite 2748; pret 3s ongeat 14, 1512, 1518; *hear* pret 3p ongēaton 1431, 2944; *discover* inf ongytan 1496; *understand* imp s ongit 1723; *seize* pret 3s angeat 1291

onhōhsnian 2 *put an end to* pret 3s onhōhsnode 1944

onhrēran I *arouse* p ptc onhrēred 549, 2554

onhrīnan I *touch* wg pret 3s onhrān 722

onirnan III *spring open* pret 3s onarn 721

onlǣtan VII *loosen* pres 3s onlǣteð 1609

onlēon I (wd of pers and g of thing) *lend* pret 3s onlāh 1467

onlīcnes f *likeness* ns onlīcnæs (= -es) 1351

onlūcan II *unlock* pret 3s onlēac 259

onmēdla m *overweening* ds onmēdlan 2926

onmunan pres ptc (wa of pers and g of thing) *consider worthy (of)* pret 3s onmunde 2640

onsacan VI *withstand* inf 2954

onsēce see **onsēcan**

onsǣge adj *fatal* nsf 2076, 2483

onsǣlan I *unbind, disclose* imp s onsǣl 489

onsēcan I (wa of pers and g of thing) *deprive (of)* pres subj 3s onsǣce 1942

onsendan I *send* pret 3s onsende 382; 3p 45; imp s onsend 452, 1483; p ptc onsended 2266

onsittan V *fear* inf 597

onsponnan VII *unfasten* pret 3s onspēon 2723

onspringan III *spring apart* pret 3p onsprungon 817

onstellan I *bring about* pret 3s onstealde 2407

onswīfan I *swing* pret 3s onswāf 2559

onsȳn see **ansȳn**

ontyhtan I *impel* pret 3s ontyhte 3086

onðēon I *thrive* pret 3s onðāh 900

onwadan VI *enter, pervade* pret 3s onwōd 915 [MnE wade]

onwæcnan VI *awaken* pret 3s onwōc 2287; *be born* pret 3s 56; 3p onwōcon 111

onweald m *possession* as 1044

onwendan I *turn aside* inf 191, 2601

onwindan III *unwind* pres 3s onwindeð 1610

onwōc see onwæcnan

open adj *open* asf opene 2271

openian 2 *open* inf 3056

ōr n *origin, beginning* ns 1688; as 2407; *front, vanguard* ds ōre 1041

orc m *cup* np orcas 3047; ap 2760

orcnēas m p *evil spirits of the dead* np orcnêas 112

ord m *point* as 1549; ds orde 556; *front, vanguard* ds 2498, 3125; *beginning* ns ord 2791

ordfruma m *leader in the vanguard* ns 263

ōretmecg m *warrior* np ōretmecgas 363, 481; ap 332

ōretta m *warrior* ns 1532, 2538

oreðe see oruð

orleahtre adj *blameless* ns 1886

orlege n *battle, strife* gs orleges 2407; ds orlege 1326

orleghwīl f *time of battle, time of war* ns 2002; gs orleghwīle 2911; gp orleghwīla 2427 [MnE -while]

orþanc m *cunning, skill* dp orþancum 406, orðoncum 2087

oruð n *breath* ns 2557; gs oreðes 2523; ds oreðe 2839

orwearde adj *without a guardian* asn 3127

orwēna adj wg *despairing (of)* ns 1002, 1565

oð prep w a *until* 2399, 3069, 3083; oð þæt conj *until* 9, 145, 219, oð ðæt 100, oþ ðæt 296, 1133, oþ þæt 56, 307, 545, 622, 644, etc., oðð þæt 66; oþ ðe 649; oð þæt adv *and then, at length* 1740, oð ðæt 2039

oþberan IV *carry off* pret 3s oþbær 579 [MnE -bear]

oðēode see oðgān

ōðer adj *other, another* nsm 503, 534, 1352, 1353, etc.; nsn 1300; asn 1086, 1583, etc.; is ōðre sīðe *another time* 2670, 3101; used absolutely in nominal function: nsm ōþer 1755, 1815, 2061; asm ōðerne 652, 2985; dsm ōþrum 814, 1228, ōðrum 1471, 2199; etc. *next, following* gs ōþres 219, 605, etc.; correl *the one . . . the other* ns ōðer . . . ōðer 1349–51; *further* 1945

oðferian 1 *bear away* pret 1s oðferede 2141 [MnE -ferry]

oðgān anom *escape* pret 3p oðēodon 2934

oððe conj *or* 283, 437, 635, 637, 693, 1491, 1763, 1764, etc.; *and* 2475; *until* 649

oðwītan I (wd of pers and a of thing) *reproach* inf 2995

ōwer see ōhwǣr

ōwiht f *aught, anything* ds ōwihte 1822, 2432

gerād adj *apt* asn gerāde 873

rand see rond

randwiga m *shield-warrior* ns 1298; as randwigan 1793

rāsian 2 *rifle, ransack* p ptc nsn rāsod 2283

raþe see hraþe

rǣcan I *reach* pret 3s rǣhte 747

gerǣcan I *reach, strike* pret 1s gerǣhte 556; 3s 2965

rǣd m *what is advisable, wise policy, good counsel, help* ns 1376; as 172, 278, 2027, 3080; *benefit* as 1201; ap rǣdas 1760 [archaic MnE rede]

rǣdan VII *control, hold sway over* inf 2858, *possess* 2056 [MnE read]

rǣdbora m *counsellor* ns 1325

rǣdend m *ruler* ns 1555

rǣhte see rǣcan

gerǣhte see gerǣcan

rǣs m *storm, onslaught* as 2626; dp rǣsum 2356

rǣsan I *rush* pret 3s rǣsde 2690

gerǣsan I *rush, charge* pret subj 3s gerǣsde 2839

rǣst f *resting-place* as rǣste 139, reste 2456; ds rǣste 122, 747, 1237, 1298, 1585

rǣswa m *leader* ds rǣswan 60

rēafian 2 *plunder* inf 2773; pret 3s rēafode 2985, 3027; 3p rēafeden (= -on) 1212 [archaic MnE reave]

rēc m *smoke* ds rēce 3155 [MnE reek]

reccan I *recount, tell* inf 91; infl inf tō reccenne 2093; pret 3s rehte 2106, 2110

reccan I *care about* pres 3s recceð 434 [archaic MnE reck]

reced m, n *hall* ns 412, 770, 1799; as 1237; gs recedes 326, 724, 3088; ds recede 720, 728, 1572; gp receda 310

regnheard adj *marvellously strong* apm regnhearde 326

regnian 2 *prepare, adorn* inf rēnian 2168; p ptc geregnad 777

rēnian see regnian

renweard m *hall-guardian* np renweardas 770

rēoc adj *savage* nsf 122

rēodan II *redden* p ptc roden 1151

reon see rōwan

reord f *voice* as reorde 2555

reordian 2 *speak* inf 3025

*ge*reordian 2 *prepare a feast* p ptc gereorded 1788

rēotan II *weep* pres 3p rēotað 1376

rēotu f (= *rōētu) *joy* ds rēōte 2457

rest see ræst

restan I *rest* inf 1793, 1857; pret 3s reste 1799

rēow see hrēoh

rēþe adj *fierce* nsf 122, nsm 1585; npm 770

rīce n *kingdom, realm* ns 2199, 2207; as 466, 912, 1179, 1733, 1853, 2369, 3004; gs rīces 861, 1390, 1859, 2027, 3080 [MnE (bishop)-ric]

rīce adj *mighty (one), powerful (one)* ns 172, 1209, 1237, 1298, rīca 310, 399, 1975 [MnE rich]

ricone adv *swiftly* 2983

rīcsian 2 *rule, hold sway* inf 2211; pret 3s rīxode 144

rīdan I *ride* inf 234, 855; pres subj 3s rīde 2445; pret 3s rād 1883, 1893; 3p riodan 3169

*ge*rīdan I wa *ride up to* pret 3s gerād 2898

rīdend m *rider, horseman* np 2457

riht n *right, what is right* as 1700; ds rihte 144, 1049, 2056, 2110; *law* as 2330; *rightly* on ryht 1555

rihte adv *rightly* 1695

rinc m *man, warrior* ns 399, 720, 2985; as 741, 747; ds rince 952, 1677; gp rinca 412, 728

riodan see rīdan

rīxian see rīcsian

roden see rēodan

rodor m *sky, heaven* gs rodores 1572; np roderas 1376; gp rodera 1555; dp roderum 310

rōf adj *brave, strong* nsm 682, 2084, 2538, 2666; asm rōfne 1793, rōfan 2690

rond m *shield* as 656, 2566, 2609, rand 682; ds ronde 2538, rande 1209; ap rondas 326, 2653, randas 231; *boss (of a shield)* as 2673

rondhæbbende m *shield-warrior* gp rondhæbbendra 861

rōwan VII *row* pret 1p rēon 539; 2p 512

rūm m *opportunity* ns 2690 [MnE room]

rūm adj *spacious, generous* nsn 2461; asm rūmne 278 [MnE room(y)]

rūmheort adj *great-hearted* ns 1799, 2110 [MnE room, heart]

*ge*rūmlīce adv *far away* compar gerūmlīcor *further away* 139

rūn f *consultation* ds rūne 172

rūnstæf m *rune* ap rūnstafas 1695

rūnwita m *private counsellor* ns 1325

ryht see riht

*ge*rȳman I *clear, vacate* pret subj 3p gerȳmdon 1086; p ptc gerȳmed 492, 1975; *allow* p ptc 2983, 3088

gerysne adj *proper* nsn 2653

*ge*saca m *adversary* as gesacan 1773

sacan VI *contend* inf 439

sacu f *conflict, strife* ns 1857, 2472; as sæce 154 [MnE sake]

*ge*sacu f *strife* ns 1737

sadol m *saddle* ns 1038

sadolbeorht adj *with bright saddles* apn 2175

sāl m *rope* ds sāle 302, 1906

sālum see sǣl

samod prep *at, simultaneously with* 1311, somod 2942

samod adv *together* 2196; samod ætgædere *together* 329, 387, 729, 1063; *as well* 1211, somod 1614, 2174, 2343, 2987

sand n *sand, shore* ds sande 213, 295, 1896, 1917, 1964, 3033

sang m *song, cry* ns 90, 1063; as 787, 2447

sār n, f *pain* ns 975; as 787; nsf 2468 [MnE sore]

sār adj *bitter, biting* dpn sārum 2058 [MnE sore]

sāre adv *grievously, sorely* 1251, 2222, 2295, 2311, 2746

sārig adj *mournful* asm sārigne 2447 [MnE sorry]

sārigferð adj *sad at heart* nsm 2863

sārigmōd adj *sad-hearted* dpm sārigmōdum 2942

sārlīc adj *painful, sad* nsn 842; asn 2109 [MnE sorely]

sāwlberend m *soul-bearers, people* gp sāwlberendra 1004

sāwol f *soul* ns 2820; as sāwle 184, 852; gs 2422, sāwele 1742; *life* as sāwle 801

sāwollēas adj *lifeless* asm sāwollēasne 1406, sāwullēasne 3033

sāwuldrīor m, n *life's blood* ds sāwuldrīore 2693

sǣ m, f *sea* ns 579, 1223; as 507, 2380, 2394; ds 318, 544; dp sǣm 858, 1297, 1685, 1956

sǣbāt m *ship* as 633, 895 [MnE sea-boat]

sǣcc f *fighting, fight, battle* as sæcce 1977, 1989, 2347, 2499, 2562; gs secce 600; ds sæcce 953, 1618, 1665, 2612, 2659, 2681, 2686; ap sæcca 2029

sæce see sacu

sǣcyning m *sea-king* gp sǣcyninga 2382

sǣd adj wg *wearied (with)* asm sǣdne 2723
[MnE sad]

sǣdan see secgan

sǣde see secgan

sǣdēor n *sea-beast* ns 1510 [MnE sea, deer]

sǣdraca m *sea-dragon* ap sǣdracan 1426

sǣgan 1 *lay low* p ptc gesǣged 884

sǣgēap adj *lofty* ns 1896

sǣgenga m *sea-walker (*i.e. *ship)* ns 1882, 1908

sǣgon see sēon

sǣgrund m *bottom of the sea* ds sǣgrunde 564
[MnE sea-ground]

sæl n *hall* as 307, 2075, 2264, sel 167

sǣl m, f *time, opportunity, season* ns 622, 1008,
1665, 2058; ap sēle 1135; gp sǣla 1611;
happiness (on sǣlum *happy)* dp sǣlum 643,
1170, 1322, sālum 607

sǣlāc n *sea-booty* ds sǣlāce 1139; ap sǣlāc 1652

sǣlād f *sea-voyage* ds sǣlāde 1139, 1157

sǣlan 1 *moor, tie up* pret 3s sǣlde 1917; 3p
sǣldon 226; *twist* p ptc gesǣled 2764

gesǣlan 1 *befall, happen* pret 3s gesǣlde 574,
890, 1250

sæld n *hall* as 1280

sǣlīðend m *seafarer* np 411, 1818, 2806,
sǣlīþende 377

sǣmann m *seaman* gp sǣmanna 329; dp
sǣmannum 2954

sǣmēþe adj *sea-weary* npm 325

sǣmra adj compar *inferior, worse* ns 2880; dsm
sǣmran 953

sǣnæss m *headland* ap sǣnæssas 223, 571
[MnE sea, ness]

sǣndeþ see snǣdan

sǣne adj *slow* compar nsm sǣnra 1436

sǣrinc m *seaman* ns 690

sǣsīð m *sea-voyage* ds sǣsīðe 1149

sǣweall m *seashore* ds sǣwealle 1924 [MnE
seawall]

sǣwong m *seashore* as 1964

sǣwudu m *ship* as 226 [MnE sea-wood]

sǣwylm m *surging sea* ap sǣwylmas 393

scacan VI *hasten, go* inf 1802; pres 3s sceaceð
2742; pret 3s scōc 2254, 3118; *pass away* p
ptc scacen 1124, 1136, sceacen 2306, 2727
[MnE shake]

gescād n *meaning* as gescād witan (wg) *understand the meaning* 288

gescādan VII *decide* pret 3s gescēd 1555

scaduhelm m *concealing shadow* gp scaduhelma 650

scamigan 2 *be ashamed, show shame* inf 1026;
pres ptc npm scamiende 2850

scaþa see sceaþa

gescæphwīle f *destined hour* ds gescæphwīle 26

sceacen see scacan

sceaceð see scacan

scead n *shadow* ap sceadu 707

sceādenmǣl n *damascened sword* ns 1939

sceadu f *shadow* ap sceadwa 1803

sceadugenga m *walker in darkness* ns 703

gesceaft f *world, creation* as 1622

sceal see sculan

scealc m *retainer, warrior* ns 918, 939

gesceap n *shape* np gesceapu 650

sceapen see scyppan

scearp adj *shrewd* nsm 288 [MnE sharp]

scēat m *region* gp scēata 752; ap scēatas 96

sceatt m *silver coin* ap sceattas 1686

sceaþa m *warrior* np scaþan 1803, 1895; *foe,
ravager* gp sceaþena 4, sceaðona 274

scēawian 2 *see, examine, look at* inf 840, 1413,
2402, 2744, 3032, scēawigan 1391; pres 2p
scēawiað 3104; subj 1s scēawige 2748; 1p
scēawian 3008; pret 3s scēawode 843, 1687,
2285, 2793; 3p scēawedon 132, 204, 983,
1440; p ptc gescēawod 3075, 3084 [MnE
show]

gescēd see gescādan

sceft m *arrow-shaft* ns 3118

scel see sculan

scencan 1 *pour* pret 3s scencte 496

scenn *metal plate (of a sword)* dp scennum
1694

gescēod see gescēoþan

sceolde see sculan

sceoldon see sculan

gescēop see gescyppan

scēotan II *shoot* pres 3s scēoteð 1744

gescēotan II *hasten to* pret 3s gescēat 2319

scēotend m *warrior* (lit. *shooter* i.e. *archer)* np
703, 1154; dp scēotendum 1026

scepen see scyppan

sceran IV *cut* pres 3s scireð 1287 [MnE shear]

gesceran IV *cut through* pret 3s gescær 1526,
gescer 2973

sceþðan VI, 1 *injure, harm* wd inf 1033, 1524;
pret 3s scōd 1887, sceþede 1514; *do harm* inf
sceðþan 243

gesceþðan VI *injure, harm* wd inf 1447; pret 3s
gescōd 1502, 1587, 2777, gesceōd 2222

scildig see scyldig

scildweall m *shield-wall (battle formation)* as
3118

scildwiga see scyldwiga

scile see sculan

scīnan I *shine* inf 1517; pres 3s scīneð 606, 1571; pret 3s scān 321, 405, 1965; 3p scinon 994, scionon 303

scinna m *evil spirit* dp scinnum 939

scionon see scīnan

scip n *ship* ns 302; as 1917; gs scipes 35, 896; ds scipe 1895; dp scypon (= -um) 1154

gescipe n *fate* ds 2570

sciphere m *attack fleet* ds scipherge 243

scīr adj *bright* ns 322; asn 496; gsn scīran 1694; *glorious* nsm 979 [MnE sheer]

scireð see sceran

scīrham adj *bright-mailed* npm scīrhame 1895

gescōd see gesceþðan

scofen see scūfan

scop m *court poet* ns 496, 1066; gs scopes 90

gescop see gescyppan

scrīfan I *decree* inf 979

gescrīfan I *decree* pret 3s gescrāf 2574

scrīðan I *wander, stalk, glide* inf 650, 703, 2569; pres 3p scrīþað 163

scucca m *demon* dp scuccum 939

scūfan II *push, shove* pret 3p scufon 215, scufun 3131; *advance* p ptc scofen 918

sculan pret-pres *must, have to, ought to* pres 1s sceal 251; 2s scealt 2666; 3s sceal 20, 24, 183, 287, 440, 977, 1004, scel 455, 2804, 3010, sceall 3014, 3077, etc.; subj 2s scyle 1179; 3s scyle 2657, scile 3176; pret 3s scolde 10, 85, etc.; sceolde 2341, 2400, 2408, 2421, etc.; subj pret 3s scolde 1328, sceolde 2708; *shall, will* pres 1s sceal 384, 424, 438, 601, 636, 1706, 2069, etc.; pres 2s scealt 588; 1p sculon 683; subj pret 3s scolde 280; *be accustomed to, be inclined by nature to* pres 3s sceall 2275; pret 3s scolde 10, 230, 1067, 1260, 3p scoldon 1798, sceoldon 2257, etc. Without an accompanying inf, expressing simple futurity: pres 3s sceal 1783, 1855, 2255, 2659, etc.

scūrheard adj *hard in battle* nsf 1033 [MnE shower, hard]

scyld m *shield* ns 2570; as 437, 2675; ap scyldas 325, 333, 2850

scyldan I *protect* pret subj 3s scylde 1658

scyldfreca m *shield-warrior* ns 1033

scyldig adj *guilty* nsm 1683, scildig 3071; *having forfeited* (wg) scyldig 1338, 2061

scyldwiga m *shield-warrior* ns 288

scyle see sculan

scyndan I *hasten* inf 2570; p ptc scynded 918

scȳne adj *beautiful* nsf 3016 [MnE sheen]

scynscaþa m *spectral foe* ns 707

scyp see scip

scyppan VI *create, cause* pret 3s scōp 78; p ptc sceapen 2229, scepen 2913

gescyppan VI *create* pret 3s gesceōp 97

scyppend m *creator* ns 106

scȳran I *settle* inf 1939

se m, þæt n, sēo f dem *the, that, that one, he, it, she*; rel pron *who, that, which*. On the difficulty of distinguishing these two uses see IIIB3 above. I. se, þæt, sēo used with a noun or nominalized adj *the, that* nsm se 84, 86, 92, 102, 159, 205, 258, etc.; asm þone 107, 168, 300, 363, 1202, 2055, ðone 202, etc.; gsm þæs 132, 989, 1030, 2316, ðæs 1105, etc.; dsm þæm 52, 143, 197, 270, ðæm 1685, þām 425, 713, 824, ðām 2039, 2083, 2139, etc.; ism þȳ 2573; npm þā 3, 282, ðā 99, 221, 2718, etc.; apm þā 1841, 2490, ðā 192, 1482, 2718, etc.; gpm þāra 9, 2779, ðāra 2734, etc.; dpm þǣm 370, 1191, þām 2788, etc.; nsn þæt 133, 191, 890, 1605, ðæt 2701, etc.; asn þæt 628, 654, 1304, 2127, etc.; gsn þæs 1220, 1467, 1809, etc.; dsn þǣm 1215, 1484, 1635, ðām 639, 2232, etc.; isn þȳ 110, 1797, 2573, ðȳ 1664, 2028, etc.; gpn þāra 681; dpn þǣm 1492, 1612, ðǣm 2145, 2669, þām 2298; nsf sēo 66, 146, 1153, 1250, sīo 2098, 2403, etc.; sīe 2219; asf þā 354, 470, ðā 189, 1977, etc.; gsf þǣre 1025, 2546, 2887, ðǣre 562; dsf þǣre 125, 617, etc.; gpf 2794; dpf ðām 2989.

II. se, þæt, sēo used independently as a dem *that one, that, he, it, she* nsm se 196, 469, 898; asm þone 1354, 3009; dsm þǣm 1363, ðǣm 12, 59, þām 2612; np þā 44; ap 488, 3014, ðā 2148, etc.; gp þāra 98; dp þām 137; nsn þæt 11, 170, 249, 309, 454, 716, 2000, etc.; asn þæt 194, 290, 435, 632, etc.; gsn þæs 350, 586, 778, 1145, etc.; *for that, because of that* 7, 16, 277, 588, 900, 1220, etc., ðæs 114, 1992; tō þæs 1616; isn þon 724, 1722, 2591, 2845; before a compar *the* (as in 'the longer *the* better') þȳ 974, 1902, 2880, ðȳ 487, 2277, 2749, þē 821, 1436, ðē 2687, þon 504, see l. 2423 note; nsf sīo 2024, 2087; nsn anticipating a noun clause þæt 2200 see note; asn þæt 798 see note, 2219, þæt eal 1185; gsn þæs 778, 2032 (see ll. 2031–8 note). III. se, þæt, sēo used as a rel pron *who, that, which* nsm se 143, 196, 370, 1267, etc.; asm þone 13, 2048, 2751; dsm þǣm 310, ðǣm 374, þām 2199, 2779; nsn þæt 453, 2500; asn þæt 766, 1456, 1466, etc.; gsn 1398, as 272, 383; nsf sīo 2258; asf þā 2022; np þā 41, 113, etc. IV. se,

þæt, sēo used as a rel pron in combination with **þe**: see **þe** rel particle. V. **se, þæt, sēo** used alone as antecedent and rel: **se** *he who* 143, 1977; **þæt** *what* 1466, 1748; **þæs** *for what* 1398; **þǣm** 2199 see l. 2199b note, 2779. VI. adverbial uses: gsn **þæs** *to that degree, so* 773, 1366, 1509, see l. 968 note; *therefore, for that reason* 1778; isn **þē** *therefore, for that reason* 821, ðē 2687, **þȳ** 2067; **ðȳ** *by that* 1273; **tō þon** *to that degree, so* 1876; **tō ðon** *until the time* 2591, 2845. VII. conj: gsn **þæs** *as* 272, 383; **þas þe** *as* 1341, 1350, 3000; **þæs þe** *because* 108, 228, 1628, **þæs ðe** 626, 1779, 1998, 2797; isn **þē** *when* 1000; as 2135; **þē . . . ðē** *for that reason . . . because* 1436, 2638–41; **þȳ . . . þē** see ll. 487b–8 note; **þē** *by which* 242; **þȳ læs** *lest* 1918; **tō þæs þe, tō þon** see **tō** prep.

sealma m *couch* as sealman 2460
sealt adj *salt* asn 1989
searo n *skill, artistry* dp searwum 1038, 2764; *war-gear, armour* np searo 329; dp searwum 249, 323, 419, 1557, 1813, 2530, 2568, 2700
searobend f *cunningly made clasp* dp searobendum 2086
searofāh adj *cunningly decorated* nsf 1444
searogimm m *precious gem* ap searogimmas 2749; gp searogimma1157, 3102
searogrim adj *cunningly fierce* nsm 594
searohæbbend m *armed warrior* gp searohæbbendra 237
searonet n *mail-coat* ns 406 [MnE -net]
searonīð m *cunning hostility* ap searonīðas 1200, 2738, 3067; *skilful contest* gp searonīða 582
searoþonc m *skill* dp searoþoncum 775
searowundor n *curious wonder* as 920
seax n *short-sword* ds seaxe 1545
sēcan I *seek, seek out* inf 756, 801, 2495, 2513, sēcean 1989, 2422; infl inf tō sēceanne 2562; pret 1s sōhte 2738; 3s 139, 2231, 2300, 3067; imp s sēc 1379; *go to, visit* inf sēcean 187, 200, 268, 645, 821, 1597, 1869, 2820, 2950, 3102, sēcan 664, 756, 1450, 1820; pres 3s sēceð 2272; subj 3s sēce 1369; pret 2s sōhtest 458; 3s sōhte 208, 376; 2p sōhton 339; 3p sōhtan 2380; subj 1s sōhte 417; *search* pret 3s 2293; *require* pret 3s 2572; *attack* pres 3p sēceað 3001
*ge*sēcan I *seek* inf gesēcean 684; *go to, visit* inf 692, 2275, gesēcan 1004; infl inf tō gesēcanne 1922; pret 3s gesōhte 463, 520, 717, 1951; p

ptc npf gesōhte 1839; *attack* pres 3s gesēceð 2515; pret 3p gesōhtan 2204, gesōhton 2926; subj 3s gesōhte 2346
secce see **sæcc**
secg m *man* ns 208, 249, 402, 871, 947, 980, 1311, 1569, 1759, 1812, 2226, 2352, 2406, 2700, 2708, 2863, 3028, 3071; as 1379; ds secge 2019; np secgas 213, 2530, 3128; gp secga 633, 842, 996, 1672; dp secgum 149, 490
secg f *sword* as secge 684
secgan 3 *tell, say* inf 51, 273, 391, 582, 875, 880, 942, 1049, 1346, 1700, 1818, 2864, 3026; infl inf tō secganne 473, 1724; pres 1s secge 590, 1997, 2795; 3p secgað 411; pret 2s sægdest 532; 3s sægde 90, 1175, 1809, 2632, 2899, sǣde 3152; 3p sægdon 377, sǣdan 1945; p ptc gesægd 141, gesǣd 1696; pres ptc (verbal noun) secggende *teller* 3028
*ge*secgan 3 *say, tell* pret subj 1s gesǣgde 2157; imp s gesaga 388
sefa m *mind, spirit, heart* ns 49, 490, 594, 2043, 2180, 2419, 2600, 2632; as sefan 278, 1726, 1842; ds sefan 473, 1342, 1737
sēft see **sōfte**
*ge*sēgan see *ge*sēon
segen see **segn**
segl m, n *sail* ns 1906
seglrād *sail-road*, (i.e. *sea*) ds seglrāde 1429
segn m, n *standard, banner* as segn 2776, asn 2767, asm segen 47, 1021; ds segne 1204; npn segn 2958
*ge*sēgon see *ge*sēon
sel see **sæl**
sēl (noun) see **sǣl**
sēl adv compar *better* 1012, 2277, 2530, 2687
*ge*selda m *hall-fellow* as geseldan 1984
seldan adv *seldom* 2029
seldguma m *hall-retainer* ns 249
sele m *hall* ns 81, 411; as 826, 2352; ds 323, 713, 919, 1016, 1640, 1984, 3128
seledrēam m *joy in the hall* as 2252
seleful n *hall-cup* as 619
selegyst m *hall-visitor* as 1545
selerǣdende m *hall-counsellor* np 51; ap 1346
selerest f *bed in a hall* as selereste 690
sēlest see **gōd**
seleþegn m *hall-thane* ns 1794
seleweard m *hall-guardian* as 667
self pron *self* nsm (strong) 594, 920, 953, 1010, 1313, sylf 1964, 2702; (weak) selfa 29, 1468, 1733, 1839, 1924, seolfa 3067, sylfa 505, 3054; asm selfne 961, 1605,

self (*cont.*)

sylfne 1977, 2875; gsm selfes 1147, sylfes 2013, 2147, 2222, 2360, 2639, 2710, 2776, 3013; *his own* selfes 700, 895; gsf selfre 1115; np selfe 419; apm sylfe 1996; gp sylfra 2040

sēlla see **gōd**

sellan I *give* inf syllan 2160, 2729; pres 3s seleð 1730, 1749; pret 2s sealdest 1482; 3s sealde 72, 622, 672, 1271, 1693, 1751, 2019, 2044, 2155, 2182, 2490, 2994, 3055; 3p sealdon 1161; *give up* pres 3s seleð 1370 [MnE sell]

ge**sellan** I *give* inf 1029; pret 3s gesealde 615, 1052, 1866, 1901, 2142, 2172, 2195, 2810, 2867

sellīc adj *strange, remarkable* apm sellīce 1426; asn syllīc 2109; nsf 2086; compar asf syllīcran 3038

sēlra see **gōd**

semninga adv *presently* 644, 1640, 1767

sendan I *send* pret is sende 471; 3s 13, 1842

sēo see **sē**

sēoc adj *sick, stricken* ns 2740, 2904; npm sēoce 1603

seofon num *seven* a 517, seofan 2195, syfone 3122

seolfa see **self**

seomian 2 *rise* inf siomian 2767; *lurk* pret 3s seomade 161, *ride, undulate* seomode 302

sēon V *see* inf 387, 920, 1365, 3102, sêon 1180, 1275; pret is seah 336, 2014; *look, look on* pret 3s seah 2717, 2863; 3p sāwon 1650, sǣgon 1422

ge**sēon** *see, look* V inf 396, 571, 648, 961, 1078, 1126, 1485, 1628, 1998; pres 3s gesyhð 2041, 2455; pret is geseah 247, 1662; 3s 229, 728, 926, 1516, 1557, 1585, 1613, 2542, 2604, 2756, 2767, 2822; 3p gesāwon 221, 1023, 1347, 1425, 1591, gesēgan 3038, gesēgon 3128; subj 3p gesāwon 1605; *see each other* inf gesēon 1875; *see (the last of)* pret 3p gesāwon 2252

seonu f *sinew* np seonowe 817

sēoðan II wa *brood over* pret is sēað 1993; 3s 190 [MnE seethe]

seoððan see **siððan**

sēowan I *link together* p ptc sēowed 406 [MnE sew]

sess m *seat* ds sesse 2717, 2756

sētan see **sittan**

setl n *seat* as 2013; gs setles 1786; ds setle 1232, 1782, 2019; dp setlum 1289 [MnE settle]

settan I *set* pret 3p setton 325, 1242; p ptc nsn geseted 1696

ge**settan** I *establish* pret 3s gesette 94; *settle* pres subj 3s 2029

sexbenn f *stab-wound* dp sexbennum 2904

sibæðeling m *noble kinsman* np sibæðelingas 2708

sibb f *peace* ns sib 1164, 1857; as sibbe 154; gs 2922; as *relationship* 949, *ties of kinship* 2431, sibb' 2600

sibbegedriht f *band of kinsmen* as 387, 729

sīd adj *broad, large* asm sīdne 437, 507; dsm sīdan 2347; apm sīde 223, 325; nsn sīde 2199; asn sīde 1733; nsf sīd 1444, 2086; asf sīde 1291, 2394; asm sīdne sefan *large spirit, magnanimity* 1726; gpf sīdra *great, deep* 149

sīde adv *widely* 1223

sīdfæþme adj *broad-beamed, capacious* asn 1917 [MnE fathom]

sīdfæþmed adj *broad-beamed, capacious* nsn 302

sīdrand m *broad shield* ns 1289

sīe (2219) see **se** I

sig see **bēon**

sīgan I *sink* pret 3p sigon 1251; *march* 307

ge**sīgan** I *fall* inf 2659

sigedrihten m *victorious lord* ns 391

sigeēadig adj *rich in victories, victory-blessed* asn 1557

sigefolc n *glorious people* gp sigefolca 644

sigehrēð n *glory of victory* as 490

sigehrēþig adj *rejoicing in victory, victorious* ns 94, 1597, 2756

sigehwīl f *victory* gp sigehwīle 2710

sigel *sun* ns 1966

sigelēas adj *of defeat* asm sigelēasne 787

sigerōf adj *glorious* ns 619

sigeþēod f *glorious* ds sigeþēode 2204

sigewǣpen n *weapon of victory* dp sigewǣpnum 804

sigle n *jewel* as 1200; ap siglu 3163; gp sigla 1157

sigor m *victory* gs sigores 1021; gp sigora 2875, 3055

sigorēadig adj *victorious* ns 1311, 2352

sīn poss pron *his* asm sīnne 1960, 1984, 2283, 2789; dsm sīnum 2160; dsn 1236; *her* dsn 1507

sinc n *treasure, precious object* ns 2764; as 81, 1204, 1485, 2383, 2431; gs sinces 607, 1170, 1922, 2071; ds since 1038, 1450, 1615, 1882, 2217, 2746; gp sinca 2428; *treasure-cup* as sinc 2023 sincfæt n *precious cup* as 2231, 2300; ap sincfato 622; *precious setting* as sincfæt 1200

sincfāg adj *treasure-decked* asn sincfāge 167

sincgestrēon n *treasure* gp sincgestrēona 1226; dp sincgestrēonum 1092

sincgifa m *treasure-giver* as sincgyfan 1012; ds sincgifan 2311, sincgyfan 1342

sincmāðþum m *treasure* ns 2193

sincþego m *receiving of treasure* ns 2884

sinfrēa m *husband* ns 1934

singāl adj *continual* asf singale 154

singāla, singāles adv *continually, always* singāla 190; singāles 1777, syngales 1135

singan III *sing, ring out* pret 3s sang 496, song 323, 1423, 3152

sinhere m *standing army, retinue* ds sinherge 2936

sinniht f *perpetual night* ds sinnihte 161

sint see bēon

sīo see sē

sioloð m *sea* (?) gp sioleða 2367 [a word of uncertain meaning which occurs only here]

siomian see seomian

sittan V *sit* pres 3s siteð 2906; pret 3s sæt 130, 286, 356, 500, 1166, 1190, 2852, 2894; 3p sæton 1164, sætan (= -on) 1602; *sit down* inf sittan 493, 641; imp s site 489

gesittan V *sit down* pret 3s gesæt 171, 1424, 1977, 2417, 2717; p ptc geseten 2104; *press, exert pressure against* pret 3s gesæt 749; wa *sit down in, occupy* pret 3s gesæt 633

sīð m *voyage, journey, undertaking, expedition, exploit* ns 501, 765, 1971, 2541, 2586, 3058, 3089; as 353, 512, 872, 908, 1278, 1429, 1966; gs sīðes 579, 1475, 1794, 1908; ds sīðe 532, 1951, 1993; np sīðas 1986; ap 877; gp sīða 318; *time, occasion* ns sīð 716, 1463, 1527, 2625; as 1579; ds sīðe 740, 1203, 2049, 2286, 2511, 2517, 2670, 2688, 3101

sīð adv compar *later* 2500

gesīð m *retainer, comrade* gs gesīðes 1297; np gesīþas 29; ap gesīðas 2040, 2518; gp gesīða 1934; dp gesīðum 1313, 1924, 2632

sīðast adj superl nsf *last* 2710; dsn æt sīðestan *at the end* 3013

siþfæt m *expedition* as 202; ds sīðfate 2639

sīðfrom adj *eager to depart* npm sīðfrome 1813

sīðian 2 *journey, make a journey* inf 720, 808; pret 3s sīðode 2119

siððan I. adv *afterwards, thereupon, since* siððan (siþðan) 470, 685, 718, syððan (syþðan, syðþan) 142, 283, 567, 1106, 1453, 1901, 1951, 2064, 2071, 2175, 2207, 2217, 2395,

2702, 2806, 2920, seoððan 1875, seoþðan 1937. II. conj *after, when, since* 106, 413, 604, 648, 656, 850, 901, 982, 1148, 1204, 1253, 1261, 1281, 1784, syððan (syþðan, syðþan, etc.) 6, 115, 132, 722, 834, 886, 1077, 1198, 1206, 1235, 1308, 1420, 1472, 1556, 1589, 1689, 1947, 1949, 1978, 2012, 2051, 2072, 2092, 2103, 2124, 2351, 2356, 2388, 2437, 2474, 2501, 2630, 2888, 2911, 2914, 2943, 2960, 2970, 2996, 3002, 3127, seoþðan 1775; correl w adv *sīððan:* syððan . . . syððan *after . . . then* 2201–7

slǣp m *sleep* ns 1742; ds slǣpe 1251

slǣpan VII *sleep* pres ptc nsm slǣpende 2218; asm slǣpendne 741; apm slǣpende 1581

slēac adj *indolent, sluggish* ns 2187

slēan VI *strike* pres subj 3s slēa 681; pret 3s slōh 1565, 2576, 2678, 2699, slōg 2179; *slay* pret 1s slōg 421; 3s 108, 2179, slōh 1581, 2355; 3p slōgon 2050; p ptc slægen 1152

geslēan VI *bring about by fighting* pret 3s geslōh 459; 3p geslōgon 2996

slītan I *tear* pret 3s slāt 741 [MnE slit]

slīðe adj *terrible, fierce* asm slīðne 184; gpn slīðra 2398

slīðen adj *cruel* nsn 1147

geslyht n *battle* gp geslyhta 2398

smǣte adj *pure, polished* asn 2217

smið m *smith* ns 1452; gs smiþes 406

snǣdan I *eat, devour* pres 3s sǣndeþ 600

snell adj *brave* nsm snella 2971

snellīc adj *brave* ns 690

snotor, snottor adj *wise* nsm 190, 826, 908, 1384, snotera 1313, snotra 2156, 3120, snottra 1475, 1786; npm snotere 202, 416, snottre 1591

snotorlīce adv *wisely* compar snotorlīcor 1842

snūde adv *quickly* 904, 1869, 1971, 2325, 2568, 2752

snyrian I *hasten* pret 3p snyredon 402

snyttru f *skill, wisdom* as 1726; dp snyttrum 872, 942, 1706

sōcn f *persecution* gs sōcne 1777

sōfte adv *easily* compar ōþ sēft *the more easily* 2749 [MnE soft]

somod see samod

sōna adv *immediately, right away* 121, 721, 743, 750, 1280, 1497, 1591, 1618, 1762, 1785, 1794, 1825, 2011, 2226, 2300, 2713, 2928 [MnE soon]

sorg see sorh

sorgian 2 *be concerned, grieve* inf 451; imp s sorga 1384

sorh f *sorrow, trouble* ns 473, 1322; as sorge 119, 1149, 2463; ds sorhge 2468; gp sorga 149, sorge 2004; dp sorgum 2600

sorhcearig adj *sorrowful* nsm 2455; nsf sorgcearig 3152

sorhfull adj *sorrowful* nsf 2119; *perilous, sorrowbringing* asm sorhfullne 512, sorhfulne 1278, 1429

sorhlēas adj *free from care* nsm 1672

sorhlēoð n *song of sorrow* as 2460

sorhwylm m *surging sorrow* np sorhwylmas 904; dp sorhwylmum 1993

sōð n *truth* ns 700; as 532, 1049, 1700, 2864; ds sōðe 51, 590, 2325

sōð adj *true* nsm 1611; asn 2109 [archaic MnE sooth]

sōðcyning m *true king* ns 3055

sōðe adv *truly* 524, 871

sōðfæst adj *firm in truth, truth-speaking* gp sōðfæstra 2820

sōðlīce adv *truly* 141, 273, 2899

specan see sprecan

spēd f *success* as on spēd *successfully, with skill* 873 [MnE speed]

spell n *tale, tiding(s)* as spel 873, spell 2109; gp spella 2898, 3029

spīwan I *spew* inf 2312

spōwan VII impers wd *succeed* pret 3s spēow 2854, 3026

spRæc f *talk* ds spRæce 1104 [MnE speech]

sprecan V *speak* inf 2069, 3172, specan 2864; pret 2s spRæce 531; 3s spRæc 341, 1168, 1215, 1698, 2510, 2618, 2724; 1p spRæcon 1476, 1707; 3p 1595; p ptc sprecen 643; imp s spRæc 1171

gesprecan V *speak* pret 3s gespRæc 675, 1398, 1466, l. 2792b note, 3094

springan III *spring, gape* pret 3s sprong 1588, *spurt* 2966, *spread* sprang 18; 3p sprungon 2582

gespringan III *arise, burgeon forth* pret 3s gesprang 884, *spurt forth* 1667 [MnE spring]

stān m *stone, stone structure* as 887, 1415, 2553, 2744; ds stāne 2288, 2557

stānbeorh m *stone barrow* as 2213

stānboga m *stone arch* ap stānbogan 2545, 2718 [MnE stone, bow]

stānclif n *rocky cliff* ap stāncleofu 2540

standan VI *stand, remain* inf 2271, stondan 2545, 2760; pres 3s standeð 1362; 2p standað 2866; subj 3s stande 411; pret 3s stōd 32, 145, 926, 935, 1037, 1416, 1434, 1913, 2679; 3p stōdon 328, stōdan 3047; *issue, arise, shine*

forth pret 3s stōd 726, 783, 1570, 2227, 2313, 2769

gestandan VI *stand, take a position* pret 3s gestōd 358, 404, 2566; 3p gestōdon 2597

stānfāh adj *paved with stones* nsf 320

stānhlið n *rocky cliff* ap stānhliðo 1409

stapol m *stairway (?)* ds stapole 926; *pillar* dp stapulum 2718

starian 2 *look, gaze* pres 1s starige 1781, starie 2796; 3s starað 996, 1485; pret 3s starede 1935; 3p staredon 1603 [MnE stare]

stæl m *place* ds stæle 1479 [MnE stal(wart)]

stælan I *avenge* inf 2485; p ptc gestæled 1340

stēap adj *high, lofty, steep* asm stēapne 926, 2213, 2566; apm stēape 222; apn stēap 1409

stearcheort adj *stouthearted* ns 2288, 2552 [MnE stark, heart]

stedenægl m *firm nail* gp stedenægla 985

stefn m *prow, stem* as 212

stefn m *time* ds niowan stefne *another time, again* 1789, nīwan stefne 2594

stefn f *voice* ns 2552

stēpan I *exalt* pret subj 3s stēpte 1717

gestēpan I *support* pret 3s gestēpte 2393

steppan VI *step, march* pret 3s stōp 761, 1401

gesteppan VI *step* pret 3s gestōp 2289

stīg f *ascending path* ns 320, 2213; ap stīge 1409

stīgan I *go, go up* pret 3s stāg 2362; 3p stigon 212, 225; subj 3s stige 676

gestīgan I *set out* pret 1s gestāh 632

stille adj *still, in place* nsm 301, 2830

stincan III *sniff* pret 3s stonc 2288

stīð adj *resolute* nsn 1533

stīðmōd adj *stout-hearted* nsm 2566

stondan see standan

stōp see steppan

storm m *storm* ns 3117; ds storme 1131

stōw f *place* ns 1372; as stōwe 1006, 1378

strang adj *strong* nsm 1844; nsn 133; nsf strong 2684. Superl strengest nsm 196, 789, 1543

stRæl m *arrow* ds stRæle 1746; gp stRæla 3117

stRæt f *street* ns 320; as stRæte 916, 1634

strēam m *stream, current* as 2545; np strēamas 212; ap 1261

strēgan I *spread, prepare* p ptc strēd 2436 [MnE strew]

streng m *string (of a bow)* dp strengum 3117

strengel m *ruler* as 3115

strengest see strang

strengo f *strength* as strenge 1270; ds 1533, strengo 2540

gestrēon n *treasure* np 2037; as 1920, 3166

strong see strang

strūdan II *plunder* pret subj 3s strude 3073, 3126

gestrȳnan I *acquire* inf 2798

stund f *time* dp stundum *at times* 1423

stȳle n *steel* ds 985

stȳlecg adj *steel-edged* nsn 1533

styrian I *stir up* pres 3s styreþ 1374; *disturb* pret subj 3s styrede 2840; *treat of* inf 872

styrman I *storm, shout* pret 3s styrmde 2552

suhtergefæderan mp *brother's son and paternal uncle* np 1164

sum pron *a certain (one), some(one)* [sum has adj infl but usually functions as an indefinite pron] nsm 207, 248, 314, 1240, 1251, 1266, 1312, 1412, 1499, 2301, 2401, 3123, 3124; asm sumne 713, 1432, 2091, 3061; npm sume 400, 1113; apm 2940; nsn sum 271, 1607, 1905; asn 675, 2279; isn 2156. Wgp: eahta sum *one of eight* (i.e. *he and seven others*) 3123, fēara sum *one of a few* (i.e. *with a few others*) 1412; sometimes perhaps with an emphatic sense: *a most important one, a particular one* e.g. 248, 271, 314, 1312, 1607, 2279

sund n *sea, water* ns 213, 223; as 512, 539, 1426, 1444; *running current* as 507; ds sunde 1510; *swimming* gs sundes 1436; ds sunde 517, 1618 on sunde *a-swimming* [MnE sound 'long inlet of the ocean']

gesund adj *safe, unharmed* asm gesundne 1628, 1998; npm gesunde 2075; apm sīða gesunde *safe in your exploits* 318 [MnE sound]

sundgebland n *surging water* as 1450

sundnytt f *sea-journey* (lit., *use of the sea*) as sundnytte 2360

sundornytt f *special service* as sundornytte 667

sundur adv *asunder* 2422

sundwudu m *sea-wood* (i.e. *ship*) ns 1906; as 208

sunne f *sun* ns 606; as sunnan 94; gs 648

sunu m *son* ns 524, 590, 645, 980, 1009, 1040, 1089, 1485, 1550, 1652, 1699, 2147, 2367, 2386, 2398, 2447, 2602, 2862, 2971, 3076, 3120; as 268, 947, 1115, 1175, 2013, 2119, 2394, 2752; gs suna 2455, 2612, sunu 1278; ds suna 1226, 2025, 2160, 2729, sunu 344, 1808; np suna 2380

sūð adv *south* 858

sūþan adv *from the south* 606, 1966

swā conj *as* 29, 93, 273, 352, 401, 444, 455, 490, 561, 642, 666, 956, 1055, 1058, 1134, 1172, 1231, 1234, 1238, 1252, 1381, 1396, 1451, 1587, 1670, 1676, 1707, 1786, 1787, 1828, 1891, 1975, 2233, 2310, 2332, 2470, 2480, 2491, 2521, 2526, 2585, 2590, 2608, 2622, 2664, 2696, 2859, 3049 (?*as if*), 3078, 3098, 3140, 3161, 3174; *when* 881, 1667; *because* 352, 2310, (*or and*), 3098; *so that* 1048, 1508, 2006, 2184, 2574; swā . . . þæt *so* . . . *þæt* 1451–3, 1732–3, 1769–72; corr swā . . . swā *so* . . . *as* 594, as . . . *as* 3168, efne swā micle swā *by just as much as* 1283, swā hwæþer . . . swā *whichsoever* . . . *as* 686–7; efne swā hwylc . . . swā *whosoever* 943, efne swā hwylcum . . .swā *whatsoever* 3057; efne swā *just as* 1571; efne swā . . . swā *just as* . . . *as* 1092–3, 1223; *so* 435; swā þēah, swā ðēh *however* 972, 2967, etc.

swā adv *so, thus* 20, 99, 144, 164, 189, 538, 559, 1142, etc.; w following adj *so, such* 347, 585, 591, 1732, 1843

swancor adj *graceful* apn 2175

swanrād f *swan's riding-place,* (i.e. *sea*) as swanrāde 200 [MnE swan, raid, road]

swāt m *blood* ns 2693, 2966; ds swāte 1286 [MnE sweat]

swātfāh adj *blood-stained* nsf 1111

swātig adj *bloody* nsn 1569 [MnE sweaty]

swātswaðu f *bloody track* ns 2946

swaþrian 2 *subside* pret 3p swaþredon 570

swaðu f *track* as swaðe 2098 [MnE swath]

swaþul m, n *flame* ds swaþule 782

swæfun see swefan

swæs adj *own, own dear* asm swæsne 520; npm swæse 29; apm 1868, 2040, 2518; gpm swæsra 1934

swæslīce adv *in a friendly manner, pleasantly* 3089

sweart adj *dark* nsm 3145; dpf sweartum 167 [MnE swart]

swebban I *kill* (lit., *put to sleep*) inf 679; pres 3s swefeð 600

swefan V *sleep, sleep (in death)* inf 119, 729, 1672; pres 3s swefeþ 1008, 1741, 2060, 2746; 3p swefað 2256, 2457; pret 3s swæf 1800; 3p swæfon 703, swæfun 1280

swefeð (600) see swebban

swēg m *sound* ns 644, 782; *noise, applause* ds swēge 1214; swēg *music* ns 89, 1063, 2458, 3023

swegl n *sky* gs swegles 860, 1773; ds swegle 1078, 1197

swegl adj *bright* apm swegle 2749

sweglwered adj *clothed with radiance* nsf 606

swelan IV *burn* inf 2713

swelgan III *swallow* wd pret 3s swealh 743, swealg 3155; subj 3s swulge 782 swellan III *swell* inf 2713

sweltan III *die* pret 3s swealt 892, 1617, 2358, 2474, 2782, 3037 [MnE swelt(er)]

swencan I *afflict, harass* pret 3s swencte 1510; p ptc geswenced 975, 1368

geswencan I *strike* pret 3s geswencte 2438

sweng m *(sword)stroke* as 1520; ds swenge 2686, 2966; dp swengum 2386

sweofot m, n *sleep* ds sweofote 1581, 2295

sweoloð m, n *fire* ds sweoloðe 1115

sweorcan III *grow dark* pres 3s sweorceð 1737

gesweorcan III *grow dark* pret 3s geswearc 1789

sweord n *sword* ns 1286, 1289, 1569, 1605, 1615, 1696, 2499, 2509, 2659, 2681, 2700, swurd 890; as sweord 437, 672, 1808, 2252, 2518, 2562, swurd 1901, swyrd 2610, 2987; gs sweordes 1106, 2193, 2386; ds sweorde 561, 574, 679, 2492, 2880, 2904; np swyrd 3048; ap sweord 2638, swurd 539; gp sweorda 1040, 2936, 2961; dp sweordum 567, 586, 884

sweordbealu n *death by the sword* ns 1147 [MnE sword, bale]

sweordfreca m *sword-warrior* ds sweordfrecan 1468

sweotol adj *clear* nsm swutol 90; nsn sweotol 817, 833; dsn sweotolan 141

swerian VI *swear* pret 1s swōr 2738; 3s 472

sweðrian 2 *subside, diminish* inf 2702; pret 3s sweðrode 901

swīcan I *escape* pret subj 3s swice 966; *fail* pret 3s swāc 1460

geswīcan I *fail* wd pret 3s geswāc 1524, 2584, 2681

swift adj *swift* nsm swifta 2264

swīge adj *silent* compar nsm swīgra 980

swīgian 2 *be silent* pret 3s swīgode 2897; 3p swīgedon 1699

swilce see swylce adv

swīn n *boar-image* ns swȳn 1111; as swīn 1286 [MnE swine]

swincan III *toil* pret 2p swuncon 517

geswing n *swirl* ns 848

swingan III *swing, soar* pres 3s swingeð 2264

swīnlīc n *boar-image* dp swīnlīcum 1453

swioðol m, n *fire* ds swioðole 3145

swīð adj *strong* nsn 3085; swȳð 191. Compar swīðre *right* 2098

swīðe adv *greatly* 586, 597, 997, 1092, *very much* 960, swȳðe 2187, swīðe *very* 1743, 1926, swȳðe 2170. Compar swīðor *very much* 960, 1139, *more especially* 1874, 2198

swīðferhð adj *strong-minded, stout-hearted* ns swȳðferhð 826; gsm swīðferhþes 908; npm swīðferhþe 493; dpm swīðferhðum 173

swīðhicgende adj *stouthearted, valiant* nsm 919; npm 1016, 1624

swīðmōd adj *stouthearted* nsm 1624

swōgan VII *resound, sough* pres ptc swōgende 3145

swōr see swerian

swulces see swylc

swurd see sweord

swutol see sweotol

swylc pron (dem) *such* ns 178, 1940, 2541, 2708; gpm swylcra 582; dsm swylcum 299; asn swylc 996, 1583, 2798; gsn swulces 880; apm swylce 1347; gpn swylcran 2231; (relat) *such as* apm swylce 1156, npn 2459; asn swylc 72; asf swylce 1797; (corr) *such . . . as* swylc . . . as swylc . . . swylc nsm 1328–9; isn swylce . . . 1249; apf 3164

swylce conj *such as* 757, 2869

swylce adv *likewise, also* 113, 293, 830, 854, 907, 920, 1146, 1165, 1427, 1482, 2258, 2767, 2824, 3150, swilce 1152

swylt m *death* ns 1255, 1436

swyltdæg m *death-day* ds swyltdæge 2798

swymman III *swim* inf 1624

swȳn see swīn

swynsian 2 *resound* pret 3s swynsode 611

swyrd see sweord

swyrdgifu f *giving of swords* ns 2884

swȳðe see swīðe

sȳ see bēon

syfanwintre adj *seven years old* nsm 2428

syfone see seofon

sylf see self

syll f *floor* ds sylle 775 [MnE sill]

syllan see sellan

syllīc see sellīc

symbel n *banquet* as 564, 619, 1010, 2431; ds symble 119, 2104, symle 81, 489, 1008; gp symbla 1232

symbelwynn f *joy of feasting* as symbelwynne 1782

symble adv *always, ever* 2450, symle 2497, 2880

symble see symbel

symle see symble adv

synbysig adj *guilty* nsm 2226 [MnE sin, busy]

syndolh n *lasting wound* ns 817

syndon see bēon

gesȳne adj *manifest, visible* nsm 2947, 3158; npm 1403; nsn 1255, 2316, 3058

syngāles see singāla, singāles

gesyngian 2 *do wrong, err* p ptc gesyngad 2441 [MnE sin]

synn f *crime* dp synnum 975, 1255, 3071; *hostility* ns synn 2472 [MnE sin]

synscaða m *evil ravager* as synscaðan 801 [MnE sin-]

synsnǣd f *sinful morsel* dp synsnǣdum 743 [MnE sin-]

synt see bēon

gesynto f *safety* dp gesyntum 1869

syrce f *mail-coat* ns 1111; ap syrcan 226; ap 334 [MnE sark]

syrwan 1 *ambush* pret 3s syrede 161

syððan see siððan

tācen n *evidence, sign* ns 833; ds tācne 141, 1654 [MnE token]

talian 2 *suppose, consider* pres 1s talige 677, 1845; 2s talast 594; 3s talað 2027; *maintain* pres 1s talige 532

getǣcan 1 *point out, assign* pret 3s getǣhte 313, 2013

getǣse adj *satisfactory* nsf 1320

te see tō

tēar m *tear* np tēaras 1872

tela adv *well* 948, 1218, 1225, 1820, 2208, 2663, 2737

telge see tellan

tellan 1 *consider, deem* pres 1s telge 2067; pret 1s tealde 1773; 3s 794, 1810, 1936, 2641; 3p tealdon 2184

getenge adj *lying on* wd asn 2758

teohh f *company* ds teohhe 2938

teohhian 2 *assign* pret 1s teohhode 951; p ptc geteohhod 1300

tēon II *drag* pret 3s tēah 553; p ptc togen 1439; *lead* inf tēon 1036; *draw* p ptc togen 1288; *undertake* pret 3s tēah 1051, 1332

tēon 2 *furnish, provide* pret 3s tēode 1452; pret 3p tēodan 43

getēon II *draw* pret 3s getēah wd 1545, wa 2610

getēon 2 *deal with, allot* pres 3s getēoð 2526; pret 3s getēode 2295

getēon I *bestow, confer*; pret 3s getēah 1044, 2165; imp s wearne getēoh ðīnra gegncwida *bestow refusal of your answers* (i.e. *refuse to answer*) 366

tīd f *time* as 147, 1915

tīdan 1 *befall* pret 3s tīde 2226

til adj *good* nsm 61, till 2721; nsn til 1304; nsf tilu 1250

tilian 2 *earn* inf 1823

timbran 1 *build* p ptc timbred 307

tīr m *glory* gs tīres 1654

tīrēadig adj *glorious* dsm tīrēadigum 2189

tīrfæst adj *glorious* ns 922

tīrlēas adj *inglorious* gsm tīrlēases 843

tīðian 2 *grant* (wd of pers and g of thing) p ptc nsn getīðad 2284

tō I. adv *too* 133, 137, 191, 905, 969, etc.; *on, over, forth* 1422, 1755, 1785, 2289, 2648; tō þæs *so* 1616. II. prep A. wd *to, towards* 28, 124, 234, 270, 298, 313, 318, 323, etc.; *by* 641, *at* 26, 172, 647, 1242, 1654b, 1990, *about* 1138, 1139, *from* 158, 188, 525, 601, 909, 1207, 1272, 1396, 2494, 2922 (te), 3001, *for* 1186, 1472, 2639, *as* 14, 95, 379, 665, 971, 1021, 1654a, 1830, 1834, 1901, 2448, 2804, 2941, 2998, 3016, tō sōðe *for a truth, truly* 51, 590, 2325. B. introducing a prep conj wg tō þæs þe *to where, until* 714, tō ðæs ðe 1967, 2410, *to the extent that* 1585; wi tō hwan *to what result* 2071, tō þon . . . þæt *so . . . that* 1876–7. C. w infl inf 174, 257, 473, 1003, 1419, etc.; w inf 316, 2556

tōbrecan IV *break, shatter* inf 780; p ptc tōbrocen 997

tōdrīfan I *drive apart* pret 3s tōdrāf 545

tōgædre adv *together* 2630

tōgēanes prep *against, towards* 666, 1542, 1626, 1893; *to* tōgēnes 3114

tōgēanes adv *towards, at* 1501

togen see tēon II

tōglīdan I *split open* pret 3s tōglād 2487

tōhlīdan I *split apart* p ptc npm tōhlidene 999

tōlūcan II *destroy* inf 781

tōmiddes adv *in the midst* 3141

torht adj *resplendent* asn 313

torn n *anger* ds torne 2401; *affliction* as torn 147, 833; gp torna 2189

torn adj *grievous* superl nsf tornost 2129

torngemōt n *hostile encounter* as 1140

tōsomne adv *together* 2568

tōweccan 1 *stir up* pret 3p tōwehton 2948 [MnE wake]

tredan V *tread, walk on, traverse* inf 1964, 3019; pret 3s træd 1352, 1643, 1881

treddian 2 *step, go* pret 3s treddode 725, tryddode 922

trem m, n *space* as 2525

trēow f *good faith* as trēowe 1072; gs 2922

trēowan 1 wd *trust* pret 3s trēowde 1166 [MnE trow]

trēowloga m *troth-breaker, traitor* np trēowlogan 2847

trodu f *footprint* ap trode 843

trum adj *strong* nsm 1369

ge**trum** n *troop* is getrume 922

truwian 2 *trust, have confidence in* (wd or g) pret 1s truwode 1993; 3s 669, 2370, 2953

ge**truwian** 2 *trust in* pret 3s getruwode 1533, 2322, 2540; (wa) *pledge* pret 3p getruwedon 1095

tryddode see treddian

trȳwe adj *loyal* nsm 1165 [MnE true]

ge**trȳwe** adj *loyal* nsm 1228 [MnE true]

twā see twēgen

ge**twǣfan** 1 *end* p ptc wæs . . . getwæfed *had been ended* 1658; (wa of person and g of thing) *hinder, deprive* inf 479; pres 3s getwæfeð 1763; pret 3s getwæfde 1433, 1908

ge**twǣman** 1 *prevent (from)* (wa of person and g of thing) inf 968

twēgen num *two* npm 1163; apm 1347; gpm twēga 2532; dpm twǣm 1191; npf twā 1194; apf 1095

twelf num *twelve* npm twelfe 3170; apm 1867; gpm twelfa 2401; uninfl gpm twelf 147

twēone num *two* dp be sǣm twēonum *between the seas* (i.e. *throughout the earth*) 858, 959, 1297, 1685, 1956

tȳdre adj *cowardly* npm 2847

tȳn num *ten* npm tȳne 2847; uninfl dpm tȳn 3159

þā adv *then* conj *when*. On the difficulty of distinguishing these two uses see IIIB3 above. I adv *then* 26, 28, 34, 53, 64, 74, 86, 399, 518, 615, 710, 720, etc.; corr w þā conj *then . . . when*: 138–40, 723, 1506, 1665, 2623–4, 2756, 2982–3. II conj *when* 140, 201, 323, 402, 419, 512, 539, 632, 1698, 1813, 2372, etc., *as, since* 201, 723, 733, 1103, 1293, 1495, 1539, 2550, 2676

þā pron see se

ðafian 2 *submit to* inf 2963

þāh see þēon I

ge**þah** see geþicgan

þām see sē

þanan see þonan

þanc m *thanks* wg = *for* ns 928, 1778, as 1809, 1997, 2794; *favour, thoughtfulness* ds tō þance *as a token of esteem* 379

þanchycgende adj *taking careful thought* nsm 2235

þancian 2 *thank* (wd of person and g of thing) pret 3s þancode 625, 1397; 3p þancedon 227, þancodon 1626

þanon see þonan

þāra see se

ge**þǣgon** see geþicgan

þǣm see se

þǣr adv *there* conj *where, if*. As with þā there is often difficulty in distinguishing the first two uses. I. adv *there* 32, 36, 71, 89, 118, 157, 284, 331, 440, 1165, 2573, etc.; as an introductory expletive: 271, 2555, etc. II. conj *where* 286, 356, 420, 508, 522, 693, 762, 777, 797, 866, 2369, etc.; *to where* 356, 1163, 1313, 2851; with present tense *where* shading into *wherever, because,* or *if* (OES §3621) 1835. III conj with past tense *if* 762, 797, 1835, 2730

þǣre see se

þǣs see se

þæt pron see se

þæt conj (used to introduce noun clauses or adverbial clauses) *that* 15, 62, 77, 84, 92, 177, 274, 290, 300, 338, 701, etc.; *so that* 22, 65, 358, 567, 571, 634, 698, 891, 954, 965, 1141, 1434, etc.; *provided that* 1099. On 'þæt ðe/þe' in 1846 and 1850 see l. 1846 note.

þætte (= þæt ðe) *that* 151, 858, 1256, 1942, 2924

þē pers pron see þū

þē isn see se

þē used as adv and conj see se VI and VII

þe rel. particle (indeclinable) *who, that, which,* etc. used as ns 192, 500, 2635, etc.; as 355, 941, 1271, 1487, etc.; gs 950; ds 1334, 2400, 2796 (on postposition); np 45, 238, 993, etc.; ap 1482, 1858; dp 1654b (to postposition), 2866 (on postposition); ns *he who* 138; þe *him to whom* 2468; in relative combinations with se (*Guide* §§ 162.4, 163.1, and 164). See notes to ll. 44, 79, 87, 108, etc.; in conjunctions þæs þe see se; þēah þe see þēah

þēah I adv *however, nevertheless* swā þēah *however* 972, 1929, 2878, swā þēh 2967; hwæðre swā þēah *nevertheless* 2442 [MnE though]. II conj *though* 203, 526, 587, 589, 1102, 1660, 2031, 2161, 2467, 2855, þēh 1613, þēah . . . eal *although* 680; þēah þe *although* 682, 1130, 1167, 1368, 1716, 1831, 1927, 1941, 2218, 2344, 2481, 2619, 2642, 2838, 2976

ge**þeah** see geþicgan

þearf f *need* ns 201, 1250, 1835, 2493, 2637, 2876; ds þearfe 1456, 1477, 1525, 2694, 2709, 2849; as þearfe 1797, 2579, 2801

þearf vb see þurfan

þearfa adj *in need of* (wg) nsm 2225

geþearfian 2 *impose by necessity* p ptc geþearfod 1103

þearle adv *severely* 560

þēaw m *custom* ns 178, 1246, 1940; as 359; dp þēawum *by customs, in the traditional manner* 2144

þec see þū

þeccean 1 *cover, engulf* inf 3015; pret 2p earmum þehton *swam* 513 [MnE thatch]

þegn m *thane, retainer* ns 194, 235, 494, 867, 1574, 2059, 2709, 2721, 2977; as 1230, 1871; gs þegnes 1797; ds ðegne 1085, 1341, 1419, 2810; np þegnas 1230; ap 1081, 3121; gp þegna 123, 400, 1627, 1644, 1673, 1829, 2033; dp þegnum 2869

þegnsorg f *grief for thanes* as þegnsorge 131 [MnE thane, sorrow]

þēgon see þicgan

þēh see þēah

þehton see þeccean

þencan 1 *think* pres 3s þenceð 289, 2601; pret 3s þōhte 691; þōhte . . . tō *thought about* 1139; w inf *intend* pres 3s þenceð 355, 448, 1535; pret 1s þōhte 964; 3s 739; 1p þōhton 541; 3p 800

geþencan 1 *remember* imp s geþenc 1474; *conceive, imagine* inf geþencean 1734 [MnE think]

þenden I. adv *then* 1019, 2418, 2985; II. conj *while, as long as* 30, 57, 284, 1177, 1224, 1859, 2038, 2499, 2649, 3027, 3100

þengel m *prince* as 1507

þēnian 2 *serve* pret 1s þēnode 560

þēod f *people, nation* ns 643, 1230, 1250, 1691, ðīod 2219; gp þēoda 1705

þēodcyning m *king of the people* ns 2963, 2970, ðīodcyning 2579, ðēodkyning 2144; as þēodcyning 3008, 3086; gs þēodcyninges 2694; gp þēodcyninga 2

þēoden m *prince, lord* ns 129, 365, 417, 1046, 1209, 1675, 1715, 1871, 2131, 2869, 3037, þīoden 2336, 2810; as þēoden 34, 201, 353, 1598, 2095, 2384, 2721, 2786, 2883, 3079, 3141, þīoden 2788; gs þēodnes 797, 910, 1085, 1627, 1837, 2174, 2656; ds þēodne 345, 1525, 1992, 2032, 2572, 2709; np þēodnas 3070

ðēodenlēas adj *having lost a lord* npm ðēodenlēase 1103

þēodgestrēon n *people's treasure* gp þēodgestrēona 1218; dp þēodgestrēonum 44

ðēodkyning see þēodcyning

þēodsceaða m *people's foe* ns 2278, 2688

þēodþrēa f *nation's calamity* dp þēodþrēaum 178

þēof m *thief* gs þēofes 2219

þēon I *prosper* pret 3s þāh 8, 2217, ðāh 2836; *be profitable* 3058; *virtuous* p ptc nsf geþungen 624

þēon 1 see þȳwan

geþēon I *prosper* inf 25, 910; imp s geþēoh 1218

þēos see þes

þēostre adj *dark* dp þēostrum 2332

þēow m *slave* ns 2223

þes dem pron *this* nsm þes 432, 1702, þæs 411; asm þisne 75, þysne 1771; gsm ðisses 1216; dsm þyssum 2639; apm þās 2635, 2640, 2732; dpm ðyssum 1062, 1219; nsn þis 290, 2499; asn 1723, 2155, 2251, 2643; gsn þisses 1217, þysses 197, 790, 806; dsn þissum 1169; isn þȳs 1395; apn ðās 1652; nsf þēos 484; asf þās 1622, 1681; gsf ðisse 928; dsf þisse 638

þicgan V *partake of, consume* inf 1010, ðicgean 736; pret 1p þēgun 2633; 3p þēgon 563

geþicgan V *partake of, receive* pret 3s geþeah 618, 628, geþah 1024; 3p geþǣgon 1014

þīn poss pron *thy, thine (your, yours)* nsm 459, 490, 593, 954, 1705, 1853, 2048; asm þīnne 267, 353, 1848; dsm þīnum 346, 592; apm þīne 2095; gpm þīnra 367, 1672, 1673; dpm þīnum 587, 1178, 1708; nsn þīn 589; asn 1849; gsn þīnes 1761; isn þīne 2131; gsf þīnre 1823; dsf 1477

þincean see þyncan

þing n *matter* ns 409; *meeting* as ðing 426; gp ǣnige þinga *in any way* 791, 2374, 2905 [MnE thing]

geþingan 1 *determine, plan* p ptc geþinged 647; *invoke* 1938

geþinge n *agreement* ap geþingo *terms* 1085; *result, outcome* gs geþinges 398, 709; gp geþingea 525

þingian 2 *settle* inf 156; pret 1s þingode 470; *make diplomatic arrangements* inf þingian 1843

geþingian 2 *open negotiations* pres 3s geþingeð 1837

ðīod- see þēod-

þīoden see þēoden

þis see þes

geþōht m *thought* as 256, 610

þolian 2 *suffer* inf 832; pres 3s þolað 284; pret 3s þolode 131; *endure* pres 3s þolað 2499; pret 3s ðolode 1525

geþolian 2 *suffer, endure* infl inf tō geþolianne

geþolian (*cont.*)

1419; pret 3s geþolode 87, 147; *remain* inf geþolian 3109

þon (44) see þonne conj

þon see se

þonan adv *thence, from there* 819, 2061, 2099, 2140, 2359, 2545, 2956, ðonon 520, 1373, 1601, 1632, 1960, 2408, þanon 111, 123, 224, 463, 691, 763, 844, 853, 1265, 1292, 1805, 1921, þanan 1668, 1880; *from him* 111, 1265, 1960

geþonc m *thought* dp geþoncum 2332

þone see se

þonne adv *then* conj *when, whenever, than.* As with þā, there is often difficulty in distinguishing the first two uses. I. adv *then* 377, 484, 1104, 1106, 1455, 1484, 1741, 1745, 1836, 2032, 2041, 2063, 2446, 2460, 3062, 3107; *then, therefore* 435, 525, 1671, 1822; *furthermore* 3051. II. conj *when, whenever* 23, 485, 573, 880, 934, 1033, 1040, 1042, 1066, 1143, etc.; corr: þonne . . . þonne *then . . . when* 484–5, 1484–5, 2032–4, 2446–7, 3062–4, 1104–6. III. conj *than* (following compar) introducing a clause: 44, 248, 1385, 1560, 1824, 2572, 2579; without clause following: 469, 505, 534, 678, 1139, 1182, 1353, 1579, 2433, 2891

þonon see þonan

þorfte see þurfan

þrāg f *time* ns 114, 1257; *time of distress* ns 2883; as þrāge 54, 87

geþræc n *pile* as 3102

þrēanēdla m *dire distress* ds þrēanēdlan 2223

þrēanȳd f *dire distress, dire necessity* as 284; dp þrēanȳdum 832

ðrēat m *troop, company* ds ðrēate 2406; dp þrēatum 4 [MnE threat]

þrēatian 2 *harass* pret 3p þrēatedon 560 [MnE threat(en)]

þrecwudu m *spear* ns 1246

þrēo num *three* ap 2278, þrīo 2174

þreottēoða num *thirteenth* ns 2406

þridda num *third* dsm þriddan 2688

geþring n *tossing* as 2132

þringan III *press (forward)* pret 3s þrong 2883; 3p þrungon 2960

geþringan III *press, surge* pret 3s geþrang 1912

þrīo see þrēo

þrīsthȳdig adj *stouthearted* adj nsm 2810

þrītig num *thirty* ap 123, 2361; gs þrītiges 379

þrōwian 2 *suffer, endure* inf 2605, 2658; pret 3s þrōwade 1589, 1721; ðrōwode 2594

geþrūen p ptc *forged* 1285

þrȳdlīc see þrȳðlīc

ðrymm m *force* ns ðrym 1918; dp þrymmum (adv) *forcefully* 235; *glory* as þrym 2

þrymlīc adj *mighty* nsm 1246

þrȳð f *strength* dp þrȳðum 494

ðrȳþærn n *mighty hall* as 657

þrȳðlīc adj *valiant* nsm 400, 1627. Superl þrȳðlīcost *finest* 2869

ðrȳðswȳð adj *mighty* nsm 131, 736

þrȳðword n *brave word* np 643

þū pers pron *thou* (*you*) ns 269, 272, 352, 366, 386, 407, 429, 445, 450, 457, etc. as þec 946, 955, 1219, 1763, 1768, 1827, 1828, 2151, þē 417, 426, 517, 1221, 1722, 1833, 1994, 1998; ds 354, 365, 525, 581, 590, 660, 949, etc.; dual git 508, 512, 513, 516; g incer 584; d sv 510; pl gē 237, 245, 252, 254, 333, 338, 393, 395, 2529, 2866, 3096, 3104; ap ēowic 317, 3095; gp ēower 248, 392, 596; dp ēow 292, 391, 1344, 1987, 2865, 3103

þūhte see þyncan

geþungen see þēon I

þunian 2 *creak* pret 3s þunede 1906 [MnE thun(der)]

þurfan pret-pres *need* pres 2s þearft 445, 450, 1674; 3s þearf 595, 2006, 2741; subj 3s þurfe 2495; pret 3s þorfte 157, 1026, 1071, 2874, 2995; 3p þorfton 2363

þurh prep wa *through, by means of* 184, 267, 276, 278, 558, 699, 940, 1101, 1335, 1693, 1695, 1726, 1979, 2045, 2405, 2454, 2661, 3068

þurhbrecan IV *break through* pret 3s þurhbræc 2792

þurhdūfan II *swim through* pret 3s þurhdēaf 1619 [MnE through, dive]

þurhetan V *eat through* p ptc np þurhetone 3049

ðurhfōn VII *penetrate* inf 1504

þurhtēon II *bring about* inf 1140

þurhwadan VI *pass through, cut through* pret 3s þurhwōd 890, 1567 [MnE through, wade]

þus adv *thus* 238, 337, 430

þūsend n *thousand* as 3050 ap þūsendo 2195, þūsenda 1829, 2994

geþwǣre adj *united* npm 1230

þȳ see se VII

þyder adv *thither* 379, 2970, 3086

þȳhtig adj *strong* asn 1558

þȳ lǣs see se VII

geþyld f as *patience* 1395; dp geþyldum *with equanimity* 1705 þyle m *court spokesman* ns 1165, 1456

þyncan I *seem, appear* (impers) wd inf þincean 1341; pres 3s þynceð 2653, þinceð 1748; 3p þinceað 368; subj 3s þince 687; pret 3s þūhte 842, 2461, 3057; 3p þūhton 866 [archaic MnE (me)think(s)]

þyrs m *giant* ds þyrse 426

þyslīc adj *such* nsf þyslīcu 2637

þȳs see þes

þysne see þes

þysses see þes

þyssum see þes

þȳstru f *darkness* dp þȳstrum 87

þȳwan I *threaten* inf ðēon 2736; pres 3p þȳwað 1827

geþȳwe adj *customary* nsn 2332

ufan adv *from above* 330, 1500

ufera adj (compar) *later* dpn ufaran 2200, uferan 2392

ufor adv *farther away* 2951

ūhta m *pre-dawn, time just before daybreak* ds ūhtan 126

ūhtfloga m *night-flyer* gs ūhtflogan 2760

ūhthlem m *tumult at night* as 2007

ūhtsceaða m *ravager by night* ns 2271

umborwesende adj *as a child* asm ns 46; dsm umborwesendum 1187

unblīðe adj *joyless, sorrowful* ns 130, 2268; npm 3031 [MnE unblithe]

unbyrnende adj *without burning* nsm 2548

unc see ic

uncer (pers pron) see ic

uncer poss pron *of us two* dpm uncran 1185

uncūð adj *unknown, not previously known* asm uncūðne 276; gsm uncūþes 960; asn uncūð 1410; gsn uncūþes 876; nsf uncūð 2214 [MnE uncouth]

under I adv *below* 1416, 2213 II. under prep *under* wd (rest): 8, 52, 310, 505, 651, 714, 1078, 1197, 1204, 1631, 1770, 1656, 2411, 2415, 2967, *under* (i.e. *wearing*) 342, 396, 404, 1163, 2049, 2539, 2605, *within, behind* 1928, 3060, 3103, *at the lower part of* 211, 710, 2559, *with* 738; wa (motion): *under, to the lower part of* 403, 707, 820, 836, 887, 1037, 1360, 1361, 1469, 1551, 1745, 2128, 2540, 2553, 2675, 2744, 2755, 3031, etc.

undernmæl n *morning time* as 1428

undyrne adj *manifest, not hidden* ns 127, 150, 410, underne 2911; nsn undyrne 2000

unfæcne adj *sincere, without deceit* asm 2068

unfæge adj *not fated to die, undoomed* ns 2291; asm unfægne 573

unfæger adj *hideous* nsn 727 [MnE unfair]

unflitme adj *undisputed*(?) isn 1097 [a word of uncertain meaning which occurs only here; cf. unhlitme l. 1129]

unforht adj *fearless* nsm 287

unforhte adv *fearlessly, without hesitation* 444

unfrōd adj *young* dsm unfrōdum 2821

unfrom adj *feeble* nsm 2188

ungeāra adv *soon* 602, *not long ago* 932

ungedēfelīce adv *unfittingly* 2435

ungemete adv *exceedingly* 2420, 2721, 2728

unglēaw adj *ineffective* asn 2564

ungyfeðe adj *denied* nsf 2921

unhǣlo f *evil* gs 120

unhēore adj *monstrous* nsm unhīore 2413; nsn unhȳre 2120; nsf unhēoru 987

unhlitme adv *without lot* (?), *involuntarily* (?) 1129 [a word of uncertain meaning which occurs only here; cf. unflitme l. 1097]

unigmetes adv *exceedingly* 1792

unlēof adj *not loved* apm unlēofe 2863

unlifigende adj *not living, dead* nsm 468; asm unlyfigendne 1308; gsm unlyfigendes 744; dsm unlifgendum 1389, unlifigendum 2908

unlȳtel adj *no little, great* nsm 885; asn 833; nsf 498

unmurnlīce adv *ruthlessly* 449; *ungrudgingly* 1756 [MnE -mourn-]

unnan pret-pres *wish* pres 1s an 1225; pret 1s ūðe 960; pret subj 3s 2855; *grant, concede* pret 3s 2874; subj 3s 503

geunnan pret-pres *grant* inf 346; pret 3s geūðe 1661

unnyt adj *useless* nsm 413; nsn 3168

unriht n *wrong* as 1254, on unriht *wrongfully* 2739 [MnE unright]

unrihte adv *wrongfully* 3059

unrīm n *countless number, huge amount* ns 1238, 3135; as 2624

unrīme adj *countless* nsn 3012

unrōt adj *sad* npm unrōte 3148

unsnyttru f *folly, unwisdom* dp unsnyttrum 1734

unsōfte adv *with difficulty* 1655, 2140

unswīðe adv compar unswīðor *less strongly* 2578, 2881

unsynnig adj *guiltless* asm unsynnigne 2089

unsynnum adv *guiltlessly* 1072

untǣle adj *blameless* apm 1865

untȳdre m *evil progeny* np untȳdras 111

unwāclīc adj *splendid, not mean* asm unwā-
  clīcne 3138
unwearnum adv *unrestrainedly* 741
unwrecen adj *unavenged* nsm 2443
up adv *up, upwards* 128, 224, 519, 782, 1373,
  1619, 1912, 1920, 2575, 2893
uplang adj *upright* nsm 759
uppe adv *up* 566
uppriht adj *upright* nsm 2092
ūre pers pron see ic
ūre poss pron *our* nsm 2647; asm ūserne 3002,
  3107; dsm ūssum 2634; gsn ūsses 2813
ūrum see ic
ūs see ic
ūser see ic
ūserne see ūre
ūsic see ic
ūsses see ūre
ūssum see ūre
ūt adv *out* 215, 537, 663, 1292, 1583, 2081,
  2515, 2545, 2551, 2557, 3092, 3106, 3130
ūtan adv *from outside, outside* 774, 1031, 1503,
  2334
ūtanweard adj *outside* asm ūtanweardne 2297
ūtfūs adj *ready to set out* nsm 33
uton (1p subj of wītan used w inf) *let us* uton . . .
  fēran *let us go* 1390, uton . . . efstan *let us
  hasten* 3101, wutun gongan *let us go* 2648
ūtweard adj nsm *eager to get out* 761
ūþe see unnan
ūðgenge adj *departing* ns 2123

wā adv *woe* 183
wacian 2 *keep watch* imp s waca 660
wada, wado, wadu see wæd
wadan VI *stride, advance* pret 3s wōd 714, 2661
  [MnE wade]
gewadan VI *advance* p ptc gewaden 220
wāg m *wall* ds wāge 1662; dp wāgum 995
wala m *reinforcing ridge (on a helmet)* ns
  1031[MnE weal, (gun)wale]
waldend see wealdend
waldswaþu f *forest track* dp waldswaþum 1403
  [MnE wold, swath]
walu see wæl
wan adj see wonn
wang see wong
wanian 2 *dwindle, dissolve* inf 1607; *diminish*
  pret 3s wanode 1337; p ptc gewanod 477
  [MnE wane]
wānigean 2 *bewail* inf 787
warian 2 *occupy* pres 3p warigeað 1358; pret 3s
  warode 1253, 1265; *guard* pres 3s warað 2277

waroð m *shore* ds waroðe 234; ap waroðas 1965
wascan VI *bathe, wash (over)* inf weaxan 3115
  [MnE wash]
wāst see witan
wæccan 3 *watch, be awake* pres ptc wæccende
  708; asm 2841, wæccendne 1268
wæcnan VI *to be born* pret 3s wōc 1265, 1960;
  3p wōcun 60; *arise* inf 85 [MnE waken]
wæd n *sea, water* np wado 546, wadu 581; gp
  wada 508
gewæde n *armour* ap gewædu 292
wæfre adj *restless, enraged* nsm 1331, 2420; nsn
  1150
wǣgbora m ns *wave-roamer* 1440
wǣge n *cup* as 2216, 2253, 2282
wǣgholm m *surging sea* as 217
wǣgsweord n *damascened sword* as 1489
wæl n *the slain, corpse* as 448, 635, 1212, 3027;
  ds wæle 1113; np walu 1042
wælbedd n *corpse-bed, bed of death* ds wælbedde 964
wælbend f *mortal bond* ap wælbende 1936
wælblēat adj *mortally distressing, excruciating*
  asf wælblēate 2725
wældēað m *murderous death* ns 695
wældrēor m, n *battle gore* ds wældrēore 1631
wælfǣhð f *deadly feud* gp wælfǣhða 2028
wælfāg adj *slaughter-stained* asm wælfāgne
  1128
wælfeall m *violent death, slaughter* ds wælfealle
  1711
wælfūs adj *eager for slaughter* nsm 2420
wælfyll m *violent death* gp wælfylla 3154
wælfyllo f *abundance of slain, fill of carrion* ds
  wælfylle 125
wælfȳr n *murderous fire* ds wælfȳre 2582; *funeral fire* gp wælfȳra 1119
wælgǣst m *homicidal creature* ns 1331; as 1995
wælhlem m *deadly blow* as 2969
wællseax n *battle-knife* ds wællseaxe 2703
wælm see wylm
wælnīð m *deadly enmity* ns 3000; ds wælnīðe
  85; np wælnīðas 2065
wǣlrāp m *flood-cord* (i.e. *ice*) ap wǣlrāpas 1610
  [MnE rope]
wælrǣs m *deadly onslaught, bloody encounter* ns
  2947; as 2101; ds wælrǣse 824, 2531
wælrēaf n *spoil from the slain, battle booty* as
  1205
wælrēc m *deadly fumes* as 2661 [MnE -reek]
wælrēow adj *fierce at slaughter* nsm 629
wælrest f *resting place for the slain, deathbed* as
  wælreste 2902

wælsceaft m *slaughter-shaft, deadly spear* ap wælsceaftas 398

wælsteng m *slaughter-pole* ds wælstenge 1638

wælstōw f *battlefield* ds wælstōwe 2051, 2984

wǣn m *wagon* as 3134 [MnE wain]

wǣpen n *weapon* ns 1660; as 685, 1573, 2519, 2687; gs wǣpnes 1467; ds wǣpne 2965, 1664; ap wǣpen 292; gp wǣpna 434, 1045, 1452, 1509, 1559; dp wǣpnum 250, 331, 2038, 2395

wǣpnedmon m *man* ds wǣpnedmen 1284

wǣr f *treaty* as wǣre 1100; *keeping* as wǣre 27; ds 3109

wǣran see wesan

wǣre see wesan

wǣron see wesan

wǣs see wesan

wǣstm m *form, lineament* dp wæstmum 1352

wǣter n *water, sea* ns 93, 1416, 1514, 1631; as 509, 1364, 1619, 1904, 1989, 2473; gs wæteres 471, 516, 1693, 2791; ds wætere 1425, 1656, 2722, wætre 2854

wǣteregesa m *dreadful water* as wæteregesan 1260

wǣterȳð f *wave of the sea* dp wæterȳðum 2242

wē see ic

wēa m *woe, trouble, misery* ns 936; as wēan 191, 423, 1206, 1991, 2292, 2937; gp wēana 148, 933, 1150, 1396

wēalāf f *survivors of calamity* as wēalāfe 1084, 1098

*ge*wealc n. *rolling* as 464

*ge*weald n *power, control* as 79, 654, 764, 808, 903, 950, 1087, 1610, 1684, 1727; dp mid gewealdum *of his own accord* 2221

wealdan VII *rule* inf 2390; pres 1s wealde 1859; pret 1s wēold 465, 1770; pret 3s 702, 1057, 2379, 2595; *control* inf wealdan 2984; pret 3s wēold 30; 3p wēoldon 2051; *possess* inf wealdan 2827; *manage* inf 2574; *wield* inf 2038; *prevail* inf 442

*ge*wealdan VII *control, wield* inf (wg) 1509; pret 3s (wd) gewēold 2703; *bring about* pret 3s (wa) 1554; p ptc apm gedēð him swā gewealdene *makes subject to him in this way* 1732

*ge*wealden see *ge*wealdan

wealdend m *ruler, lord* ns 17, waldend 1661, 1693, 1752, 2741, 2875; as 183; gs wealdendes 2857, waldendes 2292, 3109; ds wealdende 2329 [MnE wield(er)]

weall m *wall* as weal 326; gs wealles 2323; ds wealle 229, 785, 891, 1573, 2307, 2526, 2542, 2716, 2759, 3060, 3103, 3161; ap weallas 572, 1224

weallan VII *well, surge* pres ptc nsm weallendu 581; nsn weallende 847; pret 3s wēol 515, 849, 1131, 1422, wēoll 2138, 2593, 2693, 2714, 2882; *of human feelings: stir, well up* pres ptc weallende npn 546, asf 2464; pres 3p weallað 2065; pret 3s wēoll 2113, 2331

weallclif n *cliff* as 3132 [MnE wall, cliff]

weard m *watchman, guardian, keeper* ns 229, 286, 921, 1390, 1741, 2239, 2413, 2513, 2580, 3060; as 2524, 2841, 3066 [MnE ward]

weard f *watch* as wearde 319

weardian 2 *occupy* pret 3s weardode 105, 1237; 1p weardodon 2075; *guard the track* (i.e. *remain behind*) inf weardian 971; pret 3s weardade 2098; *follow* pret 3s weardode 2164

wearn f *refusal* as wearne 366

wēaspell n *tidings of woe* ds wēaspelle 1315

weaxan VII *grow, thrive* pres 3s weaxeð 1741; pret 3s wēox 8 [MnE wax]

weaxan (3115) see wascan

*ge*weaxan VII *increase* pret 3s gewēox 66; *grow up, develop* 1711

web n *tapestry* np 995 [MnE web]

weccan 1 *stir up, awaken, kindle* inf 3144, weccean 2046, 3024; *revive* pret 3s wehte 2854 [MnE wake]

wedd n *pledge* ds wedde 2998

weder n *weather* np 1136; *storm* gp wedera 546

weg m *way* as on weg *away* 264, 763, 844, 1382, 1430, 2096

wēg = wǣg m *wave* as 3132

wegan V *carry, wear* inf 3015; pres subj 3s wege 2252; pret 3s wæg 1207, 2704; *bear, sustain* pret 1s 1777; 3s 2464; *carry on, inflict* pret 3s 152, 2780; *weigh, consider* pret 3s 1931; *carry out* pres 3s wigeð 599

*ge*wegan V *fight* inf 2400

wēgflota m *wave-floater, ship* as wēgflotan 1907

wēglīðende m *seafarer* dp wēglīðendum 3158

wehte see weccan

wēl, well adv *well, rightly, very much* wēl 186, 289, 639, 1045, 1792, 1821, 1833, 1854, 2570, 2601, 2855, well 1951, 2162, 2812

wēlhwylc pron *every, everyone* nsm 266; gpm wēlhwylcra 1344; *everything* asn wēlhwylc 874

welig adj *valuable* asm weligne 2607 [MnE weal(thy)]

wēlþungen adj *accomplished* nsf 1927

wēn f *expectation* ns 734, 1873, 2323, 2910; as

wēn (*cont.*)

383, 3000; dp wēnum 2895; *a likely thing* as wēn 1845

wēnan I *expect* inf (wg) 157, 185; pres 1s wēn' 338, 442, wēne 525, 1184, 1396, 2522, 2923; 3s wēneþ 600; pret 1s wēnde 933; 3s 2239; 3p wēndon 937, 1596, 1604; *think* pres 1s (wg) wēne 272; pret 3s wēnde 2329; pret 3p wēndon 778, 2187 [MnE ween]

wendan I *go* pres 3s wendeð 1739 [MnE wend]

*ge*wendan I *change, turn* inf 186; pret 3s gewende 315

wennan I *present* (wd of thing and a of person) pret subj 3s wenede 1091

weora see **wer**

weorc n *work, deed* as 74, 1656; gs weorces 2299; ds weorce 1569; gp worca 289; dp weorcum 1833, 2096, worcum 1100; *difficulty, misery* as weorc 1721; dp weorcum 1638; *difficulty* is (adv) wesan weorce *be distressing* 1418

*ge*weorc n *work* gs geweorces 2711; *handiwork* ns geweorc 455, 1562, 1681; as 2717, 2774

weorod see **werod**

weorpan III *throw* pret 3s wearp 1531, 2582; (wa of person and g of thing): *sprinkle* inf weorpan 2791 [MnE warp]

weorð adj *honoured* nsm 1814; compar þȳ weorþra *the more honoured* 1902 [MnE worth]

weorð n *price* is weorðe 2496 [MnE worth]

weorðan III *come about, happen, arise* inf 2526, 3068; pret 3s wearð 767, 1280, 1302, 2003; p ptc geworden 1304, 3078; *become* inf wurðan 807; pres 3s weorðeð 2913; 3p weorðað 2066, wurðaþ 282; pret 3s wearð 77, 149, 409, 555, 753, 816, 818, 913, 1255, 1269, 1775, 2378, 2392, 2482, 2612; 3p wurdon 228; subj 3s wurde 2731; w tō + d obj *become* inf 1707; pret 1s wearð 2501; 3s 460, 905, 1261, 1330, 1709, 2071, 2078, 2384; 3p wurdon 2203; subj 2s wurde 587; pret 3s on fylle wearð *fell* 1544; used as an auxiliary w p ptc to form the passive voice: *to be* inf 3177; pres 3s weorþeð 414; pret 3s wearð 6, 902, 1072, 1239, 1437, 1947, 2310, 2692, 2842, 2961, 2983; subj 3s wurde 2218; pret 3s w p ptc of intr verbs: *had* wearð 823, 1234

*ge*weorðan III *be* (used as an auxiliary with p ptc to form passive voice) pret 3s gewearð 3061; *settle* inf 1996; impers w a of person

and g of thing *occur to* pret 3s gewearð 1598; p ptc geworden 2026

weorðfull adj *glorious* superl. nsm weorðfullost 3099 [MnE worthful]

weorðian 2 *honour, bring honour to, exalt, adorn* pret 1s weorðode 2096; subj 3s weorþode 1090; p ptc geweorðad 250, 1450, geweorðod 1959, 2176, gewurþad 331, 1038, 1645

weorðlīc adj *worthy, splendid* superl. weorðlīcost 3161

weorðmynd f, n *glory, worldly honour* ns 65; as 1559; gp weorðmynda 1752; dp weorðmyndum 8, worðmyndum 1186 [MnE worth, mind]

weotena see **wita**

weotian 2 *ordain, destine* p ptc apf weotode 1936

wer m *man* ns 105; as 1268, 3172; gs weres 1352; np weras 216, 1222, 1233, 1440, 1650; gp wera 120, 993, 1731, 3000, weora 2947; dp werum 1256 [MnE wer(wolf)]

wered n *sweet drink* as 496

wereda see **werod**

werefyht n *fight arising from uncompensated murder* [cf. werfǣhð] dp werefyhtum 457

werga adj *accursed, evil* gsm wergan 133, 1747

wergend m *defender* gp wergendra 2882

*ge*wērgian 2 *exhaust, weary* p ptc gewērgad 2852

werhðo f *damnation, condemnation* as 589

werian I *protect* inf 541; pres 3s wereð 453; pret 3s werede 1205, 1448; 1p weredon 1327; p ptc npm werede 238, 2529

wērig adj *weary* (wg = *from*) nsm 579; dsm wērgum 1794; wd *exhausted (by)* asf wērge 2937

wērigmōd adj *weary at heart, weary* nsm 844, 1543

werod n *company, band, host* ns 651, weorod 290, 2014, 3030; as werod 319; gs werodes 259, werudes 3154; ds werede 1215, weorode 1011, 2346; gp weoroda 60, wereda 2186

werþēod f *nation* ap werþēode 899

wesan anom *be* inf 272, 1328, 1859, 2708, 2801, 3021; pret 1s wæs 240, 2428, 3087; 3s 11, 12, 18, 36, 49, 53, etc.; 1p wǣron 536, 544, 1820; 3p 233, 548, 612, 881, etc. wǣran 2475; subj 2s wǣre 1478; 3s 173, 203, 593, 945, etc.; subj 3s wǣre 1105; fused with negative particle: pret 1s næs 2141, 2432; 3s 134, 1299, 1921, 2192, etc.; 3p nǣron 2657; pret subj 3s nǣre 860, 1167; imp s wes 269, 1170,

1219, 1224, 1480, wæs 407; non-expression of wesan: 617, 992, 1783, 1857, etc.

wēste adj *deserted* asm wēstne 2456

wēstenn n *wilderness, deserted place* as wēsten 1265; ds wēstenne 2298

wīc n *place, dwelling-place* as 821, 2589; gp (ws meaning) wīca 125, 1125; dp wīcum 1612, 3083, wīcun 1304

gewīcan I *fail* pret 3s gewāc 2577, 2629

wicg n *horse* ns 1400; as 315; ds wicge 234, 286; ap wicg 2174; gp wicga 1045

wīcstede m *dwelling-place* ns 2462; as 2607

wīd adj *wide, broad* asn 2473; gsn wīdan 1859; apm wīde 1965, *far* 877; ds tō wīdan feore *forever* 933; as wīdan feorh *ever* 2014. Compar wīdre *further off* 763

wīdcūþ adj *widely known* asm wīdcūðne 1489, 1991; gsm wīdcūþes 1042; nsn wīdcūþ 1256

wīde adv *far and wide, far* 18, 74, 79, 266, 898, 1403, 1588, 1959, 2135, 2261, 2316, 2582, 2913, 2923, 2947, 3099, 3158

wīdeferhð m, n as (adv) *always, ever* 702, 937, ealne wīdeferhþ *forever* 1222

wīdfloga m *far-flier* ns 2830; as wīdflogan 2346

gewidre n *storm* ap gewidru 1375 [MnE weather]

wīdscofen adj *far-reaching* ns 936 [MnE wide, shove]

wīdweg m *far way* ap geond wīdwegas *through distant regions* 840, 1704

wīf n *woman* ns 615, 2120; as 1158; gs wīfes 1284; ds wīfe 639, 2028; gp wīfa 993

gewif n *web (of fate), woven destiny* ap gewiofu 697

wīflufu f *affection for a wife* np wīflufan 2065

wīg n *war* ns 23, 1080, 2872; as 685, 1083, 1247; gs wīges 65, 886, 1268, 2298; ds wīge 1084, 1337, 2629, wigge 1656, 1770; *fighting force, prowess* ns wīg 350, 1042, 2316; as wīg 2348; gs wīges 2323

wiga m *warrior* ns 629; gp wigena 1543, 1559, 3115; dp wigum 2395

wīgan I *fight* inf 2509

wīgbealu n *evil of war* as 2046

wīgbil n *war-sword* ns 1607

wīgbord n *war-shield* as 2339

wīgcræft m *skill in battle* as 2953

wīgcræftig adj *strong in battle* asm wīgcræftigne 1811

wīgend m *warrior* ns 3099; np wīgend 1125, 1814, 3144; ap 3024; gp wīgendra 429, 899, 1972, 2337

wigeð see wegan

wīgfreca m *warrior* as wīgfrecan 2496; np 1212

wīgfruma m *war-leader* ns 664; ds wīgfruman 2261

wigge see wīg

wīggetāwa f *war-gear* dp wīggetāwum 368

wīggeweorþad adj *distinguished in battle* ns 1783

wīggryre m *war-horror* ns 1284

wīgheafola m *helmet* as wīgheafolan 2661

wīghēap m *band of warriors* ns 477

wīghete m *warlike enmity* ns 2120

wīghryre m *slaughter, battle-death* as 1619

wīgsigor m *victory in war* as 1554

wīgspēd f *success in war* gp wīgspēda 697

wigtig see wītig

wīgweorþung f *homage to idols* ap wīgweorþunga 176

wiht f *creature* ns 120; as 3038; (w neg) *aught, anything* as 581, 1660, 2348, 2601, 2857, (adv) *at all* 541, 862, 1083, 1735, 2854; ds (adv) *at all, in any way* wihte 186, 1514, 1991, 1995, 2277, 2464, 2687, 2923 [MnE wight, whit]

wilcuma m *welcome person* (used like an adj: hīe sint wilcuman *they are welcome*) np wilcuman 388, 394, 1894

wildēor n *wild beast* ap 1430 [MnE wild, deer]

wilgeofa m *benefactor* ns 2900 [MnE will, give(r)]

wilgesīþ m *dear companion* np wilgesīþas 23

willa m *will, wish* as willan 635; ds 3077; ofer willan *against (his) will* 2409, 2589; dp sylfes willum *of his own will* 2222, 2639; *desired thing, pleasure, wish* ns willa 626, 824; ds willan 1186, 1711, on willan *according to (his) desire* 2307; dp willum *according to one's wishes* 1821; *desirable or good thing* gp wilna 660, 950, 1344

willan anom *wish, desire, will* w inf pres 1s wille 318, 344, 351, 427, wylle 947, 2148, 2512; with negative particle fused (ne + wille): nelle 679, 2524; 2s wylt, 1852; 3s wille 442, 1184, wile 346, 446, 1049, 1181, 1832, wyle 2864; 1p wyllað 1818; subj 3s wille 979, 1314; pret 1s wolde 2497; 3s 68, 154, 200, 645, 664, 738, 755, 796, 880, 1010, 1041, 1094, 1277, 1292, 1339, 1494, 1546, 1576, 1791, 1805, 2083, 2090, 2160, 2186, 2294, 2305, 2308, 2315, 2588, 2940, *to be disposed to* 2858; pret subj 3s 1055; neg: (ne + wolde) nolde 791, 803, 812, 1523; 3p woldon 3171; subj 1s wolde 2729; neg nolde 2518; 2s wolde 1175; 3s 988, 990, 2376; 1p woldon 2636; 3p 482; w

willan (*cont.*)
  inf unexpressed: þā metod nolde *when the lord did not will it* 706, 967; pres 1s wille 318; 3s 1003, 1394, wylle 2766; subj 3s 1371; pret 1s wolde 543; 3s 1055, 3055
wilnian 2 *ask for* inf 188
wilsīð m *desired journey* as 216
wīn n *wine* as 1162, 1233; ds wīne 1467
wīnærn n *wine-hall* gs wīnærnes 654
wind m *wind* ns 1374, 1907; ds winde 217, 1132
windan III *curl, spiral* pret 3s wand 1119; *eddy* 3p wundon 212; *twist* p ptc ns wunden gold *twisted gold* (i.e. *gold formed into rings*) 1193, 3134; dsn wundnum 1382 [MnE wind]
gewindan III *escape* inf 763; pret 3s gewand 1001
windæg m *day of strife* dp windagum 1062
windblond n *swirling wind* ns 3146
windgeard m *home of the winds* (i.e. *sea*) ns 1224
windig adj *windy* ns windge 2456; apm windige 572, 1358
wine m *friend, lord (and friend)* ns 30, 148, 457, 530, 1183, 1704, 2047, 2101; as 350, 376, 2026; gs wines 3096; ds wine 170; gp winigea 1664; *retainer* gp winia 2567; dp winum 1418
winedrihten m *lord (and friend)* as 862, 1604, winedryhten 2722, 3175; ds winedrihtne 360
winegeōmor adj *mourning for friends* ns 2239
winelēas adj *friendless* dsm winelēasum 2613
winemǣg m *retainers* np winemāgas 65
winia see **wine**
winigea see **wine**
gewinn n *conflict, struggle, turmoil* as gewin 798, 877, 1469; gs gewinnes 1721; *strife, trouble* ns gewin 133, 191; as 1781
winnan III *strive, fight* pret 2s wunne 506; 3s wan 144, 151, won 1132; 3p wunnon 113, 777 [MnE win]
wīnreced n *wine-hall* as 714, 993
wīnsele m *wine-hall* ns 771; as 2456; ds 695
winter m *winter* ns 1132, 1136; as 1128; gs wintrys 516; *year* gp wintra 147, 264, 1927, 2209, 2278, 2733, 3050; dp wintrum 1724, 2114, 2277
gewiofu see **gewif**
wīr m *wire, gold filigree* gp wīra 2413; dp wīrum 1031
wīs adj *wise* nsm 1845; wīsa 1400, 1698, 2329; asm wīsan 1318; gpm wīsra 1413; nsf wīs 1927; *sound of mind* nsm 3094
wīsa m *leader* ns 259
wīscan I *wish* pret 3p wīston 1604

wīsdōm m *wisdom* ns 350; ds wīsdōme 1959
wīse f *way, manner* as ealde wīsan i*n the (good) old way* 1865 [MnE wise]
wīsfæst adj *wise* nsf 626
wīshycgende adj *wise in thought* nsm 2716
wīsian 2 *show the way, guide, lead* pres 1s wīsige 292, 3103; pret 3s wīsode 320, 402, 1663; wīsade 370, 1795; *show the way to* inf wīsian 2409; *pointed out* pret 3s wīsade 208
gewislīce adv *certainly* superl gewislīcost 1350
wisse see **witan**
wisson see **witan**
wist f *feasting, abundance* ds wiste 128, 1735
wiste see **witan**
wistfyllo f *lavish feast* gs wistfylle 734
wiston see **witan**
wīston see **wīscan**
wit n *intelligence* ns 589 [MnE wit]
wit pers pron see **ic**
wita m *wise man, councillor* np witan 778; gp witena 157, 266, 936; weotena 1098
witan pret-pres *know* inf 252, 288; pres 1s wāt 1331, 1830, 1863, 2656; with negative particle fused (ne + wāt) nāt 274; 2s wāst 272; 3s wāt 2650; neg nāt 681; subj 3s wite 1367; pret 3s wisse 169, 715, 1309, 2339, 2410, 2725, wiste 646, 764, 821; 3p wiston 181, 798, 878; subj 1s wiste 2519; *have* pret 2p wisson 246
wītan I *accuse* inf 2741
gewitan pret-pres *ascertain, tell* inf 1350
gewītan I *go, depart* (st with refl dat) inf 42; pres 3s gewīteð 1360, 2460; pret 3s gewāt 210, 217, 662, 1236, 1601, 2471, 2624; with accompanying inf: pret 3s gewāt . . . fēran *proceeded to journey* 26, gewāt . . . nēosian *went to seek* 115, gewāt . . . faran *proceeded to go* 123, 234, 1263, 1274, 1903, 1963, 2387, 2401, 2569, 2819, 2949, 3044; 3p gewiton 301, 853, 1125; go imp p gewītað 291
wītig adj *wise* nsm 685, 1056, 1554, 1841
wītnian 2 *punish* p ptc gewītnad 3073
witod see **weotian**
gewitt n *senses, intellect* ds gewitte 2703; *seat of knowledge, head* ds 2882 [MnE wit]
gewittig adj *conscious* nsm 3094 [MnE witty]
wið prep (wd, g and a) *against* 113, 144, 145, 152, 174, 178, 213, 294, 319, 326, etc.; *with* 155, 365, 424, 425, 426, 523, 1088, 2534, 2566, 2600, 3027; *towards* 439, 811, 1173, 1864, 1954, 2914; *opposite, facing* 1977, 1978, 2013; *from* 827, 2423; *near* 2925; *as far as, up to* 2673; *in* 3049
wiðerrǣhtes adv *opposite* 3039

wiðfōn VII wd *grasp* pret 3s wiðfēng 760

wiðgrīpan I *grapple (with)* inf 2521

wiðhabban 3 wd *withstand* pret 3s wiðhæfde 772

wiðre n *resistance, power of resistance* gs wiðres 2953

wlanc see wlonc

wlātian 2 wg *watch (for)* pret 3s wlātode 1916

wlenco f *daring, pride* ds 338, 1206, wlence 508

wlītan I *look, gaze* pret 3s wlāt 1572; 3p wliton 1592, wlitan (= -on) 2852

wlite m *looks, appearance* ns 250

wlitebeorht adj *beautiful* asm wlitebeorhtne 93

wlitesēon f *sight, spectacle* ns 1650

wlitig adj *beautiful* asn 1662

wlonc adj *proud* nsm 331, wlanc 341; gsm wlonces 2953; *exulting in* wlanc nsm 1332, wlonc 2833

wōc see wæcnan

wōh adj *perverse* dpn wōm 1747

wōhbogen adj *coiled* nsm 2827

wolcen n *cloud* dp wolcnum *sky* 8, 651, 714, 1119, 1374, 1631, 1770 [archaic MnE welkin]

wolde see willan

wollentēar adj *with welling tears* npm wollentēare 3032

wōm see wōh

womm m *misfortune* dp wommum 3073

wong m *plain, open ground, place, field, level ground* as 1413, 2409, 3073; wang 93, 225; ds wonge 2242, 3039, wange 2003; np wongas 2462

wongstede m *place* ds 2786

wonhȳd f *rashness* dp wonhȳdum 434

wonn adj *dark* nsm wonna 3024, 3115; nsn won 1374; npn wan 651; dsf wanre 702 [MnE wan]

wonsǣli adj *unhappy* nsm 105

wonsceaft f *misery* as 120

wōp m *wailing, lamentation* ns 128; as 785; ds wōpe 3146

worc see weorc

word n *word, speech* ns 2817; as 315, 341, 390, 654, 2046, 2551; gs wordes 79, 2791; is worde 2156; np word 612, 639; ap word 870; gp worda 289, 398, 2246, 2662, 3030; dp wordum 30, 176, 366, 388, 626, 874, 1100, 1172, 1193, 1318, 1492, 1811, 1833, 1980, 2058, 2669, 2795, 3175

wordcwide m *word* ap wordcwydas 1841; gp wordcwida 1845; dp wordcwydum 2753

wordgyd n *lament* as 3172

wordhord n *word-hoard* as 259

wordriht n *formulated obligation, instruction* gp wordrihta 2631 [MnE word, right]

worhte see wyrcan

worn m *a great number* (usually w part g) ns worn fela *a great many* 1783; as 264, 530, 870, 2114, 3154; gp worna 2003, 2542; as worn eall *a great many things* 3094

worold f *world* ns 1738; as 60, 1183, 1681; gs worolde 950, 1062, 1080, 1387, 1732, worulde 2343, 3068, worlde 2711

woroldār f *worldly honour* as woroldāre 17

woroldcyning m *earthly king* gp woroldcyninga 1684; wyruldcyninga 3180

woroldrǣden f *universal rule (of vengeance)* as woroldrǣdenne 1142

worðig m *precincts* as 1972

worðmynd see weorðmynd

woruldcandel f *candle of the world, sun* ns 1965

woruldende m *end of the world* ds 3083

wracu f *vengeance* as wrǣce 2336

wrāð adj *hostile, evil* dsm wrāþum 660, 708; asn wrāð 319; gp wrāðra 1619

wrāðe adv *grievously, utterly* 2872

wrāðlīce adv *grievously* 3062

wrǣc n *misery* ns 170; as 3078

wrǣcca see wrecca

wrǣce see wracu

wrǣclāst m *path of exile* ap wrǣclāstas 1352

wrǣcmæcg m *exile* np wrǣcmæcgas 2379

wrǣcsīð m *exile* as 2292; dp wrǣcsīðum 338

wrǣtlīc adj *wondrous, splendid* asm wrǣtlīcne 891, 2173; asn wrǣtlīc 1489, 2339; nsf 1650

wrǣtt f *ornament, treasure, work of art* ap wrǣte 2771, 3060; gp wrǣtta 2413; dp wrǣttum 1531

wrecan V *drive, force* p ptc wrecen 2962; *drive out* pret 3s wræc 2706; *recount, utter* inf wrecan 873, 3172; pres subj 3s wrece 2446; pret 3s wræc 2154; p ptc wrecen 1065; *avenge* inf wrecan 1278, 1339, 1546; pres subj 3s wrece 1385; pret 1s wræc 423, 1669; 3s 1333 [MnE wreak]

gewrecan V *avenge* pret 1s gewræc 2005; 3s 107, 2121, 2395, 2875; 3p gewrǣcan 2479; p ptc gewrecen 3062

wrecca m *exile* ns 1137; ds wrǣccan 2613; gp wreccena 898

wrecend m *avenger* ns 1256

wreoþenhilt adj *with twisted (decorated) hilt* nsn 1698

wrīdian 2 *flourish* pres 3s wrīdað 1741

wrītan I *engrave* p ptc writen 1688 [MnE write]

wrīþan I *bind, bandage* inf 964; pret 3p wriðon 2982 [MnE writhe]

wrixl f *counterstroke* ds wrixle 2969

wrixlan I wd *change, exchange* inf 366, 874

gewrixle n *exchange* ns 1304

wrōht f *strife, hostility* ns 2287, 2473, 2913

wudu m *wood, forest* ns 1364; as 1416; *spear* ap 398; *ship* ns 298, 581; as 216, 1919

wudurēc m *wood-smoke* ns 3144 [MnE wood, reek]

wuldor n *glory* gs wuldres 17, 183, 931, 1752

wuldortorht adj *gloriously bright* npn wuldor-torhtan 1136

wuldurcyning m *king of glory* ds wuldurcy-ninge 2795

wulf m *wolf* as 3027

wulfhliþ n *wolf-inhabited slope* ap wulfhleoþu 1358

wund f *wound* ns 2711, 2976; as wunde 2531, 2687, 2725, 2906; dp wundum 1113, 2830, 2937

wund adj *wounded* nsm 2746; dsm wundum 2753; npm wunde 565, 1075

wundenfeax adj *with braided mane* nsn 1400

wundenhals adj *with curved prow* nsm 298

wundenmæl n *damascened sword* as 1531

wundenstefna m *ship with curved prow* ns 220

wunderfæt n *wondrous vessel* dp wunderfatum 1162

wundor n *wonder, wondrous thing* ns 771; as 840, wundur 3033; gp wundra 1509, 1607; ap wundur 2759, 3103; dp wundrum 1452; *miracle* as wunder 931; ds wundre 931; *mystery* ns wundor 1724, 3062; dp (adv) wundrum *wondrously* 2687

wundorbebod n *mysterious prompting* dp wundorbebodum 1747

wundordēað m *wondrous death* ds wundor-dēaðe 3037

wundorlīc adj *strange* nsm 1440

wundorsīon f *wondrous sight* gp wundorsīona 995

wundorsmiþ m *wonder-smith, smith who makes wondrous things* gp wundorsmiþa 1681

wundurmāððum m *marvellous treasure* as 2173

wunian 2 *remain* inf 3083, 3128; pres 3s wunað 284; pret 3s wunode 1128; *dwell* pres 3s wunað 1735, 1923; *stand* pret 3s wunode 2242; *inhabit, occupy* inf wunian 1260; pres 3s wunað 2902 [MnE won(t)]

gewunian 2 wa *stand by, support* pres subj 3s gewunigen 22

wurð- see weorð-

wutun see uton

wyle see willan

wyllað see willan

wylm m *welling, surging, surge* ns 1764, 2269, wælm 2546; as wylm 1693; ds wylme 516; ap wylmas 2507; *surging water* gs wælmes 2135

wylt see willan

wynlēas adj *joyless* asm wynlēasne 1416; as wynlēas 821

wynn f *joy, delight* ns wyn 2262; as wynne 1080, 1730, 2107, 2727, heofones wynne *heaven's joy* (i.e. sun) 1801; ds 2014; dp wynnum 1716, 1887

wynsum adj *joyful, splendid* asm wynsuman 1919; npm wynsume 612 [MnE winsome]

wyrcan I *make* pret 3s worhte 92, 1452; *bring about* inf 930; *achieve* pres subj 3s wyrce 1387 [MnE work, wrought]

gewyrcan I *achieve, accomplish* inf 1660; pres 1s gewyrce 1491; pret subj 1s geworhte 635; *build* inf gewyrcean 69, 2802; pret 3p geworhton 3156; subj 2p 3096; *make* inf gewyrcean 2337; p ptc geworht 1696; *inflict* inf gewyrcean 2906; pret 3s geworhte (tō) 1578, 2712; *dispose* p ptc apm geworhte 1864; *bring about (that)* inf gewyrcean 20

wyrd f *fate* ns 455, 477, 572, 734, 1205, 2420, 2526, 2574, 2814; as 1056, 1233; *destined event* gp wyrda 3030 [MnE weird]

wyrdan I *destroy* pret 3s wyrde 1337

wyrm m *serpent, dragon* ns 897, 2287, 2343, 2567, 2629, 2669, 2745, 2827; as 886, 891, 2705, 3039, 3132; gs wyrmes 2316, 2348, 2759, 2771, 2902; ds wyrme 2307, 2400, 2519; ap wyrmas 1430 [MnE worm]

wyrmcynn n *serpent-race* gs wyrmcynnes 1425 [MnE worm, kin]

wyrmfāh adj *with serpentine ornament* nsn 1698

wyrmhord n *dragon's hoard* as 2221 [MnE worm, hoard]

wyrp f *change, improvement* as wyrpe 1315

gewyrpan I *recover* pret 3s hyne gewyrpte *he recovered* 2976

wyrsa adj compar *worse* asn wyrse 1739; gsn wyrsan 525; dsf 2969; *less worthy* asm wyrsan 2496; npm 1212

wyrt f *root* dp wyrtum 1364 [MnE wort]

wyrðe adj *worthy* asm wyrðne 2185; npm wyrðe 368. Compar nsm wyrðra 861

wyruld- see worold-

yfel adj *evil* gp yfla 2094

ylca pron *(the) same* gsn ylcan 2239 [MnE ilk]

yldan 1 *delay* inf 739

ylde m p *men* gp yldo 70, ylda 150, 605, 1661; dp yldum 77, 705, 2117, eldum 2214, 2314, 2611, 3168

ylde see yldo f

yldesta see eald

yldo (70) see ylde m

yldo f *old age* ns 1736, 1766, 1886; ds ylde 22, eldo 2111

yldra see eald

ylfe m p *goblins* npm 112 [MnE elf]

ymb, ymbe prep wa and d *around* ymb 399, 689, 838, 1012, 1030, ymbe 2597, 2883, 3169; *on* ymb 507, 568; *for* 439, 668; *near* 2477; *after* ymb 135, 219; *about, concerning* ymb 353, 450, 531, 1536, 1595, 2509, 3172, ymbe 2070, 2618

ymbbeorgan III *protect* pret 3s ymbbearh 1503

ymbefōn VII *clasp, clench* pret 3s ymbefēng 2691

ymbehweorfan III *circle round* pret 3s ymbe-hwearf 2296

ymbgān anom *go round among, attend* pret 3s ymbēode 620

ymbsittan V *sit round* pret 3p ymbsǣton 564

ymbsittend m p *neighbouring peoples* np 1827; gp ymbsittendra 9, ymbesittendra 2734

yppe f *high seat* ds yppan 1815

yrfe n *legacy* ns 3051

yrfelāf f *heirloom* as yrfelāfe 1053; ds 1903

yrfeweard m *heir* ns 2731; gs yrfeweardas (= -es) 2453

yrmþu f *misery* as yrmþe 1259; gp 2005

yrre n *anger* as 711; ds 2092

yrre adj *angry* nsm 1532, 1575, 2073, 2669; gsm eorres 1447; npm yrre 769

yrremōd adj *angry at heart* nsm 726

yrringa adv *angrily* 1565, 2964

ys see bēon

ȳð f *wave* np ȳþa 548, ap ȳðe 46, 1132, 1909; gp ȳþa 464, 848, 1208, 1469, 1918; dp ȳðum 210, 421, 515, 534, 1437, 1907, 2672, 2693

ȳðan 1 *destroy* pret 1s ȳðde 421

ȳðe adj see ēaðe

ȳðelīce adv *easily* 1556

ȳðgeblond n *surging water* ns 1373, 1593; np ȳðgebland 1620

ȳþgesēne see ēþgesȳne

ȳðgewinn n *swimming* gs ȳðgewinnes 1434; ds *turbulent water* ȳðgewinne 2412

ȳþlād f *way across the waves, voyage* np ȳþlāde 228

ȳðlāf f *leavings of the waves, shoreline detritus* ds ȳðlāfe 566

ȳðlida m *wave-traverser, ship* as ȳðlidan 198

ȳwan 1 *show, manifest, eventuate* pres 3s ēaweð 276, ēoweð 1738; pret 3s ȳwde 2834

geȳwan 1 *bestow* inf 2149; p ptc geēawed 1194

Proper Names

For abbreviations, see glossary.

Variants are listed under the most common form of the name, with cross-references in the appropriate place.

Line references are given to all occurrences of names with the exception of the following forms, where the words *passim* or *etc.* are used:

> Bēowulf, Bēowulfes, Bēowulfe
> Dena, Denig(e)a, Denia
> Ecgþēowes, Ecgðīowes, Ecgðīoes
> Gēata, Gēatena, Gēatum
> Grendel, Grendles, Grendle
> Healfdenes
> Higelāces
> Hrōðgar, Hrōðgāres, Hrōðgāre
> Scyldinga, Scyldunga, Scildunga
> Wed(e)ra

The family trees are set out in IVA.

Readers should be aware that normally Germanic personal names were transparently meaningful. Thus *Ecgþēow* meant 'servant of the sword', *Gārmund* 'spear-hand', *Gūðlāf* 'remnant of war', *Heoroweard* 'sword-guardian', *Wonrēd* 'lacking counsel, unreason'. We do not spell out the etymological meanings of names in the entries below, but since name-meanings sometimes seem to be relevant to the narrative in which they occur, one may find it useful to investigate them by looking up component elements of names in the glossary proper or in a standard dictionary of Old English.

Ābel *son of Adam and Eve, murdered by his elder brother Cain* as 108

Ār-Scyldingas see **Scyldingas**

Ælfhere *kinsman of Wiglaf* gs Ælfheres 2604

Æschere *chief counsellor and favourite retainer of Hrothgar* ns 1323, 1329; gs Æscheres 1420; ds Æschere 2122

Bēanstān *father of Breca* gs Bēanstānes 524

Beorht-Dene see **Dene**

Bēowulf (the Dane) *Danish king, son of Scyld, grandfather of Hrothgar* ns 18, 53

Bēowulf (the Geat) (usually spelled **Bīowulf** by second scribe) *son of Ecgtheow, nephew of King Hygelac, the hero of the poem* ns 343, 405, 506, 529, 631, etc.; as 364, 653, 2389; gs Bēowulfes 501, 795, 856, etc.; ds Bēowulfe 609, 623, 818, etc.

Breca *ruler of the Brondings and youthful companion of Beowulf* ns 583; as Brecan 531; as or ds 506

Brondingas *name of a tribe* gp Brondinga 521

Brōsingas *legendary forgers of a splendid necklace (mentioned in the Old Norse Edda)* gp Brōsinga 1199

Cāin see **Ābel** ns 1261; gs Cāines 107

Dæghrefn *warrior and standard-bearer of the Franks (Hugas), killed by Beowulf, probably in the battle in which Hygelac was slain* ds Dæghrefne 2501

Dene *Danes* np 2050; ap 1090; gp Dena, Denig(e)a, Denia *passim*; dp Denum 767, 823, 1158, 1417, 1720, 1814, 2068. Compounds: **Beorht-Dene** (*beorht* 'bright') gp Beorht-Dena 427, 609; **Ēast-Dene** gp Ēast-Dena 392, 616; dp Ēast-Denum 828; **Gār-Dene** (*gār* 'spear') gp Gār-Dena 1; dp Gār-Denum 601, 1856, 2494; **Hring-Dene** (*hring* 'ring' perhaps 'chain mail') np 116, 1279; gp Hring-Dena 1769; **Norð-Dene** dp Norð-Denum 783; **Sūð-Dene** ap 1996; gp Sūð-Dena 463; **West-Dene** dp West-Denum 383, 1578

Ēadgils *Swedish prince, younger son of Ohthere and brother of Eanmund. Helped by Beowulf (ll. 2391–6)* ds Ēadgilse 2392

Eafores gs 2964. See **Eofor**

Ēanmund *son of Ohthere and elder brother of*

Eadgils. *Killed by Wiglaf's father Weohstan (ll. 2611–25)* gs Ēanmundes 2611

Earnanæs ('eagles' promontory') *a headland in Geatland near the site of the dragon fight* as 3031

Ēast-Dene see Dene

Ecglāf *father of Unferth the Dane* gs Ecglāfes 499, 590, 980, 1465, 1808

Ecgþēow *son-in-law of King Hrethel, father of Beowulf* ns 263, 373; gs Ecgþēowes, -ðīowes, -ðīoes *passim*

Ecgwela *an early Danish king* gs Ecgwelan 1710

Eofor, Eafor-, Iofor- *Geatish warrior who slew Ongenþeow in battle (ll. 2484–9) and was rewarded with the hand of Hygelac's daughter in marriage (ll. 2997–8)* gs Eofores 2486, Eafores 2964; ds Iofore 2993, 2997

Ēomēr *son of King Offa* ns 1960

Eormenrīc *late fourth-century king of the East-Goths* gs Eormenrīces 1201

Ēotan *Jutes* gp Ēotena 1072, 1088, 1141; dp Ēotenum 902, 1145. See ll. 902b–3 note

Finn *King of the Frisians, married to Hnæf's sister Hildeburh* see I D4 ns Fin 1096, 1152; as 1146; gs Finnes 1068, 1081, 1156; ds Finne 1128

Finnas *Lapps (living in Norway and Sweden)* gp Finna 580. See l. 580b note

Fitela *nephew of Sigemund* ns 879, 889

Folcwalda *father of Finn* gs Folcwaldan 1089

Francan *Franks* gp Francna 1210

Frēawaru *daughter of Hrothgar, wife of Ingeld* as Frēaware 2022. See ll. 2026–9a

Frēsan *Frisians* gp Frēs(e)na 1093, 2915

Frēscyning *king of the Frisians* ds Frēscyninge 2503

Frēslond *Friesland, Frisia* dp Frēslondum 2357

Frēswæl *Frisian battlefield* ds Frēswæle 1070

Frōda *king of the Heathobards, father of Ingeld* gs Frōdan 2025

Froncum dp < Francan 2912

Frȳsan *Frisians* gp Frȳsna 1104; dp Frȳsum 1207, 2912

Frȳsland *Friesland* as 1126

Gār-Dene see Dene

Gārmund *father of King Offa* gs Gārmundes 1962

Gēat *(the) Geat (used of Beowulf, the hero of the poem)* ns 1785; as 1792; gs Gēates 640; ds Gēate 1301

Gēatas *Geats, a Scandinavian tribe living in what is now southern Sweden* ap 1173; gp Gēata, Gēatena (see *Guide* §22) *passim*; dp Gēatum *passim*. Compounds: Gūð-Gēatas (*gūð* 'war') gp Gūð-Gēata 1538; Sǣ-Gēatas (*sǣ* 'sea') np 1850; gp Sǣ-Gēata 1986; Weder-Gēatas (*weder* 'storm, weather') gp Weder-Gēata 1492, 1612, 2551; dp Weder-Gēatum 2379

Gēatisc *Geatish* ns 3150

Gēatmæcgas *men of the Geats* gp Gēatmecga 829; dp Gēatmæcgum 491

Gēotena gp < Gēatas (*Guide* §22) 443

Gifðas *Gepidae, an East Germanic tribe* dp Gifðum 2494

Grendel *the monster that ravages Heorot and is slain by Beowulf* ns 102, 151, 474, 591, etc.; as 424, 1334, 1354, 1586, 1997, 2070; gs Grendles 127, 195, 384, etc., Grendeles 2006, 2118, 2139, 2353; ds Grendle 666, 930, 1577, 2521, etc.

Gūð-Gēatas see Gēatas

Gūðlāf *a Danish warrior* ns 1148

Gūð-Scilfingas see Scylfingas

Hālga *Danish prince, younger brother of Hrothgar and father of Hrothulf* ns 61

Hāma *a hero of the Gothic legends of Eormenric* ns 1198

Hæreð *father of Queen Hygd* gs Hæreþes 1929, Hæreðes 1981

Hæðcyn *second son of King Hrethel, who accidentally killed his elder brother Herebeald (ll. 2435–43) and who was himself slain by Ongentheow at Ravenswood (ll. 2481–3)* ns 2434, 2437; as Hæðcen 2925; ds Hæðcynne 2482

Healfdene *king of the Danes, father of Hrothgar* ns 57; gs Healfdenes *passim*

Healf-Dene *Half-Danes, the tribe to which Hnæf and Hildeburh belonged* gp Healf-Dena 1069

Heardred *son and successor of King Hygelac (ll. 2369–79), killed in action (ll. 2202–6) by Onela for helping Onela's rebel nephews (ll. 2379–90)* ns 2388; ds 2202, 2375

Heaðo-Beardan *Heathobards, the tribe to which Ingeld belonged* gp Heaðo-Beardna 2032, 2067, Heaða-Beardna 2037

Heaþolāf *a Wylfing warrior killed by Beowulf's father Ecgtheow* ds Heaþolāfe 460

Heaþo-Rǣmas *a people living in south-eastern*

Heaþo-Rǣmas (*cont.*)
Norway ap Heaþo-Rǣmes (= -as) 519. See
l. 63 note.

Heaðo-Scilfingas gs 63, see **Scylfing**

Helmingas *family to which Queen Wealhtheow
belonged, apparently part of the Wylfingas* gp
Helminga 620

Hemming *kinsman of the Angles Offa (l. 1944)
and Eomer (l. 1961)* gs Hemminges 1944,
1961

Hengest *leader of the Half-Danes at Finnesburh
after the death of Hnæf.* See I D4. ns 1127; gs
Hengestes 1091; ds Hengeste 1083, 1096

Heorogār *Danish king, elder brother of Hrothgar*
ns 61, Heregār 467, Hiorogār 2158

Heorot *the royal hall of the Danish King
Hrothgar* ns 1017, 1176, Heort 991; as
Heorot 166, 432, Heort 78; gs Heorotes
403; ds Heorote 475, 497, 593, 1267, 1279,
1302, 1330, 1588, 1671, Heorute 766, Hiorote 1990, Hiorte 2099

Heoroweard *son of the Danish King Heorogar*
ds Heorowearde 2161

Herebeald *eldest son of the Geatish King
Hrethel, accidentally killed by his brother
Hæthcyn (ll. 2435–43)* ns 2434; ds Here-
bealde 2463

Heregār see **Heorogār**

Heremōd *early Danish king.* See notes to ll. 14,
901–15, 913–15, and 1709b–22a. ns 1709; gs
Heremōdes 901

Hererīc *uncle of the Geatish king Heardred and
probably brother of Queen Hygd* gs Hererīces
2206

Here-Scyldingas see **Scyldingas**

Hetware *a Frankish tribe* np 2363, 2916

Higelāc see **Hygelāc**

Hildeburh *Danish princess, sister of Hnæf and
wife of the Frisian king Finn.* See I D4. ns
1071, 1114

Hiorogār see **Heorogār**

Hiorote, Hiorte see **Heorot**

Hnæf *leader of the Half-Danes at Finnesburh.*
See I D4. ns 1069; gs Hnæfes 1114

Hōc *father of Hnæf and Hildeburh* gs Hōces
1076

Hondsciōh *Geatish warrior and companion of
Beowulf, killed by Grendel* ds Hondsciō 2076

Hrǣdlan, Hrǣdles see **Hrēþel**

Hrefnawudu *'Ravenswood', a forest in Sweden
where Ongentheow killed Hæthcyn* as or ds
2925

Hrefnesholt *'Ravenswood'* (same as *Hrefnawudu*) as 2935

Hrēosnabeorh *hill in Geatland, site of a Swedish attack on the Geats* as 2477

Hrēþel *Geatish king, father of Hygelac and
maternal grandfather of Beowulf* ns 374,
2430, 2474; gs Hrēþles 1847, 2191, 2358,
2992, Hrædlan 454, Hrædles 1485

Hrēþling *son of Hrethel, referring to Hygelac* as
1923 *and to Hæthcyn* as 2925

Hrēðlingas *sons of Hrethel (i.e. Geats)* np 2960

Hrēðrīc *elder son of Hrothgar* ns 1189, 1836

Hring-Dene see **Dene**

Hrōnesnæss *'whale's cape', a headland in Geatland where Beowulf was entombed* ds Hrōnes-
næsse 2805, 3136

Hrōðgār *king of the Danes in the time of Grendel*
ns 61, 356, 371, 456, 653, etc.; as 152, 277,
339, 396, 863, etc.; gs Hrōðgāres *passim*; ds
Hrōðgāre 64, 1296, 1399, etc.

Hrōðmund *younger son of Hrothgar* ns 1189

Hrōþulf *Danish prince, nephew of Hrothgar,
supposed by some to have seized the Danish
throne after Hrothgar's death.* See I D4 and
ll. 1017b–19 note; ns 1017; as 1181

Hrunting *Unferth's sword* ns 1457; as 1807; ds
Hruntinge 1490, 1659

Hūgas *a name for the Franks* ap 2914; gp Hūga
2502

Hūnlāfing *a Danish warrior* ns 1143. See note.

Hygd *wife of the Geatish King Hygelac* ns 1926,
2369; ds Hygde 2172

Hygelāc *king of the Geats.* See IVB. *Beowulf is
his sister's son, a particularly close tie among
Germanic peoples. The ultimate victor at
Ravenswood (ll. 2941–98), killed in action
(l. 2201) in Frisia (ll. 2354–9) by the
Franks (ll. 2910–21)* ns 2151, 2201, 2372,
2434; Higelāc 435, 1202, 1983, 2000, 2914; as
1820, 1923, Hygelāc 2355; gs Hygelāces 813,
2386, 2943, Higelāces 194, 261, 342, 407,
etc., Hȳlaces 1530; ds Hygelāce 2169, Higelāce 452, 1483, 1830, 1970, 2988

Hȳlaces see **Hygelāc**

Ingeld *king of the Heathobards* See ll. 2026–9a
note; ds Ingelde 2064

Ingwine *a name for the Danes* gp Ingwina 1044,
1319

Iofor see **Eofor**

Merewīowing *(the) Merovingian (i.e. [the]
king of the Franks, who is not identified by*

name) gs Merewīoingas (= -es) 2921. See l. 63 note.

Nægling *Beowulf's sword* ns 2680
Norð-Dene see **Dene**

Offa *king of the continental Angles* ns 1957; gs Offan 1949
Ōht(h)ere *Swedish king, elder son of Ongentheow and father of Eanmund and Eadgils* gs Ōhtheres 2928, 2932, Ōhteres 2380, 2394, 2612
Onela *Swedish king, younger son of Ongentheow. Married Healfdene's daughter (l. 62). Killed by Eadgils (ll. 2391–6)* ns 2616; gs Onelan 62, 2932
Ongenþēow, -ðīo(w) *Swedish king. Rescued his wife at Ravenswood (ll. 2928-33). Subsequently trapped near Ravenswood and killed by Eofor (ll. 2484–9) and despoiled after striking down Eofor's brother Wulf (ll. 2941– 98)* ns 2486, 2924, 2951, 2961; gs Ongenþēoes 1968, Ongenðēowes 2475, Ongenðīoes 2387; ds Ongenðīo 2986
Ōslāf *a Danish warrior at Finnesburh* ns 1148

Sǣ-Gēatas see **Gēatas**
Scedeland see **Scedenīg** dp Scedelandum 19
Scedenīg *the southernmost part of the Swedish peninsula (now Skåne), which was ruled by the Danes; used of the Danish realm in general* ds Scedenigge 1686
Scēfing *son of Scef (i.e. Scēaf) (an appellation of Scyld)* ns 4. See note.
Scilding see **Scylding**
Scildingas see **Scyldingas**
Scilfing see **Scylfing**
Scyld *a Danish king, founder of the royal house of Hrothgar* ns 4, 26; gs Scyldes 19. See notes to ll. 4 and 30.
Scylding *(the) Dane (i.e. King Hrothgar)* ns 1792, Scilding 2105
Scyldingas, Scyldungas *descendents of Scyld (i.e. the Danish dynasty or Danes in general)* np 1601, Scyldungas 2052; ap Scyldingas 58; gp Scyldinga, Scyldunga, Scildunga *passim*; dp Scyldingum 274. Compounds: **Ār-Scyldingas** (*ār* 'honour') gp Ār-Scyldinga 464; dp Ār-Scyldingum 1710; **Here-Scyldingas** (*here* 'army') gp Here-Scyldinga 1108; **Sige-Scyldingas** (*sige* 'victory, glory') gp Sige-Scyldinga 597; dp Sige-

Scyldingum 2004; **þēod-Scyldingas** (*þēod* 'people') np 1019
Scylfing *(the) Swede* (i.e. *King Ongentheow*) ns 2487, Scilfing 2968. Compound: **Heaðo-Scilfing** (*heaðo* 'battle, war') [referring to Ongentheow] gs Heaðo-Scilfingas (= -es) 63. See note.
Scylfingas *the Swedish dynasty or Swedes in general* gp Scylfinga 2381, 2603. Compounds: **Gūð-Scilfingas** (*gūð* 'war') ap 2927; **Heaðo-Scilfingas** (*heaðo* 'war') np 2205
Sigemund *legendary Germanic hero* gs Sigemundes 875; ds Sigemunde 884. See I D3 and ll. 875–97 note.
Sūð-Dene see **Dene**
Swēon *Swedes* gp Swēona 2472, 2946, 2958, 3001
Swēoðēod *the Swedish people* ds Swēoðēode 2922
Swerting *maternal uncle or grandfather of Hygelac* gs Swertinges 1203
Swīorīce *Sweden* ds 2383, 2495

þēod-Scyldingas see **Scyldingas**
þrȳð gs þrȳðo 1931. See ll. 1931b–2a note

Unferð *courtier of Hrothgar* ns 499, 530, 1165; as 1488

Wægmundingas *the family to which Weohstan, Wiglaf, and Beowulf belong* gp Wægmundinga 2607, 2814
Wæls *father of Sigemund* gs Wælses 897
Wælsing *son of Wæls* (i.e. *Sigemund*) gs Wælsinges 877
Wealhþēow *Hrothgar's queen* ns 612, Wealhþēo 1162, 1215, 2173; as 664; ds Wealhþēon 629
Wederas *Geats* gp Wed(e)ra *passim*
Weder-Gēatas see **Gēatas**
Wedermearc *land of the (Weder-)Geats* ds Wedermearce 298
Wēland *in Germanic legend a famous maker of weapons* gs Wēlandes 455
Wendlas *Vandals* gp Wendla 348
Wēohstān, Wēoxstān *father of Wiglaf, presumably a Swede (l. 2603). Killed Ēanmund when fighting with Onela against Onela's nephews (ll. 2611–19)* ns 2613; gs Wēohstānes 2862, Wēoxstānes 2602, Wīhstānes 2752, 2907, 3076, 3110, 3120
West-Dene see **Dene**

Wīglāf *a Wægmunding kinsman and loyal follower of Beowulf. Prince of the Swedes (l. 2603)* ns 2602, 2631, 2745, 2862, 2906, 3076; as 2852

Wīhstān see **Wēohstān**

Wilfingas see **Wylfingas**

Wiðergyld *a Heathobard warrior* ns 2051

Wonrēd *a Geat, father of Wulf and Eofor* gs Wonrēdes 2971

Wonrēding *son of Wonred* (i.e. *Wulf*) ns 2965

Wulf *a Geat warrior* ns 2965; ds Wulfe 2993

Wulfgār *an important officer in Hrothgar's court* ns 348, 360

Wylfingas *a Germanic tribe* dp Wylfingum 471, Wilfingum 461

Yrmenlāf *a Dane, Æschere's younger brother* gs Yrmenlāfes 1324

Appendix
A New System of Punctuation

§1 This title perhaps gives the impression that the 'possible way out' mentioned in IIIB3 is more revolutionary than it is. For this 'new system' can be described as involving a minimal use of modern punctuation with one departure from it: the replacement of the semicolon by the elevated point (·) found in OE prose and verse manuscripts.

The basic principle of this system is

No punctuation where the sense is clear without any.

It involves the use of the following marks of punctuation:

1 the paragraph inset, to mark major changes of theme or argument;
2 the capital letter;
3 the point (.), to indicate the end of a paragraph or of a major sense unit or the introduction of a new line of thought;
4 the elevated point (·), to mark off clauses. It indicates a less definite pause which may vary between today's comma and full stop;
5 the colon, to introduce speeches or, in the words of H. W. Fowler, for 'delivering the goods that have been invoiced in the preceding words';
6 the comma, to be used only within clauses and only when it is needed to make the sense clear;
7 dashes (–), to mark the parentheses which play an important part in Old English, especially in the poetry;
8 the question mark;
9 the exclamation mark;
10 single inverted commas, with double inverted commas inside when needed.

§2 The following marks of punctuation are used in the same way as the system outlined in IIIB3: (1) the paragraph inset, (2) the capital letter, (5) the colon, (7) dashes, (8) the question mark, (9) the exclamation mark, and (10) inverted commas. The point (3) is less common and more significant. The elevated point (4) takes over the functions assigned to the comma in

IIIB5 and 6 and often replaces the modern semicolon or full stop. The comma (6) is no longer used to separate clauses but is used only within them, e.g. to mark off vocatives and to remove possible ambiguities; see IIIB4 (1) and (2).

§3 Modern punctuation limits the multiple reference of Old English syntactical constructions, is unable to signal that the unit of Old English poetry is the verse paragraph not the modern sentence, does not permit the recognition of *apo koinou* constructions (IIIB3), forces editors to choose between commas and full stops (and so between hypotaxis and parataxis) in passages like ll. 126–9a and 194–8a (IIIB3), and perpetuates what has been called 'the awkward tension between the artificially disjointed parataxis imposed by edited texts and the provocatively allusive poetry that we manage to sense in spite of it all' (*Neuphilologische Mitteilungen*, 93 (1992), 179). In short, it destroys the ebb and flow of the poetry. The aim of the new system is to remove these problems. It seeks to eliminate unnecessary punctuation and to reduce to a minimum the number of interfering whistle-blasts from officious umpire-editors. The flexibility of the elevated point means that editors are spared the task of deciding whether *þā* is an adverb or a conjunction and whether *se* is a demonstrative or a relative where ambiguity exists, and perhaps that of adjudicating about *apo koinou* constructions, and allows readers to make up their own minds about these difficulties or to pass over them without being aware of their existence. The system is designed to allow the river of poetry to ebb and flow so that readers can appreciate its variety, hear its distinctive voice, and be gripped by its compelling attraction.

§4 There follows a version of ll. 1–114 punctuated in accordance with the principles set out above. Facsimiles of the manuscript pages which contain ll. 1–21, 21–46, and 46–68, will be found facing the appropriate pages in the text in II above. For a fuller theoretical and practical exposition see Bruce Mitchell and Susan Irvine *'Beowulf' Repunctuated*, in preparation.

[Scyld Scefing]

HWÆT!
   WĒ GĀR-DEna   in geārdagum
þēodcyninga   þrym gefrūnon·
hū ðā æþelingas   ellen fremedon.
   Oft Scyld Scēfing   sceaþena þrēatum
5 monegum mægþum   meodosetla oftēah·
egsode eorlas·   syððan ærest wearð
fēasceaft funden·   hē þæs frōfre gebād·
wēox under wolcnum·   weorðmyndum þāh
oð þæt him æghwylc   þāra ymbsittendra
10 ofer hronrāde   hȳran scolde
gomban gyldan·   þæt wæs gōd cyning.
Ðæm eafera wæs   æfter cenned
geong in geardum   þone god sende
folce tō frōfre·   fyrenðearfe ongeat·
15 þæt hīe ær drugon   aldorlēase
lange hwile·   him þæs līffrēâ
wuldres wealdend   woroldāre forgeaf:
Bēowulf wæs brēme   – blæd wīde sprang –
Scyldes eafera   Scedelandum in.
20 Swā sceal geong guma   gōde gewyrcean
fromum feohgiftum   on fæder bearme
þæt hine on ylde   eft gewunigen

---

6 eorlas] eorl   15 aldorlease] aldor . . . ase   20 geong guma] . . . uma   21 bearme] . . . rme

HWÆT! We regard this word as an emphatic extra-metrical call to attention, perhaps accompanied by a chord on a harp or lyre. We find it hard to believe that the poet or the scop introduced *Beowulf* with an apologetic unstressed *Hwæt* 'Now'.

2 gefrūnon is followed by an elevated point because the *hū* clause is in apposition with *þrym*. Compare ll. 14b–16a but contrast ll. 20–3. Cf. IIIB5.4.

4–11a Stanley observes that these lines can be taken as one sentence or as two, the second beginning at l. 7b. By this he presumably means that modern punctuation requires *funden* (l. 7a) to be followed either by a semicolon (one sentence) or by a point (two sentences). The use of an elevated point here removes this problem and indicates that we take ll. 6b–7a *apo koinou* with two principal clauses. But it might be clearer if we removed the punctuation before and after these lines.

12 Ðæm is taken as a demonstrative rather than a relative because l. 11b seems to be an independent emphatic statement, although, as the elevated point before *þæt* indicates, it is linked more closely in meaning to what precedes than to what follows it. Cf. *Se* l. 2391 which not only also follows *þæt wæs god cyning.* but in addition begins a new fitt.

13 þone, an ambiguous demonstrative/relative, is not preceded by an elevated point. This preserves the flow of the verse and suggests that in our opinion *þone* here is more likely to be a relative than a demonstrative. Cf. IIIB5.5. The same observation holds for *þā* l. 41, *þone* l. 70, and *þā* l. 113.

14b–16a We take the *þæt* clause as the second object of *ongeat*; cf. l. 2 note. Without the elevated point after *ongeat*, the *þæt* clause would be explanatory 'in that . . .'.

20–5 Here *Swā* can be seen as pointing forward to ll. 24b–5; hence the colon at the end of l. 24a.

wilgesīþas   þonne wīg cume·
lēode gelǣsten: lofdǣdum sceal
25 in mǣgþa gehwǣre   man geþeôn.
Him ðā Scyld gewāt   tō gescæphwīle
felahrōr fēran   on frēan wǣre·
hī hyne þā ætbǣron   tō brimes faroðe
swǣse gesīþas   swā hē selfa bæd·
30 þenden wordum wēold   wine Scyldinga·
lēof land fruma   lange āhte.
þǣr æt hȳðe stōd   hringedstefna
īsig ond ūtfūs   æþelinges fær·
ālēdon þā   lēofne þēoden
35 bēaga bryttan   on bearm scipes
mǣrne be mæste·   þǣr wæs mādma fela
of feorwegum   frætwa gelǣded·
ne hȳrde ic cȳmlīcor   cēol gegyrwan
hildewǣpnum   ond heaðowǣdum
40 billum ond byrnum·   him on bearme læg
mādma mænigo   þā him mid scoldon
on flōdes ǣht   feor gewītan·
nalæs hī hine lǣssan   lācum tēodan
þēodgestrēonum   þon þā dydon
45 þe hine æt frumsceafte   forð onsendon
ǣnne ofer ȳðe   umborwesende·
þā gȳt hīe him āsetton   segen gyldenne
hēah ofer hēafod·   lēton holm beran·
gēafon on gārsecg·   him wæs geōmor sefa
50 murnende mōd·   men ne cunnon
secgan tō sōðe   selerǣdende
hæleð under heofenum   hwā þǣm hlæste onfēng.

[The Danish royal family and the building of Heorot]

Ðā wæs on burgum   Bēowulf Scyldinga
lēof lēodcyning   longe þrāge
55 folcum gefrǣge   – fæder ellor hwearf
aldor of earde –   oþ þæt him eft onwōc
hēah Healfdene·   hēold þenden lifde

---

47 gyldenne] g . . . denne   51 selerædende] selerædenne

30 The *þenden* clause is taken *apo koinou* with the *swā* clause which precedes it and with the principal clause which follows it. See ll. 4–11a note. Again, it might be better not to mark off the *apo koinou* clause by punctuation.

38 **ne hȳrde ic** Here *ne* is more likely to be an adv than a conj. Hence it is preceded by an elevated point. Cf. IIIB6.3.

gamol ond gūðrēouw   glæde Scyldingas·
ðæm fēower bearn   forðgerīmed
60 in worold wōcun   weoroda ræswan:
Heorogār ond Hrōðgār   ond Hālga til·
hȳrde ic þæt * * * elan cwēn
Heaðo-Scilfingas   healsgebedda.
   þā wæs Hrōðgāre   herespēd gyfen
65 wīges weorðmynd   þæt him his winemāgas
georne hȳrdon   oðð þæt sēo geogoð gewēox
magodriht micel·   him on mōd bearn
þæt healreced   hātan wolde
medoærn micel   men gewyrcean
70 þone yldo bearn   æfre gefrūnon
ond þær on innan   eall gedælan
geongum ond ealdum   swylc him god sealde
būton folcscare   ond feorum gumena·
ðā ic wīde gefrægn   weorc gebannan
75 manigre mægþe   geond þisne middangeard
folcstede frætwan.   Him on fyrste gelomp
ædre mid yldum   þæt hit wearð ealgearo
healærna mæst·   scōp him Heort naman
se þe his wordes geweald   wīde hæfde·
80 hē bēot ne ālēh·   bēagas dælde
sinc æt symle.   Sele hlīfade
hēah ond horngēap·   heaðowylma bād
lāðan līges·   ne wæs hit lenge þā gēn
þæt se ecghete   āþumswēorum
85 æfter wælnīðe   wæcnan scolde.
   Ðā se ellengæst   earfoðlīce
þrāge geþolode   se þe in þȳstrum bād
þæt hē dōgora gehwām   drēam gehȳrde
hlūdne in healle·   þær wæs hearpan swēg
90 swutol sang scopes·   sægde se þe cūþe
frumsceaft fīra   feorran reccan·
cwæð þæt se ælmihtiga   eorðan worhte
wlitebeorhtne wang   swā wæter bebūgeð·
gesette sigehrēþig   sunnan ond mōnan

---

60 ræswan] ræswa   62] hyrde ic þ elan cwen   84 ecghete] secg hete   aþumsweorum] aþum
swerian   92 worhte] wo . . .

---

59 ðæm The semantic flow suggests that *ðæm* is a demonstrative here. If so, it is not immediately obvious why the poet used *ðæm* here and *Him* l. 76 with different referents, though perhaps the demonstrative carries more emphasis.

61–114 These lines illustrate the use of the point to mark verse paragraphs and the various situations in which the elevated point is and is not used.

95 lēoman tō lēohte   landbūendum
    ond gefrætwade   foldan scēatas
    leomum ond lēafum·   līf ēac gesceōp
    cynna gehwylcum   þāra ðe cwice hwyrfaþ.
    Swā ðā drihtguman   drēamum lifdon
100 ēadiglīce   oð ðæt ān ongan
    fyrene fremman   fēond on helle·
    wæs se grimma gǣst   Grendel hāten
    mǣre mearcstapa   se þe mōras hēold
    fen ond fæsten·   fīfelcynnes eard
105 wonsǣlī wer   weardode hwīle
    siþðan him scyppend   forscrifen hæfde
    in Cāines cynne·   þone cwealm gewræc
    ēce drihten   þæs þe hē Ābel slōg·
    ne gefeah hē þǣre fǣhðe   ac hē hine feor forwræc
110 metod for þȳ māne   mancynne fram.
    þanon untȳdras   ealle onwōcon
    eotenas ond ylfe   ond orcnêas
    swylce gīgantas   þā wið gode wunnon
    lange þrāge·   hē him ðæs lēan forgeald.

101 fremman] fre . . . man   107] Caines *altered from* Cames

Note

The comma is not used in ll. 1–114. However, it is used – only within clauses, not to separate them – in three contexts:

1   to mark off vocatives, e.g. ll. 365a and 590b;
2   to mark off parts of speech in apposition where confusion might arise without a comma, e.g. ll. 194–5 (comma after *Gēatum*) and ll. 250b–1a where *ǣnlīc ansȳn* is not the object of *lēoge* (comma after *lēoge*);
3   to mark off verbless clauses, e.g. ll. 484–7a (comma after *līxte*) and 497b–8 (comma after *drēam*).